Hinduism Beliefs & Practices

MAJOR DEITIES and SOCIAL STRUCTURES

The Sussex Library of Religious Beliefs & Practices

This series is intended for students of religion, social sciences and history, and for the interested layperson. It is concerned with the beliefs and practices of religions in their social, cultural and historical setting. These books will be of particular interest to Religious Studies teachers and students at universities, colleges, and high schools. Inspection copies available on request.

Published

The Ancient Egyptians Rosalie David
The Bhagavad Gita: A text and commentary for students Jeaneane Fowler
Buddhism Merv Fowler
Chinese Religions Jeaneane Fowler and Merv Fowler
Christian Theology: The Spiritual Tradition John Glyndwr Harris
Gnosticism John Glyndwr Harris
Hinduism Jeaneane Fowler (published 1997, compact 192-page edition)
Hinduism: Beliefs & Practices (Major Deities and Social Structures), expanded edition
Hinduism: Beliefs & Practices (Religious History and Philosophy), expanded edition
Hindu Goddesses Lynn Foulston
Humanism Jeaneane Fowler
Islam David Norcliffe
The Jews Alan Unterman
The Protestant Reformation: Tradition and Practice Madeleine Gray
Sikhism W. Owen Cole and Piara Singh Sambhi
T'ai Chi Ch'üan Jeaneane Fowler and Shifu Keith Ewers
Zen Buddhism Merv Fowler
Zoroastrianism Peter Clark

Forthcoming

You Reap What You Sow: Causality in the Religions of the World
Jeaneane Fowler

Published and of related interest

Chanting in the Hillsides: Nichiren Daishonin Buddhism in Wales and the Borders
Jeaneane Fowler and Merv Fowler
An Introduction to the Philosophy and Religion of Taoism: Pathways to Immortality
Jeaneane Fowler
Perspectives of Reality: An Introduction to the Philosophy of Hinduism
Jeaneane Fowler
World Religions: An Introduction for Students Jeaneane Fowler, Merv Fowler, David Norcliffe, Nora Hill and Diane Watkins

Hinduism Beliefs & Practices

MAJOR DEITIES and SOCIAL STRUCTURES

Volume I

Jeaneane Fowler

SUSSEX
ACADEMIC
PRESS
Brighton • Chicago • Toronto

2 4 6 8 10 9 7 5 3 1

First published 2014 in Great Britain by
SUSSEX ACADEMIC PRESS
PO Box 139
Eastbourne BN24 9BP

and in the United States of America by
SUSSEX ACADEMIC PRESS
Independent Publishers Group
814 N. Franklin Street, Chicago, IL 60610

and in Canada by
SUSSEX ACADEMIC PRESS (CANADA)
1108 / 115 Antibes Drive, Toronto, Ontario M2R 2Y9

British Library Cataloguing in Publication Data
A CIP catalogue record for this book is available from the British Library.

Library of Congress Cataloging-in-Publication Data
Fowler, Jeaneane D., author.
Hinduism beliefs & practices : v. I Major deities and social structures/ Jeaneane Fowler.
pages cm
Previously published: 1997.
Includes bibliographical references and index.
ISBN 978-1-84519-622-6 (pb : alk. paper)
1. Hinduism. I. Title.
BL1202.F68 2014
294.5—dc23

2014005777

MIX
Paper from responsible sources
FSC® C013056
FSC www.fsc.org

Typeset and designed by Sussex Academic Press, Brighton & Eastbourne.
Printed by TJ International, Padstow, Cornwall.
This book is printed on acid-free paper.

Contents

Preface and Acknowledgements

In 1997, I wrote an introduction to Hinduism for students who were meeting the religion for the first time in order to encourage undergraduates to take an interest in eastern religions. In the main, the students came from conventional Religious Education backgrounds having studied only Christianity and very few had any knowledge at all of any other religion. Rather than being a challenge, I found such a clean slate a useful starting place for an exploration of other beliefs and, indeed, of a non-religious stance like Humanism. Some students were embarking on a teaching career and specializing in Religious Education at the primary school level. These students needed background knowledge of different religions that would inform their teaching of children and their responses to questions by colleagues. The 1997 book was designed for such students, encouraging them to explore some of the concepts of Hinduism without too many obstacles on route. That book was divided into two parts: the first dealing with the phenomenology of Hinduism suited to first-year undergraduates and the second part as a second layer, exploring some of the history and philosophy in more depth. Today, many students embarking on Religious Studies courses at universities have a greater understanding of religions like Hinduism; whereas in the past it was unusual as a subject choice it is now more readily studied. Interest in eastern religions has reached the wider populace, with doctrines such as *karma* and reincarnation well known and there is now a general interest in other aspects of eastern religions that makes a new and more comprehensive book a valid exercise. With the advances of cyber space and the speed at which news travels around the world, there have been central events connected with Hindu religious belief that need addressing. It is in light of such changes that I was pleased to be invited to write a new introduction to Hinduism in which the original two parts of the first book will be extended into two volumes. Nevertheless, both books will be truly *introductions* with undergraduate students particularly in mind but also the interested general reader.

The same two purposes that informed the original book are here in this present volume and in its forthcoming companion second volume. In particular, there is a serious attempt to present *living* Hinduism but at the same time, to analyse the beliefs and traditions that underpin contemporary praxis. This first aim is intended to promote *dialogue* between the reader and Hindus and is, thus, a starting point for inter-cultural and inter-faith communion through an understanding of the major deities of Hinduism and its social structures. Examination of the major Gods, the divine in female form, and pan-Hindu and local village deities should give the reader a sufficient understanding of the divinity in Hinduism to engage in discussion with Hindus anywhere. Exploration of the social structures has the same function of exploring contemporary Hinduism through such mediums as class and caste, the rich variety of ways in which Hindus worship in the home and community, how they celebrate the important occasions in their own lives and in the veneration of their deities at festival times, and through pilgrimage. In short, the first aim is informed very much by a desire to present a *living* religion, underpinned by the traditions that inform it.

The second purpose is to explore the religious traditions that support the living religion. A deeper layer of religious history and philosophy underpinning present belief and practice will inform the second volume especially but will be by no means absent from this first volume. One issue that looms large in the current ethos of Hinduism and India is the treatment and status of women and the separate exploration of this will be a new departure from the original book and will be taken up in the current volume. With the advantage of a longer text, the present book deals more with the complexities of its subject headings with space for greater discussion of interesting intricacies. However, like the 1997 text but, again, with greater space, the richness and diversity of the beliefs and practices of what might be called many "Hinduisms" will pervade the book.

I am indebted to so many students in the past who accompanied me in exploring Hinduism and I hope that this expanded volume will serve today's students in the same way as the original book did in the past. The team at Sussex Academic Press, especially Anthony Grahame, supported the original book and made the experience of writing it an enjoyable one. That support led to several other publications with Sussex Academic Press and I am delighted to have the opportunity to rewrite the first book with the same publishers.

Wentwood
New Year 2014

I HAVE MET THEE where the night touches the edge of the day;
where the light startles the darkness into dawn,
and the waves carry the kiss of the one shore to the other.
From the heart of the fathomless blue comes one golden call,
and across the dusk of tears I try to gaze at thy face
and know not for certain if thou art seen.

Rabindranath Tagore

Introduction

The religion we term "Hinduism" is mainly an Indian phenomenon, but Hindus can be found throughout Asia, in Africa, the West Indies and Indonesia as well as in a number of countries in which they have been immigrants. Hinduism is something of a unique religion because it has no founder and so no real point in time when it could be said to have begun: it also has none of the core doctrines that are so often associated with a founder. While it would be true to say that many religions lack uniformity, Hinduism, in particular, is characterized by immense diversity. It is precisely this lack of uniformity that makes it such an attractive religion to study, for Hinduism reflects the multiplicity of shades of human aspirations in the religious and spiritual dimensions of existence. It is almost impossible to study Hinduism without coming across religious ideas that make sense in terms of one's own perspectives of religion, even if they are atheist, for Hinduism caters for all levels of thinking and all personal stages on the evolutionary pathways through life.

Then, too, Hinduism has been fed by very different cultural traditions, from its prehistoric beginnings so far back in time to modern times in which local custom may even witness the rise of a new deity to incorporate contemporary needs. From the earliest times, a predominantly village culture in a vast country meant that different religious ideas obtained and existed side by side, sometimes with minor variations but often with marked contrasts. This is another dimension in which Hinduism is different from many other religions for it accommodates changing religious and cultural perspectives as part of its psyche. Such accommodation is another reason why Hinduism is characterized by such a rich variety of ideas and practices resulting in what appears as a multiplicity of religions under that one term "Hinduism". So Hinduism, as probably the oldest religion in the world, has added many strands to its overall character in thousands of years. Additionally, outside influences have been accommodated also: the Āryan migrations in the second millennium BCE left an indelible socio-religious character on what developed into the Hindu religion as we know it today. But indigenous beliefs and practices survived and, though they were not evident in the Āryan scriptures, surfaced in one way or another as time went by if, indeed, they ever disappeared at the popular level. As a result, Hinduism cannot be slotted into any particular belief system – monism, theism, monotheism, polytheism, pantheism, panentheism – for all these systems are reflected in its many facets.

The student of Hinduism has a fascinating journey of exploration ahead but it is a journey that requires some mental preparation. Westerners are so accustomed to living life according to linear beliefs and patterns of existence: we have to have a beginning, middle and an end of things, or a method, result and conclusion, for the comfort of our own minds.

Indeed, many students will be aware of their tutors' requests for work that has an introduction, main body of material and conclusion. Our lives, too, are viewed in the linear concept of one birth, life and death. Hinduism is different in that it has little interest in, for example, a linear view of history or a linear pattern of life. What Hinduism has instead is a *cyclical* perspective of life, even of the cosmos. This means that time is viewed differently and there is a cosmic perspective to it that has pervaded Hinduism from the time of the Āryans onwards: death is not the end of the line but the door to the next cycle, to birth – and this is true of the universe as much as of the human being and all creatures. Westerners are less aware of the cyclical patterns in the rhythms of nature but the student of Hinduism would be advised to travel with this somewhat different perspective. Importantly, too, the student needs to travel with an open mind, exploring the dimensions of Hinduism like completing parts of a jigsaw puzzle and not prejudging the effect until a whole area is in place. In this book, I cannot complete the jigsaw for the student, only offer significant pieces and parts: it is impossible ultimately to capture the intangible "wholeness" of Hinduism. And the best way for the student to travel is without mental baggage for it leaves one free and unhindered: the mind will do better when it remains uncluttered by prejudices or biased conceptions. It is hoped that readers will have sufficient interest to journey further than this book and its companion volume can take them.

Although Hinduism exists beyond India, I have confined the subject matter to Hinduism in India rather than extend the study to diasporic Hinduism. My approach is primarily a study of facets of Hinduism as a religion and while it is necessary to incorporate some sociological, anthropological and ethnographic material, these are not the central aims of the study. But, unlike many western religious stances, religion and social living are melded together to provide complex patterns for living on a day-to-day basis and it would be difficult for a Hindu to distance his or her self from religious expression in social living, especially since contemporary Hindu society is what it is mainly because of religious traditions. Thus, there is an inevitable over-spilling and merging of religious and social themes. Writing some time ago, Timothy Fitzgerald criticized the treatment of Hinduism as a "world religion" or, indeed, any other religion placed in that category. His argument is that Hinduism (and other religions) should be lifted out of its "construction" as a "fictional entity" and explored sociologically.[1] His whole thesis is summed up thus:

> My point is that the World Religion approach does not begin, as it should, with the study of a particular society; it begins with 'a religion', or 'a World Religion'. The extent to which religion is embedded in the social relations of a group, or of an ideologically defined set of groups in a geographical location, is basically ignored. The 'social dimension' is presented almost as though it were an optional extra, rather than the locus of non-theological interpretation.[2]

It is precisely in the light of such a view that the title of this volume contains *Social Structures*, but that does not mean to say that religion cannot be informed by or intimately linked with sociological elements: the two are, I believe, interactive. That is not to say that I would go as far as Fitzgerald in discrediting Hinduism as a world religion, though I would concur that a sociological approach to Hinduism, especially, is a very valid pathway of exploration.

I have avoided a deconstructive approach, so popular with postmodern scholars. While I accept that a term like "Hinduism" has been constructed outside India and imposed on those within, to deconstruct it to the point at which it has no meaning at all seems to me ridiculous. "Hinduism" and "Hindu" are admittedly vague constructs, but if they are broadened to encompass a general idea of complexity and variance as to what Hinduism is and what it is to be a Hindu, I see no reason to spend endless space on their deconstruction. Brian Smith aptly presents the kernel of such deconstruction when he says: "This misleading category of 'Hinduism,' it is argued, must be deconstructed in the interests of truth in advertising and atonement for the sins of our Oriental forbears. The Indological authorities of the past created 'Hinduism,' and the Indological authorities of the present are now busy disestablishing its conceptual existence."[3] The same may be said of the term "religion", which does not really exist in the context of Hinduism as we shall see in the first chapter. Nevertheless, many within and without India are thoroughly conversant with the extraordinarily pluralist and all-encompassing religion that we call Hinduism regardless of the origin of the term. We do not imagine or construct a religion that is Hinduism; today *it exists*, albeit as a bewildering complexity of beliefs and practices. While this volume is bound to contain some "modern constructs", in other words, its critical theories, it does not set out to create them and avoids the vagaries of constructions and deconstructions. Post-structural and postmodern attempts to prevent the scholar's generalizations have their place and I have tried to avoid any such generalizations in the pages that follow, but the writer needs words as his or her tools and if the words are defined well, they should be clear to the reader.

Thus, I do not want to eschew the term "Hinduism" despite the confines that western study has so often placed on it as a term in the past. I like the analogy offered by Jessica Frazier of Hinduism resembling a rope: "It can be likened to a rope of cultural movements, woven from many threads, some longer and some shorter, entering at different points in history. These threads, which originate in different regions and different periods, entwine and influence each other creating a tradition with inner diversity and considerable flexibility."[4] I shall have more to say about the complexities of the term "Hinduism" in the first chapter of this book, but Frazier's words here aptly depict the fact that "Hinduism" depicts what are complex and multifarious beliefs and practices that will never be reduced to a unified "system", even if there are practices like pilgrimages that unite often disparate religious and social groups temporarily. The vast country of India is home to innumerable variations in what it is to be a Hindu: there are contrasts in the North, the South, and the many different regions, let alone the differences that class and caste impose on groups of individuals. Cultural and religious traditions are multiple and localized, many stemming from migrating Āryan origins but often, in the South, for example, informed by indigenous and ancient roots.

In a similar vein, the balance between textual and historical Hinduism and contemporary popular beliefs and practices is a delicate and difficult one with blurred edges, diffused interactions and sometimes total divorce. But I have tried to present both, especially since the textual evidence and the sources of mythical elements inform so many of the beliefs that colour popular praxis. On the other hand, as Tracy Pintchman points out: "With respect to the Hindu tradition, it must be said that the vast majority of Indians – past and present, Hindu or not – have no knowledge of Sanskrit and have never read a word of the Brahmanical canon."[5] Such a statement implies how divorced the textual tradition can sometimes be from living praxis.

Chapter 1 deals with *Fundamental Beliefs* that will provide a basis for the chapters that follow, but I have kept it brief, since the concepts here will be explored at greater depth in a more philosophical context in the companion volume to this book. The textual foundations of orthodox Hinduism are explored in chapter 2 as well as the texts that are accepted by popular Hinduism. Class and caste (*varṇa* and *jāti*) are the subjects of chapter 3 along with the stages of life (*āśramas*) that, along with class, are often depicted as the "religion" of the Hindus, albeit that the stages of life have almost disappeared for all but a few. Nevertheless, the second of the stages, marriage, has important implications for societal living and for women in particular. The middle section of the book is devoted to the major deities, Śiva in chapter 5, the divine in feminine form in chapter 6 and the popular deities of Viṣṇu and especially Kṛṣṇa and his favourite Rādhā in chapter 7. Having examined the nature of the deities, the remaining chapters deal in the main with the ways in which those deities are approached, the term "ritual" loosely linking the final four chapters. Thus, chapter 8 deals with worship, chapter 9 with life-cycle rites and chapter 11 with festivals and pilgrimage. Chapter 10 is devoted exclusively to the status of women in Hinduism, a chapter that I believe to be essential in view of the global outrage at the rape and murder of a young student in Delhi in December 2012. The factors informing attitudes to women as well as women's contemporary situations are explored in this chapter.

I decided for this text and its companion volume to use diacritical marks for the Sanskrit and have retained Sanskrit terms as much as possible so that the reader can become accustomed to them. A glossary of some of the main Sanskrit terms used is to be found at the end of the book as well as some suggestions for further reading. The companion volume to this book will deal with historical and philosophical traditions but the extensive nature of what we call "Hinduism" cannot be encompassed in a few books. It is an exhaustive religion that is bound to necessitate omissions in content. What is so fascinating about Hinduism is that there is always room for study of new aspects, and for greater depth of study of what is already known: as a religion of all possibilities, there can be no end to what Hinduism has to offer the student.

1
Fundamental Beliefs

As stated in the *Introduction*, many scholars believe that the term "Hinduism" is misleading for it suggests a unified system of beliefs and ideas, which is certainly not the case. It was, in fact, an "ism" given by eighteenth- and nineteenth-century European people to the multiplicity of beliefs in India that we today call Hinduism. It is not a word Hindus themselves would normally use, and the term "Hindu" itself originated as a geographical one used by fourth-century BCE Persians for those who lived beyond the river (S)indu, though use of the term may have been much earlier.[1] These days, however, "Hinduism" and "Hindu" are too well-known and current to be eschewed or replaced by other terms. As was seen in the *Introduction*, too, Hinduism is much too broad a phenomenon to be confined to the usual definitions of religion. It represents a whole spectrum of beliefs and practices that contains worship of trees and stones and the like, incorporates magic and much superstition and, at the other end of the spectrum, is characterized by highly profound, abstract, metaphysical thought. We find simple rituals at local shrines, naked *sadhus* practising asceticism, traditional ritual praxis of priests, a multiplicity of different gods and goddesses or maybe belief in none; and all this diversity is not underpinned by any core creedal statements or any historical point in time when the religion began. Rather, Hinduism has evolved from a multiplicity of ideas that, in the main, have never been discarded but have been retained alongside each other, yet each has encompassed all the transformations that time has brought about, adding to diversity. That is why it is more correct to speak of *Hinduisms* than of Hinduism in the singular. Geographically, too, it needs to be remembered that India – the home of most Hindus – is a vast country with over nine hundred million inhabitants and hundreds of different languages, leading to rich and varied religious beliefs and practices. Julius Lipner appropriately describes Hinduism as a "plural reality",[2] and Hermann Tull makes the equally apt comment that: "India is renowned for its diversity. Dissimilitude abounds in every sphere – from the physical elements of its land and people to the intangible workings of its beliefs and practices."[3] And yet, amidst all the bewildering diversity in beliefs and practices, some see a certain overall unity or wholeness to all the "Hinduisms" that obtain, what Lipner terms a "racio-cultural expression" and "multifaceted ethnicity".[4] When I use the term Hinduism or Hindu throughout this book, I am referring to one or more facets of this immensely diverse religious phenomenon.

In the five thousand and more years of the history of Hinduism few aspects have been lost and new ideas have been accommodated alongside the old ones with localized changes and emphases. This is partly why, when visiting a Hindu temple, we are likely to see pictures of Jesus of Nazareth, Guru Nanak or the Buddha alongside those of Hindu deities. It is this kind of accommodation of a multiplicity of ideas – albeit constantly changing and subject to modifications – that is at the heart of Hinduism and such a tolerance of ideas comes about because of a deep belief in the differences in the individual natures of people. No two human beings are the same and it is rather illogical, therefore, to expect two people to have the same views of God, the same level of understanding, the same beliefs, or the same needs and practices. Because each individual is an evolving, changing, entity his or her individual nature will necessitate an individual approach to God that is different from the approach of another. Constraints of class and caste as well as locational issues of, for example, village or urban life and family tradition, will inform religious belief. But it may well be that an individual has a caste-orientated set of beliefs and practices, traditional family ones that are different, and yet a personal deity that is different from the former two. The nature of the Hindu deity as absolute makes possible multiple ways in which that Absolute can be expressed. Tolerance of different views is present, though this does not mean that fierce arguments concerning religious stances do not take place, for indeed they do. I rather like Lipner's comparison of Hinduism to the banyan tree that sends down aerial roots in such a way that the mature tree becomes an intricate, interconnected mass of roots and trunks. He writes: "Like the tree, Hinduism is an ancient collection of roots and branches, many indistinguishable one from another, microcosmically polycentric, macrocosmically one, sharing the same regenerative life-sap, with a temporal foliage which covers most of recorded human history. But unlike the botanical model, the Hindu banyan is not uniform to look at. Rather, it is a network of variety, one distinctive arboreal complex shading into another, the whole forming a marvellous unity-in-diversity."[5] And, also on the analogy of the banyan tree, elsewhere, Lipner refers to Hinduism as "an interconnected, polycentric phenomenon in the flux of growth, change, and decay".[6]

With little interest in history, historical dates or a linear approach to its development, tradition is seen as the important factor that informs the present way of life in Hinduism. Countries and governments and, indeed, civilizations have come and gone, while some parts and traditions of India have remained very much the same. Many of the scenes witnessed today in India are remarkably similar to those of thousands of years ago. Troy Wilson Organ commented rather aptly of Indian tradition: "Probably nowhere else do people live in so many centuries simultaneously. Sun worship and atomic research, ox carts and jet airplanes, astrology and theoretical physics, magic and modern medicine, ultramodern multistoried buildings and mud huts – these do mix in India."[7] It is tradition that has made this possible. Tradition and culture are almost one and the same thing with little division between the religious and the secular. Indeed, since religion is not an independent phenomenon in Hinduism there is, in fact, no term for it; instead, emotive terms like *bhakti*, "devotion" and *dharma*, "what is right", depict essential aspects of religion, as do practical aspects like *varṇa-dharma*, class duty, which I shall examine in chapter 3. Organ thinks that a word like *sādhana*, which has no direct translation in English, depicts Hindu religion rather well. Its basic root *sadha* has many meanings – "to reach one's goal", "to subdue", "to gain power over", "to fulfil", "to accomplish an aim" – and involves the idea of an individual reaching the fullest spiritual potential and perfection.[8] In reaching spiritual perfection, however, no one way or interpretation is to be found. Another modern expression that is indicative of contemporary Hindu religion is *sanātana-dharma*, which means something like "eternal righteousness", indicative of the pervasive cosmic *dharma* and the necessity of the individual, the family, the community and the world itself to be in line with it. For many ordinary Hindus, tradition is played out in the rituals of the home and in the patterns of family and social living. Gidoomal and Thomson justifiably comment that: "Fulfilling your *dharma* within your family framework could be a definition of being a Hindu. It is a way of life."[9] For others it may involve deep commitment to a particular deity and a particular path of personal evolution, and for others the following of philosophical pathways with deep-rooted traditions: the possible pathways are multiple. In a frequently cited passage by S. A. Nigosian, these possible pathways are superbly depicted:

> The chief concern of those of Hindu religious conviction is not the existence or nonexistence of God, or whether there is one God or many gods. Hindus can choose to be monotheists, polytheists, pantheists, atheists, agnostics, dualists, monists, or pluralists. They may or may not follow strict standards of moral conduct, spend much time on everyday religious rituals, or attend a temple. Magic, fetishism, animal worship, and belief in demons (*asuras*) coexist, supplement, or accompany profound theological doctrines, asceticism, mysticism, and esoteric beliefs. Religious truth, according to Hinduism, is not conceived in dogmatic terms, since truth transcends all verbal definitions. In consequence, Hinduism represents an astonishingly complex conglomeration of doctrines, cults, rituals, practices, observances, and institutions.[10]

Before embarking on an exploration of these traditions and pathways, it would be prudent here to examine some of the fundamental pan-Hindu concepts that will inform the chapters that follow. Since these are concepts that are better placed in Volume II and will be taken up for more detailed discussion there, I shall deal with them only briefly here.

The Hindu concept of God

Although many people associate Hinduism with a multiplicity of deities, in fact for most Hindus there is only one supreme Absolute. This Absolute is called Brahman and everything in life, whether living or not, originates in Brahman. Every creature, every plant, every individual, every stone, every tree – everything in existence – has its source as Brahman. This means that Brahman is in all things and each entity is a part of Brahman; this is called *pantheism* (*pan* "all", *theism* "of God").[11] In the *Muṇḍaka Upaniṣad* we find the words:

Brahman alone here extends to the east;
    brahman to the west;
    it alone, to the south, to the north,

it alone extends above and below;
It is *brahman* alone that extends
over this whole universe,
up to its widest extent.[12]

Because Brahman is in all things, all things can be regarded as sacred in their essence and Hindus call this essence *ātman*. To keep the idea of Brahman as Absolute, Brahman is sometimes depicted as *It* and *nirākāra* "without form". In this case, Brahman cannot be called "God", because that would be making Brahman male rather than female. Brahman would then be describable and the concept of an Absolute would be limited. However, other Hindus accept a describable Brahman and use the term "God" or even see Brahman as female. Because Brahman is in all things in the cosmos it can be manifest in myriad forms and it is in this way that Brahman can also be seen in the many gods and goddesses of Hinduism as *sākāra*, "with form". Importantly, however Brahman is viewed, it is the source of the interconnection between all things.

Thus, while there are many manifestations of Brahman in the forms of deities, each deity is really an aspect of Brahman or, ultimately, Brahman itself. And since Brahman is in all things then there is no reason why Brahman cannot be manifest in feminine forms as well as masculine ones. The relationship between the many manifest deities and the unmanifest Brahman is rather like that between the sun and its rays. We cannot experience the sun itself but we can experience its rays and the qualities that those rays have. And though the sun's rays are many, ultimately, there is only one source, one sun. So the major and minor gods and goddesses of Hinduism amount to thousands, all representing the many aspects of Brahman.

Saṃsāra: The cycle of reincarnation

Hinduism, like Buddhism and Jainism that originated in India, accepts the concept of reincarnation, the idea that at the end of each life, the individual is born again in another existence in order to carry on his or her evolutionary path. Hindus believe all life to be cyclical, evident in the cycles of the planets, of trees and plants, of nature, of the universe, and so of humankind too. Apart from the physical body and the breath which makes us live, Hindus see the individual as composed of two elements. One is the personality self called the *jīva*, which is the living soul, the living being, the finite individual. The *jīva* is constantly changing and is the sum total of all our experiences in life, all our desires and aversions and all our conscious and subconscious characteristics. Without all these qualities, the *jīva* is simply a living being, but it becomes an egoistic personality that responds in myriad ways to the environment resulting in the biological, psychological and social self that enjoys, suffers, acts, thinks, makes choices between this and that and is subject to the experiences mediated by the senses. It is this egoistic *jīva* that reincarnates.

The other element that makes up the self is the part of the individual that is Brahman and is called *ātman*. The *ātman* cannot change, is permanent and is that which is accepted sometimes as partly and sometimes as wholly Brahman. The *ātman* does not reincarnate at all; it is simple *there* in everything that is manifest in the world. The next reincarnation of a *jīva* will depend entirely on the sum total of personality traits – conscious and subconscious – in his or her present existence. The Hindu *Bhagavad Gītā* contains the following statement: "As a man casting away worn-out clothes takes other new ones, so the embodied (Self), casting away worn-out bodies, enters new ones."[13] The verse is a clear reference to the chain of reincarnation and to the egoistic self that passes from life to life, as well as the unchanging embodied Self, the *ātman*, that passes, always the same, from one body to the next. The transmigrating self, the *jīva*, carries personality and individual potentiality engendered by all the innate tendencies and dispositions built up by the last and previous lives. It is the self that is composed of ever-changing elements, and is the self that is too engaged in the world of the senses to become aware of the true Self, the *ātman*, within. Mentally, then, the *jīva* creates its new body before it leaves its old one. The *Bṛhad-āraṇyaka Upaniṣad* (4:4:1–6) likens such passage to a caterpillar that stretches out onto a new leaf before finally releasing its grip on the last one, and a goldsmith making a new and more beautiful form from an old object. As the *Kaṭha Upaniṣad* (1:6) puts it: "A mortal man ripens like grain, and like grain he is born again."[14] Each self, then, is composed of a changeable, impermanent *jīva* and an unchanging, permanent *ātman*, the whole being the *jīvātman*, what Chandradhar Sharma described as "a mixture of the real and the unreal, a knot of the existent and the non-existent, a coupling of the true and the false".[15] What determines the state of the individual in the next existence, is *karma*.

Karma: The law of cause and effect

The problems of defining *karma* are considerable and one need only look at Wendy O'Flaherty's *Karma and Rebirth* to see how scholars apply widely different approaches and meanings to the concept.[16] *Karma* (*karman*) means "act", "action" or "activity" and refers, not only to actions undertaken by the body, but also to those undertaken by the mind. *Karman* in the context of ancient Hindu sacrificial religion was ritual action or actions that aimed at specific results – from recreation and sustaining the cosmos to wealth, prosperity and longevity for the mortals in it, particularly the rulers. Thus, from the start, we have an action/cause that is followed by a result intimately related to that action, with an emphasis on precise and correct action leading to good results and incorrect ritual leading to adverse, even catastrophic, results. By the time of the early *Upaniṣads*, certainly by the sixth century BCE, the doctrine of *karma* as we know it was in place. *Karma* came to mean action and *reaction*: all actions were believed to produce results and it is this theory that is behind the concept of *saṃsāra*, and actions in this world affected one's status in the next life. The doctrine had been extended from ritual activity to all activity.

Not all actions produce immediate results, particularly those actions of the mind, so it may be a very long time before the results of certain actions – whether physical or mental – come to fruition. This means that results of actions may come about in later existences. According to the *Bṛhad-āraṇyaka Upaniṣad*: "A man resolves in accordance with his desire, acts in accordance with his resolve, and turns out to be in accordance with his action."[17] It is the *jīvātman*, the personality with its many positive and negative likes and dislikes and positive and negative actions that causes *karma* and it is desire for and aversion to – but particularly the former – that sets up causes. Having created causes we must have effects, results. Just as a pebble thrown into a pond inevitably creates ripples that are near and far, so results of actions reverberate through subsequent lives.

So *karma* "winds through the Hindu world like an attractive, dangerous, and yet unifying creeper", as one writer puts it.[18] Each individual goes through life creating the kinds of results that will be stored up to form his or her *jīvātman* in the next existence. Each person chooses how to act or think, so each person's *karma* is his or her own and equally so the results of those choices belong to that person. If choices are good, then results in the next life will be good, but if choices are evil then the just rewards of such will be reaped also in subsequent lives. If actions are very bad then a person may actually *involve* and degenerate into a lower life form as an animal. Westerners sometimes see the operation of *karma* as fatalistic, but it is far from this, since, while an individual can do little about the *karma* he or she must reap, *karma* that is in the process of being formed, and all of an individual's future lives can be affected by present actions, thoughts and words: we shape our own future. And while it is also suggested by some that belief in *karma* serves to maintain the *status quo* in India with regard to poverty, there are many Hindus who would argue that responsibility in care for the poor is one of the means by which good *karma* can be promoted. At death it is only the body that ceases to exist, while the subtle accumulated *karma* of one's existence in the present and past lives continues into the next existence. The two concepts of *saṃsāra* and *karma* are generic to what it is to be a Hindu: regardless of individual or communal beliefs, they are fundamental beliefs. Combined, they provide a logical rationale and operative moral order for animated existence that extends from the individual *jīva* to the cosmos itself.

Nevertheless, good or bad actions were assessed in relation to conformity to the social and religious norms and the individual and social *dharmas* or duties that life had allotted each individual: there could be no deviation from such placement without incurring negative *karma*. *Karma* determines each life, its genus, the gender, the class or caste into which one is born, the type of family and the society and environment. It is a destiny of life that an individual is expected to fulfil and the nature of an individual and the environment into which he or she is born are the best possible, are *dharmically* set, and cosmically designed. To stray from such prescriptive circumstances is against *dharma*, *adharma*. In the popular conception of *karma*, the cause–result process is pertinent to this lifetime as much as to post-death circumstances: in fact, *karma* is related to this lifetime more than to past or future ones in the popular mind.[19] In villages, too, it is also believed that adverse *karma* by one individual can have a result that affects the collective community,[20] as well as collective bad actions producing collective adverse results. Susan Wadley gives an example of a pre-monsoon dust storm that caused a fire in the village of Karimpur in northern India, destroying homes, animals and humans. The cause was considered by the villagers to be accumulated sins of the villagers, leading to a collective adverse result.[21]

The *Bhagavad Gītā* endorsed the norms of social and religious action to a point, but presented a solution, that of detached action, that is to say, action that is selfless. This raises the important point that *karma* – whether good or bad – can only accrue to an egoistic self, not to the true Self that is the *ātman*. For release from the endless rebirths that *karmic* action necessitates, no good or bad *karma* should be accrued by the individual: no *karma* at all is necessary for liberation, *mokṣa*, and for some in Hinduism that concept informed a decision to withdraw from the world and all its activity and even, for some, to attempt to be totally inactive. The concept of retributive action became crystallized in the devotional texts and in popular belief, though not without the means to eradicate it by accepted devotional praxis. The late devotional scripture, the *Bhāgavata Purāṇa* succinctly states the crystallized definition: "The same person enjoys the fruit of the same sinful or meritorious act in the next world in the same manner and to the same extent according to the manner and extent to which that (sinful or meritorious) act has been done by him in the world."[22]

Dharma: What is right

In order to achieve good *karma* or, better, no *karma* at all, it is important to live life according to *dharma*, meaning something like "what is right", though the word has no real English equivalents. It is neatly defined by Barbara Holdrege who says that, from the orthodox viewpoint, "*dharma* is the cosmic principle that is transhistorical, eternal, and universal, structuring the separation of functions among the various classes of beings on each plane of existence and interconnecting them in the complex network of symbiotic relations that constitutes the cosmic ecosystem."[23] *Dharma* extends to a variety of contexts and involves doing what is right for the individual, the family, the class or caste and also for the universe itself. Indeed, overarching all right action is the *dharma* that is the cosmic norm, the *sādhāraṇā-dharma*, the eternal, universal *dharma*, which is the rhythm of the cosmos, the ultimate "rightness" of all things: any *dharma* – ritual, familial, social or cosmic – is part of an interrelated whole. The concept of *dharma* arose in priestly, *Brāhminical*, circles as far back as the eighth century BCE,[24] However, coming from the root *dhr*, "to preserve", *dharma* is sometimes translated as "duty" and is seen as essential for the preservation of daily, societal, class, but also ruling and legal, norms. It is associated very much with scriptural authority in which it was founded. Seen in this light, *dharma* is prescriptive, being the way life is lived according to one's class and caste, or even the stage one is at in life, as we shall see in chapter 4. But *dharma* also affects the future, for each individual has his or her own *dharmic* path, *sva-dharma*, dependent on the *karma* that has been accumulated. So one's *dharmic* path in the next life, just as in the present life, is the one necessary to bring to fruition all the results of past *karma* and is thus right for the individual, even though it may be a difficult path. The issue of *dharma* is sufficiently complex to be interactive and conflicting; for example, one's *sva-dharma* as a warrior is at odds with *sādhāraṇa-dharma* that upholds non-violence, *ahiṃsā*, as one of its norms. However, the family and community into which one is born will be that which mainly dictates one's *dharma*. The Hindu epics are full of accounts that illustrate how *dharma* and *adharma* are played out in ordinary lives, giving ordinary Hindus guidance in ethical living.[25]

Mokṣa: Liberation from *saṃsāra*

The ultimate aim of many Hindus is that one day the endless cycle of *saṃsāra* will be over and there will be no necessity to be reincarnated. This can only happen when there is no *karma* to cause an individual to be reincarnated because there is no egoistic self, no "I" to reap any results. When the egoistic perceptions of the world, the dualities of perception, and the desires that create the ego are all lost, *mokṣa*, "release", "liberation", from the cycle of *saṃsāra*, is realized. As the *Bṛhad-āraṇyaka Upaniṣad* (4:4:6) puts it, it is actions rooted in desire that cause rebirth:

A man who's attached goes with his action,
  to that very place to which
  his mind and character cling.
Reaching the end of his action,
  of whatever he has done in this world –
From that world he returns
  back to this world,
  back to action.[26]

The same verse comments on one who is without desire: "Now, a man who does not desire – who is without desires, who is freed from desires, whose desires are fulfilled, whose only desire is his Self [my upper case] – his vital functions do not depart. *Brahman* he is, and to *brahman* he goes."[27] To achieve such a state devoid of *karma* Hindus have many paths; it is not something that can be achieved in only one way. But when a person realizes *mokṣa*, the *ātman* – the part of the individual that is Brahman – merges with Brahman like the river merges into the sea. Instead of all the dualities that are part of the normal life – happiness and sorrow, desire and aversion, good and evil, likes and dislikes and so on – there is only unity. Just as the centre of a circle is equidistant from all points on the circumference, the one who has realized *mokṣa* is poised between all the dualities of life. In such a state, it is possible to engage in activity but not from the level of desire for one thing rather than another, or preference for this as opposed to that. As to the relationship with Brahman, sometimes this is presented as complete identity, but at other times as personal, dual and intimate. Either way, it is the *ātman* of the self that experiences that full or partial unity.

Mokṣa arose first in northern India and was antithetical to the norms of the old sacrificial actions of ritual, *karman*, as well as to marriage as necessary for society. Heaven as a post-death goal of the good man was also abandoned. *Mokṣa* meant turning away from goals and desires and an afterlife in order to focus on *total* liberation. While priests were the central protagonists of *karman*, it was from their own ranks that *mokṣa* as an ultimate goal gained ground and became attractive, with knowledge (*jñāna*) and not ritual action (*karman*) as the means to that ultimate goal. It must not be thought, however, that *mokṣa* is a goal in the mind of most Hindus. It is a *remote* possibility and most religious praxis is conducted for the purpose of more immediate and pragmatic goals pertinent to daily living, and in such a way that secular and religious life are comingled. In the next chapter, I shall examine the scriptural bases for many of these fundamental beliefs.

2
Scriptures

Ancient religion for many cultures was underpinned by belief in the power of the spoken word, very often in the form of blessings and curses. Such is certainly true of the religion of the ancient Āryans of India, in which the word was believed to be at one with its concrete manifestation. Ancient Sanskrit was the language of this group of Āryan people and was imported to India in their migrations from the plains of Central Asia, east of the Caspian Sea, in the second millennium BCE. These Āryans brought with them oral hymns that were carefully chanted in order to maintain their well-being in life. The "word" came to be *śabda*, powerful and emotive sounds for effectuating the continuation of all that was necessary for existence. Needless to say, it became an essential tradition to preserve the exact sounds and it is this tradition that is at the root of orthodox Hindu scriptures, some of which have survived the centuries of time through oral, and eventually written, transmission. Hinduism can boast of a plethora of scriptures, many like the ancient hymns of the Āryans but others rooted in stories that passed from village to village, stories of local heroes, of strange events, of wars, of interchanges with gods and demons. While the original oral corpus of Āryan scriptures has remained almost unchanged, the traditional stories have become more adaptable to regional variations, to regional languages and to changing circumstances, though not with a total loss of past traditions. We shall see in what follows, how such an immense wealth of scriptures came about in Hinduism. The scriptures of the ancient Āryans are known as *Veda*, "Knowledge" or "Wisdom", encompassing four *Vedas* and related *Brāhmaṇas*, *Āraṇyakas*, and *Upaniṣads*. So sacred are these scriptures that only certain classes of Hindu males were permitted access to them. What I want to do now is to look at each of these in turn.

Śruti: *Veda*

Written scriptures were for a very long time considered to be vastly inferior to the spoken word but those known as *Vedas* were considered particularly sacred in that they were believed to be timeless and eternally present. They were revealed to ancient sages and, thereafter, carefully transmitted with every minutia of intonation and correctness to privileged members of elite families, and remain with us today. To use Michael Witzel's analogy, "it is, in fact, something like a *tape-recording* of ca. 1500–500 BCE" that is preserved into the present.[1] There are four *Vedas*, the *Ṛg* the *Sāma*, the *Yajur* and the *Atharva*, and it was only after many centuries that they and their related scriptures were committed to written form at a time that probably pre-dated the advent of Buddhism in the sixth century BCE. Their oral origin may be as early as 3000 BCE,[2] but most seem to suggest a date of about 1500–500 or 400 BCE.[3] Some parts of the *Vedas* are clearly younger than others, the *Ṛg* being the oldest. Because the four *Vedas* and their related literature are considered "revealed", that is to say, "cognized" or "heard" by the ancient seers, the *ṛṣis*, they are classified as *śruti*. The medium of such "hearing" was mystical, a kind of inner experience of the eternal truths of the *Veda*, and it is in that sense that they are considered timeless since they are believed to have no human or even divine origin. While the *Vedic* corpus of scriptures is collectively termed *śruti*, that which is heard in this way is called *śrauta* or "scriptural". Since it was the sound of the scriptures that was so important, the *Vedas* are barely understandable in their old *Vedic* Sanskrit: recitation and correct enunciation were always considered more important.

The four *Vedas* are given the name *Saṃhitās*, "collections", in order to distinguish them from their related *Vedic* texts. The hymns that they contain are devoted to the gods but in a form that is designed to constitute ritual performance, *yajña*. It is *yajña* that ensured the welfare of the people, the land, the individual, the king, which is why the hymns were so meticulously preserved during transmission. *Yajña* was, in fact, the primary reason for the *Vedas*: the scriptures served a highly important pragmatic function.

Ṛg Veda

The *Ṛg Veda* is the oldest and longest of the four, dating possibly from about 1500 BCE, predating the Iron Age,[4] with its latest hymns being dated to about 1000 BCE. Some of its content is repeated in the other *Vedas*, so we know it precedes them. *Ṛg* means "Royal", indicative of the importance of this primary *Veda*. Its language is archaic Sanskrit and its nature experiential rather than historical or sequential in thought. It contains religious hymns collected into ten books that support a sacrificial system of ritual to gods who personified aspects of nature – thunder, the dawn, the sky and the like. The clientele attached to such ritual praxis was elitist and wealthy so we see right from the beginning that *śruti* scriptures excluded ordinary, lower-class individuals. Each hymn is set out in verses and the compilers of the hymns, the *ṛṣis*, who traditionally "heard" the hymns, were usually connected to a particular tribe or clan. Two of the most notable of these seers were Vasiṣṭha and Viśvāmitra who were responsible for many of the hymns in the *Ṛg*. The hymns tell us a good deal about the life of the upper-class Āryans. Their needs, for which they propitiated the gods, were longevity, cattle, wealth, success in battle and life after death in a heaven of cool breezes and refreshing streams. While the gods were propitiated for such needs, it was the ritual carried out by specialist priests that really produced results through *śabda*, the "sound" produced by the ritual, supported, however, by extensive animal sacrifice. The impressive speculative parts of the *Ṛg* that have become well known and the flashes of mystical inspiration that are outstanding must be left to Volume II along with the nature of the major deities of the *Ṛg*, but suffice it to say here that there were opposing gods and demons representing positive and negative forces, and deified personifications of all sorts of natural phenomena that could be controlled by ritual. Many of the mythical deities and demons were brought into India in narrative traditions pertaining to individual clans.

Sāma Veda

Sāma Veda is "Knowledge of Chants" and provided the priests with the melodies and chants that accompanied the hymns of the *Ṛg*. As the title suggests, this *Veda* contained *sāmans* or songs that could accompany different verses or hymns with the correct metrical sound. Very often a hymn in the *Ṛg* may incorporate different metres.

Yajur Veda

Yajur Veda is "Ritual Knowledge" and incorporates all the sacrificial formulas, thus containing comprehensive details of how sacrifice and ritual should be performed. It has been divided into an earlier portion, known as the *Black Yajur* and a later portion known as the *White Yajur*. There is a difference between the two in terms of style; the *Black* is mainly prose and contains the formulas that are indicative of the *Yajur*, while the *White* is characterized by *mantras*. The priest used these formulas and *mantras* as he carried out each item of ritual.

Atharva Veda

The *Atharva Veda*, "Knowledge of Incantations", or "Knowledge of Charms", is later than the other three *Vedas* though it also contains some very ancient material. Such ancient material may predate the Āryan migration into India and includes many old spells and magical charms. Other material is much later, dating to around 900 BCE. While the other three *Vedas* reflect the religious world of the upper classes, the *Atharva Veda* seems to deal with the superstitions and daily concerns of ordinary folk. It is pervaded by magic, sorcery and evil beings that pester humanity, while the gods that are mentioned are more magicians than representatives of natural phenomena as in the *Ṛg*. There is certainly much that is ancient in its content, despite its later, final compilation. What is interesting about the *Atharva Veda* is that it departs from the male-orientated nature of the gods of the *Ṛg* to include mainly female deities – a fact that, it seems to me, must surely reflect popular religion that was outside the higher-class *Vedic* ritual. Yet, the *Atharva* became accepted as the fourth *Saṃhitā*, perhaps because, as Troy Wilson Organ commented, "even a king sometimes desired to ease a toothache, to drive evil spirits from the royal chambers, to overcome the resistance of a mistress, and to get rid of a personal enemy. Even a king sometimes used a charm against a cough."[5] Thus, the *Atharva Veda* has a huge section on charms to cure diseases and possessions by demons of disease. Such charms cover coughs, fever, jaundice, discharges, constipation, urine retention, colic, dropsy, fractures, wounds and even something like jealousy.

On the positive side, the *Atharva Veda* has charms for long life and good health, though these are fewer, and there are many charms for women who want a husband, passionate love, the allaying of jealousy, conception or even to suppress a rival. Given that the religious world of the Āryan was geared to life benefits, the *Atharva* contains many charms for prosperity in the home, the field, in business, for cattle and, surprisingly, for success in gambling. Even the parts that are taken from the *Ṛg* are altered to become charms. Nevertheless, hints of more philosophical depth are also occasionally to be found.[6] While it may seem that the medical charms found in the *Atharva Veda* are rooted in superstition, this *Veda* is the basis of medical practice known as *Ayur-Veda* in India, indicative that some of the healing remedies of the *Atharva Veda* were based on empirical observations of the benefits of plants, minerals, insects and such things on health.

Brāhmaṇas

Each of the four *Vedas* has associated *śruti* material attached. The first of these are the *Brāhmaṇas*, a word that means something like "sacred praxis". If any of the *Vedas* contained mystical, intuitive experience, the *Brāhmaṇas* have little. They are dry and arid technical manuals for orthodox practice by the priests and are indicative of the increased power of ancient priests in conducting costly ritual. Since they were the only beings who knew the sacred texts and correct sounds, religious ritual was monopolized in their hands. Two major *Brāhmaṇas* were attached to the *Ṛg*, eight to the *Sāma*, two to the *Yajur* and one to the *Atharva*. They are dated about 800–500 BCE. As essentially priestly manuals, they were written by the priests themselves and, with some justification, Organ described them pejoratively as being "characterized by uncritical assertions, imaginative symbolisms, and contrived interpretations".[7] The rites of the *Vedas* now became so complicated and deliberately secretive that only the priests could conduct them, and animal sacrifice was greatly amplified. Increasingly, the priests became more important than the gods for renewed stability and welfare. Yet the *Brāhmaṇas* are not without interest: aside from their comments on ritual and the hymns of the *Vedas*, we have in them, for example, a charming story of a devastating great flood and the equivalent of the Judeo-Christian Noah. At the other end of the spectrum, attempts to link ritual action with wider cosmic events, renewing the whole creative process through ritual, was an emphasis that paved the way for later, more philosophically speculative thinking.

Āraṇyakas

The *Āraṇyakas*, "Forest" or "Wilderness Writings", are also part of the *śruti* tradition. As their title suggests, these writings were composed in the forests, away from the sacrificial ritual of the priestly circles and yet still in the priestly domains. Dated from about 400–200 BCE, they are transitional from the religiously arid and grotesquely bloody sacrifice of the *Vedas* to a more symbolic, analogical and allegorical interpretation of sacrifice. The four *Vedas* or *Saṃhitās*, and the *Brāhmaṇas* form the ritual action or *karma-kāṇḍa* portion of *śruti* tradition, the *Āraṇyakas* are the beginnings of the *jñāna-kāṇḍa*, or knowledge portion of *śruti* and they stand astride these two kinds of emphases on ritual and more contemplative philosophy. It is to the latter that I now wish to turn in the important literature known as the *Upaniṣads*.

The *Upaniṣads*

The *Upaniṣads* are the last of the *śruti* tradition. The term means something like "sitting down near" and is probably meant in the sense of a pupil sitting down with his teacher, the "near" suggestive of some secrecy in the transmission. The *Upaniṣads* mark the end of *śruti* and the "end of the *Veda*" or *Vedānta* (*Veda* + *ānta*, "end"). They are highly speculative, contemplative, mystical and philosophical but far from systematic. The transition from ritual action to the pursuit of pure knowledge is the hallmark of these texts, and they are generic to many of the fundamental principles of Hinduism to the present day. There are over a hundred of them and they were composed between about 600 and 300 BCE,[8] so there was certainly some overlap with the *Āraṇyakas*. Thirteen are normally considered to be the major *Upaniṣads* of which, the *Bṛhad-Āraṇyaka* and the *Chāndogya* are the earliest, also the *Taittirīya*. The later ones like the *Īśā*, the *Śvetāśvatara* and the *Māṇḍūkya* illustrate a shift in thought in the concept of God. These are issues that I want to take up in more detail in the companion second volume to this book. Here, I shall confine the content specifically to the nature of the scriptures.

Like the *Brāhmaṇas* and *Āraṇyakas*, the *Upaniṣads* are also attached to specific *Vedas*. They were written by the *ṛṣis*, the "seers", who travelled in the forests, debating and discussing their knowledge. That knowledge is of an intuitive kind that is a quest, described, in the words of the *Bṛhad-Āraṇyaka* (1:3:28): "From the unreal lead me to the real, from darkness lead me to light, from death lead me to immortality." Being esoteric in nature, the *Upaniṣads* were an internalizing of the *Vedic* external sacrifices. Such internalization was not just philosophical, drawing from the few philosophical strands of the *Brāhmaṇas*, but was also cosmological in that the human body was related to the whole cosmos in a unifying manner informed, especially, by the synthesis of Brahman and *ātman*. While being philosophical, there is little attempt in the *Upaniṣads* to formulate philosophical argument or defend a particular position. Rather, there are mystical peaks of thoughts without any verbal troughs that lead to them. They are infused with spiritual incandescence without material argument, "experiments in consciousness" as one source describes them.[9] Indeed, it is in the *Upaniṣads* that we find the major principles of Hinduism that are present today – the nature of the Self and its relation to God, *karma*, reincarnation, God as impersonal and personal Brahman, the foundations of *yoga*, the path of knowledge, and the foundations of devotion in the later *Upaniṣads* that focus on major deities. There is an emphasis on Brahman as a "no thing" in the sense that it is indescribable and yet *is* and is monistically identical to the true Self of all beings. The *Upaniṣads* are not, however, totally divorced from *Vedic* rites and ceremonies, which are peppered in their pages and each *Upaniṣad* begins with an invocation to the gods to assist in the search for true knowledge, but they do represent a trend to a more internalized type of worship.

Smṛti scriptures

The *Vedānta* marks the end of *śruti* or revealed scriptures. Not quite so authoritative, yet extremely important, is the whole class of scripture known as *smṛti* "that which is remembered". Four genres of scriptures, collectively the *Vedāṇgas*, "limbs" or "accessories" to the *Vedas*, constitute *smṛti* scriptures – the *Dharma-sūtras*, the *Dharma-śāstras*, two epics and the *Purāṇas*. Apart from aids to the study of the *Vedas*, *smṛti* consists of many teachings on *dharma*. *Smṛti* scriptures are not written in the Sanskrit of the *Vedas* but are still revered as God's words to humanity. It is the epics and the *Purāṇas*, in particular, which represent the religion of the populace: and since ordinary folk were not permitted to study the *Veda*, it is to such *smṛti* scriptures that they turn.

Dharma-sūtras

A *sūtra*, literally "thread", is an aphorism, a short statement written in prose in which every word and syllable has to have meaning without any repetition of thought. There were *sūtras* on a variety of subjects: the West, for example, came to know of the *Kāma-sūtra* on sexual pleasure. Three *Sūtras* are major: the *Śrauta-sūtra* deals with *Vedic* ritual sacrifice, and the *Gṛhya-sūtras* deal with religious ritual in the home, and are a source of practices of life-cycle rites, some of which are very ancient, as well as ancestor veneration. The third, *Dharma-sūtras*, are aphorisms about right conduct – *dharma* in all sorts of contexts, but particularly in relation to class and stages of life, which will concern us in chapters 3 and 4. *Dharma-sūtras* were closely connected with the *Vedas*, being regulations for the conducting of ritual, and being linked to different branches of priests, they have different recensions.[10] They are difficult to date, but probably came into being before 200 BCE, the earliest being perhaps about 500 BCE.[11] They were composed by branches of priests, were able to be learned easily by students given their aphoristic style, and pertained to the high classes of Hindu society. In essence, like the *Dharma-śāstras*, the compilers set out to clarify positions on *dharma*, especially where there were anomalies in the *Vedas* themselves, citing clearly what was considered to be *dharmic* and what *adharmic*.

Dharma-śāstras

The *śāstras*, a word itself meaning "scriptures" or "teachings" are less connected to the *Vedas* than the major *sūtras* and their compilers are not affiliated to particular *Vedic* schools. They are not written in aphoristic prose but in verse. Important were *Dharma-śāstras*, teachings about *dharma*, what is right, though there could be *śāstras* on all sorts of subjects like poetry, statesmanship or music. There were a vast number of them and they prescribed the correct conduct for different castes, for families or clans, for guilds, the army, diet, rituals in life-cycle rites and even for regions: they were rule books that covered all aspects of family, social, political life and judicial proceedings. Noticeable is the fact that different groups and even different individuals had different *dharmas*: there was no conception of all in society having to behave in the same way: such a thought would have been alien given the vastness and complexity of the Indian continent. The well-known *Manu-smṛti*, or *Mānava-dharma-śāstra*, the "Laws of Manu", was composed somewhere between 200 BCE and 100 CE and is the earliest *Śastra* that we have. It broke from tradition, like other *śāstras*, by being less steeped in *Vedic* tradition and yet sought authority for its content by the claim that all its teachings were thoroughly evidenced in the *Vedas*. Manu was a legendary figure said to be the tenth in his line and the progenitor of the present human race. While collective authorship of the *Manu-smṛti* is unknown, the text is encyclopedic in its regulatory details that tell us so much about life in classical India. Such was the influence of the *Manu-smṛti* that it became the basis of the Indian legal system that obtains to the present day. When the British arrived in India, they found it essential to translate the text in order to understand that legal system. We shall find the *Laws of Manu* to be prolific in the chapters that follow given its regulations concerning class and caste and stages of life, with precise punishments for transgressions.

Itihāsas: The two epics

Along with the *Purāṇas*, the *Itihāsas* are the foundation of all popular religion. For all those not permitted to study the *Vedas*, these two genres of scriptures in the *smṛti* tradition are at the heart of Hinduism in the present and available to all castes and to women. *Itihāsa* means "history", but not history in the western sense since mythology is well-encompassed by the term. History and mythology are recounted in two great epics, the *Rāmāyaṇa* and the *Mahābhārata*.[12] These two epics, especially the latter, deal with every human emotion and with all kinds of human experience, so it is easy to identify with characters and situations. They contain much mythology, legend, fantastic tales of gods and demons but, at the same time, they have profound teachings about *dharma* and it is often the underlying meanings that are so important and relevant to Hindus. Such importance of the *Itihāsas* and the *Purāṇas* is put rather well by Bithika Mukerji:

> With the genre of smriti literature we enter the jurisdiction of time and can see its influence as a category of existence. The massive proliferation of sacred texts seems to have kept pace with the increasing complexities in societies, the many movements of emigrations, and influxes of peoples on the plains of India. Diverse trends were integrated and became part of the same homogenous cultural pattern. It is considered unnecessary and even unseemly to seek to pick out the individual strands of this many-colored garment because the insistence on continuity and homogeneity is not without its metaphysical overtones.[13]

The two epics, in particular, feature daily in the Hindu home with parts of them being recited or used in prayers. Stories from them are told to young children, read in the villages, staged on television and in theatre and its characters and events portrayed in art and music. The *Mahābhārata* is the world's longest epic – so long that it could not possibly be the work of one author. Rather, it was composed over a long period of time with different parts being added. This process probably began somewhere about 400 or 500 BCE and ended about 300 or 400 CE, with core events perhaps centuries earlier.[14] The *Rāmāyaṇa* on the other hand, is more composite, being written about 400–200 BCE, though there are wide discrepancies concerning dating,[15] and John Brockington thinks that the *Mahābhārata* is older.[16] The final form of the *Rāmāyaṇa* was completed about 200 CE with the addition of the first, seventh and last books but, even so, is the result of many authors and poets who added to the work over a period of many generations. Even the original strand of the story probably drew upon a number of pre-existent folk tales about its hero Rāma. A long oral tradition accompanied many of the tales and legends of heroes in the epics, so there are certainly parts that can be called ancient. Some suggest that there may even be some ancient Indo-Āryan oral elements in the tale.[17] Popular religion often became absorbed by the priestly class, the *Brāhmins*, in an attempt to bring it under their control. It was they who committed the material in the epics to written form in a process of "*Brāhminization*". The tales spread far and wide and became adapted to local customs and beliefs, so that no one version of each tale exists.

Of considerable interest is the concept of deity that the epics reveal, an aspect that I shall treat briefly below and in more detail in Volume II. An important aspect of this concept of God was the rise in devotional worship that the epics encouraged. It was a devotional approach to God that has been retained to the present day and that reflected the religious life of the masses that had been a potent undercurrent to *Vedic* ritualism. The *Itihāsas* are transitional scriptures sometimes upholding *Vedic* ideas and *Vedic* gods, and at other times moving beyond the old *Vedic* gods and beliefs in Heaven to more philosophical concepts of God and belief in liberation from reincarnation beyond any Heaven. The *Rāmāyaṇa*, especially, makes mention of the old *Vedic* rituals and the Heaven to which mortals aspired. Both epics mark the beginnings of a rise in theism that was taken up so much by the *Purāṇas*, and the deities Viṣṇu and Śiva emerge in the *Mahābhārata* in a manner that paves the way for the devotional sects that focused on them.

The *Rāmāyaṇa*

The *Rāmāyaṇa* is immensely popular throughout India today. It is an epic loved by all Indians and its charming tale now even features in the Religious Education lessons in many syllabuses in schools in the United Kingdom. Of all the Hindu literature that has emerged out of religious tradition the *Rāmāyaṇa* has perhaps the greatest appeal to the everyday Hindu. Although overshadowed in literary dimensions by the other great epic, the *Mahābhārata*, Romesh Dutt justifiably commented that "as a poem delineating the softer emotions of our everyday life the *Ramayana* sends its roots deeper into the hearts and minds of the million in India".[18] There is a universality about the *Rāmāyaṇa* that appeals to all races and nations. Mahatma Gandhi regarded it as the greatest book in Hindu devotional literature and it seems to have a notable special appeal because of its depiction of everyday domestic events and situations that attract rich and poor alike. As such, it became the focus of much of the devotional movement in Hinduism and was the theme taken up by generations of poets. The *Rāmāyaṇa* spread to all parts of southern Asia and was represented in plays, poetry, song, art and sculpture and translated into many Indian languages and dialects. Special favourites of the many regionally different texts are those of Tulsī Dās, which was written in Hindi in the sixteenth century and the Tamil version of Kamban, which came about in the tenth to twelfth centuries. The epic is written in couplet form that adds to its enchantment.

The *Rāmāyaṇa* gives us a picture of the religious, social and political life of ancient India: it is a graphic description of the culture and civilization of the period in which it was written. The poet sets the story in a golden age of the kingdoms of Kośala and Videha, an ideal age of righteousness, justice, duty and morality. For two thousand years the story has been celebrated in temple ritual, religious festivals, at home shrines, and at places of pilgrimage, in recognition of the noblest of ages and the noblest of heroes and heroines in Rāma and Sītā. It is therefore not surprising that the last words which Gandhi spoke before he died were "Rām, Rām." The original and traditional author of the *Rāmāyaṇa* was said to be the poet Vālmīki, who probably lived in north-east India, the area in which most of the story is set. According to legend, Vālmīki was a robber who one day met a Hindu holy man who converted him to a more virtuous life. It was Vālmīki who, perhaps drawing on folk traditions, was believed to have woven together the original text. Later, many subsidiary stories and extra details were added. While having much of the "fairy tale" nature, Brockington thinks that "there is a kernel of historical or semi-historical fact around which the epic has developed".[19]

The story of the *Rāmāyaṇa* is a beautiful tale of devotion, duty and right relationships, and of *karma* and especially *dharma*, which is the key theme of the *Rāmāyaṇa* – the *dharma* of society, of family and of the individual. The whole epic abounds with good and evil, light and dark and few shades of anything in between. Rāma and Sītā are the ideal royal couple, Rāma is a brave, wise and good warrior, and Sītā his devoted, faithful, kind and beautiful wife. Daśaratha, King of Ayodhyā, wished to hand over his throne to his son, Rāma, but the workings of *karma* were such that the King was destined to die before this could take place. Instead of seeing his son crowned king and ruler of Ayodhyā, through the machinations of one of his wives, Rāma is banished to the forests, accompanied by his faithful wife and his brother. There they live the lives of hermits and are befriended by the holy men who live a life of meditative retreat in the seclusion of the forest. The central episode of the long narrative is the abduction of Sītā by the demon Rāvaṇa, and Rāma's pursuit and rescue of her aided by the brave monkey-general Hanumān. The story has both a happy and sad ending – happy, in that Sītā is rescued by Rāma and returns to Ayodhyā after fourteen years to be greeted by its citizens with the greatest possible joy, but sad because a probably later insertion at the end of the epic finds Sītā's chastity during her period of capture by Rāvaṇa questioned for a second time. She is banished, and when she returns to Ayodhyā, it is to a second trial by fire to prove her innocence. But Sītā, who came out of the earth at her birth, calls Mother Earth to take her back into the earth from which she came. The saintly wife of Rāma is taken in the arms of her Mother and disappears for ever.

The epic is full of mythical creatures as well as human heroes and demons and has as its basis the battle between good and evil in which all these beings participate. The good are idealized as perfect – loyal, faithful, obedient, knowing what is right, able to fulfil obligations and duty – in short maintaining *dharma*. When it was televised in 1987 in India, the television set became a shrine around which old and young gathered in villages and urban locales to watch this wonderful epic. The regional variations offer different perspectives, sometimes radically, of the hero, Rāma, and of Sītā also. Vālmīki's version, for example, brings out the meekness of Sītā, whereas Tulsī Dās' version gives her superhuman strength. Translations into local vernacular languages brought the *Rāmāyaṇa* to those for whom the Sanskrit original would have been alien and this was a process that was begun as early as the seventh century.

The concept of *avatāras*

Although the *Rāmāyaṇa* has been copiously copied in the vernacular, there are two major recensions plus all their different local transmissions. In the North, it is Vālmīki's *Rāma-kathā*, "Story of Rāma", that is the original. In Vālmīki's account Rāma is divine, as are his three brothers, and at the end of the epic, Rāma enters a river and ascends to Heaven as, once again, the great deity Viṣṇu. In this way, Rāma is presented as an *avatāra*, "descent",[20] of Viṣṇu. Nevertheless, there are no theistic elements in Vālmīki's tale and many believe that, where divinity of Rāma is overt, and the association with Viṣṇu maintained, these are later insertions. In the South, it is Tulsī Dās' sixteenth-century *Rāmcaritmānas* that clearly has a highly devotional and theistic nature and here Rāma is certainly both divine and an *avatāra* of Viṣṇu. The differences in the two major recensions and their derivative texts can be, therefore, considerable. The northern texts, for example, present the demon Rāvaṇa as a ten-headed monster, but in the southern texts, he is a dashing hero.[21]

It is late in both epics that the idea of descents of Viṣṇu emerge, and so Rāma is likely to have been portrayed as thoroughly human in the original tale of the *Rāmāyaṇa*: he was a hero sung about by travelling bards, though identified with certain *Vedic* gods from time to time in the text. John Brockington thinks that it was by the third century that Rāma became divine rather than human,[22] and only much later that he was linked to Viṣṇu through a process of partial, then full descent.[23] Mukerji rather captures this transition in his assessment of Rāma as "the touchstone of perfectability and thus trans-natural in his being, but he is close to the heart of man because he lives, acts, suffers, and rejoices as if he were nothing but a mortal man".[24] Nevertheless, the doctrine of *avatāras* became important for the followers of the deity Viṣṇu who descends into human form in both epics: in the *Mahābhārata* he is the *avatāra* Kṛṣṇa. The *avatāras* are very important in the concept of *bhakti*, "loving devotion" to a personal deity, for by becoming manifest in this way, Rāma and Kṛṣṇa have become the objects of devotion to the masses of Hindus thereby providing a more meaningful representation of the more abstract Brahman. The *avatāras* represent manifestations of the divine that represent the ideal in morality, justice, devotion to duty and perfection – the capabilities of human beings when they realize the divine particle within themselves. However, the portrayal of Rāma is as a more "fairy tale" hero than the macho warriors of the *Mahābhārata*, even Kṛṣṇa, and Rāma has little of their brute aggression, their frequent *adharmic* actions and their violation of the doctrine of non-violence.[25]

Important in the *Rāmāyaṇa* and in all scripture related to the *avatāras* of Viṣṇu, is the human nature of the *avatāras*. It is this aspect that enables people to come close to them. The life of Rāma, in particular, is a mixture of the divine and human, though his unawareness of his divinity throughout the narrative makes him all the easier to relate to. And this human nature is further enhanced by his emotion, such as when he has to leave his distraught mother and hasten away because emotion overwhelms him: this episode shows that he is capable of deep suffering. We meet Rāma in the *Rāmāyaṇa* as a mature man who has clear characteristics of honesty and uprightness, while Sītā shows kindness, obedience and chastity, characteristics that make the ideal hero and heroine to the Hindu mind. In Tulsī Dās' version of the *Rāmāyaṇa*, Rāma's extreme sorrow in exile is portrayed by relating how he has to sleep on the ground, find roots and fruit to eat, how he cries when Sītā has an ominous dream and when he hears his father has died. Rāma and Sītā have to endure great hardships, but through this suffering and privation the qualities of right action come through thereby providing a model for the millions of Hindus today.

The *Rāmāyaṇa* gives us a thorough understanding of the concept of *dharma* – "what is right", and each character in the drama has his or her own *dharma* to play out. The intrinsic nature of each character – whether god, demon, human or animal – has its own space in existence, at the same time being interdependent on all others: these are the cosmic norms that uphold the world. Such a delicately balanced arrangement cannot afford to be wildly upset as is the case with the banishment of Rāma and the abduction of Sītā. Rāma is the embodiment of *dharma*, and it is easy to see how the idea of his becoming human from the divine had the purpose of restoring good from evil, *adharma*. Such, indeed, was to be the *raison d'être* of the whole thought behind *avatāras*. The epics are very much concerned with cosmic imbalance, when the forces of evil threaten to overcome those of good. So Rāma and Sītā are perfect examples of how man and woman should be both individually and in their relationship with each other. The epics, then, bring the complex concept of *dharma* into real situations, in this way providing moral guidance in a very concrete form for the Hindu. "What is right" is learnt through the characters of Rāma, Sītā and Rāma's brother rather than through philosophical speculation. Not only, then, does such *smṛti* literature bring people close to God, but it also shows what is required of them at their very best. As the saying goes: "As long as the mountains and rivers last on Earth, that long will the tale of the *Rāmāyaṇa* be told throughout the worlds."

The *Mahābhārata*

The *Mahābhārata*, the world's longest poem, means "The great story of the Bhāratas" and it tells the story of a tremendous struggle for power between two royal families, the Pāṇḍavas or Pāṇḍus and the Kauravas or Kurus. The King, Bhārata (which is the old name for India and the name of its ancient ruler), had two sons, Pāṇḍu and Dhṛtarāṣṭra. Pāṇḍu had five sons who were very noble and good, representing *dharma* in life, while Dhṛtarāṣṭra had a hundred sons who were generally evil and who represented *adharma* in life. The story of the power struggle between these two unequal parties, the five Pāṇḍavas and the hundred Kauravas, forms the story of the *Mahābhārata* and into this story are interwoven all kinds of episodes of love, war, intrigue, relationships and all the countless situations that make up life. Like much *smṛti* literature, the stories can be told to children, to adults, to intellectuals or to the simple; it will depend on the individual level of consciousness as to what will be gleaned from the narrative. The attentive listener, however, will discern much moral, social, political and religious teaching in these stories.

The kingdom over which there is a dispute is that of Bhārata, or Kurukṣetra, in northern India close to the Himālayas. Its capital was Hāstinapura. The ruler of the kingdom was a descendant of Bhārata and father of Bhiṣma, the latter a great character in the *Mahābhārata*. Bhiṣma should have inherited his father's kingdom, but gave up the right so that his father could marry a maiden, Satyavati, whose father would not let her marry unless it was her sons and not Bhiṣma who inherited Kurukṣetra. The royal line, however, was later at the point of dying out, when Satyavati asked her only son Vyāsa to produce heirs by two sisters. One produced Dhṛtarāṣṭra who was born blind, and the other the pale Pāṇḍu. Both were Kurus, or Kauravas, descendants of Kuru, the grandson of Bhārata. Because he was blind, Dhṛtarāṣṭra could not rule, so Pāṇḍu took the throne.

Pāṇḍu was cursed so that he could not live if he had intercourse with his two wives. He renounced the throne, handing it to blind Dhṛtarāṣṭra, and retired to the forest. His first wife, Kuntī, conceived four sons by different gods, though she abandoned Karṇa, one of these sons. Three – Yudhiṣṭhira, Bhīma and Arjuna – became the Pāṇḍus or Pāṇḍavas, the sons of Pāṇḍu. Pāṇḍu's second wife, Mādrī, bore him the twins Nakula and Sahadeva, again with the help of the gods. Thus, all the Pāṇḍava brothers had divine fathers. Intercourse with Mādrī brought about the death of Pāṇḍu, and Mādrī committed ritual suicide on her husband's funeral pyre. Kuntī took the five sons back to the royal court at Hāstinapura. Dhṛtarāṣṭra's intention was to take care of the kingdom until Pāṇḍu's sons grew up, the eldest of the Pāṇḍavas, Yudhiṣṭhira, being the rightful heir to his father's kingdom. He and his brothers were brought up at the court of Dhṛtarāṣṭra, taught by Bhiṣma their great-uncle and by Droṇa the priest and master archer, among others. The five Pāṇḍava brothers excelled at everything. It was during this time that they became friendly with a neighbouring clan, the Vṛṣṇis, of whom Kṛṣṇa was chief.

Duryodhana, the eldest of Dhṛtarāṣṭra's hundred sons, became jealous of the Pāṇḍavas and sought to acquire their inheritance, even conniving to murder his cousins. Dhṛtarāṣṭra tried to conciliate the two sets of cousins by dividing the kingdom into two. Duryodhana, to whom Dhṛtarāṣṭra gave his throne, took the North with Hāstinapura as capital, and Yudhiṣṭhira the South, from Indraprasta, but tensions remained. Attempts at reconciliation were thwarted by Duryodhana and, finally, he engineered games of dice with Yudhiṣṭhira at which the latter lost all – kingdom, wealth, possessions, and the communal wife of the five brothers – because his opponent cheated. As a result, Yudhiṣṭhira had to take his brothers into exile in the forest for twelve years followed by another year during which, if their identities were discovered, they were to submit to a further twelve years of exile. If not discovered, then they could reclaim their share of the kingdom. But when the Pāṇḍavas returned after their long exile, Duryodhana refused to grant them even as much soil as could be held on the point of a needle. The climax was a massive apocalyptic battle between the two sides at the Battle of Kurukṣetra.

Superimposed on, and woven into, this basic plot is a wealth of eclectic material that deals with the years of exile in the forest, encounters with gods and demons, with hermits, friends and foes, warriors, kings, mythological tales, beautiful women, and a veritable history of the universe. Much of it juxtaposes *dharma* and *adharma* and upholds and sheds light on many Indian religious traditions. It certainly seems to uphold the *Laws of Manu* in terms of class duties, stages of life and the established aims of social living. This is an interesting point in that the background to the epic must surely have been challenges to *Brāhmin* authority making it "a religiously energized political response" by *Brāhmins* to the weakening of *Brāhmin* power and status.[26] The *Mahābhārata* does this by including so many tales of the *Vedic* deities, "textual representations of all the gods into a single, compendious whole".[27] Importantly, the *Mahābhārata* reinforced *dharma*, the social order, the role of each within that order, and the nature of what a true *Kṣatriya*, warrior, and true *Brāhmin* should be, but it has none of the black and white clear demarcations of what is right and wrong that characterize the *Rāmāyaṇa*. While the *Mahābhārata* is about *dharma*, good and evil, and is concerned with good *Kṣatriyas* as opposed to evil ones, the nature of the war is horrendously brutal with the good *Kṣatriyas*, even Kṛṣṇa, responsible for many dark acts, what Fitzgerald calls "violent apocalyptic redress".[28] In the eighteen days of the battle, the Pāṇḍavas certainly perpetrated some atrocious deeds in the name of war.

The *Mahābhārata* is sufficiently important to be called the "fifth *Veda*", though it stands firmly in the *smṛti* tradition. Like the *Rāmāyaṇa* it was televised throughout India – even in the West in the late nineteen eighties – and to watch it became an act of worship. Given its incredible length, it was obviously not written as a composite work. Probably beginning as a secular tale, and being passed down orally until it was committed to written form, Arun Kumar Mookerjee makes the important and valid claim for the *Mahābhārata* when he says that: "Bringing together for the people both the archaic and the historical material, it has given every Indian his cultural and historical identity."[29]

The crucial value of the epics is that they bring to the masses the spirit and teachings of religious texts that they were previously unable to read, all of which is transferred from timelessness to historicity and made easily acceptable through story and myth that exemplify *dharma* in existential circumstances. Although far from devoid of priestly orthodoxy, the epics are, in short, the religion of the populace. In both epics, each being – whether god, human, demon, man, woman, forest sage – has his, her or its appropriate nature and own *dharma* dictating how life should be lived, though there are many occasions when ethics are situational rather than prescribed, the war itself being an issue of the use of violence against a general Indian doctrine of non-violence.

The *Bhagavad Gītā*

The *Bhagavad Gītā*, "The Song of the Lord" (*Bhagavad* "Lord" and *Gītā* "Song"), is a superlative text. The "Lord", here, is Kṛṣṇa, traditionally the descent to Earth of one of Hinduism's greatest deities, Viṣṇu. While some of its passages are pertinent only to the time in which it was written, others transcend that time and are applicable to all ages. It is a delightful text that is at the heart of Hinduism and has been adopted in the present as a very popular text in the West and the wider world. It is likely, however, that its popularity in India did not occur until the last two or three centuries of our time. The *Gītā* is one of the texts that has been added into the *Mahābhārata*, intervening when the Pāṇḍavas and Kauravas are poised on the battlefield, ready for war. Arjuna, whose name means "Bright" or "Light", is the hero of the *Gītā* and finds himself incapable of beginning a fratricidal war. Kṛṣṇa offers his advice to the warrior Arjuna after the latter sits down in his chariot and refuses to fight. The great war that is the context of the *Gītā* places the text at a crucial culminating point in the whole of the *Mahābhārata*.[30] Kṛṣṇa's advice encompasses topics vast in breadth and depth – the nature of the self, the nature of God and God's relationship with the world, paths to God, and God's secret to his devotees.

The *Bhagavad Gītā* was written in Sanskrit. As the *Song of the Lord*, it was meant to be sung or recited, and parts, or the whole, learned by heart. It has been described as "a little shrine in a vast temple"[31] and is just a tiny portion, and is not quite like the rest, of the *Mahābhārata*. It is not a mystical text that is only for the initiate, but it does stand out as a part of the *Mahābhārata* that has profound depth, yet not such that precludes its reading by the ordinary individual. Perhaps it is indicative of a more reflective period of time, in that it speaks to a more introspective philosophy than the warmongering of the *Mahābhārata* as a whole, though the rest of the *Mahābhārata*, too, has a good deal of teaching. Many have attempted to weave a course through the pages of the *Gītā* in order to claim it as relevant to their own sectarian views, and there are certainly many ways in which it can be understood, but the *Gītā* is essentially non-sectarian. Alexandre Piatigorsky, in his introduction to van Buitenen's translation of the *Gītā*, claims it as a "*general and universal*" text with wide teaching,[32] and I think this comes close to the nature of the text. The *Gītā* deals with the nature of God and matter, with reality, with morality, with the self, and with the means by which the individual can approach God and become liberated from the endless cycle of rebirths. To find a definitive path in it exclusive of all others is to do the *Gītā* a disservice. However, since the dialogue between Arjuna, the Pāṇḍava hero, and Kṛṣṇa the God is a dynamic one, there is no continuous thread throughout. Rather, themes are repeated in order to be developed, interrupted in order for explanation of a point, or dropped abruptly for a new dimension to be examined.

At the close of each chapter of the *Gītā* is a colophon that describes it as an *Upaniṣad*, indicating that the *Gītā* remains entrenched in, and not divorced from, the *Vedānta*. The *Gītā* reflects a good deal of the *Vedāntic* spirituality and conceptual philosophy. In short, it remains orthodox and has always been accepted as such. Yet, at the same time, it synthesizes ideas of its time, converging all on the supreme Absolute, Brahman, and on Kṛṣṇa as the embodiment of Brahman, melding devotional religion with *Vedāntic* tradition, but not without criticism where it sees that fit. But on many occasions, the text uses material directly taken from the *Upaniṣads* or closely reflects many *Upaniṣadic* passages.

The *Gītā* seems to be astride both *śruti* and *smṛti* literature. It is accorded the nature of *śruti* since it is described as an *Upaniṣad* at the end of each chapter, yet is of the nature of *smṛti* like the *Mahābhārata* in which it is set. The great commentators, Śankara, Ramanuja and Madhva saw the text as *śruti* and not *smṛti*. Both types of scripture are steeped in oral tradition as the favoured means of transmitting the sacred word, but the *Gītā* is not restricted in its readership, unlike the *Vedic* material that is open only to twice-born male Hindus (the top three classes). Such readability is enhanced by the fact that, unlike *śruti* scriptures, the *Gītā*, as the *Mahābhārata*, and the *Rāmāyaṇa*, has a less structured style of language that is closer to the populace of the day than the *Vedic* material, and more suited to narrative content. Then, too, the text accords well with the trend of devotional Hinduism that gained ground during the last few centuries BCE. This was *bhakti*, "loving devotion", to a particular deity, that of the *Gītā* being Kṛṣṇa.

The elitist ritualism of the priests and the aristocracy was far removed from the ordinary person and the lofty speculation of the *Upaniṣads* even more so. Although we have only glimpses of popular religion from early literature, it is not difficult to imagine how receptive the populace would have been to a *personal* God. And this was not a god that was confined to a locality, but one that was cosmic, supreme and yet whose descent to Earth in mortal form made him close, able to be praised, visualized and to whom tangible devotion could be offered. In short, at local levels there was ample space for the development of overt theism to a God such as Kṛṣṇa. By the time of the *Gītā*, *Vedic* ritualism had begun to decline, but religious praxis continued to thrive at the popular level. The advent of the devotional popular literature originated not in *Brāhminical* circles but in the higher echelons of the ruling class of kings, administrators and warriors,[33] but its appeal was to encompass the wider populace. The *Upaniṣads* are Brahman focused and mainly transcend the world, but the *Gītā*, though steeped in *Vedānta*, is very much world involved – as, indeed, is Kṛṣṇa as a character throughout the *Mahābhārata*.

Acceptance of a deity like Kṛṣṇa made manifest a new impetus in religious belief with which the priests must have felt the necessity to accord. Since the *Gītā* accepts so much that is orthodox, especially in its conception of the Absolute, Brahman, it is not so far removed from *Vedāntic* beliefs to necessitate its rejection by orthodox circles. But at the same time, its theism embodied in Kṛṣṇa as God on Earth had immense appeal in the wider society. There is, then, something of a synthesis of ideas in the *Gītā*, but not one that is necessarily an attempt by the author to systematize the material: indeed, contradictions in the text speak only too readily of a lack of systematization throughout. The overall picture is of a harmony of ideas that permits multiple pathways, but which, unfortunately, also permits multiple choices in interpretation and the possibilities of over-emphasizing one pathway and giving lip-service to others.

Theories as to the dating of the *Gītā* vary considerably. It is certainly later than the main classical body of the *Upaniṣads* and seems also to predate most of the early major orthodox schools of Hindu philosophy.[34] A date of the fifth century BCE is accepted by some,[35] with a later demarcation of the second century BCE, which I think is the more probable. It is a certain looseness and flexibility of terminology in the *Gītā* that suggests it is much earlier than most of the philosophical systems as well as an absence of developed ideas of the *avatāra* concept, the "descents" of the deity, or even explicit identification of Kṛṣṇa with Viṣṇu, as was later the case. Some parts seem to reflect Buddhist ideas, which, if they do, certainly suggest a date no earlier than the late fifth century BCE. The author of the *Gītā* is completely unknown, though legend has it that it was the sage Vyāsa who wrote it along with the *Mahābhārata*. The oral traditions that preceded some of it must have stretched back many centuries before its compilation.

I shall leave the content of the *Gītā* to unfold in the companion volume to this book, but what I need to stress here is that it has both a varied nature of God as Absolute and as manifest, and that it has three approaches to God – the path of knowledge (*jñāna*), the path of selfless action (*karma*) and the path of thorough devotion (*bhakti*). It seems to me that the *Gītā* does not uphold any of these pathways as the only means to God, though it certainly posits the path of devotion as the easiest.[36] The universality of the *Gītā* ensures that its content has relevance for all. John Koller points out, rather aptly I think: "The *Gītā*, like most religious texts, is concerned to speak to the condition of the hearer, to reach into the heart as well as the mind, opening it to the divine power and the in-dwelling spiritual life. This the *Gītā* does, speaking to many different kinds of persons of different backgrounds, qualifications, and abilities, assuring them that, though their way may be different from someone else's, it is not therefore wrong."[37] In many ways, the *Gītā* unified disparate beliefs, at times even melding what had been considered separate pathways in the pursuit of *dharma* and liberation, though with its focus as Kṛṣṇa, it became an essential Vaiṣṇava text.

Of crucial importance in the *Gītā* is the well-known statement in 4:7 and 8: "Whenever there is a decline of *dharma*, Bharata, and a rise of *adharma*, then I manifest myself. For the protection of the good and for the destruction of the wicked, for the firm establishment of *dharma* I am born in every epoch." Here we have the germ of the whole concept of the developed doctrine of *avatāras*, so pre-eminent in the Vaiṣṇava tradition and around this statement of Kṛṣṇa is a profound philosophy of the concept of God as both unmanifest and manifest. So precious are the words of the *Gītā* that even today people gather around a visiting holy man in the villages to hear it told. As to the entirety of the epics, John Brockington's remark that "their stories and their characters are integral to every Hindu's consciousness" is particularly pertinent.[38]

Purāṇas

Like the epics, the *Purāṇas* are at the heart of popular religion: indeed, Klaus Klostermaier has commented that: "Reading the *Itihāsa-Puraṇa* one can recognize the character of the Indian people, enlarged, typified, idealized – true in an uncanny sense. The persons described, their wishes and fantasies, their joys and sorrows, their emotions and ideas are much closer to the India of our own time than the venerable age of the books would suggest."[39] The *Purāṇas* are, thus, representative of living Hinduism, containing the breadth of human experience and charming mythology. They are believed to complement the *Vedas* by additional information, the *Vedas* being unchangeable and the *Purāṇas* a more fluid, flexible material. Velcheru Narayana Rao's comment here is most apt: "It is as if the two inseparable components of language – the sound of an utterance and its meaning, the signifier and the signified – have been split apart and located in two separate groups of texts perceived as one unit."[40] *Purāṇic* content is wide and eclectic but contains a good deal of orthodox ideas and instructions on class, life-cycle rites, women, purity and impurity, pilgrimages and general aspects of worship – in short, much that would be applicable to daily life. Some *Purāṇas* like the *Agni* delve into politics and royal administration.

Purāṇas means "tales from the ancient past" or "ancient books", or as an adjective, "old", "ancient". They began as oral traditions, tales told by travelling bards, and their dialogue nature is suggestive of narrator–audience participation.[41] The popularity of the legion of tales in the *Purāṇas* has meant that they have been adapted regionally and presented in regional vernaculars, so that their presence overall is an immense tapestry of traditions. They are set in the traditional times of the four ages or *yugas*, a golden age, the *Kṛta*, followed by three successive, degenerating and unequal eons, the *Tretā*, *Dvāpara* and present *Kali* ages. In popular beliefs the *Purāṇas* are also concerned with many heavens and hells, with Earth acting as the division between the two. Traditionally believed to be of divine origin, divulged to the sage Vyāsa – he who is also said to have edited and compiled the *Vedas* – true authorship of the *Purāṇas* is the result of countless hands. They most likely arose outside the priestly circles and *Veda*, reflecting, as they do, popular beliefs and praxis. They are referred to in *Vedic* texts so a few must have been in circulation from an early date. Others came into being during the first millennium CE, the earliest of these before 400 CE.[42] The *Viṣṇu-purāṇa* is probably one of the earliest and the *Bhāgavata-purāṇa* one of the latest,[43] and they cover a time span of well over half a millennium. Their oral origins make dating precarious, as does the borrowing, intermixing and overlapping from the different traditions in the tales. Freda Matchett describes them rather well as "something fluid, a snapshot of a river of tradition, made up of many tributaries, which might look very different if the shot had been taken further up or downstream".[44] The overriding concept that links them all is a rising theism and devotional praxis. God is brought close to humanity, as deeply involved in creation. God in the *Purāṇas* is not remote but close, compassionate, and offers his grace to individuals. Hindu spiritual tradition is transformed from orthodoxy to warm experience to which ordinary people can relate, all within concrete experience of *dharma*.

While developing outside the priestly realms, the *Purāṇas* were brought into the orthodox fold and adapted by the priests who could use them to convey orthodoxy to the vast populace. Nevertheless, many individual *Purāṇas* have a sectarian bias with worship of one or other of the great Hindu deities amounting to worship of a personal God or Goddess. It is in the *Purāṇas*, then, that we find a wealth of information about individual Gods and Goddesses, some of them expanded tales of the old *Vedic* deities like Agni, the god of fire, but so much about the major Hindu deities of today – Viṣṇu, Śiva and the Mother Goddess. Because of the *Itihāsa-Purāṇa* tradition, it is possible for each individual to have his or her own chosen deity, and it is especially in the *Purāṇas* that manifestations of the deities come to life, even though they are respected as one. The *Padma-purāṇa* puts this clearly: ". . . the form of Śiva and that of Viṣṇu are identical. There is no difference between the glorious two, who are of the same form. (One can) salute Śiva in the form of Viṣṇu, and Viṣṇu in the form of Śiva. Viṣṇu is the heart of Śiva, and Śiva is the heart of Viṣṇu. The three gods Brahmā, Viṣṇu and Śiva are (just) one form. There is no distinction among the three, only the qualitative differences are narrated."[45]

Such identity obtains even though some *Purāṇas* are dedicated to specific deities, but even in this case, other deities are not excluded from such specific texts: indeed, few of the *Purāṇas* are dedicated to just one deity and they are generally eclectic in nature, especially the *Kūrma-purāṇa*. In the sense that *Purāṇa* means "history", the past is recounted but is interwoven with the changeable patterns of popular religious society that have occurred through the years. The result is a fascinating blend, a warp and weft of millennia of ideas.

Eighteen are accepted as great or *māha Purāṇas*, though not being one of the "great" *Purāṇas* is by no means suggestive of inferiority. The *Purāṇas* are expected to contain five topics (*pañcālakṣaṇa*) – the creation of the universe, its dissolution and recreation, genealogies of deities, the progenitors of each new phase of humanity in the different ages of the world, and histories and genealogies of solar and lunar kings and living beings. It is the inclusion of these five themes that differentiates the *Purāṇas* from the epics, though the themes do not in themselves constitute a major part of the content of each *Purāṇa*.[46] They also contain much information on ritual and moral codes, four aims of life, and pilgrimage – topics to which I shall return in later chapters – but the main emphasis is the overt theism that makes them the fundamental scriptures of popular religion. Devotion to God or Goddess is paramount, whether that devotion is focused on images, in temples or in any form of worship. Whereas in earlier orthodox Hinduism worship of goddesses was mainly absent, the *Purāṇas* permit focus on the Mother Goddess and on the consorts of the major deities. Indeed, worship of goddesses had probably always been present at village levels throughout the long history and even pre-history of Hinduism. Such content made the *Purāṇas* popular with women, who had always been precluded from reading the *Veda*. But the *Purāṇas* were equally classless, offering to the lowest class, who also had no access to the *Veda*, accepted pathways to God or Goddess, at the same time being attractive to the higher classes of Hindus.

The *Viṣṇu-purāṇa* tells wonderful tales of the young Kṛṣṇa, the events of his birth, his childhood as a cowherd, his sporting with, and teasing of, the cowherdesses, the *gopīs*, whom he entices with his flute playing, and his identity as the great God Viṣṇu. Here, the *avatāra* doctrine of descents is fully formed. The love of the *gopīs* for Kṛṣṇa was taken up with more passion and intimacy in the later *Bhāgavata-purāṇa*. The *Bhāgavata-purāṇa* is one of the latest of the *purāṇas* dated to about the ninth century CE, though it was written in archaic style to suggest age and authenticity and is a product of South India. It is very close to the hearts and minds of the general populace in India. As a Vaiṣṇava text, it celebrates the life of Kṛṣṇa in a highly emotional way. It is the immense *love* of the *gopīs* for Kṛṣṇa that is the major feature and that is all that is needed; that is the *dharma* to be followed, irrespective of gender, class or low societal standing. Intense love, utter devotion, total surrender to Kṛṣṇa, and pain at separation from him are the hallmarks of this highly popular devotional movement that was the wellspring for all kinds of sectarian devotional developments.

All the colourful myths and tales about the gods and goddesses as well as their appearances and characters are gleaned from the *Purāṇas*. The Hindu concepts of time, the cosmic cycles of the universe and the practices that inform daily cyclical religious and social life are to be found in them. New *Purāṇas* have come into being, especially when a particular caste adopts and even creates a mythology. Such texts are mostly written in Sanskrit and are linked to Vyāsa as author in order to legitimize the upward social rise of the caste. So there are late *Purāṇas* for weavers, goldsmiths, tradesmen, leatherworkers and so on.[47]

Devotional songs and poetry

Arising out of popular *Purāṇas* were a plethora of devotional poetry and songs. These were written in vernaculars and poured out devotion and longing for a personal deity. The process began about 600 CE and extended right up to about 1500 and was part of that whole devotional movement known as *bhakti* that enabled people of all genders and classes to focus on a chosen deity with a worship that came from the heart. Tulsī Dās' *Rāmāyaṇa* in the sixteenth century was one such devotional text that prompted devotional worship to Rāma as a personal God. Many of the authors of devotional songs, or *bhajans*, that became so important in temple worship, were low class or caste, women or even outcastes, though some were from orthodox circles. These beautiful devotional works expressed the writers' intense personal experiences of their chosen God often mystically and erotically.

Two particular groups of such poetical writers were the roaming Āḻvārs, "divers" (into mystical experiences), and the Nāyaṇārs, "leaders", the former being adherents of Viṣṇu and the latter of Śiva. Both arose in the Tamil area of southern India. It is often said of the Āḻvārs of the sixth century that they sang the Buddhists out of India. These poet–saints added vitality to religious scriptures through their own powerful, emotional interpretation and experience of the divine. The epics and *Purāṇas* formed the basis of much of their material but that content was taken to a whole new level with the intensity of joy, love, despair and ecstasy that inspired their followers. The Āḻvārs took up the relationship between Kṛṣṇa and the *gopīs* and infused it with erotic longing for the divine, while the Nāyaṇārs focused on tales and legends of Śiva and the way in which deep mystical inner encounters with the deity could be experienced. Such was the influence of these poet–saints that they crossed both regional and social boundaries. Poetry concerning the intimate relationship between Kṛṣṇa and his favourite *gopī,* Rādhā, inspired devotional literature in the north of India. The *Gīta-Govinda* of the classical poet Jayadeva is one such twelfth-century text. It depicts in erotic words the passion of Rādhā for Kṛṣṇa and the intensity of her longing when they are separated. It is Kṛṣṇa's flute that calls Rādhā, and this symbolizes the intoxicating and enchanting call of God to the soul summoning it out of its existential living to divine bliss.

Āgamas and *Tantras*

Āgama means "scripture" and has come to be indicative of the non-orthodox literature that is non-*Vedic.* Some is Vaiṣṇava, some is Śaiva, and some belong to sects that revere the Mother Goddess, as Śākta. It is this last, relating to the Goddess, which overlaps with what is termed *Tantra.* For some Śaiva sects, it is Śiva who divulges these scriptures to a sage, revealing secrets concerning his nature. This almost makes such *Āgamas śruti.* The *Āgamas* have been important in determining temple ritual and worship, as well as domestic worship and have had far more relevance in ritual and worship in the past and today than the *Vedas.* Being "remembered" by sages, they are considered as *smṛti*, but they can be difficult to understand without the aid of a teacher. Nevertheless, since they focus on a supreme describable God or Goddess to whom worship can be offered, they provide a concrete focus for the worshipper and are less dependent on the *Purāṇas* than other devotional literature. The rituals they prescribe are different from *Vedic* ritualism.

Tantra usually involves some aspect of the female, whether that is the Śākta Goddess or the male–female sexual energy where union of the two in the microcosm of man and woman symbolizes the union of male and female, or unmanifest and manifest, aspects of creation on the macrocosmic level. *Śakti* means "power" or "energy" and in many of the

Tantric sects it is the female energy that is all important, sometimes to the relative exclusion of the male. In Śaiva sects it is the relationship between Śiva and Śākti that is at the heart of theology and ritual. Much Tantric practice involves internalizing the cosmos within the human body particularly through meditation and the use of *mantras*. But the Śaiva *Āgamas* contain Tantric *mantras* also. These are *mantras* that do not necessarily stem from the *Vedas* but are pertinent to the particular sect and are available for any individual of any class, caste or gender to learn from a teacher, a *guru*, providing they are initiated into the respective sect. In this case, it was and is the *gurus* rather than the priests to whom gifts are offered at sacred sites. Some Tantra is monistic in its conception of an Absolute, as in Kashmir Śaivism in the North of India, where reality consists of pure consciousness, contrasted with the dualistic conception of God in the Śaiva Siddhānta of the South that makes human, God and the world separate. Worship of the Mother Goddess, Devī, in the Tantric tradition was relatively late, but reflected what must have been a totally endemic phenomenon in village and urban life well before the advent of Hinduism. This I shall return to when we examine the Indus civilization at the outset of Volume II and some of the important Goddesses will be featured in chapter 6 in the present book. Here, mention needs to be made of the more horrendous Goddesses like Kālī to whom bloody sacrifices need to be offered in order to ward off her terrible aspects. Again, I shall return to such Goddesses in chapter 6. Tantrism appears on the surface to be mysterious and marginal to the rest of Hinduism, but it is well to bear in mind the comment of Dominic Goodall and Harunaga Isaacson: "That these Tantric traditions were not marginal can be seen not just from the huge quantity of textual material that their followers produced, but their influence also in higher echelons of society."[48]

What is important about the vast variety of scriptures in Hinduism is their fluid and accommodating nature. Not having a founder, Hinduism has no one tradition from which springs all others: being such an immense continent, it has so many local variations in language, traditions, local myths of heroes, superstitions, and cultural variations. The evolution of its scriptures has allowed such variations to be accommodated and, indeed, often to travel the length and breadth of the country with changes and adaptations to suit different locales. Mukerji describes such phenomena as "swirls and eddies in a river",[49] which is a rather appropriate analogy of the main river of Hindu ideas that has permitted the incorporation of other streams that have reflected the search for different pathways.

3
Class and Caste
Varṇa and *Jāti*

Since Hinduism has no word that translates as "religion", we would have to look at other concepts that encapsulate for Hindus that which is the heart of their beliefs. *Dharma*, fundamentally "what is right", is one that would suffice, or *sādhāraṇa-dharma*, "universal, common *dharma*". But another that pervades the roots and growth of Hinduism is *varṇa-āśrama-dharma*. *Varṇa* is "class" and *āśrama* "stages of life". Both are sufficiently important concepts – especially the former – to warrant independent treatment in two separate chapters. This chapter will deal with class and caste, which has been the subject of countless anthropological, sociological and political studies in recent years. My purpose here is, however, mainly a religious one, though with the remit of analysing some of the data from other disciplines and field studies that support the religious perspective. When those who know little about Hinduism are asked what they do know, they are likely to respond with the two ideas of many gods and a society based on caste. The nuances of meaning of the first of these will be left to chapter 5. At the outset of this chapter, I want to differentiate between class and caste; the reasons for which will become clear as the chapter proceeds. It is class that I want to explore initially, but first, a few general remarks about class and caste are necessary.

Important initially is the fact that, while class and caste pervade Indian social and religious structures, there are immense regional variations, particularly with castes. A washerman in one region may be higher caste than his counterpart in another region and lower than yet another counterpart somewhere else. In some regions, there is a more relaxed status between classes, but in others, a clear divide between the highest class and the rest.[1] There are four classes, *catur-varṇa*, and thousands of castes that one would expect to fit neatly into the four classes, but this is not so. One reason for such differences is the variations in rules about purity, which in some areas may be more relaxed than in others. Tradition will be the determinant of such diverse praxis. In some cases, as I shall show below, people of exactly the same caste can be antagonistic to others of the *same* caste for what seem to be minute reasons. Variations in observance are endemic. In Sophie Baker's study of caste, for example, she points out: "In the northern Hindi-speaking states such as

Bihar, Uttar Pradesh and Harayana, where there is still great backwardness in rural life, general prevailing poverty and very little upward social mobility, the caste system is at its most strong, the people firmly entrenched in its laws and customs."[2] Bihar, in particular, is notable for its rigid observance of caste. And yet there are some regions of the North where class practices are more relaxed in comparison to rigidity of purity practices in some parts of the South. What is also important to state here is that class and caste – again, the latter in particular – are *active* determinants. While rooted in religious beliefs of the past and religious praxis of the present, they define activity, what groups do and do not do, in a very dynamic way. It is in this way that the many dimensions of Hinduism are revealed – indeed, the "Hinduisms" that I wrote of in chapter 1. Even those not Hindu by race can become Hindu by being adopted into the caste systems.

Class: *Varṇa*

Class is *varṇa* and there are four. I find John Koller's definition of *varṇa* rather apt for defining class in the ancient past as well as what it might be in an ideal world. He writes: "Varṇa is a way of grouping individuals according to their own natures and qualifications so that they might make maximum contribution to the social order while at the same time enhance their prospects for fulfilment and liberation."[3] *Varṇa* means "colour", or even "form", "kind, species". Perhaps, when the lighter-skinned Āryans infiltrated northern India in the ancient past, they differentiated themselves from the darker-skinned indigenous people, but they are likely to have brought with them the idea of an *ārya*, a noble, honourable man, and classified those who were not as barbarians or at best the lowest of their classes. This lowest class were the *Śūdras*, above whom were the *Vaiśyas*, the *Kṣatriyas* and the *Brāhmins*[4] in ascending order. On the other hand, colour may refer to the four colours – white, black, red and yellow – associated with sacrificial ritual.[5] Class, *varṇa*, is very much a religious phenomenon and is classically traditional: the ancient texts all understood *varṇa* to refer to the *catur-varṇa*, the four classes of society. The distribution of tribes and clans in ancient India, alongside the permeating settlers, had much to do with the stratification of society and inter-marriage with aboriginal strands must, at one time, have been endemic, thus obfuscating simplistic distinctions between groups. Agriculture must surely have been a contributive factor in differentiating between landowners, those who leased land, and labourers who were forced to work on the land. But it was the religious ideology attached to such agricultural structures that entrenched millennia of class and caste traditions. Nevertheless, it would be well to note Brian Smith's comment that: "*Varṇa* . . . was a classificatory system which attempted to encompass within it all of the major sectors of the visible and invisible universe."[6] This brings us back to usage of the term *varṇa* as "kind" or "form" and is a reminder that *varṇa* is not limited to the stratification of society.

Early textual evidence

There is scant evidence in the oldest of the *Vedas*, the *Ṛg*, for the four classes. In one place, it says that the *Vedic* god, Indra, "smote the Dasyus, and gave protection to the Āryan colour".[7] The *Dasyus* or *Dāsas* seem to have been the indigenous aboriginal peoples in India and the *Ṛg Veda* suggests in one place that they are "noseless" and slain by the god Agni,[8] probably referring to the flatter-nosed indigenous tribes. Another *Ṛg Vedic* hymn is even more disparaging: "The foolish, faithless, rudely-speaking niggards, without belief or sacrifice or worship – Far far away hath Agni chased the Dasyus, and, in the east, hath turned the godless westward."[9] Elsewhere, they are called a "hostile rabble" with the remit: "let not the lewd approach our holy worship".[10] This last comment is significant in that purity in worship and the protection of religious ritual against impurity lies at the heart of class and caste differentiation of society.[11] Nevertheless, the *Ṛg Veda* has no firm evidence of four classes other than one famous passage with which I shall deal below, but it does seem to have what Ram Sharan Sharma refers to as "slowly emerging social classes in their embryonic stage".[12] But Sharma is one who thinks that *Ṛg Vedic* society was "pre-class" and that there were no sharp class divisions.[13] What seemed to exist in *Ṛg Vedic* India were tribes and clans that prefigured later class divisions.

The *Puruṣa-sūkta*

One hymn of the *Ṛg Veda* became the foundation of the religious rationalization of class and caste divisions in India. The famous *Puruṣa-sūkta* recounts the sacrifice of a primeval being from whom the world and all its phenomena came into being. In verses 1–3 we have:

A thousand heads hath Puruṣa, a thousand feet.
On every side pervading earth he fills a space ten fingers wide.
This Puruṣa is all that hath been and all that is to be;
The Lord of Immortality which waxes greater still by food.
So mighty is his greatness; yea, greater than all this is Puruṣa.
All creatures are one fourth of him, three-fourths eternal life in heaven.

And then the crucial section for our purpose in verses 11–12:

When they divided Puruṣa how many portions did they make?
What do they call his mouth, his arms? What do they call his thighs and feet?
The Brāhman was his mouth, of both his arms was the Rājanya made.
His thighs became the Vaiśya, from his feet the Śūdra was produced.[14]

So we have here the religious origins of the class, and later caste, systems. From the mouth of Puruṣa sprang the priestly class, at the top of a hierarchical structure, the mouth being part of the most important aspect of the body, the head. Coming from the mouth *Brāhmins* are the ones that chant the sacrificial hymns of the *Vedas* that serve to maintain the harmony of the cosmos. From the arms come the *Rājanyas*, more usually called *Kṣatriyas*, and these are the rulers, those who are leaders of men and whose role is to protect society in peace and war, the arms being the medium for carrying and wielding weapons. From the thighs came the common people, the *Vaiśyas*, who were the producers of food and maintainers of productivity and trade. Finally, there are those who emerged from the feet, the *Śūdras*, at the base of society and as the servants of the other three classes.[15] The hymn is late and is likely to have been an interpolation into the text, but it has importance well beyond its appearance in the *Ṛg*, and it is iterated in later texts in such a way that it became a fixed religious foundation for social praxis. It was meant to be an ideal system in that it provided for diversity in an overall unified and interdependent society.

In time, the differentiated four classes were allied with *dharma*. It was the *dharma* of each class to function in a certain way and there was a right *dharma* for each class and the individuals within it. Responsibilities and duties of each class had religious sanction and each individual born into a class was believed to be in the best position to fulfil his or her role in life. *Karma* was linked with class *dharma* in that whatever class one found oneself in that was the result of actions in past lives: the better the previous life or lives lived, the higher the class into which one would be born. This is all well and good for the fortunate in life, but for the masses of impoverished there existed passive acceptance of their lot as a result of what they believed to be adverse *karma* from wrong actions in a previous existence. Past wrong doings were felt to be religious ones in that rites to the gods had been neglected along with class duties. The result was an indoctrination of the Indian mind for millennia. *Varṇa* came to be viewed not as a lifetime condition but as a timeless *dharma* that had to be worked out through many lives. When I said at the beginning of this chapter that *varṇa-* (along with *āśrama-*) *dharma* is what many understand as religion in Hinduism, it will exemplify only too well how deeply class is embedded in the Indian psyche both collectively and individually.

Class in the *Upaniṣads*, *Sūtras* and *Śāstras*

It was the period of the *Vedānta* that developed concepts of a transmigrating self in an interminably long process of *saṃsāra* as a result of good or evil actions in one's past life resulting in positive or negative *karma* respectively. The two concepts of *saṃsāra* and *karma* are concomitant. The *Chāndogya Upaniṣad* makes this clear: "Now, people here whose behaviour is pleasant can expect to enter a pleasant womb, like that of a woman of the Brahmin, the Kṣatriya, or the Vaiśya class. But the people of foul behaviour can expect to enter a foul womb, like that of a dog, a pig, or an outcaste woman."[16] It was a doctrine that was to be taken up again and again by the writers of the *Sūtras* and *Śāstras* and one that rigidified class and caste in religious and social life. Gautama, founder of the Nyāya school of philosophy laid down stringent rules for the duties of each of the classes in his *Gautama Dharma-sūtra*, and all the *Sūtras* and *Śāstras* from the fifth century BCE to the fifth century CE were keen to reiterate the importance of class *dharma* as well as the duties pertaining to the stages of life: these last I shall take up in chapter 4. Class duties became embedded in law. It is likely that the *Chāndogya Upaniṣad* took up the earlier regulations on class from Gautama. It is Gautama, too, who wrote extensively of loss of caste for those who do not follow their class duties. Important to note here is that because one's class – and one's caste – was associated with the extent to which duties had been carried out in former lives, each class carried a different degree of purity and goodness. And it was that degree of purity and goodness that dictated just how much access to the truth of the *Veda* one could have. The lowest class, having little of that purity and goodness could have no access at all. Kenneth Post comments here: "The consequence of loss of access to Veda is uncertainty about right action, and uncertainty about right action means that wrong action is virtually inevitable. Thus, the most important sanction with respect to human behaviour becomes the loss of access to Veda."[17] Concomitant with no access to the *Veda* is an attitude of mind that thinks those with no access are *inherently* evil and thoroughly impure. The sad point here is that there is little will to assist those impoverished outside the purer classes. How an individual looks, speaks, dresses, where he or she lives, in which region or setting, where he or she is placed in the village, what is eaten, what occupation is undertaken – are all results of perception of the *karma* and *saṃsāra* of a class or caste.

Of all the *Sūtras* and *Śāstras* related to class and caste, it is the *Laws of Manu*, *Mānava-dharma-śāstra*, or *Manu-smṛti*, composed somewhere between 200 BCE and the early centuries of the Common Era, which has been pivotal to the entrenching of class and caste regulations in the religious life of every Hindu. Mythologically, Manu was believed to be the progenitor of the human race and his laws are set for all humanity. He took up the *Puruṣa-sūkta* of the *Ṛg Veda* and amplified it into a legal code.[18] But the *Manu-smṛti* is a *Brāhmin* text that seeks to promulgate the supremacy of *Brāhmins*. Consider, then, what Manu had to say about *Brāhmins*:

> The very birth of a priest is the eternal physical form of religion; for he is born for the sake of religion and is fit to become one with ultimate reality. For when a priest is born he is born at the top of the earth, as the lord of all living beings, to guard the treasure of religion. All of this belongs to the priest, whatever there is in the universe; the priest deserves all of this because of his excellence and his high birth.[19]

If this may seem like bizarre aggrandisement forgivable at an early time, it is unfortunate that its sentiments have lasted to the present day albeit not without criticism. What Manu established so well was the idea that class dictated *sva-dharma* for any individual. *Sva-dharma* is "own *dharma*", what is right for an individual within a collective group that has the same *sva-dharma* for its individuals, depending on the class into which one is born. Moreover, Manu seemed to suggest that a person's *sva-bhāva*, "own being" or "own nature", was predetermined:

> And whatever innate activity the Lord yoked each (creature) to at first, that (creature) by himself engaged in that very activity as he was created again and again. Harmful or harmless, gentle or cruel, right or wrong, truthful or lying – the (activity) he gave to each (creature) in creation kept entering it by itself.[20]

Individuals, then, have their own natures that render them suitable to certain beliefs and lifestyles. Were a man to look Āryan and claim to be high class, according to Manu his impurity and lack of class would soon be found out because of the way the man behaves.[21] But despite the apparent predetermination of individual nature, Manu accepted that carrying out class duties enabled one to attain a higher class in the next life. Thus, for a *Śūdra*: "If he is unpolluted, obedient to his superiors, gentle in his speech, without a sense of 'I', and always dependent on the priests and the other (twice-born classes), he attains a superior birth (in the next life).[22] Book 10 of the *Laws of Manu* goes into great detail concerning the kinds of occupations that can be undertaken by each class, but the *Śūdras* are not given the tasks of religious sacrifice or study, unlike the other three classes. Sacrifice was pivotal to religious and social society and essential for maintaining the success and well-being of all. This brings me now to one of the most crucial factors that underpins class and caste in India – purity and impurity.

Purity and impurity

In a nutshell, goodness is pure and evil is impure: the higher the class the greater the purity of the individuals within it. Maintaining that purity necessitates avoiding contact with anything or anyone that is deemed impure otherwise the goodness one has is tainted. Such a notion led to all sorts of class regulations concerning personal hygiene, diet and the avoidance of contact with the dead, with animals and with anyone who has been in contact with impurity. Whatever is pure, it was believed, could so easily be contaminated, but it is food that is particularly contaminating to a *Brāhmin*. Certain people could never offer food to a *Brāhmin* – musicians, doctors, hunters, *Śūdras*, goldsmiths, actors, washermen, carpenters, money-lenders, dyers, criminals, liars, prostitutes, thieves, cruel people – according to the *Laws of Manu*. Food, moreover, has to be of excellent quality, spotless, and particularly kept separate from a dog or a menstruating woman. The kitchen is a sacrosanct place where purity is paramount. Even the *glance* of an impure person could transfer impurity, let alone the touch. Death of a relative renders a whole family impure, even those family members who live at a considerable distance. Should a *Brāhmin* come into contact with impurity, then rigorous steps have to be taken to become pure once again. Baker included the following comment in her field research: "One of the most efficacious means of purification is to drink a mixture of the five products of the cow, a paste of milk, clarified butter, curds and urine bound together with a little dung. Many a hapless member of a traditional Brahmin family has returned from three years studying law or commerce in a European university and consumed a mouthful of this vile mixture before being allowed to embrace his own parents."[23]

Cow urine is still used to sprinkle a house where an outcaste has entered.[24] The following extract from Baker's book illustrates the extent of what I mean by impurity:

> 'Desecration' offers perhaps the most apt analogy of 'pollution'. On a journey through India, one's senses can be continually reviled by the lack of general hygiene – children urinating in the gutters, men defecating along the roadside, piles of discarded rubbish dumped in public places – and the notion of anyone remaining unsullied in such surroundings seems ridiculous. In Patna, where the Ganges flows full and wide, one can observe a man sifting through the charred remains of his father, rinsing the pot of ashes in the murky water, while, alongside, a dhobi will be washing a pile of white dhotis and cotton saris. However, the Ganges is the holiest of rivers, and whatever diseased remains have been dumped there its water is always considered pure and cleansing.[25]

So pure is Ganges water considered to be that it could be conveyed to a *Brāhmin* household without it becoming impure. Certain occupations like those taken from the *Laws of Manu* above are exceptionally polluting, and the fact that a family is involved in such an impure occupation renders them impure from generation to generation.

Dvija "twice-born" Hindus

The *Śūdras*, who are the servants at the bottom of the class hierarchy, are distinguished from the other three classes by the fact that they are not "twice born", or *dvija*. To be born a second time is to pass to a state of purity that overcomes the impurity of being born of a woman: *Śūdras* do not have this privilege.[26] To be *dvija*, a Hindu undertakes a rite by which he (not she) is initiated into the Hindu faith by a teacher, a *guru*, and thereafter is able to study the *Veda* and take part in *Vedic* rituals. I shall deal with these rites in more detail in chapter 9 but here, being twice born is relevant to the degree of purity of an individual or whole class. We have to think here of the concomitance between the sacred and pure scriptures and the proximity to them of classes of people who are in various stages of impurity. Thus, it is obvious that *Brāhmins* are the purest and must keep themselves pure because of their primary access to the *Veda*. At the other end of the scale, the *Śūdras* are considered impure and cannot have access to scriptures *or* to the *Brāhmins* who have access to them. Those who are twice born go through many life-cycle rites, or *saṃskāras*, that are important in maintaining purity at critical stages of life. Again, these I shall return to in chapter 9. Suffice it to say here that the more *saṃskāras* one undertakes, the purer the individual. If a higher-class group does not carry out these *saṃskāras*, then that group becomes more impure. Conversely, the more a group undertakes *saṃskāras*, the purer, the more acceptable, respectable and *Sanskritized* or absorbed into Hinduism it becomes. And in order to maintain purity and keep impurity out, marriage came to be acceptable only within one's class or, more pertinently, caste, as we shall see below. However, the *Laws of Manu* stipulated in minute detail, as we might expect, exactly what *saṃskāras* could be practised by each class and exactly how they could be carried out. The result is a hierarchical structure that is embedded in tradition, with stringent regard for purity, and endogamy.[27] Moreover, just as *Brāhmins* were occupationally bound, the same occurred with the groups below them: men tended to practise the craft or profession of their fathers, of their clans, castes and classes, and Manu had much to stipulate about this, too. Economically, this social structure had its advantages in the interdependence of trades and services. *Vaiśyas* paid taxes and *Śūdras* provided labour.

Another important perspective of class is the distribution of qualities called *guṇas*. Many Hindus believe that everything in the cosmos is composed, in varying degrees, of three qualities: they are *sattva*, *rajas*, and *tamas*. *Sattva* is light, truth, evolution, wisdom, intellect, the kind of qualities that allow one to progress spiritually and to pursue what is right. Its opposite is *tamas*, which is dullness, inertia, the quality that tends to hold one back and that is averse to progress. *Rajas* is the active quality, the one that makes us go out and *do* things. Everything in life is felt to be a combination of these three *guṇas*, but while we have all of them in us and may experience one or another at certain times, one of these *guṇas* will be the dominating characteristic of each person's character, while there will be a less obvious secondary *guṇa*. Applied to the class system, each class is believed to have its own characteristics from the point of view of the *guṇas*. Thus:

Brāhmins	*sattva – rajas*
Kṣatriyas	*rajas – sattva*
Vaiśyas	*rajas – tamas*
Śūdras	*tamas – rajas*

The *Vaiśyas* and the *Śūdras* have no *sattvic guṇa* and would, therefore, not have the kind of qualities that could carry out the pursuit of religious practice typical of a *Brāhmin* who is endowed with so much *sattva*. Similarly, it is only the *Kṣatriya* who has sufficient active energies, combined with the necessary wisdom, to become involved in war or leadership. A *Vaiśya* would have the active energy but not the wisdom to be a warrior leader.

Class in *smṛti* literature

Many of the traditional scriptures support the four-class system, though Yudhiṣṭhira in the *Mahābhārata* was often outspoken against its injustices, and the earliest strand of the *Rāmāyaṇa* hardly mentions the class system, referring more to town and country people.[28] It is the *Bhagavad Gītā* that upholds the class system fully. To begin with, the *Gītā* claims that "No one remains even for a moment without performing action, for all are helplessly made to act by the *guṇas* born of *prakṛti*."[29] *Prakṛti* is "nature" and the verse is suggestive – as the *Gītā* in general accepts – that individual natures are fixed. Most significant are the words of Kṛṣṇa in 4:13 of the *Gītā*: "The fourfold class system has been created by me according to the differentiation of *guṇa* and *karma*."[30] Chapter 18 also delineates the different characteristics of each of the classes, and explains that each individual has to do his own duty.[31] The crucial verse, however, is verse 47: "Better is one's own *dharma* devoid of merits, than the *dharma* of another well performed. Doing duty ordained by his own nature, one incurs no sin."[32] At one point, too, this devotional and universal text says that it is easier for *Brāhmins* and *Kṣatriyas* to reach God than it is for women and the lower classes.[33] One of the reasons in the *Gītā* why Arjuna refuses to fight is that he fears the mixing of classes that will lead to the downfall of the whole of society; "confusion of *varṇa*" he calls it.[34] This is not to say that mixed-class marriage did not occur, but it was certainly socially unacceptable.

So let me bring this section on class up to date. *Brāhmins* have maintained class identity throughout India, whereas distinctions between the other classes and even those classes themselves have blurred or even disappeared. For example, Loius Dumont commented that: "Thus in the south there are scarcely any castes intermediate between Brahmans and Shudras; the warrior castes themselves are considered a part of the Shudras, and scarcely worry about this at all."[35] Julius Lipner makes a similar point: "In Bengal, for instance, there are three main upper castes: the Brahmins, the Baidyas and the Kāyasthas. There may be no dispute about the *varṇa* of the Brahmins, but it is hardly relevant to ask to which *varṇa* the other two castes belong. Some claim that the *Kṣatriya* and *Vaiśya varṇas* are virtually defunct in Bengal; others that the Baidyas are ex-Brahmins and the Kāyasthas are *Śūdras*."[36]

It is caste that is more relevant in today's world and I shall examine it in detail below. At this point, however, some mention needs to be made of the nature of each of the four *varṇas*.

Brāhmins

The word *Brāhmin*, as its form suggests, is associated with Brahman, and that association is in the prayers and ritual utterances that are the *Vedas*. The term conveys the special knowledge that the *Brāhmins* have of Brahman and the power of the sounds they use to reach Brahman and make ritual efficacious. *Brāhmin* comes from the Sanskrit root *bṛh* meaning "to grow great, become great", originally with connotations of prosperity. The *Brāhmins* were Āryans *par excellence*, the purest of beings that could conduct sacrifices and rituals to perfect effect. They came to be more powerful than the *Vedic* gods themselves with exclusive knowledge and secret powers that they handed down from generation to generation in their respective families of priests. The *Brāhmins* were the chief priests, those who oversaw the entire sacrificial rituals, though there were other specialist priests with different functions – *hotris* in charge of the fire, *adhvaryus* of materials and instruments, and *udgātṛs* in charge of the chants. *Brāhmins* who have a teaching role today are known as *paṇḍits*. Family priests are *pūjāris*. The power of the *Brāhmins* and their effect on the whole of society in terms of purity rules was massive. There were, however, some quarters of opposition to such *Brāhminism*, The *Atharva Veda*, for example, frequently mentions oppressors of *Brāhmins*, and a whole hymn of the *Ṛg Veda* likens *Brāhmins* to frogs prating on water, with disparaging names for them: "The music of the Frogs comes forth in concert like cows lowing with their calves beside them." Another part of the hymn says: "When the Frog moistened by the rain springs forward, and Green and Spotty both combine their voices . . . One is Cow-bellow and Goat-bleat the other."[37] In the sixth century BCE greater challenges to *Brāhmins* came from the unorthodox systems of Buddhism, Jainism and the materialist Cārvākas.

The *Laws of Manu* set out careful regulations for the occupations of the *Brāhmins*, "teaching (the *Veda*), reciting (the *Veda*), sacrificing for themselves, sacrificing for others, giving and receiving. But of the six innate activities, three innate activities are his means of livelihood: sacrificing for others, teaching, and receiving gifts from a pure man."[38] These were occupations forbidden for the other twice-born classes. Such occupations were the *dharma* of *Brāhmins*, which was primarily religious. Manu did, however, permit *Brāhmins* to engage in other occupations should that be necessary. Thus, they could become farmers, soldiers, money-lenders or state officers, but never, under any circumstances, domestic servants. The rest of society was obligated to ensure that *Brāhmins* were always respected as those who maintained the religion: they were gods of men and gods of gods. To murder a *Brāhmin* was a cardinal sin.

Apart from their role in *Vedic* ritual, or *yajña*, *Brāhmins* have always been involved in the rituals surrounding life-cycle rites – especially birth, initiation, marriage and death, as well as in the petitions made on the behalf of non-*Brāhmins*. The training of priests for religious roles is extensive even today and since it is a hereditary profession, these days fewer young men take up the religious role of their fathers, so priesthood is not the means of livelihood for the majority. In the past, large numbers of *Brāhmins* were landowners, their lands being the gifts of royal kings and patrons, but their ownership of land is greatly diminished in present times. Those who rely on their traditional profession may be temple priests,[39] domestic priests who officiate for non-*Brāhmins*, and those still dedicated to learning. While *Brāhmins* today may be found as schoolteachers and clerks, for example, they would be loath to take up manual work.[40] Many have gone into the medical profession, though this often renders them impure in the eyes of their families.[41] However, the many *Brāhmins* in the past who lacked the required learning of their class had little option other than taking up agricultural work.[42]

One role that has not changed is the preservation of purity: indeed, Declan Quigley comments rather appropriately in any context of past or present that "the primary function of priests is to cleanse the society of anything which threatens it with death and evil".[43] And preservation of purity involves having no contact with impure individuals, so *Brāhmins*, certainly in villages, separate themselves physically from the rest of the inhabitants. Indeed, those priests who officiate for the lower classes and castes are not usually *Brāhmins*. Clearly, a role of *Brāhmin* superiority in society has traversed the centuries to the present day. Since *Brāhmins* were assured of education, this, too, gave them superiority in society, even if today they may not be economically well off. Such superiority has never been political and temporal, but has remained spiritual. Nevertheless, the services of *Brāhmins* have only been offered to each other and the upper echelons of society but never to those of the lowest classes. The gifts that are given to *Brāhmins* for their services would render the priests impure if they came from impure groups or individuals. Gifts, *dānā*, to *Brāhmins* result in good *karma* for the donor, but are sufficiently dangerous for the recipient for some *Brāhmins* to avoid priestly work.[44] *Brāhmins* are expected, however, to give food leftovers and garment leave-offs to *Śūdras*. Today, the government donates a small income for priests who tend temples.

The *Brāhmins* have been far more versatile than other groups in the occupational field having been less territorially bound. Many have had western education aiding them to move into executive, managerial, legal and professional occupations. However, where this was once the case, attempts to override class injustice have necessitated positive discrimination in favour of the lowest classes and castes in attaining good posts. These days there is considerable discrimination *against Brāhmins* taking up government offices and similar occupations in favour of positive prejudice to low castes.[45] As a result, *Brāhmins* have become more politically conscious and are attempting to assert their rights. In urban areas, class and caste consciousness has been broken down to some extent in the complex workplace, but not so much when the worker returns home and not in the case of marriage. Baker includes the following comment about such double standards of *Brāhmins*:

> Many businessmen will eat meat curries and drink alcoholic beverages in a five-star hotel with a foreign client, particularly if a beneficial deal is about to be made, whereas in their own home they take off their shoes at the threshold, are strict vegetarians, their wives eat at a separate table during their monthly periods and sweepers are only allowed to clean the toilet if there is another servant to wipe over where they have

> walked. Even the most lowly clerk will live a life of double standards – he will ignore all caste taboos in the office, yet on reaching home take off his Western-style clothes, have a ceremonial shower and put on his traditional kurta pyjama outfit, thus reintegrating himself in his own caste.[46]

In contemporary urban India, it would be difficult to identify *Brāhmins* by their occupations. Travelling on buses and trains and an industrialized context of living necessitates avoidance of purity rules. Similarly, in tenement blocks the patterns of living do not always permit separation of caste groups. In the village, it is different: here, the *Brāhmins* are clearly discernible by their separate habitations and minimal contact with other groups.

I have not yet discussed the complex subject of caste, but in relation to *Brāhmins* it is perhaps not as complex as in the other classes. It seems they are well represented throughout India with many individuals claiming to be of the *Brāhmin varṇa*.[47] *Brāhmins* themselves are separated into many, many different castes and these are hierarchized. The highest caste is constituted of those who do not perform temple rituals but who are learned *paṇḍits*. Sometimes their ranking is dependent on the religious sect to which they belong.[48] Any that perform services for *Śūdras*, such as marriages or horoscopes, are considered very low caste or even *Śūdras* themselves. Manu probably entrenched such views and considered the best class of *Brāhmins* to be those who were wealthy enough not to be employed at all, and who, therefore, could devote their time to study. The priests who served high-caste families were next in line, but he seems to have thought less of the temple *Brāhmins* who provided services for the ordinary people, and even less of those who provided cooking, medical services or obtained money through the drawing up of horoscopes. Intermarriage between these *Brāhmin* castes is highly unlikely and there is a good deal of disputation amongst each of them about their status in relation to the other *Brāhmin* groups. One fact is certain and that is that one has to be born a *Brāhmin*; it is impossible to become one. So exclusive is the *Brāhmin* class as a whole that non-*Brāhmins* are regularly classified together by *Brāhmins* as *Śūdras*.

Kṣatriyas

Kṣatriyas, or *Rājanyas*, as they were referred to in the *Puruṣa-sukta* of the *Ṛg Veda*, probably originated as tribal chieftains. They were the warriors who expanded their kingdoms but also were expected to study the *Veda*, to sacrifice and to bestow gifts on the *Brāhmins*. In the late *Vedic* period, they held sway with the *Brāhmins* and probably became somewhat more markedly differentiated from the two lower classes. Whereas the early *Vedic* period does not contain much evidence for class divisions, Sharma thought that it was the Iron Age that introduced more marked differentiation: "When iron tools came to be used for handicrafts, large-scale clearance and field cultivation, conditions were created for the transformation of the tribal, pastoral, egalitarian Vedic society into a full-fledged agricultural and class-divided social order in the sixth century B.C."[49] Those who were responsible for labour were considered inferior to those who were non-labourers so that in the *Brāhmaṇas* there is a clear bifurcation between these two categories of society, *Brāhmins* and

Kṣatriyas being the superior sector. A symbiotic relationship developed between the temporal and political power of the *Kṣatriyas* and the spiritual power of the *Brāhmins*, the latter providing the sacrifices and rituals and enforcing the *dharma* that ensured the prosperity of the former and the former providing the necessary stability and security for the latter. Importantly, the *Kṣatriyas* were expected to maintain family ceremonies, without which, a claim to be a *Kṣatriya* was nullified. This is an important consideration in today's world where purity and impurity still obtain. Nevertheless, there were many times when the two were antagonistic towards each other. Texts like the *Laws of Manu* were profoundly *Brāhmin*, whereas there were *śāstras* that were forcefully *Kṣatriya*. A text like the *Bhagavad Gītā* clearly favours the perfect man as the *Kṣatriya* Arjuna, and it is he that Kṛṣṇa teaches, not a *Brāhmin*. Yet Manu's view was that these two superior classes had to function together: "Rulers do not prosper without priests, and priests do not thrive without rulers; priests and rulers closely united thrive here on earth and in the world beyond."[50]

Who were these *Kṣatriyas* of the ancient past? There were not that many kings or state administrators to constitute a whole class. In an old but interesting book, Ketkar pointed out that *Kṣatriyas* were not an organized body and that any group that became dominant and exacted homage from others could call themselves *Kṣatriyas* providing they accepted the *Brāhmins* and carried out the appropriate religious ceremonies. There seems to be no question of lineage here, if Ketkar's comment is right: "The man who rose, raised his whole family or tribe to Kshatriyahood; but when a tribe failed in strength, the whole tribe suffered in status."[51] War and the need for a fighting force seem in the past to have encouraged rulers to expand the *Kṣatriya varṇa* without any scruples about purity.[52] Such looseness of demarcation seems to be an aspect of modern times with observance of the life-cycle rites associated with twice-born Hindus so minimal as to make *Kṣatriyas* less recognizable. But the *Kṣatriya* lineages live on in the names of their castes.[53] Given this precarious gain and loss of status in the past, it is not surprising that *Kṣatriyas* have to some extent disappeared in the modern world. The *Rajputs* are one group of contemporary Hindus who still claim *Kṣatriya* status but, generally, the *Kṣatriya* class is now blurred in favour of a predominantly caste system. Where some may claim to be *Kṣatriyas*, others will classify them as *Śūdras*, but it would be the maintaining of ritual and support of *Brāhmins* that would bolster any claim to the *Kṣatriya varṇa*. The exception here may be the *Rajputs*: they may be found today in the army or police force and many are landlords, but they are more relaxed about their status. According to Baker "they are far less concerned by the caste conceptions of prayer and beliefs about food. Rajputs are well known for their enjoyment of consumption of all kinds of flesh, especially the wild game which they take great pleasure in hunting."[54] But if they are relaxed about food, Baker notes that the initiation rite in which boys are given the sacred thread is still practised among the *Rajputs*.[55] I shall be exploring this ceremony in chapter 9 on life-cycle rites.

Vaiśyas

Vaiśyas were peasants, commoners, the vast bulk of ordinary people who, the *Laws of Manu* stated, were exclusively expected to trade, tend cattle, cultivate and live from the land, lend money and should take an interest in the values of such things as precious stones and metals, be conversant with other countries and languages, with scales of wages, profit and loss and buying and selling, though they should not actually *make* products or learn a trade; it was *Śūdras* who would do this and work as labourers for *Vaiśyas* and the other classes. *Vaiśyas* were, however, fundamentally traders, the main tax payers in the form of produce, and may have owned their own land. *Brāhmins*, in fact, could take up *Vaiśyas*' occupations if in need; but the reverse could never happen, not even for a *Kṣatriya*. Like the two highest classes, *Vaiśyas* were also twice-born and so could study the *Veda*, sacrifice and give gifts to *Brāhmins*. Yet, given the symbiotic relationship of *Brāhmins* and *Kṣatriyas* in the distant past, it is not difficult to see that the *Vaiśyas* were very much third-class citizens, in the current sense of the term, and distinctions between *Vaiśyas* and *Śūdras* were obfuscated. Indeed, in times of difficulty Manu allowed *Vaiśyas* to take up *Śūdras*' occupations of servile work for the higher classes. This could only result in loss of class and caste status and there was a tendency from about 300 CE for *Vaiśyas* to be spoken of with *Śūdras*. It certainly seems that any status of *Vaiśyas* was gradually deteriorating to the point of a general downgrading simply because there was often so little to differentiate them occupationally and economically from *Śūdras*. In time, except for those *Vaiśyas* who excelled in trade, differentiation tended to vanish unless, of course, the sacred rites were observed. Inter-marriage between *Vaiśyas* and *Śūdras* also served to coalesce the two classes. Today, where there are *Vaiśyas*, they have become castes of businessmen, landowners and money lenders. They are known more often as *Banyas* and are in many ways, as in the distant past, the mainstay of the economy: that was their past *dharma*. Indeed, a versatility gives them what Marriott describes as "occupational breadth, mobility, and flexibility" and "tranquil but energetic commerce".[56] Where they could excel, they did so with vigour and success and Marriott makes the point that they were sufficiently flexible to exploit opportunities that came their way as traders, with a certain independence and self-sufficiency.[57]

Śūdras

The class of *Śūdras* is the most fascinating. Perhaps they were the original inhabitants of India who were added to the Āryan fold as a servile class but there were also Āryans that degenerated into *Śūdras*. Certainly, their aptitudes and natures came to be deemed such that they were outside the twice-born classes. Then, too, aptitudes and functions in society were connected with different occupations and this may have led to hierarchical stratification of the many *Śūdra* castes that arose, especially when tribal groups broke down. Yet Sharma's intensive study of *Śūdras* suggests that in the later *Vedic* period there is no evidence to suggest that some occupations like leather working were deemed objectionable.[58] Parts of the *Atharva Veda* suggest that *Śūdras* were a tribe and Sharma suggested that they may have been a migratory tribe that pre-dated the *Vedic* Āryans.[59] Through all kinds of economic and warring conflicts, particularly dispossession of land, we can say with certainty that a large number of people formed a fourth and much-needed class that supplied labour, especially to landowners. The *Puruṣa-sūkta* is the only evidence for *Śūdras* in the whole of the *Ṛg Veda*, though there is mention of *Dāsas* and *Dasyus*, as we have seen, in some *Vedic* hymns, and these are considered to be the aboriginal element in India. But the *Ṛg Veda* never refers to a class of *Śūdras*. What is clear is that, despite the *Puruṣa-sūkta*, the *Vedas* give us no account of what came to be the fourth of the *varṇas*. It is late in the *Vedic* period and the post-*Vedic* period that *Śūdras* emerged as a serving class.

When they do emerge in the literature, it seems that their tribal status was lost, as was the case with all groups. With no tribal rights, they slipped into economic depression and social disability. They had no right to participate in religious ritual, study the *Veda* (indeed, their presence when the *Veda* was being recited would be contaminating), to be educated or to take up higher occupations than complete servitude. They existed purely to provide servile labour for the upper three classes. The *Dharma-sūtras* tell us that *Śūdras* were to use the garments thrown away by the other *varṇas* and they were certainly exploited in every way by the upper classes. They had to work on land owned by others and had no say in what they were paid. As time went by, they grouped together in guilds and castes and had their own exclusive administrative rules, but there was no protection for them in legal proceedings: abuse of a *Śūdra* by a *Brāhmin* was not considered a crime. And death awaited the *Śūdra* who committed adultery with a woman of the other three classes. Killing a *Śūdra* amounted to the same as killing a flamingo, a duck, a crow, an owl, a frog or a dog and the like. The *Puruṣa-sūkta* was invoked in many of the law books to justify the maintainance of *Śūdras* as a separate servile class from the higher *varṇas* and the laws served to segregate them more and more and to limit their social living. The law books also stipulated that food touched by *Śūdras* is impure and not fit to be eaten.

From the evidence of the *Saṃhitās* other than the *Ṛg* it seems *Śūdras* were included in some religious rituals with the other *varṇa*s,[60] though their ritual was of a diluted kind. While they could never be allowed to forget their lowly status, they could actually use some *Vedic* ritual in propitiation of their own gods. But total exclusion was under way, too, in the late *Vedic* period and it is at this time that *Śūdras* were excluded from the initiation ceremony (*upanayana*) that became the twice-born ceremony that was the prerogative of the upper three classes. Such exclusion meant an exclusion also from any kind of education. It came to be believed that contact with a *Śūdra* rendered sacrifice void. Then, too, sacrifices had to be paid for and the only ones who had the means for this would have been the higher classes: the *Śūdras* were economically and socially unable to live in the same way as the other *varṇas*. The law texts certainly excluded *Śūdras*. Such exclusion had the corollary of a belief that *Śūdras* were evil: if the *Veda* was the epitome of truth and its injunctions followed in order to maintain what is right, *dharma*, without access to the *Veda*, *Śūdras* could only do what was wrong and *adharma*. Yet they were never debarred from listening to devotional *smṛti* literature, though their local dialects may, for many centuries, have precluded their understanding of it. Strictly speaking, of course, *Śūdras* were Āryans and as one of the four classes were distinctly separated from non-Āryans, those who were not divinely originated from the primeval Puruṣa. But because the *Śūdras* were born from the feet, the antipathy of the head, though Āryan, they were differentiated from other classes as impure.

The *Laws of Manu* provide our main evidence for the denigration of *Śūdras*. They never paid taxes, but were expected to provide manual labour and service to the upper *varṇas*, though Manu accepted that they could occasionally become artisans. Permitted occupations for *Śūdras* were those that provided a service for the other *varṇas* – potters, carpenters, medics, garland makers, washermen, dyers, bowl makers, jewellers, goldsmiths, armourers, perfumers, tailors, weavers, metal workers, cloth makers, leather workers. Some *Śūdras* were artists and actors, dancers, tumblers, drum and flute players. Some occupations were represented by guilds and for some *Śūdra* artisans economic stability was fairly good. Some also entered trade, which came to be accepted as an appropriate occupation for *Śūdras*. There is even evidence of *Śūdra* rulers in the Gupta period.[61] And it is likely, too, that some in Gupta times, may have risen to the status of *Vaiśyas* by economic gain and the adoption of important life-cycle rituals. Up to late medieval times, the religious rites permitted for *Śūdras* seem to have expanded and relaxed and the devotional Vaiṣṇava movements made love of God concomitant with complete purification for a *Śūdra*. Nevertheless, the law of *karma* underpinned these more enlightened ideas, suggestive that *Śūdras* were in their appropriate role with a *dharma* of servitude for sins of past lives. For a vast majority of the economically deprived that laboured on the land as agriculturalists, their lot was miserable and many were regarded as being on the same level as untouchables. So there was something of an upward movement for more affluent *Śūdras* to become on a par with *Vaiśyas*, and a downward movement of others to the level of being outside castes. Later in this chapter, I shall explore the notion of untouchables, with which India is so often associated in the western mind. The law books actually make a distinction between *Śūdras* and untouchables, though in practice, the distinction was blurred. Mixed castes, especially, were linked with untouchables, but in the caste structure, which I shall look at shortly, a *Śūdra* caste will differentiate itself from untouchable castes.

Manu's fanatical detestation of the *Śūdras* set out all sorts of horrendous punishments for those that got above their station. Any *Śūdras* working for *Brāhmins* Manu considered as slaves: they were created by God with innate servitude as their nature, unlike members of the other *varṇas*. Manu even stated that a *Śūdra*'s name should be something contemptible. He did not believe that a *Śūdra* should own anything and gave *Brāhmins* the right to seize anything their *Śūdra* slaves had. While *Śūdras* were not slaves *per se*, many were treated and lived as such and were subject to forced labour, but while they often corresponded to slaves they were not regarded so legally, and it would be a mistake, as far as I can see, to use the categories conterminously: slaves were *Śūdras* but *Śūdras* may not be slaves and some owned slaves. Marriage of a twice-born man with a *Śūdra* woman was unthinkable and Manu stated that anyone who explains the law or gives advice to a *Śūdra* will sink to Hell. In all, Manu considered *Śūdras* (and women) to be the very dregs of society.[62] Those *Śūdras* that sank to the level of slavery had no rights at all and could be beaten at will: they were items of property and not human beings. *Śūdra* women were often considered as objects of sensual pleasure for the men of higher classes, and were often nothing more than prostitutes, though they could be taken in marriage by men from higher *varṇas*.

As servants of higher *varṇas*, the *Śūdras* were indispensable. They were domestic servants and quasi-slaves, but mostly agricultural slaves or labourers and were essential for economic growth and production – a traditional labour force, very often with their womenfolk working alongside them. Many of their occupations were stigmatized as degrading: the work of the barber, for example, in removing hair and dirt from the head. As far as *Brāhmins* are concerned, any non-*Brāhmin* is regarded as a *Śūdra*, a fact reflected in early nineteenth century censuses.[63] In contemporary India, the term *Śūdra* has fallen into disuse as have the terms *Kṣatriya* and *Vaiśya*. Of notable *Śūdra* occupations today, weaving is one,[64] especially tie-and-die weaving, which is the traditional mode of producing silk garments.[65] Baker describes with vividness the *Śūdra* area of a village: "There was no drainage system in the village, only ten houses having any form of water closet. Behind the well they had a small latrine but there was no hole, just a tin door to allow a little privacy. Urine was absorbed into the ground, some running into their neighbour's courtyard where it irrigated some tomato and cucumber plants. Normally they relieved themselves in the open fields."[66] The level of pollution to a *Brāhmin* is understandably high. *Śūdras* today are called *Other Backward Classes* (OBC), *Backward Communities* (BC), *Mandal Group* or *Subaltern*, and will be found in countless castes and sub-castes, many with traditional *Śūdra* occupations as carpenters, blacksmiths,[67] weavers, shepherds, potters, and so on. They constitute about forty per cent of the population. *Brāhmins* have traditionally found them antagonistic to their own privileges and have labelled them as untrustworthy, uncouth and prone to alcohol. They could never accept food from these castes. Those unskilled but lucky enough to find employment as servants in the towns and cities have few possessions and sleep on the floor perhaps on the landing of an apartment block.[68] Lipner comments that *Śūdras* "formed a useful category, socially, religiously and psychologically, as scapegoats for a hierarchical-minded, purity-conscious élite. In many ways this rationale obtains even in contemporary Hindu society."[69]

Caste: *Jāti*

I have chosen to separate class and caste in this chapter. While the two terms are often used interchangeably – and there is some evidence that this is acceptable in India today, as well as in some past texts – my view is that *varṇa* is essentially religious and *jāti* a social network with religious undertones but something that is organically innate to a person. To westerners, the caste system of India is known as a point of fact but not with any understanding of it as a working phenomenon. Debjani Ganguly describes caste superbly as "that ubiquitous, befuddling constellation of social practices that has characterized South Asian society for at least three thousand years now, a constellation whose cornerstone is the belief 'human beings are not equal'."[70] I particularly like the connotation of caste being "befuddled", because any attempts to analyse it and make of it a factual theoretical construct can only fail. Caste can be examined in one area only to be found very different in another. Castes can combine, divide, increase and diversify but they can rarely be quantified and written of in tablets of stone. The Commerce Minister in India in 2007 said that there were 4,635 endogamous communities in India: these were 3,990 caste groups and 645 tribes.[71] But the actual number of castes is probably far greater than this. Caste is now at the heart of Hinduism and is a distinguishing feature of any Hindu. Class, *varṇa*, with the exception of *Brāhmins*, has become so blurred as to be virtually extinct. It is caste, *jāti*, which is all-important.

The proliferation of *jātis* and the blurring of classes for all but *Brāhmins* has meant that it is impossible to derive most castes from any one particular class of the four, and individuals themselves would find it difficult if not impossible to give an authentic, as opposed to legendary, history of their caste in relation to class. In any case, most *jātis* are localized. They can fluctuate, consolidate, merge, grow or disappear, but will have some kind of shared custom and ancestor to bind each together. It is, thus, a difficult term to define: perhaps a modern definition is offered in the following with caste being "a familial group that has come to encompass extended family and even those who are associated by business, marriage, political alliance or geographical cohabitation, to form a linked group that claims a shared history or traditional affiliation".[72]

Jāti has many meanings. It can refer to caste but can also mean species like kinds of animals, insects or plants and, specifically, birth. According to Ganguly, it can refer to families, genders, regional groups, nations, creatures that come from eggs, ones that come from wombs, groups of deities and species of demons – the term is very wide.[73] When applied to caste, then, it can mean a very profound differentiation in kind and nature: each caste is "one's own kind". *Jāti* depicts one's origin of birth, a birth that endows an individual with a distinct and inalienable "own being", *sva-bhāva*, something that cannot be changed. The translation of *jāti* as caste derives from the Spanish word "casta" and was used by the Portuguese in the mid-fifteenth century as a rather inadequate translation that sometimes refers to *varṇa* and sometimes to *jāti*. Despite there being thousands of castes, there is such a distinct difference perceived between one caste and another that the whole system is hierarchized but, at the same time, "awesomely complex" as one author describes it.[74] Caste may refer to one particular group[75] or it may refer to a whole collection of related groups: there are also many sub-castes within some castes. Individuals are born into their caste and marry within that caste, maintaining strict membership, possibly exclusive occupations, food traditions, rules that ensure the separation of the group from other groups, and a profound sense of the place of their caste in relation to other castes. Even amongst *Brāhmins* there are hundreds of castes with many factors contributing to the complexity of the divisions and each will have its own hierarchical status that may prohibit contact with certain other *Brāhmin* castes. Ideas of purity and impurity, then, still exist and since animals are caste related, some castes are classified according to whether they are associated with the purer kinds or the impure kinds of animals. A certain division of labour amongst castes obtains but, despite separation, there is also interdependence.

The origins of caste are obscure. Manu certainly refers to castes, perhaps to attempt to incorporate them into the *varṇa* system and to differentiate them for the sake of purity. But castes must have been in evidence well before him, the result, believed Manu, of the inter-marriage between the different classes and the various combinations of progeny possible. The progeny thereof was carefully categorized in the *Dharma-Śāstras*. However, there must have been tribal and clan elements that rigidified into social groups as well as those groups that specialized in certain occupations. Tribes were probably absorbed into the Hindu system and categorized in so far as they accepted *Brāhmin* authority and incorporated the appropriate religious rites. These tribes would have been adopted into the caste system; others were outside it. Concepts of purity and avoidance of impurity were pervasive enough to encourage separation of all the various groups, perhaps the result of the *Brāhmin* ethos spreading through the lower echelons of society.[76] Many groups also claim mythological and legendary roots in order to support their ancestry. Indeed, it was Manu who classified the status of groups socially and ritually, in order that the four *varṇas* – and, of course, the supremacy of the *Brāhmins* – should not be lost. While he blamed mixed marriages for the increased number of castes, he saw all of them subsumed under the four *varṇas*. It was particularly the lowest groups that he sought to identify and separate and the worst of these, "untouchables", he excluded as outside the *varṇa* system.[77]

The relation between *varṇa* and *jāti*, class and caste, then, is a complex one. The four classes are really also *jātis* in that they are "kinds" and partially classified by birth. But I still maintain that *varṇa* has a fundamentally religious and ritualistic foundation, whereas *jāti* has more to do with one's social status in birth and is associated with communities, unlike class. There are claims of some groups to be a specific *jāti* in such-and-such *varṇa* but for others, as stated earlier, it would be futile to inquire to which class they belong. Such distinctions are not consistent and there is much overlapping: I would be over-simplifying the case to say that the division between class and caste is a clear one. Suffice it to say that there are sufficient differences in the nuance of meanings of the terms to maintain some distance between them. Can one change one's caste? Not according to Béteille: he thinks social mobility is easier in the class system and impossible in the caste system.[78] Perhaps this is because the lowest classes have now become so blurred. Land ownership, in particular, is a means of raising one's class. Others, on the contrary, provide evidence of considerable caste change, like that of the northern Nadars of Tamil Nāḍu, who have raised themselves from low-caste toddy-tappers to fairly well off and respectable business people,[79] though they are still called *ShaaNaar*, "toddy-tappers". Others, like the *Śūdra* Yādavas have found themselves able to raise their caste status through political activism.[80] Strictly speaking, if *jātis* arose from admixtures of *varṇas*, every one of the former should have some connection to the latter, though this is not so. But there are all sorts of machinations and spurious histories of some castes to claim affiliation to a high *varṇa* that others may not recognize. If nothing else, such instances are evidence that caste status can change.

Conformity to caste rules has been presented traditionally as the best way to overcome adverse *karma* of past existences. It is still believed that outside one's caste with all its regulations and prescribed patterns of living, the fate for a future life is sealed as a lower state of birth. Caste purity, in particular, is something that is a communal tradition, not an individual one, and cannot be offended. There is solidarity in one's communal caste, along with the relative purity or impurity associated with each caste. But in its hierarchical structure, even the lowest of castes are exclusive and do not fraternize easily with other low castes. The style of life of each caste is different from that of the next and each style has its own status and tradition to uphold: as a general rule, the greater the religious rituals of the caste, the greater the status. Caste nature is maintained by strict endogamy, the punishment for marrying outside one's caste being ostracism from it and all the solidarity and protection it gives. Inevitably, new castes arise based on new occupations in a modern and industrial age but in other instances modern occupations like stonemasonry may cut across a number of castes.[81] And in the village situation, as in the years stretching well back to ancient times, there has to be a certain interdependence of castes in the provision of labour, services and crafts for the whole community, though it is in rural villages, especially, that caste groups remain more rigidly separate both in customs and spatially. The groups – generally, *Brāhmins*, non-*Brāhmins* and outcastes – in the villages live separately. In the large tenements of the city suburbs, families of different castes are forced to live side by side, perhaps five-hundred people sharing one outside tap,[82] making cross-caste interaction unavoidable.

The separation of one caste from another is often the result of a very minor difference in the same occupation, perhaps a simple difference between the way one caste and another does something – a minute difference in the way oil is gathered from the presses, or fishermen who weave nets from right to left as opposed to others who do so from left to right.[83] Natrajan's fieldwork supplies the following comment of a potter in April 1996. Natrajan was conversing with a potter, a *kumhār*, who was asked why he would not marry his daughters with other *kumhārs*. The answer was that the other potters were from a different *samāj*, or cultural community. Although also potters, they use a stick to turn the wheel not their bare hands and so are different and of a different caste.[84] Béteille points out that there is still a physiological difference between upper and lower castes. *Brāhmins* are fairer skinned, sharp-nosed and have refined features, but at the other end of the scale the outcastes are dark-skinned, broad-nosed and shorter than *Brāhmins*. Apart from physiological differences, Béteille suggests that there can be differences in dress, particularly women's dress, or dress colour, though such differentiation today is less pronounced.[85] There would also be differences in speech and even in the choice of names.[86] Ganguly comments that "at the very least, most South Asian Hindu surnames are a sure giveaway of the caste we originate from".[87] Rituals, especially, demarcate one group from another, and as Béteille rightly says: "Rituals serve to express in dramatic form not only the unity within a group, but also the cleavages between different sections of it,"[88] and concomitant with ritual are the purity and impurity regulations concerning food and the necessity to keep ritual and its participants pure.

As far as possible, people in the same caste live together side-by-side in a separate area preferring to have their own spatial framework: indeed, their caste names may be defined by such territories. This cannot always obtain in the towns and cities but still does in the villages. Again, such practice binds a caste community together and reinforces the regulations for its social and religious living. Elsewhere, new opportunities in education mean that individuals can remove themselves from their caste backgrounds to pursue varied occupations, but change in the villages is very, very slow. Nevertheless, it is impossible for a non-*Brāhmin* to take on the functions of a priest, in the same way that a *Brāhmin* would never become a washerman. And a *kumhār*, a potter, is exactly that: no one other than a *kumhār* could become a potter. Land ownership, however small, is a source of status; land labouring is not. In village life there is still the necessity for labour and an interchange of skills and labour. An exception here are the fishing communities like the Mukkuvars of Kanyakumari, who are regarded almost as untouchables but who are independent of landowners' demands, and who regularly come into contact with caste Hindus in selling their produce.[89]

Are there any benefits, then, of the caste system? It would have to be said that the insularity of a caste provides for its members a certain solidarity and protection. It also provides religious diversity with a wealth of local possibilities of approaches to different gods and goddesses within the domains of the caste territory. Here there are ways of religion that depart radically from the *Brāhmin* traditional religious praxis and this is a factor that makes Hinduism overall such a richly diverse mixture of religions under that one term: caste underpins the whole of Hinduism, maintaining an incredible social structure across a vast land. In a way, individual belief is secondary to the corporate existence of a group. Then, too, even amongst different village castes, there has to be a degree of interdependence for the functioning of the whole through providing different commodities or even for the settling of disputes.

But caste is also a repressive and constricting network that has bedded oppression into Indian life. Bithika Mukerji's noble comment that: "Reason is the inalienable right of man to be himself"[90] is counter to a caste system that has no room for individualism and little room for modernization. Indeed, Ganguly describes caste as "the very antithesis of every norm of social existence connoted by the term 'modernity'".[91] Even in the cities, where the old taboos are disappearing, every individual would know his or her caste. For many, caste will dictate all kinds of daily practices that have nothing to do with religion and everything to do with the identity of an individual within his or her group. In village life, sons may follow the occupations and habits of their fathers, who followed those of their fathers before them and endogamy ensures that little can change, though the present young generation is breaking down old taboos. There can often be no dialogue between castes when important environmental changes are needed, yet what is happening in contemporary India is a tendency to fusion for the sake of political gains. It is prudent for castes to unite in order to support political aims that would be to their advantage. But what of those who have no caste at all? I want now to explore that excrescence of human indignity that is the lot of those outside the caste system.

Outcastes

Those outside the caste and class systems constitute 16.77% of the population in India or well over 115 million people. Originally "outcastes", those outside the *varṇa* system term themselves *Dalits* "oppressed" or even "broken", "crushed". Some are *Scheduled Castes* because they are able to claim scheduled benefits from the government: the 2001 census counted 1,225 of such castes. By grouping together into networks they are able to fight for social and political rights. They are also sometimes called *Adi-Dravidas*. Mahatma Gandhi called them *Harijans*, literally, "Sons of Hari" and, therefore, "Children of God", though the term can, unfortunately, also mean "bastards". The usually known term for them is *untouchables*.[92] Legally, the Indian constitution has made discrimination against them or any other Indian citizen illegal, but in practice, it very much exists. Manu classified outcastes as those born to *Śūdra* women, and used *Caṇḍālas*, which is the name of an outcaste group, as the collective term for many outcastes. In Manu's eyes, such outcastes were the most impure of all, comparable to animals like the dog and the pig. Sharma put their origins down to what he called the "cultural lag of the aboriginal tribes, who were mainly hunters and fowlers, in contrast to the members of brāhmaṇical society, who possessed the knowledge of metals and agriculture, and were developing urban life".[93] Such a cultural difference was allied to the contempt of the higher classes for those who did manual work. Evidence from the *Laws of Manu* suggests that untouchability was already extensive in society and was probably in existence in the first millennium BCE,[94] when the equation impurity as equal to oppression already obtained. What is impure was believed to be innate and could only be contained by strict regulations and physical separation.

Manu stipulated that outcaste dwellings had to be outside the village because their occupants are *apapātras*, beings so impure that their touch was highly polluting to a purer being. More specifically, outcaste vessels could never be used by purer beings. The locational separation has existed to the present day, where *Dalits* live outside villages in rural India. According to Manu, they should live near famous trees and those most contaminating of all places, burial grounds. Sharma thought this indicative that these outcastes were originally tribes that lived beyond *Brāhmin* settlements.[95] These outcastes could keep dogs and donkeys, use broken dishes, ornaments of iron and the garments of the dead. They were not permitted into towns and villages at night, but could work in them during the day. Manu seems to have equated those outside the caste system, the *Caṇḍālas*, as *Dasyus*, probably the indigenous aborigines of India that we met earlier. Another term often used for them collectively is *Bāhyas*, those outside the class system, but there is some evidence that the borderline between outcastes and *Śūdras* was blurred. Some became outcastes because their own community expelled them – usually for breaking caste rules.

The religious practices of the *Dalits* are conspicuously different from orthodox religions. Having been forbidden to enter temples where they would pollute sacred space and offend the gods, they turned to their own local folk religions and these days have their own small temples and shrines. Such places of worship have priests drawn from their own ranks to officiate. While they are now permitted in temples, since the ancient ideas of purity and impurity perpetuate, in practice it is still believed that untouchables are polluting to temple premises, to the whole process of worship and to the deities themselves. While not prohibited from the larger temples if they wish to enter, they usually prefer their own. Yet their services are sometimes required at religious festivals, marriages and funerals to beat drums – the leather on the drum surface being a highly impure material.[96] Many in the past turned to Buddhism, Islam, Sikhism, Jainism and Christianity, but this did not change their caste status since such foreign religions anyway were considered outcaste. Caste still obtained within Buddhism and Sikhism and many reconverted to Hinduism in the nineteenth and early twentieth centuries. But mass conversions to other religions have also been recent. Outcastes are sufficiently removed from *Brāhmins* to consider that contact with a *Brāhmin* would bring them bad luck.[97] Outcastes have no religious *dharma* at all: their religion is what they wish to make of it themselves. In the eyes of the *varṇa* Hindus, they are like animals with no merit. Their *karma* has placed them on the level of animals for sins in past lives. Paradoxically, their very impurity means they can perform tasks that maintain the ritual purity of the highest *varṇas*. Dumont described untouchables and *Brāhmins* as "a totality made up of two unequal but complementary parts",[98] which is a very apt way of describing the two poles of impure and pure, yet the mutual need each has for the other.

Of all the outcastes, *Caṇḍālas* are usually considered to be the most impure and the most despised: some ancient texts record that it was a sin to look at one. Even Buddhist texts depict them with gross disparagement. The *Chāndogya Upaniṣad* listed them as below a dog and a pig in terms of rebirth. They have been called "the last refuge of all unwanted people".[99] The law books believed they were the offspring of a *Śūdra* father and a *Brāhmin* mother. But they appear originally to have been aboriginal tribes and like other tribal elements were different and ostracized. Since there are groups who have performed worse jobs in society, Prabhati Mukherjee thinks that they were despised not so much from a purity–impurity criterion as their antagonism to *Brāhmins*.[100] In the past, they had to beat a stick when they entered a town or city so that they could be avoided. They clean streets, are employed at cremation grounds, executed criminals in the past and are considered prone to liking alcohol, garlic and onions (which are *tamasic* foods) and beef-eating, which is anathema to many class Hindus given the sacredness of the cow: *Brāhmins* are usually vegetarian and a *Brāhmin* who eats meat is likely to lose his caste status. In literature and commentaries of the past, *Caṇḍālas* are always portrayed in highly disparaging terms. In contemporary India, they would not be allowed in business premises unless it were to clean lavatories.

Current views of *Dalits* by Indians are that they are untrustworthy, "unthrifty and improvident".[101] The areas inhabited by *Dalits* in rural areas are exceptionally squalid; perhaps a single mud and thatch hut in which a few families live in a general environment of squalor. A well or a single water tap could be used by scores of inhabitants and latrines are absent. Béteille considers their physical appearance to be different from the *varṇa* groups: the familiar darkness of skin, shorter stature and broad-nosed features still obtain,[102] and in his field study in southern India, he found a difference in speech and vocabulary.[103] The local well is a source of rigid fear of impurity and Baker goes as far as to comment that: "There is still probably not one village in the whole of India where the Harijans will use the same well as the upper castes."[104] Baker includes the following very interesting and illuminating comment of a *Dalit* from a market town in Bihar in northern India.

> One feels one's Untouchability most of the time. I've never shared a meal with caste Hindus and I would never draw water from their well. Some of our children do study with theirs but rarely play together after school. My father used to warn me not to let my shadow fall on a Brahmin. I think perhaps in my subconscious I'm careful in the presence of the high castes, certainly not out of respect but perhaps instinctively. We both feel used and abused by them. I would always avoid confrontation because then I wouldn't get the work I needed to sustain my family. I certainly wouldn't go into the house of one unless invited and I've noticed how sometimes they spray water in my path before I enter. It's insulting, but something one gets used to.[105]

Atrocities against outcastes are legion despite government legislation to protect them and there is no shortage of accounts of their humiliation, murder and mutilation. Even in cities of contemporary India, where they have more freedom to move around where they wish, the unskilled workers live usually on the outskirts where they are more safely separated.

It is occupation that has always distinguished between pure and impure groups and the *Dalits* have been associated traditionally with the most menial and degrading of work and with work that brings them into contact with the most polluting substances. The unskilled and uneducated who migrate from the villages to the towns for work live at the edges, both spatially and economically, undertaking menial jobs. The educated and skilled untouchables on the other hand, have become part of the rising middle class. The *Camārs* have always been associated with dead cattle and cowhide; they are the leather workers who may occasionally be employed street sweeping. The low-caste *Paraiyah* actually considers a cobbler to be of a much lower caste than his or her own.[106] *Bhangis* or *Doms* are associated with removal of dead animals, of sewage by cleaning latrines and with sweeping but also with basket-weaving and funeral work. If a *Dalit* enters a house of one of the *varṇas* to clean the lavatory, the floor where the outcaste has walked has to be thoroughly cleaned. Some *Dalits* labour on the land, often at the whim of a landlord. Some women are midwives, since birth is an inauspicious event pervaded by impurity. *Brāhmins* who have become obstetricians are still tainted with coming into contact with gross impurity. Those leather workers who play drums on special occasions are often not paid, but are given leftovers of food from the occasion. In more urban areas, *Dalits* are employed in road building and digging. The majority are agricultural labourers. Weavers, too, have sometimes been classed as untouchables though this is usually an occupation of *Śūdra* castes. Similarly, washermen and barbers may be *Śūdras* in one place and untouchables in others. Washerwomen or men in the villages wash clothes even for the low castes or outcastes.[107] Most of it is done in a river or tank. Incredibly, amongst all the groups of outcastes, the same self-separation occurs through status as is the case with caste Hindus. The following are the words of Viramma, a *Paraiyar* from Karani:

> Just as there are the rich castes, so there are the poor low castes. God gave the land to the rich high castes and he gave the poor low castes the duty of cultivating the land. The duty of the rich high castes is to employ us, us the Palli, the Pariahs, the Kudiyanar. But there are some Kudiyanar who own land, sometimes as much as 12 acres: they don't go and work. Other low castes have their particular trade. They are a little higher than us because they don't eat beef. They eat eggs, vegetables, fish, poultry, they drink milk like you. But meat is unclean, it's waste. Milk is pure. And as we eat waste, we're unclean. That's the difference between low caste and high castes.[108]

These words are a fascinating insight into how caste is viewed by many today; the same purity–impurity rules remaining, the religious roots of caste, and the traditional landowning–labouring division.

Barbers are an interesting group. Their occupation involves a grossly impure act of cutting the hair and removing the dirt from hair and face, as I said earlier. And yet, they have ritual functions in the important life-cycle rites of even the purest of *Brāhmins*. The baby's first haircut, for example, is one of the purifying religious rituals that are essential in twice-born *Brāhmin* families. These days there are barbers' shops, but it is not unusual, still, for the barber to visit the home of a *Brāhmin* to cut his hair or shave his chin.[109] His status will vary in different parts of India, depending on the extent of his functions in a religious role. Shaving armpits and cutting finger and toe nails one would associate with the utmost pollution, but the barber is a religious specialist and therefore has a certain status that renders him more *Śūdra* than outcaste. The village barber and his wife may also be called on to dress a bride and groom at their wedding.[110]

The Constitution of India has never abolished caste, but it has made the notion of outcastes and untouchables illegal. Legal prohibitions, however, have not always served to change attitudes. Nevertheless, there are stringent attempts by both the government and by the *Dalits* themselves to change their situation economically and politically. Some fusion of groups has served to consolidate protest and members of the Scheduled castes now represent the struggle in the Indian Parliament. There are now *Dalit* associations that press for education, local cooperative loans in order to obtain small amounts of land, greater work opportunities and better payment for work. There have been movements to educate *Dalits* for many years, and while the standard of that education is not always good, especially in rural areas, for some, it has meant economic stability. Caste is a huge political issue and whole elections can be fought on the basis of it. Those outside caste are learning to articulate their needs in a very powerful way. The Constitution of India has attempted to provide better education and open up administrative appointments for the Scheduled castes. Thus, new realms of occupation are available for some as teachers, mechanics, politicians and so on. However, consider the words of the same *Paraiyah* woman noted above. Viramma reflects on her status as a *Paraiyah*:

> I'll tell you that I didn't know myself why we're called that. I found out by asking different people. I thought that it was because we aren't civilized, because we don't have beautiful teeth, because we chew betel, we carry our meals in earthenware dishes, because we neglect everything to do with cleanliness and dress. Today our youngsters have caught up in this way. Girls are in nylon saris, boys in terylene shirts, aluminium bowls have replaced earthenware pots . . . We use soap to wash and *sikakai* for our hair. But we'll still be unclean . . Soap does not remove uncleanliness. . . Just because we're a little bit 'decent' now doesn't mean we're going to be allowed into people's houses; and if we touch any utensils in a courtyard or at a well, women still rinse them with loads of water before they pick them up.[111]

Influences of *bhakti*

For all those excluded from the orthodox scriptures – *Śūdras*, outcastes and women – whole waves of devotional beliefs and practices spread throughout India and included the formerly excluded. These waves were of *bhakti*, "loving devotion", to a deity: it was so intense that it was all that was needed in approaching the divine. Having said this, *bhakti* did not entirely disregard caste and gender on the level of praxis. So embedded were the ideas of impurity that total concessions to low-caste and outcaste devotees could by no means exist. Nevertheless, this great emotional movement of devotional religion was championed by poet–saints from the ninth century onwards inspiring the most popular of the *Purāṇas*, the *Bhāgavata-purāṇa*, that epitomized devotion to Kṛṣṇa. The poet–saints used their own vernacular language to take originally Sanskrit religious stories from village to village and from one region to another. They were present at pilgrimage sites and at festivals and it was the ordinary person that they especially attracted. Thomas Hopkins makes a very important point here: "Their popular appeal has reached across sectarian and social lines, challenging fixed ways of thinking and creating new alignments. Though many have been outcastes and Śūdras, they have helped make the Brahmanical synthesis work by constantly revitalizing Hindu religious life and making its highest products available to all."[112] The interesting point here is that the devotional movements were not ones that were solely for the excluded but embraced the more orthodox also. It was in this way that *bhakti* cut across the divisions of class, caste and gender.

The abundance of written devotional works in vernacular languages was inspirational to ordinary individuals in towns and villages, but there were classical texts, too, which supported the approach to God that transcended social distinctions. I have already mentioned the *Bhāgavata-purāṇa* as one of the most important, but the *Bhagavad Gītā* is a Sanskrit text that deals with the theology of devotionalism in its inclusiveness. In beautiful verses from chapter 9, Kṛṣṇa says:

> Whoever offers to me with devotion, a leaf, a flower, fruit, water, that I accept, offered with *bhakti* by the pure-minded.
> Whatever you do, whatever you eat, whatever you offer in sacrifice, whatever you give, whatever *tapas* [austerity] you practise, Kaunteya, do that as an offering to me.
> Thus you shall be liberated from good and evil fruits of the bonds of *karma* . . .
> I am the same to all beings; none is hateful to me, none is dear. But whoever worships me with *bhakti* they are in me and also I am in them.
> Even if a really evil person worships me with exclusive devotion to none else, truly he should be regarded as righteous; indeed, he is rightly resolved.
> Soon he becomes righteous and attains to eternal peace, Kaunteya: know that my devotee does not perish.
> Indeed, Partha, those who take refuge in me, even those of an inferior birth – women, *Vaishyas* and also *Shudras* – they also attain the supreme goal.[113]

The *Gītā* does not condemn *varṇa* by any means: indeed, Kṛṣṇa says that it is he who created the system, and the *Gītā* is keen to point out on many occasions that one's class duty has to be maintained. The point is that those who approach him from the heart with the utmost love are not excluded even though it is traditionally believed that their low birth is the evidence of their past evils – the "really evil person" of the extract. This does not, however, mean that one's *sva-dharma*, one's own personal duty, can be abandoned, any more that it is possible to abandon one's *sva-bhāva*, one's innate and special nature. But, in the *Gītā*, Kṛṣṇa does not preclude any fervent devotee from access to him and to the path of liberation.

The *Bhāgavata-purāṇa* has the same emphasis on the fact that caste is no barrier in devotion to Kṛṣṇa as a descent of Viṣṇu. It is mainly the Vaiṣṇava tradition that sparked these great devotional waves. The greatest of all of the Vaiṣṇava *Āḷvārs*, the poet–saints of the South, was Nammāḷvār, a *Śūdra*, who wrote over a thousand hymns. But the Śaiva traditions also have devotional elements and the cult of the son of Śiva, Gaṇeśa, the God who removes obstacles, is devoid of caste distinctions. Other Śaiva sects such as those that were Tantric were more universal in the initiating of women and *Śūdras*, even children, into their sects. Amongst such devotional sects, *gurus* replaced *Brāhmins* as those to whom loyalty, gifts and devotion were offered. *Gurus* have been a particular phenomenon of the twentieth century and continue to be of massive influence in the third millennium. Their teachings are open to all, irrespective of gender or caste. In more modern times, mention must be made of Mahatma Gandhi's devotionalism as well as his attitude to class and caste. He believed that caste was inimical to spiritual and religious growth. Gandhi was a *Vaiśya*, and brought great distress to his family by flouting the rules of his class. His eldest sister, Ralihat Behen, died at ninety very bitter at having been subject to ostracism and humiliation throughout her life because of her brother.[114] Gandhi himself was temporarily made an outcaste. Yet Gandhi actually supported the *varṇa* system, though he favoured compassion for the poor and outcastes. He wanted not to throw over the class and caste system but to change people's attitudes towards it, and fought hard to get outcastes accepted in temples, public places and at wells. According to an article in *The Guardian* in 1994, Gandhi actually came to accept the necessity of inter-caste marriage.[115]

Contemporary issues

Opposition to class and caste has been political as much as religious. As early as the twelfth century a Śaiva group known as the *Liṅgāyatas* reacted against all superstitious practices including the caste system and, relevant here, condoned marriage between *Brāhmins* and untouchables. Despite their founder being a *Brāhmin* they were fiercely anti-*Brāhmin*. They still exist in India today as a recognizable force against caste distinction. Politically, untouchable groups are realizing that they have strength in numbers and are aware that their degraded position can be changed by such amalgamation. Ram Mohan Roy (1772–1833), would have been pleased to see such fusion that would overcome the divisiveness of caste. Ram Mohan did not think that society could be socially classless but it could strive to be more religiously egalitarian. His founding of the *Brāhmo Samāj* was with the aim of instituting a more rational religious monotheism that could unite all. Its later proponents wanted the abolition of caste, the permitting of inter-caste marriage and inter-commensality. Throwing away the sacred thread for twice-born Hindus was a prerequisite initiation into the *Brāhmo*. It was a notion of universality that brought out tremendous opposition from traditionalists in the form of the *Ārya Samāj*, "Society of Nobles", founded by Dayananda Saraswati (1824–1883), with the aim of reinstalling traditional Hindu beliefs and practices in a rather aggressive way. They sought, too, to bring back into Hinduism those who had left for other religions. In terms of caste and class, they believed, as does tradition, that there are class differences in character and intelligence, but not necessarily birth. While their methods were aggressive, they are renowned for welfare work of all kinds.

In post-modern India, economic changes have meant that caste has had to be relaxed in occupational opportunities. It is no longer impossible for a low-caste individual to rise to a considerable status, though endogamy still exists and entrenches caste distinctions. Wherever possible in the towns people congregate together, live together by caste, and the many caste associations emphasize caste solidarity. Nevertheless, non-*Brāhmins* can be found working in offices alongside *Brāhmins* and such economic changes are beginning to have effect in the villages. Manufacturing in the towns and cities have made commodities less village based and have made available cross-caste employment. Land ownership, especially, has passed from *Brāhmins* to non-*Brahmins* and even, in some cases, to Scheduled castes that have banded together for economic strength: land is now less associated with specific castes. *Brāhmins* have less control and less respect than they had in the past, their power having shifted to non-*Brāhmins*. Whereas they once had a monopoly on education in the Sanskrit texts and then western education, now, education is more widely available to all and that empowers some to rise on a more equal footing with higher-caste individuals. Yet, Béteille warns that while possibilities are there for economic and political positions, caste is still an issue in setting limits of choice in economic advancement.[116] And for the low-caste individual who has been blessed with upward economic advance, there is still some embarrassment about caste. Consider the following words of Mark Juergensmeyer about a successful low-caste man living in a middle class suburb: "This man was quick to inform me that he is quite proud of his caste and cultural background, and supports lower caste religious and political organizations as much as a person in his situation can. But he seems to share the feeling of embarrassment and fear of disclosure that one finds among many lower caste moderns of Model Town, although one of their upper caste colleagues insists that 'everybody knows who and what they are'".[117] Many have to live a double life – intermixing at work with other castes, but slipping into private caste life beyond the working environment.

Politically, the hitherto backward or oppressed classes have realized the strength of fighting for their causes. *Dalits* have their own party, the Bahujan Samāj Party, the BSP. In opposition is the Bharatiya Janata Party, the BJP, which fights for traditional Hindu values, including *varṇa-dharma*, though it claims to remove social injustices. One of the problems of such upward movement of Backward and Scheduled castes through a political government policy of positive discrimination or "reservation" in their favour[118] is that there is a good deal of resentment by higher-caste Indians. Because of the policy of reservation, these latter have less chance of getting jobs despite a sound education and good qualifications. Really speaking, in striving to create social equality for lower castes and *Dalits*, there has to be *inequality* in opportunity: it is now the higher castes that have to fight for equality. Despite a *Dalit*, K. R. Narayanan, reaching the office of Indian President in the last decade, there is a long way to go to address the remaining depth of the iceberg. Especially in the villages, *Dalits* still find themselves in a very weak economic position. Centuries of psychological ingraining of their inferior nature and the superiority of others cannot be overcome in a few decades. And to fight one's cause or just one's corner, an articulate and educated case is needed. Small wonder, then, that the village *Dalit* will still cross to the other side of a street to avoid a *Brāhmin* and will find himself unable or disinclined to be outspoken at a village meeting, even if he were invited. The younger generation is braver and more outspoken, as well as being able to see the advantages of fusion with other castes for political and economic gain. But fusion with other castes and caste politics have led to a desirability of maintaining caste for political gain, so entrenching it further, albeit in a secular rather than religious nature. Thus, Banerjee-Dube points out that "the perception of caste as a religious institution with ritual attributes has given way to conceptualizations of caste in terms of aggressive identities and contesting hierarchies".[119] It remains an interesting anomaly that positive discrimination is bringing about the rise of the lowest castes to the disadvantage of the highest-caste *Brāhmins*.

Caste today in India is understood as "cultural difference". Natrajan, for one, is critical of the term as white-washing the caste system with what seems to be an acceptable term. He challenges the rationalizing of "cultural differences" or "cultural ethnicities" as negatively delineating castes into separate natural groups. In other words, "cultural ethnicity" is a nice way of referring to *jātis*. He calls it the "culturalization of caste" that attempts to make caste a natural phenomenon. He also calls it "differentialist casteism".[120] This seems to suggest that, since caste is so endemic it needs to be turned into a positive and natural phenomenon to be accepted with a certain degree of pride! The term *samāj*, "cultural community", then becomes a euphemism for the negative system of caste. Natrajan thus describes the *samāj* as "a site of contested hegemonies constituted by struggles over the meanings and materiality of caste, group identity and interests".[121] Banerjee-Dube thinks caste is a "muddle". He writes: "The muddle again has been mainly on account of a basic disharmony between a legal order committed to total equality and a social order defined by stratification."[122] Caste may be an anachronism to those who wish to build an open, progressive and secular Indian society, but social protest is a potent tool that encourages caste as a means to an end. Rajni Kothari, for example, argues that caste has been politicized.[123] And yet, traditionalists are now finding that they are forced to form political coalitions with low-caste majority groups.

I began this chapter by pointing out the great regional variations in attitudes to class and caste. In the North, attention is given to divisions between Hindus and Muslims and caste is slower to change, but in the South, the lower castes have changed the political scene dramatically since the nineteen sixties. Universal franchise helped this to come about.[124] More than pertinent here are Varshney's comments: "Weighed down by tradition, lower castes do not give up their caste identities; rather, they 'deconstruct' and 'reinvent' caste history, deploy in politics a readily available and easily mobilized social category ('low caste'), use their numbers to electoral advantage, and fight prejudice and domination politically. It is the upper castes, beneficiaries of the caste system for centuries, that typically wish caste did not exist when a lower caste challenge appears from below."[125] Nevertheless, as Varshney points out, lower-caste politics "has pressed the polity in new directions, and introduced a new colouring of phrases, diction, and styles in politics".[126] In South India, particularly: "Democracy is no longer a gift from above".[127]

The tension between tradition and new socio-political forces in India is bound to persist in the present and well into the future. The blame for millennia of oppression must lie at the foot of the *Brāhmins*, but class differentiation is not to be castigated by those in the West who do not let it pass through their minds. It is easy to see the extremes of it in India, but it is becoming less covert and more obvious in the West, too. We are differentiated in the West by the kinds of places where we shop, our diet, our leisure activities, our types of homes, the education of our children, our peers and social grouping, language, speech and so many cultural characteristics. Our servant culture has been fairly recent in our history, as well as a black/white divide, and we are currently in danger of creating an indigenous/immigrant divide. In India, the divisions are more obvious: in the West, they are much more subtle. But while those divisions in India are more obvious and I have attempted to extract the threads of religious and social hierarchy in the writing of this chapter, it has to be said in the final analysis that the societal matrix of differentiation of status in India is a complex knot of interacting traditions, customs, religious laws, regional preferences and shifting patterns of economic development.

4

Stages of Life

Āśrama-dharma

The previous chapter dealt with the *dharma* of *varṇa*, class, but concomitant with *varṇa-dharma* is *āśrama-dharma*, which is concerned with stages in life. The whole, *varṇa-āśrama-dharma* is how many Hindus might describe their religion even though most of the *āśramas* are barely observed. *Varṇa* and *jāti* dictated the ways in which one could live life according to one's birth and one's nature: the *āśramas*, on the other hand, were prescriptive proximate goals of living that came to relate to various stages in individual life. *Varṇa* and *āśrama* were combined to provide what was right, a particular *dharma*, for each member of society, with *Brāhmins* particularly expected to observe the *āśramas* to a greater extent. Just as there are four *varṇas* so there are four *āśramas* in what became a rather oversimplified and much disputed system to encompass ways in which life should be lived at various ages. The *āśramas* were certainly a *Brāhminical* phenomenon that, alongside *varṇa*, were an institution to be protected by priest and king alike – the former to control religious prerogatives and the latter to control subjects through religious social organization. Nevertheless, such "control" was often theoretical and occasionally contradictory, the parameters of praxis being more flexible and the boundaries blurred.

The four *āśramas* eventually crystallized into first, the life of a celibate student, then that of the householder, the stage of the retired forest dweller and, finally, the mendicant. How this came about was much more complicated than the simplicity of such a definition suggests, as we shall see. The *Bṛhad-āraṇyaka Upaniṣad* saw the process as designed especially for *Brāhmins* for their progress to Brahman. The text speaks of one who is the true, liberated Self:

> He is the one who is beyond hunger and thirst, sorrow and delusion, old age and death. It is when they come to know this self that Brahmins give up the desire for sons, the desire for wealth, and the desire for worlds [the householder stage], and undertake the mendicant life. The desire for sons, after all, is the same as the desire for wealth, and the desire for wealth is the same as the desire for worlds – both are simply desires. Therefore, a Brahmin should stop being a pundit and try to live like a child [the celi-

> bate student stage]. When he has stopped living like a child or a pundit, he becomes like a sage. And when he has stopped living like a sage or the way he was before he became a sage, he becomes a Brahmin [knower of Brahman].[1]

Clearly, it is *Brāhmins* that the text has in mind here and the passage possibly referred to *Brāhmins* who lived in *āśramas* or hermitages and followed a separate religious life from *Brāhmins* elsewhere. *Dharma* texts like that of Manu's extended the concept to a more rigid definition and prescriptive life for each of the stages, but such rigidity was not evident in the earlier phases. We saw in the last chapter that the class and caste of an individual were believed to be dictated by conduct in previous lives, so each life became a stepping stone to progress. The *āśramas* in their fully evolved form provided more proximate stepping stones during each of these existences, but in origin their nature was much more fluid and it is to these origins that I now want to turn.

The *āśramas*

The word *āśrama* comes from the Sanskrit root *śram*, meaning "to make an effort", "exert energy". The same word denotes a hermitage, monastery or dwelling set aside for religious devotion, where it has more the meaning of "halting place", "stopping". Either way, the word is suggestive of spiritual effort necessary for nurturing the individual in the best possible pathways for spiritual evolution. In essence, *āśrama* is a term that was used primarily by *Brāhmins* in an attempt to codify the various characteristic ways of *Brāhmin* life. Later, it was extended to other areas of society. Patrick Olivelle neatly combines the two usages of the term when he says that it referred to "exceptional Brahmins who dedicated their lives in an extraordinary manner to religious exercise (*śrama*), living, in all likelihood, in areas somewhat removed from villages and towns".[2] And for Olivelle, it was a new term, one created in *Brāhmin* circles to depict such spiritual individuals who were probably, at the same time, also householders rather than ascetics.[3] In such communities, the regular, compulsory *Vedic* sacrifices that were the hallmark of *Brāhmin* life were continued, as did married life, the producing of children and study – indeed, the householder was held in the highest esteem given its support of *Vedic* ritual and *Brāhmin* ideology and maintenance. But these *Brāhmins* had removed themselves from mainstream living rather like the respected ancient seers, the *ṛṣis*. Others had adopted celibacy and an ascetic existence.

Of the four traditional *āśramas* – the *brahmacārin*, the celibate student; *gṛhastha* the householder; *vānaprastha*, the forest dweller; and *saṃnyāsin*, the renouncer – the first, third and fourth were all celibate stages. According to Olivelle, there were always four: "The earliest and the only evidence we possess indicates that the system originally included all four institutions. The system did not form through a process of aggregation. It was a theological scheme of four invented by one or more bold theologians and not something that simply came into being through an unconscious historical process."[4] The "bold theologians" were those *Brāhmins* who wished to systematize and legitimize the diversity of living praxis in their *Brāhmin* world. But, essentially, the motivation was originally religious rather than social. It was religious in the sense that it was perceived as *dharma*, especially the *dharma* of a *Brāhmin*. But the traditional *Brāhmin* householder had been challenged by different *Brāhmin* modes of living, and it was these that were brought into the religious fold of *dharma*. Again, Olivelle:

> The *āśrama* system, it appears, sought to bring rival and often mutually exclusive life styles within the orbit of *dharma* by extending the use and meaning of *āśrama*. To call a mode of life an *āśrama*, therefore, was to give that life a theological meaning within the context of *dharma*. It meant more specifically that vedic injunctions provided for such a mode of life and that it was legitimate and as ideal a life style as the primordial *āśrama* of the *ṛśis*. The proponents of the system, in effect, were telling their Brāmaṇical audience that the life of a celibate ascetic or student is as good as the life of a holy householder.[5]

Once associated with religious *dharma*, the way was paved for the four *āśramas* to become an accepted and necessary institution.

The *āśrama* system arose, like so many other new religions, practices, ideologies, and spiritualities, in a time of social turmoil around the middle of the first millennium BCE. A greater division occurred between village and urban existence and the *Brāhmin* superiority came under challenge from all these radical changes. It is Olivelle's belief that the *āśrama* system arose at this time from challenges within *Brāhminism* itself, rather than reaction to the presence of non-*Brāhmin* groups extraneous to Hindu tradition.[6] I do not see why both factors could not have played a significant role in the foundation of the *āśrama* system and, it seems to me, there must have been some attempt to bring rising ascetic praxis into the fold of *Brāhminical* Hinduism albeit in an innovative rather than a conservative and defensive way. Kaelber concurs that there was a deliberate attempt of *Brāhmins* to bring asceticism into the fold of orthodoxy: "Engaged in a grand process of inclusion, the *sūtra* and *śāstra* literature sought to bring at least theoretical order to the multiplicity of ascetic lifestyles present in ancient India as well as to the often conflicting aims and inclinations expressed through those lifestyles."[7] Yet, Olivelle makes the valid point of the division that was occurring between urban and village *Brāhmins* and, at the same time, emphasis that was shifting from worldly goals and religious ritual to liberation from the cycle of births and deaths through celibate renouncing of the world. He thinks it was the urban *Brāhmins* that were responsible for the *āśrama* system in order to incorporate changes in their own perspectives, in particular, the celibate life instead of the householder one.[8] We are reminded here of the words of the *Bṛhad-āraṇyaka Upaniṣad* above, that desire for wealth, sons and worlds should be given up for the mendicant life. As Olivelle says: "In every case the value system of the vedic world is inverted: wilderness over village, celibacy over marriage, economic inactivity over economic productivity, ritual inactivity over ritual performance, instability over stable residence, inner virtue and experience over outward observance. Both in ideology and in life style these reversals represented a radical challenge to the vedic world."[9]

Such radical challenge must have been internal as well as external. Inevitably, there was a tension between on the one hand, the pathway of the householder, the legitimate path of marriage as a means to sacrifice to the gods, bring sons into the world and support ancestors, as well as support and maintain the social order and, on the other, the opposite of these in ascetic praxis that concentrated only on liberation, *mokṣa*. The householder's path was one of action, *karma*, the ascetic's one of knowledge, *jñāna*, and Kaelber is right to say that: "It is this opposition, this conflict, this tension between two soteriological visions and the effort to somehow resolve that opposition, which gave birth to the *āśrama* systems."[10] The *āśrama* system sought to encompass the various aspects of human life into a legitimate scheme, permitting an element of individual choice that was unlike life in the *varṇa* system. Effectually, *dharma* was extended to cater for changes in religious society, and *āśrama-dharma* became central to Hinduism alongside *varṇa-dharma*.

Since the *Bṛhad-āraṇyaka Upaniṣad* is possibly the oldest of the *Upaniṣads*, we can assume that its thought underpins practices of the time that are suggestive of early *āśramas*. A date somewhere in the fifth or fourth centuries BCE is likely for the origins of the *āśramas*. The *Ṛg Veda* does not mention them, though it does mention householders and ascetics and even students, suggestive that each of the *āśramas* was a mode of living well established before being religiously institutionalized. The first reference to the system seems to have been in the early *Dharma-sūtras* of the first four centuries BCE. What is important about such early references is the fact that the *āśramas* were not then *stages* of existence but *alternative* life styles. So we have an *original* system of choice of *āśrama* followed by a *classical* system of four prescriptive *āśramas* in one life – the latter often not without grudging acceptance.

The original system

From the beginning, it is fairly clear that only twice-born Hindus could participate in the *āśrama* system, that is to say, *Brāhmins*, *Kṣatriyas*, and *Vaiśyas*. Kangle notes that in Kauṭilīya's *Artha-śāstra* "the four *āśramas* are represented as four different ways of life to be adopted according to one's aptitude and bent of mind, rather than as successive stages in the life of the same individual".[11] It is clear to see from all that was said in the last chapter about *varṇa* and *jāti* that this kind of attitude to aptitude and individual nature could easily be set alongside *varṇa*. The *Dharma-sūtras* permit choice of lifestyle but as a *permanent* choice for twice-born males. A period of studentship was the forerunner to such choice with the student leaving his home after *Vedic* initiation for that of a teacher, under whose tutelage he would become conversant with the Hindu traditions and with the nature of each of the *āśramas*. These student years in the early *Dharma-sūtras* do not appear to constitute an *āśrama*, the celibate student life choice *after* study being one of the *āśramas*. At the end of his student years, the twice-born male could choose in which *āśrama* he wished to spend the remainder of his life. By giving the student choice, the ascetic and celibate stages were given equal importance with the householder way of life. If Olivelle is right, this is exactly what many progressive *Brāhmins* wanted.[12] There is no suggestion that the appropriateness of each *āśrama* has anything to do with the age of an individual or that the celibate student life should not be taken up as an *āśrama* throughout the whole of an individual's life. However, only one choice could be made.

The positing of celibate and ascetic *āśramas* alongside and equal to the householder way of life must have been anathema to the conservative *Brāhmins* who wished to uphold the established traditions of household sacrifice, study and payment and support of *Brāhmin* priests. Indeed, it was only as a householder that certain important *Vedic* rites could be conducted. Without the householder, traditions were in danger of breaking down, especially since no children would be produced in order to hand down teaching and rituals. There is plenty of evidence in the *sūtras* that the conservative thinkers upheld the importance of marriage and of procreation as *Vedic* injunctions.

The classical system

The classical system of *āśramas*, first formulated by Manu, saw the four of them as ideal stages of life for each twice-born male. The student stage that was the forerunner to choice of *āśramas* itself became the first of the four of them. After this stage, the young adult male passed to the householder stage when he was expected to marry and raise a family. Then, when his social and family commitments had been fulfilled, he was expected to retire to the forest after which, finally, he entered the full renouncer's stage. This is clearly a system that has to do with progressing age and there is a strict order here, unlike the original system when order after the preparatory student stage was not evident. But the classical system was also one that could be incorporated easily into the *varṇa* system. We saw in the last chapter how *karma* from past lives was believed to inform the status of an individual in the present existence, and not just the status but the "own being", or *sva-bhāva*, creating a particular life *dharma*, a *sva-dharma* for each individual. The classical *āśrama* system contributed to such concepts, taking up the nature of the individual and the appropriate style of living for him (not her). Another important aspect is the fact that the householder *āśrama* was critical to the classical system. Removal of choice of *āśrama*, meant that there was no legitimate means of avoiding the second stage: indeed, only one who had completed the second stage could enter the final *āśrama* of renunciation. This was done by a special rite that would make no sense without having been a married householder as will become clear when I examine the nature of each of the stages below. By the time of the *Dharma-śāstras* in the centuries following the Common Era, the classical system of *āśramas* had prevailed as a series of stages, a ladder to liberation to be engaged in during a lifetime and each stage was given much space as to how it should be lived.

The classical system, then, was a progressive one that pertained to age and individual development. Just as it is impossible to return to youth, so it was impossible to return to a previous *āśrama* once that stage had passed. The whole process was a pathway to liberation. Women were not part of this process. Since they could not participate in the first *āśrama*, which was a prerequisite for the other three, there were no means for them to participate. The *āśrama* system was distinctly for males and twice-born males at that: *Śūdras*, like women, were also precluded in both the original and the classical systems. The links with the fourfold class system are obvious here. The *Bhāgavata-purāṇa* contains passages that encapsulate this link:

> From the Person of the cosmic Man, the classes of society (*varṇas*) viz. Brāhmaṇa, Kṣattriya, Vaiśya and Śūdra sprang (respectively) from the mouth, arms, thighs and feet (of the Cosmic Person). And they were severally characterised by their own righteous duties and conduct.

> The order of householder originated from my loins, and that of life-long celibates from my heart, the order of forest-dwelling hermits from my chest and the order of *Sannyāsins* from the crown of my head.
>
> The natures of persons belonging to the different classes and orders of society follow the source of the limbs (of the Cosmic Man) from which they are evolved. The lower the limb (as source of evolution), the lower the nature of activities, the higher the member of the body (as the source), the nobler the activities.[13]

There are so many associative links in these verses, not just between *varṇa* and *āśrama*, but also between either of these and *sva-bhāva*, individual nature, and also *sva-dharma*, individual duty. The whole *varṇa-āśrama-dharma* concept as foundational to Hinduism is clear here. Indeed, initiation into each stage by a rite, a *saṃskāra*, linked the *āśramas* with the life-cycle rites performed by twice-born males from early times.[14]

By the time of Manu's *Śāstra* at the end of the first millennium BCE, the classical system had just about passed to its now-known character from its original form of choice, after a period of five centuries. Indeed, it is this *Śāstra* that provides the first evidence for the classical system. Manu laid down careful duties for each of the stages as he had done with the four *varṇas*, though not in a way to suggest the centrality of the *āśramas* in relation to the *varṇas* or other issues. He does not list them formally, which is suggestive that there may have been competing ideologies and that he did not regard the *āśramas* as critically important.[15] Manu divided human life into four parts though not with any strict delineation of the ages that each should be. There were already traditions about the student stage and the ages that were most appropriate for it to begin and end. But the classical *āśramas* were clearly chronological. Troy Wilson Organ rather neatly describes the rhythm of these four stages: "They constitute a rhythm of inner-direction and outer-direction. The student is inner-directed; his task is to prepare himself for the life ahead. The *grihastha* and the *vanaprastha* are both outer-directed: the former supports the entire society; the latter shares his experiences for the good of all. The *sannyasi* is inner-directed; having contributed to society at least as much as he received, he prepares himself for the final release."[16] Each of the stages was linked with specific life-cycle rites, to which I shall return in chapter 9, and if not thoroughly prescriptive, represented what the ideal man, especially a *Brāhmin*, should undergo. Since rites accompanied the passage from one stage to another it meant that it was impossible to revert once a stage had passed. But we should not think of the classical system as set in tablets of stone. It was an ideal system and there must have been many deviations from it as well as license within it, with subgroups in each of the stages. Yet there were attempts to systematize every aspect of lifestyle in each of the *āśramas*.

The classical system supported *Brāhminism* in a way that the original system of choice did not. Since in the classical system every male had to become a householder, then *Vedic* praxis, and support to *Brāhmins* could not be avoided. *Brāhminical* theorists were more satisfied with that than with the possibility of three quarters of males choosing a celibate existence outside the householder tradition and outside the traditional practices. But the classical *āśrama* system was not so purist that there could not be modifications. The third *āśrama*, for example, could be omitted for those who had paid their debt to society and wished to go straight to the final, renouncer stage.[17] Then, too, there were still those who believed that liberation could come about only by focusing on the *ātman* within, the true Self that is Brahman. To such, worldly concerns and a householder life were unacceptable.[18] Nevertheless, the classical system was religiously based and remained so in the minds of some, though it also became a social phenomenon in determining social living.

Thus we have two systems of *āśramas*, the original with choice and the prescriptive directional stages of the classical one. It is likely that there was no abrupt end to the former but a considerable overlapping of the two for some time. In Olivelle's monumental work on the *āśramas*, he sums up the system by saying that "the strategy of the creators of the original system to use the concept and the term *āśrama* to evaluate the religious status of different ways of life became successful probably beyond their wildest dreams. Not only did the system they designed become a central institution of Brāhmaṇical theology, the very concept of *āśrama* came to define the theologically proper way to live one's life. By the early middle ages, living outside the four recognized *āśramas* came to be regarded as tantamount to living in sin."[19]

Brahmacārin: The celibate student

Whether in the original *āśrama* system or the classical, this *āśrama* was essential in the preservation of the *Vedic* traditions. It is at this stage that the student "preserved the centrality of the Veda in one's existence", making "the Aryan religion a going concern" writes Julius Lipner, who adds also "and, if one wants to be a little cynical, it maintained the authority of the Brahmins who were the guardians of this religion"[20] – a point that is to my mind completely valid. The word *brahmacārin* means "one who is on the path to", "walks the path of" or "applies himself to Brahman". The similar *brahmacarya* means "studentship". Given that the pursuit of Brahman is the goal, the one on this path is expected to be celibate. To become a *brahmacārin* is to begin an important stage of life that is in essence a rebirth: the *brahmacārin* has a second birth into the Hindu religion whereby he (not she) is introduced to the *Veda* and to intensive study of it that is to last throughout life. In the classical *āśramas* it was, and still is, the first stage that is undertaken during adolescence. In the original system, it was the precursor to choice of *āśramas* and could be an *āśrama* for life if the student so chose. In this case, the student would have been instructed in the ways and duties of each of the *āśramas* in order to make an informed choice.

No student could venture on study of the *Veda* without undergoing initiation. I shall leave full discussion of the initiation rite, *upanayana*, until chapter 9, but here it needs to be noted that it represented the passage from childhood to adolescence, from the home of the parents to the home of a teacher, an *ācārya* or *guru*, and a time to take seriously *Vedic* religious traditions, sacrifices, knowledge and duties pertaining to class. The special mark of the initiation rite became the sacred thread, the *yajñopavīta*, which is a cord that passes from the left shoulder across the body and is worn continuously. In the past, this was not a thread but a girdle of grass, a kind of chastity belt and a symbol of celibacy. Since the student was to be a *tapasvin*, one who practised *tapas*, "austerity" (lit. "heat"), the boy would take vows to this end. Depending on *varṇa*, a boy as young as five would go through this rite and leave home to live with a teacher. There, he would serve the teacher in all sorts of ways, and learn. At the end of his studentship, he would take a ritual bath and return to his parents, becoming a *snātaka*, one between *brahmacārya* and the next stage of householder. In the original system, should the adult student wish to spend the rest of his life studying in such a way and continuing to serve his teacher in his teacher's home, then he could choose to do so, but he could not change his mind after deciding which pathway he preferred. Texts vary as to the appropriate age for the child to leave home but the higher the *varṇa* the younger the age and the younger the cut-off age when it would be too late. The *śāstras* that reflect the classical system of *āśramas* mostly give eight years old for *Brāhmins*, eleven for *Kṣatriyas* and twelve for *Vaiśyas*. According to the *Āśvalāyana Gṛhya-sūtra*, for initiation the boy was expected to dress in a new unwashed garment, wear special ornaments (for the ceremony only) and have had his hair partially shaved: *Brāhmins* wore reddish-yellow coloured garments, *Kṣatriyas* light red, and *Vaiśyas* yellow. They also had staffs of different wood and girdles of different materials depending on *varṇa*.[21]

Fire and water are features of the intricate initiation ceremony but perhaps the most poignant part is the point at which the teacher places his hand on the student's heart with the fingers stretching upwards and says: "Into my vow I put my heart; after my mind may thy mind follow; with single-aimed vow do thou rejoice in my speech; may God Brihaspati [heavenly priest of the gods] join thee to me."[22] Traditionally, the *Gāyatrī-Mantra* – a central *mantra* of the *Ṛg Veda* – was recited to the boy. So important is this key *mantra* of the *Ṛg Veda* that the teacher and student are sometimes covered in a white cloth while it is taught to the student in whispers. The period of instruction lasted about twelve years and it is *dharma* that informs the process, the student gaining knowledge in his own *dharmic* duties and the religious rituals that accompany them. But the student was also the teacher's servant, gathering wood for the teacher's sacred fires, begging for his own food and for his teacher's and performing general tasks, perhaps tending cattle or helping in the home. His teacher was to be venerated as his father and as a god. As Thomas Hopkins aptly comments: "Studentship was no casual period of leisurely academic study, but a time of rigorous discipline during which the student learned a way of life: rituals, values, duties, and patterns of behaviour. He was well prepared when he left his teacher to perpetuate both the content and the style of the tradition."[23] While the period of studentship was supposed to be about twelve years, in practice, it was often far less, especially for twice-born non-*Brāhmins*. "Patterns of behaviour" would include how to dress and how to behave, and the student would be utterly forbidden to engage in any kind of frivolity or self-aggrandisement externally or psychologically. The *brahmacārin*'s periods of study were regarded as ascetic discipline, and something that should be retained throughout life regardless of the way in which life was lived. Such austerity necessitated celibacy because the *brahmacārin* was himself in a ritually sacred state in contact with a sacred teacher, and because he was reading, learning, reciting and memorizing sacred scripture. Celibacy was believed to serve the purpose of retaining semen and utilizing it for spiritual purposes.

While the *āśrama* system is embedded in the notion of what it is to be a Hindu, it is barely practised today except by some *Brāhmins*, though the *upanayana* ceremony is often maintained and cherished. Even in the distant past, a period of five months in one year was considered adequate training of the *brahmacārin*. Today, for those who go through the initiation, it is rare for them to leave their homes and reside with their teachers. *Brahmacārya* was always more associated with *Brāhmins* whose livelihood often depended on their knowledge of scriptures, but for *Kṣatriyas* and *Vaiśyas* other occupations meant that there was less need of formal spiritual education. These days, a formal education in school and university – hopefully celibate – is how high-class Hindus view the first *āśrama*.

Gṛhastha: The householder

Marriage and the sacrifices that took place in the home were a *Brāhminical* institution long before any system of *āśramas*. As the mainstay of society, it was and still is, an essential stage of life. At the close of the first *āśrama* of the classical system, before leaving his teacher the now adult male was expected to give his teacher a gift, perhaps a monetary one, or something simple like a parasol and then, after a ritual bath that formally ended his studentship, he returned to his parents. Usually, the parents lost no time in arranging a suitable marriage so that the second *āśrama* was begun as soon as possible, but there is a period between the first and second *āśramas* of the classical system when, strictly speaking, the male is outside the *āśrama* system as a *snātaka*.

The *brahmacārin* as the celibate student was the means by which *Vedic* traditions were learned by twice-born males. But it was the householder, the *gṛhastha* that passed on that tradition from one generation to the next. Without the householder there could be no future generations. Consequently, it was hailed by the majority as the most important of all the *āśramas*. It is the householder that supports the *brahmacārya āśrama*, the sacrifices to the gods, the *Brāhmins* and the mendicants. The *Mahābhārata* endorses it as the highest duty outweighing the other three *āśramas* put together. *Brāhmins*, especially, were expected to pay three debts: one to the ancient seers for the *Veda*, which could be fulfilled by daily study and recitation of the *Vedas*; one as ritual offerings to the gods, fulfilled by performing daily sacrifices, particularly the *homa* sacrifice in the household's permanently maintained sacrificial fire of a married couple; the last as producing sons to provide offerings at funerals and to ancestors.[24] Manu made it clear that these three debts had to be paid before the *Brāhmin* could entertain passing to other *āśramas*. The original *āśrama* system had enabled the householder stage to be missed entirely, rendering the three debts stipulated in the *Vedas* as of little importance in choice. The classical system, however, reinforced the debts and the necessity of the householder state that had been clearly regulated in the *Vedas* as the only lifestyle in which all three debts could be paid. Without the householder, then, there would be a breach of *dharmic* regulations.

As far as the *Vedas* were concerned marriage was essential in order to carry out certain daily sacrifices – mainly five of them to the gods, the ancestors, worldly life, human existence and Brahman – that could not be performed by the unmarried man. In addition there were the sacred fires to maintain by married couples as part of the sacrificial offerings, so the pre-eminence of the married householder was well established: in short, it became the foundation of the other *āśramas*. Its completion in late middle age meant that the two renouncing *āśramas* were relegated to old age in order to give the second *āśrama* full scope. Kangle makes the point that Kauṭilīya in his *Artha-śāstra* said that all transactions begin with marriage,[25] and it is no mean point given that all that on which society depended came from the productivity of the family. While some of the household rituals necessitated the participation of the wife and could not be carried out without her, since women, like *Śūdras*, were excluded from the *āśramas*, their marriage and household status was rarely considered as an *āśrama*. A few sources suggested that *Śūdras* were entitled to consider the householder life as an *āśrama*, with *Brāhmins* expected to undertake all four, *Kṣatriyas* the first three, *Vaiśyas* the householder and hermit stages, leaving *Śūdras* with just the householder stage,[26] but this was one view in fairly fluid attitudes to the *āśramas*.

In the original system, once marriage and the householder *āśrama* had been entered on, no other *āśrama* could be open to the male: since celibacy was paramount for the other three *āśramas*, the choice of *gṛhastha* was a lifetime one and one that was praised as much as the celibate choices. In the classical system, however, the later *āśramas* were expected of a *Brāhmin* after he had fulfilled his obligations as a householder. The *Laws of Manu* heap praise on the householder *āśrama*: "But the householder is said to be the best of all of them, according to the rule of the revealed canon of the Veda, for he supports the other three. Just as all rivers and streams culminate in the ocean, even so people in all stages of life culminate in the householder."[27] Manu certainly saw the necessity of sustaining the householder *āśrama*: "Just as all living creatures depend on air in order to live, so do members of the other stages of life subsist by depending on householders. Since people in the other three stages of life are supported every day by the knowledge and the food of the householder, therefore the householder stage of life is the best."[28] Here, the overlap between *āśrama* and *varṇa* is obvious, the duties of both being circumscribed by one's place in the social order and the particular stage at which one is in life. By the time of Manu's *Dharmaśāstra*, the *āśramas* were expected to be undertaken in due order and the duties of each *āśrama* were meticulously set out.

The religious and social obligations of the householder, though duties, were meant to be enjoyable, to involve pleasure and to be concomitant with social and material well-being. Sons are considered a great blessing for in their turn they support the life of the whole family and ensure the continuation of the religious traditions. But more important than anything else, householders supported the whole of society. In contemporary India, the progression from the first to the second *āśrama* – if, indeed, the first is undertaken at all – is likely to be prolonged until the adult male has gained economic status with a job: only then it may be thought prudent to marry.

Vānaprastha: The forest dweller

The *vānaprastha āśrama* is a stage of retirement with the dweller, *prastha*, leaving home for a life in the forest, *vāna*. Life in the forest is termed *vānaprasthya*. In the original system of *āśramas*, where choice was permitted, the twice-born male could proceed straight to this stage after his initiation period as a student. There was not much to choose between the life of the forest dweller and the full mendicant of the final *āśrama*. Both lived silently and celibately in the original system without a roof over the head or any kind of shelter and with clothes made from the wild. But the forest dweller would be permitted a single fire, unlike the full mendicant. That meant that the *vānaprastha* could still prepare his food, but it was a frugal life devoted to spiritual rather than temporal existence.

In the classical system the forest dweller represented the third *āśrama*, that entered into after the householder stage, but there is little clarity in the ancient texts to establish exactly when this should be and there are so many similarities with the fourth *āśrama* that the third really became obsolete. But Manu devoted a whole chapter to this stage stating that:

> But when a householder sees that he is wrinkled and grey, and (when he sees) the children of his children, then he should take himself to the wilderness. Renouncing all food cultivated in the village and all possessions, he should hand his wife over to his sons and go to the forest – or take her along. Taking with him his sacrificial fire and the fire-implements for the domestic (sacrifice), he should go out from the village to the wilderness and live (there) with his sensory powers restrained.[29]

Clearly, the forest dweller was expected to continue with daily sacrifices but to live an ascetic lifestyle. Divorce from society was not yet total, since the forest dweller was often the source of spiritual advice in what John Koller believed to be "a vital part of the social fabric".[30] The break from family responsibilities is not total since the wife can accompany the *vānaprastha* and they may undertake pilgrimage and still visit temples, so there is a gradual decrease in the involvement with the world in favour of a contemplative existence. It is a progressive detachment when the affairs of the home are handed over to sons and a gradual move towards complete asceticism takes place. Yet Manu expected the *vānaprastha* to wear wet clothes in the winter and expose himself to the heat of fires in the unbearably hot summers – both extremes without any shelter. This may have been a more ultimate aim of the forest dweller rather than an early change of lifestyle. Since Manu saw the second, householder, *āśrama* as pre-eminent and the stage at which the three *Vedic* debts were paid, he seemed to accept that the third *āśrama* could be omitted in order to proceed straight from the second to the fourth stage of renunciation. Further, Manu accepted that once the three debts had been paid, a man could hand over his responsibilities to his eldest son but continue to dwell in his own home.[31] This is, in fact, what many do, remaining at home to give advice when needed. Perhaps this is why the third *āśrama* of *vānaprastha* became almost obsolete.[32] Where it was practised, the third stage acted as a kind of bridge between that of the householder and the final *saṃnyāsin*.

In the third stage today there may be increased involvement in religious life of the temple, in meditative practices and private devotion. Pragmatically speaking, Lipner has perhaps the final word on this *āśrama*: "Human nature being what it is, however, the reality does not always mirror this ideal, the proverbial obstacle to the latter's realisation being the resistance of the mother-in-law to relinquish control over household affairs and the allegiance of her son's affections."[33] Given the prominence of the householder stage, it is inevitable that there are tensions between it and renunciation that is expected to follow. The householder has external goals to follow and the ascetic and renunciation *āśramas* completely different internalized goals. The classical *āśrama* system aimed at balancing the stages of life to create a harmonized life that provided full scope for worldly and spiritual proximate goals with an ultimate goal of final liberation but in practice, many move no further than the householder stage. The *vānaprastha āśrama* was always a nebulous stage that, these days, is more akin to retirement in the same house and environment, if it exists at all. Thus Kaelber's comment is to the point when he says that "it has 'melted into' the householder *āśrama* rather than into that of *saṃnyāsin*".[34]

Saṃnyāsin: The renouncer

Saṃnyāsa, is "abandonment" of life, the "casting away" or renunciation of the world. It was, and still is, a mode of life that has nothing to do with the *āśramas*, having been in the backdrop of Indian life from very ancient times. It is characterized by the practice of austerities or *tapas*, a word meaning "heat", the kind of heat that occurs with intensity of austere practice and discipline. Early *Upaniṣads* recognized this ascetic lifestyle that was separate from the rest of society and could be entered into at any time of life and without any special precursors: thus, even the married householder could become a wandering ascetic, should he so choose. The Buddha was one such man, who left his opulent married life in a palace to become a mendicant. For these renouncers, the term *saṃnyāsa* was not used; in fact, *saṃnyāsa* was a later term used specifically by *Brāhmins* to depict the final *āśrama* of the classical system.[35]

With the formulation of the original *āśrama* system, to become a renouncer, a twice-born male had to have been initiated into studentship and have undergone the long period of instruction in *Vedic* traditions before making the choice to enter *saṃnyāsa*. But, as Olivelle states: "The system clearly did not reflect social reality" since all kinds of individuals, embarked on the path of renunciation, even those who were no longer celibate.[36] While some individuals would have become renouncers at a young age, especially in the original *āśrama* system, it is logical that *saṃnyāsa* would be better associated with old age and with the advent of the classical system that idea had become more formalized. There remained unorthodox individuals who took up the renouncer's path but the *Brāhminical* classical system gave the new term *saṃnyāsa* to orthodox renunciation, and prescribed a formal, ritual role in the normative life of a twice-born male, with emphasis on obedience to *Vedic* injunctions as essential prerequisites.[37] Thus, renunciation became thoroughly Sanskritized. While there were ascetics who were not in the Āryan fold, the aim of *mokṣa* and final release is more likely to have come from within *Brāhminism* itself, just as subsequent regulations and prescriptions for the stage of *saṃnyāsa* were set out by *Brāhmins* in order to keep other ascetic *Brāhmins* firmly in the orthodox fold. Once that happened, *Śūdras* and women were not permitted to be renouncers. Neither had been through the formal training of a twice-born male, but in practice: "There is ample historical evidence, however, to show that Śūdras and low-caste people in general did become ascetics and that their ascetic status was recognized by the civil authority."[38] Although females were generally forbidden to become ascetics, they in fact existed: often widows, they were even used as spies for the court, their wanderings permitting them free access anywhere.[39] Some texts indicate that female high-class widows were also acceptable as ascetics, and that they were praised for their choice,[40] but they were outside the *Brāhminical* system.

In the original *āśrama* system a twice-born male could choose the renouncer's path rather than any other. In the classical system, the householder stage was essential to *saṃnyāsa*. Such was the importance of total renunciation that it was begun by special rites. Since *saṃnyāsa* was *total*, thereafter, there would be no ritual praxis whatever – quite different from the third *āśrama* of the classical system. Final offerings are made to ancestors, the head and beard are shaved and the last ritual bath taken. The central point is the giving up of the fires that were the mainstay of normal daily, occasional and optional ritual. These were permitted and expected for the third *āśrama* of the *vānaprastha*, and were obligatory for the householder. But to give up fire meant that it had to be formerly and formally used at the householder stage, so anyone undertaking the fourth *āśrama* would have to have been a householder. Some texts like the *Artha-śāstra* insist that before becoming a *saṃnyāsin* judges were to decide whether adequate provision had been made for the family. Kangle thinks this may have been in order to check a "fashionable tendency" to leave the householder stage on "the slightest pretext".[41]

The goal of the fourth *āśrama* was the ultimate one of *mokṣa*, final release and liberation from the cycle of rebirth. According to Manu, renunciation is a stage of desirelessness that brings about *nivṛtta*, "dissolution" of the self and its involvement with the world that results in liberation – quite the opposite of the *pravṛtta* of necessary desire-filled involvement with the world of the householder. Society cannot exist without the latter and neither could *dharmic* order be maintained at the worldly and cosmic levels, but with the classical system, both can be accommodated. Nevertheless, if the three debts have not been paid, in Manu's view, *mokṣa* cannot be realized.[42] Because the focus is totally on liberation, the *saṃnyāsin* is alone: all ties with family are now broken. The special fire ceremony marks the occasion, though it is described variously in the texts. In this, all the ritual implements for the sacrificial rites are abandoned after the last fire ceremony. Sacrifice is internalized in the breaths of his own body, so there is no need of fire. After a last sacrifice in the fire, the renouncer extinguishes it. Henceforth, any worldly and ritual possessions are abandoned, celibacy is absolute and vows of truthfulness and non-injury to any creature are taken.

Early usage of the term *saṃnyāsa* actually referred to this abandonment of fire.[43] The tensions between the important householder stage and that of ascetic renunciation I have emphasized above and are reflected in the inconsistent prescriptions for the *saṃnyāsin* in texts that deal with them.[44] There are inconsistencies particularly in terms of what should or should not be given up in the process of initiation into the classical fourth stage. What is mainly expected is that the sacred thread that is the mark of the twice-born male is given up and offered to the gods in the last fire that the *saṃnyāsin* will ever light. He is permitted to wear a loincloth, an ochre garment and sandals, and to carry a begging bowl with which he can beg food once a day, a staff and a water jar. Meditative practices accompany his solitary life with an emphasis on *vairāgya*, restraint. *Dharma* does not obtain at all other than concentration on the final goal and preparation for death, so the *saṃnyāsin* is casteless and without any ritual status. In renouncing the world, the *saṃnyāsin* renounced all *dharmas* since even desire to fulfil one's *dharma*, to perform sacrifice, to maintain laws of purity, and the like, are to *act* in a positive way but, nevertheless, to accrue *karma*, albeit positive *karma*, and necessitate its results in a future life. The *saṃnyāsin*, however, should have no desires and should reap no *karma*. It is the householder that supports such mendicants in supplying food, the rest of their diet being the roots, plants and fruits of the forest. The *Laws of Manu* delineate the life and attitude that should accompany the *saṃnyāsin*:

> He should not welcome dying, nor should he welcome living, but wait for the right time as a servant waits for orders. He should set down his foot on a place purified by his gaze, drink water purified by a straining cloth, speak words purified by truth, and act in ways purified by mind-and-heart. He should endure hard words and never despise anyone, not become anyone's enemy for the sake of this body. He should not respond with anger against someone who is angry, but speak a blessing when he is threatened; nor should he speak untruthful words shed at the seven gates. He should live here on earth seated in ecstatic contemplation of the soul, indifferent, without any carnal desires, with the soul as his only companion and happiness as his goal.[45]

No longer permitted to maintain his sacred fires, the *saṃnyāsin* cannot cook his food, cooked food being synonymous with the trappings of a worldly life, nor should he stay more than one night in any place, except in the rainy season. The renouncer does not become an individual either:[46] individuality is the result of desire and egoistic thought and the *saṃnyāsin* is expected to transcend such thought – he should not desire to die any more than he should desire to live, as the *Laws of Manu* stated above. Indeed, renunciation according to Manu is synonymous with *mokṣa* and the term *mokṣa-āśrama* used by Manu is suggestive of a state in which individuality in the form of egoistic thought of any kind must be absent. The *saṃnyāsin* is regarded as having died in life. When he dies biologically, no funeral rites are performed to mark his passing. Burial rather than cremation is likely to be the case, since having divorced himself from his family there is no one to perform the usual funeral rites, though his family will regularly perform memorial rites from the time of his initiation into *saṃnyāsa*. In short, there was no return for the *saṃnyāsin*; those who attempted to return were treated as the worst of untouchables.

While ascetic renunciation was not confined to how *Brāhminical* Hindus would have wanted it, it did become more of an expected tradition of *Brāhmins* than others. Olivelle thinks this was the case by the fourth or fifth centuries CE and by the eighth and ninth centuries it seems the fourth *āśrama* was believed to be applicable only for *Brāhmin* males.[47] And in that time, too, as in contemporary life, the fourth *āśrama* became much modified. Despite *Brāhminical* objections, monasteries, *maṭhas*, became institutions in which *saṃnyāsins* retired to live a contemplative and spiritual life. These were almost exclusively *Brāhmin* and with gifts of land and generous donations became powerful economic forces.[48] Those who enter the fourth or even the third *āśrama* today are exceptionally rare, even if it is into a monastery as opposed to being a wandering mendicant. While there may be some change in lifestyle – a slowing down and a more reflective mode of living – few would want to leave home and society for the rigours of ascetic life. Thus, the *āśrama* system remains something of an ideal rather than what is now practised. There must have been many deviations from the classical system of four *āśramas*. In the ideal system, the twice-born male traversed a circuitous pathway from celibate young student devoted to study of the *Vedas* to celibate old man, devoted to the internalizing of that study. In Hopkins' words: "Having passed through life in the world and performed his duties to society, the *saṃnyāsin* was reinitiated into the celibate state of *brahmacārya*, and became again like a child, and sought to regain the identity with Brahman that was his true permanent condition."[49]

So how much of a gap was there between theory and praxis? It would seem that, typically of Hinduism, attempts at systematizing were not suited to the word in practice and Kaelber's point is sound: "It is important to realize that the classical system, like its predecessor, was a diligently crafted and evidently theoretical formulation. The system embodied normative prescription rather than social fact. It struggled to present a neat comprehensible, and acceptable sequence, a montage of goals, lifestyles, and practices that often defied the efforts of system-seeking priests."[50] Perhaps this is why *āśrama-dharma* remains an important *concept* in Hinduism, but not one much practised.

Puruṣārthas

Puruṣārtha, meaning a person's (*puruṣa*) aim or goal (*artha*) is a term used to depict fundamental goals of human existence. There are four of them, just as there are four *varṇas* and four *āśramas*, but the *puruṣārthas*, unlike the first two, are a separate concept: even though there is much to link them with the *āśramas* in particular, that link is spurious. The *puruṣārthas* are to be found in many of the *Dharma-śāstras* and certainly in the *Mahābhārata* as the norms that should inform social living. Originally, there were three of them, *tri-varga*, *artha*, which is wealth, *kāma*, which is enjoyment and pleasure, and *dharma*, what is right. A fourth, *mokṣa*, liberation or release, was added later constituting the *catur-varga*, "four goods", or, with Organ, four "means by which one becomes a full man".[51] I am placing them here in this chapter alongside the *āśramas* since they are proximate goals for life, as are the *āśramas*, but the link between the two is an artificial one – endemic among writers – and one that it would be erroneous for the reader to maintain as fact. It is probably because the first three *puruṣārthas* are best placed for fulfilment in the *āśrama* of the householder that the link between the two has been cemented and because, as I have done here, placing the *puruṣārthas* in the context of the *āśramas* is rather appropriate. Attempts to match each of the *puruṣārthas* with each of the *āśramas* is, however, nonsensical and the ancient texts are silent on any such an association. The *puruṣārthas* came into being in the few centuries before the Common Era, and Hartmut Scharfe dates their first combined appearance in a *Gṛhya-sūtra* of about the third or second centuries BCE.[52] I have placed them in the order *artha*, *kāma*, *dharma* with *mokṣa* logically last in view of its being added later and its ultimacy, but the order of the first three is varied in the old texts.

Lipner thinks that the first three may have been originally associated with sacrificial ritual, *artha* being the wealth and means by which the whole sacrificial system was financed, *kāma* being the satisfaction that could be gained through good results of the sacrifices, and *dharma* the *karmic* merit for individuals and society through the correct conducting of the ritual.[53] In time, however, if this was the original meaning, it was one that was lost to more temporal social living that depicted a balanced life and what the aims of life should be.

Artha: Wealth

In Kauṭilīya's *Artha-śāstra*, *artha* is defined as "the sustenance or livelihood of men".[54] It was one of the *tri-varga* from early times and it came to mean, and to be the aim of, acquiring material possessions, wealth, success, food, a home and physical well-being. It could refer to one's home, one's profession, one's status in life, power, fame, the goods one can amass and the family one has, and was a more individualistic goal than other prescriptive social regulations. *Artha* also includes commerce and agriculture, jurisprudence and polity and the kinds of actions and attitudes that bring about wealth and success. *Artha* is an old word that can mean "wealth" or "worldly goal" or just "goal". In the *Ṛg Veda* it means the goal at the end of a journey or the outcome of an enterprise and "matter" or "objective", "matter in hand".[55] It is clear here how easy it is to associate *artha* with the second of the *āśramas*, the householder stage. Dandekar was of the opinion that *artha* is concerned with ends irrespective of the means that were used to achieve those ends.[56] There is ample evidence of this in the warfare of the *Mahābhārata* where seemingly unethical methods are used to achieve victory in what can only be described as grossly unfair praxis. Given that the *Artha-śāstra* was focused mainly on the monarch, it is not difficult to see how acquisition of wealth, lands, success in battle, would have been the focus. Dandekar considered *artha* to be the second of the *puruṣārthas*, but since wealth supports the costly priesthood and rituals, as well as society at large, it is often placed first. *Dharma* without *artha* seemed difficult to achieve, and we only have to cast our eyes back at *varṇa-dharma* to see how such a concept operated in practice, for poverty meant that one had been evil in a past life and one's *dharmic* path was grim. One thing is clear, *artha* legitimized work in whatever form that might take and productivity as the mainstay of any society; wealth was believed to be a *karmic* blessing that could be used for the individual, his family, the priesthood and as support for religious traditions. In the closing chapters of the *Mahābhārata*, the Pāṇḍava brothers argue as to whether *artha*, *kāma* or *dharma* is the superior. When Yudhiṣṭhira, the eldest of the Pāṇḍava brothers and the embodiment of *Dharma* is persuaded to become king, he is told that the *dharma* of a king involves becoming wealthy through war, and lying, cheating and spying as the means to win wars. Ideally, *dharma* should overarch the pursuit of *artha* suggestive that the means would not justify the ends, but texts such as the *Mahābhārata* tell us otherwise.

In the modern world, there is plenty of evidence of the pursuit of *artha* but not always of any *dharma* that might accompany it. Ideally, says Lipner, "dealings must be honest, employment considerate, wages just, competition not ruinous, advertising sensitive and fair", so that "the accumulation of wealth is not time-serving; it neither kills the spirit nor becomes an end in itself".[57] These are sensitive ideas that are far from fact in modern India.

The Kauṭilīya *Artha-śāstra*

Three texts dealt with the first three *puruṣārthas*: thus, there is an *Artha-śāstra*, a *Kāma-śāstra* and a *Dharma-śāstra*. Each dealt with its subject as a science. Any separation and superiority of one over the other was denied by Manu: "Religion and profit are said to be better, or pleasure and profit, or religion alone, or profit alone here on earth; but the fixed rule is that the triple path is best."[58] Kauṭilīya, a royal minister, was the author of the *Artha-śāstra*, dated in its earliest form perhaps to the third or fourth century BCE and in its final form some centuries later, though recent research is suggesting a much later date than BCE.[59] But Kauṭilīya's remit is different from the more individual interpretation later given to *artha*. For Kauṭilīya, *artha* was necessary to maintain – or, more precisely, rule – the earth with the king and governmental administration as the central means of that maintenance. It was polity with which Kauṭilīya was mainly concerned; polity in which the ends justified the means. As Klostermaier writes: "Success in power politics, as history teaches us, does not depend on sensitivity and piety, but on determined ruthlessness to acquire power, to keep it, and to increase it. That is *artha*."[60] Noticeable, then, is the *Kṣatriya* nature of the text, in which it is the ruler's perspective of society with which the text deals.

The *Artha-śāstra*, thus, is a text that focuses on rulership, on kingly power and polity, so *artha* is essentially involved with politics. As Kangle says: "It is intended to teach a ruler how he should conduct himself in the various situations that are likely to arise in the course of his rule."[61] But that conduct need not be ethical! "Creating the illusion of a danger from *rakṣasas* is particularly recommended for the purpose of inducing the enemy king entrenched in a fort to come out for their propitiation and of murdering him when he has come out for the purpose."[62] I do not want to peruse the contents of the *Artha-śāstra* here, but suffice it to say that it is almost solely concerned with the broad matters of state. Yet it came to be applied to human behaviour, too, especially in the social living of the householder stage of life.

Kāma: Pleasure, desire

Westerners are often surprised at *kāma*, pleasure, or desire – and sensual and sexual pleasure, at that – as being one of the basic aims of Hindu life. But Hinduism does not have the repressive darkness of some religions and makes enjoyment of life a legitimate pursuit. Strictly speaking, however, the pursuit of *kāma* in isolation from *dharma* is not acceptable according to Manu, as was seen in the case of *artha*. *Kāma* is relevant to both mundane life and to cosmic contexts. One can be involved with the multiplicity of desires that constitute daily life or, the single ultimate goal of liberation. Vedic ritual sacrifice, *yajña*, was centred on desire for results, *phala*, not just for longevity, cattle, sons, victory in war, but desire for cosmic renewal of creation, of the appropriate seasons and rains. In all cases, such ritual had a desired result, and much personal ritual in contemporary times has the same basic desires in mind – health and wealth for the family and children, but especially in women's rituals, the well-being and longevity of their husbands. A section of the *Laws of Manu* maintains that there is no such thing as no desire and that it is right to engage in sacrificial rituals with an intention, a goal or desire, for a successful outcome, and if desires are right, then Heaven is the outcome.[63] Parallel with the necessity of desire is the necessity of getting rid of it, for the pattern desire > *karma* > *phala*, whether positive or negative, is perpetuated unless the cause of the cycle, desire, is lost. The *Bṛhad-āraṇyaka Upaniṣad* (4:4:7) makes this clear and it is a major theme of the *Bhagavad Gītā* in its doctrine of *karma-yoga*, actions without desire or, more explicitly, actions without a desire for a result.

Kama is primarily sexual enjoyment but also the enjoyment of other pleasures such as music, dance and literature. They are, says V. Raghavan "part of the web of passion, desire, and longing that constitutes existence".[64] Again, it is easy to see how this particular *puruṣārtha* is associated with the second *āśrama* of the householder, as was *artha*. Strictly, speaking, it is only within married life that *kāma* can reach its full expression, though just as *artha* was directed to the monarch, so the king was expected to experience *kāma* with courtesans, so it was particularly pertinent to kingly existence. In all, *kāma* provided a healthy and positive attitude to sex. *Kāma* was the god of love and a particularly strong and virile deity that gave impetus to the notion of *kāma* as expressive of the power of sexual enjoyment for both male and female. The god *Kāma* dates back to the *Ṛg Veda* where he is found as the primal energy, primal desire, that brings about form from formlessness. All the senses were included under the rubric of *kāma* as well as all possible sensations and, balanced by *dharma*, it is seen as a necessary dimension of human existence.

The extent to which *kāma* was given religious sanction is evident in the powerful devotional literature that used explicit and ecstatic sexual longing and passion as symbolic of the depth of love of the devotee for the divine, the longing of the soul for God. In Tantrism, the word is used abundantly as overtly sexual, as in Śaiva Tantrism where the divine is the fusion of the male and female. At a cosmic level, *kāma* as desire is frequently the cause of the universe. It is found, for example, in that great hymn of the *Ṛg Veda*, the *Puruṣa-sūkta* that sees all as a product of the One: "Thereafter rose Desire in the beginning, Desire, the primal seed and germ of Spirit."[65] In other words, desire on the microcosmic level stems from the origin of desire at the beginning of creation. The right kind of expression of *kāma* is even identified with Kṛṣṇa in the *Gītā*: "Of the strong, I am strength devoid of desire and passion. In beings I am desire unopposed to *dharma*, lord of Bharatas."[66] Providing desire is focused on God in the *bhakti* traditions, the fruits of that desire will be the object, God, so obviating a worldly *karmic* result. The *Gītā* uses the word extensively, but never sexually. There is also an argument put forward by Bhīma, one of the Paṇḍāva brothers in the *Mahābhārata* that desire is the prerequisite for *artha* and *dharma* and for pleasure.

Vātsyāyana's Kāma-sūtra

There were a number of texts that dealt with sexual pleasures but the most well-known is *Vātsyāyana's Kāma-sūtra*, "Aphorisms of Love".[67] This lengthy text is a compilation of traditions about sexual pleasure – the very fact that it is a compilation dependent on earlier sources being expressive of the widely accepted attitude of Hindus to sex. Its date is later than the *Artha-śāstra* and could belong to the fourth century CE.[68] The *Kāma-sūtra* does not deal only with sexual pleasure but with the way in which a cultured and refined man should live his life, the kind of house and garden he should have ". . . in the garden, a swing, well covered and under the shade of a tree, as also an earthen platform strewn with the falling flowers of the garden . . .".[69] How and when he washes, shaves, clips his nails, eats, engages in activities – drawing, painting, sculpting, playing music – has an afternoon nap, pays social calls, are all included in the *Kāma-sūtra* to instruct the high-class male. Then there is all the advice on preparation for sexual enjoyment, sexual positions and the best measures for full enjoyment. Lest it should seem that no appropriate notice is taken of *dharma*, Koller notes that *Vātsyāyana* defines *kāma* thus: "*Kāma* broadly speaking, consists in engaging the various senses with their appropriate objects, but always under the control of the heart and mind directed by the conscious self."[70] *Vātsyāyana* always considered *dharma* as the most important of the *puruṣārthas*.

There must have been numerous tensions between the two extremes of sensuous pleasure and the ascetic traditions that sought to transcend the senses. Theoretically, *Brāhminical* Hinduism accommodated both, with the balanced *āśramas* on the one hand, and the *puruṣārthas* on the other, though they were never designed as complementary systems. Marriage and procreation were endorsed by the *Vedas* in a way in which asceticism was not, so sexual enjoyment and pleasure in marriage had religious sanction. Indeed, celibate ascetics were often accused of choosing such an unnatural life because they were impotent![71] But *kāma* provided legitimate means for sexual and aesthetic enjoyment in life – a means that extended into the whole realm of art and literature.

Dharma: What is right

Dharma can be widely translated. I usually prefer a meaning "what is right" and that can be meant in any context – duty, correct religious ritual, observance of *varṇa* and caste rules, social mores, food regulations, morality, right conduct, laws, politics – indeed, the extension of the term to encompass many aspects of Hinduism from the individual to the cosmic dimension of the universal, *sādhāraṇa-dharma*, is possible. *Dharma* stems from the root *dhṛ* with the meaning "to support, maintain", so the different *dharmas* maintain the whole complex structure of religious and social living in such a way that order in society and cosmos is continued. As we shall see in the companion volume to this book, *dharma* evolved from the old *Vedic* concept of *ṛta*, which was cosmic order. Koller comments that: "This universal aspect of dharma is not lost when the concept takes on greater social significance, for all ordinary human dharma is only an aspect of the universal dharma and is justified not in itself, but only in the function of the universal dharma, the ṛta of the Ṛg Veda."[72] Thus, *dharma* as support is reciprocally of society and cosmos.

The rationale underpinning *dharma* is one of balance and harmony in the idea that if each fulfils his or her (but mainly his) duty then the harmony of society is guaranteed. Fulfilling *dharma* extends not just to humans but to non-humans as well: so even the gods were subject to *dharma*. The fulfilment of *dharma* may well be associated with desires, as in the context of *artha* and *kāma*, but it can also be fulfilled with a lack of desire – action from the inaction of a still, inner Self – as was Kṛṣṇa's understanding of *dharma* in the *Gītā*. Of course, it is Manu that preserves the respective *dharmas* like no other. Doniger and Smith state so unequivocally in their translation of the *Laws of Manu*: "No modern study of Hindu family life, psychology, concepts of the body, sex, relationships between human and animals, attitudes to money and material possessions, politics, law, caste, purification and pollution, ritual, social practice and ideals, and world-renunciation and worldly goals, can ignore Manu."[73] Manu was the authority on *dharma* in all its dimensions. It is the epics of the *Rāmāyaṇa* and *Mahābhārata* that transfer theoretical *dharmas* into practice. This is so much the case with the lives of the characters in the former and is the thread that runs through the latter. It is in these epics that the individual is able to identify with correct *dharmic* roles. The *Mahābhārata* closes with the words:

> From dharma comes success and pleasure:
> why is dharma not practised?
> Never reject dharma – not for pleasure, not from fear,
> not out of greed.
> Dharma is eternal. Discard life itself,
> but not dharma.[74]

As one of the *puruṣārthas*, *dharma* regulates the others, ensuring that no excess of practice can occur so that normative *dharmic* behaviour is continued: *dharma* should make ethical behaviour in any context the norm. In the *Taittirīya-āraṇyaka* are the words: "Dharma is the foundation of the whole universe. In this world people go unto a person who is best versed in dharma for guidance. By means of dharma one drives away evil. Upon dharma everything is founded. Therefore, dharma is called the highest good."[75]

Mokṣa: Release

The three *puruṣārthas* of *artha*, *kāma* and *dharma* operate in time. The fourth, *mokṣa* (a noun from the root *muc* "to liberate, release"), pertains to what is beyond time, to release and liberation from the perpetual cycles of birth and death that are the result of *karmic* residues. *Mokṣa* was a later addition to the other *puruṣārthas* and was a necessary addition when ascetic withdrawal with the aim of transcending the world of desires in order to focus on, and arrive at, Brahman became the ultimate goal for many. It is sometimes referred to as the highest wealth, for it is *ultimate* release. While the term *mokṣa* itself does not appear much in the *Upaniṣads*, it is there that we find the evolving thought of merging with Brahman to be liberated from the desire-filled self. It became the goal of the fourth *āśrama*, *saṃnyāsa*. *Mokṣa* represented inactivity (*nivṛtti*) of the egoistic self as opposed to the normal activity (*pravṛtti*) of the self involved in life. The tension between these two pathways is rather obvious, even if the three world-involving *puruṣārthas* are believed to be preparations for *mokṣa*. Even *dharma* does not always sit comfortably with this final *puruṣārtha* and in the *Gītā*, Kṛṣṇa actually says: "Renounce all *dharmas*: take refuge in me alone. I will liberate you from all evils; grieve not."[76] However, the *Gītā* has many contradictions: elsewhere, class *dharma* is firmly upheld, and Kṛṣṇa's teaching incorporates the importance of Arjuna carrying out his *sva-dharma*, his "own *dharma*" as a warrior.[77] Perhaps light can be shed on Kṛṣṇa's statement here by comparing it with the *Uddhava Gītā*, where Kṛṣṇa says: "A person should perform all *dharmas* for my sake. Surrendering the mind and thoughts to Me, one should delight in doing *dharma* to Me."[78] *Dharma* need not be abandoned, just focused on Kṛṣṇa. Or perhaps Kṛṣṇa's words reflect a monist view, whereby, as in Advaita Vedānta, the Self is Brahman and all else, including *dharmic* actions, is illusion. However, other Vedāntic philosophers, as Roy Perrett points out, uphold the maintaining of *dharma(s)*.[79] There is no one pathway to *mokṣa* (as the companion volume to this book will seek to explore), and neither is there a single concept of what *mokṣa* is. How it is defined will inform the extent to which it is linked with the *āśramas* and the *puruṣārthas*.

The western mind is likely to find conflicting aims here between worldly wealth and pleasure and the ultimate goal of liberation, especially in the political domain and there is no one view as to whether *mokṣa* is separate and opposed to *artha* and *kāma* – even if these are conducted within the realms of *dharma* – or whether *dharmic* action is legitimately a preparation for, and therefore to be linked with, *mokṣa*. It seems to be a dichotomy between "religion" (*mokṣa*) and "politics" (*artha* and *kāma*) but, in many ways, these two English terms are theoretical constructs that do not sit well in Hinduism and Hinduism has no definitive answers to any antagonism between the two. Indeed, as Perrett points out, Hinduism itself has very different views of the relative relationship between the two: taking just the classical Hindu philosophies, he suggests "different philosophers give different answers".[80] The *āśrama* system clearly does not separate political gains from the ultimate religious goal; it simply places the stages at appropriate times in life on the path to *mokṣa*. Similarly, *artha* and *kāma* are given their appropriate spaces in life on the same pathway. *Dharma* seems to be the overriding bridge that unites *āśramas*, *puruṣārthas* and *mokṣa*. It seems to me that *Brāhminical* attempts to bring all aspects of Āryan life into the religious domain, with *dharma* being the overarching principle, is suggestive that separating religion and politics, or religion and social living, is unsound. While the philosophical understanding of *mokṣa* may in some cases divorce that ultimate goal from any active living, the overall *Brāhminical* view is to include all *dharmas* rather than separate them from *mokṣa*. The symbiotic relationship between king and politics and priest and religion in Hinduism has historical weight and William Sax is one who thinks this relationship between politics and religion is present in more recent times: "Our understanding of South Asian society and history is sometimes muddled by the rigid distinctions we make between 'religion' and 'politics'. The resurgent appeal of Hindu nationalism, the involvement of Hindu renouncers in contemporary Indian politics, and the continuing relevance of religious issues to political discourse throughout South Asia, show that such a discussion is of limited utility."[81]

5
Gods and Goddesses
Śiva

Of all the Hindu deities, the God Śiva is by far the most complex. Explorers of Hinduism in the past, who came across myths relating to Śiva, had difficulty refraining from all kinds of vilification of what they considered to be a depraved god that was associated with equally depraved praxis. I have to confess that, while I have no such vilifying thoughts myself, getting this complex deity across to the reader without engendering horror of the God is no easy task. It is the delicate balance between the mythology of Śiva and the philosophy and metaphysics that underpin that mythology that creates the problem. Indeed, it could be said that those who are devoted to Śiva range – just as in Hinduism as a whole – from the simplistic to the most profound. The first task really is to understand the nature of myth. Myth can relate to different levels of individual consciousness permitting ways of understanding many dimensions of a religion: so myths can be accepted simplistically or highly philosophically. The myths about Śiva are legion: they also vary from one location to another, from sect to sect and in popular and Sanskrit accounts and so are multiform. Wendy Doniger O'Flaherty comments on the complexity of such mythology: "There are many myths dealing with each theme, and many themes within each myth. There is no way to begin with any 'basic' myth or any 'basic' theme".[1] Thus there is an incredible inconsistency in the same myth recorded in different places, at different times and for different people. Individuals take what best suits their situation and level of being. Transposition of events takes place in different accounts of the same myth and one account may seem hopelessly confused with others. Myths may even refer to a deity's actions in different eons of time. Justifiably, Namita Gokhale describes myths as "elastic and energetic and in a constant state of reinterpretation and reinvention",[2] so there are no definitive versions for me to present to the reader.

My approach in treating the deities, particularly Śiva, is not to recount the myths unless they are relevant to an underlying point. Devdutt Pattanaik says that myths "are conceived in dreams and expressed through symbols as a reaction to man's inexplicable yet desperate need to validate his presence in the cosmos. They do not teach, they generate experience."[3] It is such an experiential dimension that I prefer to encapsulate in the reader's mind leaving the reader to explore the myths in more detail in other sources. I shall try, rather, to explore the essence of the respective deities, and this will be especially the case with Śiva.

Those who are followers of Śiva are known as Śaivites or Śaivas, but the differences in praxis are remarkable; some extend to the female energies of Śiva known as *Śakti*, with which I shall deal in the following chapter. But I shall start with Rudra, the precursor of Śiva – indeed, the same deity, with many of the same characteristics. Essentially, these characteristics are dual, total opposites in nature, dark and light, ferocious and kind, violent and benign, pertaining to death and to life, active and passive, dissolving and creating. These opposite tendencies are the key to understanding Rudra, Rudra-Śiva and Śiva. Rhythms of sacrificial worship accompany such dualities with praise for the positive and pleas against the negative. The imagery of this complex deity will reflect not only the dual nature but also the different ways in which humans will interact with this inscrutable deity. First, I want to explore the early nature of Śiva as Rudra.

Rudra

Rudra is a god that features in the *Vedas* but is highly likely to pre-date them and to be indigenous to India rather than being imported from elsewhere. The connection of this god with Śiva lies in the fact that both deities have strikingly opposite characteristics in their personalities. Rudra is the darker of the two and, when Śiva comes to the fore in later times, his darker side often earns him the title Rudra. Conversely, when the gentler aspect of Rudra predominated, he was called Śiva, "auspicious" – not always as a proper name, but often just descriptively. So Rudra is important in that he prefigures what Robert Zaehner called "the uncanny, paradoxical, and fascinating figure of the later Śiva".[4] The minimal picture that we have of Rudra in the early *Vedas* suggests that the migrating Āryans saw him as epitomizing the antagonistic surrounding forces – hostile tribes, jungle vegetation, and what seemed to them dark religious praxis. The name Rudra is variously interpreted as the "Fierce One", the "Wild One", the "Howler", the "Roarer", the "Weeper", the "Red One". Each of these meanings has a different etymology in explanation of the name, many accompanied by appropriate myths and all indicative of the dark character and difficult nature of this strange god.

As probably a non-Āryan deity, Rudra seems to have been outside the orthodox gods of the *Vedas* and only gradually accepted as Āryan, even then, retaining pre-Āryan characteristics along with Āryan ones. This may be one reason for the persistent opposites of character. Perhaps he was associated with a non-Āryan mountain deity,[5] certainly with goblins and demons, with fertility rites, and was possibly a powerful tribal god with which the Āryans had to contend. One way of dealing with this was to absorb these non-Āryan characteristics in the later deity Śiva, so bringing this fierce tribal deity into Sanskritized orthodoxy. The nature of Rudra as an "outsider" features markedly in the early myths about him. Notably, too, is the prominence of Śaiva cults in the South of India, an area where Āryan influence was slow to infiltrate. What we have in Rudra is a mixture of different origins grafted into one personality in whom the disparate organic foundations are still present.

Rudra in the Vedas

Rudra is only a minor god in the *Ṛg Veda* with sporadic references and only three hymns dedicated to him. Yet, "the rich ambivalence of his character", as Wendy Doniger O'Flaherty puts it,[6] was to encompass diverse strands of divine character that developed into the major deity that is Śiva. The main descriptors of Rudra in the *Ṛg* are of a terrifying god, destructive, fierce, the slayer of cows and men, whose swift arrows bring death. He personified the destructive forces of nature such as disease, storms, lightning, fires, anthropomorphizing the wild elements of the environment. It is not surprising, then, that the few hymns dedicated to him in the *Ṛg Veda* implore him to stay away though, paradoxically, he may be implored to bestow good health. But he hardly seems to be popular and veneration of him remains predominantly apotropaic:

> Let the weapon of Rudra veer from us; let the great malevolence of the dreaded god go past us. Loosen the taut bows for the sake of our generous patrons; O bountiful one, have mercy on our children and grand-children.
> O tawny and amazing bull, O God, do not become incensed or kill us.[7]

And yet, Rudra is the best of healers, as this earlier verse shows:

> We would not wish to anger you, Rudra the bull, by acts of homage or ill praise, or by invoking you together with another god. Raise up our heroes with your healing medicines; I hear that of all healers you are the best healer.[8]

Such ambivalence in the character of Rudra is the key to understanding the later development into the great God Śiva. But it is the benevolent aspect of Rudra that is often to the fore with Śiva. Thus, the aspects of Rudra as a healing physician, the granter of prosperity to all creatures, the lord of songs and sacrifices and the remover of sins are features of the God Śiva. It is the later *Vedas* that develop these two opposite characteristics of Rudra. In some parts of the *Yajur Veda*, Rudra is ubiquitous, the Lord of all areas, forests, fields, copses, gullies and even barren earth. He is present in all things – streams, ditches, lakes, rivers, clouds, lightning, cow pens, cattle sheds, rain, drought, mist and dust. He is described as sweet-scented, a divine physician for humans and animals and one that lends ease to ewes and lambs. But Rudra does not lose his terrifying aspects in the *Yajur Veda*, for he is also described as the Lord of thieves and cut-throats, a wanderer and vagabond and one who is the best of tricksters. There is much that is unpleasant about this god as the personification of the darker elements of life and its unpredictable vicissitudes. These darker elements are personified in the *Rudras* and *Maruts*, and the *gaṇas* and *pramathas*, hosts of equally malicious beings that accompany Rudra, who is their Lord. In the *Yajur Veda* homage is paid to Rudra as one who roars and screams in the hope that he will spare the worshipper, his children and his descendants. This fierce nature is intensified in the *Atharva Veda* as the god that kills.

Such *Vedic* views of the god Rudra are more pertinent to the pre-Āryan tribal peoples than to the Āryan priestly circles but his inclusion in the *Vedas* represents an attempt to bring this inscrutable god into the *Brāhminic* fold. Yet it seems that in the *Brāhmaṇas* even the gods fear Rudra. We find many myths about the birth of Rudra, and wider mythology indicating that his cultic importance was increasing, though there is a tendency not to mention the name of this dangerous god. However, we find eight names for Rudra in the *Brāhmaṇas*, four (Rudra, Śarva, Ugra and Aśani) depicting his terrifying aspect, and four (Bhava, Paśupati, Mahā-Deva and Īśāna) his gentle aspect. Chakravarti's comment here is rather apposite because "on the one hand, the tendency towards identifying and blending originally distinct and apparently local Vedic gods with one another, and, on the other hand, the origin of the conception of Rudra-Śiva in the pantheistic system of the post-Vedic period" is evident in passages from the *Brāhmaṇas*.[9] What we have, then, in the *Vedic* conception of Rudra is the expedient apotropaic veneration of a dangerous god, who himself is an amalgamation of a number of tribal gods, and who is in the process of being incorporated into the Āryan concepts of divinity, what Chakravarti terms "the metamorphosis of an Āryan god into a god who has both Āryan and pre-Āryan features".[10]

The many dimensions of Rudra

It is in the *Upaniṣads* that Rudra becomes a more transcendent God, portrayed, at times, as the greatest God. In the late *Śvetāśvatara Upaniṣad* Rudra is supreme:

> There is only one Rudra; he has not tolerated a second who would reign over these worlds by his sovereign powers. After drawing in all beings, he stands as the protector at the end of time turning west towards men.
> Eyes everywhere and face everywhere, arms everywhere and feet everywhere, he forges with his two hands, he forges with the wings, producing the heaven and earth, the one God . . .
> Who is higher than *brahman*, the immense one hidden in all beings, in each according to its kind, and who alone encompasses the whole universe . . . [11]

The *Śvetāśvatara Upaniṣad* tells us that Rudra dwells in the mountains, is thousand-headed and thousand-eyed, and while often depicted as auspicious, *śiva*, the darker side of Rudra is evident with references to his arrows of death and he remains a God to be appeased: "The arrow, O Mountain-dweller, that you hold in your hand to shoot – make it benign, O Mountain-protector; hurt not man or beast."[12] And again: "Do not hurt us in our offspring or descendants, in our life, in our cattle or horses. Do not slay in anger, O Rudra, our valiant men."[13] Importantly, this same *Upaniṣad* depicts Rudra as *Sthāṇu*, "the post", standing like the trunk of a tree,[14] a descriptor that will be taken up, also, as an epithet for Śiva.

There are many myths about the birth of Rudra and he has many titles. In congruence with his fierce nature, he is depicted as clothed in animal skins – a black antelope skin often symbolizing the ascetic and a tiger skin, symbol of the hunter, around his loins. Serpents are coiled around his neck. He is an ominous-looking god who can change his appearance to terrible or benign forms. He is usually depicted as ruddy, tawny, sun or copper-coloured, or even blood red, and with a blue throat. This last was acquired when gods and demons churned the ocean in search of the nectar of immortality. All sorts of things came out of the process including a deadly poison that would have killed all, but not Rudra. He drank the poison without it harming him, though his throat remained permanently blue. Sometimes, Rudra is described as radiant with limbs covered in shimmering gold, and wearing a golden necklace bearing many forms and colours. His hair is braided. At other times, he is in the form of a bull or a tawny boar.

Rudra is presented in the *Śvetāśvatara Upaniṣad* as omnipresent:

> You are a woman; you are a man; you are a boy and also a girl. As an old man, you totter along with a walking stick. As you are born, you turn your face in every direction.
>
> You are the dark blue bird, the green one with red eyes, the rain-cloud, the seasons, and the oceans. You live as one without a beginning because of your pervasiveness, you, from whom all beings have been born.[15]

Thus, Rudra has many roles, many names and many forms, his omnipresence and pervasiveness in the cosmos meaning that he can be anything anywhere, different things at the same time, and yet no-thing and nowhere. In a potent statement, Stella Kramrisch said: "The names and forms of Rudra interlace. Their total pattern is an inexhaustible concatenation of evocations locked together by his innumerable qualities and actions in the cosmos from aeon to aeon, and anchored in his immutable being beyond manifestation."[16] Some of the names and forms that he takes will pass to Śiva but, as stated earlier, in the earlier stages, *śiva* is used as an adjective to describe Rudra's benign form.

The fierce and benign opposite characteristics of Rudra are important in our understanding of the deity Śiva who is the God of opposites *par excellence*. Chakravarti says of Rudra: "He combines in himself the malevolent and benevolent, the terrific and pacific, the demoniac and angelic features. These are the germs which afterwards developed into Rudra-Śiva."[17] Rudra on the one hand has the arrows of death and destruction and, on the other, a healing plant and soothing water. He will hurl disease and then cure, wound and then soothe, destroy dwellings but is still the protector of dwellings and homes. His malevolent side incorporates all the worst in humanity – treachery, pillage, thieving, plundering. So savage is he that his name was often not mentioned for fear of offending him: he would be referred to as "that god". Thus, destruction is Rudra but also creation. Alain Daniélou rather pertinently writes: "Anyone who performs a function of destruction participates in the Rudra principle. Life, which can exist only by destroying life, is a manifestation of Rudra."[18] Rudra, as Śiva later, reconciles all opposites but perhaps not quite in the powerful metaphysical way that is the case with Śiva.

Rudra is associated with many other *Vedic* gods. His children are the *Maruts*, the gods of the storm, who are usually associated with the god Indra. They roar like lions and have horrendous teeth. Similar were the *Rudras*, born of the anger of the god Brahmā, according to one myth. They were terrifying destructive forces, personifying injury, anger, greed, doubt, old age and disease. In his role as protector of dwellings, Rudra was Vāstoṣpati, and as Lord of Creation, he was Prajāpati. As Lord of Creatures he was Paśupati, the divine herdsman, but he was often amalgamated with other deities especially with Agni, the god of fire, fire being a destructive force and Rudra being the ferocious and destructive aspects of fire. Agni was an important *Vedic* god and the association of Rudra with Agni meant that Rudra gained prestige. The direct opposite of Agni as fire was Soma, sometimes equated with the moon, cool, watery and shadowy. Soma was both a god and a consciousness-heightening plant used during priestly ritual. Thus, in passages of the *Vedas* that refer to Soma-Rudra, we have both the ferocious and soothing character of Rudra. At other times, Rudra is Śarva the archer with his cruel arrows that harm and kill. Such identifications with different gods and functions are indicative of the expanse of powers of the god. "His contradictions, his polarities operate on all levels of his ambience, radiating from his center", wrote Kramrisch.[19] So, for example, he creates, but he also destroys in order to recreate.

As I noted earlier, Rudra, like the later Śiva, is an outsider among the other gods. It seems the gods themselves feared, loathed and dreaded this threatening and disruptive deity. Rudra was, nevertheless, associated with some female deities towards the end of the *Vedic* period.[20] He was never accepted at the sacrifices to the gods: indeed, he received only the leftovers of the sacrifices, offerings that the other gods did not want. Thus, he will accept any offering from a worshipper. Whereas the other gods were clothed in splendid attire, Rudra was dressed as a hunter, as wild in appearance as in character. Such rough attire was the symbol of the ascetic as, indeed, was the humiliation of eating only the left-overs of the sacrifice. Rudra's character, then, absorbs also the ascetic nature, a nature that will be paramount in the God Śiva, but there are elements of the Great *Yogin* in Rudra, particularly in his character as *Sthāṇu*, the motionless pillar, noted above.

Rudra features at the beginning of time when, according to one of the creation myths, he interrupts with his arrow the sexual intercourse between a primal man and his daughter, causing some of the father's seed to fall and form existence. Rudra here symbolizes the creator, the cause of relative time, though he existed outside that time in absolute Time. He becomes both the cause of manifest existence, manifest existence itself and the reproductive power in nature. In another myth, Rudra becomes the cause of the rhythms of life and death and rebirth, the instigator of periods of restful quiescence, the spells of death in the cycles of living. Rhythms of the earth are in the domain of Rudra's functions, too. He may be on the fringes of the other gods but he is close to creatures and to humans, present everywhere. As Kramrisch put it:

> The universe resounds with Rudra's presence; he is sound and echo, intangible vibration and infinitesimal substance, too, of every particle of dust and foam. His presence is immanent in verdant trees and the soft green grass. He is the rustling, withered leaves and the silent dead. Unmistakably, the healthy and the afflicted are hallowed by his sign, while his innumerable arrows flit across the universe. At certain spots his presence is acutely felt. These are fords (*tīrtha*), and at them he is the ferryman. He ferries across to the other shore, into the far beyond of which he is the guardian. He is the liberator, but – paradoxically, he is also the ferryman from death to life.[21]

Rudra, said Kramrisch, is found wherever life is "felt acutely", present in sunshine as in shade, in disease and its cure, in anxiety and its loss and in all components of life.[22] We must turn, now, to see how much the fully developed concept of Śiva as one of the greatest Gods of Hinduism, reflects the characteristics of Rudra.

Śiva

As with Rudra, there are many myths surrounding the complex deity that is Śiva. Such myths are contradictory, inconsistent and altered through time to conform to sectarian divisions. But, what all the myths show, is the mysterious nature of this God. Śiva is both terrifying and yet an object of devotion for many Śaiva sects. The complexity of this God is summed up well by T. S. Maxwell when he says: "Shiva is all man and half woman, saint and sinner, ascetic and lover, dual, triple and fivefold godhead."[23] The opposite characteristics that were present with Rudra are there, too, with Śiva but they are intensified and deepened in Śiva. The versatility of this deity is quite incredible. It is in the *Purāṇas* that the full richness of myth is manifest. There, the *Śiva-purāṇa* has many myths that focus on Śiva and the gods associated with him, but there are five other *Purāṇas* – the *Liṅga*, the *Skanda*, the *Matsya*, the *Kūrma* and the *Brahmāṇḍa* – that feature Śiva. Nevertheless, many other *Purāṇas* include myths about Śiva. What they reveal is that Śiva has many, many, bewildering forms.

Śiva means "kind", "auspicious", "benevolent", "protector". In the *Vedic* context the word is often used as an adjective, and it is not until the *Śvetāśvatara Upaniṣad* that we find Śiva used as a proper name for the peaceful aspect of Rudra. Śiva begins to emerge as a deity in about the second century BCE. The transformation of Rudra into Śiva is never really complete, though the latter came to be the object of deep devotion that could never be offered to Rudra. It is in the *Śvetāśvatara Upaniṣad* that the god Rudra changes to become *the God*, Rudra-Śiva or simply Śiva. The transformation is clear: Rudra becomes the God of metaphysical heights and depths that is Śiva:

> One sees him as the beginning, as the basis and cause of the joining, as beyond the three times [past, present and future], and also without parts. He, from whom the unfolding of the world has come forth, is higher than and different from the time-confined forms of the tree [of life].
>
> After we have first venerated that adorable God displaying every form, the source of all beings, as residing within one's heart, and then recognized him as the one who bestows righteousness and removes evil, as the Lord of prosperity, as abiding within ourselves (*ātman*), as the Immortal residing in all beings –
>
> We will find this highest Great-Lord among lords, the highest God among gods, the highest master among masters, the God beyond the highest as the adorable Lord of the universe.[24]

Clearly here, Rudra has been transformed in character, in status and in majesty to immeasurable heights. While he has many characteristics, he is also portrayed in the same chapter of the *Śvetāśvatara Upaniṣad* as having no qualities, as *nirguṇa*, and as present as the soul of all creatures. The transformation from a threatening deity to a transcendent one had taken place though the darker side is always a possible manifestation and it is then that Śiva becomes Rudra. While Śiva's roots in Rudra are non-Āryan, texts like the *Śvetāśvatara Upaniṣad* gave Śiva what Chakravarti describes as "the Āryan touch of sophistication",[25] but the pre-Āryan god of the mountains, the earth-orientated god is still there in Śiva despite the sophistication given to him in some texts. Indeed, Śiva was and is popular in the South of India, where the original, indigenous people, the elusive, non-Āryan Dravidians, embraced non-orthodox conceptions of deity that were more receptive to an elusive and all-encompassing God like Śiva.

Śiva became the God of outcastes, of *Śūdras* and especially of wandering ascetics. The Śaiva *Āgamas* reflect this non-*Vedic* trend with their emphasis on the direct experience of God without the need for rite or priest. Indeed, Śiva himself appeared as an outcaste would dress. In one myth, Śiva appears as a beggar with a bell attached to his leg resembling the bells worn by outcastes to warn others of their polluting approach. In the epic the *Rāmāyaṇa*, the demon king who abducts Sītā is a worshipper of Śiva and, as we shall see below, he is very much associated with demons and other horrendous creatures. Just as Rudra could be ferocious and benign, so Śiva can also be the "Terrible One", Bhairava, with hair around his head like flames, naked, covered in ashes and accompanied by the unclean animal, a dog. Bhairava is an outcaste, venerated by outcastes. He carries a begging bowl that is actually the skull of the god Brahmā which, according to myth, stuck to his hand when Śiva cut off one of Brahmā's heads. Bhairava takes many forms, all horrific – a skeleton, or a fat, staring horrible form, for example. Bhairava is Śiva's hit man, the form of Śiva that creates death and havoc.

Of Śiva's many forms, the most prominent are Bhava, "Existence, Being"; Śārva, "Divine Archer"; Paśupati, "Lord of Animals"; Ugradev, "Fierce Warrior"; Rudra, "Wild"; Mahā-Deva and Maheśvara, "Great God and "Great Lord"; and Iśāna, "Ruler". But since Śiva is everything his names and forms are many. His names may reflect his appearance as three-eyed (Tri-locana), blue-throated (Nīla-kaṇṭha) or five-faced (Pañcānana) but there is always something of a dichotomy between anthropomorphic descriptions of Śiva and the more abstract portrayal of him that is beyond form. It is this factor that makes a study of Śiva such a difficult one: on the one side there are the abundant myths about an anthropomorphic character with many opposing sides to his being, and on the other, a transcendent essence that absorbs and is all opposites. Zaehner rightly said that "he transcends humanity, and the violence of the contradictions that he subsumes into himself gives him a sublimity and a mystery that no purely anthropomorphic figure could evoke".[26] While there are many and varied anthropomorphized images of Śiva, it is normally his symbol, the *liṅga* that is the object of devotion in temples. This is a subject to which I shall return below. Śiva remains illusive and any attempt to pin down some kind of ordered account of the deity is dispelled by the abundant myths that make him now this, now that. Śiva is not the kind of God that we expect. In a rather pertinent modern description of Śiva, Pattanaik says of him: "Shiva means auspicious one. Yet, everything about him seems inauspicious: he dwells in isolated hills, dark caves and dense jungles. He dances amidst funeral pyres, rattling bells and drums, wearing animal hide, if anything at all; he stinks like a goat, smears himself with ash, carries skulls, drinks poisons, smokes narcotics, enjoys the company of ghosts, ghouls and goblins, demands worship during the dark half of the lunar month."[27] Śiva is, as Rudra, an outsider, different, the God that incorporates all manifestation in the cosmos whatever the nature of that manifestation: that includes the darker forces.

Occasionally, Śiva's image is of one with five heads, each head depicting an aspect of his personality, but he is variously anthropomorphically represented and there are differences in such representations in North and South India. According to Maxwell, Śiva carries the trident or *triśūla* and cobra in northern iconography, but in the South, the axe and deer are more common.[28] As will be seen below, Śiva is the greatest of ascetics and so is often depicted as an orthodox *Brāhmin* in ascetic pose, still, deep in meditation, the Great *Yogin* or *Mahā-Yogin*. Yet he can also be portrayed carrying a skull on the end of a staff or a club symbolizing that he is separated from orthodox Hinduism as an outcaste. He is often described as "sky-clad", that is to say, naked. He sometimes carries a bow, a drum in the shape of an hour-glass and a cord with which he binds those who have done wrong. Śiva has three eyes, his third, in the centre of his forehead, being that which will destroy the world. In one myth, his consort Pārvatī, playfully came behind him and covered his eyes. The world went black until his third eye opened with blazing fire, destroying all in front of it. His blue throat, I have noted above, a feature that makes Śiva readily identifiable and that symbolizes liberation from death. The deadly, terrible burning mass of poison is the opposite of the nectar of immortality that the gods and demons had hoped to procure from the churning of the ocean.

It is clear to see that Śiva embodies just about all the opposites of character imaginable and it is in the multiplicity of myths about him that these characteristics are portrayed. They have been acquired and absorbed from earlier gods. Rudra, of course, supplies Śiva's dark and wild side, and since Rudra was often equated with deities like Indra and Agni, we find Śiva absorbing the lascivious features of Indra. O'Flaherty believes that Indra was a phallic god of fertility and that it is from Indra that Śiva inherits his eroticism.[29] There are, indeed, times when they are said to be synonymous,[30] but Indra does not have the opposite qualities of asceticism as does Śiva. Śiva has also inherited aspects of Agni, the god of fire. Fire, heat, is considered as *tapas*, the ascetic fervour of the *yogin*, as well as the fire of destruction and the heat of sexual desire. Again, all three are aspects of Śiva's personality. The creator god Brahmā's powers and characteristics are also reflected in the personality of Śiva. O'Flaherty devotes a whole chapter to what she calls the opposition to, and identity between, Śiva and Brahmā.[31] Primarily, both are creators, though Śiva is very much the God of death and dissolution in the process of renewal. But these two deities are close in nature. It is not my purpose here to draw on the canyon of myths that would support such a statement. Suffice it to say that, as O'Flaherty puts it: "The two gods participate in aspects of each other so deeply that they exchange roles almost at random."[32] Nevertheless, they were frequently at loggerheads with each other, as the severing of Brahmā's head by Śiva serves to show. Another god that informs some of Śiva's nature is Kāma, the god of desire and love. It is the erotic nature of Śiva that features in the similarities, though there is much evidence of opposition, too. Finally, Śiva is often associated or even identified with Sūrya, the sun. In view of his association with fire and heat, this is not surprising. What we have in Śiva, then, is a complexity of nature drawn from many sources both in complementarity and in opposing natures. But it is only Śiva in whom the direct opposites obtain to the full.

As we have seen, in the *Vedas*, *śiva*, "auspicious" or "gentle", was the adjectival descriptor used of the benign aspects of Rudra and the same use of the epithet occurs, too, in the *Śvetāśvatara Upaniṣad*. But the process by which Śiva became a God was well underway and in the *Śvetāśvatara Upaniṣad*, Śiva becomes a personal God to whom prayer and praise can be offered. Śiva is identified as the Absolute, Brahman, and as the pure, inner Self of all beings. He is Lord of all manifest existence, which stems from his Being:

> The one God who covers himself with things issuing from the primal source, from his own inherent nature, as a spider, with the threads – may he procure us dissolution in *brahman*.
> The one God hidden in all beings, pervading the universe, the inner self of all beings, the overseer of the work, dwelling in all beings, the witness, the spectator, alone, devoid of qualities . . .".[33]

The all-pervasiveness of Śiva means that he is in all forms, can take any form and at the same time is transcendently without form. The interconnectedness of all things through Śiva in the *Śvetāśvatara Upaniṣad* is suggestive of a monistic and non-dual view of the universe, in line with much *Upaniṣadic* teaching, but at the same time allowing room for devotion to a personal God. In the *Mahābhārata* Śiva is sometimes portrayed as the supreme deity but at other times in the epic he is subservient to Viṣṇu. Thus, we expect Vaiṣṇava texts to identify Viṣṇu as Brahman and Śaiva texts to do the same with Śiva. The *Purāṇas*, especially, extol their preferred God. Nevertheless, given the unorthodox nature of Śiva, it is not surprising that he remains, like Rudra, separated from other deities. Frequently, his destructive nature made him a God to be feared rather than adored. Since he is unorthodox, he is able to be absorbed into local myths to create new strands to his character and powers; some of these will be fierce and some gracious. Overall, whereas many of the *Vedic* deities faded into insignificance, Rudra-Śiva gained in importance to become one of the greatest deities in Hinduism.

As we shall see below, Śiva is very much associated with fertility. Rudra features in the early mythological ideas of creation as the primeval archer who breaks up an incestuous act to allow the male seed to deposit itself to bring about manifestation. Rudra represents the reproductive power in manifest existence and Śiva represents the dissolution, but importantly, the subsequent creation of manifest existence after quiescence. The moon, a symbol of fertility, is to be seen on Śiva's forehead, and the *liṅga*, the phallic symbol of Śiva, though hardly at all associated with fertility in present-day Śaiva worship, must surely reflect some influence of fertility cults in the ancient past.

I said earlier, the key to understanding the complex God that is Śiva lies in his opposing nature both at the phenomenal and the metaphysical levels, what O'Flaherty describes as "correlative opposites that act as interchangeable identities in essential relationships".[34] The fire of ascetic practice and the fire of desire are a prime example here. O'Flaherty describes Śiva as a "mediating principle":

> The mediating principle that tends to resolve the oppositions is in most cases Śiva himself. Among ascetics he is a libertine and among libertines an ascetic; conflicts

> which they cannot resolve, or can attempt to resolve only by compromise, he simply absorbs into himself and expresses in terms of other conflicts. Where there is excess, he opposes and controls it; where there is no action, he himself becomes excessively active. He emphasizes that aspect of himself which is unexpected, inappropriate, shattering any attempt to achieve a superficial reconciliation of the conflict through mere logical compromise. Mediating characters of this type are essential to all mythologies which deal in contradictions.[35]

Śiva is the balance and fulcrum between opposites. He could swallow deadly poison because he is the source of life, for example. As the fulcrum between all opposites, he reconciles them and at the same time unifies them. The opposites in Śiva are complementary, just as we need light to appreciate what dark is. Of the three *guṇas*, Śiva is associated with *tamas*, darkness and inertia. It represents his role as the Dissolver in life, *tamas* being the darkness, blackness and death into which the universe falls at the end of a phase of manifestation. Śiva is the centrifugal force, the dissolving force that pulls things apart, dispersing existence, expanding the universe until it is no more. Yet from that blackness it is Śiva who brings creation and life once again. Just as in birth each being is slowly proceeding towards death, so the universe is slowly expanding out to the point of total blackness and the point at which manifest time ceases to exist. This is what Kramrisch described as "a limitless pool of indistinction".[36] But by means of that blackness, creation can once again unfold, with Śiva as its instrument. It is a positive rather than a negative process, as Daniélou points out: "Ultimately Śiva is the death of death, that is, eternal life. On the other hand, it is from destruction that life arises. Life exists only by devouring life. Life is the image of the giver of death."[37] The dissolution of the universe in order to recreate it is Śiva's gift to the world. Śiva is death that ends suffering, but at the same time he is the source of life. He is associated with the stage of deep, dreamless, restful sleep in life, which is the dissolved universe in miniscule.

Śiva is manifest time with all its tiny moments, and absolute Time, *Kāla*, beyond the existence of the cosmos. *Kāla* also means "death" and "black", the blackness that absorbs all life and manifestation, and the blackness that ends a single being's life. At the dissolution of the cosmos, time stands still, absorbed in Śiva who is ultimate Time, Great Time, or *Mahā-kāla*. Fire is the means by which Śiva dissolves the final stages of the world's manifestation: he is fire and all-devouring Time at the same time. Maxwell thinks that the snake coiled around Śiva's arm represents the eternal time-cycles of manifest and unmanifest existence.[38] For Śaivites, Śiva is the greatest God, he that pervades and holds within himself the entire universe. In the words of the *Muṇḍaka Upaniṣad*:

> His head is the fire, his eyes the sun and moon;
> His ears are the quarters; his speech the Vedas disclosed;
> His breath is the wind, his heart the universe;
> And with his feet he is, indeed,
> The inmost self of every being.[39]

The asceticism / eroticism of Śiva

India has a long history and even pre-history of asceticism and I shall return to the very early evidence of asceticism in Volume II with an exploration of the ancient Indus civilization. The typical ascetic is he who has long matted hair, soiled clothes, is sometimes naked, and who lives on the fringes of society and outside orthodox religious praxis. The *Ṛg Veda* has a record of such a man.[40] Being outside orthodoxy, such ascetics were often derided, especially since the householder was highly regarded in Hindu society as was the producing of children and honouring of the gods: ascetics rejected these basic religious and societal aims. As the greatest of all ascetics, Śiva was different to other deities and his asceticism – with the traditional ascetic appearance – was often offensive to non-Śaivites. But Śiva has another side, too, and that is his eroticism that outclasses anything to which Kāma the god of love could aspire. The *Purāṇas* abound with the enmity between Śiva and Kāma but the tension on the anthropomorphic level reflects more of a symbiosis on the metaphysical one.

The abundance of myths about Śiva generally portray either his ascetic nature or his erotic nature. I noted above the phenomenon of fire as both ascetic fervour and austerity, *tapas*, and as sexual desire, and it is perhaps easy to see from this example how two at first seemingly opposing characteristics can, in fact, be complementary. Śiva as the God at the fulcrum of all opposites is the balance between asceticism and desire or eroticism. But the tensions between the two are also obvious and brought out in a myth in which Kāma attempts to aim his lustful arrow to disturb the deep meditation of Śiva. Śiva reduces Kāma to ashes with that fire-devouring third eye of his. And yet, Śiva plays the role of Kāma because the seed produced by desire is that which causes creation. Śiva in his meditative, inactive state cannot create: it is his erotic state that can do this, conjoined with his feminine energies that I shall examine below. Suffice it to say here that Śiva, the God who unites all opposites, is as much feminine as masculine.

On the ascetic side, Śiva is the Great *Yogin* the *Mahā-Yogin*: the stillness that he is, is the goal of Śaiva *yogins*. In that stillness and stasis, Śiva represents the Unmanifest, the *nirguṇa* Brahman and the ultimate peace of Non-Being. Śiva is the Lord of *Yoga*, the perfect ascetic who can be reached in the cavern of the heart through direct experience by those deep in meditation: there is no need for orthodox ritual in order to experience Śiva deep within – another reason why Śiva is beyond orthodoxy. There are many myths that describe the austerities performed by Śiva that last for thousands of years. In such ascetic practice, the sexual seed is believed to be drawn upward, as opposed to normal erotic emission, and it is this upward flow that produces the power of the *yogin* and the power of Śiva as the supreme *Yogin*. O'Flaherty points out that in the *Vedas*, *tapas* as desire was praised because it produced progeny, but in the *Upaniṣads*, *tapas* as ascetic fervour produced the ultimate goal of liberation from the endless round of rebirth.[41] Yet Śiva has a consort, the Goddess Devī, though variously named, as we shall see below, and is thus pictured as a householder and an erotic one at that, his love-making prolonged for a hundred years. As O'Flaherty points out: "Śiva resolves the paradox in his own character by embodying a philosophy found throughout Hinduism: that chastity and sexuality are not opposed but symbiotic, that the chaste man is procreative by virtue of his chastity, and that the man who lives happily with his wife is performing a sacrament in his very life, if he but realize it."[42] And yet, Śiva is not chaste but produces no real offspring from his own seed. The offspring of Śiva are not normally produced: it is as if reproduction is impossible for the Great Ascetic. Nevertheless, Śiva represents the balance between asceticism and eroticism just as he is the balance between all other opposites.

The Gods and Goddesses of Hinduism, whether major or minor, are mostly portrayed anthropomorphically as supra-human but with human tendencies. Gods are often represented in myths as blatant seducers of women. Śiva's relationship with his wife, Pārvatī (Devī), is portrayed as like any other marital pair with its quarrels and misunderstandings, as well as its powerful love and occasional antagonism. Pārvatī in her own right is a great ascetic and when the myths tell us that they both perform *tapas*, the power produced is dangerous. But it is usually Śiva's erotic behaviour that is dangerous, his ascetic phases being associated more with his benign personality.[43] There is danger in their combined love-making or their combined ascetic meditation since both are withdrawal phases when the world is without protection.[44] But both are extremes, opposing ends of the swing of a pendulum that can only go so far before it has to return in the opposite direction. Quiescence and activity are the phases of unmanifest and manifest existence, both held in Śiva along with all the phases in between.

As I said above, Śiva's offspring are not the product of union with his consort. One, Skanda, the god of war, was born when some of Śiva's semen fell into a sacrificial fire and then into the river Ganges. The other, more famous, God is Gaṇeśa, or Ganapati, the elephant-headed God. He was born from the flakes of skin that dropped from Pārvatī one day when she bathed. Gaṇeśa is an immensely popular God, prayed to before undertaking any venture, whether beginning a business, marriage, taking an examination, and so on. Other sons of Śiva are born in equally unnatural ways, many becoming demons opposed to the gods.

The tensions between asceticism and eroticism are not always obviated by lifting the concepts to the level of metaphysics. The same tension is found as in the *āśrama* tradition with the householder and ascetic being contradictory phases. It is the iconography of Śiva that portrays the ascetic/erotic nature of the God. He is often ithyphallic (having an erected penis), the *ūrdhva-liṅga*, indicative of his *yogic* powers *and* his erotic abilities. Popular myths tend to concentrate on the erotic tales, the more conservative Sanskrit accounts of Śiva on his ascetic chastity, but both asceticism and eroticism run side by side in the majority of myths about Śiva. We must turn, now, to examine the major symbol of Śiva, the *liṅga* or phallus.

The Śiva *liṅga*

Śiva is mainly worshipped as his *liṅga*, his phallus, a practice that could be regarded "as a part of the general evolution of the human mind and part of the history of religion",[45] regardless of how modernity may view such practice. The phallus in such worship represents the creative energy. The Sanskrit word *liṅga* means "sign", or "characteristic", that by which something is known. Metaphysically, Śiva cannot be known in his ultimate being, but his sign, his *liṅga*, represents his metaphysical transcendence: what is perceptible is a symbol of the imperceptible. The association of Śiva with the *liṅga* was fairly late, in the time of the epics,[46] but there is plenty of evidence for phallus worship in early pre-Āryan religion. The *Ṛg Veda* refers disparagingly to those who worshipped the phallus and says that they were slain by the god Indra.[47] Seals found at ancient pre-Āryan sites of the Indus Valley – a subject to which I shall return in Volume II – show an ithyphallic figure. Such early religious praxis was based on fertility, so it would be fairly true to say that in its early form *liṅga* worship was involved with ideas of reproduction, fecundity and fertility. Chakravarti notes the synonymy between *liṅga* and *lāṅgala*, this latter meaning "plough",[48] with its obvious association with fertility. But there is no sense of fertility in contemporary religious praxis where the *liṅga* is present: the connection between the *liṅga* and fertility has been lost over the centuries.

There are many popular myths to explain why the *liṅga* of Śiva is separated from him. The most basic of these myths are those relating Śiva's encounter with sages in the Pine Forest, the Deodar Forest. Śiva entered the Pine Forest naked in the guise of a beggar and the wives of the sages fell madly in love with him to the consternation and anger of their sage husbands, who cursed Śiva so that his phallus dropped off. The severed phallus created all sorts of havoc and destruction until the sages begged Śiva to stop it. The outcome was that Śiva taught the sages to worship the *liṅga*. There are many variations of this basic myth and many layers placed on it as well as many separate myths in which Śiva, for one reason or another, is bereft of his penis either through being cursed or by self-castration. Philosophically, Śiva devoid of his penis is the remote ascetic, while the *liṅga* is the creative energy that allows the world to be manifest. Devoid of the *liṅga*, Śiva is often *Sthāṇu*, the "post", that is to say, he is immobile, withdrawn, contained within himself: it was, as noted earlier, also a name for Rudra. As *Sthāṇu*, then, Śiva is not maintaining creation, so *Sthāṇu* is indicative of destruction, whereas the *liṅga* symbolizes creative energy. One myth describes Śiva's *liṅga* as a flaming tower that extended to eternity above and below with no beginning, middle or end. The god Brahmā changed into a swan in order to fly upwards to find the top of it but could not, while Viṣṇu turned into a boar and burrowed down into the earth but, similarly, could not find its base. Here, Śiva's superiority is represented as the *Axis Mundi* of the universe, a never-ending pillar of light of which he is the core.

The *liṅga* of Śiva represents the essential characteristics of Śiva as creator, dissolver and liberator. When visible, Śiva's *liṅga* is usually erect, indicative of *ūrdhva-liṅga*, the semen travelling upwards and controlled rather than expelled. This is the mark of Śiva as the supreme ascetic, the Great *Yogin* and the quiescence that precedes creative activity. The *liṅga* is to be found in the heart of Śaiva temples. They are sometimes made of stone and some are regarded as *svayambhū*, "self-existent", that is to say, having existed spontaneously without human intervention: these are considered especially sacred. Similarly, pebbles that have assumed the same shape are regarded as *svayambhū*. Some *liṅgas* are hand carved and can be of any material. Some carry the head of Śiva on the top or front; others have four heads of Śiva facing the four directions, or five heads symbolizing the five elements and five senses. Some sects like the Liṅgāyatas carry a small *liṅga* around their necks in a casket. Śiva's *liṅga-śarīra*, his "subtle body", or hidden cosmic essence, is believed to be manifest in the *liṅga* pointing to his absolute unmanifest state.

Some myths suggest that the severed *liṅga* of Śiva is the means by which he obtains sexual satisfaction, as if the *liṅga* can behave independently of its owner. On the other hand, the severed *liṅga* symbolizes fertility of the earth and the productivity arising from its fall, as if it were divine seeds of creation. Thus, as O'Flaherty puts it, concerning Śiva's castration in the Pine Forest, "the falling of the *liṅga* does not render Śiva asexual but extends his sexuality to the sages and to the whole universe".[49] The *liṅga* is certainly male creative energy, but that energy is transformed into the cosmic dimension of the energy necessary for creation of the cosmos. Those who venerate the *liṅga* in Śaiva temples do so without seeing any sexual connotations in the object of worship or their patterns of worship. Richard Davis puts this point rather well when he says that a devotee may well "glimpse beyond" the symbol to "Śiva's more all-encompassing nature". The symbol or icon becomes translucent: "While it had a substantive presence in itself, it also allowed a viewer in the proper spirit of devotion and knowledge to glimpse with a devotional eye through it – imperfectly, since all human encounters with transcendence will be limited – to the transcendent reality of the deity as well."[50] Śaivites are well-known for meditative and *yogic* praxis. Their goal, in this case, is to focus on the abstract reality of Śiva as Brahman, knowledge of which will bring liberation. Transcending the purely visible, the goal is to attain that point of focus that overcomes all opposites, the essential nature of the being of Śiva.

The base of a *liṅga* in a temple is hidden, indicating that its roots are in the formless void, the unmanifest that is not known and that simply *is* when the cosmos is not manifest. But what is visible is believed to incorporate the divine presence. Davis gets to the heart of such a concept when he says: "Śaiva siddhāntins speak of a Śiva *liṅga* as possessing 'Śivaness' (*śivatva*), an attribute that sets it apart from ordinary stuff of creation, which is inert and inanimate. In an important sense, the object that is infused with or identical with God cannot be composed of ordinary matter; it must undergo a transubstantiation. This requires a combination of divine grace and human ritual labor."[51] Śiva may well appear manifest in such a symbol, but he is ultimately unmanifest and undifferentiated. The Śiva *liṅga* stands independently in the womb, the *garbha-gṛha*, of a Śaiva temple, with pictorial images elsewhere. In other temples, like those dedicated mainly to Viṣṇu, a separate shrine containing a *liṅga* may well be present, but always separated from the other deities. Devotees will be of different types but the *Liṅga-purāṇa* says there are two: "The spiritual liṅga is not perceptible to the deluded person who conceives things only externally and not otherwise. The gross liṅga made of clay, wood, etc., is perceptible only to the non-yogin as the subtle and eternal Liṅga is perceptible to the Jñanin [one with ultimate knowledge]."[52] But the *liṅga* is treated as if it were a special guest in the temple, so it is bathed, given flowers and food offerings, decorated with ornaments and praised with hymns and music.

Hermaphrodite Śiva: *Ardhanārīśvara*

If Śiva is that in which all opposites unite, then he must also be male and female. I shall be examining the *Śakti*, female "energy" or "power" of Śiva in the next chapter, but it is necessary to include some of that information here as it pertains to the character of Śiva. The male *and simultaneous female* nature of Śiva is represented in iconography that is hermaphrodite, androgynous, half male and half female: this is called *Ardhanārīśvara*. The female part of Śiva is the energy and power that makes creation possible when it is separated from the male. The androgynous form represents the quiescence that precedes creation and yet the creative impulse with all its potentiality for manifest existence. Śiva's major consort, Pārvatī, while mostly portrayed as inferior to Śiva (though she may be distinctly superior), is his power of manifestation in the cosmos.

The androgyne portrays Śiva on the right, often partly nude, draped in skulls, while the female side is on the left, may be partly clothed, and garlanded with lotuses. Śiva is still, static and upright, whereas Pārvatī is fluidly represented. It is a paradoxical icon, as O'Flaherty suggests: "Iconographically, the image of the androgyne is the symbol of sexual union but also representative of a situation in which union is physically impossible."[53] In the androgyne, Śiva is both the unchangeable unmanifest that is pure consciousness and, in his female half, the energy of creative power. Śiva is time and Pārvatī is space. When they separate into their distinctive personalities, creation takes place. For many Hindus, the female power, the *Śakti*, became the focus of devotion in the form of the Mother Goddess – a being that was accepted as superior to any other divine being, including Śiva.

Symbolically, the female side, Pārvatī, is represented as the circular *yoni*, the female generative organ, the vagina. The *yoni* is the pedestal in which the erect *liṅga* stands. It may not always be associated with the *yoni*, in which case it simply acts as a base for the *liṅga* and as a basin in which to collect and drain off the liquids poured over the *liṅga* during worship in the temple or home. When not a visible base, the *yoni* may be simply a circle of stones around the bottom of the *liṅga*. Together, the *liṅga* and the *yoni* represent the unity of all existence, its totality in manifestation and the unmanifest being of Śiva that is Brahman. In the myths about the *liṅga* and *yoni*, Śiva's castrated *liṅga* causes havoc in the world of gods and humans, a destructive force of fire that only the Great Goddess can control with her own womb that is water: water calms fire. Notably, however, the *liṅga* does not penetrate the *yoni*; it emerges from it and as Kramrisch wisely commented: "The knowledge of ultimate reality and of contingent reality, in which the former dwells, has the *liṅga* in the *yoni* as its visual equivalent."[54] It would be a grave mistake to view these symbols at a gross, sexual level. Śiva is inert but is the essence of life, *Śakti*, is matter, energy, nature imbued with the life principle: the two combined make existence possible but an existence that always has the potential to revert to the stillness of a pure consciousness that is the ultimate Śiva when physicality returns to its metaphysical reality.

Symbols of Śiva

All Hindu deities are replete with symbolism and their icons portray aspects of their natures by means of such symbols. Indeed, Hinduism perhaps more than any other religion uses symbols to project the mind beyond the concrete to abstract ideas. Symbols have layered meanings, and it will depend on the nature of the individual in what way such symbols are interpreted: for some, they will be understood simplistically; for others profoundly, with all the variables in between. Since Śiva has both an ascetic and an erotic nature the symbolism of his appearance has the opposites that are portrayed in his character. The ascetic accoutrements are horrific, the erotic ones, beautiful, but there may be some overlap in these at deeper levels. There are regional differences in the ways in which Śiva is represented iconographically, particularly between North and South India, but some of the most obvious symbols associated with Śiva are as follows:

- ***Serpents*** are portrayed as the sacred thread of Śiva, as well as being a necklace, bracelets and in his clothing. While these are horrific symbols, O'Flaherty notes the sexual symbolism of snakes in general. Additionally, cobras, she says, are believed to have rubies in their hoods that act as lanterns for Śiva and Pārvatī during the nights. Moreover, cobras are often portrayed as encircling the *liṅga* with its tail deep in the *yoni*.[55] There were probably serpent cults in early India and these may have been absorbed into Śaivism.[56] In *yogic* praxis, the snake symbolizes the inner energy at the base of the spine. Through meditative praxis this energy rises to higher points with the aim of total liberation. Snakes are poisonous, but no poison can harm Śiva as his blue throat reminds the onlooker: he could drink the destructive poison that no other god could. Snakes strike according to the will of Śiva because he is their Lord. Thus, the bow of Śiva is featured as a snake. Yet there are positive aspects to the snake: it can shed its skin and seemingly rejuvenate itself, suggestive of continued life and strength.
- ***Ashes*** are smeared over Śiva's body as a symbol of his asceticism and his rejection of the world. Ash is associated with the cremation grounds, places of horror. Again, O'Flaherty notes the more erotic association of ashes when used for control of fevers, especially those occurring from love.[57] Ashes are also smeared on Śiva's *liṅga*. The three parallel lines on the forehead of Śiva and of Śaivites are symbols of the ash.
- ***The third eye*** symbolizes Śiva's paramount ascetic nature. With that eye, with connotations of the familiar "evil eye", he reduced the god of love, Kāma, to ashes, indicative that he is against eroticism. From the eye issues fire, symbolic of Śiva's fierce aspect, the fire of utter destruction that could not only destroy Kāma, but the whole world at the end of time. The fire from the third eye is like the sun that can blaze in destructive force. Yet, the third eye can be beautiful and shining when it is the *tilaka* mark on Śiva's forehead in his benign and attractive form, just as Śiva's calm gaze restored Kāma to life. In his benign form, Śiva is symbolized by water and the moon (Soma), quite the opposite of fire. The third eye symbolizes Śiva's absolute power over the three worlds of Earth, Heaven and the Underworld or the space inhabited between Earth and Heaven, as well as the three times – past, present and future. It is also the symbol of supreme spiritual intuitive perception and absolute knowledge. There is a tension in the myths about this third eye with some portraying it as the light of the continuation of creation when it is open and others as the destructive fire that causes dissolution.
- ***The crescent moon*** on Śiva's forehead, and later in his matted hair, symbolizes Soma, the liquid of immortality. A whole book of the *Ṛg Veda* is devoted to this substance imbibed by the priests during ritual in order to heighten consciousness. In early Hinduism, the moon was regarded as the place to which the dead went.

The moon was also the controller of plants and vegetation, as was Rudra in the *Vedas*. The crescent moon is indicative of the cycles of time, the phases of life and death, the decay and revival of vegetation and the activity and quiescence of the cosmos. The shape of the crescent moon bears some resemblance to the horns of a bull according to some.[58]

- ***The skull*** carried in Śiva's hand is stuck to it as penance for cutting off one of the heads of the creator god, Brahmā. It was eventually released in Banāras and thereafter placed on the top of a pole sometimes as a mace. The skull is the symbol of the ascetic's begging or drinking bowl. A garland of skulls also adorns Śiva in his ascetic aspect, a reminder of the mortality of human life and the transience of all things.
- ***The trident*** or *triśūla* is said to represent the three deities of Brahmā, Viṣṇu and Śiva, the forces of creation, preservation and dissolution, respectively, though all three roles are manifest in Śiva. But the trident is also a weapon, like the spear and axe that Śiva uses to destroy the universe at the end of time.
- ***Animal hides*** are the dress of the ascetic Śiva, a black antelope skin as the upper garment and an elephant hide on his lower half. He is usually seated on a tiger skin. But Śiva may also carry an antelope in his hand, a symbol of his protection. Dogs, mainly despised creatures, accompany Śiva on his ascetic wanderings.
- ***Matted hair*** is a symbol of the ascetic and Śiva's is sometimes piled up into the shape of a *liṅga*, with the crescent moon on the right side.
- ***The earings*** Śiva wears are a masculine one in his right ear and a feminine one in his left, indicative of his containing and uniting of both male and female within his nature.
- ***The River Gaṅgā***, the sacred Ganges, flows from the hair of Śiva representing the phases of everlasting time.

Nandi the bull

Śiva has as his mount a white bull called Nandi. He may be seen seated or standing on Nandi, or simply leaning against him with his arm placed on a hump or horn of the bull. Even when Pārvatī is featured with Śiva, Nandi is there in the background or the two beings may have their hands on the bull: he is part of their family. As we shall see in the second volume to this book, the bull featured widely on seals in ancient Indian cities. It was probably an animal that was venerated, probably for its power and fertility. It is likely that some of the cults that continued such praxis were incorporated into the early worship of Rudra and then of Śiva. In Śaiva shrines, Nandi is to be found seated and facing the *liṅga*, both protecting and adoring his Lord with utmost constancy, and devotees touch its flanks in passing as an added blessing. Looking at Śiva through the horns of Nandi is believed to be the best possible perspective of the *liṅga*. Nandi is calm and gentle – not at all the image one would have of the male bull. The symbolism here is one of control of the senses, particularly the sexual drives.

The entourage of Śiva

Śiva in his fierce aspect does not act alone. He is accompanied by *gaṇas*, hosts of all sorts of ghouls and goblins, spirits, ghosts and demons. Gokhale rather aptly says of these creatures: "All these dark, troubled and troublesome forces are the various energy emanations of negativity and uncontrolled, unharnessed vitality that are present in every life situation."[59] Śiva is associated with death and dissolution: he grants death as a resting place, a quiescence in the endless cycle of rebirth. Since he is associated with death, it is the cremation grounds that Śiva likes to frequent along with his entourage. The cremation grounds are revolting but they are to be celebrated in that they mark the end of life and the passage to new life. Siva's association with such places is rather like his detachment from the poison that turns his throat blue; he transcends such places, is aloof from them and is unmoved by the horrors of ghouls and ghosts around him. Indeed, he liked to dance with them in cremation grounds. Kramrisch noted here: "Śiva liked his ghostly entourage. It attracted to his presence those who had nothing to fear, who had mastered the onslaught of the multiple categories of threatening powers that were fatal to those who were less than heroes, and who could not control the frightening phantoms because they had not controlled themselves."[60] It is from the funeral pyres that Śiva obtains the ash with which he smears his body. We should remember that his name means "Auspicious One", so in his frequenting of the cremation grounds he makes what is dark and inauspicious auspicious, all the time remaining spiritually pure. Thus should be his devotees in times of fear and struggle. Śiva does not turn the devotee away who is low caste, outcaste or demonic providing they are devoid of ego. Historically, there were probably demon cults in popular religion, and whereas the priests may have wanted to ignore such a phenomenon as ignorant, it is likely that its persistence necessitated the inclusion of demons as part of Sanskritized mythology. Śiva would have provided an ideal deity with whom demons – once the enemy of the gods – could be associated. This is another example of how Śiva absorbed non-*Vedic* elements as an "outsider". Kramrisch called the demonic entourage of Śiva "part of Rudra's being, tremors, resonances of his nature, by-products of tensions that sustain his contradictory wholeness".[61]

The many facets of Śiva are represented in his iconography. While the *liṅga* is by far the most widespread symbol, there are many aspects from the myths surrounding Śiva that are celebrated in art. These may show him bedecked with spectacular jewellery and rich garments that obscure the *liṅga*. Śiva's manifold nature is depicted by more than one head – mostly three, but also four or five. Southern India boasts the *Dakṣiṇāmūrti*, literally, the south-facing image, which celebrates Śiva as the master of *yoga* and all sacred knowledge, as well as music. This image is so-called because Śiva is represented in myth as sitting in his abode in the Himālayas, facing South: it is from here that he divulges spiritual knowledge. Other artistic representations show Śiva seated on a lotus, one hand in the meditative position, or *mudra*, in his lap, one holding scriptures, one a rosary representing eternal *dharma* and another in the *mudra* of giving, bestowing wisdom on his devotees. Like other deities, many arms represent extended powers. Occasionally, Pārvatī is featured on the left side of Śiva and significantly smaller to suggest his supremacy.

The dances of Śiva

As the God in whom all opposites are reconciled, Śiva has both the still motionless *Sthāṇu* in his character as well as its opposite of intense movement, this latter being epitomized by dance. In Kramrisch's words: "As sign of cessation, Sthāṇu, the post, stood for the arrest of time, a state beyond death. The symbol shape of Śiva Sthāṇu, the branchless stem, stands opposite to the image of dancing Śiva, his many arms, his flowing hair filling the cosmos with the rhythms of his being. Sthāṇu standing by the moving universe is a symbol of the timeless state attainable in *samādhi*. Śiva, the Lord of Yoga, dwells in timeless eternity, while Śiva, the dancer, performs his aeviternal dance at the end of each aeon across which Kāla speeds."[62] Śiva's dances are many and are of different forms – joyous; celebration of slaying demons of ignorance or of a major demon; dances with his consorts; an evening dance; dances of preservation and destruction of the universe. His dances may be ecstatic, graceful, wild, violent, playful, sportive or happy. Yet Maxwell makes the following valid point: "It will be noticed in all these dancing figures that the face of the god is calm, the eyes usually half-closed: his inner nature, upon which he meditates even in the most violent of his activities, is the ultimate peace which he brings to his devotees."[63] The most well-known dances are the two that preserve the world on the one hand and destroy it on the other. These two apparently opposing forces are complementary: he periodically brings an end to the universe in order for it to be re-created. The symbols of such are evident in his ashes of death and his erotic creativity. Śiva is the great Creator but also the Dissolver just as a single man is a procreator but is subject to death.

The *Naṭarāja*

The most famous dance of Śiva is that of the *Naṭarāja*, a cosmic dance that incorporates the whole cycle of time from creation, symbolized by the drum in his left hand, to dissolution symbolized by the fire in his right. Sivaya Subramuniyaswami entitled his work on Śiva as *Dancing with Śiva* to reflect the fact that every engagement in life is interaction with Śiva: "Thus, dancing with Śiva is everything we do, everything we think and say and feel, from our seeming birth to our so-called death. It is man and God forever engaged in sacred movement."[64] It is *activity* and *motion* of Śiva that is so evident in the figure of the *Naṭarāja*, an activity so stunning that images are now widely available in the West. Originating in the North of India probably in the eighth or ninth centuries, the image spread throughout India and is now particularly popular in South India. The magnificent swaying figure of the God is a joy to behold and yet is full of symbolism that points to the inscrutability and power of this supreme God. Creation is portrayed as beginning and ending with dance, movement, movement and sound being the primordial aspects that begin creation. The rhythms of life, its pulses from moment to moment are all symbolized in the *Naṭarāja*. Śiva is Lord of the Dance, Lord of Life and all its movements of mind and body so the *Naṭarāja* is a dynamic image of eternal rhythm and of everything that exists from the smallest of atoms and molecules to the massive ranges of mountains, the great oceans and the apparent eternity of space and cosmos. The dancing Śiva keeps all this in motion. Hints of the origins of a dancing god may well date back to the Indus civilization that I shall be examining in detail in Volume II. I do not want to press the association of Śiva with any so-called Proto-Śiva on seals from the Indus Valley too closely, but there is evidence that dance was part of the early religious culture of pre-Hinduism.

The *Naṭarāja* image is animated and dynamic in a pose that is traditionally known in Indian dance as "fear of a snake". So the body is twisted to one side with the left leg raised as if it is avoiding or has trodden on a snake. The arms, too, are animated, full of swaying rhythm. All the activities associated with other Gods are here in the *Naṭarāja* – creation associated with Brahmā, preservation and evolution associated with Viṣṇu and then the dissolution that allows creation again with Śiva himself. Every part of this image is symbolic:

- ***Four arms*** represent the universal power of the God.
- ***His left arm*** crosses the body like the raised left leg and like the trunk of an elephant, showing strength and pointing to his raised right foot. Śiva's son, Gaṇeśa, had the head of an elephant and is associated with good fortune, blessing and the removal of obstacles.
- ***Fire*** in his raised left hand is indicative of the fire that will destroy the universe but is also the fire that will destroy ignorance and release the soul from its slavery to manifest existence. Thus it is a positive symbol, indicative of pure spiritual Knowledge.
- ***His lower right hand*** is raised in blessing and hope with the *mudra* "fear not", signifying protection and support: fear of repeated births and deaths is deemed the greatest fear of all.
- ***A raised right foot*** twisted across the body is the symbol of liberation – a positive sign.
- ***A demon*** or dwarf under Śiva's left foot represents ignorance, a negative symbol unlike the raised left foot. The name of the demon is Apasmāra Puruṣa, which means "The Being without Memory", hence the ignorance it represents. Śiva epitomizes the balance between opposites, that point where opposites no longer exist. This is what the conqueror of ignorance can attain.
- ***A drum*** in the upper right hand is shaped like an hour-glass in two parts symbolic of male and female. It has thongs attached, is held in the middle and when shaken the thongs hit the skins of the ends of the drum like a rattle. It is symbolic of the sound, the vibrations of energy, that begin creation and of Śiva as the source of sound and creation. The drum, then, is the "rhythm at the heart of the universe" as Stephen Cross puts it.[65] Its beat during the *Naṭarāja* supplies the pulse of the universe, sustaining all activity and movement and all manifestation. The drum in his right hand is balanced perfectly with the fire of his left denoting the opposites of creation and destruction, life and death, manifestation and the unmanifest.
- ***A circle of flames*** around the whole image represents pure energy but is also representative of the flames of destruction at the end of time. It is said, too, to symbolize the sacred sound of *Oṃ*, the first sound to be made in the regenerating universe.

> The fact that Śiva's head touches the circle of flames is also suggestive that it is manifest existence that stems from Śiva as the unmanifest Absolute. Thus, it represents matter, nature and the revolving wheel of births and deaths.

The whole animated image of the *Naṭarāja* is contrasted by the beautifully passive and tranquil face of Śiva, still, though faintly smiling. This facial pose is the opposite to the animation of the dance: it is the still state of the Unmanifest, the point that needs to be attained by the devotee. In Cross' words: "Here, utterly still at the centre of the dance, is the inner witness, the omnipresent Self, the unmoved Mover, the still point at the centre of the ever-changing world."[66] The whole image is, then, full with contemplative aspects, what Maxwell describes as "a superb symbol of the divine forces which demand utter self-surrender on the part of the individual, presented in ritualized artistic terms which engage the mind of the devotee as compellingly as does the temple dance itself".[67]

The *Naṭarāja* that creates and sustains the universe is transformed into the wild dance of its dissolution at the end of time. Śiva then dances the world into oblivion in a dance called the *Tāṇḍava.* Then the mountains are scattered by the violence of his dance, the stars are flung apart and flames absorb all phenomena. In this final stage his terrifying entourage assist, as does his female consort, Devī. This is the dark, *tamasic* aspect of Śiva that brings about involution. The myths that describe the *Tāṇḍava* describe Śiva with a thousand arms, a thousand eyes, a thousand feet, terrible fangs and a face no longer benign.

All iconographical representations of Śiva, and even the *liṅga*, are but physical symbols of a supreme God that is ultimately indescribable. The *Śvetāśvatara Upaniṣad* states that Śiva has no sign, no *liṅga*, for he is beyond all manifestation, a totally transcendent Absolute without qualities, without perceptible form and without parts.[68] In this case, Śiva is Brahman, ultimate reality and it is this that the *liṅga* symbolizes. For Śaivas, Śiva is the supreme God, superior to any other. It is he that will perform the three major cosmic functions of creation, preservation and dissolution without the aid of the other two deities of Brahmā and Viṣṇu. The *Mahābhārata* contains the following statement concerning this identity of Śiva with all that is utmost and beyond time:

> He is the cause of the continuance and the creation (of the universe). He is the cause of the universe and the cause also of its destruction. He is the Past, the Present, and the Future. He is the parent of all things. Verily, he is the cause of every thing. He is that which is mutable, he is the unmanifest, he is Knowledge; he is Ignorance; he is every act; he is every omission; he is righteousness; and he is unrighteousness.[69]

We have to gather information about Śiva from the many myths that portray the immense diversity of character of this major Hindu God. It seems to me that it is always important to look behind the myths for the transcendent Śiva in order to reconcile the multiple facets of the God's character that have arisen from so many complex and contradictory mythical traditions. In deepening the understanding of the transcendent Śiva it is possible to reconcile opposing concepts, to see Śiva as that in which all opposites cease to exist, as the fulcrum and balance between opposing polarities. O'Flaherty says that "Śiva's complexity allows him to penetrate into the deepest corners of Hindu devotion."[370] This is precisely why the God is so important since Śiva seems to encompass almost every definition possible of multi-faceted Hinduism.

6

Gods and Goddesses

Śakti – The Divine as Female

The conception of divinity as female in Hinduism is not confined to its fringes but is a central belief for millions of Hindus and is immensely important. In contrast to Śiva, the juxtaposition of myth and metaphysics is a little clearer, though both stand parallel to each other occasionally with few obvious bridges between them. It is not my purpose here, to recount the multiplicity of myths surrounding different goddesses, the complexity of which is a subject more suitable to a whole book than an isolated chapter. Rather, what I want to examine are the more conceptual underpinnings of beliefs in female goddesses.

The dualities of goddesses

In the same way as with Śiva, the dualities of the concept of goddess are the key to understanding them. Indeed, duality is of the essence of the manifested world, non-duality being associated only with the ultimate Absolute that is Brahman. But even Brahman is both unmanifest, *nirguṇa*, and manifest, *saguṇa*. As an unmanifest Absolute, Brahman is beyond all description and all opposites, but when manifest, what is One can become dual or many and, in particular, can express duality as either male or female: indeed, it might be said that to be one rather than the other would place limitations on divinity. I think it was Vivekananda who said that the bird of humanity cannot fly with just one wing, and goddesses are as necessary to the understanding of divinity in Hinduism as are gods. Both are aspects of divine manifestation but it is the goddess that is closer to the hearts and minds of many ordinary people. This is likely to have been the case since the times of the very earliest settlements in India that long pre-date the Āryans and the beginnings of Hinduism. I want to leave discussion of the important Indus culture until Volume II, but it should be noted here that this culture, dated to the third and second millennia BCE, revealed ample evidence of female figurines that were part of domestic religious ritual, as well as seals that depicted a fertility culture that is partly representative of goddess worship. The male-dominated Āryan religion does not reflect the worship of the divine in female form that was probably endemic at the popular level, but with the evolution of the concept of Brahman, manifest duality as male and female divinity became possible. Thus, T. S. Maxwell is to the point when he says: "the breaking away of the Goddess from the masculine rule of the gods became possible with the rise of the neuter brahman concept in the Upanishads."[1]

Women, it would seem, are more naturally attracted to the divine in female form: they are natural participants in the female essence that is divine and human in the same way that there is a natural understanding between mother and child. One of the most important and popular texts extolling the Goddess, the sixth-century *Devī-Māhātmya* (also known as the *Durgā-Saptaśati*),[2] has the statement: "All the various knowledges, O Goddess, are portions of you as is each and every woman in the various worlds. By you alone, the Mother, has this world been filled up."[3] The *Devī-Māhātmya* is a critical text in the presentation of the Goddess for, as Thomas Coburn puts it, it "is surely the earliest in which the object of worship is conceptualized as Goddess with a capital '*G*'".[4] In some aspects of Hinduism the Goddess is viewed as superior to all the gods, even to the great Hindu Gods Śiva and Viṣṇu. Such a view is particularly evident in Tantric sects of Hindus, to which I shall return later in this chapter.

Manifest divinity in female form is ubiquitous. In her introduction to *Hindu Goddesses*, Lynn Foulston writes: "The Goddess pervades the world and everything in it – in every living being, in the rivers that water the land, in the land itself, in the smallest blade of grass or the tiniest insect. Beyond and above, within and without, nothing exists or stirs in the cosmos that is not infused with the power of the Goddess."[5] The Goddess, whether local goddess or major pan-Indian Goddess, is as multi-faceted as we saw with the character of Śiva and thus exemplifies the broad spectrum of beliefs that we know as Hinduism, reflecting its richness and variety of perspectives of deity and associative religious praxis. What might surprise the reader is that goddesses can be represented by many forms – portrayed as human or represented by just a stone or a tree.[6] Like Hinduism in general, sophisticated philosophical belief may surround one goddess only for another to be reflected by simple superstition. Multitudes of different forms represent the goddess as well as a multiplicity of names and myths. Different regions prefer different names, some being widespread in use, others localized and pertaining to a small village or urban area. In terms of pan-Hindu Goddesses the nature of the Goddess will be epitomized by her name, such as Kālī as the embodiment of time, or Lakṣmī, the Goddess of wealth and prosperity, but they may have a preferred, different name in other places. Goddesses that are peculiar to a small area may take their names from a local myth and would not be recognized elsewhere, and even a small community may have many goddesses housed in different shrines or approached at different natural places in the area. What all this variety points to is a plurality of experience of divinity, and is one of the major reasons why Hinduism cannot be defined simplistically.

Nevertheless, the Great Goddess, Mahā-Devī, is the essence that informs all goddesses: they are all her multiple manifestations. While most Hindus understand the Goddess to be One but possessing many forms, Kathleen Erndl makes a very interesting comment when she says that in her experience of "ordinary Hindu devotees", they "move with apparent ease between universality and particularity in their ritual and devotional lives, speaking of the Goddess (singular) in some contexts and of particular goddesses (plural) in other contexts and often even in the same sentence."[7] She emphasizes that the identity of the Great Goddess is "multivalent and capable of multiple understandings and interpretations which may be extremely idiosyncratic".[8]

Given the archaeological evidence from the Indus civilization and later discoveries, we know that worship of the goddess was ancient and pre-Āryan. As such, it has continued to feature deeply in the Hindu religious psyche. The non-Āryan forms of female divinity were associated with nature, vegetation and fertility, as were goddesses in other ancient cultures. We find this emerging in the representations of *yakṣīs*, the female correspondents to male spirits of the trees and earth.[9] Since the early peoples lived mainly in villages, they were dependent on the rhythms of the seasons, on fertility of the land, and were close to nature. It would have been natural for such a life-pattern to be reflected in worship of goddesses. And since forests and wildernesses were wild places, these goddesses themselves were portrayed as wild and ferocious. Devdutt Pattanaik writes rather artistically: "In the forests, long before civilisation's stifling influence, ancient Indian tribes heard Devi's wild, unrestrained, virginal laughter. She was found residing in trees, with birds and beasts. She was Bagalamukhi, the heron-faced goddess. She was the turtle-riding Yamuna and the crocodile-riding Ganga – proud, turbulent river-goddesses. She belonged to all. She was Renuka, mistress of the earth. She was Yellamma, everyone's mother."[10] While there are few goddesses in the *Ṛg Veda* in comparison to the number of gods, one, Pṛthivī, is praised in several hymns that extol the earth, a fact that prompted David Kinsley to write: "An underlying implication of perceiving the earth as a great and powerful goddess is that the world as a whole, the cosmos itself, is to be understood as a great, living being, a cosmic organism."[11] This is something that the *Devī-Māhātmya* reiterates, as will be seen later in this chapter. But as we know, nature can be benign, majestic and beautiful or cruel and destructive – dualities that are prevalent in the natures of many goddesses. Nowhere is this more obvious than in the life-giving nature of water, for example, and yet it has powerful torrents that destroy.

Thus, many early goddesses have been associated with nature especially with mountains: they probably reflect the tribal religions that pervaded the Indian soil long before the Āryans, and were persistent even after the Āryans had settled. These goddesses were to be seen as equally dangerous as the hostile wilderness and jungle environments beyond the pale of the villages. The dual nature of these goddesses reflects on a microcosmic level the very environments in which people lived and on a macrocosmic level the dualities necessary for all existence – positive and negative, as well as benign and fierce, traits. In a way, such dualities corresponded to the very nature of human beings themselves and made sense to the ordinary individuals with ordinary lives. That is perhaps why goddess worship today is the focus of those of low castes or those outside the caste system – potters, weavers, blacksmiths and tanners, for example. It is likely, then, that many of the major Goddesses had their roots in primitive pre-Āryan tribal beliefs and were associated with agriculture, propitiated as such and sometimes were the receivers of blood sacrifices. To an extent, the more male-orientated *Vedic* religion and society submerged the goddesses into what to orthodoxy were alien, unrefined and unacceptable praxis – the religious beliefs and practices of the common people. It was a process that Pattanaik sees as a "psychological shift" that made women subservient to men and goddesses to their spouses when civilized urban growth replaced the village and agricultural patterns of living.[12] This was all to change from about the seventh century CE onwards with the rise of the popularity of goddess worship, aided perhaps by Tantrism, to which I shall return at the end of this chapter.

The *Vedas* were not entirely without goddesses, but they did not have the powerful natures associated with goddesses of later times. *Vedic* goddesses were more amorphous and lacking in distinct anthropomorphic characteristics as, indeed, were some of the *Vedic* gods. These goddesses tended to personify aspects of nature like the dawn, the star-filled night, the sun and the earth. There is a beautiful hymn extolling the goddess of speech in the *Ṛg Veda*, making this goddess paramount in the universe: "I breathe a strong breath like the wind and tempest, the while I hold together all existence."[13] It is a hymn not without influence in later developments in worship of the Goddess. Another significant, though amorphous goddess in the *Vedas* is Aditī, who is the mother of *Ādityas*, the sun gods. She is presented as the cosmic womb that generates all, protects all and grants happiness like a mother to a child. Her attribute of motherhood persists long after her *Vedic* context. The dual nature of *Vedic* goddesses, however, is evident. Mandakranta Bose describes such goddesses as "a parcel of character attributes and functions that were imagined as the essence of femininity, including not only life-affirming attributes but also the potential for destruction".[14] The very best goddesses were bountiful – Uṣas, Pṛthivī, Vāc, Aditī, Sarasvatī, but there were a few malevolent ones, Nirṛti and Rātrī being the most noticeable.

Given the idea that all emerges from One, manifestation is partly good and partly evil, partly benign and partly ferocious, partly positive and partly negative. There is no concept of a totally evil deity or a totally beneficent deity, though some may lean towards one aspect more than another. Rather, each manifest deity embodies both positive and negative qualities and this is something that the myths about the deities demonstrate all too well. But it is particularly in the goddesses that such dual personality is evident. The powerful, ferocious goddess was a problem for the orthodox priests, and through a process of *Brāhminization*, they were transformed into benign, subservient and orthodox wives of other gods. In other cases, where the ascetic, non-householder traditions prevailed, any form of womanhood, be it deity or human, was believed to impede man's path to liberation. Here, women and individualized goddesses were not acceptable and were inimical to spiritual evolution. Benign Goddesses are mainly pan-Indian and the consorts of major Gods. Lakṣmī, the consort of Viṣṇu, is a typical example, as is Rādhā, Kṛṣṇa's lover and, to a lesser extent, Sītā, the consort of Rāma. These are "pure" Goddesses, accepted and worshipped by the orthodox, with their purity maintained by specialist priests. They are kind to their devotees, gentle, and willing to accept the prayers of the worshippers. The orthodox Goddesses are anthropomorphized in attractive forms, as devoted wives to their divine husbands and as role models for women to follow their *dharmic* paths. Sītā is a particularly good example of such a role model as the perfect wife. And yet, Lynn Foulston's study of goddesses in Orissa shows that it is not to the pan-Indian Goddess Lakṣmī's temple that people flock but to that of the more popular and powerful goddess.[15] Any attempt to Sanskritize or *Brāhminize* many of the popular goddesses does not wholly succeed.

The goddesses who are close to the people are anything but role models. They are usually fierce, powerful, and independent of any male deity. These goddesses symbolize what is dark and negative in life as well as the battle against evil. They transcend orthodoxy and the norms of *dharmic* Hinduism, flying in the face of the *Dharma-śāstras*. They are casteless and, if married through Sanskritizing, do not appear as supportive to, or pictorially smaller than, their spouses. Rather, they stand on their spouses or are in the process of sexual intercourse, but in the dominant position on top. This would never be represented in the case of a goddess like Sītā, for example. And as ferocious goddesses they are not represented as beautiful and soft: rather, they are often portrayed as warriors, with all the bloody appendages that accompany such a role, including the radically impure practice of animal sacrifice. Indeed, power and impurity appear to be concomitant aspects of many goddesses. In the main, it is the pan-Hindu, *Brāhminical* Goddesses that are pure and the locally confined goddesses that are non-*Brāhminical* and impure, though some of the pan-Indian Goddesses have their darker sides, too. Both pan-Indian and local goddesses are frequently conceived of as Mother, whether granting prosperity and protecting devotees as the pure Goddess or fighting injustice as the warmongering impure Goddess. It is especially the powerful Mother Goddess as a slayer of demons that demotes the male into a subservient and almost powerless position.

While goddess worship certainly obtained in India from the earliest times, its textual evidence for the more powerful aspects of female divinity is slim until about the fifth or sixth centuries CE.[16] Numerous elements informed its final expressions and many of these elements, as I have pointed out above, were pre-Āryan and non-Āryan. But its rise as a powerful medium in Hinduism is late.[17] It is likely that goddess worship began to hold ground parallel with the *bhakti* movements in the first two centuries CE.[18] After that time, the goddess became more and more popular right up to its pervasiveness of modern times. Textual sources do not do justice to the immense variety of goddesses that span the length and breadth of India. Orthodox textual sources such as the *Devī-Māhātmya* of the sixth century CE and a few *purāṇas* of a much later period, especially the *Devī-bhāgavata-purāṇa*, which repeats and enlarges much of the *Devī-Māhātmya*, provide the basis of orthodox myths for the Mother Goddess, but it is field work undertaken in local studies that enriches the understanding of goddesses in rural and small urban settings. What I want to do now is examine the whole concept of *power* that lies at the heart of divinity in female form.

Śakti and *Devī*: The Mother Goddess

The word for "goddess" in Sanskrit is *devī*, which comes from the root *div*, "to shine". Thus, it is the power of the sun, for example, to radiate heat and light. The supreme Goddess is Devī, and at the same time *Śakti*, the immensity of power that is the essence of the Goddess and that energizes the entire universe. Swami Chidbhavananda depicted *Śakti* as the immanent Reality of the universe: "She is the immediate cause of the perceptible world. The experiences of beings are all in her domain. To know her first therefore in her entirety is the means to know the Reality."[19] *Śakti* means energy, ability, power, force, strength, might, effort and is the energizing principle of the cosmos.[20] In the *Vedas*, *śakti* means "power" but more in the sense of ability or capacity to do something,[21] though goddesses there like Indrāṇī and Vāc are also associated with creation, the creative "power".[22] *Śakti*, thus, mostly came to be understood as divine power.[23] Such female divine power is essentially linked with creation, but not in such a way that it is remote, for the Mother of the universe is also the Mother of humanity. As Erndl puts it: "However one speaks of the Goddess, singularly, or goddesses, plurally, she is connected with *śakti*, the dynamic creative power or energy pervading and sustaining the universe."[24] Those who accept Devī in this way are called Śāktas and their understanding of her is as the ultimate power behind the universe that has existed for all time and beyond all time. Śāktas transform the creative power of the universe into tangible forms as goddesses, a point emphasized by Bose: "Giving shape to perceptions of the constant forces of the cosmos, the Hindu imagination locates the feminine energy at the heart of primordial creativity, which it shapes into anthropomorphic figures of protective authority and compassion."[25]

There are many myths relating to the birth of Devī but the most important and prevalent is that pertaining to the killing of the buffalo demon, Mahiṣa. This demon became so powerful that he could not be destroyed and was in the process of destroying the gods. In desperation, the gods created Devī from the energies – in particular, the anger – of all of them so that she became more powerful than the gods themselves. In a similar myth, Devī already exists and the gods give her their weapons in order to kill the demon and in yet another, Devī destroys two other demons, Śumbha and Niśumbha. The point here is twofold: first, the gods do not have the necessary power to overcome the demons themselves and, secondly, no beautiful, gentle goddess could accomplish the task as opposed to a powerful warrior in every aspect. In this sense, Devī is no ordinary Goddess: she is *Mahā-Devī,* the "Great Goddess", the Power, the *Śakti*, that creates the universe, makes it what it is, and absorbs it at the end of time. Devī here is the source of all goddesses and unifies them, so that each seemingly independent goddess is but an expression of her being. This was something that the *Devī-Māhātmya* articulated.

So here we have a very different Goddess from the benign ones that are the spouses of the Gods. Noticeably in her battles, Devī acts independently of the gods: she does not even use them to assist her but creates female warriors instead: this is female power at its most potent and independent. And that female power can take many, many forms – hence the multiplicity of goddesses each of which represents an aspect of Devī: many of these are known as Mā, "Mother". The *Devī-Māhātmya* depicts Devī as three of the most important Goddesses: "O Goddess, you are insight, knowing the essence of all scripture, you are **Durgā**, a vessel upon the ocean of life (that is so) hard to cross, devoid of attachments. (You are) **Śrī**, whose sole abode is in the heart of Kaiṭabha's foe (Viṣṇu); you are **Gaurī** whose abode is made with the one who is crowned with the moon (Śiva)."[26] Here, the consorts of Śiva and Viṣṇu are identified as Devī, as well as the Goddess Durgā, of whom, more below. It is especially Durgā who is identified with Devī in the text. The *Devī-Māhātmya* does not just identify various major Goddesses as her own being, but the powers and characteristics that they possess. Chapter 5 of the *Devī-Māhātmya* says much the same, identifying Devī as well with volition, consciousness, intelligence, sleep, hunger, reflection, power, thirst, forgiveness – in short, every dimension of human and divine existence. In chapter 11 of the *Devī-Māhātmya*, Devī is portrayed as the feminine power of all the Gods. She is ubiquitous, taking multitudes of forms, but Devī is the ultimate Reality of the cosmos: "I alone exist here in the world; what second, other than I, is there?", says Devī in the *Devī-Māhātmya* and when she is accused of needing the aid of manifestations of herself in order to defeat her enemies, she continues: "O wicked one, behold these my manifestations of power entering back into me!"[27] It is the earliest text to raise the feminine deity to exalted Goddess.[28]

However, when we examine the goddesses of local settings it is not the metaphysical Devī that is in the forefront of religious belief and praxis but the character of the local goddess correlated with the needs of the local people. And yet many women wear the *bindi*, the red dot applied to the centre of the forehead, which is a symbol of *śakti*. It is a symbol of fertility, of femininity, and of identity with the essence of the Goddess. Local goddesses may have no accompanying literature to explain their origins or nature, so the metaphysical traits of the Goddess are left to Sanskrit, fairly orthodox texts like the *Devī-Māhātmya*. Positing the unity of all the goddesses is one way of Sanskritizing and legitimizing worship of the many. Thus, Kinsley pointed out that such unity is asserted "by assuming the existence of one transcendent great goddess who possesses most classical characteristics of ultimate reality as understood in the Hindu tradition and then subsuming all particular goddesses under her as partial manifestations of her."[29] What we are left with, then, are juxtaposed concepts that are localized and varied – the many – and the metaphysical ultimate Reality of Mahā-Devī – the One. As the latter, Devī in some texts is even the creator of the great Gods Viṣṇu, Śiva and Brahmā and is the source of their respective powers and functions. In short, such texts present all the deities as inferior to Devī: they are her creations and operate by her will. It is the *Devī-bhāgavata-purāṇa* especially that projects such superiority of Devī. She is Brahman in such a profoundly Śākta text, in the same way that Viṣṇu is Brahman in Vaiṣṇava texts or Śiva in Śaiva texts. As Brahman, she is *everything* that exists and is both with qualities, *saguṇa*, and without qualities, *nirguṇa*. The *Devī-Māhātmya* presents Devī as both efficient and material cause of the universe but, at the same time, sees the whole universe as her form, her power abiding in all phenomena. She is implicitly *nirguṇa* Brahman, while her manifestations in *saguṇa* forms contribute to her character as a nurturing, friendlier form as well as a warrior Goddess.[30] The power of this Great Goddess is explicit in the *Devī-Māhātmya*: "You are the primordial material (*prakṛti*), of everything, manifesting the triad of constituent strands [*guṇas*], the night of destruction, the great night, and the terrible night of delusion"[31], that is to say, of periodic cosmic dissolution, final cosmic dissolution and the darkness of delusion. And in a previous verse of the same chapter, Devī is presented as the genetrix of all and one that clearly is responsible for the roles normally assigned to Viṣṇu, Śiva and Brahmā:

> By you is everything supported, by you is the world created; by you is it protected, O Goddess, and you always consume (it) at the end (of time).
> At (its) emanation you have the form of creation; in (its) protection (you have) steadiness; Likewise at the end of this world (you have) the form of destruction, O you who consist of the world!
> You are great knowledge (*mahāvidyā*), the great illusion (*mahāmāyā*), the great insight (*mahāmedhā*), the great memory,
> And the great delusion, the great Goddess (*mahādevī*), the great demoness (*mahāsurī*).[32]

But if Devī is cosmic and metaphysical, she is especially worldly and anthropomorphic, and it is in this latter sense that she is mainly known in some form or other throughout India. It is as Mother, Mā, Ambikā or Ambā, that many who venerate the divine as female envisage the Goddesses, whether they are pan-Hindu or localized. Usha Menon's study of goddesses in Oriya shows that most devotees refer to the Goddess as Mā, "Mother", whatever form the manifestation of the Goddess takes, be that ferocious-looking Kālī or the gentle Pārvatī. That is because she "generates and regenerates all life".[33]

The philosophy underpinning the concept of *Śakti* is gleaned from a school of thought known as Sāṃkhya.[34] This school posits two realities, an ultimate, spiritual one known as *puruṣa*, and a material one known as *prakṛti*. In Sāṃkhya thought these are completely separate and the goal is to transcend the latter for the supreme experience of the former. Śākta sects accept the concepts of *puruṣa* and *prakṛti*, viewing *puruṣa* as male and *prakṛti* as female, though it will be the female that is predominant. *Puruṣa* as male is static, inert and impotent without the female energy, *Śakti*. The Goddess *animates* and *energizes* the male at the same time being the energy and manifested active reality of the cosmos. The metaphysics of the Goddess amount to her three "energies", for want of a better word – *śakti*, *prakṛti* and *māyā*, though there is no consistency in Hindu texts as to the degree one or all are emphasized or even linked. Essentially, these three energies constitute the capacity for, and actuality of, the whole of creation. All three energies involve Devī in the world, in life and all its manifestations, in the rhythms of existence, in the dualities and transient changes that characterize all phenomena, and in the variety and variations of species. The important point about these three aspects is that they are perceived differently in Śāktism as opposed to sects that elevate male deities. John Stratton Hawley makes this point when he writes that according to the *Devī-Māhātmya*, "*māyā* is not complementary or subordinate to Viṣṇu, as other texts would have it. Nor is *prakṛti* balanced – or superseded – by the principle of maleness, *puruṣa*, with which it is so often paired. Nor is *śakti* paired with, or subsumed in, the male God Śiva. In Devī, these qualities stand on their own, constituting reality in a manner that is independently female."[35]

The association of the Goddess with *śakti*, *prakṛti*, and *māyā* varies. The *Purāṇas* tend to view them as combined in the Goddess who is completely equal to Viṣṇu or Śiva. Here, both male and female are complementary and necessary for creation. It is in Śākta sects that we find the Goddess often elevated to identity with Brahman and superior to male deities, in contrast to male Gods being identified with Brahman in Vaiṣṇava and Śaiva sects. In the Śākta *Devī-bhāgavata-purāṇa* especially, the Goddess becomes ultimate Reality, the *nirguṇa* Brahman and *nirguṇa Prakṛti*, indescribable formlessness. Creation is her *saguṇa* form, when the Goddess becomes the combination of *guṇas*, entering all that she has created. So, as *Śakti* she is the impulse for creation, creation itself, and its sustaining factor.

Prakṛti

Prakṛti is Nature, the material substance that permits form and identity of everything in existence. Everything that is manifest, whether positive or negative, is *prakṛtic* and composed in varying combinations of the three *guṇas*, *sattva*, *rajas* and *tamas*. For Śākta sects, *prakṛti* is what the Goddess *is* and what she becomes: one is the creative source, the other is creation, the manifest world itself. Because the Goddess as Creator is female, this makes her the Mother of all. Others believe that as *prakṛti* Devī animates and energizes *puruṣa* to produce Nature, but Devī is sometimes portrayed as the creator of *puruṣa* also: even if she is not, there is no pre-eminence of *puruṣa* over *prakṛti* as in Sāṃkhya philosophy: matter is not denigrated in favour of spirit. Some Śākta sects that see the Goddess as pre-eminent refer to Devī as *Mūla-prakṛti*, "Primordial matter". As primordial matter in which the potentiality of all things is held, she is that which exists when the cosmos is withdrawn as much as the creator and nourisher of it when it is manifest. And since *prakṛti* consists of the three *guṇas*, Devī as ultimate *sattva* is called *Mahā-Lakṣmī*; as *rajas*, *Mahā-Sarasvatī*; and as *tamas*, *Mahā-Kālī*. The whole concept of *prakṛti* here makes the world thoroughly divine even though it is characterized at times by death and decay, by grossness and evil. We shall see this epitomized when I examine the natures of Goddesses like Durgā and Kālī below.

Māyā

Māyā is usually understood as delusion or illusion, but in Śāktism, the former is probably the better meaning. Devī is sometimes referred to as *Mahā-māyā*, or *Mahā-mohā*, "Great Delusion", in that she is the creator of the whirlpool of thoughts, ideas, actions and consciousnesses of those caught up in the world she has created, of which she is the substratum, and in which she manifests herself. Devī is, in the words of Pattanaik "the delusion that makes life alluring yet elusive".[36] She is presented as the cause of knowledge in the world but also the cause of ignorance that is veiled illusion about the world, the dualities of the Goddess clearly evident here. The crux of *māyā* is egoistic perceptions of the self that hide divinity and reality through being fascinated with the world of sense perceptions. But *māyā* is not a negative force as much as a description of a reality beyond which is the supreme Goddess who will also provide the knowledge for release from the endless cycle of rebirth. And it is through *māyā* that the Goddess can be known. The *Devī-Māhātmya* describes her as "the gracious giver of boons to men, for the sake of (their) release",[37] and says: "She is the supreme, eternal knowledge that becomes the cause of release from bondage to mundane life; she is indeed queen (governing) all who have power."[38] *Māyā* is the source of the universe according to the *Devī-Māhātmya*,[39] a universe that whirls around in a pit of egoism.[40] All that can happen in the life of an individual stems from the *māyā* of Devī: the material pleasures such as wealth, *artha*, and pleasure, *kāma*, are possible because of *māyā*, just as disease and natural disasters are the negative possibilities. Since all aspects of creation stem from her, it is not surprising that she eclipsed the third member of the Hindu triad of Gods, Brahmā, as the Creator of the universe: temples to Devī in one form or another are prolific, yet only one exists dedicated to Brahmā. Nevertheless, as Pintchman points out concerning the Goddess: "Who she is can and does change from text to text, depending on sectarian biases, but her identity as a creative force manifest in cosmogony and the foundation and source of all that is persists across sectarian contexts."[41]

Because she is the creator of all that exists and is present in all that exists, duality is of the essence of the Goddess. She is, thus, both goddess, *Devī,* and demon, *Asurī.* She can be pleasing yet terrible. The individual may well be caught up in the whirlwind of sense experience and the dualities of life, but it is Devī who supplies the knowledge that enables her devotees to transcend such dualities and to tread the path that leads to liberation. Such, indeed, is the positive role that Devī encompasses, but she is also *active* in the world in the sense that she will take on the role of a warrior to protect and preserve the cosmos that is her creation. Her main positive role is to sustain life and nourish the earth. Kinsley made the graphic point that: "Crops, food – all living things that teem upon the surface of earth – are the natural bubblings of the great fertile power that resides in the earth and is identified with Devī."[42] Similar to Viṣṇu and his *avatāras*, Devī incarnates from time to time in order to uphold the balance of good in the cosmos. It is then that she may take on more terrible forms as the warrior needed to overcome demons. She herself then becomes bloodthirsty and ferocious, occasionally dividing herself to produce other even more bloodthirsty aspects of herself. Devī will tear her enemies apart with her own teeth and hands and those who revere her in this form will sometimes offer her blood sacrifices, though such practices are more usually appropriate for the female forms that issue forth from her.

Śakti power is not confined to independent Goddesses like Devī for it also extends to the consorts of the major Gods, and I shall examine both types of Goddesses below. The idea of the Gods having submissive and supportive consorts was prevalent long before all these were subsumed into a unifying principle of female power, *Śakti*. But if they were inferior to their spouses, they were nevertheless occasionally shown to have immense powers, though this never went as far as that characterizing the independent Goddess. Devī is dependent on nothing other than her own power, but the consorts of Gods are locked mainly in a reciprocal relationship with their partners, though they may be represented as providing the *śakti*, the power, by which their male counterpart acts. On occasion, the consorts may display aspects of ferocity that emulate the independent Goddesses, but they are mainly benign. And it is when they are benign that they can act as role models for women in a way that the independent, fierce, Goddess cannot. Where a major God incarnates, his spouse accompanies him. For example, Rāma as the *avatāra* of Viṣṇu naturally means that his devoted wife Sītā is also identified with Viṣṇu's divine consort Śrī or Lakṣmī: indeed, in some Śākta traditions, Sītā takes precedence over her husband.

In Śākta sects, the relationship between male and female, God and Goddess, *puruṣa* and *prakṛti*, is representative of the cosmos in its unmanifest and manifest states. The union of God and Goddess, most usually Śiva and his consort, produces creation, their separation the dissolution of the universe. Śiva is the abstract Absolute and *Śakti* the power that creates from that Absolute. As was seen in the chapter on Śiva, the androgyne Śiva symbolized the intimacy and necessity of the male and female, *puruṣa* and *prakṛti* principle. The fusion of the *liṅga* of Śiva and the *yoni* of his consort is also a combination of male spiritual and female material reality that makes manifest existence possible. This kind of relationship is accepted even by Vaiṣṇava and Śaiva sects and is articulated especially in later *Purāṇas*.

Devī as the benign Mother Goddess is represented as a beautiful young maiden with lotus eyes and a beautiful, soft smile. She has a third eye to represent her divine consciousness. Her power is represented by many arms in which the dualities of the Goddess are apparent, her left hands holding auspicious objects like a pot, plants, mirrors and musical instruments, while in the right hands she holds weapons, fire and skulls. Around her are thousands of attendants while she herself, as Queen of Heaven, sits gracefully on a throne, regally dressed. Many hymns praise her great beauty and wonderful appearance. It is usually her manifestations that produce the opposite, terrifying appearance, as will be seen below. But even as Devī she can display a body on fire with flames that will consume the universe; thousands of eyes brighter than millions of suns; horrible teeth grinding harshly in thousands of heads. Yet for her devotees, she is the champion of their needs, rescuing them in distress. In the words of the *Devī-Māhātmya*: "O Goddess, who takes away the sufferings of those who take refuge in you, be gracious; be gracious, O mother of the entire world. Be gracious, O queen of all, protect all; you are the queen, O Goddess, of all that does and does not move."[43] It is the *Devī-Mahātmya* that brings to the fore for the first time all the strands of the divine as female and the importance of the text cannot be overestimated. Coburn puts this superbly:

> The synthesis that is accomplished in the *Devī-Māhātmya* is therefore extraordinarily and uniquely broad. It reaches deep into the Sanskritic heritage, identifying the Goddess with central motifs, names, and concepts in the Vedic tradition. It appropriates one familiar myth on behalf of the Goddess, and enfolds several less-known tales into its vision. It locates the Goddess in relation to a full range of contemporary theistic and sectarian movements, familiar ones such as those of Śiva and Viṣṇu, and more recent ones such as those of Skanda and Krishna Gopāla.[44]

Needless to say, the *Devī-Māhātmya* that extols this Goddess contains what Coburn depicts as "the best known devotional words in contemporary India" and is "one of the major verbal artifacts that has been left in the Indian subcontinent".[45] The Goddess is clearly multi-pervasive. What I want to do now is explore the natures of some of the main Goddesses. In my view, most of them display the dualities so characteristic of female divinity, even if they are benign. Let us begin, then, with a seemingly benign Goddess, the consort of *Śiva* as Umā or Satī.

Umā / Satī

The consort of Śiva is originally Satī, a name meaning "True" or "Faithful wife", also called Umā, "Peace of the Night". She is also later reincarnated as Umā-Haimavatī, "Descended from the Himālaya", clearly a mountain Goddess, being the daughter of Himavat, King of the Himālayas, and is also called Pārvatī, "Of the Mountains". It is these Goddesses that absorbed other local goddesses under the principle of *Śakti*, but they were not independent as they were primarily the consorts of Śiva. The name Umā can be applied to both Satī and the incarnation of Satī as Pārvatī. The blissful union of Śiva and Satī is the perfection of the Absolute, the ideal and perfect balance. Such a balance, however, is disarranged by the more forceful dual nature embodied in Satī. Mythologically, Satī is said to have been angered by her father's neglect to admit her wild husband to an important sacrifice to which all the other gods were invited. Incensed, Satī attends the sacrifice herself and when she discovers her father's intention was to insult her husband Śiva, immolates herself. When Śiva discovers her body he picks it up and carries it throughout the universe in intense grief, causing massive catastrophes in the cosmos. These are only prevented when Viṣṇu hacks pieces off Satī's body until it becomes nothing. Where the pieces are said to have fallen, places of pilgrimage have been established. Satī's death as a faithful wife became the basis for the practice of a widow going to her death on her husband's funeral pyre: to commit such an act of immolation was accepted as an act of great devotion and one that would aid the husband in his future birth, as well as a wife keeping her supportive *śakti* with him. Outlawed now in India, it is not unknown for the odd occurrence of it to take place. Satī's role was not, however, to disappear, since she was to reincarnate as another consort of Śiva, Umā/Pārvatī.

The *Mahā-vidyās*

The image of Satī as the dutiful wife is dispelled totally by her opposite characteristics when she learns that she and her husband have been excluded from her father's sacrificial celebrations. Śiva forbids her to go alone and it is then that we see the ferocious form of Satī. She transforms herself into a dreadful image and then divides herself into ten beings. These are the *Mahā-vidyās*. *Mahā*, here means "great" and *vidyā* is "knowledge", suggestive of beings with supreme knowledge or wisdom. It is they who destroy Satī's father's grand sacrifice. The *Mahā-vidyās* are a good example of the collective unity of goddesses, and they are rarely found represented separately in Hindu temples, with the exception of Kālī. They appeared on the Hindu scene rather late, somewhere around the tenth century CE[46] as forms of Mahā-Devī and they are particularly popular in Tantrism. As Kinsley pointed out: "They inhere in each other and represent different facets of a single, multifaceted being.[47] While they are associated with Satī, they may be linked instead to other forms of Devī. Interestingly, they seem to mirror the ten *avatāras* of the Viṣṇu tradition. Some, like Kalī, are pan-Indian, others are little known. The ten are the ferocious Kalī, who is always the first and is also independent of the others; the fierce, dark Tārā, well-known in Buddhism; Ṣoḍaśī who is a beautiful young girl but who carries malevolent weapons and is often depicted astride Śiva in sexual intercourse; Bhuvaneśvarī, who is pleasant but has both beneficent and fierce weapons in her four hands; Chinnamastā, who has cut off her own head; Bhairavī, who has a fierce appearance and is grotesquely clothed; Dhūmāvatī, the old, stern and dishevelled widow; Bagalāmukhī, who has the head of a crane and holds a club while pulling out the tongue of an enemy; Mātaṇgī who is beautiful but holds menacing weapons in her four hands; and finally, the only really benign one of them all, Kamalā, a form of the Goddess Lakṣmī. The first three are usually regarded as the most important. While they are represented as one group, these are malevolent goddesses in the main and are connected with Śiva who, as was seen in the previous chapter, has that violent and dangerous streak which, clearly, is also manifested in the Goddesses or goddesses with whom he is associated. What I think is important to point out here is that female divinity, even when represented as mainly benign, incorporates also the duality of ferocity.

The *Mahā-vidyās*, it seems to me, reflect the original non-Āryan characteristics of early goddess worship. They are unorthodox, dangerous and not at all role models for orthodox woman: they break free from the normal perceptions of benign and gracious Sanskrit

Goddesses and they are less confined as consorts of Gods. If they are associated with Śiva, he is portrayed as inferior. He is impotent in the face of Satī's power when the *Mahā-vidyās* are created from her. Thus, the *Mahā-vidyās* are mainly independent and dominant – they sit on the corpses of males, on the Gods who are empowered only through them and have intercourse on top not beneath the male. But they are not portrayed as consorts and do not produce offspring: they are, again, untypical of what is expected of women. "These goddesses", wrote Kinsley, "if they allow males in their presence at all, demand to be served by them."[48] Their mainly fierce natures, their frequent association with cremation grounds and corpses, their sexual aggression, liking for blood and associations with pollution make them profoundly anti-social and impure. To be a devotee of a *Mahā-vidyā* one has to overcome fear of death and find the goddess in the negative as much as the positive.

Umā / Pārvatī

Satī is reincarnated as Pārvatī and becomes once again the consort of Śiva after many years of severe austerities. She emerges in association with Śiva about the time of the classical epics (from about 400 BCE–400 CE) and, like Satī, is featured in *Purāṇic* literature. She has little independence apart from her association with Śiva and her role is more of a symbol of the householder life, bringing Śiva out of extreme asceticism and involving him in worldly affairs for the sake of the gods and the world. Familial iconography shows Śiva happily seated with Pārvatī and their two sons born, not from conjugal intercourse, but through extraneous means. In this sense, Pārvatī is the Goddess of the harmonious household, of motherhood and the family. She is a gentle Goddess, her many names reflecting her beauty, and her iconography displaying her graceful and benign form. Yet as the *śakti* of Śiva she is the aspect of him that creates. She is the energizing force behind all manifestation in the cosmos and she is identified as Mahā-Devī in some texts but, aside from her association with Śiva, Pārvatī is not venerated as an independent Goddess. But Pārvatī can also be a powerful ascetic in her own right, equalling the *tapas*, the austerities, of Śiva. She can sometimes reveal her darker side and is represented in some myths as causing a violent Goddess, usually Kālī, to emerge from her being. Indeed, she is often depicted as dark in colour, like Kālī. However, as Kinsley pointed out: "So out of character is Pārvatī on the battlefield that another goddess, it seems, must be summoned to embody her wrath and dissociate this fury from Pārvatī herself."[49] Pārvatī in one myth so despised her dark colour as to have got rid of it and acquired a golden complexion, earning her the name Gaurī, "Bright, Golden One."

Yet there is a description of Pārvatī's form in the *Kūrma-purāṇa* where it is anything but benign and beautiful: "It was ablaze with thousands of flames in clusters resembling hundreds of world-destructive conflagrations (at the end of the world). It was terrible due to its curved fangs and was irresistible. It was embellished with clustres of matted hair. It wore a crown and was holding a mace, a conch, a discus and an excellent trident in its hands. The terrible form was frightening everyone."[50] Earlier in the same chapter we find Pārvatī describing herself as the powerful *Śakti* of Śiva: "Know me to be the Supreme Potency abiding in the great god Maheśvara. I am non-different from him, unchanging and the absolute, whom those desirous of salvation perceive. I am the *Ātman* of all conceived beings. I am Śiva, the auspicious spouse of God in all respects."[51] Since Śiva is the great ascetic, often withdrawn from the world, Pārvatī as his *Śakti* performs all the active functions that he does not and is sometimes equated with *Prakṛti* in the same way as Devī, paralleling Śiva's spiritual *Puruṣa.* As Kinsley said: "Pārvatī as *śakti* not only complements Śiva, she completes him."[52] He is creator, she creation; he the subject, she the object; he the sun, she the light; he fire, she water; he the day, she the night. Their complementary nature is essential for all manifestation.

Despite the recounting of her powerful *śakti*, Pārvatī is usually just the dutiful wife, what O'Flaherty described as "the quintessence of the lowly mortal woman worshipping the lofty male god".[53] As such she is both the devotee of Śiva herself and the mediator of other devotees of Śiva causing him to extend his grace towards the suppliants: without Pārvatī, this would be impossible given the remote asceticism of Śiva. She represents the *dharma* of the householder, balancing the extreme ascetic tendencies of Śiva – a patient force that obviates the destructive aspects of her spouse.

Durgā

Durgā is a pre-eminent and popular Great Goddess. Pattanaik describes her as "the most splendid manifestation of Devi. Virginal and sublime, containing within her the power of all the gods combined, she is the invincible power of Nature who triumphs over those who seek to subjugate her."[54] She is a fierce and independent Goddess and it is she who is Devī in the *Devī-Māhātmya.* The meaning of her name is illustrative of her nature, "Beyond Reach", though she has many other names. She is the great buffalo slayer of the *Devī-Māhātmya*, being the favourite form of Devī. The myth of the defeat of Mahiṣa dates to about the fourth century CE and by the sixth century[55] was widespread, making Durgā an immensely popular Goddess. All that applies to Devī in the *Devī-Māhātmya* is applicable to Durgā. The ferocity of this Goddess is a reminder of her origins in non-Āryan spheres and indigenous tribes. She seems to be the opposite of anything orthodox. One of the names for Devī in the *Devī-Māhātmya* is Caṇḍikā, meaning "The Violent and Impetuous One", suggestive of veneration of an early tribal goddess perhaps with this name.[56] Born from the anger, the *tejas*, of the gods as Devī, Durgā inherits all their powers. But it seems that aside from the *Devī-Māhātmya* Durgā's origins are complex and varied:[57] in Bhattacharji's view: "She took a long time developing into her present dimensions".[58] Textually, her origins are variously given, and she may sometimes originate also from Viṣṇu or from Pārvatī. But her best-known origin is as the slayer of the demon Mahiṣa, and the necessity of being born from all the gods because of their inability to defeat the demon themselves. Rather like the *avatāras* of Viṣṇu, Durgā is said to reappear when the need arises: "Once again, when there has been no rain, no water, on earth for a hundred years, then, remembered by sages, I will come into being without being born from a womb."[59] It seems fairly clear from this extract that Durgā is associated with fertility and the goodness of the land and vegetation but she also incarnates to destroy enemies: "Then, taking on bodily form, I will bring about the destruction of enemies."[60] Nevertheless, this is a Goddess that incorporated many different facets from a range of other local goddesses. According to Bhattacharji:

> The process of Durgā's growth in stature was long and steady. One by one she absorbed the main traits of regional mother-goddesses, household deities who were worshipped for different things by different tribes. Some were fierce and awe-inspiring, others were mild, benign and motherly, yet others were embodiments of lofty ideas – all these were fused into one composite supreme goddess – Durgā . . . A supreme goddess who commanded the whole-hearted allegiance of various types of people, had to combine in her personality all the different traits that would satisfy these manifold demands.[61]

All these facets in her origins combine to make Durgā an unorthodox Goddess that appeals to the fringes of *dharmic* society outside of which she clearly stands. She takes on the role normally associated with males as a great warrior. She is never a consort of any god, not even in the sense of being the *Śakti* of a god. She has no divine family and is never born in the normal sense of the term. Durgā is surely no role model for Hindu women who wish to remain within orthodoxy. She dwells not in the household but in the mountains; she eats meat, drinks wine and becomes intoxicated. Indeed, this is "a goddess who stands outside the civilized order of dharma: her presence is to be found only after stepping out of the orderly world into the liminal space of the mountainous regions where she dwells."[62] Since Durgā occasionally accepts animal sacrifice, she is really in the category of an impure Goddess and the *Devī-Māhātmya* also suggests that this should occasionally be blood that is drawn from the devotees' own bodies.

As an independent deity, Durgā is not, like Satī and Pārvatī, associated with Śiva, nor for that matter with any other God.[63] There is an account of her being born from Viṣṇu in the *Devī-Māhātmya*, but the connection here is not one to be pressed: indeed, in the *Devī-Māhātmya*, she puts Viṣṇu to sleep and he is only roused from that sleep when she leaves him, but she is called "illusive Viṣṇu's *māyā*" in the *Devī-Māhātmya*.[64] In some iconography, however, Durgā carries the trident of Śiva and the conch and discus of Viṣṇu, at the same time standing on the severed head of a buffalo suggestive of her superiority to both Gods.[65] Nevertheless, she does have the dark aspects that correlate with those of Śiva, as well as being the force that is incarnated when negative cosmic energies threaten to overpower the positive ones, just as Viṣṇu does. Her battle is one that supports knowledge as opposed to ignorance, though not through the normal channels of *dharmic* stereotyping. She is the warrior *par excellence* that can accomplish what all the gods together cannot and she came to be venerated especially by kings and warriors before battle.

Ajit Mookerjee describes Durgā as "one of the most spectacular of all personifications of Cosmic Energy".[66] In her early iconography as the demon slayer she is the epitome of a divine warrior seated on a ferocious lion, her many arms each wielding a weapon. But she is more frequently portrayed as a great beauty, leaving it to the fierce emanations of herself to show the more grotesque features. Her complexion is normally golden, though it can become ink black when angered. Such dualities in Durgā's personality and appearance are clear from the *Devī-Māhātmya*: "You are *śrī*, you are the queen, you modesty, you intelligence, characterized by knowing, modesty, well-being, contentment, too, tranquillity and forbearance are you. Terrible with your sword and spear, likewise with cudgel and discus, with conch and bow, having arrows, sling and iron mace as your weapons, gentle, more gentle than other gentle ones, exceedingly beautiful."[67] Above all, however, there is an abundance of textual evidence extolling her virtues, benevolence, superiority and beauty. Durgā is a Goddess that serves the needs of her devotees and takes up their causes: she is "Beyond Reach" in the cosmic and metaphysical sense, yet she is eminently close to devotees who need her, like a mother. She is as she is, needing no-one, yet fulfilling the needs of others and those of the cosmos as well as of the gods, who are inferior to her. She is a cosmic queen who protects her subjects. Durgā is at once her own self and Mahā-Devī who is Brahman and ultimate Reality. As a manifestation of Devī, she is nonetheless equal to and is Devī and is the *śakti*, *prakṛti*, and *māyā* of the cosmos just as Devī. She is the substratum and embodiment of the three *guṇas* as much as one who is intent on saving the dejected and distressed that take refuge with her.[68] For her devotees, Dūrga is the Great Mother: "Nurturing and energy (*śakti*) are the attributes that have made her the highest goddess in popular estimation, a divinity to whom one can surrender and at whose hands one may seek boons and protection."[69]

The *Mātṛkās*

In another spectacular battle against two demons, Śumbha and Niśumbha, recorded in the *Devī-Māhātmya*, Devī is aided by seven *Mātṛkās*, "Mothers", though their external appearances are anything but motherly. According to the *Devī-Māhātmya*, they were created by each of seven major gods who were watching the battle. Each of the *Mātṛkās* was the *Śakti* of a god, bearing the same weapons and symbols of that god. They are, thus, recognizable from their association with male gods. Nevertheless, they are inextricably bound with Durgā and, as we saw above, when the demons accuse her of having too many female helpers and not being strong enough herself to defeat them, she refers in the *Devī-Māhātmya* to the goddesses being her own powers that she recalls back into her own self,[70] suggestive that they are collectively her own being. This, indeed, is how some *Purāṇic* mythology views the *Mātṛkās*: they are violent and dangerous emanations of Devī, representing the darker duality associated with Durgā rather than the consorts of the original gods that created them. They became particularly important in Tantrism, as will be seen below.

The *Mātṛkās* are wild, restless and unorthodox. They are a bloodthirsty group of women who can bring disease and destruction: they thrive on the blood of the battle. While their nature may seem somewhat bizarre, it has to be remembered that life in Indian villages was and is still accompanied by disease and death and for many was and is dangerous and violent. The *Mātṛkās* represent this aspect of life. They emerge as a group in the first century CE and are textually attested in the *Mahābhārata*, becoming popular after the period of the epics.[71] They must surely be non-Āryan in origin, given their completely unorthodox natures and the fact that they are said to speak different languages and to dwell in wild places. They are akin to local, village goddesses, and are likely to have been the localized goddesses of the past, close to the village populace and their tribulations. Their like does not obtain in the *Vedas*, and as Stuart Abbott points out, they came to feature widely in

Śāktism and Tantrism: "In this process the untamed creative and destructive powers associated with groups of wild female deities such as the Matrkas came to be incorporated into the broad theological and cosmological worldviews centred upon the concept of *sakti*, as promoted by *Saktism* and *Tantrism*."[72]

Since, as a group, the *Mātṛkās* are believed to promote the stability of cosmic rhythms and the right paths for the universe, they have been somewhat Sanskritized, but they do not lose their terrifying natures in the process. Kinsley believed that the *Brāhminization* of the *Mātṛkās* occurred through their association with the *Śaktis* of the main gods and the reduction of their number to seven, though originally they may have been independent of the gods and far more numerous.[73] Their names, which at one time were varied, became standardized in this process as did their function in upholding cosmic *dharma*. As well as being ferocious and terrifying, the *Mātṛkās* represent human vices – pride, envy, greed, anger, lust, ill-temper and ignorance: indeed, their natures are inauspicious and negative. They live at dangerous places like crossroads, cremation grounds and dark caves or mountain recesses. Some are attractive, but most are frightening to behold. They are believed to be especially harmful to children – another aspect that links them to local village goddesses whose children were so often the recipients of disease or were the occasion of difficult births, which were felt to be manifestations of the anger of the local goddess. While none is important individually, as a group the *Mātṛkās* represent the dark aspects of life that harm the village community and, especially, its children.

Kālī

Kālī is one of the most important Goddesses in Hindu Śāktism. Mookerjee describes her as "one of the most intoxicating personifications of primal energy in the cosmic drama".[74] Tantrism, especially, celebrates this iconic Goddess, as do devotees in Bengal in particular. This is astounding, given her horrific appearance and nature. David Kinsley said of her: "She represents, it seems, something that has been pushed to its ultimate limits, something that has been apprehended as unspeakably terrifying, something totally and irreconcilably 'other'. She seems 'extreme'".[75] The name Kālī is the feminine form of *kālā*, "time", significant of the devouring aspect of time to which everything is subject. The name is also connected with blackness, and therefore with dissolution: indeed, Kālī is as dark as soot. She is the darkness of the past that has gone and of the future that is to come. She is first mentioned in the *Devī-Māhātmya*, where it is said that she comes forth from the brow of Durgā during the battle to destroy the enemies of the gods. That brings her onto the scene in the sixth century CE, but there are earlier references to her as a minor goddess.[76] However, it was very late that she came to pre-eminence in Bengal.[77]

Kālī is an independent Goddess who needs no consort. If she is ever associated with a God, that God is Śiva, but not in the role of the supportive *Śakti*. Rather, she is the *Śakti* that incites the more dangerous aspects of Śiva, his wildness, destructiveness and drunkenness that are inimical to the cosmos. Kālī acquiesces in the anti-social behaviour of Śiva. Such a destructive nature is sometimes represented iconographically with Kālī standing on the lifeless body of Śiva, she the energy of the cosmos and he the inert consciousness; he the *nirguṇa* unmanifest and she the *saguṇa* manifest universe. Such association is especially prevalent in Tantric sects. Like Śiva, her favourite haunts are the cremation grounds and they both share the connection with Time, *kālā*, the blackness that envelops all things at the end of time. Like Śiva, Kālī dances, too, and for Śākta sects, it is she that dances the creation, preserving rhythms and eventual dissolution of the cosmos. She is depicted as enjoying the mad, deranged dances in which she is joined by Śiva. It seems natural, then, for the two deities to be linked together, a process that occurred somewhere about the eighth century.[78]

It is highly likely that Kālī evolved from the many non-Āryan, tribal, wild goddesses from the villages that peppered the wilderness and mountainous areas over large and disparate territories. There were thieves and bandits, raiders, criminals and bloodshed in the world of these wild goddesses and Kālī became the epitome of them all, even being the Goddess of bandits (indeed, she is the source of our word "thugs"). An early name for her was Cāmuṇḍā, a terrifying goddess whose appearance and wild antics were no less dreadful than those of Śiva. She must surely have been an outcaste among goddesses until she was *Brāhminized* in the *Devī-Māhātmya* as issuing forth from Durgā. But she remains an "earthy" Goddess, nude, fertile, sexual and full of life-giving energy. She is unorthodox and therefore popular with those outside the normal patterns of orthodox, *dharmic* Hinduism, the low caste and outcastes of society as well as village tribal elements. Kālī is a great Goddess but an impure one, always associated with contaminating blood and death. Durgā could also be involved with blood sacrifice, meat-eating and imbibing intoxicants but she is mainly represented as a beautiful Goddess: Kālī, on the other hand, takes unorthodox behaviour to a whole new level. She is a challenge to *dharma*, a challenge to the neatly delineated systems of societal norms: it is impossible to suppress the darker sides of life in contemplation of Kālī. She is free, liberated, unconventional and uncontrolled. Her mythical origins are always as a result of anger, making her the receptacle of anger and the one who manifests it.

It was surely with some difficulty that Kālī as a typically non-Āryan deity was accepted into mainstream Hinduism. The *Vedic* goddess Nirṛti, a dark-skinned demon associated with disease and death, has some similarities with Kālī and is something of a precursor but, it seems to me, there is nothing so dreadful as this powerful Goddess Kālī in both appearance and character in any of the previous textual sources. It is the *Devī-Māhātmya* that hurls Kālī to prominence. When Durgā is engaged in battle, she suddenly becomes so angry that her face becomes black as ink and from her forehead springs Kālī, also black in colour:

> From the knitted brows of her forehead's surface immediately came forth Kālī, with her dreadful face, carrying sword and noose.
> She carried a strange skull-topped staff, and wore a garland of human heads; she was shrouded in a tiger skin, and looked utterly gruesome with her emaciated skin, her widely gaping mouth, terrifying with its lolling tongue, with sunken reddened eyes and a mouth that filled the directions with roars. She fell upon the great Asuras in that army, slaying them immediately. She then devoured the forces of the enemies of the gods.[79]

Kālī then proceeds to grind most of the enemies between her teeth or crushes and tears them apart. Such is her role in defeating a number of demons and their armies in the *Devī-Māhātmya* and other sources. She begins as subservient to Durgā but evolves further to being a Goddess in her own right. Given the abundance of myths associated with any of the deities, we also find Kālī originating from the anger of Pārvatī or Satī. In the case of the former, the mild Goddess Pārvatī displays her ferocious duality when she enters Śiva's body, uses the poison from his throat and emerges as Kālī in order to destroy a demon. And Kālī enters spectacularly into the kill as what Kinsley called Pārvatī's "personified wrath, her alter ego, as it were", her "dark, violent nature in embodied form".[80] As I said earlier, even the benign Goddesses have their dual, dark side and it is this side that exhibits massive power, so great a power that it eclipses the male Gods. Similarly, when Satī becomes infuriated with her father's insult in not inviting her and her spouse to the great sacrifice, her anger produces the ten *Mahā-vidyās*, and Kālī is the first of these to emerge. In the *Rāmāyaṇa*, Kālī is also born from Sītā in order to defeat a demon.

Kālī is the complete opposite of the benign Goddesses. She is the Jungian demon within that has to be faced in order to be whole as an individual, even if in some Tantric sects she is sometimes represented as benign and beautiful as an object of meditative visualization. Mookerjee says that Kālī has "an overwhelming intensity, a mighty strength, a force to shatter all obstacles. She is there for swiftness, for immediate and effective action, for the direct stroke, the frontal assault that carries everything before it. Awe-inspiring, determined and ruthless, she destroys evil force."[81] If this is translated into an inner meditative process, one that faces and overcomes the darker inner fears and dualities, then it can be seen that Kālī is, in fact, a source that unites the inner self to liberate it. In myths, Kālī is rarely docile and yet, even when she is dancing at a cremation ground, her face is often smiling and relaxed. She is a union of opposites that leads to liberation. Awful as she is, and dreadful as are her deeds, she opposes evil, facing it head on. Nevertheless, Kālī is portrayed as getting so frenzied during battle that she becomes drunk with victory and almost destroys what is good in the attempt to destroy evil. According to Menon's research in Oriya, Kālī is too inauspicious a deity to be worshipped in the home: "She could never insure the material prosperity of the household nor the maintenance of the lineage."[82]

In appearance, Kālī is horrendous to behold: naked (literally sky-clad), adorned with bones, skulls and blood, and personifying malevolence and savagery, she symbolizes all that is terrible in life and dispels all the illusions behind which human life wishes to hide. Her nakedness, especially, is symbolic of the Self that is no longer held by sensory impulses and the illusionary *māyā* that clouds reality: Kālī is ultimate Reality that is unhidden. She is gaunt and wild, laughs like a mad woman, rides a ghost and frequents cremation grounds often surrounded by goblins and jackals, though she loves the battlefields, where she eats the flesh of her enemies and drinks their blood, or tramples, crushes, burns and breaks the bodies of her enemies. She is sometimes full-breasted, despite her otherwise gaunt appearance and this is indicative of her fertility, her life-giving properties as much as her destructive ones. But at other times her breasts are long and pendulous, matching her gaunt body. Her earrings are infant corpses. There is much that is like Śiva, with serpents adorning her and a crescent moon on her forehead. She eats raw or rotten flesh and gets drunk on wine. Kālī's appearance and ornamentation are replete with varied symbolism depending on her sectarian devotees, and depending on which particular icon is to the fore. As an example of the various facets of such icons the following will suffice:

- **A black complexion** represents Kālī as time and darkness (*tamas*), the formlessness that absorbs all things: black absorbs all other colours and obliterates all shapes into shapelessness.
- **Dishevelled long hair** symbolizes illusion "the fabric of space-time which organizes matter out of the chaotic sea of quantum-foam".[83] It also symbolizes her total freedom and unconventional nature. It is sometimes represented as flames.
- **A garland of fifty heads** represents each letter of the Sanskrit alphabet and, therefore, wisdom and knowledge. Sanskrit letters are sacred sounds and sound was believed to be the first manifestation of the universe. Kālī, then, represents primordial potentiality for sound and manifestation, as well as that manifestation itself. Notably, all the heads are male and all are freshly bleeding; and they are smiling! They are reminders of recent death that will be transformed into life.
- **A girdle of human arms** is symbolic of the workings of *karma* and the capacity for action. The girdle is a statement that Kālī can cut her devotees free from their *karmic* bindings.
- **Her three eyes** are red and indicative of past, present and future, and sun, moon and fire. The third eye represents wisdom. Occasionally, she sends forth flames from her eyes, but her eyes are often sunken.
- **A lolling red tongue** symbolizes the *rajas*, active *guṇa*. Kālī eats meat and drinks wine – both polluting substances.
- **White fangs** for some represent the *sattva guṇa*, the quality of lightness and evolution. But her mouth is portrayed with blood on it, blood that drips from the sides over her face. And yet, she smiles and looks calm.
- **Four arms and hands** indicate her power. The right hands have benevolent symbols and the left malevolent. Her hands are sometimes like claws with long nails. Occasionally, she is shown with just two arms or with six or eight. According to Kinsley: "Kālī's four arms represent the complete circle of creation and destruction, which is contained within or encompassed by her. She represents the inherent creative and destructive rhythms of the cosmos."[84]
- **A severed head** in one left hand illustrates the annihilation of the ego. The head is freshly cut and bleeding, indicative of the ridding of past *karmic* bonds. In a way, it is a positive symbol that indicates the end of bondage for a devotee.
- **The sword** in the other left hand represents the cutting of the bondage that binds an individual to the world of the senses. It is the sword of knowledge. The sword, too, is stained with fresh blood, suggesting the immediacy on which the path of knowledge of Kālī can be entered. Sometimes her hands will hold the trident, like Śiva, and perhaps the noose of Yama, the Lord of Death.
- **One right hand**, the upper one, is raised dispelling fear, the gesture of assurance. Fear of death is the great human fear and Kālī's raised hand assures the devotee that she can assist in overcoming this fear.

- **The other right hand** encourages spiritual fortitude and offers favours and blessings. This hand assures the blessings of permanent bliss rather than the fleeting happiness of worldly gains.
- **Serpents** often drape her body, rather as in the case of Śiva. One she seems to use as a sacred thread, others as a necklace. She sometimes lies on a bed of snakes. Tantric sects see the serpents as representing spiral energy within the body known as *kundalinī*. Ananta/Śeṣa the thousand-headed cosmic serpent associated with Viṣṇu is often above Kālī's head. Since serpents can shed their skins and form seemingly new bodies, they symbolize transformation of the self to the Self. Kinsley wrote of these creatures: "Serpents are liminal figures in that they pierce different cosmic zones, the earth and the underworld. As beings who live both on the earth and in the earth, they move between cosmic planes and also between states of being, between the realms of the living and the dead. Kālī is at home with these mysterious, powerful, liminal beings, which suggests her transformative nature and power."[85]
- **Cremation grounds** are the places where the body is dissolved, burnt up in the fires of dissolution. Similarly, all the attachments, desires and aversions of the individual are burnt up in the symbolism of the cremation ground. According to Kinsley: "The heart of the devotee is where this burning takes place, and it is in the heart that Kālī dwells. The devotee makes her image in his heart and under her influence burns away all limitations and ignorance in the cremation fires. This inner cremation fire in the heart is the fire of knowledge, *jñānāgni*, which Kālī bestows."[86]

We should not see Kālī from these horrendous images as a Goddess purely evil and demonic – a Hindu Satan: she is anything but. Her appearance and iconography are thoroughly symbolic of the inner metaphysics of transformation of the egoistic self to a blissful transcendent being: this is what Kālī offers her devotees through facing the dark and negative as much as the light and positive. That delicate point that results when the two are in union is the enlightenment of the Self that has transcended all opposites. Kālī is a liminal Goddess on the fringes of society, pointing out the dark places to which the mind is afraid to go. Her association with death is meant as a source of light, and is meant to demonstrate that death is transformative and purposeful.

While Kālī may incorporate aspects of earlier wild goddesses, she emerges as unique. She is a terrifying form of *Śakti*, independent and dominating rather than being submissive to the only God with whom she is sometimes associated – Śiva. Her iconography has softened a little, and she is sometimes venerated as Mother, perhaps at just a stone block or mound that represents her. She is the foremost of the *Mahā-vidyās* and, indeed, the other *Mahā-vidyās* are sometimes portrayed as emerging from Kālī. She has about eight main forms and nine main names and in present-day India she takes on local forms and characteristics.[87] One of her most popular forms is *Dakṣiṇa*-Kālī. This is her benign form and in Elizabeth Harding's graphic book about Kālī worship she explains that such a form is easily recognizable because Kālī will have her right foot forward and hold her sword in her left hand. Conversely, if Kālī has her left foot forward and holds her sword in her right hand, she is in her terrible form.[88] She is both a Mother that protects and gives and one that harms and takes away, this latter aspect evident in her need for blood sacrifices. But many of her devotees see her as Mother despite her malevolent appearances and the fact that nothing in her iconography portrays her as a mother. They see themselves as her children and are thus able to accept anything the Mother decides to throw in their path, good or bad: but there are some places in India where Kālī becomes the beautiful Mother and her darker side is lessened.[89] In the Śrī-Vidyā sect of southern Indian Śākta Tantrism, for example, Kālī is represented as Śrī-Kula, a much more benevolent and gracious Goddess rather akin to Lakṣmī, and is venerated in *yantras* and *mantras* as impersonal. In the Śākta Tantrism of the North, however, Kālī is the more terrifying Kālī-Kula Goddess, though both of these sects project Kālī to the absolute power, the *Śakti*, behind the whole universe.

Śaiva myths portray Śiva as having to subdue Kālī's uncontrolled rampages, but Menon's research in Oriya suggests that her Śākta worshippers there believe she regains control of herself, particularly when she reminds herself of her wifely duty to Śiva or when her devotees remind her of her maternal and nurturing nature by calling her Mā.[90] The frequent portrayal of Kālī stepping on Śiva is, for the Oriyans, the point when she *chooses* to become calm, though for other Śāktas it shows Śiva's dependency on his female counterpart or even her superiority over the prostrate Śiva. As Menon reports, there cannot be a "bad mother" and if she is addressed as Mā "the human devotee taps into sensibilities that cannot help but be nurturing".[91]

It is as a fierce Goddess that Kālī is associated with power, and it is only when benign Goddesses take on a fierce aspect that they, too, become powerful. Thus, we find many fierce goddesses associated with the impurity of blood, death and cremation grounds, but not benign and pure goddesses. Kālī receives blood sacrifices regularly, as do other localized fierce and impure goddesses. In the distant past, Kālī also received human sacrifices. The idea here is probably one that believes the goddesses have to be nourished themselves in order to protect their devotees and this is a facet more likely to be associated with female deities than male ones.

We may want to avoid Kālī's disgusting images and habits and concentrate on safer, more attractive categories of living but it is exactly the former that we are asked to face. Kinsley put this so well when he said: "Kālī in her rude way deconstructs these categories, inviting those who would learn from her to be open to the whole world in all of its aspects. She invites her devotees . . . to dare to taste the world in its most disgusting and forbidden manifestations in order to detect its underlying unity and sacrality, which is the Great Goddess herself."[92] Kālī shakes one's confidence, upsets one's conditioned thinking, overturns the structured patterns of society and looks beyond attachments to what seems terrifying and yet is the answer to the spiritual journey through the loss of individuality in the union of opposites, the end of all illusion and the end of time-consciousness that brings the eternity of transcendent consciousness.

Just as Devī is *śakti*, *prakṛti* and *māyā* – power, manifest Nature and delusion, respectively – so Kālī embodies these three aspects but in a much more dynamic way. Her *māyā* is revealed as the negative that most wish to avoid, but which is a facet of human and non-human existence: yet at the same time it is all existence, the many that come from the beginningless One that is Kālī. Similarly, *prakṛti* can be harsh and uncontrollable, disastrous and dangerous and Kālī reflects this more violent side of Nature, too. But it is Kālī as *Śakti* that is more volatile and powerful than any other of the *Śakti* forms, at the same time as being the primordial, *nirguṇa*, power behind the universe, devoid of form and any dualities. Kālī wants the individual to see beyond the world in any of its manifestations. She wants them to see through the repressed fears and terrors that lie deep in the subconscious to ultimate Reality, the highest Brahman. Creator and Destroyer, the dualities in Kālī are the secret to what she offers: to take note only of the exterior is to miss the inner secrets of the Goddess. Such, indeed, is the pathway adopted by the Tantric devotee. Non-Tantric devotees approach Kālī as a child to a mother; Śaivites unite her with Śiva; in Kashmir Śaivism Kālī is ultimate Reality, *nirguṇa* when unmanifest, Kālī when manifest. Bengali poets like Ramprasad (1718–75) praised her in verse, and Ramakrishna (1836–86) served her at the Dakṣineśvara Temple in Bengal. Ramakrishna saw Kālī as the Mother who would bestow liberation on her devotee. Bose writes that for such individuals: "Thus, from a figure of menace Kālī becomes central, and the dance of death becomes the beat of life. Philosophically as much as emotionally, no inversion could be more radical."[93] Her devotees do not see her ugliness only her beauty, "her dark skin glows with light, her hair dances to cosmic rhythm, and her face radiates grace".[94] Kālī is a Goddess whose multiple symbols point towards liberation, *mokṣa*. In Tantra, especially, as Kinsley put it: "The goal is to identify completely with Kālī, who is the symbol of the absolute, beyond name and form, beyond individuality and specificity."[95]

Time consumes all of us and all things, and Kālī represents that unconquerable, inexorable aspect of all existence. Harding puts this well when she says of Kālī: "As the eternal, indifferent Time she confronts man with his pitiful finite attachments, swallows them up, and produces them again in a different form, in a different time."[96] There will always be things in life that will not conform to order, to what seems to be right and how we want things to be: Kālī makes sure that we recognize this. Standing outside the prescribed patterns of Hindu living, Kālī opens the eyes of her devotees giving a whole new perspective of what it is to be Hindu.

Śrī / Lakṣmī

Balancing the ferocity of Goddesses like Kālī are pan-Indian Goddesses who are predominantly benign. Such is the Goddess Śrī who is usually called Lakṣmī and who is one of the most popular Goddesses amongst the major orthodox deities. The term Śrī is found in the *Vedas* with connotations of majesty, power, glory, handsomeness, and is used in the context of earthly kings, but it also means beauty, prosperity and wealth and it is in this sense that it is applied to the Goddess Lakṣmī who is associated with all kinds of auspiciousness and good fortune. "Lakṣmī", writes Constantina Rhodes, "is the epitome of luminous energy in action: without a doubt, the goddess of prosperity is the quintessential devī."[97] Lakṣmī means, loosely, "fortune", and it is as the Goddess of Fortune that she is known. While there are no temples to Lakṣmī exclusively, she appears alongside other deities in many temples, and shrines for her are prolific since she is widely venerated for success and happiness. Such fortune may originally have been concerned with agriculture, particularly the corn harvest[98] with, according to Kinsley, "many and obvious associations with the sap of existence that underlies or pervades all plant and animal life".[99] She may have had some connection with fertility and the dark side of the *Vedic* goddess Nirṛti and her non-Āryan nature, but it is as an Āryan Goddess that Lakṣmī becomes prominent,[100] initially having much to do with the fertility of the land, of plants and vegetation, a legacy of her nature in pre-Āryan times.[101] Her *Vedic* profile sees her granting gold, cattle, horses and food to those who propitiate her. Even today, she is worshipped for her ability to aid the fertility of the land in the village setting.

In her early evolution, Lakṣmī was linked with different gods – Soma, who is associated with the moon and life-giving sap; Indra, who is generally the chief of the gods and the most regal, as well as being the god of rain; and Kubera, the lord of wealth and prosperity. Such links highlight the propensities of Lakṣmī's associations with fertility, royalty and prosperity. Mythologically, she is said to have emerged when the gods and demons churned the ocean aided by Viṣṇu in the form of a tortoise, and it is with Viṣṇu that Lakṣmī is mostly associated, underpinned by Śrī as a splendid force in the *Vedas*. Rhodes thinks that this *Vedic* perception of Śrī lends to Lakṣmī her power and vitality: "Śrī is an abstract quality, and although as a feminine noun the term carries the connotation of a divine feminine force, it is not yet associated with any particular form or personification of divinity. Rather, there is a magnificent ambiguity in the term for 'splendor' is recognized as taking the form of whatever it manifests, as in the blossoming abundance of the earth, the life-giving waters, bounteous grains, and fatted cattle."[102] Lakṣmī is the "particular form" and embodiment of the power and vitality of Śrī.[103]

From about 400 CE, Lakṣmī became associated with Viṣṇu as his consort. I shall be returning to examine the nature of this highly prominent God in the next chapter but here, it is as the consort and *Śakti* of Viṣṇu that Lakṣmī is now well known. As Viṣṇu's consort, Lakṣmī is the epitome of great beauty, the perfect wife, and is often featured with the symbol of beauty, the lotus: indeed, Lakṣmī is also known as Padma, "Lotus", and her iconography abounds with lotuses. She is pictured with lotus-shaped wide eyes, so prized by women in India. As a symbol the lotus is connected with organic growth and plenty, not just on a microcosmic level but also on the level of macrocosmic creativity and the generating and maintaining of the pulses and rhythms of life. Lakṣmī epitomizes this in her role as Viṣṇu's *Śakti*. Since, too, the lotus grows in muddy water, its outstretched leaves untouched by the mud beneath it and its flower centred magnificently on the flat leaves, Lakṣmī is also a Goddess that signifies spiritual purity, and beauty that is unsurpassed. Elephants as symbols of regal power and also of rain and fertility were associated with Lakṣmī in her earlier evolution, emphasizing her illustrious and prosperous nature. Indeed, her early appearance is as a slender and splendid beauty, radiant and golden like the sun and she is sometimes represented as seated between elephants that are showering water over her: again, her links to fertility are strong here, since elephants can only exist where there is a plentiful water supply.

In association with Viṣṇu, Lakṣmī is docile, pictorially much smaller than her great husband and she provides wifely duties such as massaging his feet. This is not to say that she is undervalued. What Lakṣmī does is to emanate power but, unlike the uncontrollable and unorthodox power of Kālī, Lakṣmī remains in the orthodox, *dharmic*, societal norms: she can be a role model for those women who wish to follow the orthodox prescriptiveness of societal life for a woman. Śrī-Lakṣmī's wealth is not just of the material kind, for it is also the wealth of liberation from suffering and rebirth that lies in her power to grant, so she has an important role that can be met without transgressing her orthodox position. Her power in this way is symbolized by her third eye representing her great wisdom and super-consciousness. Her power may also be symbolized by her many arms; more usually, however, there are just two, the left pointing to the earth, which is the gesture of granting boons and the right showering coins. She sits or stands tall and gracefully on a lotus and while she has no independent temples dedicated to her, this image is ubiquitous on calendars, in shops, businesses and homes throughout India. She is believed to be manifest only in the best and most auspicious places, so houses are cleaned before some festivals in order to attract her.

The name Lakṣmī is prefixed by many forms to show her various roles as the companion of kings, as victory in battle for what is right, as the support for the good and virtuous wife, or as fame and as good fortune. However, there is an opposing side to Lakṣmī, an opposite, Alakṣmī, who is the goddess of all that is opposite to Lakṣmī and who is to be found where places are not clean or where lust, pride and envy rather than righteousness are present. But Lakṣmī herself, like most *devīs*, can display her dark and fierce side: "She may bear a lotus, discus, and conch, but also a necklace of severed heads. She may be attended not only by smiling, sweet-natured, plump young elephants who shower her with life-giving rains, but also by poisonous cobras whose hoods sway menacingly as they stand poised by her side."[104] These words of Rhodes are applicable to Tantric Lakṣmī in which she is the means to spiritual liberation. As beneficent, Lakṣmī is associated with Viṣṇu, but as the dark, ferocious Goddess, with sword and trident, she is associated with Śiva.[105]

Lakṣmī also appears as the last of the *Mahā-vidyās* under the name Kamalā and with her current functions as the one who bestows abundance and good fortune. Amongst these ten goddesses, she is the most benign and somewhat out of place until her role as the consort of Viṣṇu gave way to her character as a slayer of demons in Tantric sects. Outside the group of *Mahā-vidyās*, Kamalā is a popular Goddess in her own right: amongst them, however, and being listed last of them, she is deemed the least important. But it is in relation to Viṣṇu that Lakṣmī is best known as a mediator for, and mother to, the devotee who approaches her and Viṣṇu. Whereas in her early history Lakṣmī was associated with a number of gods, once the association with Viṣṇu took place, she became steadfast to him. Viṣṇu is a deity that descends in a number of forms, *avatāras*, in order to restore the balance of good in the world. When he does so, then Lakṣmī descends with him. She is Sītā to his Rāma and Rādhā to his Kṛṣṇa. There is a relational necessity between Lakṣmī and Viṣṇu, an interdependence and intimacy, a unity, and at the same time a complementary nature that is inseparable. In the *Viṣṇu-purāṇa*, Viṣṇu is said to be speech and Lakṣmī meaning; he understanding and she intellect; he creator and she creation; he the support of the earth and she the earth itself; he the tree and she the creeping vine that clings to it; he the maleness in males and she the feminine in females; he love and she pleasure.[106] The *Purāṇas* mostly combine the male/female divinities in such a way as essential components for the creation of the universe. The *Kūrma-purāṇa* is one early text to depict Lakṣmī as Viṣṇu's power to create. She is Viṣṇu's *śakti*, his *māyā*, but as *prakṛti* she is creation in her own light.[107] In the *Bhāgavata-purāṇa*, Lakṣmī becomes "Great Lakṣmī", Mahā-Lakṣmī, the *prakṛtic* matter that makes the universe possible.

The motif of Viṣṇu as Creator and Lakṣmī as Creation is taken up by some schools of Hinduism in such a way that Lakṣmī becomes pre-eminent, Viṣṇu being inactive as compared to the active *Śakti* that is Lakṣmī. *She* creates with but a tiny fraction of herself being manifest existence, while remaining totally transcendent beyond creation. Here, it is Lakṣmī that creates, sustains and dissolves the universe not Brahmā, Viṣṇu, and Śiva. Such is the view of the Pañcarātra school of Hinduism and this, it seems to me, gathers up the earlier concept of Lakṣmī as the dynamic power of manifestation evident in growth and decay, life and death, the cycles of rhythmic time – in short, pulsating life of the earth, its inhabitants and its vegetation. In Śāktism, Lakṣmī becomes Mahā-Lakṣmī, the Great Goddess, the Mother, the source of the three *guṇas* that make all manifestation possible. In some Tantric sects she is equated totally with the *nirguṇa* Brahman. In Śrī-Vaiṣṇavism the intimate connection between Viṣṇu and Lakṣmī is emphasized, as its name suggests. Here, Lakṣmī is the mediator for the Śrī-Vaiṣṇava devotee in approaching Viṣṇu, obtaining Viṣṇu's grace for that devotee and being warmly approachable in worship. It is small wonder that Lakṣmī is one of the most venerated Goddesses throughout India.

Sarasvatī

Another beautiful, benign and very popular Goddess is Sarasvatī. Since she was originally a river goddess; her name means "Flowing One" or "Watery One". Rivers were always considered to be feminine, like the great river Ganges, who is identified as the Goddess Gaṇgā. The Sarasvatī, or Sarsuti, was one of seven sacred rivers, no longer in existence but is believed in myth to flow underground. The connection between rivers and the divine is important, a point put well by Foulston when she says: "Connections between the divine and water or rivers in India have been important in the development of the idea that India itself is a sacred place. It emphasizes the interconnection between the physical and the divine, especially as the sacred rivers, in Hindu mythology, are said to flow from the realm of the gods. The life-giving property of water is suggestive of divine grace being poured onto the land."[108] Notably, Sarasvatī is thus connected with fertility like so many other early goddesses, her watery nature being the source of vegetation and produce. Since water is also connected with purity, Sarasvatī was a Goddess who could heal, cleansing through her sacred waters.

Sarasvatī is linked with the God Brahmā as his daughter or consort. She is his power, his *Śakti*, and as time went on her association with water gave way to one with speech, Vāc, in particular with the primordial sound that begins creation. Her father (or, at times, husband), Brahmā is the Creator, but she is the active power that makes creation happen through the medium of sound. And from that association came one that linked her with knowledge, poetry and music and all that is cultural and beautiful. It is because of Sarasvatī that we can make sense of the manifested world for she provides the knowledge that makes understanding possible. She evolved into a Goddess of learning and wisdom and became known as the Mother of the *Vedas*. Through her, language developed and writing became possible. Since the popularity of Brahmā waned in the light of his role as the power of creation being usurped by the *Śakti* Goddesses, Sarasvatī is mainly found separate from and independent of her consort. Although Sarasvatī is sometimes portrayed as one of the five *śaktis* of Kṛṣṇa, she has become essentially an independent goddess without a consort, "on a plane elevated from mundane family life or common relations".[109]

Dressed in white and unadorned by jewellery, Sarasvatī is an image of purity and a lack of ostentation. She is pure *sattva*. Wisdom is her emanated aspect and she needs no other adornment. Her vehicle is a white swan, a symbol of spiritual transcendence, and she is sometimes pictured sitting on a lotus with a lute in her hands. She usually has two arms but is sometimes featured with four or even eight, these carrying besides the lute, a book, a rosary, an elephant hook, a bell, a water pot and a plough, as well as more aggressive things such as a bow, an arrow, a mace, a spear, and a discus. It seems that even this beautiful Goddess has faint elements of a dual aggressive character and in some myths she is shown to be exceedingly angry – enough so to curse the gods. But it is not as such that she is loved throughout India. Pattanaik comments: "Schools and libraries were her temples; books, pens, artistic tools and musical instruments were the ritualistic emblems of her worship. Those who worshipped her were blessed with the light of knowledge that drove away the demons of ignorance and unhappiness."[110] On her festival day, school children throughout the whole of India venerate this beautiful Goddess of learning, and prayers are often offered to her in schools each morning. Whenever and wherever human thought produces the best in science, art, poetry, music and artistic genius in any form, Sarasvatī is believed to be there. She is very orthodox, the water pot and rosary symbolic of the important religious rites that are necessary in a *dharmic* society. Kinsley's remarks on Sarasvatī were particularly apt and attractive: "Sarasvatī, astride her swan, suggests a dimension of human existence that rises above the physical, natural world. Her realm is one of beauty, perfection, and grace; it is a realm created by artistic inspiration, philosophic insight, and accumulated knowledge, which have enabled human beings to so refine their natural world that they have been able to transcend its limitations. Sarasvatī astride her swan beckons human beings to continued creation and civilized perfection."[111]

Local goddesses[112]

While the great pan-Indian orthodox Goddesses have their place in the Indian mind, it is to the local goddess that most turn and to which devotees offer their attention and affection. And it is goddesses rather than gods that are predominant at the local level. The local village goddess is the *grāma-devatā*. Foulston graphically writes: "Huddled under trees, at the edge of a water tank or at the centre of a bustling settlement, the divine feminine in the form of local goddesses pervades and characterizes local Hindu religion. Found in a variety of different locations and situations, they, more readily than the lofty orthodox goddesses, supply the daily spiritual sustenance that keeps heart and soul together for the mass of the Hindu population."[113] What such worship and practice display is a rich diversity with changing patterns to match the changing lives of the devotees. Such a fact means that just one goddess may have different names in different locales or have a different form from that in another area. The goddess is shaped by the local community in form and nature.

It would seem that the more orthodox the goddess, the more remote she is from the lives of ordinary people.[114] It is unorthodox goddesses that are to be found peppered everywhere in Indian towns and villages. Local goddesses often arise from tragic incidences of deaths of local women – a suicide, a *satī*-burning, death in pregnancy and the like. Such events are crimes committed against women that need appeasement and so they are worshipped and cared for at local shrines. Alternatively, myths evolve concerning a woman's anger that is so powerful as to result in some transformation of the woman into goddess-type behaviour.[115] At other times, unusual natural phenomena are explained by goddess presence.[116] Such goddesses are close to the local inhabitants and are felt to be intimately known, leaving the great orthodox Goddesses often as mere onlookers. It needs to be remembered, too, that temples were barred to low-caste Hindus in the past and the goddess in a local shrine, therefore, seemed more concerned with the needs of local, low-caste inhabitants. Orthodox Goddesses have cosmic battles to fight and cosmic roles to play: local goddesses are often linked with a particular caste, supplying the needs for that caste, and are asked for help in the mundane things of life.

Local goddesses may not have anthropomorphic images but be represented by an odd stone, a tree or a water pot, or maybe not at all until festival times. The same goddess may, thus, be different in representation in different locales. Occasionally, a trident is placed in the ground with a face on the centre. Nevertheless, in some senses all these goddesses are linked under the same cosmic *Śakti*, at least theoretically. This is something that textual sources may uphold, but that may not be to the fore in the minds of localized inhabitants. As Foulston says: "Possibly the devotees of local goddesses are less concerned with the relationship between all goddesses but more interested in how their goddesses are particular to them."[117] However, one link between the orthodox and the local goddesses is clear; the latter display the same duality of temperament – benign and fierce – as was seen with so many of the orthodox goddesses. In the vicissitudes of ordinary life, the average Hindu has need of some outlet to answer the harshness that accompanies local living: it is the goddess that is thought to provide the answers, and is the first to be approached when problems arise. In some cases, however, the unifying *Śakti* is more evident, since some local goddesses are believed to be incarnations of major Goddesses like Durgā or Kālī, sometimes with textual evidence.[118]

Such links with orthodox deities are often an attempt to bring a local goddess into line with orthodoxy. Marrying a local goddess to a Hindu orthodox God – Śiva in particular – serves to tone down her behaviour and obviate some of the unorthodox praxis that accompanies her worship. The fierce Goddess Mīnākṣi housed in the temple at Madurai in Tamil Nāḍu is one such example. She is wedded to Sundareśvara, a form of Śiva, and thus is domesticated, but she is never subservient and remains the dominant partner. Local goddesses, therefore, generally display a level of independence. They are fierce, impure, accept blood sacrifices and can mete out harm to local inhabitants if not appeased or if displeased. Even if they are allied with a major orthodox Goddess, they are usually nothing like that Goddess in character and retain localized traditions. Indeed, if they become too benign and orthodox, their power to help their devotees is believed to be radically diminished. I must point out, however, that there are warrior-type male deities who also accept blood sacrifices. A male god like Tamil Nāḍu's Murugan has all the characteristics of the ferocious goddesses including possession.[119]

The variations in every aspect of their nature, origins, representation, mythological background and methods of worshipping local goddesses are immense. There may be no literature to accompany the nature and status of a local goddess, and her cult must rely on oral transmission often relating back to an unusual event or a dream someone has had about her. When a goddess is adopted locally, the surrounding inhabitants are more likely to focus on her to the exclusion of others. That is why each individual, though perhaps within a whole group, will focus on his or her *grāma-devatā*. Such a village deity will be deemed able to help in finding a suitable marriage partner, some lost cattle, cure an illness and the like.

Whilst it has been generally believed that villages grew up around a particular local goddess, and that the goddess creates the village and is the centre of it,[120] Foulston's research in Indian village settlements has shown that goddesses can, in fact, be brought from outside the village.[121] Nevertheless, the goddess as the "mother" of the village is common in southern Indian use of the name Amman, "mother" as part of the name of a goddess. The village goddess protects the inhabitants from demons, disease and death and provides fertile crops with the appropriate rains for their growth. In return, the inhabitants care for the goddess, worship her and are attentive to her needs. This reciprocal relationship is spatially confined to the village: beyond it, there is no protection for an individual and the power of the goddess does not obtain. Many goddess shrines are situated on the boundaries of the villages where the goddess can protect inhabitants from outside negative forces. Protection of the village demands of the goddess some degree of power and, as I explored earlier, power is equated with fierceness and impurity: a benign goddess will not have the necessary power to combat the petty demons that might threaten the village. But while powerful, these goddesses are not as wild as Kālī; they are simply not pure and orthodox. It is the manifest anger of the goddess in terms of drought and disease that makes her non-benign, though at other times, she may well be auspicious, nourishing and protective. Thus, these local goddesses have the dual personality that is so characteristic of almost all female divinity. Obeisance to the fierce side frequently involves animal sacrifices as food for the goddess in order for her to maintain her protective power.

Protection against disease has always been the most important role of the goddess, particularly against smallpox in the past, though that is no longer a threat in India. What is interesting is that the goddess is deemed to *cause* disease because she is angry, and that anger is believed to be the result of neglect of her by the locals. Foulston's research suggests that goddesses do not wantonly cause disease as some earlier writers believed: they may have the latent power to cause disease, but they mostly protect against it.[122] "Therefore", writes Foulston, "with regard to disease, to describe them as malevolent is to distort their nature in a way that is detrimental to their overall character."[123] Goddesses like Māriyamma" and Bhadrakālī who used to be associated with smallpox no longer are, and their protective roles against other diseases like measles and chickenpox are much more to the fore. The roles of these goddesses, it seems to me, are not so ambivalent as often suggested, but are rather reflections of the negative and positive occasions in life, the fragility and difficulties of human existence in poor environments. The goddesses provide an answer to such aspects of life and there seems good evidence that devotees do not, in fact, find their *grāma-devatā* a wilful, unpredictable and malevolent force. It is at their festivals when, if at all, their fierce natures are pacified in animal sacrifices.

The fact that most local goddesses are independent of males maintains their power. Attempts to make these goddesses respectable often involve "spousifying" them to ensure that they become more orthodox females, but even then, they may not always be subservient to a husband even if their purity levels are a little increased. Since many goddesses are related to low castes or outcastes, they are automatically impure, for their attendants and devotees are themselves sources of pollution. Some goddesses no longer accept blood sacrifices and the earlier practice is represented by *kumkum*, the red paste – perhaps on a pot or smeared on a melon that in former times may have been a skull. And the red hibiscus flowers favoured by goddesses may also be reminiscent of blood offerings of the past.[124] The bottom line here is that local goddesses are mainly impure and even if they no longer accept blood offerings, their patterns of worship reflect such earlier praxis. This is particularly so at festival times for the goddesses, when traditional rites have changed less. For example, a goddess like Jeṇakai Māriyamma" in Cholavandan has become much *Brāhminized* in appearance and nature, but at her annual festival a fire-walk takes place in her honour. Indeed, there is often a good deal of duality in the pure–impure characters of, and devotions to, many of the goddesses.

Goddesses can arise and decline, depending on need. A now thoroughly *Brāhminized* goddess is Santoṣī Mā, whose images are beautifully adorned to match her beautiful, milky-white countenance expressive of her essentially benign character. And yet, Santoṣī Mā as a goddess is said to regularly possess a local woman in Khurdapur – a clear indication that she has not been and perhaps cannot be thoroughly *Brāhminized*. What catapulted Santoṣī Mā to widespread fame was the film *Jai Santoṣī Mā*, which was released in 1975. To *Brāhminize* her she was said to be the daughter of Gaṇeśa, the elephant-headed son of Śiva, but her appeal to the masses of Hindus, especially to the illiterate, was without precedence, without caste differentiation, without the need of an intermediary priest and without elaborate offerings. Santoṣī Mā is the goddess of the people, sensitive to their daily needs – whether that is the need of a refrigerator or any other modern need. And this goddess takes possession of local people to answer their needs directly. Indeed, Santoṣī Mā's name translates as "The Mother of Satisfaction". Further, goddesses may not be specifically connected with a locale. In the western Himālayas, there are many small shrines to goddesses whose names are unknown: they are expressions and manifestations of the forces of nature and are closely connected with the landscape, having less to do with protection of a demarcated domain.[125]

Much has been said in this book about attempts of *Brāhmins* to bring anything outside their authority under orthodox control, and much will be said on this point in chapters that follow. The contrast between local goddesses and orthodox *Brāhminical* Goddesses is considerable but some interesting points emerge in relation to the attempts of orthodoxy to Sanskritize goddesses, especially local ones, and bring them into line. Shree Padma has a fascinating thesis that turns Sanskritizing of local goddesses right around in the context of social movements from villages to urban settings. The *Devī-Māhātmya*, as we have seen, is the first text to unite all goddesses as aspects of the one Great Goddess, the source of all creation. But instead of orthodoxy being the source of the unification of the Goddesses as one, Padma sees *local* goddesses as representing basic and unifying powers of existence: "Hence, the identification of the Goddess with śakti has as much to do with protective power of local goddesses still venerated by so many of India's villagers and, increasingly, by its urbanized populace as well as it has to do with the philosophical and metaphysical musings of Brahmanic tradition."[126] Padma's view is that it is non-Sanskritic *local* goddesses that are the rationale for the uniting of all the goddesses as one. Since the majority of Hindus worship local goddesses: "Veneration of local goddesses is actually the "great tradition" in question, given its historical longevity, geographical ubiquity, and cultic predominance. Sanskritization is simply a means of making these cults 'user friendly' in urban contexts."[127] She sees this as a process of "de-Sanskritization" when Sanskrit goddesses are transformed into characters that are more like local goddesses in the process of movements from villages to urban areas. The villagers take their beliefs concerning local goddesses with them and these beliefs are accommodated in urban settings by de-Sanskritizing "higher" goddesses to make them suitable to their local goddesses and to their wider beliefs: "In the current context of urbanization, the function of the goddess as a symbol of the village and its most powerful protectress shifts focus from village to family, from crops and cattle to one's job, and from one's children's health to their economic future."[128]

Padma's thesis is a rather neat example of how local goddesses are sufficiently fluid in character to provide new manifestations appropriate to new needs without shifting the underlying belief that they are all the same unified goddesses. Thus, quite the opposite of *Brāhminization*, a form of Dūrga can find herself transformed into a local goddess[129] with a little disguising of the original village goddess[130] and shifts in the reasons for veneration for altered types of protection: "What is 'great' about the Great Goddess is her perceived ability to care for her devotees in their worldly pursuits and desires."[131] What this suggests is that Great Goddesses are adapted to local goddesses, rather than the other way around through *Brāhminization*.

Padma's thesis is an interesting one, endorsed by the fact that local goddesses can take any animate or inanimate form and yet still be perceived as one by locals everywhere. But it seems to me that we have to remember that local goddesses are limited to a spatial area and their powers do not reach beyond their locale. Then, too, the unity of the goddesses is something of a metaphysical principle that may owe a lot to the same, developed idea of the unity of male gods as ultimately Brahman. On the broader canvas, there may well be an overlap of influence between local beliefs and *Brāhminical* concepts. Pintchman seems to think that the rise of the goddess's worship has needed the orthodox backdrop for "although the impulse to elevate the feminine principle may be largely non-Brahmanical, the means by which it is elevated are borrowed directly from Brahmanical orthodoxy".[132] This is a rather neat Sanskritizing of the goddesses, a blend of old and synthesized new, and Pintchman thinks this leads to "a certain amount of structural continuity within the Brahmanical tradition".[133] Thus: "The impulse to revere goddesses highly, then, which appears to be more part of the non-Brahmanical traditions of India than of Brahmanical orthodoxy, is absorbed into Brahmanical structures so that tensions between the orthodox system and unorthodox systems are mitigated."[134]

Tantra

Tantrism is an intricate warp and woof in myriad patterns that blur normative sensation and knowledge. It is esoteric and secretive, and few can claim to have penetrated – a term that is meant sexually as well as metaphysically – its depths. It centres mainly on the intimate relationship between *Śakti* and Śiva, the former being the active aspect and the latter the passive one. The divine female and male here are the duality of existence, at the manifest level of reality. Their true fusion is beyond duality, complete union, and is ultimate Reality. However, all dualities, not just the female and male, are contained in the Śiva-*Śakti* synthesis. The word *tantra* is associated with weaving and comes from the Sanskrit root *tan* meaning "to spread out" or "expand": thus, loosely, it means "woof". Tantra now refers to the many systems, doctrines, diverse practices and texts that come under the umbrella heading that it now assumes. Main branches of Tantrism will differ in the emphasis placed on the synthesis of Śiva and *Śakti* or on one rather than the other. It is the uniting and transcending of dualities that lies at the heart of Tantrism and such processes involve highly ritualistic praxis. A male practitioner of Tantrism is a *sādhaka* or a *tantra-yogin*, and a female a *sādhikā* or a *tantra-yoginī*. The goal is to become *siddhi*, that is to say, to achieve perfection, in some cases along with extraordinary powers. Tantrism is usually divided into three main aspects – Right-handed, Left-handed and Kaula. The distinction between Right and Left is one between orthodoxy and unorthodoxy: the right hand is used by Indians and others for pure actions and the left for polluting ones.

Tantrism is regarded by many as heterodox simply because it does not accept the *Vedic* and *dharmic* religious laws for society. It is casteless and its rites involve impurity and impure substances. Georg Feuerstein writes of the origins and unorthodoxy of Tantra:

> Tantra originated and flourished at the margins of Hindu society and gradually helped shape it. Tantra provided a home for all those who longed for direct spiritual experience but found orthodox Hinduism (Smārta Brāhmanism) far too restrictive and exclusivist. The Tantric circles were open to members of all castes, and at least for the duration of the rituals Brahmins and untouchables drank from the same cup, ate from the same plate, and freely mingled their bodily juices, for during the *cakra-pūjā* all were transformed into sacred beings – gods and goddesses – free from all cultural stereotyping and societal constraints.[135]

In line with theories of *śakti*, it is the female that is responsible for all creation. Śiva, as male, is unchanging and inactive, the totally transcendent Absolute that remains formless. It is his *Śakti*, the power inextricably inseparable from him, which provides the pulse for creation and the subsequent rhythms of all life. While Śāktism and Tantrism are really two separate beliefs, the prominence of the *Śakti* force in Tantrism means that there is much mutual overlapping of doctrine. What is important about the influences of Tantrism on Śāktism is the non-*Vedic* nature of the goddesses venerated, as well as the projection of the goddess as supreme and, in some cases, superior to the male deity. Essentially what we understand as reality is the result of the intimate relation between the quiescent male and the active female. The intimate duality of male and female in Śiva-*Śakti* is expressed in the intimacy between ordinary and ultimate reality, between microcosm and macrocosm, being and becoming, spirit and matter, ordinary consciousness and pure consciousness, change and changelessness, time and infinity.

While Tantrism began somewhere about the middle of the first millennium,[136] from what I have said earlier about non-Āryan goddesses of early times worship of the goddess was prolific amongst the ordinary populace. It is not surprising, then, that some of this tradition developed into Tantrism. We have seen above that the *Śakti* force can take on virtually any form and this is something that Tantrism accepts. Stuart Abbott explains this rather well: "Within the Tantric worldview the universe is understood as the unfolding of a complex web of feminine power, which manifests as subtle energies and gross material forms. Accordingly, Hindu Tantric traditions conceive of the macrocosmic universe and the microcosmic human body in terms of *sakti*, ultimately both are expressions of the divine feminine power."[137] This is not to say that male deities are not present in Tantrism for indeed they are: both male and female deities are personifications of specific energies that aid the Tantric adept on the path to liberation. While these deities are not the goal *per se*, they are the means to the goal.

The *Mahā-vidyās*, those ten mainly malevolent goddesses, are prominent in Tantrism, where they are invoked to reveal the secrets of the cosmos: indeed, it is Tantric texts that are our main source of information on them. In Tantrism, each has a particular universal function and is an aspect of transcendental wisdom: combined, the ten become a whole. Mookerjee puts it thus: "The Śakti-cluster of the Mahāvidyās as a whole reflects this dynamic unity of existence, in which all aspects of life, the darkest, the purest, the most forceful and the inert, are combined to form a whole, a vision of unity in diversity."[138] The *Mahā-vidyās* can offer the Tantric adept not only spiritual progress but magical powers. Kālī is always listed as the first of the *Mahā-vidyās* and, as we know, she likes to frequent cremation grounds. For some Tantric practitioners, such places help to rid the self of aversions in life. Desires and aversions are inimical to liberation and, while it may be possible to suppress desires, it is infinitely more difficult to overcome aversions, especially ones involved with the darkness and fear of death and corpses in cremation grounds. But the Tantric attempts to do exactly this, with the aid of different aspects of Kālī. Other Tantric sects take a softer approach to Kālī. Kinsley noted that in some Tantric texts Kālī has become less associated with death and is more positively portrayed as softer and more beautiful. He wrote: "These positive features are apt, because Kālī no longer is a mere shrew, the distillation of Durgā's or Pārvatī's wrath, but is she through whom the hero achieves success, she who grants the boon of liberation, and she who, when boldly approached, frees the *sādhaka* from fear itself. She is here not only the symbol of death but the symbol of triumph over death."[139] Kālī is the *Mahā-vidyā* that reveals ultimate Reality for the Tantric devotee: it is no surprise, therefore, that she is the dominant deity of Tantrism, and Gods like Brahmā, Viṣṇu and Śiva are said to emanate from her "like bubbles from the sea, endlessly arising and passing away, leaving their source unchanged."[140] It is in Tantrism that Kālī is portrayed as sexually aggressive, dominating Śiva, who is subservient to her wishes.

The beautiful Goddess Śrī is pre-eminent in the Śākta Tantric sect of Śrī-Vidyā. Similarly to Kālī, the Goddess here is seen as the ultimate Reality who is superior to her consort and, as the source of the creation, preservation and dissolution of the universe, acts independently of him. She is a mainly benign Goddess whose fiercer side, though she possesses it, is predominantly latent. She is a good example of the more orthodox kind of Tantrism that does not so readily defy normal *dharmic* prescriptions. But Śrī has also subtle forms that are pertinent only to Tantrism. Subtle forms of the goddesses like Śrī or the ten *Mahā-vidyās* are represented in secretive diagrams called *yantras* and the equally secretive meditational and visualization sounds that are *mantras*. Both are means to participate in the power of the goddess and are subtle forms of the ultimate Reality that is *Śakti*: they *are* the goddess. In Abbott's words:

> In contrast to exterior, exoteric, forms of devotional religious practice associated with the goddess's gross form, worship using these esoteric *Tantric* forms involves the practitioner taking an individual and personalized approach to religious discipline. These powerful forms of the deity are understood as expressions of her transcendent nature, as her *śakti*. As visual and sound forms of the deity, they are felt to be the purest and highest expression of the feminine Absolute, filled with cryptic symbolism through which the *Tantric sadhaka* aims to gain insight into the true nature of reality.[141]

Mantric sounds have a particular effect on consciousness and their repetition alters states of consciousness[142] and when the practitioner repeats his or her *mantra* the goddess becomes present in the body. At the same time, a whole text may be *mantric* and recited as part of ritual. The *Devī-Māhātmya* is one text that readily lends itself to exploration of *mantric* power in its words, and so has been adopted widely in Tantrism.[143] The most widely known *yantra* is the Śiva-*Śakti* one in which Śiva is symbolized by five triangles pointing upward and *Śakti* by four pointing downward, creating an image of forty-nine triangles that are representative of the unified cosmos.

The *Śakti* that is the Goddess is believed in Tantrism to be coiled in the body as *kuṇḍalinī*, literally, "snake" or "serpent power". It is the spiritual force of the Goddess that is, for most human beings, completely dormant at the base of the spine. The Tantric, however, seeks to awaken this dormant energy, causing it to rise through a series of centres, lotuses, or *cakras*, to fuse eventually with the male principle that is Śiva, in the head. Key to the understanding of this process is the Tantric belief that the microcosm of the body and mind is a mirror of the macrocosm of the cosmos. Thus, the goddess without is also the goddess within. As Feuerstein puts it: "We can access the cosmos by going within ourselves because objective and subjective realities coevolve from and subsist in the same Reality. In the transcendental dimension, they are absolutely identical."[144] Thus, it is the body and mind that is the key to liberation in Tantrism and the geography of the body has to be known intimately for this to happen. A complex cosmogony of goddesses belonging to subtle realms hidden to ordinary mortals parallels the inner spirituality of the body,[145] and these subtle realms are increasingly experienced by the Tantric adept through visualization of appropriate goddesses. There is no gender barrier to such practice and perhaps this is why Tantrism does not compartmentalize women into traditional roles. Male and female are both capable of the heights that Tantrism can offer and both the male and female body are, ultimately, expressions of female divinity: body and mind are ultimately divine.

Nevertheless, since the *Śakti* energy can be wildly ferocious and gruesome, relating to the goddesses can be a dangerous and terrifying experience: one only has to think of the natures of the *Mahā-vidyās* to see that this would be the case. Conjuring up such goddesses within the body and mind can be fraught with danger. Complex rituals accompany such praxis and, given its dangers and complexities, are passed on from *guru* to practitioner through initiation only when the *guru* can see that a practitioner is ready for the first or a new stage. Having a *guru* to guide the individual is the only way in which the deconstruction of the self and the rebuilding of the spiritual dimension can take place safely. Only then is one released from the dualities of existence for total freedom and union in the One. But on the path to that goal, the *guru*'s instruction is critical and, as a teacher, he is to be viewed as father, mother and even god. Initiation, *dīkṣā*, cuts the ties that bind a disciple to the world of ignorance and begins his or her path of true knowledge. It is an individualistic and secretive pathway, whereby an initiate is given his or her own special goddess with an accompanying *mantra*, carefully explained by his or her *guru*. The practitioner's pathway will involve stringent disciplines that vary according to the sect: rituals and visualization techniques will normally play a part. As Feuerstein puts it: "Tantric practitioners endeavour to gather all their energies into a laser beam focused on the Divine."[146] The pathway is one on which the subconscious conditionings are gradually weaned away in a process of purification of the self to reveal the full spiritual Self that is one with the Great Goddess. The secrecy surrounding the language, imagery and rituals is such that they are only available to the initiate, but to become the goddess on whom one's entire being is focused is to attain her nature and her powers and that is done by identifying with her and visualizing her fully within one's body.

The *pañca-makara*

Much is made by writers on Tantrism of the *pañca-makara*, five items or principles that are considered impure by orthodox Hindus. They are fish, meat, parched grain (probably intoxicating or hallucinogenic), wine and illicit sexual intercourse (all beginning with the letter *m* in Sanskrit). The Left-handed Tantric sects use these five impure substances literally and focus very much on the fierce aspects of Kālī. These sects are unconventional and are practised marginally in Hinduism. Their aim is to transcend dualities by facing what is normally unclean and forbidden, but also to gain the powers concomitant with the transcending of dualities. Their rituals appear to involve elements of magic and their practice of "coupling", sacred copulation, for them is one of the most important of the five substances, though it is accompanied by extensive ritual, sometimes in cremation grounds, and only under the supervision of a *guru*. Sexual fluids, even menstrual fluids, are believed to be particularly powerful and desirable, and cremation grounds are the places where life is in between living and dead and are openings to the spiritual realm. Kinsley lifted the sexual coupling to a more philosophical level when he wrote: "In the context of Tantra, sexual attraction, sexual behaviour, and sexual intercourse suggest the underlying texture of reality, which is the manifestation of the dynamic, energetic, creative, and harmonious interaction of Śiva and *Śakti*."[147] Sexual intercourse for the Left-handed Tantric sects is representative of the union of Śiva and *Śakti*.[148]

Right-handed sects, on the other hand, interpret the five substances mentally and symbolically, concentrate on the benign aspects of the goddess, particularly Śri, and adopt more conventional practices. But their goal is the same, the transcendence of dualities. A third major Tantric sect is the Kaula path of Tantrism, which is something of a blend of the Left and Right paths. In some Kaula sects the female is the means of transmission of teachings, in others it is the male who receives and transmits the tradition. The Kaula path is explicit in accepting any individual regardless of caste – just as the Ganges receives streams from any territory without distinction. Unity is the goal of Tantrism, the immediate unity of the practitioner with his or her personal, individualized goddess and then the ultimate unity that is the ultimate Reality of the union of Śiva and *Śakti*, the fusion of *Puruṣa* and *Prakṛti*, of passivity and activity, of unmanifest and manifest.

This journey in exploration of the Goddess brings to the fore the feminine tendencies of creativity and at-one-ness with the rhythms of Nature, the shifting tides of life and death and the waxing and waning of all things. The Goddess is felt to be close to these more earthly, worldly patterns, even if at times she does battle to restore the harmonies of those rhythms and reminds us that we cannot control and tame Nature. It is because she can contain all, that she can be truly Absolute. Since the Goddess is manifold and believed to be present in the multiple forms of the prolific goddesses in India, she unites them all as one, just as she unites everything female. It has to be asked, however, whether seeing divinity as female alongside the male in Hinduism has done anything to improve the status of women and the stereotyping of them as the support of their husbands and families, dutiful, loyal, faithful – millions of Sītās. I am writing this on New Year's Eve in 2012, with the news full of a young medical student who had been gang raped and murdered in India. While such atrocities occur in every country, in India such attacks are rife and victims mostly dismissed and not protected. Rape and sexual harassment (called "eve-teasing") are endemic and acceptable behaviour for men. In an article in *The Observer*, Jason Burke writes: "Few now doubt that India, and particularly Delhi, has a problem with rape and sexual violence against women. In recent weeks the issue has changed from being 'a privately accepted fact' to a 'public cause', said the local *Indian Express* newspaper. Now many are talking about a turning point."[149] Will such a dreadful event galvanize Indians to demand greater care and protection of women? It is to be hoped that the current demonstrations now happening will make this possible. It would have to be said that having divinity as female has not, actually, done much for the freedom and value of women. Females cannot, in view of such atrocities, share in the *Śakti* divinity in the eyes of men. It is a subject that I want to take up in chapter 10.

7

Gods and Goddesses

Viṣṇu, Kṛṣṇa and Rādhā

The Vaiṣṇava religions

When it comes to worship of a personal God, it is in Vaiṣṇavism that we find all the warmth and devotion that accompanies worship of a deity who is believed to be the closest to humankind. Such a focus on a personal God is at the heart of Vaiṣṇavism, making it one of the most popular of all aspects of Hinduism.[1] In many ways, such a focus is monotheistic, singling out one particular aspect of deity for intense focus. It is Viṣṇu in his incarnations or "descents" who provides the means for such devotions. Vaiṣṇavism is far removed from the metaphysical focus on an impersonal Brahman even if the deities on which it centres are considered as manifestations of Brahman. And the devotion offered in Vaiṣṇavism is of an intensity that transcends ordinary devotion, to become *loving* devotion, devotion of the fullest possible kind that involves the whole being. This is *bhakti*, the path of devotion that leads directly to God. I want to delay looking in depth at *bhakti* until Volume II, though it is impossible to examine deities such as Viṣṇu and, in particular, Kṛṣṇa without setting them within this broader framework. The personal nature of the deities means that they are accompanied by a plethora of often highly attractive myths; myths that bring the deity even closer to the devotee. I have used the term "religions" in the heading of this section because there are many different kinds of Vaiṣṇava groups, some regional like the Bengal Vaiṣṇavas, others attached to historical figures, for example. Each is fuelled by different types of devotional literature, some of which I shall be examining in Volume II. In the triune of Gods, Viṣṇu, Śiva and Brahmā, it is Viṣṇu who is the most human, the easiest to approach, and the one who has the most beneficent personality and it is to the nature of this deity that I now want to turn.

Viṣṇu

The name Viṣṇu is usually taken to mean "The One Who Pervades", "The Pervader" and the reason for this will become clear as we look at his character in the sacred texts and in his iconography.[2] Such a concept of pervasion suits the God's connections with the sun and light, with water, and with his essence that is present in all things whether animate or inanimate. This is a God who spreads in all directions, encompassing, surrounding and entering all things. Nevertheless, the name is not without difficulties and may even be from a non-Āryan source. Such a ready pervasion of Viṣṇu in the universe is the central factor that makes him a God permanently available to his devotees. And such availability makes Viṣṇu a focus of devotion far more than a God who is approached through ritual. It should not be thought, however, that the immediacy and closeness of the God renders him inferior to other deities. For many Vaiṣṇavites, Viṣṇu is, at the same time, the Absolute, Brahman, being both unmanifest and without attributes and manifest with attributes: the perfection and absolute nature of the God must, necessarily, involve both, though some Vaiṣṇavites will lean toward one rather than the other perspective. As the essence of all things, Viṣṇu is manifest at the deepest level of all that exists, but he is also manifest in his temple images and especially in his periodic "descents" to Earth.

The origins of Viṣṇu are complex in that there is no linear development of his rise to prominence. He is something of a syncretic character, gleaning aspects of his nature from various other major and minor deities. He was certainly linked with the Bhāgavata religion, which itself derived from a number of gods called Bhagavān, "Lord", who were probably associated with worship of the sun and with the bestowing of wealth.[3] Indeed, Klaus Klostermaier makes the valid point that: "Vaiṣṇavism, taken as a more or less unified religion, represents the constant effort to bring the growing mass of mythology together under one principle and harmonize the heterogeneous elements from various local traditions."[4] As a composite character who fused in himself the natures of other gods, Viṣṇu's status became steadily enhanced. It was a fusion with popular devotional gods of the Bhāgavata cults as well as with the more speculative source posited by the well-known hymn of the *Ṛg Veda*, the *Puruṣa-sūkta* of 10:90, which we have met in earlier chapters and on which I shall elaborate below. Many different expressions of Vaiṣṇavism could obtain first, because of Viṣṇu's composite character and, secondly, because this was a God who manifested himself in animal and human form on Earth, but it was the merging of different *devotional* traditions, in particular, that facilitated the full expression of devotional Vaiṣṇavism. What we have, then, are origins of Viṣṇu that are very different in nature from those of Śiva and, thus, two rather different expressions of Hinduism, though both stem from ancient folk traditions. Inevitably, a process of *Brāhminization* took place in the case of Viṣṇu as it did with Śiva, particularly the linking of Viṣṇu with that important *Puruṣa-sūkta* hymn of the *Ṛg Veda*. But it is more than likely that these devotional practices existed outside the folds of orthodox *Brāhmin* religion, Viṣṇu being the medium for their inclusion into orthodoxy.

Three major early gods became associated and amalgamated with Viṣṇu. These were Vāsudeva-Kṛṣṇa, Kṛṣṇa-Gopāla and Nārāyaṇa, this last sometimes called Hari, "Lord". The Bhāgavatas focused their devotion on the first two of these and the Nārāyaṇa devotees formed what is known as the Pañcarātra sect from more orthodox sources. Vāsudeva ("God of Gods"), was worshipped as far back as the sixth or fifth centuries BCE.[5] It was through tribal affiliations that he became associated with Kṛṣṇa, the principal *avatāra*, "descent", of Viṣṇu by about the second century BCE. Vāsudeva-Kṛṣṇa was worshipped as

Bhagavān, "Lord", in a thoroughly devotional and theistic manner. Such was the early devotional praxis identified with Vāsudeva, Kṛṣṇa and, later, Viṣṇu, whose names became synonymous along with the title Bhāgavan. Such theistic, devotional developments were in stark contrast to the lofty metaphysics of the *Upaniṣads* and the ritualistic cultic emphasis of orthodox Hinduism.

Nārāyaṇa was originally the seer who is said to have been the first to sing the *Puruṣa-sūkta* hymn of the *Ṛg Veda*, the same hymn that gave the basis for the class system in Hinduism. This famous hymn in 10:90 of the text posits a cosmic Puruṣa, of whom all creatures are just one quarter, with three quarters being eternal in Heaven. Notably, this Puruṣa pervades the earth on every side filling it as all that has been, is and is to be. It is this notion of pervading the universe that was to become so applicable to Viṣṇu. In the *Śatapatha Brāhmaṇa*, Nārāyaṇa is explicitly identified with the Puruṣa of the *Ṛg Vedic* hymn and clearly presented as the pervasive force in all things in the cosmos.[6] Associated with water, Nārāyaṇa came to be seen as the deity presiding over the waters that existed at the dissolution of the universe, floating as a child on a leaf until it was time for creation. Such association with creation and destruction came to be facets of Viṣṇu, whose name was joined to that of Nārāyaṇa: indeed, the latter is one of the most popular names of Viṣṇu today. Nārāyaṇa is linked with the cosmos and its creation, as well as with sacrifice. Since Viṣṇu became God of the universe, of creation and dissolution, as well as being infused in all that exists, it is easy to see how his present character is informed by this early god as Nārāyaṇa. As we shall see, too, like Nārāyaṇa, Viṣṇu is associated with the waters that obtain during the quiescence of the cosmos, when both are the womb from which creation emerges.[7] Nārāyaṇa is also inseparably paired with another sage, Nārā, both renowned for their austere practices. They were seers of *Ṛg Vedic* fame, originally separate but later joined as brothers in some traditions and as father and son in others. The point of the two is their inseparability. Thus, later, Nārā came to be representative of man and Nārāyaṇa of God, the two equally inseparable. Indeed, Sukumari Bhattacharji suggests that it is this relationship and inseparability that forms the basis of the concept of *avatāras*.[8] In the *Mahābhārata*, Nārā is believed to be Arjuna and Nārāyaṇa Vāsudeva-Kṛṣṇa. The God who moves on the waters becomes Viṣṇu, as we shall see from his iconography, and it is he who pervades the cosmos during its dissolution. By the time of the *Mahābhārata*, the names Nārāyaṇa, Vāsudeva, Hari, Viṣṇu and Kṛṣṇa had become synonymous.

The Viṣṇu of the *Ṛg Veda* is a minor god with very few hymns addressed to him. But what is important is the myth of his *three strides*, a myth that has accompanied him in his complicated evolution and which is partly responsible for the rise of the god to such a high status. The *Ṛg Veda* 1:154 refers to his "thrice setting down his footstep, widely striding", his "three wide-extended paces" and his "triple step" by which he covered the expanse of Earth and Heaven. Many link this triple expansion with the path of the sun from its rise, its zenith and its setting. Jan Gonda's point here is interesting. He connected the three steps with the sun's energy "because the pervading, omnipresent, and fecundating stream of light and energy seems to fit in better with the character of the divinity as far as it appears from the textual evidence".[9] Since Viṣṇu is likened in 1:154 to a bull and a dreaded beast that dwells and roams in the mountains, he seems to have some connection with a wilder nature but, elsewhere (7:99:3), he is presented as the source of rich food, the cow in milk and fertile pastures, a god who is benevolent to humankind. There is an idea surrounding this deity of atmospheric expansion alongside benevolent granting of the fertility of the land through the pervasive energies of the sun. Whatever the three strides were meant to represent – perhaps Earth, atmosphere and Heaven (or fire, lightning and the sun) – they certainly encompassed the realm of humankind and, at the same time, the Heaven of Viṣṇu to which beings aspired. Moreover, sacrifice was deemed essential to the well-being of mortals and Viṣṇu is portrayed in the *Ṛg* as the protector of it, ensuring its efficacy and the benefits that would follow. Benjamin McClintic believes that Viṣṇu is much more evident in the *Vedic Saṃhitās* than extrinsically stated. He thinks Viṣṇu is implicitly in the backdrop of many hymns, being implicit in the forces of fire, lightning and the sun: "In this sense", he writes, "Viṣṇu is always present, if most usually as an obliquely-signified force lurking in the background of the Vedic hymns."[10]

The *Ṛg Vedic* explicit portrayal of Viṣṇu, then, in the half dozen hymns in which he occurs, connects him with solar energy, other solar gods like the Ādityas, fertility, vegetation[11] and ritual, but the three strides go further, expanding Viṣṇu across the cosmos that he pervades and maintains for humankind's benefit as the interconnecting force of the universe. He is not portrayed anthropomorphically and yet he is a beneficent and kindly god that gives riches and prosperity to his devotees. He is not a warlike god according to the *Ṛg Veda* and aids gods like Indra when needed. Indeed, the close association between Viṣṇu and Indra probably assisted the rise of Viṣṇu in that he was able to take on the declining facets of Indra.

All these factors informed the rise of Viṣṇu to prominence in the pantheon of Hindu deities. But it was the myth of the three strides and its associative concepts that remained embedded in the developing Hindu psyche and accompanied Viṣṇu in his rise to pre-eminence. The myth is embellished with greater significance in the post-*Vedic* texts, symbolizing his great power, his annihilation of evil, his power to support Heaven and Earth and the intervening space, and his power to pervade all that he traversed, benefiting gods and humankind. Gonda made the pertinent point here that: "The general idea originally underlying this central mythical act seems to have been the eternal phenomenon of the pervading and omnipresent, mighty and blessing stream of celestial light, warmth and energy", and hence a universal character to Viṣṇu.[12] The extension and pervasion of himself over and in the universe gave Viṣṇu his important creating and sustaining characteristics. His first two strides are said to be visible, but not the third, which is Viṣṇu's highest Heaven, incomprehensible to all but the gods themselves, and the good among departed souls. Viṣṇu unites all three, interconnecting them into a purposeful whole. Such a purposeful whole, it seems to me, was one characterized by the secure order of things in their rightful places, of order in society – in short, a whole that was informed by *dharma*: it is no wonder, then, that Viṣṇu slipped easily into orthodox *Brāhminism*.

Beyond the *Ṛg Veda*, these early characteristics are enhanced. In the *Brāhmaṇas*, the myth of the three strides is developed into connection with a dwarf – later to be developed even further into one of the *avatāras* of Viṣṇu. In the *Śatapatha Brāhmaṇa* (1:2:5), we find Viṣṇu aiding the gods in a bid for sacrificial ground by disguising himself as a dwarf and then expanding to cover the whole of Earth. Of course, the *Brāhmaṇas* were highly concerned with ritual sacrifice, and it was Viṣṇu who was associated with such sacrifice[13]

– one fundamental reason for his rise in status. Indeed, many of his alternative names are prefixed with *yajña*, "sacrifice". It is sacrifice that gives the gods their powers and the sacrificers their returned favours from the gods, and by identifying Viṣṇu with the sacrifice, his rise to the greatest of gods was assured, along with the belief that his strides were the source of power for all the gods. His rise, too, it seems to me, must have been due to the temperate nature of the god. This was not a god to be feared or appeased: rather, his whole nature seems to have been concerned with care for the cosmos and the beings within it. This must surely have weighed heavily in the eyes of his devotees in making him popular. So Viṣṇu's character suited both orthodox views and popular needs. At the same time, his rising character gathered to itself many pre-Āryan and *Vedic* strands that combined to fulfil all kinds of scattered sectors of early Hinduism. By the time of the epics, Viṣṇu was the creator, sustainer and destroyer of the gods, humankind and the universe they inhabited. Everything stemmed from his manifested energy and owed its existence to Viṣṇu, though his supremacy alternates with that of Śiva and Brahmā. What I want to do now is examine the more metaphysical aspects that came to be associated with this supreme God, Viṣṇu.

The metaphysics of Viṣṇu

In the *Mahābhārata* and the *Purāṇas*, Viṣṇu is presented as one of three major deities combined in what is called the *Tri-mūrti*, or three forms, along with Śiva and Brahmā. Here, Brahmā is the Creator, Viṣṇu the Sustainer and Śiva the Dissolver. The three are linked with the three *guṇas*, Brahmā as Creator with the activity and impulse of motion of the *rajas guṇa*, and Śiva with the *tamas guṇa* of inertia that brings dissolution of the universe. Viṣṇu is associated with the *guṇa* of *sattva*, which is indicative of goodness, light, knowledge and evolution: thus, he sustains the universe and helps it to progress in the right ways. He does this through his all-pervading power. However, for Vaiṣṇavites, Viṣṇu becomes supreme as Brahman and superior to any other deity. In this case, he takes over the powers of the other members of the *Tri-mūrti*. He is the Creator from whose navel, or a lotus that blossoms from his navel, Brahmā mythologically emerges, like the action that emerges from an inner power, essence or thought. The navel was considered to be the centre of the body and Viṣṇu's navel is, thus, the centre and source of existence. While the *Mahābhārata* generally upholds the supremacy of Viṣṇu, there are occasions in it when Śiva is portrayed as superior. The Vaiṣṇava *Purāṇas*, of course, see Viṣṇu as supreme just as the Śaiva *Purāṇas* do Śiva. The *Viṣṇu-purāṇa* begins by equating Viṣṇu with Brahman in whom inheres all the potential for manifest existence. Space and time, matter and spirit exist united in the unmanifest Brahman that is Viṣṇu. In this state the three *guṇas* are in total equilibrium. Creation occurs when matter (*prakṛti*) evolves through the activation and eventual separation and subsequent combinations of the *guṇas*.

While creation is manifest, Viṣṇu pervades and sustains it, his essence being central to the existence of all things, creatures and beings. It is Viṣṇu that permits the interconnectedness of the universe, the communication of consciousness between beings and the cohesion between phenomena that makes sense of the universe. He is the centripetal force, binding atoms together to create reality. Because Viṣṇu pervades all space – the earth, the atmosphere and the heavens – he is able to gather and bestow the fruits of all three. He is the pillar of the universe, its axis through and around which the universe is supported. Such a concept is often depicted iconographically with the God standing upright and poised like a pillar, reminiscent of his earlier connections with the sacrificial post. His sustaining aspect is also concerned with the preservation of harmony and order in the world – the *dharma* of the eternal rhythms of the cosmos, of life and of societal norms.

Periodically, according to the *Mahābhārata*, Viṣṇu is said to sleep at the end of each world age. The world is destroyed by fire and subsequently flooded, while Viṣṇu sleeps on the serpent Śeṣa in the depths of the ocean until, in his essence, it is time again for the thought of creation. The universe thus passes through phases of manifested creation and dissolved quiescence. Śeṣa, the cosmic serpent, means "Remainder", that is to say, it symbolizes what is left when the world ceases to exist. He is also called Ananta, "Endless" or "Infinite" and it is this serpent that destroys the world with his fiery breath at the end of each age, preceding the deluge of waters that covers all. His coiled form on the ocean (in some myths, at the bottom of the ocean), represents the eternal revolutions of time, and it is on these that Viṣṇu sleeps with Śeṣa's thousand-hooded heads forming a canopy above the slumbering Viṣṇu. Here, we have the symbiotic nature of Viṣṇu and Nārāyaṇa, who, as I noted above, was connected with the waters of dissolution, floating on them as a child on a leaf. The image of Viṣṇu here is an anthropomorphic one, but one that conceals the metaphysical principle of potentiality held in a quiescent state until a new creation begins – a process that is cyclical like Śeṣa's coils. All that once existed is dissolved in the waters; all is still, formless, unfathomable, non-evolved, unmanifest, yet with latent possibility: the subtle germ for all creation of a new age still exists. Serpents, or *nāgas*, were likely to have been venerated in some areas and we see here how such cults have probably been absorbed into the growing mythology of Viṣṇu. The enemy of snakes is the eagle and here, too, we find a half man, half eagle being Viṣṇu's mount, Garuḍa, perhaps containing a semblance of an ancient cult of animal worship.[14] When a new age is to begin, Viṣṇu generates a lotus from his navel and in that lotus is Brahmā, who is the active energy by which the world can once more be generated.

Viṣṇu's iconography

Viṣṇu has a thousand names, indicative of the many facets of his nature. The repetition of these names is itself an act of meditation. Some of the names like Aśvattha, the name of a tree, are indicative of his ancient connection with vegetation.[15] Similarly, the *tulasī* plant is grown in many Vaiṣṇava homes and is exclusive to ritual worship of Viṣṇu. The lotus, especially, connects him with vegetation and he is sometimes portrayed seated on one. Some other names are connected with the sun. Hari, one meaning of which is "pale yellow", for example, was a word sometimes used to refer to the sun, fire and lightning, amongst other things, in the *Vedas*.[16] Indeed, Viṣṇu is mostly dressed in yellow robes. His name as Vaikuṇṭha is also indicative of his Heaven, said to be at the summit of Mount Meru and a place of exquisite beauty and richness. This gives us an immediate insight into how this God is portrayed, for he is essentially an anthropomorphic figure that readily lends him to artistic representation. Viṣṇu is royal, kingly, sometimes featured sitting on a throne to represent his rulership of the universe and the royal function of protecting his domain. He is also featured upright, seated on, or standing by, his vehicle Garuḍa, or resting on Śeṣa. Viṣṇu is dark blue, though according to myth, his colour varies depending on the cosmic age. He is charmingly handsome with long thick hair and a robust, beautifully proportioned body. The upright figure of Viṣṇu is particularly significant. Maxwell comments on this posture: "The reason for this immobility of the central cult image is associated . . . with the concept of unruffled tranquillity and effortless existence, expressive of the unqualified state of Being. . . . The stillness of these images represents the deity in his transcendent, original nature, prior to his work of Creation, in the pure state of his own being."[17]

Apart from his yellow loincloth and his sacred thread, Viṣṇu is usually naked but wears all kinds of ornaments on his arms, ankles and around his neck and waist. His unusual earrings are in the shape of a legendary figure that may be a crocodile or some kind of sea monster. A special jewel, *kauṣṭubha* is featured in his necklace. It came to the surface of the ocean when it was churned by the gods and demons at the beginning of a world cycle and symbolizes consciousness, but on a more mundane level is believed to be wish-fulfilling. A garland of flowers is also around his neck and extends down as far as his knees. A diadem on his head is in the shape of a cone.

Viṣṇu's main icon is one with four arms (though he may have eight, sixteen or just two) and in each of his hands he holds a symbolic item, each indicative of some aspect of his divine nature. The number four features in so many aspects of Hinduism – four classes, ages, directions, aims of life, stages of life. The main emblems adorning his body are:

- **A conch**, *śaṅkha*, in the lower right hand symbolizes the five elements. It is called Pāñcajanya. This white shell has a spiral, revolving base emerging from a single point indicative of creativity and cyclical existence. It came to symbolize the elements – fire, air, water, earth and ether. As a sea shell, its source is the ocean and water – a medium associated with Viṣṇu from early times and from his amalgamation with other gods, particularly Nārāyaṇa. Water, as I noted above, is the medium from which each new manifestation of the world, of creation, occurs. The vibrations made by the sound of the conch are said to resemble the primordial sound of the universe. The conch was also used at the start of battles and in many ceremonies and, today, in temple worship, when new temples are consecrated, and at major festivals.
- **A discus**, the *cakra*, called Sudarśana, is Viṣṇu's weapon, which he holds in his upper right hand. It has a hub with spokes and therefore is more like a wheel than a discus, with the hub tapering to the perimeter. It has the ability, like the boomerang of the Australian aborigines, to return to the hand of its wielder. Maxwell suggests that in tribal ritual a chariot wheel was raised on the end of a pole to symbolize the sun: there may thus be some loose connection with the earlier solar deities and Viṣṇu if this is the case.[18] The *cakra* is also associated with the mind, especially with the mind that whirls with sense perceptions, but also the mind that is the means to liberation, alongside the *cakra* that cuts asunder the bonds of ignorance. Whereas the conch is connected with the waters of creation, the discus is connected with the idea of destruction.
- **A mace**, the *gadā*, in the lower left hand symbolizes the power of knowledge and

the power of Time that destroys all things. But it is also a weapon, a club that sounded like thunder when wielded and was used to destroy demons. Its name is Kaumodakī and, notably, it was given to Viṣṇu by the god of waters, Varuṇa – again, indicative of Viṣṇu's ancient association with water.

- **A lotus**, *padma*, in the upper left hand is a powerful symbol in Indian thought. The purity of the flower that emerges on the spread leaves of the plant, despite the muddy waters in which it thrives, is like the purity of the soul in the murky realms of the world of senses. The *sattvic* lotus symbolizes the beginnings of creation and is the mythical source from which Viṣṇu produces the creator God Brahmā. As such, it is womb-like and, indeed, is a feminine noun. Again, Viṣṇu's connection with the old god Nārāyaṇa of the waters is relevant in this context.

Occasionally, when represented with eight arms, Viṣṇu carries a sword and shield and a bow and arrows, somewhat indicative of his warrior nature in conquering demons but also symbolic of the interaction of the senses in the world of phenomena as well as the battle to destroy the egoistic self that is inimical to true knowledge and liberation.[19] Outstanding, is the wonderful smile of the God in all his iconography: it is a smile that has multiple meanings to attract the variations in consciousness of his devotees.

Frequently, Lakṣmī, the consort of Viṣṇu stands at his side, though is represented much smaller than her husband. Sometimes she is divided into two as Śrī-Devī, the sky and Bhū-Devī, the earth, or Śrī-Lakṣmī and Sarasvatī. But Lakṣmī is also represented as a golden curl of hair, the *Śrī-vatsa* on Viṣṇu's chest. It symbolizes, like Lakṣmī herself, good fortune, though it may simply mean "Favourite of Śrī". It is also present on Kṛṣṇa and signifies that the bearer has special powers and greatness.[20] Lakṣmī is the *śakti* energy and creative power of Viṣṇu for those sects that combine both male and female deities. In some Vaiṣṇava religion, it is Viṣṇu that remains supreme, even though his consort accompanies much of his iconography. But the *Viṣṇu-purāṇa* depicts Viṣṇu and Lakṣmī as the male–female principles that inform all life, he day to her night, he meaning to her speech, he creator to her creation and so on. For some sects, Viṣṇu is Puruṣa, pure Spirit, and Lakṣmī is *Prakṛti*, Matter, their conjoined principles making all existence possible. In his *avatāras*, which I shall take up below, Lakṣmī is believed to incarnate alongside her husband. The emphasis jointly on both Lakṣmī and Viṣṇu is particularly evident in the Śrī-Vaiṣṇava religion of southern India. Whether alone or with his consort, Viṣṇu resides in Vaikuṇṭha, his heavenly abode high on the mountains, usually Mount Meru. Vaikuṇṭha is a perfect and radiant paradise, with a spring of honey, an ocean of milk and expansive brightness. It perhaps represents the highest step of the three mythologically assigned to Viṣṇu from *Vedic* times, for it is said to exist beyond the sun. Vaikuṇṭha is called the eye in the sky and it is there that the faithful end their long journey through countless lives. Vaikuṇṭha is the *highest* Heaven because it is higher than the usually known Heaven, Svarga, the place to which those with good *karma* go to use up their accumulated merit before being born again on Earth.

As a God that had assimilated so many of the attributes of early deities, Viṣṇu became the one supreme God who, nevertheless, could be approached in a variety of ways. He could even be merged with Śiva under the name Hari-Hara. Viṣṇu as Hari is "Remover", he that removes the sorrows of people, their ignorance that clouds their path to liberation, and their egos that blind them to his nature. At the same time he is within the sun that lends its warmth to all, the rains that nourish, and is the God who is benevolent to all his devotees. At the end of the long evolution of this God from ancient times to his modern greatness, Viṣṇu has entered the hearts of multitudes of Hindus, in whatever form they wish to approach him.

Viṣṇu's *avatāras*

By the time of the later parts of the great epic, the *Mahābhārata*, the idea of Viṣṇu descending to Earth in various ages had gained considerable ground and in the *Purāṇas* the concept was developed to its full, but there are many myths surrounding these descents. I can only offer here some of the major "incarnations", and the main myths with which they are associated. The term *avatāra* can be divided into two – *ava*, which means "down" and the verb *tṝ*, "to attain, cross over", the whole bearing the idea "to descend", resulting in the noun *avatāra*, "descent". However, while the idea of such descents of Viṣṇu existed well before the *Purāṇas*, the term *avatāra* was a fairly late one. Kṛṣṇa in the *Bhagavad Gītā*, for example, explains that he has come to Earth for the benefit of *dharma* but the word *avatāra* does not occur in the entire text. It was probably during the first centuries CE that the idea of Viṣṇu's descents evolved and was probably the result of the amalgamation of Viṣṇu's character with some of the old tribal gods. In short, it was easy to see local gods and heroes as manifestations of Viṣṇu and this may account for some of the legendary descents of Viṣṇu in animal form. Each descent was thus incorporated at a different time but the major ten descents seem to have been in place by the eighth century. Some of the descents – the Dwarf, Fish and Tortoise – are not linked with Viṣṇu at all in the early texts and probably reflected old tales of mythical creatures. It is the term *avatāra* that renders a systematized concept to Viṣṇu's descents, especially in the *Purāṇas*.

The *Bhagavad Gītā* provides us with the earliest rationale for the descent of the divine when Kṛṣṇa says:

> Being unborn, also an imperishable *Atman*, and being Lord of all beings, controlling my own *prakriti*, I come into being by my own *maya*.
> Whenever there is a decline of *dharma*, Bharata, and a rise of *adharma*, then I manifest myself.
> For the protection of the good and for the destruction of the wicked, for the firm establishment of *dharma* I am born in every epoch.[21]

Since the *Ṛg Veda*'s account of Viṣṇu's three strides states that he undertook them for distressed beings, the idea of his taking earthly form in order to counteract evil originated there. There may have been some mutual influence between Vaiṣṇavism and Buddhism, given that there were many tales of the Buddha's past lives in both animal and human forms. Of course, the idea of reincarnation in countless cycles of birth and death depending on one's positive or negative *karma* must have made more plausible the idea that a benevolent God could himself incarnate. Unlike the *Upaniṣads* that stressed in the main the unmanifest impersonal Brahman, the idea of a God that becomes manifest on Earth for the sake of humankind, lends itself to a much more *personal* conception of deity and this is, indeed, what we find with the popularity of the concept of *avatāras* as well as different expressions of a descended deity who is yet One. By the time of the rather late *Bhāgavata-purāṇa*, the incarnations of Viṣṇu were thought to be thousands – seers, priests, saints, lawgivers, gods.

The earliest manifestations seem to have been the Boar, the Man-Lion, the Dwarf and the hero Kṛṣṇa.[22] This may contradict the theory of those who see the ten major *avatāras* as reflecting an evolutionary theory of the development of life from fish (water bound), tortoise (amphibian), boar (mammal), man-lion (half animal half human), dwarf (little man) with the latest *avatāras* fully man, unless there was a conscious intent of *Purāṇic* sources to place the order in this way. It is far more likely, I think, that the creature descents reflect ancient tribal animal worship that became subsumed under Viṣṇu. In any case, while I only want to deal with the ten major descents, the lists vary considerably in the later texts. A swan, for example, heads some of the early attempts at a list, not a fish. The popular *Bhāgavata-purāṇa* mentions twenty-two, though is inconsistent throughout with the number given, and says at one point that the *avatāras* of Viṣṇu are really as numerous as the many rivulets and streams that flow into an inexhaustible lake. Other texts may give as many as thirty-nine. The first book of the *Mahābhārata* deals with partial *avatāras*, the word "partial" being *aṃśa*, something like an atom, a minute particle of the energy of a deity that manifests itself on Earth, and it seems that these minute divine manifestations can be numerous. Important thinkers and figures of the past and present are accepted as such. What is essential to note is that whether a descent is full or partial – thoroughly divine like Kṛṣṇa or a particle of the divine – the essence of divinity is believed to be unchanged. If Kṛṣṇa is accepted as an *avatāra* of Viṣṇu then both are coexistent without any lessening of the nature of Viṣṇu when he is incarnate on Earth.

The *Gītā* gives us a clear rationale for the *avatāras*, as I have shown above, but later texts like the *Bhāgavata-purāṇa* claim that the rationale for the descents is sport or play, *līlā*. I have always found this a problematic concept in Hinduism and explanations of it generally fail to be convincing. *Līlā* implies the cosmic sport of God and that the created world is an expression of that play or sport, albeit play that is done with unbounded freedom, total independence and sheer joy. The *Bhāgavata-purāṇa* links *līlā* with the concept of *avatāras* to suggest that God appears in various forms to protect humankind but as part of his play, his sport. The text, however, does not underplay the role of protection: it simply makes that protection as easy as play. We shall see how this is especially applicable to Kṛṣṇa below.

When Viṣṇu descends to Earth in human form, he lives a human life, is born, takes wives, has children, and dies and therefore has a tangible reality albeit that legends and myths of all kinds of great feats of strength and battles with demons accrue to his earthly existence. But the visible reality of the life of the God on Earth is the whole attraction of a personal God. Rāma of the *Rāmāyaṇa* became deified as one of the *avatāras* of Viṣṇu, and the tale of his life is replete with the sufferings and anguish of human existence, of difficult choices, hardship and personal struggle. If Rāma were not conceived of as real, human and divine, personal devotion to him would not be quite as fervent. Kṛṣṇa, as we shall see shortly, is a different matter, human but not losing the *līlā* of which I wrote above. But it is the *personal* nature of the descended God that is pre-eminent and that engenders a personal devotion, a close relationship with the devotee that, through his grace, he comes to protect, to save and to teach about the nature of God. As a living being, God on Earth is best positioned to appeal to the hearts of the masses.

Daśāvatāra: The ten *avatāras*

The first four *avatāras* are said to have appeared in the first of the four ages of the present cycle of the universe, in the *Satya-yuga*. As the Fish, Tortoise, Boar and Man-Lion, they are possibly bound in ancient totemism and mythological tales that have been handed down and eventually attached to Viṣṇu. The human *avatāras*, on the other hand, are more likely to have resulted from local and tribal heroes. The myths vary in connection with the major ten *avatāras* and space does not permit me to give anything more than a brief outline of the predominant myth or myths associated with each. I shall keep them in the so-called "evolutionary" order and one, Kṛṣṇa, is of sufficient importance to necessitate an independent section. The ten *avatāras* or *daśāvatāra*, then, are:

The Fish (*Matsya*). Each new age is begun by a first man, Manu. The Manu in the Fish story is the seventh of these, a sage. Each morning he bathes in a small stream. There, one morning, he rescues a tiny fish, who asks for Manu's protection. Manu places the fish in his small water pot but, as the days go by, the fish grows and grows, eventually needing an urn, a tank, a pond, a river and, finally, the ocean to contain it. It is then that Manu understands that the fish is Viṣṇu in disguise on Earth. It is the end of the age and a deluge of waters is about to engulf the world, so Manu is instructed to build a ship in which sages, species and seeds are protected. When the deluge comes, a long horn from the Fish is used to fasten the boat safely with Śeṣa acting as a rope between the two until a new age begins. In a variation of the myth (and there are a number of these in the *Purāṇas*), Viṣṇu as the Fish recovers the *Vedas* from the waters when they have been stolen by a demon during the long night of the creator god Brahmā. Viṣṇu as the Fish teaches the *Vedas* to Manu ready for the next regeneration of humankind. In the original form of this myth in the *Śatapatha Brāhmaṇa* (1:8:1) there is no connection with Viṣṇu. The *Mahābhārata* does not mention the Fish and the connection with it and Viṣṇu is therefore late.[23]

The Tortoise (*Kūrma*). When the world is again in the process of creation, the gods realize that they have lost the nectar of immortality in the depths of the waters. They join forces with the demons to recover it and Viṣṇu agrees to become a giant Tortoise so that his back, which makes up the entire vault of the heavens, will act as a rotating pivot. His great serpent, Śeṣa, acts as the rope around a gigantic churning stick consisting of Mount Meru (or another mountain, the Mandara). It is this "rope" that the demons and gods pull to churn the ocean. As in the case of Viṣṇu as the Fish, the *Śatapatha Brāhmaṇa* equates a different god, Prajāpati, with the Tortoise, not Viṣṇu. But it is Viṣṇu who is identified as the Tortoise in the *Purāṇas*. The churning of the ocean, which is made of milk, is an important Hindu myth that gives the origin of so many facets of Hinduism. It was not just the nectar of immortality that came from its depths but the origins of other things are ascribed to it – the physician of the gods, who holds the cup of nectar; Lakṣmī, the Goddess and consort of Viṣṇu; the goddess of wine; the moon; a beautiful nymph, a wonderful horse and a wonderful elephant; the jewel worn by Viṣṇu; a tree that yielded what one desired; the cow of plenty; a conch shell that when blown assures victory; a perfectly accurate bow; and then, too, the deadly poison that Śiva drank. Variations in the myths include a number of other items and beings as well.

The Boar (*Varāha*). When a demon king takes the whole of the world to the bottom of the ocean, Viṣṇu becomes a huge Boar, slays the demon and raises the world to the surface on the end of one of his gigantic tusks. Myths about such a boar occur in earlier texts and, again, it is Prajāpati, the creator god, who is associated with it in the *Śatapatha Brāhmaṇa*, where it is he and not Viṣṇu that dives down to rescue the earth. Thus, the Boar is only later associated with Viṣṇu with accounts conflicting like most of the myths related to the *avatāras*. Basham thought that the early myths involving a boar reflected a non-Āryan cult that worshipped the pig.[24]

The Man-Lion (*Nṛsiṃha*). After Viṣṇu as the Boar kills the demon, the latter's twin becomes king of the demons. He had received a boon that he could not be slain by human or beast or by day or night and this led him to tyrannize all. His son, Prahlāda, is a devout devotee of Viṣṇu, and though the King tries to kill Prahlāda many times, his son's devotion is so great that he always survives completely unharmed. The exasperated King is told by his son that Viṣṇu is everywhere: the King points to a pillar in the court and Prahlāda says Viṣṇu is even in that. It is twilight, neither day nor night; the pillar bursts apart and from it comes neither man nor beast, but Viṣṇu as half a man and half a lion. He then slays the demon king. There are no early associative myths of a man-lion and it is with the *Mahābhārata* and later texts that Viṣṇu is so defined as an *avatāra*.

The Dwarf (*Vāmana*). In the second age, a demon named Bali had conquered Heaven, Earth and the underworld. Viṣṇu approaches Bali as a dwarf and asks to be granted as much land as he could cover in three strides. Bali agrees to the modest request whereupon Viṣṇu grows to an enormous size and covers Earth with his first stride and Heaven with his second. But he does not take the third stride, so allowing the underworld to Bali. Viṣṇu is found as a dwarf in the *Śatapatha Brāhmaṇa* but there the account does not make him an *avatāra*: that is something put forward later in the epics. Already associated with three strides in the *Ṛg Veda*, it is not difficult to see how this particular myth became Viṣṇu's own, especially since his earlier three strides, like the Dwarf myth, show him as encompassing and pervading the whole universe. Preciado-Solis puts forward the rather interesting comment that just as Viṣṇu as the Dwarf encompasses the whole universe, so does the infant Kṛṣṇa,[25] as we shall see below.

Rāma with the Axe (Paraśu-Rāma). This Rāma is a *Brāhmin* who seems to have come from a time in the second of the four ages when the warrior class, the *Kṣatriyas* were too powerful. Rāma with the axe is appropriately named, since he is reputed to have destroyed the *Kṣatriyas* many times when they had become too powerful. He was contemporaneous with Rāma-candra below, and is featured in the *Mahābhārata* along with him. This *avatāra* is a somewhat angry and violent man in the myths where he occurs, but he is also the upholder of *dharma* and justice, rallying against kings and warriors who misuse their powers. He was not a worshipper of Viṣṇu according to the *Mahābhārata*, but of Śiva, which is odd given that he is later an *avatāra* of Viṣṇu, though he is not portrayed as such in the

Mahābhārata. It is just as odd that he and Viṣṇu's other *avatāra*, Rāma should have been such profound enemies on many occasions. Brian Collins highlights the strange anomalies of this character:

> Paraśurama, the *Mahābhārata* hero best known for decapitating his mother and exterminating twenty-one generations of Kṣatriyas in a campaign of "varnicide", is possessed of a list of seemingly opposing attributes. He is at once an *avatāra* and a *cirajīvin* ("long-lived one"), a Vaishnava deity and a Śaiva devotee, a Brāhmaṇa and a Kṣatriya, a Vedic sage and a Tantric hero. His story, with themes of matricide, violations of *varṇāśramadharma*, extreme violence, and exile, presents problems for sectarian communities who would assimilate him into their theo-cosmology, even if they find it necessary to list Paraśurāma as an *avatāra* to establish their lineage or facilitate the spread of their influence.[26]

Rāma. I have already dealt with Rāma as the hero and potential *avatāra* of the *Rāmāyaṇa* in chapter 2 in the context of *Scriptures*. Some further points in relation to Viṣṇu are pertinent here. Rāma is a solar deity, much in line with the benevolent character of Viṣṇu. Bhattacharji notes the complementary agricultural connections of Sītā, who was born from a furrow when the earth was ploughed.[27] She is Nature, the earth, fertility and vegetation. These two aspects of sun and earth are syncretized in the evolving character of Viṣṇu as we have seen above. Like Viṣṇu, Rāma is dark in colour and usually clothed in yellow. He is not like Viṣṇu, many-armed, but has the appearance of a strong, handsome man, a warrior holding a bow. He is a *Kṣatriya* hence, perhaps, his rivalry with Rāma with the Axe. His dark colour suggests, as with Viṣṇu, that he was originally not of the Āryan tradition.

Kṛṣṇa. Kṛṣṇa is the most important of the *avatāras* of Viṣṇu and will be dealt with in detail below. He is a full manifestation and *avatāra* and the one that is the most anthropomorphic. This combination of a fully human and fully divine figure is not evident in the same way as Rāma, for Kṛṣṇa does not weep or become distressed. While his life spans the normal phases of birth, childhood, youth, marriage, manly pursuits and eventual death, we are always left in no doubt about the divinity of this being. "Each phase", says Bhattacharji, "satisfies the soul's craving for one particular hierophany, to satisfy particular inclinations of individual needs."[28] Kṛṣṇa manifests himself in the third of the four ages at a time when *dharma* is beginning to degenerate.

Buddha. Accepting the Buddha as an *avatāra* of Viṣṇu is usually explained in two ways. First, it is possible that it might have been an attempt to incorporate the Buddha into Vaiṣṇavism in order to absorb those who preferred Buddhism to Hinduism so rendering Buddhism less of a threat. Given the syncretic nature of Viṣṇu and his ability to absorb under his character and remit the characteristics of other deities, I am rather inclined to favour this reason. Secondly, however, there is the less satisfactory claim, in my view, that Viṣṇu disguised himself as the Buddha in order to draw away the unfaithful from *dharma* and bring about their destruction, so hastening the end of the fourth and final cycle of time. Such a view is that put forward by the *Purāṇas*, especially the *Bhāgavata-purāṇa*. Below, I shall be examining a very important text, the *Gīta-Govinda*, in the context of Kṛṣṇa and one other reason for Viṣṇu being presented as the Buddha is put forward by its author Jayadeva as

Viṣṇu's compassion for animals. Buddhism takes the doctrine of non-violence, *ahiṃsa*, to a far greater level than Hinduism, by eschewing its animal sacrifice. It is an attractive idea though little recognized.

Kalkin. The *Kalkin*, first mentioned in the *Mahābhārata* as a *Brāhmin*, is the descent of Viṣṇu yet to come at the end of the fourth age of the *Kali Yuga*. *Kalkin* means "white horse" and is the steed on which Viṣṇu will ride in order to end the evil age and restore the world to its pure state in a new one. Kalkin was originally unconnected with Viṣṇu and, indeed, was a devotee of Viṣṇu. His status as an *avatāra* is rather late. The idea may have been influenced by the Buddhists' Buddha to come, the Maitreya Buddha, which long pre-dated the *Kalkin*. Interestingly, one of the early *avatāras* outside the ten was a horse-headed one whose fame was the recovering of the *Vedas* from the oceans. There may be some conflation here of the many myths of a *kalkin*, a white horse, the horse-headed saviour of the *Vedas* and even some Christian conceptions of the end of time – all subsumed in Viṣṇu.

Time has added partial *avatāras* like the sage Kapila who is said to have founded the Sāṃkhya school of philosophy; composers of scriptures like Vyāsa, who is reputed to have compiled the *Mahābhārata* and to have arranged the *Vedas* into branches; saints such as Caitanya, who lived in the sixteenth century and even those of more recent times like Mahatma Gandhi and Ramakrishna – in short, many renowned and great men. All *avatāras*, whether partial or full, reveal some dimension of what God is like, full ones like Kṛṣṇa bringing God to the personal level and intimately associated with his devotees. It is an act of compassion and a will to rescue *dharma*, whether of gods or humankind, that motivates the divine to take a tangible form. Viṣṇu is the kind of God that incorporates so many differing dimensions that make him attractive – in whatever form he is approached – to his devotees. I rather like the words of Devdutt Pattanaik in this context, when he writes: "For Vishnu, there is a time for everything – a time to play, a time to work, a time to fight, and a time to give it all up. There is a time to conform, a time to reform, a time to rebel, a time to renounce."[29] All these aspects are thoroughly evident in the main *avatāra* of Viṣṇu as Kṛṣṇa, that immensely popular deity loved by the majority in Hinduism.

Kṛṣṇa

Kṛṣṇa is the major deity who epitomizes the ethos and practice of *bhakti*, loving devotion to a personal God. He is quite exceptional, maintaining orthodoxy and yet transcending it. He is radically unconventional in that he transgresses the norms of *dharmic* society, appealing straight to the heart and the soul of the individual without any need of an intermediary. Like Viṣṇu, Kṛṣṇa absorbed in his character the many tales and legends of earlier local heroes, which perhaps accounts for a good deal of his unconventional characteristics and behaviour. There is no denying the immense popularity of this God since he is worshipped in the length and breadth of India. Like Viṣṇu, of whom he became an *avatāra*, Kṛṣṇa is dark blue in colour, perhaps indicative of his originating from a non-Āryan rural background long before he was adopted into Āryan orthodoxy. Kṛṣṇa means "black", or "dark blue", and this is the interpretation Kṛṣṇa, himself, gives of his name in the *Mahābhārata* (12:330:14). He is the greatest of the *avatāras* of Viṣṇu and the most human of them, being subject to some behaviour that is not really consonant with divinity. He could certainly cheat for his own ends, or in battle, for example. The highest possible love and devotion is offered to this personal God, Kṛṣṇa, but that love is not divorced from the kinds of love in human experience: rather, it is identified with it. What is important about Kṛṣṇa is that he can be approached as a mother would love a child, as a lover would love a lover, as a God who steals the hearts of married women, as a friend, as a great hero and warrior, or as a transcendent Lord and God or, indeed, overlapping aspects of some or all of these ways of approaching him. Kṛṣṇa is never worshipped as a father, however. With the rise of such unorthodox approaches to divinity came the means by which any individual could understand divinity through intense love – in whatever experience of love that meant.

There seems little doubt that Kṛṣṇa existed and that he was a warrior and hero of some fame. The *Mahābhārata* shows this aspect of Kṛṣṇa many times; his prowess in battle against demons, giants, monsters and evil men was exceptional and, as we shall see below, this characteristic began in his early years. He is portrayed as exceptionally strong and, it seems, he was a formidable wrestler.[30] Such feats of strength, combined with divine magical powers, are replete in the myths and legends surrounding Kṛṣṇa. He was no *Brāhmin* but an obvious *Kṣatriya* once he was accepted into the orthodox pantheon. He was mostly joined in his exploits by his elder brother Balarāma, the two forming a divine pair sometimes said to be incarnations of Nārāyaṇa and Nārā, the former, as we saw above, being another name for Viṣṇu. Kṛṣṇa is also paired with Arjuna in the *Mahābhārata* and in the *Bhagavad Gītā*. According to myth, the gods approached Viṣṇu complaining of demons oppressing Earth. Viṣṇu plucked two hairs from his body, a white one that became Balarāma and a black one that became Kṛṣṇa. The *Purāṇas* recount their joint exploits, as does the *Mahābhārata*, but the latter reveals a Kṛṣṇa emerging into a great God, not so much the end-stage of his evolution to the point of being India's favourite God.

The origins of Kṛṣṇa are complicated. There is mention of one Kṛṣṇa in the *Chāndogya Upaniṣad* (3:17), in connection with his teacher Ghora Āṅgirasa. This Kṛṣṇa is said to be the son of Devakī whom later texts also claim is his mother. However, any attempts to trace definitive origins of Kṛṣṇa must remain highly speculative. [31] Kṛṣṇa is an old name and where the name occurs in *Vedic* sources is unlikely to provide reliable links. Kṛṣṇa was probably a tribal hero and legends about him and his prowess are likely to have been widely circulated. It seems fairly certain, however, that he belonged to the Yādava, pastoral tribe and was their chief as well, perhaps, as their personal god. The Yādava tribe is likely to have been aboriginal (*daityas*): indeed, *Vedic* evidence suggests that *Brāhmins* pejoratively called them such.[32] The Yādavas fused with the Vṛṣṇi tribe, a tribe that had a god named Vāsudeva and this name was later assigned to both Viṣṇu and Kṛṣṇa. Flood notes that worship of Vāsudeva dates back to the fifth or sixth centuries BCE. He thinks that Kṛṣṇa was a deity of the Yādava clan, and that when the two tribes coalesced, Kṛṣṇa fused with the Vṛṣṇi's Vāsudeva, so becoming Kṛṣṇa-Vāsudeva.[33] On the other hand, Vasudeva, the husband of Devakī, is presented as a patronymic of Kṛṣṇa the Yādava prince in the *Purāṇic* tradition, though this is likely to have been a false connection perpetuated by tradition.

Worship of Kṛṣṇa-Vāsudeva is important in the Bhāgavata religion that I explored in relation to Viṣṇu above and it seems that here we have the kind of monotheism that is associated with Kṛṣṇa as the supreme God and Lord in a text like the *Gītā*. Indeed, so widely different are the characteristics of Kṛṣṇa as a God that it seems to me likely that we are talking of very different and variant origins for each of the Kṛṣṇas that we have: the mischievous baby and youth, the erotic lover, the great God of the *Gītā*, the warrior, are all disparate characteristics that probably had different origins. For example, early in the first millennium CE a nomadic tribe of herdsmen, the Ābhīras, seem to have engaged in the worship of a god who was the god of herdsmen, Kṛṣṇa-Govinda. Was this, then, the source of the legends of Kṛṣṇa's life as a cowherd? A definitive chronological pathway from a local god or hero Kṛṣṇa to the Kṛṣṇa of Hinduism today is impossible to trace and we have to reckon with syncretic origins that stem from fragments of legends and snippets of history.

All the same, the Vāsudeva/Bhāgavata cult is an important foundation in the evolution of Kṛṣṇa as God. Bhagavats were probably hero-gods connected to tribal areas and Vāsudeva a supreme deity in the Bhāgavata religion. When Kṛṣṇa became also Vāsudeva, he would have amalgamated and united different cultic spheres into a composite whole, at the same time permitting the absorption of the many myths and legends that had developed separately about local divine heroes. To date the origins and early rise of Kṛṣṇa is impossible but we can hazard a guess that tales of the exploits of him as a local hero were probably circulating somewhere around the sixth century BCE. By the fourth century BCE, Kṛṣṇa was widely worshipped and continued to evolve in popularity until later additions to the legends and myths about him, particularly his divine childhood, projected the God to pre-eminence.

So what are our sources for examining this popular God? Aside from doubtful references to Kṛṣṇa in the *Vedas*, the *Mahābhārata* takes up his heroic nature in some parts and his divine nature in others though the citations here are of doubtful chronology. It was in the early centuries of the first millennium CE that texts like the *Harivaṃśa* and the *Purāṇas* expanded the myths about Kṛṣṇa into their fullest form. The *Harivaṃśa* or "Genealogy of Hari", Hari here being Kṛṣṇa, was composed as an appendix to the *Mahābhārata* and gives a full account of the birth of Kṛṣṇa, his childhood, and his life with the cowherds and cowherdesses in Vṛndāvana, where he is reputed to have spent his childhood and youth. Of the *Purāṇas*, the *Viṣṇu-, Padma- and Brahma-vaivarta-purāṇas* also elaborate on Kṛṣṇa's life, but the most important is the *Bhāgavata-purāṇa* in that it is the most widely read and doctrinally accepted. Another text, the *Gītā-Govinda* of Jayadeva, dated to the twelfth century, is a pivotal text for the *bhakti* movement and for the portrayal of Kṛṣṇa as the divine lover. From such sources we can fairly safely say that the Kṛṣṇa the heroic God is much earlier in conception than Kṛṣṇa the child God and the erotic youth. The different texts clearly reflect the different pathways by which Kṛṣṇa came to pre-eminence, some like the *Viṣṇu-purāna* omitting details of his involvement in the Great War of the *Mahābhārata*, or even the nature of Kṛṣṇa in the *Gītā*, preferring to concentrate on Kṛṣṇa the cowherd. This demonstrates how important the cowherd tradition of Kṛṣṇa became. Thomas Hopkins aptly commented: "For the tradition that followed the *Vishnu-purāṇa*, the meaning of Krishna's incarnation was found in Vṛindāvana with the *gopīs*, not with Arjuna on the battlefield of Kurukṣetra at the time of the Bhārata war."[34]

Since it is the later sources that I shall be taking up to examine the life of Kṛṣṇa, it is worth making some mention of Kṛṣṇa's role in the *Mahābhārata*. Here, he is all things –

hero, warrior, chieftain, God incarnate, an advisor to Arjuna, a great teacher – but there is no record there of his childhood. Such variations occurred because his nature as a God was still developing. In the *Mahābhārata* he occasionally acts as a central figure around whom the antagonism between the two sets of brothers develops, though he is not the central figure of the epic. His exploits are typical of the mythical hero but his advice on some occasions was underhand and unethical and he could be manipulative in exciting revenge on his enemies. His home was not the pastoral Vṛndāvana but Dvārakā, where he lived with his brother. One gains the impression that there is so much more to come from this character who is an ideal hero more than anything else in the *Mahābhārata*. It is to the later literature that we must now turn to examine the fuller portrayal of the life and character of Kṛṣṇa.

Kṛṣṇa's birth and life

When Viṣṇu plucked a black and a white hair from his body, according to myth, he placed them in the womb of Devakī, who was married to Vasudeva of the Yādava tribe. The King of the Yādavas was Kaṃsa, and Devakī is described variously as the sister, cousin or daughter of Kaṃsa. The latter had imprisoned his own father so that he could rule Mathurā in his place. At the wedding of Devakī and Vasudeva, a voice from the skies (or the words of a seer in variant texts), revealed to Kaṃsa that he would be killed by the eighth son of Devakī, so Kaṃsa imprisoned her and her husband Vasudeva. Each time she bore a son, Kaṃsa killed it. Vasudeva had another wife, Rohiṇī who lived in a nearby cowherd settlement of Gokula, and when Devakī was expecting her seventh child, the gods transferred it to Rohiṇī's womb. This light-skinned, seventh child was Balarāma (also called Baladeva, Balabhadra and as a divinity, Saṃkarṣaṇa), born from the white hair of Viṣṇu. The links between Balarāma and vegetation are strong: he is said to have developed farming, teaching farmers how to plough, use grain and dig canals for irrigation. He was a man of the fields, of the land, and generally of the simple life. But he was also a fierce warrior and, according to the *Viṣṇu-purāṇa* (5:37:54–6), he was an incarnation of the great serpent Śeṣa.

Kṛṣṇa's birth was even more dramatic. It happened on the eighth day of the last two weeks of the month of Bhadrapada, our July–August, a time still celebrated in the annual festival of Kṛṣṇa Jayānti. When the child was born, it was a boy, destined to be killed. But the guards fell asleep, the prison gates opened and a voice told Vasudeva to take the child across the river Yamunā (which miraculously parted for them to cross), to Gokula and the home of the cowherd Nanda and his wife Yaśodā, who had, herself, given birth to a baby girl. As they crossed the Yamunā in a storm, the serpent Śeṣa is said to have covered the baby with his hooded snake's head. Vasudeva was instructed to exchange the babies on the other shore. The exchange made, Vasudeva returned unnoticed to his prison with Yaśodā's baby girl. When Kaṃsa arrived the following day, he killed the baby girl, but she rose to the sky, being the terrifying goddess Kātyāyanī, and informed Kaṃsa that the eighth child had survived and lived far away. Not far enough for many, however, for Kaṃsa slaughtered all the baby boys in the region. Nanda and Yaśodā were sufficiently alarmed to move with their baby boy, along with Balarāma, from Gokula to Vṛndāvana, another cowherd community where the boy was brought up. This boy was Kṛṣṇa, born from the black hair of Viṣṇu. As Yādava princes, both Kṛṣṇa-Vāsudeva and Saṃkarṣaṇa-Balarāma came to be worshipped as gods, especially by a tribal subgroup of the Yādavas known as the Sātvatas. The regional migrations of the Yādavas must have coincided with those of the forest-dwelling Ābhīras, the latter bringing with them their tales of a cowherd god that coalesced with the Kṛṣṇa-Vāsudeva cult to bring us the delightful tales of Kṛṣṇa as an infant, child and youth.

The tale of Kṛṣṇa's birth is immensely popular and representations of their crossing of the Yamunā are prolific in Hinduism today. Since he was born from the black hair of Viṣṇu, he was dark in colour. His babyhood and childhood were as magical as his birth and it is this aspect of his life that renders Kṛṣṇa so immensely popular. There are many delightful stories of his childhood in Vṛndāvana, particularly those that demonstrate his immense strength and his ability to destroy demons. One kick of his little foot smashed a huge cart, and demons sent to destroy him by Kaṃsa were also destroyed. He was a naughty little boy, stealing the milk, buttermilk, curds and grain from the cowherds' houses. When his foster mother in exasperation tied a rope around him with the other end around a pillar in order to keep him in one place, he pulled down the pillar and threw it at two demons, killing them. On another occasion Yaśodā tried to take dirt out of his mouth, but when she looked in his mouth she saw the whole of the cosmos there – rather like the image we saw of Viṣṇu covering the whole universe.

Both boys, Kṛṣṇa and Balarāma, proceeded into their youth as exceptionally strong boys who frequently enjoyed very naughty pranks – all endearing to their devotees of modern day. There are attractive variants of all these myths about Kṛṣṇa but all serve to demonstrate the divine nature of the child, a miniature God, his strength and divinity evident really before he should have been able to walk and talk. Preciado-Solis describes the image of Kṛṣṇa created by these stories as "an image of divine humanity, of the infinite and eternal incarnated in a human frame. This divinity in human form is even more dramatically expressed when the human form is that of a mere baby, for then the symbol is more potent."[35] The many tales are vividly attractive, charming, often tender and indicative of what Kṛṣṇa is all about – intimate love. He chases his own shadow, loves to make his bangles jingle, plays spontaneously and is infinitely happy, even if he is naughty enough to pee in someone's clean house. This is God in the form to which devotees can relate, a God that is inexpressibly approachable.

As we follow Kṛṣṇa into his youth, the same elements of freedom and spontaneity, spiced with a little naughtiness, are evident. David Kinsley offered the following superb comment about Kṛṣṇa's youth: "The boastful, brash, and indomitable spirit of Kṛṣṇa's play makes the world around him sparkle with aliveness. His youthful play lights up the world around him as a blazing fire lights up the darkness. The playful actions of Kṛṣṇa and his companions burst forth to tumble and romp like the wind in the trees, unpredictable and free."[36] This is a youth who defies conventions, who is unconditioned and who appears exceptionally *real*, despite being divine. His strength is phenomenal, almost as if he plays with his victims, so easy is it to defeat them; so he dispenses with the monsters sent by Kaṃsa to kill him with ease. On one occasion, and in a well-known myth, the god Indra sends torrential rain to Vṛndāvana since he feels the inhabitants have neglected him. Kṛṣṇa effortlessly picks up the local mountain on his little finger and shelters people and cattle underneath for seven days and nights until Indra relents.

As a youth, Kṛṣṇa is fond of practical jokes, especially teasing the cowherdesses, the *gopīs*, on one occasion stealing their clothes while they bathed. His world is one of joy and laughter, of beauty in his being, as Kinsley said, "a presence to be intimately enjoyed in love rather than adored in humility".[37] Kṛṣṇa is a God that is readily celebrated in drama, art, poetry, music and literature. As the youthful cowherd, he is sometimes portrayed playing his celebrated flute, standing by a cow with animals and birds all around him. He has forest flowers around his neck as well as a jewelled garland and a peacock feather on his crown. His black curly hair adorns his face, with lilies around his ears and he always, always smiles. His large eyes are like lotuses. These features are often portrayed in his famous pose in which he is bent slightly at the waist, one leg bent and crossed over the other, and his head slightly inclined. He is dressed in a golden yellow robe. It is no wonder that he enchanted and attracted every woman, married or not, in Vṛndāvana. His exploits as an amorous lover I want to treat separately below, since they are an important part of the image of Kṛṣṇa. It is an aspect of Kṛṣṇa that developed in the first few centuries of the first millennium CE – his famous flute calling to him the young girls and even married women of Vṛndāvana.

In his more mature years, Kṛṣṇa leaves the cowherd community to return to Mathurā and destroy the demon Kaṃsa, which was one of his purposes in his earthly life. Kaṃsa entices Kṛṣṇa and his brother back to Mathurā by organizing great wrestling matches. There, however, while Kṛṣṇa emerges as the champion wrestler, albeit a seemingly simple cowherd youth, Kaṃsa finally meets his death at the hand of Kṛṣṇa, who replaces Kaṃsa's father on the throne and frees his own imprisoned parents. In the *Bhāgavata-purāṇa* it is said that all the women in Mathurā fell in love with Kṛṣṇa. Strangely, however, Kṛṣṇa and his family are forced to leave Mathurā and flee West to the coast because new enemies and adverse circumstances leave him weakened. There on the coast, Kṛṣṇa builds his capital Dvārakā and fortifies it well. He lives with a harem of a thousand wives. His death is somewhat ignominious and simple. His tribe becomes decimated by internal strife to the point of its own destruction and the city he created later slips into the sea. A hunter mistakes Kṛṣṇa for a deer, and as Kṛṣṇa is sitting in meditation in the forest, the hunter shoots him in the heel – the only vulnerable place on Kṛṣṇa's body. His time to depart had come and he returned to his natural abode as Viṣṇu.

In the texts that write of the purpose of Kṛṣṇa's life, it is oft repeated that his presence on Earth serves to promote the love of and devotion to God. In the *Bhāgavata-purāṇa*, Kṛṣṇa brings Heaven to Earth in his idyllic setting of Vṛndāvana and at the same time lifts Vṛndāvana to the realms of Heaven. His flute especially symbolizes this. The sound of his flute intoxicates those who hear it, calling the hearer to him, calling the soul to God, as some texts say. Maids leave their milking for that sound, women their cooking and baking: whatever action is being undertaken, the sound of the flute intervenes and nothing else matters. Even the gods are called by Kṛṣṇa's flute. In chapter 10 of the *Bhāgavata-purāṇa* it says that the sound of Kṛṣṇa's flute delights the reeds and the river from where the flute came, clouds hover over Kṛṣṇa while he plays to give him shade, and cooling droplets of water fall on the God. Rivers slow down at the sound of the flute, lotuses grow, deer stand still in the forest and all of nature is attentive only to the notes of the flute. It is a time when all is God-focused, when all that is mundane is forgotten in the sheer joy of absorption in the God Kṛṣṇa.

The *Bhāgavata-purāṇa*

The tales of Kṛṣṇa's babyhood, infancy and youth, which are set in an idyllic rural and natural Heaven on Earth have been the inspiration for the deepest of emotional and devotional love of God that India can express. And that devotion is no less valuable because it is infused with emotion, for it reaches the depths of experience in the human psyche. Sheridan offers the following words of wisdom: "If a religious visionary beholds God in a pre-eminently personal form and has at the same time a profound conviction of God's identity with the self and the universe, then a truly creative religious moment has occurred."[38] The *Bhāgavata-purāṇa* is a late work that combines profound theism involving a highly approachable anthropomorphic God on Earth with the concept of a supreme God that surpasses all understanding. The *Bhāgavata* is sufficiently eclectic to include both ideas, but whereas the supreme and indescribable God that is Kṛṣṇa is brought out in a text like the *Bhagavad Gītā*, the *Bhāgavata-purāṇa* brings out the warmth of the personal God Kṛṣṇa in a text that is fairly uniform in thought, reflecting the views of a specific group of devotees. While Kṛṣṇa is a multi-faceted God who is both Viṣṇu and the darling of the cowherdesses, the *gopīs*, he is very much the God of the common people, and the *Bhāgavata* is the central text that exemplifies that. Bengal Vaiṣṇavism accepts it as the central text of all scripture, believing that it even incorporates the essence of all the teachings of the *Vedas* and *Upaniṣads*.

The date of the *Bhāgavata-purāṇa* is somewhere around the ninth or tenth centuries, though opinions vary, but it is usually accepted as later than most other *Purāṇas*. Most suggest no earlier than 500 CE and no later than about 950 CE, but probably later in this timescale than earlier, thus in the tenth century. Its provenance was likely South India in the Tamil region and Sheridan is of the opinion that it was probably written by learned *Brāhmins* who were devoted to Kṛṣṇa but who wanted to make their religion more orthodox in relation to other parts of India and so Sanskritized it in the *Bhāgavata*.[39] The *Bhāgavata* does this by describing the many facets of Kṛṣṇa from his transcendence to his amorous sexuality with the *gopīs*. But the emphasis is on devotion. As Thomas Hopkins justifiably pointed out, "Any determination of the origin or significance of the *Bhāgavata* must ultimately depend on this element, which gives the work its purpose and consistency."[40] Devotion to Kṛṣṇa as the *avatāra* of Viṣṇu is the *raison d'être* of the text as well as illustrating that *bhakti* is the truly efficacious means to spiritual liberation. It is by means of the *Bhāgavata* that the tales surrounding the life of Kṛṣṇa have pervaded the whole of India and have been accepted and respected by many Vaiṣṇava schools. In particular, it is the tenth canto, which details the life of Kṛṣṇa, that is the most popular and the most reproduced. But while there was an attempt to make the *Bhāgavata* acceptably orthodox, the *Bhāgavata* steps outside such orthodoxy to promote devotion as a means to liberation irrespective of class and caste status, or gender. The cowherd women of Vṛndāvana were low caste, yet their devotion to Kṛṣṇa, as we shall see below, transported them to a liberated Heaven on

Earth, even though their sexual and adulterous relationships with Kṛṣṇa were anything but orthodox.

There are parts of the *Bhāgavata* that reflect the non-dualism of the *Upaniṣads*, so identifying the inner Self as *ātman* with the supreme Self that is Brahman, but it never denies the reality or the plurality of the world that Viṣṇu pervades and unites.[41] Kṛṣṇa in the *Bhāgavata* is Lord, Bhagavān, a name given to Viṣṇu but essentially is Kṛṣṇa in the text. The *Bhāgavata* sometimes sees Kṛṣṇa as subordinate to Viṣṇu, sometimes as equal and the same, and sometimes as superior. Different sects will focus on one of these views rather than another. There are times, too, when Viṣṇu or Kṛṣṇa as Bhagavān are seen as superior to Brahman.[42] But Kṛṣṇa is certainly held to be superior to Viṣṇu on many occasions. In one verse of canto 10, for example, we find: "Of all things that exist, their essence lies in their cause and Lord Kṛṣṇa is the ultimate cause of all these causes. Hence, tell me if there is anything apart from him."[43] Kṛṣṇa replaces Viṣṇu at many points of the text, transcending the *Tri-mūrti* of Viṣṇu, Śiva and Brahmā as superior to, and the ultimate cause of, their respective roles. Kṛṣṇa is a *complete* God, not just the qualityless *nirguṇa* Brahman, but also the personal God that transcends even Brahman. To be devoid of qualities is to be incomplete. In the words of the *Bhāgavata*: "Without the presence of and apart from the Lord, there is nothing which is seen or heard of, has happened in the past or present or can happen in the future: nothing immobile or mobile, great or small is different from or without the presence of the Lord. For only he is everything and real."[44] For Vaiṣnava traditions like the Gauḍīya, Kṛṣṇa is superior to every other deity including the unmanifest, Brahman without qualities: he is both unmanifest cause of all and the manifest and personal God, Bhagavān Kṛṣṇa, who draws devotees to him and who informs every single quality in the universe.

These more metaphysical characteristics of the *Bhāgavata-purāṇa* are perfectly balanced with the highly anthropomorphic accounts of the physical life of Kṛṣṇa. We find both the great Lord that is central to the teaching of the *Gītā*, which I want to explore below, and the emotional warmth of God as a living being who laughs, plays, plays tricks and makes love. As a cowherd, a *gopa*, Kṛṣṇa lived like many other commoners, a simple rural life taking the cows out at dawn and bringing them back at dusk. The simplicity of his life demonstrates that the approach to God need not be elaborate and overtly ritualistic but simply full of love in whatever way love is understood. The ultimate goal of liberation is not to be found in withdrawing from the world but in participating in, and sharing love with, a personal God. And the world in which devotees offer their love is a real one. Kṛṣṇa's life is not regarded as illusionary but as a happening in real time. The real emotions that are inspired in his devotees – wonder, joy, blissful happiness, intense love, spontaneity, absolute freedom – are what stem from the *līlā* of Kṛṣṇa, the divine play in which Kṛṣṇa loses himself, just as devotees must also lose themselves in him. His *līlā* is what brings the universe into being; it is also expressed in the act and art of sexual love and I now want to turn to a different aspect of Kṛṣṇa – his erotic activities with the *gopīs*.

Kṛṣṇa and Rādhā

The erotic and sexual relationship between Kṛṣṇa and the *gopīs*, especially between Kṛṣṇa and one of them, Rādhā, is about as unorthodox as it is possible to get. And yet, such overt sexuality in the tales of Kṛṣṇa has become thoroughly acceptable in the Vaiṣṇava religion. Far from the idea that one had to break down attachments and desires in the self, Kṛṣṇaism taught deep attachment to Kṛṣṇa as the path to liberation. In Lee Siegel's words: "The supreme Bhagavat took on the form of the lover so that the devotee could gain access to the sacred, the infinite and eternal, through the expression, rather than the suppression of earthly desires."[45] There was clearly a considerable tension between *bhakti* and eroticism – indeed, a tension that one writer called an "irreconcilable dichotomy"[46] – because, while some texts depict Kṛṣṇa's sexual exploits as adulterous and illicit, others overcome the problem by making Rādhā, Kṛṣṇa's favourite *gopī*, his wife. In the earlier texts, *gopīs* were ordinary village and country girls who were unrefined and not high caste. Later texts refined these rougher girls somewhat, perhaps to lessen the tension between profane erotic sexuality and sacred love. But Siegel's words are important in that they suggest that the devotee becomes, so to speak, the *gopī* that is so transfixed by love, *premā*, for Kṛṣṇa that nothing else matters: the *gopī* is a symbol of the total surrender to the divine. Kṛṣṇa's flute calls the *gopīs* to him as if they are caught up in the pulse of the whole cosmos. Similarly, the tension between sheer eroticism in the moonlit meadows of Vṛndāvana and a more metaphysical understanding of it is to be found in the equating of Vṛndāvana with Heaven – a Heaven that appeared on Earth and that was, therefore, a magical place where magical liaisons could take place, albeit such liaisons were never regarded as illusory. All that is mundane seems to have been left aside in this Heaven on Earth.

It is in the *Viṣṇu-purāṇa*, the *Harivaṃśa* and the *Bhāgavata-purāṇa* that the *gopīs* are the constant companions of Kṛṣṇa, singing and dancing with him and sporting sexually with him. By the time of the *Bhāgavata-purāṇa*, the erotic aspects had reached something of a crescendo, with explicit sexual intercourse and nudity quite acceptable. Passionate love between lovers is put forward as the most expressive act between humans and, therefore, in the relationship between human and divine. But it is not only erotic love that is given prominence but *separation*. Just as the lover yearns for the beloved when separated, so the *gopīs* experience the same yearning for Kṛṣṇa when he is absent from them. These two concepts of passionate love and passionate longing are at the heart of what the tales expound. *All* women, whether married or unmarried, lose their normal boundaries of behaviour to give way to their intense love for Kṛṣṇa: they defy all the social norms that normally bind them.

Such sexual ecstasy is particularly evident in the circular dance, the *rāsa* dance, to which Kṛṣṇa playing his flute calls all to join. *Rasa* means "taste", "flavour", "mood", "sentiment", or "pleasure" in the sense of the taste of love; "aesthetic relish", is the neat term in one source.[47] Siegel states that: "The concept of *rasa* links the psychological and physiological aspects of love – *rasa* is both the emotional pleasure of love and the biological manifestation of that pleasure, i.e. semen."[48] But, as Siegel goes on the say, for many Vaiṣṇavas *rasa* was lifted to a religious transcendent experience of Kṛṣṇa. He notes that the Bengal Vaiṣṇavas understand *rasa* as a "joyful essence" that is manifested in Kṛṣṇa.[49] Semantically, *rasa* is spiritual aesthetic experience, while *rāsa*, or *rāsa-līlā*, is specifically the circular dance, ecstatic play, which is an expansion of *rasa*.[50] We should not approach the idea of the *rāsa* dance, then, without lifting it from the purely sexual to the commensurate metaphysical, for it is a means by which the bliss of the divine is experienced. "It is", says Eric Huberman, "the abstraction of a pure feeling, which takes you out of space and time, and therefore is akin to the realization of Brahman."[51]

Kṛṣṇa is said to have engaged in the *rāsa* dance several times. On each occasion, though standing as the fulcrum in the centre, he stands between all the girls, multiplying his *yogic* energy, or taking on multiple forms, so that each woman believed he was with her alone. The total aesthetic and physical feeling of each woman is clearly, from the viewpoint of the *Bhāgavata-purāṇa*, the bliss of fusion with ultimate divinity and liberation from past sins:

> Their inauspicious *karmas* being consumed by the fire-like intense agony of unbearable separation from their dearest Lord, and with their auspicious *karmas* being exhausted by the ecstatic bliss of the embrace of the Immortal Lord enjoyed in their meditation on him, the cowherd women who became united with that Supreme Soul, even as a beloved would do with her paramour, and with all the *karmic* bonds of mundane existence being instantaneously sundered off, they cast off their mortal coil constituted of the three *guṇas*.[52]

If once the *gopīs* become proud because of their privileged relationship with Kṛṣṇa, he disappears: then, they experience the agony of separation from him. But each one also experiences sexual union with him. While we may want to allegorize the sexual detail, the *Bhāgavata* makes it clear (11:12:13) that the *gopīs* have no idea that Kṛṣṇa is God: yet they offer him totally selfless love, *premā*, and it is the *rāsa* dance that epitomizes this. The whole environment in which the dances take place is exquisitely beautiful and harmonious, especially at the time of the autumn moon – a perfect environment for this graceful and charming God. Vṛndāvana, when Kṛṣṇa is present, is Heaven on Earth. Thus, *rasa* becomes the aesthetic, spiritual and highest experience of divinity. In Graham Schweig's view, the *rāsa-līlā* is "one of the most beautiful love poems ever written".[53]

The *rāsa-līlā* has remained an important expression of devotion to Kṛṣṇa in contemporary times. For example, Manipur in the eastern Himālayas has a strong Vaiṣṇava tradition strengthened by the great Hindu *bhakta* Caitanya. Here in Manipur, the *rāsa-līlā* is famous and has incorporated local dance traditions into it: "This is a characteristic example of the way in which mainstream Hindu traditions take a localized form in this region which is so distinct in language and ethnic make-up from areas to the west."[54]

The *Gītā-Govinda*

Of all the *gopīs*, Kṛṣṇa's favourite was Rādhā. For some Vaiṣṇavas, this particular relationship epitomizes all life, like the Śiva–Śakti relationship: "Rādhā and Kṛṣṇa are the deepest mystery, indwelling all other mysteries and all other aspects of reality."[55] Anthropomorphically, this intimate relationship is depicted by the fact that Rādhā is often with Kṛṣṇa at the centre of the *rāsa* dance, she, too, *yogically* pervading all that is around her. Their sexual union is ultimate bliss and the message here is that they bring divine bliss to ordinary beings. God is believed to be at his fullest when he is both impersonal but intensely personal. Experience of the latter is full and profound. Only Kṛṣṇa of all the Hindu Gods is the divine Lover. Kṛṣṇa's relationship with Rādhā goes well beyond the passionate love and longing–separation motif, for it is full of frivolity, temper tantrums, pretended indifference on both sides. Rādhā is portrayed with all the characteristics of a maiden hopelessly in love – mood swings, putting her clothes on in the wrong way like her necklace around her waist. Kṛṣṇa does the same, meaning to chew a betel leaf but chews a lotus instead. Their love-making is abandoned, frenzied; they are cocooned in their own special world. It is a divine–human love affair, where the human is in Heaven and the God is on Earth.

Such an erotic relationship between Kṛṣṇa and Rādhā does not occur at all in the *Bhāgavata.* Its full expression is to be found in the Bengali Jayadeva's *Gītā-Govinda.* This text is a Sanskrit poem, a *kāvya*, about Govinda, or Kṛṣṇa, and is a twelfth-century work that is fundamental to Vaiṣṇava devotionalism. Lee Siegel's work on this is entitled *Sacred and Profane Dimensions of Love* and this rather overtly states the problem of the balance between the erotic and the sacred that surrounds the Kṛṣṇa legends. As Siegel points out, such tension occurs because sensual passion and religious devotion can overlap in the emotions,[56] and the *Gītā-Govinda* "is literally about carnal love but it is also literally devotional".[57] Thus, it would be a mistake to try to interpret the *Gītā-Govinda* entirely in an allegorical way. Poets such as Jayadeva would have been highly educated, orthodox, cultured and probably *Brāhmin*: Jayadeva's profound devotion to Kṛṣṇa and Rādhā throughout the poem is self-evident. The *Viṣṇu-* and *Bhāgavata-purāṇas* predated Jayadeva's work and so must have provided some inspiration to the poet as well, perhaps, as poems repeated in oral transmission. What was different in Jayadeva's work was the emphasis on Rādhā that had been missing from the earlier works, though she occurs in the *Brahma-vaivarta-purāṇa* as the respectable wife of Kṛṣṇa. The whole poem deals with just one day in the relationship between the two lovers, beginning with Rādhā's sorrow at being separated from Kṛṣṇa and ending with her ecstatic reunion with him.

Carnal love juxtaposed with spiritual devotion is not an easy interplay, though Siegel warns that: "The *Gītāgovinda* is not a sacred *or* profane work, it is a sacred *and* profane work. The ambivalence reflects a coalescence of traditions: literary, erotic, folk, religious."[58] Sensual human love is not presented as opposed to love of God but a way of understanding it. Siegel comments: "The human and divine became inextricably interwoven in love, in *bhakti*, no longer *bhakti* simply as 'devotion', but *bhakti* as fervent, passionate love."[59] The presence of Rādhā in the *Gītā-Govinda* effects a change in the nature of God as Kṛṣṇa, for he *suffers* in separation from her. There are times when he worships Rādhā and is submissive to her, perhaps, as Siegel suggests, reflective of the power of Devī, the Mother Goddess tradition in Bengal.[60] But the religious effect is to bring the divine even closer to humanity.

I doubt, then, whether writers are on the right track in their attempts to symbolize the carnal, erotic interplay between Kṛṣṇa and Rādhā, the passion of the two symbolizing the intensity of love of God; Kṛṣṇa stealing the clothes of the *gopīs* symbolizing that the soul must be naked before God; Kṛṣṇa multiplying himself to make love to each of the *gopīs* representing his love for every individual, and so on. Chaudhuri refers to such attempts as "feeble antics".[61] And yet, Jayadeva was profoundly devotional, and what he created in the *Gītā-Govinda* was a devotional poem steeped in *bhakti* and so there must be also a measure of symbolism in what he wrote, especially in the idea of complete surrender to Kṛṣṇa with utter love. Siegel probably has the right balance here, I feel, when he writes: "*Gītagovinda* is unequivocally about the joy and sorrow of carnal love, about a god who in love is purely human; but it is also a work consecrated to that god as God. The holiest of holies is encountered in the human heart; the most sacred mystery is experienced in the moments, however fleeting, of human love."[62]

Kṛṣṇa as love

The erotic and overtly sexual relationship between Kṛṣṇa and the *gopīs* or between Kṛṣṇa and Rādhā has nothing to do with the same sexual praxis associated with Tantra. This is the case because love is not diminished in any way: quite the opposite, in fact, for love is in itself an ultimate Reality that reaches into the depth of the being, "celebrated in the body, in the heart, in the soul", as Siegel puts it.[63] And it must be remembered, too, that erotic passion as a mode of worshipping Kṛṣṇa is only one aspect of love. The paternal love for the child Kṛṣṇa, the love of a servant to Lord Kṛṣṇa, the love of the companion to friend Kṛṣṇa and the bliss of the meditator focusing on the transcendent Kṛṣṇa are all there, too, as means of approaching Kṛṣṇa with devotion according to the individual nature and consciousness of the devotee. In all these moods, love for Kṛṣṇa who himself loves is central. If, in selfless love, one concentrates on Kṛṣṇa as the fullest expression of love, then the two will be unified, especially since we become what we are in the mind. Unity is strived for by the orthodox ascetics who attempt to drive out desire and passion, but it can also be attained in the unorthodox passion that the devotee has for Kṛṣṇa and it was this unorthodox love of God that appealed so widely in Vaiṣṇava religion. Love unites lover and beloved and concentrates not on a distant goal but on the essence of that love itself. And in the *Gītā-Govinda*, Kṛṣṇa demonstrates every facet of the lover who feels he will die without his beloved: he *loves* wholly, passionately, and even lustfully. His love is full *premā*, love that is complete in all its dimensions and that is how the devotee needs to love Kṛṣṇa too. Love became the path to God.

Kṛṣṇa draws out the love of the devotee and that love may be expressed in any way in which the individual finds he or she is able to relate to him. I have been in Hindu temples and witnessed women sitting quietly in a corner repeating Kṛṣṇa's name in rapt meditation, in another temple hearing communal chanting of his name: both are features especially of the Gauḍīya Vaiṣṇava tradition. Kṛṣṇa is a God that laughs, smiles, loves, is beautiful and is enticing. As Kinsley commented: "He is loved with abandon and loves with abandon,"[64] and this unorthodox spiritual perspective opened the hearts of so many Vaiṣṇavites.

The *Bhagavad Gītā*

For those who find it difficult to relate to a highly anthropomorphic Kṛṣṇa as a child, a youth and a lover, the *Bhagavad Gītā*, "Song of the Lord", offers a completely different vision of Kṛṣṇa. Just as Viṣṇu pervades the whole universe, is its cause and support, so Kṛṣṇa in the *Gītā* becomes the supreme Brahman in both its manifest, *saguṇa*, and unmanifest, *nirguṇa*, senses. The *Gītā* is set into the *Mahābhārata*, the great tale of the Bhārata descendants and of the enmity between the Pāṇḍavas and the Kauravas that resulted in the great war at Kurukṣetra. Kṛṣṇa in the *Gītā* is the Paṇḍava Arjuna's charioteer, and as the battle is about to begin, Arjuna loses heart, sits down in his chariot and refuses to engage in a fratricidal war. It is then that Kṛṣṇa begins to teach him and from that teaching we can glean the nature of Kṛṣṇa as a transcendent God. Typical of a synthesizing nature of the *Gītā* the nature of God is seen as the totally transcendent Absolute of the more mystical parts of the *Upaniṣads* – an Absolute to which nothing can be ascribed and of which nothing can be said – as well as being the deity that is manifest as the world and in the world, and also manifest in human form as Kṛṣṇa. Many times, the *Gītā* will focus on all three, seeing no contradiction whatever in there being different aspects of the One or THAT which is beyond the One. Since Kṛṣṇa is a "descent", an incarnation, then it stands to reason that it is the personal God that is the main focus. But the God that pervades the *Gītā* is at least threefold. First, at its ultimate, it is Brahman that is without any attributes, that is no-thing, inconceivable and indescribable. Secondly, that absolute Brahman is also present in the manifest world that is the expression of Brahman, its creation and manifestation. In later tradition, there is a further manifestation as Viṣṇu, the deity with visible attributes as far as the divine world is concerned, attributes that Arjuna is at one point permitted to see – though overt identity of Kṛṣṇa and Viṣṇu is not yet fully developed in the *Gītā*. Last, there is Kṛṣṇa, the manifestation of Brahman on Earth, descending in mortal form in order to correct the imbalance of evil over good. But if there is one aspect that perhaps transcends others, it is the concept of the *personal* God, the God to whom devotion can be offered, the God who loves his devotee. In the personal God, the *Gītā* unites the indescribable with the devotional and the cosmic with the personal, but at the same time, does not deny pathways that incorporate different conceptions of God.

The *Gītā*'s concept of God is a lofty one. The Kṛṣṇa of the *Gītā* is a personal God of immense depth and metaphysical heights, quite the opposite of the portrayal of Kṛṣṇa's character in the *Mahābhārata*. *Bhakti* develops with increasing momentum in the *Gītā* but it is not the only pathway to liberation that is presented. The traditional path of knowledge, *jñāna*, is accepted in the *Gītā* alongside *Yoga*, but there are occasional criticisms of total renunciation of the world. Rather, selfless disinterested *action*, or *karma-yoga* is far more acceptable, particularly if actions are centred in Kṛṣṇa. However, given that Kṛṣṇa is the incarnated God in the text it is his nature that pervades its pages and he is the focus whatever the path. Thus, Kṛṣṇa says: "He who sees me everywhere and sees all in me does not become lost to me and I do not become lost to him."[65] In chapter 7, Kṛṣṇa says he is the "Source and dissolution of the whole universe" (verse 6). He says: "Nothing is higher than me" (verse7), and that he is the taste in water, the light in the moon and sun and the primeval sound in all the *Vedas* (verse 8). "As the great wind moving everywhere always exists in space, so know thus, all beings exist in me." (9:6). Kṛṣṇa is "unborn, beginningless and Great Lord of the Worlds" (10:3), and the source of all from whom everything evolves (10:8).

It is the manifest Kṛṣṇa on Earth that provides the focus for *bhakti* as opposed to his more transcendent forms. And yet, he says in 8:22 that through *bhakti* the ultimate deity is known: "That supreme Puruṣa, Pārtha, within whom all beings dwell, by whom all this is pervaded, is truly attainable by exclusive *bhakti*". But it is devotional worship of Kṛṣṇa that offers the reader a very special relationship. In 9:26 he says: "Whoever offers to me with devotion, a leaf, a flower, fruit, water, that I accept, offered with *bhakti* by the pure-minded." And in verse 34 of the same chapter: "Fill your mind with me, be devoted to me, sacrifice to me, bow down to me alone. Thus, having integrated the self, with me as the supreme goal, you shall come to me."

Chapter 12 of the *Gītā* is devoted to the path of *bhakti*, yet Kṛṣṇa makes it clear that other paths, even the hardest path of focus on the unmanifest Brahman, are valid. But by the end of the *Gītā*, we have a more defined praise of the path of devotion as making the devotee "Brahman-become" (18:54), when Kṛṣṇa says:

> By devotion he knows me, what and who in truth I am: then, having known me in truth, he enters me forthwith.
> Continually doing all actions taking refuge in me, by my grace he obtains the eternal, imperishable abode.
> Mentally renouncing all actions in me, having me as the highest goal, resorting to *buddhi-yoga*, always have your thoughts fixed on me.
> Fixing thought on me, by my grace you will overcome all obstacles . . . [66]

And in the culminating verses of the *Gītā*, we find the kernel of *bhakti* when Kṛṣṇa says:

> Hear again my supreme word, most secret of all: *you are beloved by me* . . .
> Fix your mind on me, be devoted to me, sacrifice to me, pay homage to me, then, in truth I promise you, you will come to me, *for you are dear to me.*
> Renounce all *dharmas*; take refuge in me alone. I will liberate you from all evils; grieve not.[67]

The devotion that is advocated in these verses has nothing to do with the later visions of Kṛṣṇa as a babe, child, lover. This is a different Kṛṣṇa, Kṛṣṇa the Lord, the Brahman, the source of all things, the pervader of all things. Here, the concept of deity is more orthodox, accepting of the orthodox pathways to God, but at the same time promoting the simpler means of dedicating every action to Kṛṣṇa, every thought and every ounce of one's being. But it is the words *you are beloved by me* and *for you are dear to me* that are at the heart of *bhakti* for they are indicative of God's love for man and, in the *Gītā*, woman and those of low caste. It is reciprocated love from devotee to God and the special love from God to devotee that reaches right into the heart and accounts for the popularity of this all-encompassing God. Apart from the *Bhagavad Gītā*, there are other "Songs", *Gītās*, and one, the *Uddhava Gītā*, takes the level of devotion to Kṛṣṇa much further, stressing that true devotion involves seeing Kṛṣṇa everywhere, in all things, and in all beings.[68]

Rādhā

Some attention should be paid here to Rādhā, the favourite *gopī* of Kṛṣṇa and the heroine of the *Gītā-Govinda*. Perhaps she originated with the cow-herding Ābhīras, who may have infused their pastoral tales into the Kṛṣṇa myths.[69] Since the *Bhāgavata-purāṇa*, written at the end of the first millennium, does not mention her, but the twelfth-century *Gītā-Govinda* gives her such prominence, we can assume that she rose to popularity during the space between, though there are casual references to her earlier.[70] In the *Brahma-vaivarta-purāṇa*, Rādhā appears properly for the first time: there, she is Kṛṣṇa's wife, not simply one of the *gopīs*, and Hindi poets, especially, saw her as such. It was later works that made her a simple cowherdess and one of the many amours of Kṛṣṇa, albeit his favoured one in the *Gītā-Govinda*. It is in poetry and song, especially, however, that Rādhā and her relationship with Kṛṣṇa are celebrated, particularly in northern India. Indeed, Bengali Vaiṣṇavas of Gauḍīya Vaiṣṇavism often favour Rādhā rather than Kṛṣṇa or at least as equal. For many such Bengali Vaiṣṇavas, Rādhā remains a mistress, even someone else's wife – something that enhances her character in a way that a subordinated consort cannot. Gauḍīyas raise Rādhā to the status of divine and offer her worship alongside Kṛṣṇa.

While many texts ignore or diminish Rādhā as a simple *gopī,* for some, she became identified with Devī. The *Devī-Bhāgavata-purāṇa*, as its title suggests, promoted the Great Goddess, and for some sects Rādhā filled this role as Bhagavatī.[71] She became the *Mahā-Śakti*, in some cases greater than Kṛṣṇa himself. However, like Sītā in the *Rāmāyaṇa*, Rādhā is not venerated independently even though she, again like Sītā, is elevated to the status of Goddess. In the *Nārada-purāṇa* she is presented as one with Kṛṣṇa and is his complementary essence, and though one with him she is independent as creation. Then, she becomes the universal Mother, other great Goddesses becoming her offspring as manifestations of her own being.[72] For Bengali Gauḍīya Vaiṣṇavas she is Kṛṣṇa's highest *Śakti* or divine energy. While Rādhā is beyond the phenomenal world as *Prakṛti*, she yet manifests herself as *prakṛti*, as well as being the *māyā*, the whole creative interplay of manifested existence: these – the three aspects of *śakti*, *prakṛti* and *māyā* – are facets of Devī, as was seen in the last chapter concerning the Mother Goddess. But just as Śiva and Pārvatī were two sides of a coin, interdependent and complementary to each other, for Gauḍīya Vaiṣṇavas, Kṛṣṇa and Rādhā form the same powerful combination, the one necessary to the other. Nevertheless, since the potency of Rādhā's love for Kṛṣṇa overshadows his love for her and renders Kṛṣṇa captivated by her, she can often be accepted as superior.[73] As Huberman comments, "ultimately, Rādhā rules in Vṛndāvana".[74]

For the wider Vaiṣṇava communities, Rādhā is what she is in the *Gītā-Govinda*, a beautiful and endearing creature who is at that awkward age between girlish giggling and womanish allurement. As Kinsley commented: "Her naïveté, girlish boldness, and womanly modesty combine to create an irresistible charm that is at once endearing and amusing."[75] But it is her love and passion for Kṛṣṇa that is utterly inspirational to devotees like Gauḍīya Vaiṣṇavas, despite the fact that it is the *Bhāgavata-purāṇa*, which makes no mention of Rādhā, that is their foundational text. Rādhā's is a love that overrides all boundaries, transgresses all *dharmas*; it is a love that is direct, spontaneous, free, and so it is a wonderful example of selfless love and of the full loving-devotion that characterizes *bhakti*.

It is in this way that Rādhā is an inspiration to devotees of Kṛṣṇa and herself. In Gauḍīya Vaiṣṇavism especially, Rādhā is the "sweetness" in "an already delicious recipe", as Steven Rosen puts it.[76] As such, Rādhā was inspirational, too, to classical dancers, poets and dramatists, and particularly to the singers of religious songs, *kīrtan*. Rādhā showed how love of God can be equally intense and full in company with that God or in separation.

Love is the key to the Vaiṣṇava tradition that extols just Kṛṣṇa, Kṛṣṇa and Rādhā, or even Rādhā alone. In the case of Kṛṣṇa the individual is invited to love him in whatever way he or she understands to be the best and fullest expression of love in life. Whatever love moves the soul more than any other is the love that can be directed towards the divine and that divine being can be singly male, jointly male and female, or singly female. The other critical point here is that this love of God is *personal*; it needs no intermediary and no prerequisites. It is a direct emotional experience of worship of God that is open to all, whatever class or caste, to outcastes, to men and women and to the rich and the poor in wealth and spirit. It is no surprise, then, as we leave these Gods and Goddesses for more earthly considerations of life in the home and community, that it is Kṛṣṇa who wins more hearts than any other divinity.

8

Ritual in the Home and Community

Worship

Ritual

Worship of the divine in Hinduism, whether at national or local festivals, at a temple, an outdoor shrine or a home shrine, is characterized by immense diversity. The very nature of Hinduism with its multiplicity of approaches to, and aspects of, the divine facilitates this. Such worship is part of the ritualistic dimension of religious life and much is *nitya*, "obligatory", for many of those who call themselves Hindus. Lawrence Babb defines ritual as "a form of symbolic activity that conveys information",[1] and there are certainly dimensions of ritual that would fall under the remit of such a definition for many Hindus. For others, however, the symbolic aspect of ritual is hidden beneath an overt acceptance of it as a tangible reality, when symbolism gives way to firm belief that a ritual action to a real divine image has a real outcome. It is also likely to depend on the time and occasion of ritual as to how it is perceived and for what purpose it is undertaken. It may be simply what an individual has always done; it may be casually enacted in the excitement of a festival; or it may be the focus of an urgent need by an individual. Ritual may even be felt necessary to ward off evil or malevolent forces and in this sense would often need to be very real rather than symbolic for the participant.

Nevertheless, ritual itself is rife with symbols that stem from an early age. Ritualism characterizes the religious history of Hinduism from *Vedic* times to the present and there has been no shortage of scriptural texts to prescribe it. The way in which the divine is approached has varied according to different schools of thought and modes of belief. Many times in previous chapters of this book the word *dharma* has occurred for what is right in terms of class and caste, stage of life, purity of religious practice, and it is fundamental to the way in which deities are worshipped. But, also, what is right for one individual may not be for another – it would not be considered *dharmic*, for example, for women to participate in certain rites: I shall have more to say about this later in chapters 9 and 10. Thus, it could be said that individuals do not have total freedom in choosing how they worship: *dharma* may, to a certain extent, dictate this for them. Yet, with a plethora of temples and shrines to a bewildering number of deities in India, worship is widely and contextually different and it is by no means the case that each individual worships just one deity: indeed, temples will often include a variety of deities and a visitor to a temple may worship at a number of the shrines for radically different reasons. Similarly, a home shrine may have more than one deity on which to focus.

Much of the religion that takes place in the home or temple is pragmatic in that it seeks to enhance and protect the immediate family: it has *śānti*, "peace" as its hoped-for outcome. But such ritual worship is particularly embedded in the widespread devotional praxis of Hinduism and it is *devotion* to deities that is the focus, bringing the devotee into contact with the divine in a highly personal way. Essentially, worship of a deity in any form is an approach to what is considered wholly sacred and there are ritualistic measures for preparing the individual for such an encounter – an encounter in which the normally profane enters the realm of the highly sacred. Much ritual, then, will be involved with purifying the profane to make it fit for the divine presence. Gavin Flood aptly comments that "it is ritual action which anchors people in a sense of deeper identity and belonging".[2] Such deep identity is often caste bound, location bound, gender bound but, at the same, provides security and a sense of communal solidarity. While Hinduism has explored and adopted many new pathways over its long evolution, *Vedic* ritual has not been lost entirely for, as we shall see, it still informs much of the formal ritual that takes place in temples as well as some aspects of worship in the home.

Traditionally, there have been three major approaches to the divine in Hinduism. The path of knowledge, *jñāna*, is the more intuitive, meditational and contemplative one, often characterized by withdrawal from the world in order to focus on an indescribable Absolute, the *nirguṇa* Brahman. Here, ritual is minimized. In contrast, the way of *karma* focuses on involvement in the world but in such a way that the ego is not involved: all one's actions are done *for* God.

The *Bhagavad Gītā* deals with this path in detail, as with the third pathway, *bhakti*. *Bhakti* is the most popular pathway because it is not so sectarian and is often classless, casteless and is open to women without constraints. Devotion and love are the key features of this last pathway as well as the rich mythologies of the two great epics and the abundance of myths in texts like the *Purāṇas*. *Bhakti* is an emotional path that allows full expression of spirituality sometimes devoid of ritual as, for example, when people come together for the singing of well-known devotional songs. In a way, such *bhakti* is monotheistic practice, for the devotee focuses on his or her chosen deity, *iṣṭa-devatā*, though the family as a whole may have a different deity, the *kula-devatā*, "family deity". In addition, the local community may focus on another deity, the village deity, perhaps. This last is the *grāma-devatā*, but no conflict would be seen in one individual offering veneration to all three anymore than at a temple where worship is offered to different deities at different shrines by one individual. There are times, too, when a particular deity may be more appropriate to life's circumstances than other deities, and so that god or goddess may be approached for a special reason. These are all aspects of approaching the divine in devotional *bhakti* that need to be borne in mind as this chapter proceeds. Before I examine the nature and format of such worship in detail, it seems prudent to deal first with the objects of worship as the images of deities.

Images

To use the term "idol" for the iconography of gods and goddesses in Hinduism is wholly pejorative and misrepresents the representation of divine energy that the term "image" more readily conveys. An image that is representative may be in the form of a visually perceptible three-dimensional iconic figure, or it may be a picture, or even symbolically aniconic. For many Hindus, the image is a symbol of the deity, which is to say that the deity in question is accepted as being beyond the tangible image that represents it, just as a real individual exists beyond a photograph of him or her: an image can elicit an emotional response, in the same way as a photograph. The term "idol", on the contrary, confines the god or goddess to the object itself. An image is called a *mūrti* and it represents the power or part of the essence of a deity that becomes infused in the image. Nevertheless, it would depend on the level of consciousness of an individual how far the actual presence of the deity would be evident in an image. Many see the image as a manifest object that points to the unmanifest Brahman or manifest deity that underpins it. Others accept that the deity is actually present in the image when it is being worshipped, albeit that it is not confined to the image. Thus, it is a nice point how far the image symbolizes the deity or actually *is* the deity in the eyes of its devotees. Certainly, some of the power of a deity is accepted as being present in an image, and given that the same deity may be present in many temple and home shrine images, the multiple forms of its power and character are obvious. This leads Chris Fuller to say: "Hence an image itself cannot be equated with its corresponding deity; the object of worship is not the image, but the deity whose power is inside it."[3] Fuller calls this a "double relationship" between a deity and its image.[4]

The tendency to regard an image as a real being is more pronounced in Vaiṣṇava sects, especially in the case of Kṛṣṇa as a baby and young child, when he is believed to take up real residence in his images as part of his *līlā*, his divine play.[5] In the devotional sects of Hinduism that incorporate such images, the divine is believed to have five aspects, the supreme Brahman; the manifest Brahman; the *ātman* within each self; the *Ātman* that pervades the universe; *and* its presence in its image that is the focus of worship. Such a view is tantamount to saying that God is in all things and present anywhere and everywhere. Thus, as Diana Eck points out, the *mūrti* can be "the deity itself taken 'form'". Indeed, the word *mūrti* is suggestive of a definite shape, form, figure, manifestation or even incarnation.[6] A *mūrti*, then, can be an "embodiment of the divine" that is "charged with the presence of the god",[7] or a "crystallization",[8] a "divine power made manifest in form".[9] Vasudha Narayana pertinently writes of the "paradox of nonmatter", the fact that a material image can be at the same time accepted as "fully, completely god" as it is in Śrī-Vaiṣṇava and Caitanya sects, when it is composed of non-earthly "super" substance, "a bit of heaven on earth".[10]

Vedic religion had no evidence of images, though the earlier Indian civilization on which the Āryans probably superimposed their beliefs certainly did. It is an aspect that I shall explore in detail in Volume II. In the *Vedic* period, the altar was the focus of sacrificial offerings and ritual, and "worship", in the way we normally understand the term, did not really exist. We have to wait for the devotional movements in Hinduism before that change came about. How far indigenous worship of images remained a feature of ordinary life in the interim we have no way of knowing.

Since the deity is manifest in an image, that image is constructed with the utmost precision and not left to the whims of the artist. Each orthodox image has to conform to scriptural representation in order to evoke legitimate worship but, more importantly, to invite the deity to infuse it. The *mūrtis* may be made of stone, of wood or metal, but devotional literature like the *Purāṇas* stipulated exactly what proportions, colours, poses and gestures were authentic. Although the different texts are by no means uniform in their stipulations, there was a gradual process of standardization that eliminated differences. When an image is installed, sometimes different deities are invited to inhabit different parts of the image. This is done when the ritually pure priest touches the image.[11] The main deity is also ritualistically invited to dwell in it in a ceremony. Such rituals vary between different sects but no image is authentic without the appropriate ceremonial ritual.

The major normal rite in installing a *mūrti* is that of *prāna-pratiṣṭhā*, "establishing the breath", waking up the deity, in other words, infusing the deity with life-breath. The process is enacted in the presence of sacred fires and with ritual *mantras*. The image is then enlivened by the presence of the deity for the benefit of the devotees and the latter, for their part, should treat the image as if it were the deity in reality. Still, there are those who see the images only as a representation, a tangible focus for devotion or for inner contemplation and meditation, rather than being the explicit presence of the deity. For others, the image is the deity's physical body.[12] Yet an image is not permanently sacred for when it is well aged, damaged or if it is a temporary image for a festival, the essence of the deity is "cast out" of the image. Accompanied by prescribed ritual *mantras*, the image is taken in procession and disposed of in a river or the sea. It is clay and paper images that are cast into water, while metal images may be melted down and wooden ones burnt. Needless to say, a permanent wooden image would need renewal more frequently than a heavy stone or bronze one. There are regional differences in the way images are presented particularly with stone images, white marble being favoured in the North and dark stone images in the South.[13]

When a deity is installed, after the life-breath is established in the image, the eyes of the deity are opened. The whole image is completed by the artist before the critically important eyes are painted in or are completed but covered with honey and *ghī* until this last rite of opening the eyes. The opening of the eyes is the point in time that the deity gazes on the devotees and the first time that the deity is *really* seen. Eck says: "The gaze which falls from the newly-opened eyes of the deity is said to be so powerful that it must first fall upon some pleasing offering, such as sweets, or upon a mirror where it may see its own reflection."[14] While some images are distinctly anthropomorphic, the power of divinity is frequently represented by many arms, many heads, huge eyes, and sometimes three eyes. Again, Eck comments: "They stretch the human imagination toward the divine by juxtaposing earthly realities in an unearthly way."[15] Divinity cannot be portrayed ordinarily and must arrest the emotions of the devotee, bringing the individual into intimate emotional contact with the god or goddess.

Once the deity is enlivened and its eyes opened, the image is treated as if it is royalty, as if the divine has come to Earth. Just as a king or queen is fed with choice foods, rested, entertained with song and dance, offered gifts and attended to with no time or honour spared, so the image is the royal and divine guest that is washed and dried, dressed in finery and garlanded with flowers and jewellery, given food, fanned with a flywhisk, a *caurī*, when it is hot and warmed with a shawl when it is cold. Tradition has set down sixteen ways in which a deity is ritually honoured. These are an invocation to the deity; offering of a seat; water to wash the feet; water to wash the hands; water to sip; bathing the image; dressing the image in a fresh garment; putting the sacred thread on the image; anointing the image with, for example, a paste of sandalwood; offering flowers; offering incense; offering light; offering food or a gift; bowing to the deity; circumambulation of the image in a clockwise direction; singing praise of the deity; saying farewell. These sixteen are often considerably shortened in many cases, though fire and food remain key aspects. The deity pervading the image is often rested in the afternoon and put to bed at night. The *Bhāgavata-purāṇa* has a whole section devoted to ritual worship of images. Presented as part of the *karma-yoga* mode of worship, we find the following example for devotion to Viṣṇu:

> My votary should lovingly decorate me appropriately with clothes, sacred thread, ornaments, decorative drawings on my body (on cheeks, chest, etc.), garlands of *Tulasi* leaves and sandal pigments.
> My worshipper should offer to me with faith and reverence various articles (of worship) such as water for washing feet and rinsing the mouth (for sipping), sandal-paste, flowers, *Akṣatas* (grains of unbroken rice), scented fumes, light and articles of food.[16]

The bathing of the deity is a ritual known as *abhiṣeka* and it may be done with a variety of mixed substances such as milk, the juices of fruits, pastes and oils rather than water.[17] Occasionally, whole temples are bathed in this rite. It seems that the bathing may be more intense for a male deity than a female, and yet Foulston makes the graphic remark: "A bright yellow cascade of turmeric water obscuring the face of the goddess and then replaced by a torrent of white milk, is an arresting sight."[18] Cleaning up such a conglomeration of liquids after a whole temple is bathed in such a way is an extensive and expensive business.

Purification of shrine, temple, priests, attendants and devotees is absolutely critical. Bathing in running water is the most basic method of such ritual purification but, in any case, a little water is sipped three times by the devotee before approaching the shrine of the deity. Sometimes, the bathing of an image is purely symbolic – a flower dipped gently in water is lightly touched on the face of the deity. Face, teeth and feet are "washed", just as a guest would wish after travelling through the dusty streets. Such royal treatment is extensive on the occasions when *mūrtis* or their replicas leave their shrines and are processed through the streets on specially constructed chariots that become the temporary abode of the deity. Such chariots may be built like temples or constructed to match the mythical animal vehicle of the respective deity. On such occasions there may well be elephants and horses and immense crowds who gather from near and far to witness the ritual's spectacle. Images are taken out on their festival day, to show the extent of their lands, or they may be moved to a cooler location in the hot season – all as may occur with royalty. But they are also taken out so that as many people as possible can have the devotional experience of gaining sight of the deities as an aspect of divine grace. The processions of images are an immensely popular feature of devotional Hinduism in India. *Mūrtis* that are of an immovable nature, constructed in stone or bronze as "root images", are designed not to be moved, so they remain in their shrines. Those that are movable may be duplicates of the presiding immovable deity of a temple, brought out for special rituals. As stated above, temporary images are made from disposable materials for the duration of a festival. Such icons would be enlivened and ritually consecrated like their original, but will have their deity ritually cast out at the end of the festival. Importantly, during the temporary existence of the mobile image, the deity it represents resides in the temple at the same time. Akos Östör believes that the function of the mobile image is to be able to concentrate on a particular aspect of the deity: "The intensity of worship itself separates the manifestations of the same deity; the god that dwells in the Himālayas is also the god of the local temple, the object of seasonal worship, and the inhabitant of the local jungle or hill."[19] Such multiple manifestations of a deity are in keeping with the belief that no deity is confined to time and place but has the ubiquitous power to be in many temples and shrines at the same time, yet is beyond them all.

Aside from the worship of images of deities in the manner I have just described, some may use images for an inner focus on divine activity within the body. Such, for example is the kind of practice that takes place in Tantric sects of Hinduism. Each deity – and in Tantrism this is mainly female deities – has a particular characteristic, a particular power, and the Tantric adept uses focus on a *mūrti* in order to stimulate that power within his or her own self. Then, again, there are many Hindus who revere a deity through an image without identifying the presence of the deity actually within the image: praxis is highly variable. What is important is that, in the context of devotional Hinduism, images are a medium for the full expression of devotion. In view of the widespread availability of glossy prints of Hindu deities in anthropomorphic form, worship of a deity may be focused on such a print in the private devotion of the home.

Aniconic images

Many images of gods and goddesses are not icons at all. The *liṅga* represents Śiva, and the *ṣālāgrām* stone represents Viṣṇu, especially in home shrines. These are just a few examples of such aniconic objects of worship, and the object would be treated in the same way as a full *mūrti*. Again, for some it may be felt to embody the real presence of the deity and for others it may be purely symbolic as a focus for devotion on what is beyond. Some of these aniconic objects of veneration are the recipients of blood sacrifices – as are some goddess icons – but vermilion paint or *kumkum* powder tend to have replaced the blood of the original animal sacrifice. The popular God Gaṇeśa is often represented by a paste of turmeric and water formed into a pyramid and placed on a betel leaf. Gaṇeśa and other deities are often represented by a *kalaśa*, a husked coconut placed on a pot with five mango leaves as a coronet around it. This aniconic form is especially used to represent goddesses, the pot being thought of as the womb which, like the pot that holds water and grain, is essential for life.[20] The eyes and mouth of the goddess may be painted on the coconut when it is placed on top and the pot itself highly decorated. It is also an aniconic representation of deity that can be found at the apex of temples, in homes and at certain ceremonies such as marriage. Foulston describes a festival procession in Cholavandan in which the pot, or *ghaṭa*, (known as a *karakam* in the South) in this aniconic form of the goddess represents the *śakti* or power of the goddess.[21] The invocation of the power of the goddess into this pot Foulston describes as "one of the most important rituals in goddess festivals across India",[22] and Östör states that in Bengal the pot is filled with the body elements of earth and water, so that the pot in which the goddess resides is representative also of the presence of the goddess in the body of the devotee.[23] It is in the village setting that aniconic images such as stones are particularly prolific in what are the most simplistic of shrines.

Certain species of animals and vegetation are singled out as sacred. A deity may be represented theriomorphically in full or part animal form. The cow is a sacred animal that is respected and venerated and allowed to roam unharmed. Many will touch its back as they pass it, but it has to be said that Gandhi became a vegetarian because he believed that cows were ill-treated. Monkeys are also venerated and allowed to roam freely in some temples. The *pipal* and *banyan* trees are especially sacred. The *tulasī* or *tulsī* (basil) plant is frequently to be found in homes that favour Viṣṇu but never for Śiva, who favours the *bel* tree. *Tulasī* is usually grown in the courtyard of a home, placed on a special stand and tended carefully with overt worship. The *tulasī* is venerated as a goddess, one capable of many cures and particularly of averting evil forces from the home. At some festivals, even the tools of one's trade may be the object of worship.

Pūjā

Having discussed the nature of images, whether iconic or aniconic, what I want to do now is approach the deities from the perspective of the worshipper, the devotee. It is texts like the *Āgamas* and the *Purāṇas* that prescribe the best ways in which the devotee should approach the divine. This approach is known as *pūjā*, something that Fuller describes as "the core ritual of popular theistic Hinduism".[24] There will be many reasons why a devotee will wish to come into the presence of the deity. In the words of Subramuniyaswami, writing from the Śaiva point of view:

> Our worship through *pūjā*, outlined in the *Śaiva Āgamas*, may be an expression of festive celebration of important events in life, of adoration and thanksgiving, penance and confession, prayerful supplication and requests, or contemplation at the deepest levels of superconsciousness. *Pūjā* may be conducted on highly auspicious days in a most elaborate, orthodox and strict manner by the temple *pujārīs*, or it may be offered in the simplest form each morning and evening in the home shrine by any devotee.[25]

Pūjā, therefore, is highly varied but, essentially, just as the deity is treated as royalty, so the devotee is the subject, the inferior supplicator, the one who offers gifts and hopes for grace. *Pūjā* has the basic meaning of "worship" as it is understood in the West, but it is not by any means confined to such a translation: it can also be used in the senses of respect, veneration, honour, adoration, and the like, so that one can honour and respect parents with this same word, *pūjā*. Artists and musicians may speak of their art as their life-long *pūjā*, expressing their dedication to their art.[26]

Pūjā gradually replaced *Vedic* sacrifice, *yajña*, as a more devotional rather than ritualistic religion emerged. The term was used in devotion to Vāsudeva about the second century BCE, which seems to be the earliest citation of the word for devotion, but it did not have scriptural acceptance until much later in the sixth century CE.[27] A decline in the importance of *Brāhminical* praxis made it exigent for devotional ritual to be taken up by the priestly class, Sanskritized and systematized. Gradually, *pūjā* became the main focus of religion, eclipsing the old ritualistic emphasis. With *yajña* the emphasis was on sacrifice; with *pūjā* the ethos changed to a concentration on images, temples, home shrines, pilgrimage and personal devotional approaches to the god or goddess of one's choice. And, as Subramuniyaswami's words above demonstrate only too well, there is a massive variation in the ways in which *pūjā* is expressed, whether at temple or home shrine.

However, there are still links with the past. Where *yajña* focused on sacrificial fire, *pūjā*, too, makes use of fire in its rituals. In *pūjā*, fire is still used as what Eck calls "an aniconic image of the divine",[28] and it continues to be used in temple and home ritual as well as life-cycle rites. Fire is that which transports offerings to the gods, and that is the same in the old *yajña* as in contemporary *pūjā*. Sometimes, written messages to the deities are burnt in the sacred fire and thus are transported to the heavenly realms.[29] Traditionally, a domestic fire was put in place when a couple married. It was a sacred fire around which prescribed domestic rituals were performed each day, each fortnight, at times of the full and new moon and at harvest time. These rituals were set out in the *Gṛhya-sūtras*. A sacred fire is sometimes used in the home for personal or collective *pūjā*. It is called a *homa*, which is specially erected with materials that are considered pure, like wood and leaves from the mango and *bel* trees. Pure liquid foods like *ghī*, clarified butter, are poured onto it during the ritual. The food placed on the sanctified and purified fire is an offering to the gods. In all, the *homa* is a simple ritual done in the home rather as rituals were carried out at the sacred fire that was the hearth of every married couple in earlier times, though at special times, a *Brāhmin* may be invited to the home to perform a ritual. The point here is that there are vestiges of the old *Vedic* sacrificial fire in the *homa* ritual.

Another link with the *Vedic* past is animal sacrifice, which was the mainstay of *Vedic* religion. It is rarer than previously practised, but animal sacrifice (*bali*) still exists today especially in Bengal and eastern India, mainly with worship of goddesses. It is believed that the soul of the sacrificed animal proceeds straight to Heaven, but this does not allay the criticisms of many enlightened Hindus. Most commonly, it is goats and cockerels that are sacrificed, though occasionally pigs and, rarely, buffaloes. Foulston makes an interesting point here when she says: "A vegetable offered as a suitable substitute indicates that *ritual* is as important as taking the victim's lifeblood. Technically, the pumpkin or melon is already dead before it is cut and offered to the goddess, though ritually it is treated in the same way as an animal sacrifice."[30] It is the independent, fierce goddesses – both major ones and minor local ones – that are mostly connected with animal sacrifice. These fierce deities are believed to require blood as a cooling device for their heated natures. Certainly at festivals, these fierce deities are offered blood and copious numbers of sacrifices take place in order to supply it. At Kālī's great temple in Kolkata, she receives sacrificed black goats each day, and other fierce goddesses may be thought to require daily blood offerings. At a great festival like Durgā Pūjā, many more such sacrifices will occur.

Since high-caste *Brāhmins* have nothing to do with blood, which is highly polluting, it has to be assumed that where animal sacrifice occurs, it is mainly supported by lower castes. And to keep the main deity unpolluted, blood sacrifices may be carried out before a substitute form of a deity in an area removed from the central temple shrine. Fuller notes such practice, for example, in the case of the Tamil goddess Māriyamman. She remains unsullied in her temple shrine, while sacrifice is offered to her powers that have been transferred into a pot of water at a distance by men possessed by the goddess. The priest who cares for the main image is unlikely to be present at such sacrifices. Fuller proffers this interesting comment: "The climax of a Tamil festival for a goddess like Mariyamman is the sacrifice, but it requires her to be split into high and low forms. The high form, manifested in the immovable image at the pure centre of the temple and served by a higher-ranking priest, is offered vegetarian food in the context of *pujā*, whereas the low form, manifested in, say, a pot of water and possessed men of lower rank, receives the sacrificial offering at an exterior site." The important point about such praxis is that "the polar opposition between high and low forms remains the critical feature".[31] It is possible to distinguish, then, as Fuller does in the case of Tamil Nāḍu, between *pūjā* and animal sacrifice – *pūjā* being offered to superior deities with vegetarian foods by vegetarian *Brāhmins*, and animal sacrifice to inferior deities by meat-eating non-*Brāhmins*.[32] This, in fact, is probably the way most Hindus themselves would view the existence and practice of animal sacrifice. The number of victims and locations of practice are certainly decreasing, but since popular beliefs, especially in the village setting, absorb fears of diseases, malevolent forces, ghosts, demons and have to cope with the vicissitudes of life, the idea that one can fall prey to such evils if the local goddess is not kept happy with blood sacrifices tends to sustain the belief in its importance.

Some parts of *Vedic* scriptures are also retained in *pūjā*. Significant is the *Gāyatrī-Mantra*, which is recited every morning and evening by twice-born Hindus: "Let us meditate on the lovely splendour of the god Savitṛ; may he inspire our thoughts" (*Ṛg Veda* 3:62:10). Choudhury's comment here is most apt: "The *Gāyatrī* is a *mantra* that glorifies the Sun (Savitṛ), symbolizing the power of light that illumines the earth, the sky and the heaven, and that seeks illumination of the human mind with higher intelligence (*dhī*), i.e., spiritual enlightenment."[33] It is preceded by *Oṃ*, the sacred sound that is spoken at the outset of any ritual or scriptural reading. Sophie Baker calls *Oṃ* "a password for making contact with God".[34] *Oṃ* or *Aum* is said to be the primal sound of the whole cosmos, the seed of all other sounds. Equated with Brahman, when used in *pūjā* it brings the devotee into direct contact with divinity, which is why Baker's use of the word "passport" is so pertinent. *Oṃ* is repeated as a meditative *mantra* but no scripture or ritual and no ritual activity is conducted without first uttering this sound. Parts of the *Vedas* are still recited on important occasions, though the reciting of any scriptures is an act that brings merit to the listener as much as to the reciter.[35] A text like the *Rāmāyaṇa*, for example, in particular the version by Tulsī Dās, is so well known in some parts of India that even the illiterate can recite parts of it. In his field study, Babb witnessed groups of men gathered together for the purpose of listening and singing from the text at least once a week.[36]

Pūjā for the devotee means, to use Eck's expression, "playing house" with God.[37] In other words, the image of the deity, whether icon or aniconic, is woken up each morning by gongs or bells, washed, dressed and entertained and fed at the appropriate times, before being retired for the night. In the home, simple forms of this routine are carried out in the morning and evening. They are very simple, ordinary practices that bring the deity into the sphere of the home. Crucial before any *pūjā* is purification. Water is the medium for this since it is an agent that absorbs any impurity. The water used to wash a deity must itself be pure, having been taken directly from its source with appropriate ritual, ritual that transforms the water into the same as that of the sacred Ganges. Once the deity has been washed with it, it is considered sacred. It is then sprinkled over the devotees or, if sufficient, a little is poured into the right hand for drinking. It is running water that is considered to be the most pure and while bathing in it is ritually purifying, it will suffice to pour a few handfuls of cold water over the head. For some sects there are measures of ensuring inner purification by the reciting of *mantras* and formulas and by *yogic* praxis. Amongst the populace, in particular, there is a wide belief in evil spirits of all kinds – indeed they feature widely in the myths about the gods and goddesses and in the epics. Purification is one way of ensuring that devotees do not bring with them such malevolent aspects when they approach their deities: to do so would offend the deity and make *pūjā* fruitless or even harmful. Certain grains like rice, and mustard seeds are thought to be particularly good for dispelling evil forces. There are prohibitions also that safeguard *pūjā*, for instance on the wearing of shoes. Shoes from the outdoors carry the dust of the street that can make a sacred area profane, particularly if they are made of the polluting substance of leather. But removal of shoes is also a mark of respect so they are not worn during *pūjā*. I shall return to this subject of impurity in the context of women in chapter 10.

Pūjā, though an individual rather than corporate action, may involve a group of people getting together to sing *bhajans*, devotional songs that praise and honour a particular deity. It is a more informal way of devotional practice. But *pūjā* is generally an individual act, with no particular time necessary for those who wish to visit a temple: individuals come and go as they please. The standard way of showing respect to someone in India is by means of bowing, *pranāma*, meaning "salutation, greetings", and the greater the respect one wishes to show, the lower the bow – even to the point of full prostration. For a highly superior deity or person, the inferior one will touch the feet of the other in order to indicate that the feet, though polluted by dust, are superior to the most unpolluted forehead of the individual performing the greeting. Alongside the bow the palms are brought loosely together and raised to the forehead, an action also called *anjali*. *Pranāma* may be reduced to a simple bow. This would be a normal way of greeting from person to person, with the words *Namaskar* (Sanskrit) or *Namaste* (Hindi), "I bow to you", spoken as this is done. The action is recognition of the divine *ātman* in the other person, that aspect of an individual that is the same as one's true Self. When these actions are done before a deity there is a special link between god or goddess and devotee. It is the action of *pranāma* that welcomes the deity at the commencement of *pūjā*, after having invited the deity to be seated. In general practice, the salutary greeting is minimalized or maximized depending on the status of the individuals concerned and it is not difficult to witness where deference is due, the superior making hardly any gesture at all.

It is customary to fast before *pūjā*, the intention here to purify the body and the mind: temple priests would certainly do so. The garments in which the deities are daily dressed are of uncut and unstitched silk and are coloured according to the respective deity. Viṣṇu and Kṛṣṇa, for example, favour yellow. Each day, they need a fresh garment. The water for washing the face and feet and hands, for sipping and bathing are essential parts of *pūjā* to the deity, along with the sacred thread, that is given to goddesses as much as gods. Fresh flowers are important in *pūjā* and, again, different deities are associated with specific plants and flowers. No one smells the flowers before they are offered to the deities because such action is believed to be polluting, and it is the deity that wishes to accept the flowers' fragrances. Incense and camphor are necessary requisites for *pūjā* in that they are purifying agents. The ritual may be elaborate or simplified but the ingredients of water, flowers and fire/light are fundamental and, if a priest is present, the sacred *mantras* appropriate to the deity. The food offered is critically important, for the person preparing food infuses his or her own pollution into the cooked food. Cooked rice, for example, absorbs the pollution of whoever cooks it, whereas substances like purified butter do not.

A central aspect of *pūjā* is light. *Āratī* is the special part of *pūjā* by which a priest waves a lamp in front of the deity, in whatever form that deity is represented. The lamp is waved in a circular mode that sometimes describes the *Oṃ* symbol. After waving the lamp in front of the deity, the priest takes it to each of the worshippers and they pass their hands over it and then bring their hands up to their foreheads, infusing the light, so to speak, into themselves. This symbolizes the receiving of divine blessing and protective grace. The lamp may be the special *āratī* tray, normally having five separate and open declivities in which five lights are lit, representative of the five elements (water, earth, wind or air, fire and ether), though occasionally a single flame of camphor may be used. So important and widespread is this aspect of *pūjā* that the two terms, *pūjā* and *āratī*, have become synonymous. It is an aspect of temple worship that occurs many times during the day. Accompanying *āratī* is usually the sound of drums, bells, gongs and the singing of devotional songs or *mantra* chants in what is perhaps a unique congregational gathering as opposed to independent worship. In some ways this part of *pūjā* that incorporates flames is resonant with the use of fire throughout *Vedic* ritual and other household and temple ritual. Apart from the symbolism of the *āratī* ritual, in that it unites deity and devotee, the devotee has a chance to see the face of the deity lit up by the flame – a special viewing of the deity. *Āratī* may also be performed before representations of famous teachers, religious leaders and *gurus*. The *āratī* hymn, too long to include here, is an exquisite hymn sung mainly in northern India.[38]

When the devotee passes his or her hands over the *āratī* flame and lifts the subtle contents to the head, it represents another significant aspect of *pūjā*, the receiving of *prasāda*. *Prasāda* means "grace", "blessing" or "favour". Once an offering is made to the deity – whether of flowers, water or food – the deity is believed to take the essence of the offering and the "remains" are then shared between the devotees. While leftover food is normally considered as polluting, the subservience of the devotees to the deity renders the food or water – even the water from bathing the deity – sacred and acceptable: it is a gift from the benevolence of the deity that is ritually accepted. Worshippers have usually fasted before *pūjā* and so this consecrated food breaks their fast. Normally, leftover food, or *jutha*, is contaminated and highly polluting, particularly if it has been partly eaten by someone else. Only those of the lowest castes and those outside the caste system, as well as wives who eat their husband's leftovers, will eat the *jutha* of others. But when food is offered to a deity, the leftovers, the *jutha*, is then distributed to the devotees as *prasāda*. This is so sacred that it is a great privilege to receive and eat it. Fuller goes as far as to suggest that the receiving of *prasāda* of any kind divinizes the devotee,[39] but if any such divinizing takes place, I do not think that there is in any sense a notion of equality between deity and devotee: the whole transaction is one of exalted superior to an inferior. The *prasāda* may be in the form of water as in many Vaiṣṇava temples, where the water used to bathe the deities is so sacred that it can be sipped or sprinkled on the head. Or it may be ash, as in Śaiva temples. Babb thinks that the receiving of *prasāda* transcends caste differences: "Whatever the normal cleavages within the group, for a moment it has become unified as one pole in hierarchical opposition to divinity."[40] And yet, as he notes elsewhere, it is impossible for a *Brāhmin* to accept *prasāda* from the deities of lower castes.[41] In contrast, however, a deity continually receives food from its inferiors.[42]

The devotee is given a ritual mark during or after performing *pūjā*. This is called a *tilaka*, and is a spot of paste that is either made of sandalwood or *kumkum*, vermilion powder. It may be mixed with grains of uncooked rice and, according to Baker "represents a third eye which seeks out and detects on behalf of the bearers any evil they may encounter".[43] Extraneous to *pūjā*, some males wear the red dot representing *śakti* on the forehead with two white vertical lines joined at the bottom either side of the dot. This is the sacred mark of those who worship Viṣṇu.

Pūjā may involve specialized artistic symbolic patterns or *yantras*, which are most evident in Tantrism. Here, the devotee focuses on the *yantra* for contemplative and meditative purposes. As we shall see below, many temples are built on the idea of *yantras*, but *yantras* are also to be found on the floor in front of deities, where they become part of the ritual. Other such floor patterns are called *rangoli* or *ālpanā* patterns, made with coloured powders or, in the case of *ālpanā* patterns, which are associated with Bengal, they are made with rice paste. *Rangoli* patterns are especially associated with the god Gaṇeśa and these often include a *swastika* as an auspicious sign. Gaṇeśa is the deity that removes obstacles and creates auspiciousness.

While *pūjā* involves a more or less set process of ritual from the invocation of the deity right through to the giving of *prasāda*, there are variations and different emphases, different symbolism applied and different approaches to ritual by devotees. Some never visit a temple and keep their home *pūjā* very simple or even minimal. Some follow *gurus* like the popular Sai Baba, for whom set ritual would not be needed, though *anjali* would certainly be applied to a famous *guru*. People might touch a *guru*'s feet in respect, or remove the dust from the *guru*'s feet before touching their own head. *Brāhmins* will be more traditional in maintaining the format of their worship, particularly in questions of purity. Other castes may be less intensive about their religious praxis. Baker describes the filthy balcony on which a *Vaiśya* family performed *pūjā*,[44] though this family had a family priest who came to conduct a daily forty-minute morning *pūjā*. The men of the family, however, seem to have paid but a token visit to morning *pūjā* with a quick *añjali*. At the other end of the class scale, Baker describes the communal worship and rejoicing of a *Dalit* community in Bihar, which had none of the formalities of normal temple worship and engaged in animal sacrifice as part of their merry ritual. The womenfolk sang: "Life is just like a river – swift current, strong flow and God on the other side. We will cross this river to meet Him, our ultimate goal."[45]

Darśan

When the image has had life breathed into it and has had its eyes opened, it is believed that it can see the devotees before it. For the devotee, too, being able to see the deity and if possible be seen by the god or goddess, is one of the most important aspects of *pūjā*. To see the deity is to take *darśan*, take the gaze of the deity, who gives its gaze.[46] It is a reciprocal action of each "seeing" the other. Eck puts the dual process succinctly when she says: "The central act of Hindu worship, from the point of view of the lay person, is to stand in the presence of the deity and to behold the image with one's own eyes, to see and be seen by the deity."[47] Thus, the word *darśan* can mean "audience", "viewing" or "sight of", "seeing". It is rather like gaining audience to a royal personage, the result of which is the grace of that royal person being bestowed on the visitor. The bell that is rung in temple or home shrine announces the arrival of an individual or individuals who require audience with the deity, letting the deity know that such audience is requested.

In busy temples, devotees may struggle to have *darśan* of a deity that remains deep in its inner sanctum and nothing more than a brief glimpse of the image is achieved – one reason why mobile deities are so immensely popular – but occasionally it is possible for a devotee to sit quietly, cross-legged, in front of the deity for some time. (The soles of the feet, it is worth mentioning, are never directed towards the deity). In one's home shrine, of course, *darśan* is a comfortable and easy process. So when individuals visit a temple, their purpose is to have *darśan* of the deity. Since the deity is woken in the morning, bathed, dressed and fed, an appropriate time for *darśan* is when the deity is ready for an audience, dressed in exquisite finery, bejewelled, and ornamented with flowers. Hindus will travel the length and breadth of India to have *darśan* of deities in famous temples or at famous sites, as we shall see in chapter 11 in the context of pilgrimage. Famous *gurus* and Hindu saints may also be the recipients of *darśan* by devotees or by those who wish to pay respect and honour to such holy persons. Nevertheless, many Hindus never visit a temple, or do so rarely, preferring to concentrate their *pūjā* on their chosen deity in their own home.

Pūjā in the home

For many Hindus, *pūjā* remains a personal approach to deity in the home. A priest may be called in daily to perform ritual but he would not be necessary and many do without such services. Naturally, there is immense variation in the ways in which *pūjā* at home is conducted and this will be dependent not only on sect, locale, caste and tradition, but also on the pragmatic considerations of the working family. Some may have the time and means for *pūjā* to be elaborate; others may resort to a much more simplified format or may not have the inclination to spend much time in the rituals on a daily basis. For those who can, *pūjā* begins the day, as is expected by the *Śāstras*, in the case of all twice-born householders. *Pūjā* should also end the day. In addition, there are special days when the home shrine may be cleaned and extra prayers said. For Hindus in the North of India, this is Monday of each week and in the South, it is Friday. Thursday is a popular and auspicious day on which some women fast and do special *pūjā* to Lakṣmī for the well-being of their families and Friday is a popular day to fast in honour of Santoṣī Mā. The fast is a vow, a *vrata*, which women make for the welfare of their husbands, children, or perhaps for the community. The *vrata* is important in that it is something over which women themselves have complete control and no mediation is needed by any male. Such vows may involve all-night vigils and women may group together for the purpose of chanting, singing and dancing. Pattanaik poses an interesting comment here: "A *vrata* favours the simple joys of domestic life and rejects the austere lifestyle of world-renouncing monks. The aim of a *vrata* is not *moksha* or salvation; it is *artha* and *kāma* – material power and sensual joy. Young girls pray for good husbands, married women pray for the health and happiness of the household."[48] His words are suggestive of an area of *pūjā* that offers some female empowerment, albeit that the outcome is confined to family well-being. In tune with the female context, *vratas* usually involve goddesses rather than gods. Meditative *pūjā* using a rosary, a *japa-mālā* of a hundred and eight beads takes the form of chanting the name or names of one's chosen deity with the purpose of focusing the attention entirely on the deity. Some carry *mantras* in small capsules that they wear on their person as a protective amulet.

Wealthy families may be able to afford a separate room devoted entirely to their shrine, but mostly, the shrine is kept in the cleanest room in the house, which would be the kitchen. Given that purity of food and cooking is so essential, it makes sense to place the home shrine there. The *pūjā* should be communal with the whole family gathered together and the male head of the home conducting worship if there is no priest invited. Very often, however, it is the mother, or head woman, of the home who conducts *pūjā* on behalf of her whole family. Women, in fact, have much more freedom in the home for religious practice. Women are the mainstay of religious devotion in the home and perhaps, as Tracy Pintchman points out, according to Hindu men and women, women are more religious than men and have a "special aptitude for ritual performance".[49] Girls learn about such rituals from the older women in the family from a young age. Anne Mackenzie Pearson's field research into women's attitudes to rites such as *vratas* suggests that in most cases women believe that they are more religious than men and that they are the fulcrum around which religious praxis revolves. Many suggested that this was, pragmatically, because they had more time or could manage their time in order to engage in religious activity.[50]

The *Śāstras* state that the first words mentioned when waking should be the name of God: thus, *Oṃ Rām, Rām, Rām*, or another deity, would be a short *mantra* used to set the tone of the whole day. As in temple *pūjā*, home ritual is always preceded by bathing as an act of purification and food is not eaten until the deity has first partaken of it. The *Gāyatrī-Mantra* is also an important statement that begins the day either prior or during *pūjā* and is also chanted at evening *pūjā*. *Āratī* is also part of daily worship. When there is time, *bhajans* may be sung and a scriptural reading may take place, but meditation and prayer for the well-being of the family by the head female of the home is very common. The deities of the home shrine are treated as those in the temple, with the same attention as that which would be given to a royal guest, but the relationship between them and the family members is much more intimate. Traditionally, married couples were expected to maintain a sacrificial fire in their homes on which they offered simple *homa* sacrifices. Cooked food was offered into the fire as sacrifice to the gods, also a little wood coated with some *ghī* as another sacrifice. These were two of the five great sacrifices incumbent on every married householder. The other three were water and *piṇḍas*, rice balls, for ancestors, offerings to spirits and creatures, and hospitality to guests. All such sacrifice in the home signified a daily spiritual renewal of the male householder.

Home shrines are usually bright and colourful and the same offerings of food, water, fragrance and light will be in evidence as in the temple. Despite having a chosen deity, an *iṣṭa-devatā*, there will usually be a number of deities present on the shrine, as well as immediate ancestors and/or pictures of modern *gurus*. There may also be prints of deities in other rooms: anywhere except the bathroom or lavatory is acceptable. Printed posters of deities are now widely available and are extensively utilized in the home shrine and rooms of a house. There will be differences according to the chosen main deity and the accoutrements associated with that deity. Gaṇeśa, for example, is particularly associated with flowers and leaves and especially with sweets and fruits. Viṣṇu's favourite plant, the *tulasī*, the plant of the basil family, is found exclusively at his shrines. Devotees may wear necklaces of *tulasī* beads and they are also used as rosaries.

The *swastika* symbol is frequently seen at home shrines and in temples as a symbol of the sun and prosperity. The *swastika* is in the shape of a cross with "crooked" branches facing in a clockwise direction. The crooked arms of the *swastika* point away from the centre, symbolizing the fact that the human mind is incapable of understanding the supreme Brahman by any direct means. It also points in all directions, suggesting the divine presence in all manifest existence and, like a circle, it has no beginning and no end. In popular belief, *swastikas* are a symbol of good fortune. Red *swastikas* are a particular feature of the festival of Dīvalī when they will feature in the decorations of the home. *Bel* or *bilva* leaves and fruit are favoured by Śiva, though the leaves can be offered to other deities, especially Durgā, though not to Viṣṇu. They form a natural cluster of three, like Śiva's trident. Berries of the *rudrākṣa* tree are also favoured by Śiva, as is *bhang*, the narcotic drink made from the leaves of Indian hemp (*Cannabis Indica*). The resin from its dried leaves is sometimes smoked as *ganja*. *Japa* to Śiva may involve repetition of his one thousand and eight sacred names or just the simple *mantra*, *Oṃ namah Śivaya*. Worship of the Mother Goddess is almost always in the vernacular, especially with use of the famous poetry that extolls her beauty and power. The lotus is also mainly associated with goddesses and homes that favour her are often decorated with its designs. The banana plant and mango leaves are usually to be found on the shrine of those who perform *pūjā* to the goddess.

Pūjā in the temple

As was seen in chapter 1 of this book, Hinduism is a multi-faceted expression of religion that covers almost every way in which humanity can approach the divine. In Champakalakshmi's magnificent work on the Hindu temple, supplemented with outstanding photography by Usha Kris, she offers what I think is a very pertinent remark about Hindu temples: "The temple, in more than one sense, represents the multiple facets and complex processes of this development through its architecture, sculpture, iconography, rituals and institutional organisation – it is like a text to be read and understood in the various contexts of its evolution into a monument of enduring value."[51] Temples were not part of the *Vedic* tradition, but consummate with the representation of the divine in form as images, icons or aniconic objects, particularly the first of these; temples and shrines were needed as the abode, *mandira*, of the deities. They are not places of communal worship, but are places where any individual may go independently to gain *darśan* of their chosen deity or of a deity they think is appropriate to their particular circumstances in life: while there may be throngs of people at a popular temple, worship is not corporate or congregational. It will probably have a number of shrines to different deities and the devotee can visit just one, some or all. The busy devotee might only spend a few minutes at one shrine. Narayanan aptly comments: "The temple complex is like a buffet table; worshippers will walk in, pick and choose which deities they want to worship that day, and proceed there."[52]

Despite the individualized nature of *pūjā* at a temple, the temple offers both integration and unity: "The architecture of Hindu temples provides a concrete manifestation of this characteristic polycentric structure: their multiple shrines are designed in such a way that they allow attention to many gods to be integrated in a complementary way into focus on one. In so doing they form a practical way for communities and families with members who have diverse devotional affiliations, to be united at a single religious location in a single experience of worship."[53] A temple is an "abode of God", a *deva-gṛha*, or "house of God", *devālaya*, a place where the important image, treated as a special and royal guest, is honoured. Housing a deity, a temple becomes a sanctuary, an area of sacred space in which the standard sixteen-point ritual to a deity is conducted. Each temple reflects not only the deity who presides in it, but the nature of the surrounding locale along with its inhabitants. It is a sacred world, "a small world in which people, both human and divine, may live, eat and interact".[54]

Temples have been built at sites deities are thought to frequent. Myth has supplied an abundance of such sites. Mountains are usually believed to be the home of the deities and are especially favoured, as are rivers and groves. Womb-like caves are also symbolic of the abodes of deities. The earliest permanent stone temples are dated to the first century BCE, but it was not until the sixth century CE and later that temples became more prolific and elaborate.[55] With the literary phenomenon of the *Purāṇas*, which incorporated such a wealth of popular mythology, the impetus for temple construction was stimulated. We have to view the evolution of temples as concomitant with devotional *bhakti* that made deities tangible, anthropomorphic images that could be seen, and that needed a spatial context in which to be housed. As in the case of images, a shift occurred from sacrificial *yajña* to devotional *pūjā*, and that shift necessitated concrete images in concrete shrines that reflected the devotional mythology that had transformed popular religion. And yet, while being influenced by popular *Purāṇic* tradition, it was the *Brāhmin* and *Kṣatriya* classes and the wealthy elite, who created temples.[56] However, early temples were square and flat-roofed, with a pillared porch at the front,[57] in other words, they were simple shrines.

As the temple evolved in complexity its construction became textually codified.[58] Special rites ensured that the place where it was built was free of any spirits or evil forces, though it would be an auspicious place that would be chosen.[59] The consecration of a new temple is a ritualistically elaborate event. Eck describes how the priests consecrate a temple by being hoisted to the top of its tower, from where they sprinkle water over the temple from the great height.[60] Temples are built to conform to a *maṇḍala*, a sacred design that corresponds with the cosmos, so that it is a microcosm of the universe. While the central deity is housed in an inner sanctum, other deities are assigned appropriate places in the temple design. As Eck says: "The temple is an architectural pantheon, with each portion of the structure inhabited by the gods."[61] Every stage of the construction of a temple is a sacred rite, accompanied by established ritual. The architect of a temple is highly regarded and is usually a *Brāhmin*. At the centre of the temple is a shrine room, a "womb house", a *garbha-gṛha*, and it is here that the major deity of the temple is housed. This central shrine is mostly cave-like, dark, windowless and lacking in decoration – a cave in the temple that is as a mountain. Foulston depicts rather well the metaphysical symbolism of this embryonic shrine:

> On the one hand, the *garbhagṛha* protects the most sacred element of the temple, and on a metaphysical level it reinforces the concept that ultimately creation is derived from darkness or nothingness: what is manifest originated from what is unmanifest. Here, is the very essence of the temple and, by parallel, the very essence of the cosmos. The journey into the temple for the devotee is a passage, not only from the secular world outside to a sacred world within, but perhaps on a more important and metaphysical level, it is a journey into the self. The temple provides an accessible contact between divinity and humankind and, as such, is a place of transcendence where the devotee can become infused with the purifying power of divinity.[62]

So powerful and sacred is the *garbha-gṛha* that most often only the priest is allowed to enter: it is he that performs all the rituals of *pūjā*. Devotees in North Indian temples are more likely to enter the inner shrine, whereas in the South, they cannot venture further than the threshold.[63] Above the shrine room a tower is usually built and is the *axis mundi* of the temple, the place where power rises and descends. There may well be other towers in the temple complex, but none will be as high as that above the shrine room. In the North of India, the tower above the shrine room is curved at the sides (curvilinear), and the top is rounded. In the South, however, the tower has straight sides and is pyramidical. The vertical ascent, or *vimāna*, from the shrine room in both resemble mountains with their tips directly above the important central shrine. The ground plan of a northern temple is called the *vāstu-puruṣa maṇḍala*, *puruṣa* being the primal being, *puruṣa*, in the *Ṛg Veda* who was sacrificed to form manifest existence. This primal man is fitted diagonally into the square of the ground plan of the temple, his navel being the centre, and the shrine with various deities positioned around the square. Southern temples are different, with no *puruṣa*, but a series of layers that incorporate inhabitants of the cosmos from major deities to minor ones, humans to demons. These layers are spheres of existence and the more one penetrates the inner layers the more spiritual and sacred the journey becomes. The temple reflects the abode of the deities in the heavens, particularly the abode of the main deity that resides in the inner sanctum, so in journeying inwards one is moving towards an immensely sacred point. The basic plan of such temples is, then, a *yantra*, a sacred design.

The highest tower of the northern temples that have curvilinear sides is called a *śikhara*, a "mountain peak". The top of these temples has a sun disc. Placed exactly over the *garbha-gṛha* it is designed to represent a mountain, with other, shorter *śikharas* in front that resemble the foothills of the mountain. This is the northern *nāgara* style of temple building, which is usually accompanied by a considerable amount of ornamentation. The extensive mythologies in Hindu scriptures are pictorially represented on the walls of northern temples. The deities portrayed here are not worshipped and so the artists who make the stone reliefs in the past and the present[64] have more artistic licence for their creations, carving reliefs that recapture central mythological tales from texts like the *Mahābhārata*. A perfect example of such a temple is the Kandarīya Mahādeva Temple dedicated to Śiva at Khajurāho. This temple has a walkway all around it by which devotees are able to circumambulate the entire structure before entering the outer entrance hall, and then the assembly room – both directly in front of the shrine room – so that they can have *darśan* of Śiva's *liṇga*. Some of these temples in the northern *nāgara* style have ornate and complex designs, though the *śikhara*, the main curvilinear tower, is always the major feature. Northern temples, however, have been subject to past loss through Muslim invasion and so they are not as prolific as those in the South. As we come South in India, the Deccan tends to have a hybrid style that features some of the characteristics of the North and some of the South.

In southern India, the style is different. Here, the *drāviḍa śikhara* is a straight-edged pyramid erected over a square shrine room around which there may be one or more tiers with many niches or miniature shrines containing images of deities. The outstanding feature of the southern style of temple building is the *gōpuras*, "gateways", that appeared from the twelfth century onwards. These massive towering gateways to the temples have all kinds of divine and celestial beings sculpted on them. Entrances to these temples may be on their four sides, but most temples, though not all, face east in the direction of the rising sun that can light up the shrine room. This is an important factor since the first temple *pūjā* of the day is at sunrise, wakening the deity, so to speak, with the rising sun. *Gōpuras*, therefore, are the main entrances that face east and the whole temple complex is usually enclosed in a plain perimeter wall. Some temples to Viṣṇu, however, face South. The Srī Ranganātha Temple near Madras is one such temple. It has seven concentric walls, a kind of labyrinth, that leads to the central shrine of Viṣṇu. As Kinsley commented:

> The central shrine, the centre of the world and of reality, Vishnu himself, is to be found only by those who specially and specifically seek him out. . . . The seven concentric walls represent the sheaths of a human being. The outermost wall represents the merely physical, transient sheath. The innermost wall, housing Vishnu himself, represents the human's eternal, unchanging soul, the Atman. Progressing ever inward, ever

> more deeply inside one's nature – ever downward, as it were – the devotee penetrates the various enclosures, each marked with its guardian deities, finally reaching the source, the navel of the earth, the centre of existence, Lord Vishnu himself, with whom the devotee is essentially identified, from whom the devotee has emerged, and whom he or she seeks ultimate union.[65]

Kinsley's words are a perfect example of the transition from profane to sacred that is the experience of visiting a Hindu temple.

The ornamentation of a temple is usually designed to protect the temple from malevolent forces: the function of the deities secondary to the major deity or deities would be as guardians at each side of the temple. Maintaining the purity of the temple is critical. Shoes would never be worn inside, nor would menstruating women be permitted to enter. All products used in ritual are what are considered to be pure ones, like the products that come from the cow or water from a sacred river. Again, turmeric and sandalwood are believed to be particularly purifying. The area outside the temple is polluted, as are its many inhabitants, and every possible attempt to keep such pollution from the sacred area means extensive purifying ritual. Orthodox ritual is presided over by priests as a mediating force between the microcosmic human domain and the macrocosmic divine world. Such a ritualistic mediating and intermediate level has been called a "mesocosm" by Robert Levy.[66] Temples will have their own families of priests. There may be only one priest at a small temple but at the largest ones, many would be necessary.

The temple priest is a *pūjāri* and he will have to maintain the purity of the temple at the same time carry out specific purification rites to ensure his own purity before performing *pūjā*. The body is particularly polluted with its excrement, urine, sweat, saliva, and contact with dead animals, birth, death of relatives or a menstruating woman – all having highly polluting properties. It is essential, then, for the priest to ensure that none of this pollution enters the purity of a temple. Babb comments here: "To maintain a high degree of purity is to become involved in a complicated and incessant battle against life itself, which seems constantly to be intruding into the sanctity of the shrine or the time and place of ritual."[67] In the light of this comment it is not surprising that, apart from the attention to the deities, priests must be knowledgeable in the use of *mantras* that will dispel the more subtle forms of pollutants of malevolent spirits as much as ensuring the utmost purity of every utensil used in ritual procedure. At the same time, the priest himself has to be absolutely sure that he, too, has performed the appropriate rituals and procedures to ensure his own purity. He will bathe before ritual and wear fresh clothes, if possible made of silk that absorbs pollutants less than cotton. His *mantras* and chants will help in his purifying rituals. Nevertheless, human nature being what it is, such purifying rituals are not always evident. Indeed, Fuller found such to be the case in his study of the priests at the Mīnākṣī Temple in Madurai.[68]

The *pūjāri* will perform *pūjā* on behalf of the devotee and offer *prasāda* at the conclusion. While the priests who tend the temples of the great pan-Hindu deities need to be of the *Brāhmin* class, there are a variety of castes within the *Brāhmin* class as a whole, and not all *Brāhmins* would be priests. But there would also be priests who are not *Brāhmins* at all. These latter would serve lesser temples and shrines. Special temple officials called *paṇḍas* serve temples that are places of pilgrimage, while *purohits* are family priests.[69] A *purohit* (literally "placed in front"[70]), is a hereditary priest and specialized, but because he works to provide a service to others, he is inferior to those *Brāhmins* who do not work. As Michael Witzel comments: "His theoretical dominance as a member of the first class, thus, has always been compromised by his dependence on the two lower classes."[71] Certain interdependence has to inform temple life at times. Baker comments on life around a village temple: "When there is a religious ceremony involving the whole village, who is responsible for what job follows the same pattern as for previous generations. Who constructs the deities, who sweeps around the temple, who sweeps inside the temple, which family of Brahmins bathes and dresses the deity, who carries the deity in the procession, who plays in the village band, who is permitted to approach the deity and give offerings of food at specified times – there is a part, a particular role to be played by all the community, by the barber, the carpenter, the sweeper, everyone."[72] It is an interesting comment on the interdependent diversity of communities in the village setting. In some locales, there are no *Brāhmin* priests at all, and if needed they have to be brought in from neighbouring areas. But in some communities, simplified rituals are carried out without the aid of a priest, the major absence being the chanting of Sanskrit *mantras* and verses that the priest supplies. But where a *Brāhmin* priest is present at a temple, the temple, as well as the deity that resides within it, is regarded as higher in status than one in which a priest is absent. Again, it is a question of the relative purity of a priest-officiated temple as opposed to the less pure one where he is absent. Wherever a priest is present at a shrine or temple, the participation of the devotees is diluted, with the priest sometimes officiating whether or not devotees are present.[73]

In contrast to the *Brāhmin* priests are the colourful local village priests who are not *Brāhmins* but who mediate between the local inhabitants and the deities at the village shrines. In the village setting, all kinds of superstitions abound. Evil spirits are believed to be ubiquitous and the deities of the many shrines may occasionally seek to harm rather than protect the local inhabitants. It is the role of the village priest to determine what is wrong, which forces are responsible and to prescribe the means by which the danger, illness, bad luck, and the like, can be assuaged. He is the medicine man of the locale, too, providing cures for the many ailments and diseases that plague the inhabitants including unfortunate bites from scorpions or snakes. He seems, says Babb, "to radiate an aura of easy familiarity with the world of minor gods and goddesses and malevolent spirits. He seems to have a reassuring confidence in his ability to deal with matters that produce awe and fear in others."[74] Such a village priest is believed by the locals to be able to counteract possession by demons and to combat witchcraft, and he has at his disposal many *mantras* for the purpose. Far more important than the remote great Gods and Goddesses of Hinduism, this local priest is near to the fears and ailments of a whole community. A certain amount of bargaining with the local deities takes place in the light of these practices. They are surely propitiated for well-being, security, prosperity, children and healthy lives and if negative outcomes occur, they are believed to do so because their propitiation has been neglectful or inappropriate. The greater pan-Hindu deities are much less seen in this way: they are superior and remote and it is often the little shrines and temple/shrines that are more frequently visited.

The aspects that are the most arresting in visiting a Hindu temple are those that affect the senses – the colours, sounds and smells. Apart from the shrine room, temples appear alive with activity. Designed to enclose sacred space, temples also expect the devotee to pass through the purifying stages noted earlier in order to come near to the divine. Individuals may go to the temple for a specific purpose or they may not have anything special in mind. They may just ring a brass bell to summon the deity and then proceed to the central shrine where the priest will take their offerings, usually flowers and/or fruit, and give them *prasāda*. Since visits to temples are individualistic, it may mean a devotee just wishes to sit quietly in the temple. And since visits are optional in regard to time and intention, no one is specifically expected there. Temple *pūjā* for the devotee is personal and where one may be meditative, others may be more obvious with their personal prayers. It is an informal setting despite the sacred nature and it is not expected that people should be quiet or that children should not be allowed to move around and play. It is *darśan* of a deity that would be the real purpose, whether to give praise to the deity, or to pray for a particular outcome. Circumambulation of the deity or whole shrine is usual. Sometimes such circumambulation, or *pradakṣiṇa*, is around the whole temple before entering the temple compound itself. It has to be clockwise so that the right hand (which is regarded as pure) and not the left hand (which is impure) is facing the deity at all times.[75] Such circumambulation is regarded as very auspicious.

While there are many Hindus who never visit temples and whose approach to Hinduism does not involve image worship or even *pūjā* at all, certainly at the popular level, it is devotional theism that has captured the hearts and minds of the bulk of the Hindu populace. In such *bhakti*, love and devotion to God are the main characteristics of *pūjā* whether at home or in the temple. And that devotion may take the form of singing and dancing, as well as the usual offerings to the deity that characterize most worship. Offerings need not be elaborate and in the *Bhagavad Gītā* it says: "Whoever offers to me with devotion, a leaf, flower, fruit, water, that I accept, offered with *bhakti* by the pure-minded. Whatever you do, whatever you eat, whatever you offer in sacrifice, whatever austerity you practise, do that as an offering to me" (9:26, 27). Each temple will usually have a presiding deity that emphasizes one particular dimension of that deity in contrast to another to the same deity elsewhere. The name of the temple is likely to reflect that special dimension and both – the name of the deity and the temple – are likely to be grounded in an episode of scriptural myth. Thus, since deities have multiple names, one of the names may be applicable to one temple rather than another. So even though a deity is thought to be present in the temple image, whether iconic, theriomorphic or aniconic, it is at the same time recognized that a particular deity is elsewhere, too, in other temples and even in home shrines. Fuller makes the salient point that:

> Gods and goddesses do not actually need offerings and services, because they never are dirty, ugly, hungry, or unable to see in the dark. Hence the purpose of worship is not to satisfy non-existent divine needs, but to honor the deities and show devotion by serving them as if they had such needs. By this method alone can human beings adopt a truly respectful attitude toward the deities. Such an explanation of how *puja* pleases deities is logically consistent with a relatively emphatic distinction between a

deity and its image, the container of divine power, because then the deity itself is not directly touched by the offerings and services made to the image.[76]

Eck, too, comments that: "Whisking away the flies and offering a drink of water is *our* language, and not God's necessity."[77] What *pūjā* provides is the kind of anthropomorphic theism necessary for worshippers themselves but, at a deeper level, the more devotion and care that is lavished on a deity, the more an individual is able to transcend his or her own self in total absorption in the god or goddess, thus, for a time, transcending the profane and mundane. This, it seems to me, is the experience the temple offers as does *pūjā* in its purest forms.

Song and dance are features of temple *pūjā* but they are generally not organized occasions in that they have no set format and people come and go and join in if they wish. Sometimes the name of the deity or a special *mantric* phrase associated with the deity is chanted repeatedly. This is *kirtāna*, whereas at other times well-known hymns or poems of praise, *bhajans*, are sung. *Bhajans* are especially important in devotional Hinduism and are very often sung in the vernacular – indeed, were sometimes composed so. Famous poets whose love of a particular God and especially a Goddess, have had their poetry and devotional songs immortalized by being transmitted from generation to generation and by being learned even by the illiterate. In his field research, Babb notes how groups of friends will get together for the purpose of singing such *bhajans* and that such groups seemed to cut across caste.[78]

Dance has traditionally been more formal. I dealt with the *rāsa-līlā* associated with Kṛṣṇa and Rādhā in the last chapter. It is still performed as an expression of spiritual devotion and Pika Ghosh captures the essence of this in Gauḍīya temples: "Enhanced awareness and application of this spiritual dimension of form and movement has, in part, allowed for dance to become such an important medium for enacting and exploring the biographies of the gods, with the performers often transforming into the characters they revere through their performance, as in the *rasalila* dramas of Vrindavan, where the actors are momentarily venerated as the manifest divine."[79] Temple dancers who, in the past, were married to the deity of the temple, performed intricate dances. Such dancers were *deva-dāsīs*, "servants of God" who, from medieval times, became specialists in temple ritual and dance. Unlike other women, they were highly educated, even though they were courtesans. In 1947, the Deva-dāsī Act was passed in India in order to end what was seen as temple prostitution. It forbade dancing not only in temples but in processions or festivals, indeed, at any ceremony.[80] However, it is a law that is ignored by all. *Deva-dāsīs* were experts in classical dance and music as well as being well-conversed in sexual arts. They danced and provided sexual services at temples, the courts of kings and houses of the rich. Often looked on by outsiders as prostitutes, their double identity is neatly portrayed by Vasudha Narayanan: "The *devadāsīs* sang songs of love and praise to both deity and the patron. The music and dance frequently contained double entendres – the words could refer to the king or the deity, and the emotions could be construed as *kama sringara* (physical, sensual love) or *bhakti* (devotion).[81] Despite the law, they still perform at the Jagannātha Temple in Purī and elsewhere.

While major temples are generally open to members of all castes, local and especially village temples tend to be frequented by members of exclusive castes. In town locales or villages, there would be deities specific to a certain caste and in this case ritual would be conducted according to the way of life of the caste group. While it is illegal in India to prohibit outcastes from entry into a temple, there are, nevertheless, temples where they are still not allowed in practice. Regardless of the extent to which a low-caste Hindu may undertake ritual purification, castes are hierarchically pure or polluted. People tend to remain within their own caste praxis, visit their caste temples and, like most of those outside the caste system, would prefer to be associated with their own deities, their own temples in their own restricted locales, and with what André Béteille terms "a more or less distinct ritual status in a hierarchical system".[82] Outcastes are still regarded as highly polluting and no *Brāhmin* priest officiating at a temple would be comfortable with their proximity to himself or the enshrined deities.

I shall be exploring temples in the context of festivals and pilgrimage in chapter 11, but a few comments here are in order to exemplify some of the aspects dealt with above. Temples to the Goddess in her many forms are very popular in villages and small towns. Such goddesses are felt to be close to the inhabitants of their immediate locale, offering protection and assistance in times of need. Sometimes, such areas also have a temple for one of the Sanskritized Goddesses like Lakṣmī, but a temple of that kind would be less popular. Throughout India, however, wherever there is a temple whose presiding deity is Viṣṇu, a shrine to Lakṣmī is also to be found there. As Viṣṇu's consort, she is inseparable from him, even if her shrine and image are smaller than his. In Śaiva temples, the Goddess is mostly to be found behind the *liṅga* of Śiva, though she is usually symbolized, too, in the *yoni*, the female organ in which the *liṅga* is based. As to the Great Goddess herself, Devī, it is said that there are a hundred and eight major temples dedicated to her in India. Since caves are believed to symbolize the womb, some temples to Devī are deep within them and on the sides or tops of mountains. Within such temples, Devī is usually found in aniconic form. But it is Kālī who is one of the most popular forms of the Great Goddess and is the focus of thousands of temples. Perhaps the most striking is that at the Dakṣineśwara Temple in Bengal that is associated with Sri Ramakrishna, whose descendants perform regular *pūjā* there. The founder of the temple was a woman, Rani Rasmani, and the temple was dedicated and consecrated in May 1855. At the age of nineteen Ramakrishna, who attended the dedication ceremony, was invited to become the first priest of the temple.[83]

Major temples dedicated to Viṣṇu are to be found all over India, most associated with mythological events related to the God. Sukumari Bhattacharji describes Vaiṣṇava religion as "quiet", with simple offerings of leaves, flowers and water at the temples.[84] Vaiṣṇava temples, therefore, lack the frenetic atmosphere of temples dedicated to Kālī, especially the animal sacrifice. The most magnificent Vaiṣṇava temple is probably that at the seventeenth-century Śrīraṅgam in South India, which is a massive complex that is really a temple city. The Temple of Viṣṇu Jagannātha at Purī is one of the most important Vaiṣṇava temples of North India. Here, outcastes and foreigners are certainly prohibited from entry, despite the peaceful nature of much Vaiṣṇava religion. Frédérique Marglin thinks the exclusion of non-Hindus is because the temple maintains a highly pure kitchen and will not permit food in it that is foreign: "Now, my understanding of this is that just as foreign food is banned because it is not grown indigenously, so, too, are foreigners – people – banned, because they did not have the good fortune of being nurtured on Indian soil, holy soil." As she pertinently continues to say, since *Jagannātha* means "Lord of the Universe", why should anyone be excluded?[85] The presiding deities of the Temple are Kṛṣṇa in the form of Jagannātha, Balabhadra his brother, and Subhadrā his sister, and this is a temple where *devadāsīs* sing at the threshold of the inner sacred shrine. Another massive temple complex dedicated to Viṣṇu is in the South in Andhra Pradesh. This temple complex, the Tirupati, built on seven hills, Klostermaier believes is the "arguably richest temple in the world".[86] The abundance of temples to Kṛṣṇa are founded on myths associated with his life. The temple at Mathurā, in Uttar Pradesh in North India commemorates his birthplace, and there are two temples at the site of the old city of Dvārakā, where Kṛṣṇa spent the close of his life. But it is especially his life with the *gopīs* that is celebrated at temples in Vṛndāvana and elsewhere.

In the South, in Tanjore, Tamil Nāḍu, is the eleventh-century Bṛhadeśvara Temple of the *drāviḍa* style that houses the largest Śiva *liṅga* in the whole of India. In addition, its tower is massive, standing at over two hundred feet. The ubiquitous nature of the *liṅga* means that Śiva has shrines and temples in villages, towns, forests, beneath trees and in caves. In the North of India, at Bhubaneśvar, Śiva is housed in a magnificent temple bearing the curvilinear *śikhara*, as Liṅga-Rāja, "Lord of the *Liṅga*". On the opposite coast in the West is the Great Cave Temple dedicated to Śiva on the island of Elephanta. Built in the sixth century, the cave is constructed in the rocky edifice and all its pillars and iconic figures of Śiva are spectacularly carved out of rock.[87] Both North and South India boast temple towns, massive temple areas that include the temples themselves and also all the buildings that are necessary for the administration of the main temple. In the North, such temple towns are places like Vārāṇasī, Mathurā, Purī and Bhubaneśwar, some of which I shall revisit again in chapter 11. But it is in the South of India, in places like Śrīraṅgam, where the whole town is the complex of the temple.

Temples are not just expressions of past cultural style and tradition because their construction is still being sponsored by different wealthy individuals and families or by various religious bodies. Temples, and the images they house, are the external expressions of what it is to be a Hindu in the devotional framework. Champakalakshmi neatly expresses this symbiotic nature between the deities and the structures that house them when she says that "the temple and the image are inseparable elements of a single scheme or project, meant to convey different levels of meaning through design, organisation and orientation of the structure and its decorative sculpture."[88] There is also a symbiotic nature between temple and devotee. George Mitchell makes this point when he says: "The temple is the most characteristic artistic expression of Hinduism, providing a focus for both the social and spiritual life of the community it serves".[89] Yet, at the other end of the scale, images and aniconic representations of deities are to be found in much smaller structures or, indeed, in no structure at all, perhaps just beneath a tree, and it is to these smaller shrines that I now want to turn.

Pūjā at shrines

In contrast to the many temples where those who wish for *darśan* of a deity can only gaze briefly into the shrine room, there are countless small shrines that offer much more immediate access to the deity because the structure of such shrines is so basic as to be open to the elements, though some will have a roof. Thus: "Shrines reflect rural villagers' sense that they have a direct physical connection to the specific land on which they live."[90] Whereas priests will attend the deities of temples, there may be none at all at most shrines and *pūjā* at them may not be daily. In some small shrines, it may not even occur on a weekly basis. The simplest of shrines which, just like a temple, is called a *mandira*, may be just a stone at the base of a tree, or sandal-paste and vermilion marks on a tree. Somewhere between temples and shrines are somewhat better-constructed shrines that are clearly *garbha-gṛhas* like the temples, and are big enough for a priest to enter, but around which there is no other edifice. Foulston terms these temple/shrines, with an important distinction from temples: "Therefore, the sacred heart of the temple, the sanctum, becomes integrated into the community, rather than there being, as is evident with the temples, a forced separation between the devotee and the object of his or her devotion."[91] At a temple/shrine, a devotee has a much more personal encounter with the god or goddess, being able to see perfectly well into the shrine room and, in some cases, being able to enter the shrine room itself to offer devotion directly to the deity.[92] But where a *pūjāri* is present – often found seated at the entrance to the shrine – his function is to perform *pūjā* on behalf of the devotee and to care for the deity. Newer shrines in India sometimes have women priests despite the perceived pollution of menses.[93] In contrast, a shrine that is a small heap of stones would not be attended by a priest. Either way, shrines are often shabby in appearance, despite the care that is expected to be lavished on the deities they house. Shrines occur generally at auspicious places, or at places that have been at one time noticeably inauspicious, like crossroads, where deaths may have occurred.

While shrines may be very simple, in some cases the deities that occupy them are still attended to with the accepted traditional *pūjā* offerings of water, food, clothing, incense and unguents that are smeared on even if the deity is an aniconic stone. Red powder, *kumkum*, these days is a sign that the deity at one time is likely to have accepted animal sacrifice. Devotees will offer flowers and sometimes money at the shrines that pepper the roadsides. Choudhury comments on such small shrines: "Although they may look insignificant, these roadside shrines are the nerve-centres of rural religious life and are intimately linked with local people's everyday life of vows and thanksgivings, births and deaths."[94] Low-caste women often establish their own small shrines to goddesses known only in their own locale.[95] Foulston describes a shrine in Khurdapur in Orissa, North India that is simply two side walls and a flat stone roof,[96] which is very typical of small-shrine structures. Some deities are represented by trees, the tree becoming the sacred shrine. Trees are often associated with temples and many are revered. Such veneration may reflect pre-Hindu customs given the frequency of trees worshipped on seals from the Indus cities – a topic that must be left until Volume II but, widely, trees are regarded as symbols of fertility. Occasionally, a simple shrine may be placed at the foot of a sacred tree like the *bilva* or *pipal*. Unattended shrines deep in caves reflect the similar use of natural phenomena as appropriate sites for shrines.

Shrines can suddenly appear anywhere if someone believes that a deity wishes to make its presence known. The number of devotees at a shrine is not an issue and it would not be uncommon to see just a garland of flowers on a clay mound, a termite mound, or a stone – all of which represent the devotion of one or more individuals. Like the majority of great temples, shrines usually face East, though some village goddess shrines face North, perhaps, as Foulston suggests, because of their fierce and benign natures.[97] In the case of village goddesses there may be no shrine at all until one is temporarily built for a festival.[98] In the village cultures, it is felt prudent to have boundary shrines, mainly to fierce goddesses who will protect the village. These shrines may be fairly inconspicuous and not frequently attended, but they are an important feature of the identity of the village as having a corporate protective deity.

While many shrines are dedicated to local deities, there are times when the pan-Indian great Gods and Goddesses are also to be found represented in local shrines. Śiva in the form of Pañcānana, "Five Faces", is believed to be a healer, and though he is normally represented by his *liṅga*, a stone with no particular shape and painted red may be used as the focus for recovery from ill health or for other blessings, especially in Bengal. Hanumān, the monkey general and semi-divine character from the *Rāmāyaṇa*, is an immensely popular divinity throughout India, so much so, that shrines to him are everywhere, making him surely one of the most popular images. Shrines to Gaṇeśa appear everywhere, too, for this is the God who removes obstacles. Shrines to him are to be found at roadsides, on hill and mountain footpaths, at road junctions – all intended to help the traveller on his or her intended path. Students pray to Gaṇeśa for success before taking an examination, as do businessmen before any undertaking. However, it is goddess shrines that are the most prolific in local areas, especially villages, each shrine dedicated to a goddess whose name is often unique to the locale.

Pūjā to local goddesses

Pūjā to local goddesses, particularly in village settings, is much more relaxed than in the temples, though the same basic rituals are evident with offerings of water, food and flowers. Each village will probably have its own major deity, its *grāma-devatā*, the "village deity", very often a goddess, and it is this deity that will be felt to protect the settlement and its inhabitants. Since some are housed in simple shrines, they may not be frequented regularly and, strictly speaking, there is no restriction on caste or gender for *pūjā* at such shrines: neither is there any particular time for *pūjā*.[99] Important to some locales are the more unusual ways of contact with, and devotion to, a deity. Possession of an individual by a goddess is a regular occurrence despite not being accepted by orthodox Hindus. Even a goddess like Santoṣī Mā, for example, who has now been incorporated in the orthodox fold, takes possession of a local woman in a small village settlement of Khurdapur in the North of India. Foulston describes rather well the rationale underpinning such practice: "The relationship between the possessor and the possessed is a very intimate one, and one that is mutually beneficial. Without a mortal body, the sacred goddess would not be able to leave her sanctum nor have such a closely interactive relationship with her devotees."[100] The spectacle is sufficiently popular for people to travel fair distances to observe it. The purpose of the visits of devotees is largely propitiatory: they need the goddess's blessing for all kinds of ill health and personal problems. But the most important factor here is the intimacy of the goddess with her devotees since she is able, through the medium of a possessed woman, to have physical contact with those who need her.

Some women marry themselves to their favourite goddess, becoming *matammas*, whether or not they are married or widowed. These *matammas* are often possessed, and give regular audiences to local people by which, while in trance, the goddess is able to work or "play" through them as mediums. Some women reach the status of *matajis*, women imbued with *śakti*. They are respected as "mothers", akin to the goddesses who possess them and who offer help to those who come to them for assistance in all kinds of situations. Kathleen Erndl writes of "the ambiguous fluidity between human and divine identities and powers in the phenomenon of Hindu goddess possession". Possession rituals, she says, are "traditional cultural resources which create an arena for women's empowerment in the varied and rapidly changing context of contemporary India".[101] Of the *mataji* Erndl says: "A transformation takes place through repeated possession, so that the woman becomes more 'goddess-like', more and more divinized, even in her nonpossessed state."[102] *Matajis* may become highly respected, found *āśrams* and have regular devotees. The renunciatory state normally associated with men may also be undertaken by some of these women.

By and large, but not exclusively so, goddesses possess females. Nevertheless, Sarah Caldwell describes the possession of a priest by the Goddess, the fierce Bhadrakāḷī or benign Bhagavati, in southern Kerala by which a man becomes the oracle of the Goddess.[103] Susan Wadley also records cases of possession of males by village goddesses, with the interesting anecdote of a male dressed as a goddess taking a pot around to each home in the village in the middle of the night, collecting the "inauspiciousness" from each dwelling. The pot – not in the least altruistically – is then taken to the edge of the village and flung into a field belonging to a neighbouring village.[104] Wadley notes, too, that lower-caste men may become officially possessed and, hence, ritually authoritative.[105] Similarly, Kathleen Erndl describes possession of a male of the potter caste by the Goddess.[106] Possession, then, is essentially an idiosyncratic, fluidly experiential phenomenon that is independent of caste, gender, marital status or region.

A more extreme expression of devotion is hook-swinging whereby metal hooks are dug into the skin of the back and the devotee is suspended by them or drags a festival car. Sometimes skewers are pushed through the tongue or cheeks. Babb offers a particularly vivid account of one he witnessed in Madhya Pradesh in Central India:

> The procession moved circuitously through the village, pausing briefly at each major intersection of the village lanes. At each stop a lemon was cut at the feet of the leading woman. As the procession moved along, the metal rods carried by the possessed dancers were put to use. One of the dancers pushed his rod through the fleshy part of his upper arm. Another used his rod to pierce his tongue, and then from time to time swung the rod through a 90-degree arc, twisting his tongue grotesquely out of his

> mouth. In each case a lemon was stuck on the sharpened end of the rod while it remained in the flesh of the dancer.[107]

In an equally extreme form of *pūjā* , hot coals are carried in a pot sometimes on the heads of women who, it is claimed, are unharmed by the burning pot. Fire-walking is another extreme form of festival praxis. Here, devotees walk across a pit of hot coals with bare feet. Again, it is goddesses who are believed to demand this kind of powerful devotion from their devotees. Sometimes the pit is a long, narrow pathway over which the devotee passes once, or it may be square and the devotee has to cross it a number of times. Ritual preparations for such an event are meticulous by both priests and participants and to pass over the coals successfully they must have absolute faith in the goddess who will protect them and render them so sacred that they cannot be harmed. Indeed, in South India, the fire pit is known as the "pit of flowers".[108] Foulston's vivid account of her witnessing of a fire walk in South India is a remarkable affirmation that it takes place without the participants – men, women *and children* – incurring no harm whatsoever.[109]

In many parts of India, but particularly in the South, snakes, or *nāgas*, are venerated. There are some snake goddesses like Nākamāl. Snakes and serpents have always featured widely in mythology, in which they are believed to dwell in *Pātāla*, the netherworld below Earth, and have been venerated for their fertility, though feared for their venom. Since snakes often conceal themselves in the roots of trees, it is here that shrines to them are to be found. The usual *pūjā* offerings are not given at these shrines. Instead, milk and eggs are deemed more appropriate. The goddess of snakes, Mana-sadevī, has no specific image but is represented aniconically as an earthen pot and a clay snake. Bulbul Sharma notes that legends about her powers are popular at festival time, when they are repeated by folk singers.[110] Since *gurus* are venerated widely, photographs of them are found everywhere, "from the lowly motor-rickshaw driver . . . to the wealthiest corporate manager hanging a picture of his guru prominently in his wood-panelled office".[111] Such *gurus* – equated with gods – may be the object of *pūjā*.

In conclusion, *pūjā* is essentially a devotional approach to divinity. Östör captures the basic simplicity of what *pūjā* is all about when he says: "The ideal way to treat a guest is the way to treat the gods: guests are like deities, and gods are guests among men."[112] In this way, it is not difficult to know how to relate to one's god or goddess or to the deities that are the main focuses of others. Words like honouring, respecting, serving are as applicable to a guest as to a god. There is a certain amount of *exchange*, too, in the concept of *pūjā* and this is not just the tangible gift of the deity's grace with *prasāda*, but also the intangible, reciprocal relationship between deity and devotee that takes place with that intimate moment of *darśan*.

9

Ritual in the Home and Community

Life-cycle Rites

Life-cycle rites, in Sanskrit *saṃskāras*, are a major focus in the ritualistic lives of many who would call themselves Hindus. In a conclusion to his work on *saṃskāras* Rajbali Pandey came to the following superb conclusion about life-cycle rites:

> Life has been a great mystery to man. Its origin, growth, decadence and disappearance have always exercised his thoughts and emotions. The Hindu *Saṃskāras* were just an attempt to fathom and to facilitate the flow of this mystery. Through observations and experiences and through faltering and confidence of ages the ancient Hindus realised that life was an art like any other art in the world. It required cultivation and refinement. Man born and left to himself was a mass of elements, crude and brutal and slightly removed from his fellow citizens of the forest. His life stood in need of as much care, protection and cultivation as a plant in a garden, crops in a field and an animal in a cattle-farm. The *Saṃskāras* involved conscious efforts to meet this need. The seers and the sages of yore, to their light and resources, tried to transform crude animality into refined humanity.[1]

Such interesting observations from Pandey place life-cycle rites not only in the context of social needs but also in the journey of individuals and society in their religiously evolving consciousness. As social observation shifted to religious prescription in an attempt to cultivate and refine, so accompanying ritual developed, and it is this ritualistic dimension that I want to explore in the present chapter.

Saṃskāras

Long before religious texts set down regulations for conducting life-cycle rites there must have been customs and traditions that surrounded the important transitions from one stage to another in life. It is interesting that most of the rites that became textually prescribed are to do with pregnancy, birth and early childhood and I think this must surely reflect a time in the far distant past when childbirth was a dangerous process that so often took away the life of the mother, the child, or both. Primitive ideas of malign forces would have contributed to the belief that certain practices could ward off dangers at critical times in life. We are not looking for origins of *saṃskāras* in elite religious circles but more so in the beliefs and practices extant in the lives of ordinary folk and, frequently, these are likely to have been informed by superstition. They were rites that originated in the home for the protection of its inhabitants. Life-cycle rites are rites of *passage*, the times in life when one passes from one state to another, as from foetus to life, from adolescence to maturity, from unmarried to married and from life to death; closing the door on one aspect before opening the door of a new one. However, when exploring such rites of passage today, it is clear that the social dimension in which they must have been rooted long, long in the past is retained, for they are usually joyous social occasions with the exception, naturally, of the passage from life to death.

The term *saṃskāra* has connotations of purity, of completing and refining the body and individual so that it is transformed into a new state.[2] It is not an easy word to define given its long history and tradition and perhaps the closest western idea comes in the form of "sacrament" in the sense of a religious ritual that has an inner, spiritual dimension. In the context of its scriptural usage in Hinduism, I am inclined to favour a meaning that comes close to "a purificatory rite". That would be a meaning that chimes well with so much that has been said earlier in this book about the necessity for purity in all aspects of life. Gavin Flood favours a meaning "put together" or "constructed", noting that *saṃskāras* assist in creating social identities.[3] According to Mary McGee, the term also means "to perfect, refine, polish, prepare, educate, cultivate and train".[4] She favours a rather pertinent meaning of "rites of incorporation",[5] given that the rites cause the one undertaking them to unite with, or be admitted into, an organization. Such "admittance" is a new stage of life, essentially "incorporation" into new responsibilities. Succinctly: "*Saṃskāras* incorporate individuals into an ideal centre of duties and responsibilities (*varṇāśramadharma*), traditionally governed by an organic ethos of interdependence. From a religious perspective, *saṃskāras* constitute and sanctify the individual and corporate body simultaneously."[6]

However, *saṃskāra* has very wide meanings indeed[7] and is even used in cooking but, in the light of the suggestions above, the term perhaps has the basic idea of a change, a progression forward in a positive sense, so that one who has undergone a *saṃskāra*, becoming a *saṃskṛta*, is changed, processed, refined and cultivated. For our purposes here, I think Pandey's definition is apt: "It means religious purificatory rites and ceremonies for sanctifying the body, mind and intellect of an individual, so that he may become a full-fledged member of the community."[8] Such a definition encompasses both the notions of refining and purifying as well as incorporating an individual into a new area of communal life. As we shall see in what follows, *saṃskaras* are a cultural, social and religious aspect of Hindu life that renders an individual fit for a new role, a new purpose, a new status that is recognized by society as a whole. The plural is important because it is indicative of a process, a gradation of stages reflecting evolution through life. As McGee says, "*saṃskāras* are more than just rites and ceremonies; they constitute an idea, a belief about human beings and their development in the world".[9] Without such rites, an individual is not fit for social living, is lacking in culture, perfection, refinement and purity. But importantly, too, without the *saṃskāras*, an individual is unable to progress and journey to wholeness.

In time, what began as social and popular custom became religious tradition, an inevitable Sanskritizing of the rites that accompanied the householder through domestic religious life. It was the *Gṛhya-sūtras* that set down all sorts of rules for domestic life, including those rituals pertaining to life-cycle rites. While there were variations between these texts, the important stages of life were marked by set formalas and *Vedic mantras* in detailed form, with later works adding more detail to the rituals. The *Dharma-sūtras* that were so interested in class and caste and stages of life had their contribution to add to the transition from boyhood to manhood and from single to married status that marked the second and third stages of life respectively and the *Dharma-śāstras* also incorporated some *saṃskāras*. The *Purāṇas*, too, record a great deal concerning the correct procedures for *saṃskāras*.

As I have said, *saṃskāras* represent a social, cultural and religious progression through life, preparing an individual for his or her role at each stage and even for the stage beyond death that is Heaven, rebirth, or life with ancestors, or a combination of all three (and, more remotely, *mokṣa*). Given that the textual prescriptions for them were set out by *Brāhmins*, it is not surprising that the rites are class and caste bound and male dominated. They were also an excellent means of shaping society according to *Brāhmin* teachings, and of maintaining tradition and, above all, *dharma*. I do not mean such statements as necessarily pejorative for the *saṃskāras* gave religious sanction to all aspects of life, delineating a progressive spiritual journey for the individual and stabilizing social norms as intentionally religious. Pejoratively, however, the *saṃskāras* were essentially elitist and separatist: they were only for the twice born and enabled *Brāhmins* to maintain class hierarchy and communal identity by preserving the pure classes and isolating the impure. Gavin Flood comments that "the rite of passage is an interstructural situation between social positions"[10] and it is the "social positions" that are key here, in that *saṃskāras* mark out restrictive sections of society making clear boundaries between them that cannot be crossed.

On the other hand, ordinary folk have left their imprint on life-cycle rites. The origins of the *saṃskāras* amongst ordinary folk are thoroughly evident in the many customs so that the rites permeate – albeit in diluted form – to all areas of society. The superstitious motifs that serve to ward off evil forces are pervasive in the rites; indeed, popular superstition might be said to be predominant on a number of occasions. These I shall point out when I examine each of the *saṃskāras* below but the number of practices that serve to encourage that which is beneficial, or dispel that which is dangerous, is legion.[11] Indeed, while the main purpose of the *saṃskāras* is generally given as means of transformation from one stage to the next, I am inclined to argue that it is the warding off of evil forces and overcoming dangerous moments in life that are at the heart of the rites. My reason for saying this is the fact that the bulk of rites of passage are concerned with conception, pregnancy and the young baby.

In some cases, however, the passage from one stage of life to another is a rebirth and that is especially the case with change from adolescence to manhood, from single to married life, from death to afterlife and, of course, from foetus to baby. Indeed, from his field work in Bengal, Ralph Nicholas is of the view that: "All of the *saṃskāra* rites are based upon the latent paradigm as it is culturally defined in Bengal. They transform the natural and moral qualities of a person by refining and purifying the substances of which the body is made in an action that is symbolic of rebirth. A *saṃskāra* is an ancientropic act that 'completes' a person by moving that person bodily toward the most organized, self-controlled condition he or she is capable of achieving."[12] Of the major *saṃskāras* this is certainly true, though I doubt whether the claims made here are relevant to the pre- and post-natal rites where safety and the avoidance of harmful forces seem to me the major concerns.

With the exceptions of birth and marriage, the *saṃskāras* are not applicable to women or to lower castes. A woman's natural state is not considered as pure as that of a high-caste male, so she is unable to undergo the transformations to perfection that the *saṃskāras* offer her male counterpart. For a woman, the only real and important *saṃskāra* is marriage, as will be seen below. Mensies, seminal fluid and birth are pervaded by impurity that the *saṃskāras* can never wash away for a woman, whereas the *saṃskāras* for a man are totally cleansing and purifying. But it is the lowest castes that are completely excluded from any kind of "rebirth" from one stage to the next. Once the *saṃskāras* became codified – and, indeed, compulsory for high-class Hindus – the rigidified stratification of society was further maintained. Again, as was seen in earlier chapters, that issue of purity and impurity entrenched the difference between the purer higher castes and the impure lower ones; in this instance, by the rites of passage that refined the individual. Effectively, the exclusion of the lowest class, the *Śūdras*, as well as women from *saṃskāras* meant that the *dharmic* patterns of life of the included and excluded were clarified in such a way that social norms were to a great extent thoroughly prescribed.[13] Flood makes this clear when he says of rites of passage: "They are the expression of *dharma* in time; the way in which *dharma* works in a person's life, marking the exit from one dharmically determined social state and the entrance to another."[14] *Saṃskāras*, then, provide initiation into prescriptive modes of living that uphold the *dharma* appropriate to an individual and his or her social structure. The life-cycle rites were obligatory only for twice-born classes, though the *Gṛhya-sūtras* permitted *Śūdras* to perform the life-cycle rites associated with pregnancy, birth and post-natal rites, but without the *Vedic mantras* that accompanied rites of the twice born.[15] These days, *Śūdras* have developed their own life-cycle rites, which are undertaken by their own priests, though Julius Lipner has found that some *Brāhmins* will actually perform rites for those whom they consider to be "touchable".[16]

Saṃskāras were at one time associated with sacrificial religion but, as that declined in favour of devotional movements, the *saṃskāras* became rites more associated with the proper progress of an individual from birth until death.[17] And yet, as Sharma pointed out, both sacrifice and life-cycle rites propitiate the gods for success, wealth and happiness. No *saṃskāra* would be complete without first offering *pūjā* to Gaṇeśa, for example. Just as the sacrificial rites were and are accompanied by stringent purity of vessels and personnel, so each individual in each *saṃskāra* is purified by water before undergoing the transition from one stage to the next. Fire, too, is an essential element of the life-cycle rites, with the god of fire, Agni, protecting and guarding the rite against misfortune and malevolent spirits.

While the *saṃskāras* were prescribed in sacred *sūtras*, in practice there has always been variation in the way the rites are conducted depending on regional differences, caste traditions, as well as the traditions in particular families. The number of life-cycle rites also varies from region to region. Sixteen are usually standard and it is these on which I shall concentrate below, but in much Bengal custom, only ten are practised. As we shall see, some are more important than others, some have dropped out of usage on the whole, and some, rather than being performed at a scripturally prescribed time are conflated into almost a single ceremony. The *sūtras* themselves differ in the number of *saṃskāras* that should be performed, and one *Śāstra* has as many as forty-eight. Some omit the final death rite as too inauspicious to be linked with the others: in any case, transformation in the case of death was not regarded by some as furthering and refining personality for a new stage of life. The greater number of *saṃskāras* pertained to an earlier age and later settled to sixteen in most texts. Some texts place marriage first as the central rite that makes the others possible. Importantly, contemporary customs in the popular domain have adopted practices that are inherently familial and pertain to local tradition, journeying far from orthodox Sanskrit praxis. The sacred fire – the hallmark of the twice-born householder, for example, around which *saṃskāras* were centred – hardly exists in any homes.

Horoscopes

Whatever the ceremony, it is felt to be critical that it is undertaken at an auspicious time. Even secular occasions like opening a business, undertaking a journey or organizing a political event are entered into at favourable times if at all possible. However, this was not something that concerned the authors of the *sūtras*, for it was from about 400–900 CE that astrology became a respected science that determined auspicious and inauspicious times in the calendar year. Back in *Vedic* times, its use was confined to determining the best times for sacrifice. Alongside belief in malevolent forces came the idea that at some times they were more prevalent than others. Master astrologers – usually *Brāhmins* – were capable of discovering just when these auspicious and inauspicious times were. Even the *Gṛhya-sūtras* prescribed that marriage should take place on an auspicious day when the sun was in the northern hemisphere and the moon was waxing to fullness – the bright half of the month. In contemporary India, many literate families have an annual almanac that will assist them in determining auspicious and inauspicious times.

A horoscope is especially important at birth and will be prepared by a skilled astrologer who will be able to map out the kind of life the baby will have, his or her temperament, and specify what times in life will be dangerous or particularly good. It will be a very important document employed in the choice of a bride or groom. Nirad Chaudhuri made the following remarkable comment about horoscopes: "In a Hindu, faith in his horoscope was far stronger than his faith in any god or goddess or even God, and this faith was evinced in every act of his life. If a particular prediction in a horoscope came untrue that made no difference, for it could always be explained away by assuming an error in giving the exact time of birth."[18] There must be, of course, exceptions to such a degree of acceptance of astral effects on the lives of individuals, but it is true to say that there are considered to be days, hours even, that are more propitious than others for the undertaking of an event.[19] For four months of the year, in the rainy season in India, Viṣṇu is believed to sleep on his great serpent Śeṣa. It is an inauspicious time when the nights are longer, the weather cooler, and the sun is in the southern hemisphere. At this highly inauspicious time, people would try to avoid undertaking journeys and especially would not arrange marriages.

The time at which an individual is born is the *karmically* appropriate time for that birth: in Thomas Hopkins' words, "it is the time at which cosmic forces, as represented by the positions and interrelationships of the stars and planets, are most closely attuned to the karmic condition of the transmigrating self. . . . The purpose of the horoscope is not to record an unchangeable future but to indicate the karmic factors each person must deal with if he is able to improve his life; it is a guide to personal strengths, weaknesses, dangers, and opportunities that call for the exercise of foresight and will."[20] Placing horoscopes into the framework of *karma* and the concomitant *dharma* of an individual, as Hopkins does, lends the practice a more rational basis than the word "horoscope" initially suggests. This is not to suggest that individuals are bound by their *karma* at birth, for the horoscope, though indicating the *karmic* destiny of the moment, offers sufficient information about the life ahead to encourage living life according to the best possible means in order to change the *karma* of the future, especially of a future life. In short, horoscopes were and are another means of maintaining *dharma* and social order.

Rites for conception and pregnancy

The *saṃskāras* concerning conception and pregnancy are now rarely used and need not detain us too long, but a few important points need to be made. Of the generally recognized sixteen rites, eleven are concerned with the baby and the young child, marking specific stages in their development. It is my belief that these *saṃskāras* involved with early life reflect the fears, taboos and superstitions of the ordinary populace; they became Sanskritized and accepted into established ritual praxis. Raising children is an important aspect of the second *āśrama*, the stage of a householder. Birth, like death, is seen as a time of considerable pollution and danger, when the child unborn and then born, is at great risk and is vulnerable to evil forces. So the first three *saṃskāras*, though rarely observed these days, are devoted to the safety and welfare of the unborn child.

The rites begin at conception for, during the wife's fertile period, the husband is expected to chant *Vedic mantras* and invoke certain deities. The act of procreation is, thus, consecrated and sacred and is the requirement of a married couple: it is their *dharma*. The wife was considered to be fertile between the fourth and sixteenth days after menstruation and the later the conception in this time frame, the more prestigious and fortuitous the offspring, according to the *sūtras*. Some days were inauspicious for conception, and intercourse in the daytime highly dangerous for conception and its outcome. In contemporary India, the population crisis is such that the government has encouraged contraception, though it is still opposed by some.

The second rite occurs during pregnancy and is also rarely practised today. It has always been believed that the pregnant wife must be safeguarded from evil forces, particularly witches who wish to harm the foetus. The physical and mental health of the pregnant woman becomes a priority and the *sūtras* recognized such and sought to protect her. The safety of the child was of great importance but securing a male child was also a main aim, as it is today, so the second rite may be focused on promoting the birth of a boy before the foetus quickens in the womb. Pregnancy for a woman gives her status, fulfils her main role in life, particularly if she has a boy. Also rarely used now is the rite of parting the hair, the third of the *saṃskāras*. This, again, had a superstitious origin, and was believed to ward off malevolent spirits. The parting of the hair (done usually by the husband) was believed to bring well-being to mother and child, avoid any harm from evil forces, and ensure a safe delivery. Traditionally, the husband should whisper lovely words to his wife while parting the hair and give her gifts of jewellery.

Birth rites

Any fluid that is emitted from the body – excreta, urine, semen, blood, menstrual blood, saliva – is regarded as highly polluting. The birth process, especially, is second only to death in its impurity. It is so polluting that it affects all members of the household. Aside from the dangers of pollution are the exacerbated dangers of evil forces that wish to harm the mother and, even more so, the baby. Witches are at hand to harm with their "glance", what we would call the "evil eye", and so the mother will be protected by all kinds of different customs from what she wears to the taboos on her departure from the home for any reason. Seclusion is usually the best policy. Given the amount of pollution associated with childbirth, midwives are usually outcastes in rural areas.

Birth rites are conducted in order to ensure the safety of mother and child. It is hoped that the child will be a boy for sons are critically important to the family in all sorts of ways. The preference for boys stems back to *Vedic* times, the *Atharva Veda*, for example, containing charms and rituals to that effect. It seems it was customary in early times for midwives to place a girl on the ground after birth, but a boy would be held aloft in celebration.[21] Without a son, it would be difficult to secure a safe passage of a deceased father to the afterlife through the precise death rituals that ideally only a son should perform. Without those rituals, the deceased would remain forever a ghost, a *preta*. But the birth of a boy was believed by some to allow ancestors to progress from the realm of the ancestors to Heaven,[22] and so a married male had the duty of producing boys in order to fulfil his debt to his ancestors. Then, too, the line from ancestors through to descendants would disappear without male progeny since the focus is on patrilineal descent with only rare exceptions. Any male who wished to progress to the third of the four *āśramas* would have to have at least one male born to him. Boys, too, are an economic advantage in the home, being able to work and support the family. A girl, on the other hand, leaves her natal family for that of her husband's and incurs the expense of marriage and even a dowry, albeit that dowries today are supposed to be illegal. It is customary, then, for more *saṃskāras* to be performed for boys than for girls. Women who have sons are afforded an enhanced status in the family and in *Vedic* times the family hoped for the prescribed ten sons, though *smṛti* literature reduced that number to eight.[23] So serious is the case of a woman without sons that a man will consider a second marriage. And yet, Gloria Raheja cites Hindi proverbs that speak of the heartache of losing a daughter when she marries. One such proverb states: "One has to somehow endure a daughter's birth; there's crying when she's born and crying when she goes away."[24]

In *Vedic* times, girls were not so unwelcomed. They were educated in the same way as boys, had access to the *Vedas* and were in many cases regarded by their families with pride. They could even perform sacrifices without the presence of males.[25] There is no evidence of infanticide in the *Vedic* and classical texts and it is to modern times that we owe such horrendous practice. The title of a recent article in *The Hindu* claimed "India loses 3 million girls in infanticide".[26] There are many orphanages in India that are full of girls: they are abandoned because parents cannot afford to keep them – particularly given the dowries necessary for marriage. Infanticide in these figures includes abortion, something that was regarded scripturally as a dreadful crime. Despite the encouragement of contraception, the need for boys in the family has meant an increase in feticide. The amniocentesis test that was introduced in the nineteen seventies and later ultrasonography are used widely to ascertain the sex of a child and females are frequently aborted. Sex-selective abortions mean that the population is changing to a predominant ratio of males. The Preconception and Prenatal Diagnostic Techniques (PCPNDT) Act of 1994 made selective abortion illegal and in a further attempt to curb the practice, it was amended in 2002 to make medical professionals legally responsible should the test be carried out for gender selection. Nevertheless, the practice is rife. Indian law allows abortion under certain circumstances. If a woman's life is at risk or there is the possibility of grave risks to a woman's mental and/or physical health, for example in a case of rape or underage pregnancy, or if the foetus is likely to be severely handicapped, abortion is permitted up to the twelfth week. However, abortion can also occur if there is failed sterilization. Up to twelve weeks, only one medical practitioner is needed to make a decision on abortion, two after twelve weeks and up to twenty weeks. Abortions cannot legally be performed outside government hospitals nor can equipment such as ultrasound apparatus be sold to unregistered persons or premises.[27]

Despite these laws, abortions continue, both "legally" and illegally. Indeed, the gap between theoretical law and praxis is a very wide one in the vastness of the Indian nation. The case of a doctor in Delhi who was forced by her professional in-laws to go through ultrasound testing and who was then subjected to repeated harassment to abort the twin girls she was carrying was reported in a sensitive documentary on BBC television in Britain in June 2013. The woman's evidence seems remarkable, but is common:

> Once sex-determination was done it was very open that they wanted me to abort if not both the girls at least one. There was a lot of abuse, physical, mental. Nobody would talk to me and I wouldn't be given anything to eat: I was almost starved. My husband – we had a fight one day and he just pushed me down the staircase and it was about two flights of stairs. And once he pushed me down [I was] having this leaking and abdominal pain. So they said: "You're aborting now, good." They denied me medical aid.

The point here is that the family in question on both the bride and groom's side are professional, educated people. In the view of this woman, it is exactly the educated classes who are able to pay for ultrasounds and abortions:

> The sex ratios are lower in the educated class, not in the poor. But the poor they go on giving birth to daughters until they get a son. There are other forms of abuse; they neglect their daughters; they abandon them; there may be in some cases female infanticide. But still it is not to the extent which we are doing. There are people who have undergone six abortions, eight abortions for the heck of a son. Of course it's illegal, but it's not being implemented. It's a multi-billion industry. The authorities which go to the clinic, they are bribed off.[28]

In some areas of India, the desire for sons is particularly enhanced. Veena Oldenburg claims that in the Punjab it was imperial policies that, while designed to protect women, actually "created a more 'masculine' economy and deepened the preference for sons that fostered the overt or hidden murder of girls".[29] Such is the expense of a girl that Oldenburg describes infanticide as "preemptive dowry murder".[30]

To return to the events of birth, it is sometimes the case that the pregnant woman returns to her natal home for the occasion, though she may also remain in the home of her new family. Traditionally, a room is selected for the birth on an auspicious day and there are rites that dispel any harmful presences: the house needs to be protected at all times from harmful forces. As soon as the baby is born a number of rites may occur, the most popular being a little *ghī* and honey being placed on the baby's lips or tongue. These are to encourage strength and intelligence. Names of those who have lived long lives may be mentioned in order to encourage longevity.[31] The father whispers a secret name into the right ear of the baby, and sometimes the sacred sound *Oṃ*, while giving it the *ghī* and honey. The important horoscope of the baby will be drawn up at the time of the birth or, popularly, at the naming ceremony. The birthday of a child is sometimes calculated from the time of conception and sometimes from the day of birth. As I stated above, there is likely to be celebration if the outcome is a boy, but not for a girl, even in a rich family. However, for a while the mother, baby and family are all impure and no one would enter the house or eat any of the food from it. Women in some traditions may gather outside to chant songs when a boy is born.[32] It is not until the sixth or twelfth day after the birth that the purity of the family begins to be restored. The woman can bathe and change into new, fresh clothes and also eat solid food. The house has to be thoroughly cleaned and the cotton linen sent to the *dhobī,* the washerman. Having given birth, the woman is given a good deal of post-natal care and she may remain in bed for several days, being given foods that are felt to be restorative and healthy.

Saṃskāras for infancy and childhood

Six life-cycle rites are associated with the young baby and very early childhood. The first of these is name-giving, which is done at the home or in the local temple on the eleventh or twelfth day or before the child is a few months old and certainly before six months. It is an important rite in that it introduces the baby into Hinduism, and the name given is different to that whispered in the baby's ear at birth. Women who die in childbirth are believed to haunt new-born babies because they are jealous and so, in the early days after birth, great care is taken to protect the new baby. There are even some goddesses, like the *Mātṛkās*, who could cause harm to the baby.[33] In the *Gṛhya-sūtras* there were stipulations about how many syllables should be in a name and even the consonants and vowels in it – an even number of syllables was deemed correct for a boy and an uneven number for a girl. Manu stated that the class of the baby should be reflected in the name – divine for a *Brāhmin* and contemptuous for a *Śūdra*.[34] The *Purāṇas* also took up such rules on name-giving. Sometimes, children are given false unpleasant names in order to scare away harmful forces, the real name being given later when the child is weaned. Such a case may occur where there have been tragedies associated with the family.[35] The second and real name these days is one embodying a pleasant quality regardless of class, and may be decided astrologically. The second name may be kept secret for twice-born males until the rite of *upanayama*, when a boy comes of age. Such a practice is, again, to keep away harmful spirits who, not knowing the real name of the child, cannot harm it. On the other hand, McGee comments that the real name given at this time marks the child as an individual and begins its socialization into the surrounding world.[36] Name-giving is one of the most popular of the childhood *saṃskāras* and is important enough with higher classes to be presided over by a *Brāhmin* priest, though *Brāhmins* are not essential for the ceremony.

The next childhood *saṃskāra* is the baby's first outing – a time when all sorts of inimical forces are feared and so the rite has its basis in superstitions. As the mother and the household become pure, there is no longer a fear of pollution and the parents and family can enjoy a more festive celebration of the birth. The important part of this first outing of the baby is its first vision of the sun with its life-giving forces that is part of the ritual. However, fear of harmful forces may cause the parents to delay this first outing for some time. This fear is sufficient for some to make their babies look ugly and flawed. Babb found in his field research in Madhya Pradesh that lamp black (*kājal*), was applied around a baby's eyes on its first outing, along with black spots on the body and amulets containing protective herbs tied on with black cord.[37] Again, it is the "glance" of spirits of those who have died in childbirth who wish to take the lives of beautiful babies that is particularly feared. Fuller comments: "The evil eye – commonly known as *najar* in north India and *dishti* in the south – is treated as a widespread menace throughout India, and the harm is caused, often unconsciously, by the gaze of envious people. All kinds of trouble can be brought by the evil eye, and any display of good health, splendour, or success is likely to attract it."[38] Such fear is not by any means remote superstition but real, pervasive fear that informs all aspects of life.

When the child is weaned onto solid food at about six months old, this is another occasion for a *saṃskāra*, though the rite may be purely symbolic and the baby weaned much later. The food given is likely to be vegetarian, though at one time it was meat, fish and rice. Rice mixed with curds, honey and *ghī* is fed to the baby accompanied with extracts from the *Vedas*. It is another festive occasion, with food for the family and guests and gifts for the child. Chaudhuri noted that in his experience, the child is given his second and real name at this ceremony, but it is to be kept secret until coming of age.[39] The boy's first hair cut is another *saṃskāra* carried out in the first year or as late as the sixth or seventh year. Again, the rite is rooted in superstition for, once cut, it was believed possible that evil forces could work magic on it and so the cut hair is mixed with cow dung and then buried in a cow stall, or rolled in dough and cast into a river. Cutting the hair is done to promote good health and a long life, rather like a tree is pruned.[40] It is a *saṃskāra* that gradually took place in the temple as well as the home. The hair was shaved off but retaining the top hair and this was to become an important symbol of a twice-born Hindu at the ceremony. Babb notes the popularity of the rite, sufficiently important for it to be timed with festival occasions or one of the religious fairs that takes place at the full moon in January–February.[41] When performed early enough in the child's life, the ceremony finally sees the end of any pollution associated with childbirth.

Two more *saṃskāras* occur in the life of the child. The first of these is ear-piercing, which is of later origin than the other childhood *saṃskāras*.[42] In its early days it was performed when the child was very young but later came to be carried out, if at all, at the same time as the *upanayama* ceremony for boys, though ear-piercing was applicable to both boys and girls, the latter undertaking it primarily for ornamental reasons. If the rite takes place for *Brāhmins* today, it is done by a qualified practitioner. It was probably not without its dangers and infections, and accompanying religious rites may have been incorporated for protection. Learning of the Sanskrit alphabet is the final *saṃskāra* of childhood. This, too, was a later addition to the original ones.[43] It was an introduction to reading and writing of the sacred language that prepared a boy for his proper introduction to study at his *upanayama*. It occurred at what we might consider primary-school age, between about four and seven years old. It is carried out on an auspicious day during the light half of the year. In the contemporary world it may be simply more pragmatic to celebrate the child's first day at school.

Only four *saṃskāras* remain and, thus, the bulk of them are concerned with childhood. It seems to me that with few exceptions, these childhood *saṃskāras* are rooted in popular tradition and, frequently, superstition. I do not think that we can discount this important aspect of the propitiation of good forces and the attempt to overcome the adverse forces that are believed to surround life. These are not life-cycle rites that are centred on transformation and change from one stage to another: rather, they are rites that are believed to protect and guard against evil at appropriate times in the life of a child. Many of these rites, however, have become redundant in contemporary India for all but the most pious of *Brāhmins*. One further point is, I think, important to make and that is that ceremonies for girls were not considered necessary. Discrimination against the female gender begins before the child has left the womb and is maintained during the childhood years. It is only the boy, too, that will undergo the initiation into Hinduism, *upanayana*, which is the main passage from childhood to adolescence and manhood.

Upanayana

I have dealt with some aspects of *upanayana* in chapter 4 in the context of the four stages of life, *āśrama-dharma*, including the origins of the rite and the kind of life that existed for the boy after the ceremony. Here, in this chapter, there are additional issues that I want to raise. *Upanayana* inaugurated the first of the four stages of life and along with the second, marriage, constitute the two most important of the *saṃskāras*. The importance of *upanayana* and its massive implications for a boy is neatly put by Pandey:

> Here we find that the conception of race was cultural, and it was on the basis of cultural fitness that one could seek admission into, and claim the full rights and privileges of, the community. Without the Upanayana none could call himself a twice-born. One who would not undergo the Saṃskāra was excommunicated and debarred from all the privileges of the race. The initiation was a passport to the literary treasures of the Hindus. It was also a means of communion with the society, because without it none could marry an Aryan girl.[44]

With this *saṃskāra* we find a legitimate use of the ideas of change and transformation as the key aspects of the rite of passage, as Pandey's words pertinently show. *Upanayana* means something like "drawing near to", "initiation into" in the sense of a student drawing near to the teacher, but also there is a strong sense of a rebirth[45] into a different life, the orthodox Hindu life. The *upanayana saṃskāra*, therefore, made one *dvija*, "twice-born", as opposed to *Śūdras* and those outside the caste system, who were *advija*. Only *Brāhmins*, *Kṣatriyas* and *Vaiśyas* could become *dvija*, though in contemporary India the *saṃskāra* tends to be confined to *Brāhmins* and wealthy Hindus. To be twice-born – the first at one's natural birth and the second at *upanayana* – is to become an elite member of Hindu society and have a right to education. It was essentially an orthodox rite that maintained *dharmic* societal patterns of privileged living. Pandey made this clear: "The underlying purpose was to enlist all the possible young men of the community and stamp them with the peculiar culture of the race."[46]

Before the ceremony, the boy would have had a certain amount of freedom, though I would think it already possible that some degrees of separation from lower castes might already be in place in view of the stringent aspects of purity and impurity in the contexts of daily living: class separation must already have occurred to a certain extent, particularly in contemporary times when the rite is often performed just a few days before marriage. But for the young boy in the past, rebirth meant responsibility and the beginnings of adulthood as well as education in the societal *dharmas* that would preclude his contact with others, curtail his eating habits, ensure his distance from women and introduce his elite education in learning *Vedic* chants and texts, including the important *Gāyatrī-Mantra* and the rites and methods of sacrifice – all of which differentiated him from the uneducated, *advija* individual.

All these factors exclude females, though this was not the case in ancient India when girls were educated in exactly the same way as boys and also went through the *upanayana* ceremony: that was the case until the beginning of the first millennium CE. By the ninth century the education of girls was restricted to rich and royal families, and to the courtesan dancing girls attached to temples.[47] While before this time it was regarded essential for a girl to be well-educated in the *Vedas*, such education gradually became rare for females. In time, with the lowering of the marriage age for girls to the extent that there was no space for education, together with the insistence on only males being able to perform funeral rites for their fathers, female education diminished into non-existence. The idea gradually gained ground that girls were a liability rather than a blessing. But for boys, the *upanayana saṃskāra* became compulsory as a means to ensure cultural advance for the male and for society, so sanctifying the boy and separating him as a cultured and pure being from inferior and impure castes. But education of girls declined over the centuries to the point that, by the time of British rule in India, it had practically disappeared.[48] Since only dancing girls were literate and educated, it was believed that education for females was morally dangerous.[49]

The education of the adolescent boy under the supervision of the teacher was very stringent according to the texts and it is doubtful whether all but few took them as seriously as tradition prescribed. Certainly, it was probably only *Brāhmins* who wished to train as priests that took such study seriously. *Kṣatriyas* were more interested in administration and martial interests, whereas *Vaiśyas* had little interest in such elite training and tended to pursue the family trades. "Twice-born", then, became a term applicable in the main only to *Brāhmins*, and the other two classes that should have been twice-born lost status to the extent that distinctions between them became blurred. The life of the *brahmacārin* covered every dimension of life from social interaction to spiritual evolution, what to wear, eat and how to behave, as well as being conversant in the many *Vedic* sciences that had developed: it was not an easy regime and, if done properly, needed a full twelve years to accomplish, which is why it was started at an earlier age for *Brāhmins*, a little later for *Kṣatriyas* and later still for *Vaiśyas*. However, in the past it fell to a few *Brāhmin* boys to undertake the rite and the full prescribed education, and they sometimes began study at the age of five.

I have dealt with aspects of the ceremony itself in chapter 4. Suffice it to say here that the rite became more complex as time went by until it became codified in more elaborate form with distinctive regulations for materials used and the appropriate ages to begin and end for each of the classes. Interestingly, the mother and the child ate together before the ceremony, a practice that has been retained today. Once education was over, the boy would eat with the men and not the women and his closeness to his mother would be distanced. The rite has to include the sacred fire, as all important rites in Hinduism, and purification through bathing. The head is also shaved, perhaps for the first time at the rite, coalescing the two *saṃskāras* of tonsure and *upanayana*. After bathing the boy has a loin cloth for his lower body, a triple-cord girdle tied around his waist and an antelope skin around his shoulders. Then he is given the important sacred thread, *yajñopavīta*. Notably, this thread was unknown to the *Gṛhya-sūtras*;[50] it was later texts that stipulated how it should be made, with different materials and different colours for each of the classes, though customs vary considerably. Full of symbolism, the thread is knotted to represent one's ancestors, has three threads, each one having three strands – the three representing the three *guṇas*, as well as the three debts of the twice-born male to the ancient seers, to ancestors and to gods. And the knot that ties the whole thread symbolizes Brahmā, Viṣṇu and Śiva.[51] The thread is worn over the left shoulder and under the right arm, but is changed to the right or simply placed around the neck for some other ceremonies.[52] The sacred thread is worn day and night and a new one has to be put on before the old one is removed: thus, the male is never without it. It became associated with *Brāhmins* and less so with the other twice-born classes.

The boy's education into *Vedic* texts begins during the rite when he learns the *Gāyatrī-Mantra* that he will recite daily for the rest of his life. At the ceremony, it is whispered into the initiate's right ear by his intended *guru*. Once the ceremony is over and the boy begins his induction and education into Hindu life, life should be taken very seriously and the class and caste taboos maintained. Many, however, prefer a lax approach. Most *Brāhmins*, for example, maintain a stipulated vegetarian diet, whereas *Kṣatriyas* do not. The status of the sacred thread is still maintained on the one hand by the serious *Brāhmins* who wear it, but aspiring lower classes have now adopted it also.[53] The Hindu Ārya Samāj reform movement, founded in the late nineteenth century, has adopted the sacred thread ceremony for *all* classes, including outcastes and women. A ritual known as *śuddhi* invests the thread and includes the *Gāyatrī-Mantra* and other *Vedic* chants.

In contemporary India, few would want to spend many years in stringent assiduous study and the *upanayana* ceremony has become for some an introduction to state secondary education. For others, it is delayed right up to a few days before marriage. The boy does not go away from home to study with a *guru* but only makes a symbolic gesture of doing so, pretending to journey to the sacred city of Vārāṇasī for instruction but being persuaded not to go by his family. Equally symbolically, he makes a semblance of begging his food by carrying a begging bowl. But it is an occasion of festivity and gifts for the boy or, in many cases given its deferral until just before marriage, to the young man. In view of such changes, it seems to me that the rite is no longer the change and transformation that some sources would have us believe. It certainly was so in the past, but could not be said to be so in a day and age when it has become a formality prior to marriage. Many of the aspects of the traditional *saṃskāra* are retained – shaving, bathing, the fire altar, *Vedic mantras*, the *Gāyatrī-Mantra* and the sacred thread would all be essential aspects. Baker describes a simple ceremony in Tamil Nāḍu in which boys of ten underwent *upanayana* in which, following *pūjā*, a local *paṇḍit* came to invest the boy with a sacred thread, but the ensuing stringent education was dropped. In a few cases, however, a boy may have some lessons in *Vedic* texts outside of school hours, but even *Brāhmins* of a high caste are hardly likely to undertake the long period of study necessary for the present-day financially precarious life of a priest.

Traditionally, there have been no such rites for girls and, as noted above, it was not considered necessary in the past for them to be educated. However, puberty rites for girls, which have no basis in orthodox praxis, are gaining ground in popular practices. The *ṛtu kāla* ceremony celebrates the girl's first menses in the same way that some celebrate the first time a boy shaves with the *keśānta kāla* rite. Boys and girls here will be given gifts – the girl her first *sari* and the boy his first razor. New clothes and jewellery will also be given.[54] Sarah Caldwell gives a fascinating description of the rite to celebrate first menses in Kerala:

> The symbolism of the rite celebrates the fertility of the young girl, likening her to the budding coconut and the ripening paddy, the mainstays of Kerala diet. The tender young buds of the coconut tree, lovely and promising as the breasts of a young virgin girl, are placed before her in a large measure of raw paddy rice, and she is presented with the auspicious items given to a bride. But menstruation, while signalling the potential for fertility and birth, also implies a danger: the intense emotions of sexual

desire believed to accompany physical maturity may lead the girl to disaster if they are not restrained and controlled until her marriage.[55]

The juxtaposition of celebration and danger here is particularly interesting in that it informs so many of the attitudes to women that I shall examine in chapter 10. Vijaya Nagarajan describes a Tamil custom by which women create a *kolam* outside their front doors to announce publicly that a girl has her first period.[56] The *kolam* is an intricate design constructed in ground rice flour and is particularly evident on special occasions, but is also used to make a public statement that a house is auspicious or, if it is absent, inauspicious.[57]

The *upanayana saṃskāra* is, then, not what it used to be, which in some ways detracts from the pejorative elitism that it once had. Indeed, it has become universal for those who wish to undertake it, regardless of caste. Women are excluded from it but since men no longer regard it in the same traditional way of the past, a woman need have no inclination to fight for inclusion. In a wry remark, Altekar wrote: "She looks with a contemptuous smile on a dogma, which would declare that she is ineligible for spiritual salvation because of her sex. *Upanayana* has become a meaningless formality even in the case of boys; women naturally feel that they have nothing to gain by becoming re-eligible for it."[58]

At the end of the period of study, another *saṃskāra* marked the transition to adulthood just prior to marriage. The student had lived a life of austerity and ends it by having his beard shaved. If he had started his student life at five, then, with twelve years of study behind him, he would be ready for this last *saṃskāra* of his unmarried life at the age of sixteen. The rite marked the point when the student returned to the home of his parents. He became a *snātaka*, "one who has bathed", and a *vidyā-snātaka*, "one who has bathed in knowledge". But it is no longer practised, or at most may be incorporated in the limited *upanayana*. Part of the rite was the payment of the teacher by the student, and in the past that could be anything from an umbrella to a cow. The shaving of the beard, bathing, dressing in fine new clothes marked the transition to what would become the householder stage of life in a marriage that came soon. Only remnants of the rite remain today.

Marriage: *Vivāha*

While I am not of the view that the *saṃskāras* examined so far are predominantly to do with change and transformation in contemporary Hinduism, marriage is certainly so and for a woman represents the most dramatic change of her whole life. Indeed, marriage is the most important of all the *saṃskāras* for the status of marriage is the foundation of religious tradition and praxis and of the means for a male to fulfil his three debts to ancient seers who formulated the religious tradition and *dharma*, to his ancestors, by having male heirs, and to the gods. Domestic rituals could not be undertaken by an unmarried man and there is in the marriage union a profound religious and sacramental element. Marriage begins a whole new life for a couple who have an example of perfection in the role models of Rāma and Sītā in the epic, the *Rāmāyaṇa*, as to how that life should be shaped. Marriage, *vivāha*, is the fifteenth life-cycle rite, the only one remaining being death.

There is considerable variation in marriage customs, even in the same caste, and the

Gṛhya-sūtras themselves give a variety of formats, particularly for the different classes, but there is a basic framework on which most texts agree, leaving the colourful details to custom, family and local traditions. But it is a special time in all cases, with the bride and bridegroom treated as if they were Rāma and Sītā or Viṣṇu and Lakṣmī; they are deities during the proceedings. There are usually many customs leading up to the actual ceremony and these will be particularly varied in nature, depending on family tradition. Once the wedding arrangements have been agreed, a betrothal ritual takes place either just before the wedding or a long time before. The bride and groom may not actually have met each other and may not do so until the day of their wedding. The emphasis is not on the couple itself, but on the new relationship that will come into being with two respective families. Marriage between two families may be mutually beneficial in status or the status of one side may be weakened or strengthened as a result. This kind of status balance will need to be compensated for in the marriage arrangements. Since the lineage of a family is considered to derive only through males, the choice of a suitable woman to enhance or maintain the line is essential: the purity of the line is an important consideration. Marriages between two families are times of consolidating cultural and familial identity as well as reinforcing religious custom and ritual. For the man who takes a wife, his status is very much enhanced: he enters on the second of the four *āśramas*, the householder stage, which is arguably the most important of the four stages of life. But he is described as "half a man" for religious purposes of domestic ritual, the other half being his wife, who is the means by which he can legitimately perform domestic religious rites. Once he produces male heirs, he is believed to release ancestors to Heaven and his own passage to a safe afterlife is secured by the son or sons that he bears. He becomes fully a man.

These are considerations that do not affect the woman in a marriage. For her, the transformations are massive. She acquires a little status as a married woman but until she bears a son she has no status at all in her new home. She will have to wait until she is much older, has borne her children, sees new young brides coming into the familial home, is post-menopausal and is the oldest woman in the home: only then will she have some autonomy. Such a situation obtains widely in the North of India in comparison to elsewhere.[59] The woman is transferred at marriage to a completely new family and placed in a situation that is irreversible and in which she has no independence. Indeed, independence of women is regarded as dangerous and she is, therefore, to be the subject of control. Marriage is the woman's *upanayana*, and with it comes defined duties of a sacrament with the purpose of providing male offspring and the means by which religious rites to the gods could be properly performed.

The ideal marriage is called a *Brāhma* marriage – one appropriate for *Brāhmins* – in which the girl is given as a gift by her father to a very suitable man without any exchange of gifts or money, except that the father of the bride would give his daughter some items of jewellery to take with her. Mutual respect of two families and honour between them are the key aspects of such a marriage.[60] The *Brāhma* marriage obtains today, but so does exchange of bride-price and dowry, though illegal. I shall return to these last issues below in more detail since they are practised widely. Suffice it to say here, that giving the woman away freely is the ideal. So-called love-marriages where a man and a woman themselves decide to marry are not the norm. Nevertheless, it may well occur that a couple meets at college or university and the parents agree to the match providing caste and other considerations are compatible. It is not possible for a couple to live together without severe consequences.

In the distant past, it was possible for women to choose their own husbands and this was certainly exemplified in the epics. Polygamy is evident in the tales of the epics, and there was also evidence of polyandry, that is to say when one woman married several brothers. Draupadī in the *Mahābhārata*, for example, married the five Pāṇḍava brothers. Such was the emphasis on having sons that women who were barren or had only girls could find their husbands taking another wife – or even more if no sons were produced. Polygamy and polyandry are very rarely practised today,[61] but, surprisingly, it was not until the mid-twentieth century in the Hindu Marriage Act of 1955 that polygamy became illegal. *Vedic* texts prove that women had a vastly better experience of independence in ancient India. Girls were not married until they were about fifteen, sixteen or even later and had had an education. They could probably select their own partners, but by the time of the *Dharma-śāstras* such marriages were frowned on. There is no evidence of the custom of dowries in the *Vedic* period but the evidence we have suggests that the educated and independent woman was from the higher classes, whereas the rest were nothing but chattels. But even a queen was the property of her husband if the evidence of Yudhiṣṭhira's gambling away his kingdom and his queen is anything to go by in the *Mahābhārata*.

In the *Manu-smṛti* we find Manu's views of marriage to be fairly tolerant. The father should give his daughter to a handsome and high-class man of the same caste, though this could be before she is of marriageable age, and if such a suitable husband could not be found, then according to Manu, it would be better for the girl to remain in her father's home: he was not averse to women remaining unmarried. Manu even allowed a woman to choose her own husband at a time from three years after the start of menses.[62] But Manu had extensive views on how to choose a bride, even down to avoiding a girl if her name happened to be that of a constellation, a tree, river, bird, snake, mountain, and the like, or if she was a redhead and had a hairy body![63] And yet, the well-known statement of Manu regarding women's dependence is as evident in praxis today as it was meant to be in the past: "Her father guards her in childhood, her husband guards her in youth, and her sons guard her in old age. A woman is not fit for independence."[64] Manu found mixed-class marriages abhorrent, the worst being a *Brāhmin* woman to a *Śūdra* male.

Historically, marriage is obligatory for girls. Being barred from the third and fourth ascetic *āśramas*, and having no *upanayana*, their only real transformative life-cycle rite was marriage; it was their obligatory *upanayana*, and by about the third century BCE all girls were expected to marry. From about the same time, the marriage age for girls began to lower, a process that continued for several centuries. It was a fashion that had an immediate effect on the education of girls, and on their literacy. The *smṛti* writers from 500–1000 CE deduced that puberty of a girl took place at the age of ten and that it would be prudent for them to marry before this time. As the threshold for marriage reduced from puberty to pre-puberty, girls were married at the age of nine or ten. This came about because of the fear of sexuality that was concomitant with menses and it was believed that it would be safer to protect a girl's chastity by pre-puberty marriage. *Kṣatriya* families were perhaps the exception, for they were slower to adopt the lower age range, perhaps because, as warriors, they were well aware how young girls could easily become widows,[65] but *Brāhmin* families set the trend of girls being married while they were still children. There was another distinct disadvantage for females, too, for their inferiority of age in a relationship gave them an equally inferior psychological status to their husbands. Ideally, it was thought that a male should marry at twenty four and a girl at eight. There could be little positive dialogue and relationship between them and that assisted the deterioration of the status of women over the centuries. Then, too, widowers could marry pre-puberty girls, but girls could never remarry. On the basis that marriage was the *upanayana* for girls, given that boys underwent the rite sometimes at five, it was felt that girls could be married at five, too. There is even evidence of marriages being provisionally arranged *before* a child was born.[66]

By the time of British rule in India, the average age for a girl to be married was eight or nine, and though it rose slightly in following years, pre-puberty marriage was still the norm. Attempts to raise the age of female marriage to fourteen in the early twentieth century faced considerable opposition from orthodox quarters, but raising the age of a girl's marriage is, today, believed to be an economic advantage, as we shall see. In 1955, the legal marriage age was raised to eighteen. It is still considered rather degrading if a woman is well into her twenties before marriage. The national average age of marriage for girls is up from 18.3 in 2001 to 20.6 in 2008 but, despite the law on marriage age, a National Family Health Survey reported that more than fifty per cent of women were married before eighteen and there are still cases of child marriage despite the Prohibition of Child Marriage Act of 2006.[67] However, with the difficulty of the registration of marriages in a country like India, the enormity of customs and the level of illiteracy, it is impossible, in practice, to implement the Act: there is an immense gap between theoretical law and actual praxis. A report by the Asian Human Rights Commission suggests that child marriage "is notably STILL a problem in India, with a substantially large number of the population being married under the legal age of consent".[68] These issues are important in the context of how women are viewed in the India of today. Centuries and centuries of devaluing and manipulating half of the humanity of India has informed present practice, as will be seen further in chapter 10.

Hindu marriages are mostly arranged and the arrangement has to take notice of caste, horoscope, family backgrounds, education, finance, health and appearance. As was noted above, the couple may not actually meet before the wedding but if they do, it will be in carefully supervised meetings. It is usually the girl's parents that search for an appropriate husband in the higher castes, but amongst lower castes it is the groom's family that searches for the bride, though customs vary widely. Today, it is an advantage for a girl to be educated and so higher education qualifications are an additional asset in that they make her more attractive on the one hand and allow her an education to a high standard on the other. A working woman, these days, is an economic advantage in her husband's family. Marriages are fairly strictly caste bound. If a man marries a woman of a lower caste, it is at least "in the grain", or *anuloma* (literally "with the hair") and is reasonably acceptable though not favourable. If, on the other hand, a higher-caste woman marries a lower-caste man, that is very much against the grain, or *pratiloma* (literally "against the hair"). The purity of the offspring is the issue involved here, as well as the maintenance of caste status. A disgraced marriage brings disgrace to the whole family.

Marriage with near relatives is taboo: near relatives constitute the *gotra*, an old word originally meaning "cowshed" or "a herd of cows",[69] today meaning "clan", a clan that is believed to be linked by the same ancestor. Marriage cannot take place between two people of the same *gotra*: even though such marriages are not illegal in India, tradition deems it wrong. *Brāhmins* were believed to be descendants of ancient seers who gave their names to *gotras*, so the origin of the clans is likely to have been in the *Brāhmin* class, from where it spread to other classes in time.[70] A *gotra* is not a caste, and there may be a number of castes in the same *gotra*, so whereas most will marry into the same caste, they do not marry anyone of the same *gotra*. In southern India, unlike the North, however, cross-cousin marriage is permitted. Altekar believed that inter-caste marriage disappeared by the ninth century CE because the cultural gap between classes had become so great that there could be no harmonious marriage between them.[71] Only *Brāhmins* continued to follow the *saṃskāras* and, in the main, retain vegetarian practice. *Kṣatriyas* and *Vaiśyas* on the other hand, while gradually abandoning the *saṃskāras* and *Vedic* praxis, became distinctly non-*Brāhmin* and so were no longer twice-born. Since *Brāhmins* wanted to keep their purity, they became strictly endogamous, and that became a practice that was adopted in time by all castes. Such is the effect of inter-caste on the whole family and caste community that the *Hindustan Times* reported a recent case where a violent mob from the landowning *Ror* caste in Pabwana village in North India ransacked the houses and shops of the *Dalit* community there because one of their *Ror* women had eloped and married a *Dalit* man of the locality. Caste rules had been broken, and the *Rors*, though not especially high caste, took revenge for the insult to their caste identity, destroying the water tanks of the *Dalits* in their attack.[72]

Inter-caste marriage would be a marriage of two different family traditions and cultures and would be ostracized as such but in modern Indian urban settings it is now by no means unknown, despite the cross-cultural differences. The cultural differences of mixed-faith or mixed-caste marriages are considerable. Research undertaken by Mattison Mines in Chennai, the capital of Tamil Nāḍu in South India suggests that mixed-faith marriage is far more common in the urban setting amongst upper-middle class elites, and inter-caste marriage has increased.[73] This may be especially so for wealthy families whose children have experienced more independent living in university or college education. But, according to Mines' research, there are problems of what he calls "psychological self-amputation" for children of inter-faith marriages given the bifurcation of their religious identity.[74] These offspring themselves are more likely to engage in inter-faith marriages, so increasing the instances of such unions. Arunima Mazumbar writes in *The Times of India* of a couple about to be wed. Both are *Brāhmins* but of different castes and from different parts of India, the man from Bengal and the woman from Tamil. The North and South and caste divisions mean that the northern Bengali family will eat fish and meat, whereas the Tamil family are vegans. The disparities are such that some couples have to have a marriage and relationship counsellor to give advice on the complete change of customs for a girl entering a different family tradition. Mark Juergensmeyer notes how difficult it is living and working in a modern urban setting where castes mix together, but invitations to weddings are an embarrassment when the traditional do not want contact with lower castes or, for that matter, the lower castes or former "untouchables" who have become economically advanced do not want a reminder of their previous status.[75] Then, too, food restictions are important at weddings, and it is down to the bride's family to ensure that preparations match the expectations of the groom's family.

Pandey was of the view that the careful choice of a partner for bride or groom was "primarily eugenic", in that the best possible progeny would be produced.[76] Considerations of dowry and bride price, while illegal, play a considerable role in the world of today. Manu may not have liked redheads, but today generally the darker the skin the less favourable the possible partner, probably reflecting the old Āryan/Dravidian divide: looks generally *do* matter. Advertisements for brides and grooms are now frequent in newspapers, and will often ask for a beautiful girl and a handsome boy. The salary of a prospective groom would be an important consideration. But the match is as much of two families as of two individuals. However, despite traditional arranged marriages, the status and relative culture of a family rather than caste are becoming increasingly important amongst middle classes.[77]

Dowries

Dowries, the financial or "valuable security", as the Indian legal system puts it, are now against the law in India and have been since the Dowry Prohibition Act of 1961: it is illegal to ask for a dowry, to pay dowry, or to accept it, and those doing so face at least five years imprisonment and a hefty fine. However, as long as no demand is made, the law does not apply to gifts given to the bride or groom by the bride's family. Such gifts should be listed and should be customary and should not be excessively beyond the financial means of the giver. In 1983 and 1986 legislation to prevent dowry deaths – suspicious injury or cruelty to a wife who dies within seven years of her marriage – was passed and made any harassment and coercion for post-marriage dowry demands illegal. It was an attempt to protect women, though subsequent false harassment claims of women are not by any means unknown. The Domestic Violence Act of 2005–6 also made it illegal to coerce a person by demanding dowry. According to Oldenburg, in the latter half of the nineteenth century, dowry was more legitimately the possession of the bride, her insurance, if you like, but not something demanded by the groom's family. It was a safety net but one, Oldenburg graphically states, that became "twisted into a deadly noose".[78] The British blamed the misuse of dowries on the uncivilized Hindu culture itself. But Oldenburg thinks the economic manipulations of the British were more the culprit.[79] One point about which Oldenburg is clear is that there is a firm consensus of views in India "that the custom of dowry has a causal relationship to prejudice against women".[80] Regardless of the law, dowries are perpetually paid by a bride's family. It is not the groom that asks for dowry but the groom's family, and that means that there are a number of people to be satisfied. The "valuable security" mentioned in the law means movable property like clothing, jewellery, money, items for the home, even land and cattle in rural areas. And despite the Dowry Prohibition Act, dowry deaths became "increasingly commonplace" during the latter half of the twentieth century.[81] Originally a *Kṣatriya* practice indicative of high status, dowry is now regarded widely as a necessary practice to indicate status and pride amongst Hindus.

In contemporary India, women can still find themselves ill-treated and killed if dowry demands are not continued to be met after the marriage or if the dowry fails to live up to expectations. In the sensitive documentary on BBC television mentioned earlier in the context of ultrasounds and abortion, the same professional woman in Delhi related how her husband and in-laws made excessive demands on her only three days after her marriage: "They wanted a car; they wanted a flat; they wanted more jewellery for their family members." As noted earlier, the in-laws were not uneducated by any means: indeed, they were highly-educated, highly-qualified medics. The same programme shows the "bonanza" of gifts given by a bride's family – bed, sofa, dressing table, LCD TV and a whole host of other items.[82] This in fact, is the norm and the differentiation between "dowry" and "wedding gifts" is not too difficult to make given that the gifts are only one way – bride's family to groom's. The cost of a dowry can be financially crippling: Wadley comments that a dowry is "often equivalent to the household's yearly income, an enormous sum for both the poor and the not-so-poor peasant farmer".[83] Even in the best of marriages, when no dowry is asked for, the girl is expected to be given costly jewellery and other gifts. Nicholas found this kind of marriage to be the norm in his study of marriages in Bengali families. At the same time, he found that the well-educated of the highest castes regard it as undignified to give lavish dowries, especially given the merits of their daughters.[84] But a good husband with a good salary can demand a fair-sized dowry in the marriage market and it was this factor that saw the hike in dowry costs over the last century. Conversely, a girl with a very good education and a good professional job would already be a financial asset to her in-laws and so dowry would not be set so high.

The prohibition of dowries did not prevent dowry deaths when wives whose fathers could no longer deliver extortionate payments after the marriage of a daughter: the "accident" in the kitchen when a wife is burnt with kerosene is still not unknown. In 2011, there were 8618 dowry deaths.[85] Increasing prosperity in India seems to have caused a rise in dowry demands as a means to become richer, and where women are burned in dowry deaths, court cases are so slow even for the simplest of cases that justice hardly occurs.[86] The husband is then able to remarry and claim another dowry. Dowry considerations add to the painstaking arrangements that occur before a marriage can take place. In addition to the religious reasons for having boys, the financial strain of having girls is so great that girls can add nothing to the economy of the home; they only take from it. Again, discrimination against women begins before they are born.

Bride price

Amongst the lower castes, bride price, though also illegal, is the opposite of dowry with the father of the bride receiving a price for her. The groom or his family agree to pay the bride's family for the girl. It may be paid in money or in goods and can be quite substantial. Sudeshna Maitra is of the view that women in some areas are able to work and provide economic help to the groom's family: in this case she is valuable. Additionally, brides may be scarce in a region, making them a valuable commodity.[87] Bride price is a custom that hails back to ancient times, being known as Āsura, and was castigated by all Hindu scripture, but it still obtains amongst the lower castes: Babb found it the norm in his field research in rural Madhya Pradesh.[88] Like dowry, bride price is neatly concealed under the notion of gifts. By and large, so-called gifts given to women at their marriage from their fathers should be theirs to keep, their "insurance" for the future, but are in fact appropriated by their husbands' familes. These gifts are what are known as *strī-dhana*. *Strī-dhana* could be property, though it is more likely now to be classed as wedding gifts, but a wife will hardly be in a position to retain them in the home of her in-laws. Her so-called gifts, her *strī-dhana*, are not really hers in the eyes of her in-laws and are given away to her husband's sisters, or are passed on at other celebratory occasions,[89] though *strī-dhana* also includes gifts to the bride from the groom's family. Effectively, the hierarchy of the conjugal home means that a mother-in-law and the males of the family leave a new wife with little that can be called her own even though *strī-dhana* is traditionally the bride's portion of the wealth of the natal home.

The ceremony

During the four months of the rainy season, Viṣṇu is believed to sleep on his great serpent Śeṣa and since he absent, the whole period is regarded as inauspicious. It would be imprudent to embark on any venture, including marriage. The nights are longer, the sun is in the southern hemisphere, and the days are cooler. However, once Viṣṇu wakes from his sleep in October/November, the beginning of the hot season, his protection of the cosmos is resumed and on the twelfth day he marries the goddess of the earth, represented by the *tulasī* plant. *Tulasī Vivāha* begins the marriage season, a season, Babb thinks, that coincided with a lull in agricultural work.[90] There are vast regional differences in the marriage ceremony, and I can only point here to some common factors. While marriage is obligatory for twice-born Hindus and its ceremonies are codified in various texts, local custom and family tradition have produced considerable variance. But marriage is essentially a religious rite, a solemn sacrament and is therefore formally complex. Werner Menski makes the following pertinent comment in the light of such diversity: "Far from being a uniform, static tradition, this is a complex conglomerate of sanskritic and local/caste customary practices that show quite considerable flexibility, in view of the particular circumstances of the spouses and their families, with virtually no interference from the state law."[91]

The bride and groom, treated like deities, are highly auspicious, though the bride, especially, is vulnerable to malevolent forces and there are multiple rites that are designed to ward off such evil forces. Susan Wadley, in fact, records the custom of circling coins or bowls of grain over the couple's heads in order to take away any inauspiciousness. The coins or grain are then passed to a lower-caste person. This last is deemed able to accept the inauspiciousness given that he or she already has considerable impurity.[92] Generally, the bride, as a future wife and the mother of sons, is the epitome of well-being, prosperity, success and happiness during her wedding.[93] Expressive of the divine nature of the couple is their anointing in the ceremony in the same way as deities are, with oil and turmeric, though such anointing may have a variety of purposes.[94] Deities, especially Gaṇeśa the god of good fortune, will feature in the proceedings. The wedding is conducted within a specially erected canopy, a *maṇḍap* or *maṇḍva*, which acts as a temple for the occasion. It is set up at the home of the bride, for it is the bride's family that will meet the expenses of the wedding. Before the ceremony, the bride is ritually bathed and the hands and feet are decorated with henna dye, making very attractive and long-lasting *mehndi* patterns. For the wedding, the bride will wear a red (or similar) sari, red being a highly auspicious colour and one associated with the Goddess of Good Fortune, Lakṣmī. She will also wear an immense amount of traditional jewellery, particularly on the head and face. It is traditional, too, for the bride to look particularly sad at her wedding and she is usually helped by her sisters as she walks to take her place under the canopy with her husband to be.

The ceremony involves the bride being given away not just to the groom but given away from her familiar natal home to the conjugal family into which she is venturing. It is that conjugal home that will influence the rest of her life and to which she will be expected to adapt in every way. It is a physical transformation as much as a psychological one, and is often traumatic. Whatever her life may be like in her new home, the new bride has to enjoy or endure silently. Being "given away" is a very literal transaction, for the bride is a gift to the conjugal family and cannot be taken back. The expense of the giving away of a daughter is colossal – the ceremonies are extensive and the dowry, as we have seen, usually excessive, too, reflecting the immense importance of the occasion as a sacred *saṃskāra*. In *Vedic* times and subsequently, the wife was expected to be a *pati-vratā*, one who lived for her husband's happiness; the scriptures speak highly of such a wife. Religiously, a man or a woman are an incomplete half when single, becoming the necessary and complementary whole once married. Only then, in the past, could certain religious household rites be carried out and the second *āśrama* of the twice-born Hindu, arguably the most important, be entered on.

The ritual of the ceremony, as I said above, varies enormously. At some, a *Brāhmin* may not even be present, since that would be added expense, but twice-born Hindus would be very likely to engage the services of a priest to oversee proceedings. Some of the common components of the ceremony are as follows, though none is actually necessary and the order will vary:

- **The groom's departure** with his family for the bride's home is usually accompanied with much festivity. The party may well be met before arrival and accompanied the remainder of the way with a band and/or dancers. Traditionally, the face of the groom is covered, and he is elaborately dressed.
- **A reception** at the bride's home often includes an auspicious ritual drink called *madhuparka* offered to the groom by the bride's father. The bride's father treats the bridegroom as if performing *pūjā* before a deity, washing his feet and giving him special offerings.
- **Reciting of the genealogies** of the bride and groom.
- **The girl being given away by her father** is the proper rite by which the father transfers responsibility for his daughter to the groom.
- **The sacrificial fire** signifies that Agni, the god of fire, is present. He is the celestial witness of the marriage of the two, and sacrificial offerings will be made during the ceremony.
- **Tying together** bride and groom in some form usually takes place, perhaps with a part of the garment of the bride with that of the groom, joining their wrists together with a thread, or joining their hands to represent the intended union. The bride is also adorned with a thread, a *tali*, around the neck. It is a kind of pendant necklace in some cases or simply a thread. It is an important aspect of marriage

ceremonies today and is a symbol continuously worn by women as a sign of their auspicious status as a wife. If her husband dies, a wife usually removes this thread. The groom may also touch the heart of the bride to symbolize their intimacy and fusion as one, though this may take place after the ceremony.[95]

- **The groom leads the bride by the right hand** for her to step on a stone three times, to represent the solidity and firmness of the marriage, and the bride's commitment to her future duties as a wife.
- **Circumambulation of the fire** in a clockwise direction or of the pavilion under which the couple marry has the bride following the groom. This circumambulation is known as *pherā* and may be done three or seven times: if seven, like the seven steps that follow, the rite represents the most important part of the ritual. When the circumambulations are complete, the bride will have moved from sitting on her family's side of the pavilion to that of her new conjugal family.
- **The most important *sapta-padī***, seven steps northward around the sacred fire are the heart of the ceremony. The first step is for power, the second for strength, the third for wealth, the fourth for fortune, the fifth for descendants, the sixth for happiness and the seventh for friendship, though the list varies considerably. At the seventh step, the bride becomes a wife. The rite is sufficiently important to be included in the Hindu Marriage Act, which agrees that the seventh step constitutes the completion of the marriage.
- **Vedic mantras** will be recited at twice-born ceremonies.
- The bride is often taken out to look at the sun or, if the ceremony is in the evening, the Pole Star. Like the boy in the *upanayana* rite, she pledges her firmness and steadiness like the Pole Star.

While the critical parts of the ceremony may only take a few hours, festivities and other rituals may involve several days. The groom promises to care for his wife and to be faithful and affectionate to her, as well as respecting her management of their home. For her part, the bride promises to support her husband and be faithful to him, non-extravagant, and to render her wifely duties without expecting anything in return. She promises to respect her husband's family and friends and perform her domestic duties well. Celebrations may go on for days until, in a ceremony known as *gauna*, the bride leaves her natal home for the role of wife in the conjugal home. Traditionally, the marriage is not consummated for three days, though Baker gives an account of a *Kṣatriya* wedding in Rajasthan in which the bride's and groom's faces remained covered for the entire ceremony and the first time the couple were able to see each other was at the consummation of their marriage immediately after the ceremony.[96] Often, a couple may not even have seen a photograph of their partner-to-be. In other cases, the couple are allowed to meet in an officially arranged occasion as a chance for each to scrutinize the other. McGee depicts the underlying meaning of the ceremony rather well when she says: "The marriage ritual effects the transformation of these two individuals into one body, one dharmic unit, with new responsibilities; they are incorporated into each other's lives as well as into the larger community of householders."[97]

The *vivāha* ceremony, while widely different depending on so many societal and customary influences, is necessarily different when it comes to caste. *Brāhmins* often have a more highly elaborate ceremony that maintains religious customs with established *Vedic* ritual. But being high-caste *Brāhmin* does not mean that the cost of a traditional wedding can be easily met. Baker records the words of a *Brāhmin* grandfather in Tamil Nāḍu: "We have nothing at all saved. . . . I have heard there is a law against dowries, but it is never enforced. If it were, I should be an extremely happy man." He had to think of paying for the wedding of his granddaughter since her parents were impoverished. Sometimes, all a family can do is say how much they can afford for wedding and dowry and hope that a suitable groom's family would accept that.[98] Marriage for Hindus should be an experience that takes place just once in a lifetime so some make it a highly extravagant affair, others simpler and more religiously focused. For some it is an opportunity to demonstrate wealth and status, regardless of caste, and Menski notes that there is an increasing trend for low-caste marriages to be made much more elaborate than hitherto,[99] though with the absence of *Brāhmin* officiators and *Vedic* ritual, low-caste marriages are inevitably traditionally simpler. When we come to the lowest class of *Śūdras*, it seems, according to Richards' research that there is often an unhappy mismatch between arranged partners and this is even more so the case with those outside the four-class system.[100]

The bride's departure for her conjugal home is a traumatic time for her natal family, but especially for her. The journey takes place soon after the wedding day, though may be delayed to avoid an inauspicious day. In some cases, the bride's brothers may accompany her on the journey. But the trauma of the journey is nothing in comparison to the trauma of adjusting to her new home and the complexities of a new family. Lindsey Harlan and Paul Courtright pertinently comment on the tension that awaits a new bride: "While she is expected to obey and please her husband, she is also expected to serve the interests of his family as a whole. She has to walk a delicate and at times perilous path between her husband and the other members of his family, especially the other significant women, his mother and sisters. Her conjugal family may seek to limit and structure her time with her husband to keep her from earning his loyalty and affection at the expense of his devotion to the family."[101] Her mother-in-law will train her to behave and do exactly as she wishes. Raheja points out that the new bride will be encouraged to distance herself from her husband on the one hand and her natal home on the other, especially her brothers.[102] However, ties with brothers, particularly, normally remain close in many regional traditions,[103] and may provide a subtle hint of protective influence and threat, should their sister be ill-treated.[104] There are also festivals that honour brothers. Nevertheless, the new wife will have to participate in new habits, perhaps venerate new deities; the ancestors of her new family will become hers, and all the time, she will be expected to do a good deal of work in the new home exactly as her mother-in-law demands, so her real time for independent visits to her natal home may be limited. Separation from the natal home is more of a practice in the North where it is felt to be important to avoid future marriages to close kin. In South India the woman retains closer ties with her former home. While sacred texts praised a dutiful wife, they also laid down her subservience to her husband and her role as his servant, whatever his nature, whatever his shortcomings. Perhaps Pandey was right when he said: "Those, who regard marriage as the solution of the problem of happiness, suffer from a great misconception. Those, who marry for pleasures are sorely disappointed."[105]

Adultery and divorce

Extra-marital sex is not acceptable as a general rule in Hinduism, for it brings shame on the family and community. Sex is rare before marriage and if a girl offends the family by being irresponsible with a male, the honour, or *izzat*, of the family is at stake, and it will be the girl's brothers who would retrieve her and often exact revenge on the male for the sake of family honour. Families have the responsibility of making sure a girl does not go astray, which is why marriage just after puberty was so favoured. As for adultery, the law is clear: "Whoever has sexual intercourse with a person who is and whom he knows or has reason to believe to be the wife of another man, without the consent or connivance of that man, such sexual intercourse not amounting to the offence of rape, is guilty of the offence of adultery, and shall be punished with imprisonment of either description for a term which may extend to five years, or with fine, or with both. In such a case, the wife shall not be punishable as an abettor."[106] Thus, the sanctity of marriage is such that adultery is a punishable offence but, noticeably, the woman is not punished. Her lot in life, however, would be very difficult indeed after such an event and she may in some cases be totally ostracized. And yet, Wendy Doniger pointed out that it is really only when a wife has a lover that a crime is believed to have been committed. If a husband takes a mistress, that is "simply the way of the world".[107] The bottom line here, however, is that women cannot be punished for adultery and men are rarely punished even though they are assumed to be the guilty party. While it may seem favourable to women, the law as it stands really treats a woman as property. Baker, however, describes the treatment of male adulterers in a *Dalit* village in Bihar: "Often the community would hand out its own justice. If a man was found to be unfaithful to his wife, he was likely to be publicly beaten and then forced to ride on a donkey's back while being jeered. His head would be shaved around the temples, and until it regrew everyone would know what he had done." Subsequent repetition of the offence could mean that the man would be driven from the village.[108] Thus, marriage in Hindu custom is regarded as sacred and its sanctity is important not just for a couple but for a family and the wider community.

In view of the sanctity of marriage, the attitude to divorce is a strict one, especially in more orthodox Hinduism. In the distant past of *Vedic* Hinduism, if a wife could not bear a son, her husband could invite his brother to sire a son with her. Or, if a husband died, and there was no son, it was deemed the duty of a brother to produce a son with her. These situations are known as levirate "marriage" or *niyoga*. In later times, when *niyoga* was forbidden by the first century CE, it would not be the brother who was expected to perform the role of surrogate husband, but a *Brāhmin* priest. Alongside *niyoga* was also the possibility for divorce, but this, too, was forbidden in later times for twice-born Hindus, though divorce has always obtained amongst the lowest castes. In the past, it became impossible for women to have a second husband, whether their husband were alive or dead. Despite the Hindu Widow Remarriage Act of 1856, divorce was and is rare, for a divorced woman would be a disgrace to a family and affect its honour, particularly amongst the upper castes. A second marriage, whatever the caste, is regarded as inferior to the first. The traditional dominance of a husband over a wife meant that she should remain with her husband whatever his shortcomings and if he dies before her, she should continue to pray for his well-being beyond the grave. Not so men: the *Laws of Manu* made it clear that widowers were expected to remarry.

Twentieth-century India saw a few states passing laws permitting divorce and in 1955, the Hindu Marriage and Divorce Act made divorce possible for all Hindus under certain, limiting circumstances. The Act allowed divorce by mutual consent: after filing for divorce, a six-month waiting period is necessary before advancing to the second stage of marriage dissolution. Attempts to get rid of the six-month wait in amendments to the Act in 2010 have failed. Concrete grounds for divorce, however, are set out clearly as such things as insanity, impotence, change of religion by the spouse, desertion or if the husband keeps a mistress.[109] Divorces are rising among middle-class Hindus but are infinitesimal in comparison to those in the West. Divorce is still regarded as threatening to religious and social stability. A divorced woman is inauspicious without her husband and she can easily become ostracized, though such patterns are beginning to change in the urban scene. Babb found that an abbreviated marriage ceremony could be used if a divorcee or widow remarried. He found divorce fairly common among lower and middle-ranking castes in his research in Madhya Pradesh but absent among higher castes.[110] Nicholas, too, found divorce to be rare amongst high castes,[111] and with others, it was more of an annulment tantamount to saying that the marriage "never happened in the first place"[112] and that it is a statement "about the failure of the achievement of the goals of the marriage *saṃskāra*".[113] Divorce or remarriage, it seems, is not a problem for those who are not twice-born; it is a rare advantage of being low caste. The strictness of sexual rules for women obviously does not apply to men, given that "India may become the epicentre of the AIDS crisis of the twenty-first century" and it is "'respectable' middle-class professional families among those infected".[114] Extra-marital sex must, then, be prolific amongst men.

Death: *Antyeṣṭi*

Death rites in India have undergone considerable change with modern crematoria changing the traditional patterns of sending the departed on their way. Like the other *saṃskāras* there is a tremendous variety of praxis that is dependent on region, caste, and family tradition, as well as the urbanization of large numbers of the population. And yet, side by side with modernity are the established practices of the *saṃskāra*, for it is the important last *saṃskāra*, the *antyeṣṭi*, or "last sacrifice". Given the variation of traditions, I can only offer here some of the broader outlines as well as the philosophy behind the practices. "Sending the departed on their way" were words chosen as apposite, for death for almost all Hindus is not the end of existence. It is but a transformation into a different mode and one that the family of the deceased can effect by the important rituals that they perform: the happiness of the deceased in the future world is completely dependent on these rites. And unless such rites are performed, the deceased may also want to cling to the family members, hang around the home, be jealous of the life still being lived by those alive and cause harm. He or she must, then, be sent on their way and given all the necessary needs to make sure that they do not return. A *preta*, a ghost, is not what the family wants. Neither does the family want a deceased member to be saddened by not reaching the realm of the Fathers, the ancestors, so a possible *preta* needs to be transformed to an ancestor, a *pitṛ*, a process that takes about twelve to seventeen days. In short, there must be clear demarcations between the living and the dead and some of the old texts do not even include death as a *saṃskāra* in order to create a textual difference between rites for the living and the dead.

Death is regarded as highly polluting and extremely dangerous and in a home where death has occurred there is a radical change in the interaction with society. The family is separated from those outside because it becomes so polluted and no one would dream of eating in a house in which someone has died or of having contact with the family which, to use Babb's phrase, is in "a situation of ritual crisis".[115] The deities of the home are likely to be removed or covered but are certainly not approached so that normal religious practice is also suspended. It is the sons of the deceased who are so important in rites of passage concerning death. The death may be even more problematic if it is untimely as in an accident or if the person is away from home when it occurs. Ideally, the dying person should be at home and every attempt is made to facilitate this even by hospital medics.[116] Dying at home means that all the correct rituals can be undertaken: that is a good death.

With a firm belief in ancestors prevalent when someone dies, the question has to be asked how such a belief can exist alongside *karma* and reincarnation. There have always been tensions in ideas of afterlife in Hinduism, mainly because Hinduism has had a history of accommodation of ideas rather than replacement. Thus, the *Vedic* concept of Heaven and a less well-articulated Hell has been accommodated alongside later beliefs in reincarnation, liberation at *mokṣa*, and a profound belief in a heavenly realm of ancestors. In addition, there is a ghost-like world that is the immediate state beyond death before death rites supply a body that can enjoy a more concrete life in the hereafter. It would seem that belief in ancestors comes to the fore at times of death, only to be replaced by a more general and antagonistic belief that good and evil *karma* have to be used up in a post-death existence and a subsequent rebirth. Good *karma* accrues by correct ritual praxis in life, so it would follow that correct ritual praxis surrounding death will provide good merit for whatever follows in the life beyond death, whether with ancestors, in Heaven or in a rebirth. What is important is the transition from a partly in and partly out of the world existence of a ghost, to a full passage to what follows, with no return. Babb sums up these points neatly when he says: "This marginal state of the deceased is the crux of the matter in the rites of death, not the prospect of ultimate reward or punishment, and much of the ritual may be seen as an effort to loosen the ties that still hold the ghost of the deceased to this world both in the interest of the soul's well-being and the safety of the living."[117] To this I might add the ostracism of the family through impurity, so making it exigent to emerge from it with the returned purity necessary to take up normal life.

The pollution surrounding death is so immense that all food is rendered unclean and it is necessary for the family to eat a very restricted diet. Any food that has already been cooked is polluted and needs to be thrown away. Ideally, a dying and dead person is removed from the house to the courtyard to avoid extensive pollution to food. Traditionally, the hair of the living must not be cut or shaved and the family should sleep on the ground. It is not just the immediate family that is polluted but also the family beyond, who may not even have had contact with the home of the deceased. Out of courtesy, it has become polite in some circles to avoid telling the family at a distance that death has occurred so that, ignorant of the event, these spatially distant family members can retain normal existence.[118]

While traditions vary greatly, and I do not want to dwell on such details, the following summary of the main aspects of death and funeral should suffice:

- **Preparation**. If possible before the individual dies, he or she is laid on the floor, sometimes in the courtyard outside, Mother Earth being a protective medium,[119] and is purified by being bathed (in Ganges water if possible), sipping some water and sometimes being sprinkled with the five sacred products of the cow. For some, the *tulasī* plant is placed in the mouth.[120] Gifts may be offered to the priest who attends the death and who offers *Vedic* prayers and *mantras* in the case of a twice-born Hindu. New cloths cover the body and it is anointed with sandalwood paste – all designed to assist the deceased on the journey ahead.
- **The moment of death**. If the deceased has died inside the home, it is traditional to open the doors to allow the soul to escape. Since the last thoughts of a dying person inform the state into which he or she is reborn – again, a tension between rebirth and ancestor status – the family's and/or priest's words at the time of death are very important. A priest may not be present, except in the case of a *Brāhmin* death, so the family may want to chant or sing *bhajans*. Popular are extracts from the *Bhagavad Gītā* and the *Rāmāyaṇa*. The priests who officiate at cremation grounds are highly respected, though partly feared, given their continued association with the dark, liminal times between life and death and the impurity of their vocation.[121]
- **Mourning**. Mourning begins from the moment of death and lasts until the family is purified and can resume normal duties. It is at this time that the eldest son becomes the chief mourner: though other males in the family can play this part, every man wishes for a son to undertake the rituals for him. Essentially, it is someone in the deceased's male line of descendants who should perform the ritual, that is to say, males of the conjugal family of a woman, and the natal family of a man. Once a woman marries, her husband's ancestors become hers.
- **Preparation of the body for cremation**. The body is ritually washed and dressed in new clothes or draped in a white or coloured sheet. If it is a woman who has died before her husband, she will be dressed in her wedding sari; a widow would be dressed in white. If a husband dies before his wife, he may be covered in her wedding sari.[122] The hair and nails of the body are cut and the body is then placed on a stretcher with the addition of such things as coconuts, flower garlands and a gold or silver coin in the mouth. Twice-born male mourners will change their sacred threads so that it is crossing from the right shoulder, and they will circumambulate the deceased in a clockwise, auspicious direction.
- **The journey to the cremation ground**. Sometimes with head shaved and simply dressed in a *dhoti* and without shoes, the main mourner bathes before leaving with the corpse for the cremation ground. He will lead the mourners who follow ranked from eldest to youngest. The body is placed on a pyre usually with its feet,

and therefore the head, facing South towards Yama, the ruler and judge of the dead, though there are variations. The mourners will again circumambulate the deceased, touching the feet of the corpse rather like they touch the feet of a deity in *pūjā*. Indeed, at this time, the corpse is treated like a deity. *Piṇḍas*, balls of rice, are sometimes put at points on the journey to the cremation ground and at the site itself.

These fit the corpse for its transfer to the hereafter, the ghost-like state of the deceased needing to be given a "new" body, and the *piṇḍas* beginning the sustenance for this process. They may also help to ward off any malevolent forces before the burning, but they may also be offered only after the cremation not prior to it. The stretcher carrying the corpse is carried quickly by men, led by the chief mourner and it is customary to chant the name of a deity, Rāma or Hari on route. There may well be halts on the way for customary rituals. Women do not usually attend a cremation: they often follow at a distance for a while and then return to clean the house.

- **The cremation**. Cremation, *śmaśāna*, is the norm for disposal of the body and has been so since *Vedic* times. A pyre is built at the spot where the body is to be cremated, ideally at the banks of a river like the great funeral *ghāṭs* at auspicious confluences of rivers and by especially sacred rivers like the Ganges. The funeral pyre, constructed of wood or cow dung may be organized by outcastes at the *ghāṭs* but otherwise by friends and relatives of the deceased. Circumambulation of the deceased again takes place, along with sprinkling of water. There are widely different customs that pertain to the final stages of the cremation but what all have in common is the intention to protect the soul from the malevolent forces at the cremation ground, to assist the departed soul on its way and to separate the departed soul from the living. The skull of the corpse may be broken in order to release the vital breaths from the body, or this action may be symbolized in the breaking of an earthenware pot. Either way, the act is a symbol of the breaking of the ties between living and dead.

  Fire is believed to release the soul from the body, commensurate with the Hindu belief that the soul is immortal but the body is not. The fire should be lit by the chief mourner, usually the deceased's son, before sunset and the whole process up to this point is immediate, the same day as the death. Given the heat of India, such speedy cremations are a hygienic way of disposing of the dead. Agni, the old *Vedic* god of fire disposes of the body and releases the soul in order that it can have a new body in the hereafter. Agni was the medium by which *Vedic* sacrifices were transformed from gross matter to the subtle essence for the gods: the same principle is evident in the fire that reduces the corpse to ashes. A prayer is said as the body is burning, for example the following from the *Atharva Veda*: "May the organ of vision proceed to the sun. May the vital air merge in the atmosphere. May you proceed according to your virtuous deeds to either heaven or earth or the regions of the waters, whichever place is beneficial to you."[123]
- **The return home**. After the cremation the men are expected to bathe before returning home. They leave the cremation ground without looking back and in the

reverse order in which they came, the youngest first and the eldest last. In some traditions they do not return home before the sun has set or even before the following day. Rites are performed by them during this time, rites that also serve to separate the dead from the living.[124] At home, restrictions on diet and cooking mean that friends and relatives may supply food. It is customary for the family not to eat from the moment of death up to this point, but even after the cremation, they are not expected to eat sweet foods or indulge in enjoyment, following for at least ten days a period of abstinence and asceticism.

- **Post-cremation impurity**. After the cremation, the family is highly polluted. The *Gṛhya-sūtras* made this period shorter for *Brāhmins* and increasingly longer for each of the lower classes, *Śūdras* remaining impure for one month. Diet is restricted and religious rites abandoned.
- **Scattering of the ashes**. On the third day after the cremation, the ashes and bones of the dead are collected and scattered in a river, if possible the Ganges. They may even be posted for the purpose of reaching the Ganges.[125] Sometimes, however, when there is no nearby river, they are buried and a small mound is placed over them, but immersion in water has the effect of cooling the remains, not from the heat of the pyre but from any inauspicious ferocity that could be harmful, and from any living elements of the *preta*. The gathering of the bones and ashes is called "picking the flowers", *phūl cānnā*.
- **Offerings to the dead**. In a last attempt to create a new body for the deceased and send it on its way, it is given water mixed with sesame, and the balls of rice or wheat, *piṇḍas* – sustenance that forms the new body. If crows come to peck at the *piṇḍas*, then it is believed to be a sign that all is well with the *preta*; if they do not appear, then the ghost is unhappy. The deceased are sometimes believed to take the form of birds before departing; a belief well-documented in *Vedic* texts.[126] In some parts of Tamil Nāḍu especially, crows are fed at cremation grounds for this reason. Other articles that are deemed necessary for the journey of the deceased may also be included, like lamps to light its way.[127] These rites of offerings are called *śrāddha* and they will continue daily, transferring merit from the actions of the living to the dead.
- **Uniting the deceased with ancestors**. At about the tenth or twelfth day, or even longer, special *śrāddha* rites are conducted in order to unite the deceased *preta* with the *pitṛ*, his or her ancestors. Such *śrāddha* rites are ancient, predating any belief in *karma* and *saṃsāra*, according to Kinsley.[128] Ten days after cremation is the popular amount of time for this process, symbolizing the ten months' growth of an embryo before birth. The deceased now has a subtle body like his ancestors, with whom he can enjoy his post-mortem experience. These final *śrāddha* rites release the family from their period of impurity, symbolized by the men shaving or cutting their hair, or at least touching it with a razor. According to some popular belief, it takes as long as a year for the deceased to reach the ancestors and an important *śrāddha* rite, *sapiṇḍī-kāraṇa*, therefore, takes place a year after the death and annually after that, though many perform this rite on about the twelfth day,[129] but *śrāddha* rites are also performed on the new moon dates after the death. There is also a

> general *śrāddha* ceremony for the dead in the dark part of the month leading up to the festival of Navarātri. Once the impurities of the family have been removed, a feast can be held to which *Brāhmins* are invited and are given gifts.

Many of the rites associated with death are the products of superstition and the fear of evil spirits. Troy Organ notes that mourners sometimes drop seven stones from their inauspicious left hand as they return from the cremation. This has the purpose of confusing the evil spirits who follow them and stop to count the stones, but are notorious for their inability to count![130] The prolific appearance of devils and monsters, evil demons and malevolent spirits in Hindu mythology has added to the richness of the ritualistic dimension in all the *saṃskāras*. The ceremonies for death are speedy since it is believed that evil spirits can enter a body as its soul departs and the quicker the body is out of the home, the better. Since many believe that unsatisfied *pretas* are likely to possess the living, death rites are also exigent in preventing harm from those on the other side. Then, too, cremation grounds are the abodes of all kinds of evil forces so protection of the mourners from these forces is evident in so many of the rites.

Not all Hindus are cremated for burial is reserved for the greatly sainted and for young children both of whom are regarded as sinless and pure. Those ascetics who have led a life of spiritual concentration on Brahman do not have to be reborn. They have reached the end of their spiritual journey and attained *mokṣa*; merging with Brahman is their fate. Such is the end for *sādhus*, *gurus* and *saṃnyāsins*: spiritual fire has purified them and so they have no need of Agni to take them to a heavenly realm. Some are weighted with stones and immersed in the Ganges instead of being buried. As the body sinks, disciples chant hymns and blow conch shells to celebrate the union of the soul with God. There are, however, a few sects like the Liṅgāyatas that practise burial and, according to Klostermaier, the poorest folk who cannot afford a cremation find the deceased being simply thrown into the nearest river.[131] Wood for a funeral pyre is particularly expensive.

When the period of death rites is over, the close male relatives cut or shave their hair in order to remove the pollution of death. The house has to be thoroughly cleaned and a washerman is given all the linen to clean, the washerman being traditionally low enough in the social strata to handle polluted materials. Only when the house has been thoroughly cleansed can the household deities be returned.

Ancient *śrāddha* rituals are conducted by families to commemorate their ancestors. As long as anyone deceased is believed to have crossed safely to the land of the ancestors, the *pitṛ-loka*, then the men of an immediate family – sons, grandsons and great-grandsons will gather together to honour their ancestors of the previous three generations. Basham pointed out that such a *śrāddha* rite united the family, consolidated it and defined it, the participants being *co-piṇḍas* bound together by their ancestors and the offering to their ancestors of *piṇḍas*. In this case, it is safe to link the living with the dead.[132] Four pots are filled with offerings for each of the four male ancestors at these rites. A newly deceased becomes the foremost of these ancestors, the foremost "father", and whoever used to be the fourth is no longer honoured. Honouring the ancestors is one of the three duties that a son is obliged to do: it is the *dharma* of a son to do so, which is one reason why sons are so important. Ritual water or *tarpaṇa* is expected as a gift to the ancestors in this special annual rite. No merit accrues to the performer, but since it is sinful to neglect it, punishment is believed to be the outcome for those who do not.[133]

The *satī*

It seems appropriate in the context of death to mention the *satī,* the woman who sacrifices herself on her husband's funeral pyre. Not only will its placement here serve to conclude this chapter but, I think, it will lead us neatly into the role and status of women in Hindu society in the following chapter, chapter 10. Often transcribed as *suttee* (which gives roughly the right pronunciation), the *satī* is "one who has great virtue", "a virtuous woman", "a true woman". Grammatically, a woman cannot "commit *satī*", as in commit suicide, she has to *be a satī.* Paul Courtright poignantly says that: "In the perfect Hindu moral universe, there would be no widows."[134] It is a very valid point, since it is regarded as religiously sinful if a woman outlives her husband. I do not want to pre-empt what I wish to say about Hindu women in the next chapter but it needs to be said here that a wife is expected to ensure the well-being of her husband through ritual and prayer in such a way that he has a long life. If she dies before him, then she has failed in her religious duties as a woman and wife.

The immolation of a woman on her husband's funeral pyre seems to have originated with the warrior class, the *Kṣatriyas*, and while it was voluntary, it may have been accepted as obligatory by some of the earlier *Kṣatriya* families. The past *Kṣatriya* warriors of Rajasthan are still famed for their valour as, too, are their wives, who chose to die rather than be captured by their enemies. It is here in Rajasthan that pride in the seclusion of high-caste women still largely obtains. The custom spread to the *Brāhmin* class and, by the eighteenth century, became a sign of high-class status in northern India. But it is in the myth of Śiva's wife Satī that we find the passion of the practice. Satī took her own life by immolating herself when she was humiliated at her father's great sacrifice to which he refused to invite her husband Śiva. This action of the famous Goddess became the actions of a virtuous woman at the death of her husband and Lindsey Harlan notes that in Rajasthan *satī* stones marking the places where widows immolated themselves are often associated with Śaiva-Śākta shrines.[135] The practice was unknown in the *Vedas*, equally unknown in the *Dharma-sūtras* and Manu says nothing about it. Altekar thought the practice gradually became fashionable by about 400 CE[136] and it came to be believed that a *satī*'s sacrifice was so great that she could obliterate the sins of her husband and her own and that the couple would be blissfully united in Heaven. The custom, therefore, began to be popularized in northern India but was rare in the South until the twelfth to fourteenth centuries.[137] It was also increasingly followed by lower classes.

While some believed that a *sāti* rendered herself a goddess by her action, there seems to be no consensus of opinion on the life expected for her after death. Thus, she may be with her husband, she may be liberated, attain *mokṣa*, or she may enable them both to have an excellent rebirth, or a wonderful life in Heaven, but *satīs* are generally believed to be inseparable from their husbands. It seems, too, that they are able to grant well-being to their living families.[138]

The custom was abolished by the British in 1829 and it has become a criminal offence to attempt to be a *satī* or to encourage or venerate a *satī*. It did not and has not, however, completely died out. But it was not as frequent as is generally thought, despite "*suttee*" being such a well-known term in the West. Thus, Altekar warned: "But even if we suppose that the actual number of Satīs was twice the number officially recorded, the conclusion becomes inevitable that only an infinitesimal number of widows in the general populace were immolating themselves."[139] Klostermaier, too, makes the point that numbers of immolations were nowhere near the number of dowry deaths that occur in contemporary India.[140]

Traditionally, the *satī* has been considered as superhuman, a woman who is like, or becomes, a goddess in her sacrifice. Even men used to prostrate themselves before her as she went to her death. Many are recorded as going to their deaths calmly and not uttering any cry at all during what must be an agonizing death, though critics claim a *satī* is probably too drugged to do otherwise.[141] Yet, traditionally, a *satī* moves through the crowd to the pyre distributing gifts and blessings in a coherent and regal manner. She is colourfully and regally dressed and parades to the pyre to the accompaniment of music. Courtright comments that this is her chance to accompany her husband "in a single and spectacular display of violent self-annihilating devotion" or continue to devote herself to her husband through penance and devotion in life.[142] He also aptly writes: "From the perspective of her as a person, she is a victim, the one wrung out of the system, the one who is backed into the corner of choosing between a death of life in the fire or a life of social and ritual death as a widow."[143] I shall be examining the plight of widows in the following chapter, chapter 10, where it will be seen that for some their lives are, indeed, a death in life.

Despite being illegal, there have been fairly recent cases of *satīs*. In September 1987, a young wife from a Rajasthan village – Rajasthan being one of the regions in which the custom was popular in the past – successfully became a *satī* and a shrine was erected in her honour. Such shrines in many parts of India are visited by pilgrims. The *satī* had the full support of her family and her village, who prevented the authorities from stopping her. Those who decry such actions claim that the family left behind are able to benefit through inheritance and the *Brāhmins* who officiate at such a funeral are well paid. There is also the financial benefit of promoting a *satī* pilgrimage site. Defenders of the custom say that in making a *satī*'s death a criminal offence, all semblances of religion and spirituality have been stripped from the act. Some who defend the practice say that *satīs* are also often thought by some to have murdered their husbands in previous existences and could atone for sin by immolation. It has to be said, however, that those who successfully managed to escape the fire were regarded as untouchable and ostracized, giving them little option. In many cases, the pyre was often built in such a way that it was impossible to escape.

Those who defend a *satī* cite a woman's *pati-vratā-dharma* her *dharma* to live her whole life in devotion and servitude to her husband: she is half of her husband and he of her, and they should not be separated. Traditionalists claim that it is a highly religious act that can only be undertaken by a woman of intense spirituality. The husband is the focus of a wife's whole being and her action as a *satī* is the highest devotion she can give. There are women who have attempted to be *satīs* but who have been denied what in their eyes is the privilege of self-immolation. These women become *satī-mātās*, "*satī* mothers", who live ascetic lives with great respect from the community around them and they are often believed to have miraculous powers.[144] So intense is the *śakti* and heat, or *tapas*, of a *satī* that she is believed to ignite the fire from her own energies.[145] In death she was believed to protect a whole community:

> Becoming illustrious, the *satī* makes everyone illustrious. The *satī* not only epitomizes female virtue but serves as an emblem of the entire community's virtue. More than this, she removes whatever moral failings individual community members may have: she renders them sinless. She makes tangible the community's claim to purity and the status that purity conveys. *Satīs* are, in short, status symbols and, as such, are especially valuable to communities that seek to raise their social status by emulating the traditions of higher-status groups.[146]

These words of Lindsey Harlan are perhaps positive with a hint of the pejorative, and I would not wish to leave the reader with the view that becoming a *satī* is the kind of religious and spiritual practice to be applauded. More apposite, I think, especially in the light of the chapter that follows on the status of women, are the words of Altekar: "Such a belief should have given rise to the custom of burning or burying the husband also along with the wife. Man, however, wielded supreme power in society almost everywhere and was not prepared to sanction a custom adverse to his own interest and comfort."[147] There has never been a case, as far as I know, of a man immolating himself for the good of the community.

In conclusion, it must be said that there is an immense divergence and variation of traditions surrounding the *saṃskāras* despite the codifying of them by the old law makers. There may well be an underlying philosophical ethos to *saṃskāras*, a point put well by McGee when she says: "The social life of humans on this terrestrial world is but a small part of a much larger and vital cosmos comprehended by the Hindu tradition. *Saṃskāras* help to situate human life within the larger cycle of the cosmos."[148] But there are more overt practices that serve pragmatic rather than philosophical ends. What is clear is that some of the primitive and superstitious beliefs have survived in the Hindu psyche and have been retained in the *saṃskāras* that we have seen. This is particularly the case with death rites. Facets of remote antiquity have traversed the long span of time to the present day and have accommodated widely different beliefs on route so that tensions occur with the philosophies that underpin the practices. The tension between old and new, ancient and modern is a strange one in the outcome of accommodated ideas, from the mystic chants of the priests in the old Sanskrit, to the telescoping of ceremonies for the sake of convenience. Pandey was pessimistic here when he said: "The natural consequence is the apathy and indifference of the masses towards the Saṃskāra, which have become a sealed book to them."[149] Minor rites have disappeared but what have not are the underlying currents of attitudes and superstitions. In the following chapter, I shall examine the roles of women in the home and community and it would be impossible to claim here that the ritualistic element of the *saṃskāras* has not informed the way in which women are viewed and treated from birth until death. These attitudes we must now explore.

10

Women in the Home and Community

The status of Hindu women in India

The impact of Śāktism in Hinduism might suggest that women, who are considered by Śāktas, particularly, to be the essence of the Mother Goddess in human form, would have a high status throughout Hinduism. The proliferation of goddesses in local worship, might also suggest a similar elevation of women in society as a whole. But the dichotomy between the sacred female and her dangerous sexuality – no less evident in many of the goddesses themselves – has focused primarily on the negative perceptions of the female in humanity. Mandakranta Bose makes a very pertinent and graphic point when she writes of "women who are left hanging between deification and subjugation".[1] While it may be expected that the position and status of women in society improves as society evolves, in Hinduism quite the reverse has taken place and over the last two thousand years, that status dramatically declined. When I began writing on Hinduism many years ago, the status of women showed some signs of improvement and I had hoped that new research would reveal evidence of major roads forward. However, the advent of technology into cyber-space has meant that attitudes to women in India are quickly viral. The dreadful brutal rape and murder of a student in Delhi in December 2012 quickly became world news. Today, any book on Hinduism has to address this incredible attitude to half of the humanity of India. If we cast our minds back to the chapter on Hindu goddesses it will be seen that goddesses are dangerous, violent and powerful unless they are wedded to a major god, whereby they become subservient and obedient, their powerful sexuality curbed. It is no less the case with girls and women, which is why puberty was dreaded as a time when girls could become out of control and the need for pre-puberty marriage was deemed to be essential. It is *control* of the female that lies at the heart of the treatment of women. Lindsey Harlan's and Paul Courtright's comments here are most apt:

This notion of controlled *śakti* as promoting social order finds expression in the widely

> shared understanding that women should never be independent. Women should not be left to their own devices but should be supervised and protected by men. The main concern behind this notion is not that women will go about indiscriminately killing and maiming like the frenzied Kālī but that they might succumb to sexual temptation, which will destroy their purity and the purity of their lineage. . . . For society to prosper, women's power must be channelled toward procreation and the protection of the family.[2]

Thus, the prevalence of the divine in female form does little for the status of women and, as Thomas Coburn says in the context of the mightiest text extolling the Goddess "one of the clear early lessons from feminist study is that one cannot assume that the existence of goddesses, or Goddess texts, in a given culture correlates with favourable social status for women".[3] Is this because goddesses are too isolated from human women to raise their status? As one author puts it "it seems that goddesses who stand outside of social structures rarely serve to liberate those who are within them; the analogy between them is perhaps too strained to become relevant to the everyday life of women".[4]

There is plenty of textual evidence that praises a woman as half of her husband, as skilled in undertaking household duties, as running a home economically, and as worshipping her husband as a god even if he is a poor husband in every respect. A woman, according to Manu, has no independence: "A girl, a young woman, or even an old woman should not do anything independently, even in (her own) house. In childhood a woman should be under her father's control, in youth under her husband's, and when her husband is dead, under her sons'. She should not have independence. A woman should not try to separate herself from her father, her husband, or her sons, for her separation from them would make (her own and her husband's) families contemptible."[5] *All* the *Dharma-śāstra* authors agree that a woman should have no independence since she is not suited to it. Basham's comment summed up the view of a woman rather well when he wrote: "She was at once a goddess and a slave, a saint and a strumpet."[6] However, according to Manu, the fathers, husbands, brothers and brothers-in-law on whom a woman was dependent, should honour and adorn her, for only then would the home rituals be fruitful and the gods rejoice in its residents.[7] The wife who bore sons was particularly respected. A remarkable ambivalence, then, informs attitudes to women. Even philosophically, the creative *māyā* of the Goddess is as much the source for delusive ignorance as for liberating knowledge – a point brought home by Tracy Pintchman.[8] She comments, too, that the Goddess can create but also destroy and is also the very world that the ascetic wishes to denounce. Her point is that there is always ambivalence in attitudes to the female whether she is divine or mortal.[9]

In ancient India, girls were educated, could participate in *Vedic* study and perform sacrifices without a male, being completely equal to men in religious praxis. Women could be relatively independent, distinguish themselves professionally, were not secluded, and could remarry if their husbands died. However, women could not own or inherit property.[10] Economic and geographical upheavals in northern India, and the challenging rise of Buddhism and Jainism witnessed a decline in the status of women from the sixth century BCE to the third century CE. All the restrictions on women that came about with the law codes – early marriage, the woman's *dharma* to serve her husband, marriage as her only *saṃskāra* –contributed to the demise in her status.[11] Despite the fact that some of the orthodox law-code writers like Manu believed that a time could come when the rules they had prescribed were no longer beneficial to society, the attitudes of society to women remained fairly static up to present times.[12] With the decline in status came the view that women were not ritually pure and their status dropped to the same level as *Śūdras*.

The epics have differing views of women. In the *Mahābhārata*, there are powerful and dynamic women like the common wife of the five Pāṇḍavas. Such women are given a good deal of textual space and heroes in the *Mahābhārata* are named with their matronyms as much as patronyms.[13] In Vālmīki's *Rāmāyaṇa*, however, the portrayal of Sītā is of a completely subordinate and obedient wife who has the well-being of her husband totally at heart, though his original text showed her as having more spirit. It is later strands of Vālmīki's text, as well as the much later *Rāmcaritmānas* of Tulsī Dās that makes her meek and mild. John Brockington, in fact, traces the demise of the status of women in the different phases of evolution of the *Rāmāyaṇa* with an emphasis on a woman's subservience to her husband, and her chastity, occurring in the second phase that began about the third century BCE. By the early centuries of the common era that decline had increased sufficiently for women to be regarded as temptresses.[14] By the time of the fourth stage of the evolution of the text, which began in the fourth century CE, a wife was simply an adjunct of her husband, widows had clearly become inauspicious, women could only eat after men had done so, and the custom of the *satī* becomes evident.[15]

In most scriptures, women are ignored. As one writer puts it: "In these texts women do not speak as the author, are not spoken to as subject, nor are they considered in their possibilities and value as reflective religious agents, rather than in relation to the value that they bring to men."[16] The rise of the *bhakti* movements gave them some religious respite, even to the extent that they could achieve salvation as women as opposed to being reborn as male, but there was less impact in the societal context. Then, too, control of women was emphasized more amongst the two highest classes: indeed, Joanna Liddle and Rama Joshi argue that "control over women's sexuality was essential to the development of the patriarchal caste hierarchy, both for the maintenance of the caste and for the legitimation and control of inheritance".[17]

We have to wait for the nineteenth century for painstaking campaigns for education for girls and women and the opening up of professions like medicine and teaching for women. Women campaigned alongside Mahatma Gandhi and by the end of the twentieth century there were women's movements on a wide scale. But in the nineteenth and twentieth centuries there was also a rise in conservatism amongst *Brāhmins*[18] and regulations for all aspects of a wife's daily life – from how and when she should bathe, what she should wear, to how she should sit or walk – were the subjects of some slightly earlier religious texts.[19] The aim was to maintain as much purity as possible in a home that included a basically impure woman. For some, that included preventing the woman from using any foreign materials during the period of British rule in India: she could not, for example, drink coffee. Purity and honour were essential in conservative strands of Hinduism.[20] The general result is, as Bose strikingly comments, "women as a biological category are strictly defined and their lives as social creatures hedged around by rules for every occasion".[21]

A woman is not *sva-tantra*, that is to say, she does not have her "own thread". In Bose's words, "the insistence upon domestication of women within an elaborate web of family roles and duties requires so complete a submersion of the individual in the needs of the family collective that self-sacrifice becomes the highest possible duty".[22] Her role is in the home and the efficient running of the household is her affair even if she is a working woman. It is generally believed that there are, according to Subramuniyaswami, "physical, mental and emotional differences" between the sexes such that a woman bears children, stays in the home and a man provides economic security: "As long as the husband is capable of supporting the family, a woman should not leave the home to work in the world, though she may earn through home industry. The spiritual and emotional loss suffered by the children and the bad *karma* accrued from having a wife and mother work outside the home is never offset by financial gain."[23] The *Bhagavad Gītā* (3:35) stresses: "Better one's own *dharma* devoid of merit, than the well-discharged *dharma* of another. Death in one's own *dharma* is better; the *dharma* of another is fraught with danger." Since it was not acceptable for a man to take on the *dharma* of another – in the case of the *Gītā*, its hero wanted to change his *Kṣatriya* class and become an ascetic – how much more so is it advisable that a woman should not take on the *dharma* of a man?

Whereas a woman like Sītā of the *Rāmāyaṇa* is seen as totally pure and perfect, women are also the temptresses that are inimical to the progress of a man to liberation, *mokṣa*. Such ambivalent views of women still obtain but the one that predominates is negative: women can so easily be regarded as inherently immoral. Consider the words of Liddle and Joshi here: "The importance of domesticity and the relics of seclusion mean that many people regard any woman who leaves the house for paid employment as a 'loose woman', so that it is impossible, for instance, for a woman to share transport with a male work colleague."[24] In an article in the *Japan Times*, Cesar Chelala makes the following pertinent remark: "The recent rape cases in India are not isolated incidents. They are just manifestations of a discriminating situation that starts in the womb, in a society that persists in treating women as second-class citizens. Unless this fact is accepted by Indian society, and appropriate laws are enforced, any measures to overcome this situation will only be palliative, and will not solve this important problem facing the country."[25] In a report of the Asian Human Rights Commission by Meredith McBride, the following passage is stark:

> For every woman who obtains a job, two women are killed at birth, abused in childhood, burnt over dowry, or sexually harassed at work. India's development is greatly impaired by violent crimes perpetrated against women. It follows to note that women and other minorities are disproportionately affected by the government's failure to maintain the rule of law, and this directly violates a number of international covenants, most importantly the United Nations Convention on the Elimination of All Forms of Discrimination against Women.

The same document states that India is the second worst place for women to live according to one survey (the Gender Inequality Index) and fourth in another (Trust Law, a legal news source by Thomas Reuters), in the latter case just behind Afghanistan, the Congo and Pakistan.[26]

The purity–impurity issue of a caste or family is what dictates discrimination against women in the case of the highest orthodox and conservative castes and any group wishing to rise in status would have to take on board the same kind of cultural patterns. In another interesting comment, Liddle and Joshi state: "The ideal of female subservience reinforces the containment of women's power in the gender hierarchy. In this way, women's sexual respectability determines the social respectability of men, the family and the entire caste."[27] Indeed, the upper-class attitudes to women and of women themselves are not all that far removed from the traditional views articulated by Manu. Sophie Baker found the insular nature of *Brāhmin* women in a family in Tamil Nāḍu to be evident in her research: "They were an enclosed, compact unit of individuals reliant just on each other. They rarely entered into any discussion unless it was related to their religious duties or their economic problems. They showed neither interest nor curiosity about the world beyond their home and temple."[28]

One of the reasons for the increased seclusion of women was the practice of *pardā* or *purdah* as it is sometimes spelt in the West. *Pardā* means "curtain", and refers to the seclusion of women in the home from contact with any males beyond the immediate family. Harlan and Courtright found that some women appreciate the seclusion because it gives them some freedom from the males of the family:

> Although many women find *pardā* frustrating and speak wistfully of their natal villages where as daughters they could walk about unveiled, many also say that *pardā* allows them to speak and act more freely than would otherwise be possible given the other conventions of deference that women must obey. In *pardā* they feel they can be relatively relaxed and can have the space to complain about and be critical of men and their rules.[29]

While the custom was certainly influenced by the Muslim occupation of the northern area of India, it seems to have obtained amongst higher classes in the pre-Muslim period.[30] It is a sign of respectability amongst higher classes. However, it never gained credence in southern India where Muslim influence did not extend. But even where *pardā* does not obtain, it is customary for a woman to veil her face in the presence of men: a daughter-in-law, for example, would veil her face in the presence of her father-in-law and other males in the family. Just as there are differences between North and South, there are also differences between village and urban customs, the latter having little sign of *pardā*. With low-caste women the customs are much, much more relaxed. Women here have more freedom, and often need it because they are required to work to support their families: the constraints of the higher-caste Hindu families are not theirs.

The pollution that women are believed to have as part of their being is an important factor in discrimination against them. Sexual contact with a man of a lower caste would bring a level of impurity into the family *and* into a caste as a whole, polluting and diluting the exclusivity of the caste. Control of a woman is essential to ensure that her sexuality does not get out of hand and harm the social group. Certainly, offspring of an illicit union would need to be avoided at all costs in order to preserve the caste. The author of the *Bhagavad Gītā* has its hero Arjuna complaining that if he fights in the impending battle the women in the family would become corrupt and from corruption in women arises mixing and confusion of classes, a path that leads to Hell and deprives ancestors of Heaven when rites for the dead are not performed: "Because of the evil deeds of those who destroy families causing confusion of *varnas*, the eternal *dharmas* of caste and family are destroyed" (2:43). Some temples are frequented only by women and avoided by men – and certainly *Brāhmin* men – for fear of pollution.

A woman is ritually impure in view of her menses,[31] her sexuality, and her role in giving birth. Even in ancient times when women had more freedom and education, a woman was rendered untouchable during menstruation,[32] that is to say her touch or even her voice were polluting.[33] Since procreation is a religious duty, so is sex, but a woman has a time when she is able to step back from sexual contact as well as other duties during menses and in the past, she was totally excluded from all the family and removed from the home to an area outside. Women can never enter temples when menstruating nor can they perform *pūjā* at home. Interestingly, in a new temple dated from the mid-nineteen seventies, in a village about fifty miles from Madras and dedicated to the goddess Ādipārāśakti, menstruating women are allowed to worship.[34] Once periods start, girls are expected to remain in seclusion in their homes for several days, though such taboos are now more relaxed in some sectors. With strict *Brāhmin* families, however, these rules are maintained and women leave the house, cannot have contact with men, sometimes even with their children, and definitely not with the kitchen. For some, not having the usual contact with the home is often a welcome break from the general chores. A ritual bath is taken at the end of menstruation to purify the woman: soiled clothing can only be washed by an outcaste *dhobī*, a washerman or woman. Laurie Patton recounts the remarkable case of a young male *Brāhmin* hired by a female to teach Sanskrit at a major Indian university. The *Brāhmin* requested that female students absent themselves from his classes when menstruating because they would expose him to impurity. I love the woman's reply: "Sir, perhaps I might ask you to consider where our respective institutions might be in fifty years. I can as much as guarantee you that my university will be here and standing, and probably teaching Sanskrit then. However, neither I nor you can guarantee that your *pathshala* will survive that long. Given that this is the case, I suggest you comply with the university system, where no such concerns about monthly cycles apply."[35]

In contemporary India, women are gaining greater independence through economic opportunities. While the status of a man, his family and his caste is dependent greatly on the respectability of his wife, his wife need no longer be secluded: she is able to provide economic advantages through professional employment and that employment increases status. Liddle and Joshi believe that men still control women in such situations, using employed women as an asset for their own status.[36] However, women are now making good progress in infiltrating professions that bring them economic independence, and education is more open to them. But financial difficulties in a family may mean that only the boys of a family will be educated to any extent and once a woman is married, her continued education and career are highly likely to be curtailed. Some children in poor families are needed to provide physical labour in support; they are likely to be illiterate and girls generally only receive a basic primary education if any. Recruitment for higher education tends to be from higher classes who can afford it, though grants are available for scheduled castes in particular. The professional, educated woman has some self-identity that gives her esteem and a little autonomy, but control by men is a hidden undercurrent with many a working woman being a commodity in marriage. Such undercurrents are clear in the following passage by Liddle and Joshi:

> For women, gender disadvantage is paramount inasmuch as education is used to improve their marriage chances and to maintain them in domestic dependence, as well as to provide men with material and social advantages; inasmuch as women are offered fewer opportunities and less choice in employment, as segregated, have access to fewer resources, are compelled to comply with higher standards and are hampered from performing their professional work through restrictions on their movements and interactions and through sexual harassment; and insofar as women have to do all the domestic work on top of their paid work, that paid work is designed for male lifestyles and therefore inhibits women's family life, and that domestic work is organised for male benefit and therefore inhibits women's professional work.[37]

Women often cannot study alongside men, there being colleges that are exclusively for women who are taught by women, but there are no all-male colleges. And yet a number of departments of major universities in India are chaired by women, and what is very noticeable is the number of women who study and lecture in Sanskrit with a growing number of *strī-purohits*, women ritual specialists.[38] Much primary education is free and compulsory in regions like Tamil Nāḍu for those living near a government school. Teachers in these schools would come from any caste or even be *Dalit*. It is in such schools that girls mainly receive their first education in their native language, though higher education is taught in English, which many never learn. For a girl to read or write just a little is satisfactory for most parents. As to secondary education, there are a number of schemes to encourage girls to finish high school but, as so many things in India, such schemes do not have the full effect and there is a fifty-per cent drop-out rate of girls from secondary education: while it is usually only the "creamy layer" of girls – those from wealthy high classes – who get the best out of education.[39]

India's laws have not lagged behind those of other countries in legislating for gender equality in every dimension of life – political, economic, educational, recruitment, inheritance, divorce – the list is long.[40] The problem lies in the implementation of the laws so that equality in practice is almost non-existent. Women still earn far less than men for the same job, for example. In 2005, The Hindu Succession Act Amendment followed earlier changes made to the 1956 Act in some states by allowing daughters to inherit ancestral and jointly-owned property alongside sons. This improved gender equality slightly,[41] but, again, implementation remains a problem and in northern India, in particular, women are often deprived of their inheritance rights.[42]

Professional women sometimes have the support of their family to engage in their work, but others have to battle against the domestic role that is felt to be their lot. And in the work place, Liddle and Joshi found discrimination against women in all the areas of work they examined.[43] They also found that employers believed women are less suitable for work because of their domestic constraints: they are simply not as good as men and cannot be as successful, whereas men can give unlimited time to their work with support from the home, have no constraints in the home and are free to move elsewhere if necessary.[44] The working woman still maintains the home with all its domestic chores, cultural traditions maintaining that it is not the man's role to do domestic chores or child rearing. Then, too, many mothers-in-law in a joint family can be very antagonistic towards the working woman who does not wish to come under the sway of a dominatrix in the home situation. And yet, the traditional role of the superior woman of the home has had to be abandoned in the case of many joint families of professional women.[45] But, on the other hand, the same authors have found that women in business often do very well in engaging with male business men and are recognized as hard-working and conscientious, often more so than men.[46]

At the other end of the class system are the low-caste or *Dalit* working women. They are sweepers, midwives, cleaners of latrines, washerwomen, makers of cakes of cow dung, tenders of cattle. Women do not work in agriculture other than occasionally helping their menfolk in sowing seed or weeding, but they have been traditionally prohibited from working on the land unless accompanied by a male member of the family. Agricultural work in the fields is considered degrading for a woman. The lower the status of a woman the more likely she is to be a servant to others: in urban areas, low-caste women often do manual factory work or even work on a building site. Even middle-class women in urban areas may work in full or part-time wage labour.[47] In urban areas, extended families may find themselves living in a rented flat with shared incomes. The work a woman does enhances or impedes her caste status, so if it is professional it is respectable and accepted, but if menial it is degrading: in the case of the former, the status of the husband, family and caste are considerably enhanced.

From all that has been said it would be impossible to claim that women have equality with men in all but a few random examples. And this is so despite the fact that India sought to give women equal rights with men far earlier (in 1953) than western countries like the United Kingdom. India, too, can boast being one of the first countries to have a woman as Prime Minister, and women have certainly distinguished themselves in most professional areas. Theoretically, women should have equality but in practice, they do not. There should be no discrimination on grounds of religion, gender, race, caste and place of birth according to Indian law, and *Article 5* of the Constitution of India states that all parties should take appropriate steps: "To modify the social and cultural patterns of conduct of men and women, with a view to achieving the elimination of prejudices and customary and all other practices which are based on the idea of inferiority or the superiority of either of the sexes or on stereotyped roles for men and women"[48] Yet, at the same time, the Indian government does not wish to interfere in the personal affairs of a community; in other words, patterns of discrimination can be maintained. As Meera Khanna, Vice Chairperson of The Guild of Service in India comments: "Like many schemes of the Government the spirit is willing but the implementation is weak."[49] And Rekha Singh iterates: "But passing of law is one thing and its absorption in the collective thinking of society is quite a different matter. In order to prove themselves equal to the dignity and status given to them in the Indian Constitution they have to shake off the shackles of slavery and superstitions. They should help government and the society in eradicating the evils of dowry, illiteracy and ignorance among eves."[50]

Constraints on women come from many dimensions. To begin with, there are economic constraints in that families often cannot afford the education of a girl. Even where some secondary education is possible, higher studies are too expensive for anyone except the wealthiest. Then there are mobility constraints on women. They are not expected to go out in the evenings or to share transport with a male. Field trips, research conventions, educational tours are as difficult for a professional woman as it is for a low-caste woman to work unchaperoned in the fields. A woman alone in such situations loses her respectability and is classed as immoral, even if she could manage the household routine that is her responsibility in order to, say, attend a conference. Shikha Dalmia comments: "A woman who has to wait for her father or brother to pick her up from college or work – rather than taking a cab or a bus – can't just meet whoever she wants, wherever she wants, whenever she wants. Everything she does becomes subject to time, place, and manner restrictions by her family and its moral code."[51] Since women are dependent on men in this way, it reinforces patriarchal dominance and the idea that a woman is a commodity of the family and caste.

At present, the protection of women by the males in their families is essential since one of the greatest constraints on women is their fear for their personal safety. The fear of sexual assault is great among women and they would for the most part be anxious about travelling alone anywhere. Sabrin Sidhu of the Delhi Headquarters of the United Nations for women claimed that 95 per cent of women in Delhi are scared to go out alone.[52] The effect of this is put forcibly by Liddle and Joshi: "As long as the threat is there they will restrict their activities. The threat is one of the most effective mechanisms by which men can control women's sexuality, encouraging them to restrict their own movements and to confine themselves to the home." Even more forceful is the same authors' comment that "although it is men who threaten women with sexual assault if they stray too far from home, it is the women who are accused of sexual immorality, not the men." [53] Sidhu states that two out of three men believe that women's dress provokes them.[54] The idea of immorality justifies the sexual control by men over women, and is used by men to persuade women that it is *their own fault* that they are subjected to this harassment.[55] I shall have occasion to draw attention to this bizarre but accurate reasoning in the case of the defence of the men who perpetrated the Delhi rape and murder last December, which I intend to examine below. As Liddle and Joshi claim elsewhere: "Women who refuse to seclude themselves at home as private sexual property may come to be regarded instead as public sexual property, available for any man to degrade or proposition."[56]

A term for sexual harassment in India has come to the notice of the West: it is "eve-teasing", which sounds fairly innocuous but is, in fact, a volatile and inimical force against women. Consider Liddle and Joshi's following comments on the extent of this practice:

> Eve-teasing occurs even at the highest levels in the professions. . . . it is a recurring problem for women in all the professions that we examined. It is often associated with positions of male power, but perhaps its most interesting feature is the way in which subordinate men can use the mechanism to exert power over their women superiors, illustrating one of the most powerful ways in which gender privilege can be used to overcome any other system of hierarchy and power.[57]

Crimes against women in India are legion. Women can be the subject of acid attacks, beatings, coerced sex in marriage and rape, apart from epidemic sexual harassment. McBride, in her Asian Human Rights Commission Report cited earlier, points out that while reported rapes have increased in number in India, convictions have dropped by a third because police are failing to conduct investigations and prosecutions. It has also taken more than six hundred days or even up to five or ten years for a rape case to come to court.[58] McBride also has an interesting comment on violence against women:

> The reality according to recent studies . . . is that educated and working women are more likely to experience domestic violence, and this form of violence is not unique to any specific region, caste, socio-economic group or religion. This implies that it is not lack of education that makes women more susceptible to violence, but rather the widespread acceptance of violence towards women. The "culture of silence" and accepting attitude towards violence are the most problematic parts of tackling this issue. A dramatic attitudinal change amongst both sexes is required.[59]

McBride's report reiterates the fact that men – even the judiciary and law-makers – believe that sexual harassment and rape are the fault of the woman's behaviour such as her provocative clothing, her smoking, drinking of alcohol, visiting clubs and bars and being out late at night: such a woman becomes "loose" and "immoral". These behavioural factors of women make rape more justifiable in the eyes of men. It is no wonder that a rape victim feels shame and responsibility for the violence against her as, so often, will her family: a family with a violated girl or woman would find it almost impossible to obtain a husband for her, an unmarried daughter further adding to their shame. As McBride says: "In the recent case of the brutal gang rape and murder in New Delhi, police did not take action for 20 minutes after finding the victim, as they haggled over the proper jurisdiction for her case, leaving her naked and bleeding on the streets."[60] Six-hundred rape victims in Delhi in 2012 had the courage to report the violence against them, but there was only one conviction. The Asian Human Rights Commission has found, too, that perpetrators of rape are sometimes the state police themselves or men in similar official positions, and women fear approaching police in case they become victims of those supposed to protect them.[61] The level of corruption amongst the police is so high that bribes make it easy for a culprit to get away with crime.

Rape in India is not confined to secluded places: Dalmia in her news article claims that most rapes take place in public places like parks, streets and on public transport.[62] It was in such a public place that the gang rape, torture and murder of the twenty-three-year-old physiotherapy student took place in December 2012 in New Delhi, called India's rape capital. Defending the perpetrators of the crime was just one lawyer who defended three of the accused with a defence that stems from his view that it is the victim's *own fault*. This is what he had to say in the British Broadcasting Corporation Television documentary:

> We have a different culture . . respectable girl and non-respectable girl means if you see someone, if you feel respect about her, she's respectable. If she would be respectable this will never happen to her. Respect is a very strong shield which can't

> be crossed by anybody at all. And respect comes by character: respect comes by your behaviour: respect comes by your actions: respect comes by your circumstances.

When asked if the student was responsible, the lawyer replied:

> She was responsible for this. You cannot say that only the rapists are responsible. She is also responsible equally, and entirely the boy who put her in such scenario. You have to protect yourself.[63]

The attitude of the lawyer is a pertinent summary of what I have been saying earlier, and here is an intelligent, professional man echoing the views even of politicians and religious leaders that the victim is at fault. The tragic death of the student has sparked a good deal of protest in India, with mass demonstrations not only by women, but by men also. If India wishes to be taken seriously in its economic advancement then it cannot permit half of its citizens to remain in fear of progressive activity in society. At the very least, the local and governmental authorities in India are attempting to address the issue, encouraging and training police to be more vigilant and conscientious in dealing with violence against women. There are few women police officers so it is male officers to whom accusations have to be reported but now there is a dedicated women-in-distress line to deal with cases of rape and an attempt to fast-track such cases. But, despite being fast-tracked, the Delhi rape case was concluded on the ninth of September, 2013 and four men were found guilty of rape and murder.[64] In March, 2013, a new law came into being in India aimed at protecting women against sexual violence and imposing the death penalty for repeat offenders in the case of rape or for rape that leads to death. Since the Delhi rape case, reports of cases of sexual violence against women have nearly doubled and are endemic in newspaper reports. But how can one change a deep-rooted patriarchal idealism that is rooted in socio-religious praxis and has been for over a thousand years? Prejudice against women begins for Hindu women when they are in the womb and it says little for a religion if it perpetuates unchanging and non-evolving religious norms that are detrimental to the personal evolution of the female population.

So how are women to remain "respectable" as the lawyer pointed out was so necessary? Deference and modesty is a key answer. The wife normally imbibes both in her relationship with her husband and his family. Deference to the older members of the family is expected and from women to men, women sometimes covering their faces before older men, as was noted earlier. Women have traditionally been expected to rise in the mornings before their husbands and retire after them, as well as eat after the men of the family have eaten. Without such respectability and modesty, a woman becomes a strumpet. A girl who goes to a club for a simple birthday celebration, leaving at a respectable time, is regarded as a prostitute.[65] And yet prostitutes in ancient times and later were highly valued as educated, immensely refined, accomplished and very articulate. Temple prostitutes, *devadāsīs*, have theoretically disappeared, having become illegal in 1947, but their singing and dancing skills have remained and they still obtain as temple and ritual performers. Saskia Kersenboom is an "insider" as a successor to temple dancers and records the rituals, dances and songs at the Śrī Subrahmaṇyasvām" Temple in Tiruttaṇi, providing certain evidence that the *deva-dāsī* is not extinct but still present and highly and eternally auspiciously active.[66]

In many areas of the religious sphere, women have been able to break free from the fetters of patriarchy. It is women in the main who perform the home *pūjās*, and devotional Hinduism provides for them an expressive outlet supported by the abundant *Purāṇic* literature with its rich mythology and ample dimensions that allow both literate and illiterate women to participate in religious experience. *Purāṇic* literature is more attractive, "homely", as Altekar described it,[67] and women over the centuries have been popular audiences to recitations of the many stories contained in this devotional literature. In Kṛṣṇaism, too, women found that the adultery of the *gopīs* was something in which men had to acquiesce, almost transforming themselves into females to approach Kṛṣṇa as God. It was a religious liberation for women if not a social one, and women, as a result, find equality of access to God through devotional religion whatever their caste. Within the textual, ritual or life-cycle rite customs, women have frequently added their own rituals, chants, songs and additional ceremonies to mark occasions as mainly women dominated.[68] In urban contexts, women from different caste backgrounds may even gather together for such things as festival celebrations.[69]

Within the massive devotional expressions of Hinduism emerged poet–saints. They sang praises to the deities in an emotional outburst and included famous women like Āṇṭāl in South India and Mīrābāī in the North. The poetry of the Āḻvārs of the South was characterized by inclusivity and universalism that did not alienate women. Such poetry is often claimed to be the Tamil *Veda* and whereas the ancient *Vedas* were not accessible to women, effectively excluding them from salvation, the Tamil *Veda* obviated this, making salvation for women in their present lives viable. Similarly, the development of later Śrī-Vaiṣṇava devotionalism that grew out of the Āḻvār tradition in the South included women in its theology, though with hints of the traditional view of them as temptresses.[70] But Śrī-Vaiṣṇavas accept that liberation can be attained as a woman if she surrenders herself to God with single-mindedness: that is all that is needed, and the natural ability of a woman to give love and to be devoted makes her preeminent in the approach to God; after all, she is a natural expression of *śakti*. The subject of the *bhakti* poets is not one that I want to explore until Volume II, but Bose's comment here articulates so well the powerful force of women's poetry: "The poetry of women's spirituality in particular is utterly overwhelming in its emotional authority. Transcending social constraints, the women poets of Hinduism find freedom in a direct, unmediated relationship with God, whom they feel, imagine and express in their poetry."[71]

In more contemporary times, the reverence of modern *gurus* has no gender differentiation. Like the poets of the past, many modern *gurus* make Hinduism accessible to all, not excluding anyone on the basis of race, gender or caste. Mahatma Gandhi had supported women's education and right to equality in public life. Like many, he saw the relationship between Rāma and Sītā as the ideal marriage, but with both being complementary to each other, not Sītā being subservient and obedient to Rāma. It is in Tantrism that women have not only religious equality but sometimes superiority, for they can themselves become *gurus* with many followers. Tantra's attitudes to women are far more liberal than those of traditional Hinduism and Kinsley suggested this was perhaps because Tantrism had its origins outside Hindu orthodoxy in pre-Āryan spheres.[72] In addition, it is not unknown for women to be priests in attendance of small shrines, or to participate in temple *pūjā* with their husbands.[73] The phenomenon of possession of women by a goddess has created a certain empowerment of those who are possessed, as well as of the women who attend at possession times. Kathleen Erndl writes of the "importance of the 'hanging out' time before and after the actual trance session" that provides space for women of all backgrounds and ages to linger together legitimately.[74] "Such spaces", Erndl writes, "may be seen as cracks in a patriarchal system, that is, spaces that exist at least in part because of patriarchy but which provide sites for women's creativity and interconnection, sites for thoughts and activities that can never be completely controlled by patriarchal norms and which furthermore have the potential to resist, transcend or transgress patriarchy."[75]

It would seem, then, that women have an outlet for independent expression through religious praxis, particularly in visits to the temple and their home *pūjā* but, more importantly, it is not impossible for a woman to feel that she is spiritually just as capable of religious salvation and liberation as any man. Women are so often the specialists in ritual in the home and have easy access to handbooks of ritual procedures in vernacular languages for rites they may want to conduct. These would give them all the necessary *Vedic mantras* for ritual performance of, for example, *saṃskāras*.[76] It is by no means unknown for women to become ascetic renouncers, *saṃnyasinis*, celibates or Tantric ascetics.[77] Tantric texts look positively at women regardless of their caste and women can be *gurus*, consorts in sexual ritual or even incarnations of goddesses. In Tantrism they are more readily accepted as *saṃnyasinis*, celibates, *brahmacarinis*, *yoginīs* dedicated to the practice of *yoga*, teachers at *aśrams*, beings possessed by goddesses and, at the same time, they can be married or widowed.[78] The essence of Tantric praxis for women is devotion to a deity, and since her very being as female embodies *śakti*, she is admired. Celibacy may be a life-long choice of a female whose aim is liberation, *mokṣa*, though some women leave their marriages to pursue the same goal. Others may practise Tantric ritual within the medium of their married life, either actively sexual or celibate.[79] Here, devotion to their husbands is as much an aim as to a *guru*. Some women are what McDaniel calls "professional consorts", ritual sexual partners in the more secretive areas of Tantrism.[80] It is in the social milieu, however, that a woman's freedom is heavily curtailed and what I want to do now is examine life in the home, in the family, looking at the different dynamics that pertain to family life.

The family

There are great variations in family structure across regions, classes and castes, urban and village cultures as might be expected. Male-dominated, patriarchal families obtain far more in the North of India than in the South. It is in the North that traditions are more orthodox and always have been. In the South there is more flexibility and less patriarchy. In the North, a married woman is more likely to be separated from her natal family both in distance and in tradition, whereas in the South, contact with the natal family is more acceptable. In the patriarchal setting a woman's spirituality consists of her service to her husband and his family. The man's role is to provide for his family and to maintain family status and tradition. Sītā of the *Rāmāyaṇa* is the ideal wife for a high-caste man, and loyalty, obedience and a strong sense of the particular *dharma* of the male and the female would be expected. Feminists might want to find strong streaks of independence in Sītā but, for the most part, she epitomizes how the relationship between husband and wife should be. Each has a *dharma* to fulfil and the fulfilment of that *dharma* will reflect on the wider family, its position in the community and its caste status. Stepping outside one's family *dharma* brings shame to the entire family. The dynamics of a family are also constantly changing with new wives, status-changes, as when a woman bears sons or finds herself the senior woman of a patriarchal joint family.

Way back in *Vedic* times, when high-class women were married at a later age and were educated, they were probably afforded considerable respect in the home. As brides became little more than children or adolescents, however, it is easy to see how the status of the woman in a home declined. Co-operation as necessary co-partners is enjoined by many of the teachings about marriage with the happiness of man and wife each dependent on the other and, ideally, man and woman once married should look on their relationship as indissoluble. They were expected to perform certain sacrifices daily – sacrifices that could only be performed by a married couple. In many contemporary homes, it is the women now who take care of the religious duties and who undertake much of the activities associated with festivals. It falls to the women, as Kinsley said, to "create and maintain a source of auspicious power so strong that all those within the sphere of the home will be protected from harm".[81] This is a very important point: on the one hand it gives women a massive responsibility, but on the other, it confines their role to one of subservience to the welfare of the family at all times. As Kinsley stated, it is the home that becomes "the locus of Hindu women's spirituality".[82]

Hindu families are nuclear or joint. In the joint family, where several people live in the same household, a man is subject to the wishes of his father and his wife to her mother-in-law: a new wife marries a whole family in the joint family, and she will have more tasks to undertake than any of the other women in the household: as the newcomer, she will carry out the bulk of the domestic work. A man does no household chores at all; it is simply not the cultural *dharma* of a man to take on domestic duties and, as we saw earlier, this obtains even if the woman is working full time. Nevertheless, there are other women in a joint family who can take care of the children of a working woman and who, if necessary, can bear some of the burden of chores. So how does a modern professional woman handle such a situation? Many educated professional women have married later in order to pursue their studies and are not the late-adolescent bride who can more readily come under the control of a mother-in-law. It has meant that changes have been necessary and the more confrontational relationship between a woman and her mother-in-law has sometimes given way to a more amicable and mutually satisfactory one.[83] If women can avoid living in the joint family, they often will, in order to avoid the mother-in-law problem. Ultimately, however, in a joint family, younger women are subservient to older women and women are subservient to men. The pressures on a new bride in a joint, patriarchal family are considerable. The following words are the recent statement of a young bride in North India. When asked what it means to be a good wife, she responded:

> That you listen to everyone, do what your in-laws say, do everything on time, cook the

> food, listen to them and all this. And she can't do anything without their consent. You have to ask permission for everything; you can't do anything on your own free will, without this consent. After marriage a girl has to leave behind all her own wishes and desires: she has to go along with the wishes of her husband. If it's his wish, it will happen, otherwise it won't. Otherwise arguments and quarrels happen. If she does what she wants there will be constant arguments in the home.[84]

The older a woman becomes in such a family, the greater the relaxation on her chores and restrictions on freedom. Susan Wadley found in her field research in rural North India, that high-class women were especially restricted in their movements and that teenage daughters might find it difficult to travel to high school in a nearby town.[85] The joint family, being mainly patrilineal with father and sons, means that there is an overall male dominance in the home. The men share the economic running of the home and share, too, the immovable property of the family. The status of the males has much to do with the correct behaviour of the females, so the woman cited above is encrusted in a tight traditional role. The lower the economic status of a family the more chance there is for a little freedom for its women.

The nuclear family consists of just the married couple and their children. It is ideal in that there are no hierarchical tensions of the extended family, but neither is there the support for a working woman, who still has to look after her children and run the home as well as work. The wealthy can rely on servants to manage the chores and child care; others juggle their responsibilities with great difficulty. In North India it is the poorer families who tend to live as a nuclear family in rural regions for they cannot maintain the prestige that accompanies the traditional high-class home.

Whatever the structure of the home, women will be responsible for every aspect of its domestic running. Very few men would take responsibility for even a fraction of domestic chores, and Liddle and Joshi are on the nail with their comment that: "It seems that the very thought of domestic work undermines their masculinity."[86] As noted above, for men a working woman is often viewed as an economic commodity, someone who can bring financial help as well as carry out all the domestic chores to benefit the life of the man and also raise his status. Yet, it would be rare to find a husband earning less than his wife: that would certainly undermine male dominance.[87] Male superiority is perpetuated in so far as boys grow up in an environment where it is abundantly evident. They witness the control and dominance of women and expect to behave in the same way when they mature and marry, so entrenching discrimination against females.

Traditionally, women have been expected to do everything possible to ensure the well-being of their husbands and the longevity of the male has always been an important aim. The perfect woman and wife is the *pati-vratā*, she who is utterly devoted to her husband, and unconditionally so. Even the daily *pūjā* conducted by women in the home – praxis in which they have almost total autonomy – has the goal of the well-being of the husband and family in mind rather than the spiritual journey of the wife. The woman is still what Bose describes as "a service provider".[88] Culturally and religiously, the wife should die before the husband. When a man dies before a woman, high-class society blames the woman. It is negative *karma* caused by the woman that brings about her husband's death. Women, therefore, carry out a good deal of religious rituals for the sake of the well-being of their husbands and families, particularly the males of the family. Wadley's research in rural North India found that: "Most women perform yearly rites to gain sons and to ensure both their brothers' and their husbands' long lives. Women's ritual behaviour reinforces the ideology of the male-dominated system and reproduces it in the next generation as women teach their daughters and daughters-in-law."[89] The welfare of the husband, in particular, is the wife's duty, her *strī-dharma*. She can fulfil this duty with her domestic chores and correct behaviour, but also religiously by fasts and vows. In fact, the *strī-dharma* of a woman was laid down in the law books and though no longer strictly legal in contemporary India and declining in praxis, would certainly be maintained by high-caste Hindu families. A *Kṣatriya* woman in the Banāras area of India commented that: "*Strīdharm* begins at the point at which we become married. The meaning of this is that one should give support to one's husband and family."[90]

Many women make vows, *vratas*. A *vrata* is both a vow and a religious ritual and Kinsley referred to it as "one of the mainstays of Hindu women's spirituality throughout India".[91] Women will fast or abstain from something in order to propitiate a deity for the well-being of their families. They may group together to do so in a communal gathering or may simply undertake a *vrata* alone. The same *Kṣatriya* woman above from the Banāras region observed fifteen different *vratas* every year, as well as other rituals as, for example, at festival times.[92] She stressed that performing *vratas* has a positive spiritual effect on the performer, "peace of mind or contentment, the restraint of negative emotions, the activation of purity of heart",[93] indicative that for some women there may be an underlying spirituality gained form a *vrata* as much as a pragmatic outcome for the family. Kinsley believed that the *vrata* is a form of religious asceticism or *yoga* and is what he termed "very much a part of the normal rhythm" of the lives of Hindu women.[94] Anne Mackenzie Pearson's research into *vratas* revealed that for many women *vratas* are intensely spiritual. She was told by one informant: "*Vrat* is a kind of worship of God . . . By keeping a *vrat* I will be closer to God. On the *vrat* day meditation on God is heightened, for one eats little, so we remember God more often. The heart remains pure that day."[95] The communal gathering of women for *vratas* provides an opportunity to be free of normal restraint: even a priest is not necessary.

Some *vratas* will be annual events, some associated with festivals and some are more general and individual, but the point of the *vrata*, which is usually accompanied by the recitation of an appropriate myth in communal gatherings, is that *not* to take part in it renders a woman likely to be responsible for the early demise of her husband or sons. While *vratas* are not obligatory, women see them as so, often believing that without them the well-being of their families cannot be assured.[96] It is, therefore, an auspicious ritual that seeks a positive outcome in the health and prosperity of the woman's family. But it is the family that is the focus of the vow – the longevity of a husband; love in marriage; a future happy marriage and a good husband; avoidance of widowhood; the welfare of children; the welfare of widows and their life after death.[97] Lawrence Babb records a "sixteen Mondays" *vrata* in central Indian village life, by which the vow extends to fasting for sixteen Mondays in succession, again, for the welfare of husbands.[98] Unmarried women may also carry out a *vrata* in the hope of finding a good husband and, strictly speaking, even men could perform a *vrata*, as, perhaps, when beginning a new business venture. There are *vratas*, too, that are associated with different deities like Hanumān's weekly *vrata*. But the ritual tends to be confined to women. It may seem an apotropaic act, but, Kinsley made the important point here that "it seems clear that *vratas* and other rituals undertaken by women in the domestic sphere express and create a feeling of women's religious space, in which they are in control of the most meaningful area of their lives".[99] Priests may be invited for part of the *vrata* ceremony, but they are not essential and it is women who perform the *kathā*, the traditional relating of the myth in prose or poetic form that is special to the *vrata*. Bose comments that *vratas* "provide a very special space reserved for women, in effect a refuge where they achieve a significant measure of self-sufficiency".[100]

Life in urban cities and towns is, of course, relatively different to that in rural villages and, as I have pointed out, high-caste rules for women are stricter in North India than in the South. Also, the lower the caste of the woman the greater freedom of mobility she will have. However, the attitudes to women infiltrate down from the higher classes, their so-called respectability and status dictating the way in which they believe respectable women should behave. This seems to have informed the ways in which women are viewed in the modern cities, if the comments of the lawyer defending the men accused of the Delhi rape and murder are concerned. Both men and women will need to address their gender conditioning, before changes can appear in the depths of societal thinking.

Dress

The way a woman dresses is critical to the amount of respect she can expect. Western dress in the great cities is a difficult issue, and could elicit sexual harassment. The traditional sari for women is designed to disguise the sexuality of a woman's body and its five or six-metre length is worn in different styles in different regions of India. It is expected to cover the legs, though the midriff and arms may be bare. The loose end of the sari serves as a covering for a woman's hair or face in the company of elders, of men, or when performing *pūjā*, though in some parts of India women use an extra piece of material called a *dupatta* for covering the head. A woman shows respect and gains respect by such deference. The sari is worn differently in different parts of India. In the North, it is draped once around the waist, pleated, and the pleat is tucked into the waist. The long part left over, the *pallu*, is then draped over the left shoulder in the North, whereas in the Gujarat style the *pallu* is taken to the back and draped over the front of the right shoulder. Bengali women do not pleat their saris and in a region like Maharastra, women pull the sari through the legs and tuck it in the back of the waist.

In northern India, especially in the Punjab, women prefer to wear light, loose trousers fitted into a tight band at the ankles called *salwar*, and a long loose-fitting tunic called a *kameeze*, which has slits at the side, though such a style is to be found throughout India. The *salwar*, in particular, are sufficiently loosely fitting to hide the shape of the woman and, bearing in mind the conservatism of northern India in comparison to the South, this style of dress covers the body to give a woman a respected concealment. The *dupatta* or *orhna* is particularly favoured with the *salwar-kameeze*. Northern India – an area which is composed of six different states – has been influenced by Muslim styles and is fairly conservative in dress. It is with northern India that Pashmina shawls, fashionable also in the West, are specially associated. In some regions of western India like Rajasthan, women wear a long skirt with a short-sleeved blouse, the *lengha-choli*, and a long piece of material added around the waist and over the shoulders. Similar is the *ghagra*, the pleated or gathered skirt that may be worn a little shorter than ankle length or at full length. Also in western India, women may wear a divided skirt with a belt at the waist and flared at the bottoms. An ankle-length skirt is worn underneath the sari in some parts of India, along with the bolero-type blouse, the *choli*, which exposes the midriff.

Traditionally, dress is supposed to be unsewn like the sari, though blouses for women are always stitched. While men, particularly young men in the cities, wear western-style trousers and shirts that are ready-made, outside the towns and cities the older men, especially, will wear the traditional *dhoti* wrapped around the lower half of the body. The *dhoti* is popular in northern India: it was a garment immortalized by Mahatma Gandhi and, like Gandhi wore it, it is wrapped around the waist and then tucked up between the legs. A visitor to Delhi will find men wearing the traditional *kurta-pajama* trousers covered with a long tunic. In the South of India, men wear a *lungi*, a piece of cloth wrapped around the lower body but left long and not tucked. Some men still wear turbans – a Hindu mode of dress as well as Sikh. Leather, as polluting, is not usually found in the home of a *Brāhmin*, though with modern sandals, they may well find their way into a few homes.[101] Cotton clothing is also believed to be impure and avoided by those who can do so, but low caste and poor families will certainly wear cotton. However, cotton is the main material for clothing in northern India and also in the warmer climate of southern India. A poor *Dalit* woman may only own as little as two saris and she and her children would be mainly barefooted, though it would be a mistake to think that all *Dalits* are impoverished. Some rise to professional levels and can afford to dress well. While most women may wear a sari, the style in which it is worn, its patterning and ornamentation will reflect the caste of the wearer. The saris of high-caste women will be of good fabric that is usually expensive and will be longer and broader than the cheaper factory-produced saris. The more ornamentation there is on a sari, the higher its cost and the greater the status of the wearer. Certain colours and motifs are connected with different regions and communities.

Jewellery is immensely important to a Hindu woman. In the past, a woman had no right of inheritance to immovable property, but it was considered that movable property like her jewellery was her own, though as we saw in the last chapter, she is often expected to give this away in the conjugal home. Jewellery, as clothing, is considered as a woman's *strī-dhana* and she should, in theory, have complete control over it. Nevertheless, if the woman becomes a widow, she is expected to relinquish every bit of her jewellery for it is a sign of good fortune and the widow is an inauspicious being. Wearing jewellery is a status symbol for a woman, especially a married woman, and it is another symbol of the respect she is accorded. Bracelets and bangles, rings, necklaces, earrings, toe-rings and nose-rings are popular and an auspicious bride is thoroughly laden with them all. In some parts of India, the nose-ring and toe-ring are both signs that a woman has a husband and are signs of a marriage that is blissful. Similarly, in some parts of India hair can be worn in such a way that it states a woman's devotion to her husband: this is usually in the form of a braid or a chignon.[102] The poorer the woman, the less jewellery she will have, perhaps just a few plastic bangles.

The red dot worn by women in the middle of the forehead is the *bindi*, or *pottu* as it is called in the South. Red is the colour of blood, of fertility and *śakti* energy and a female wearing such a mark usually indicates that she is post-pubescent. The *bindi* can indicate whether a woman is old or young, married or, as yet, unmarried, and the degree of respect she needs to be accorded.[103] In southern India, some married women wear two *pottus*, the second near the hairline.[104] Women may also wear a dot of colour in the parting of their hair, indicative that they are married. The ornamentation of a woman – her *bindi* or *pottu*, her wedding pendant, and toe rings, for example – are indicative of her auspiciousness, an auspiciousness, Nagaran believes, that is transferred to the well-being of her husband, and for some, the *bindi/pottu* is a symbol of this.[105] The absence of these is a sign of inauspiciousness as in menstruation or mourning.

In short, the ways in which individuals dress are statements of who they are, the degree of respect they can demand and expect, their social class, the region from which they come, the caste or tribe to which they belong and their status and wealth. While the traditional dress of one region may be adopted and adapted by another there is much in dress that differentiates an individual, and for women is indicative of the kind of respect she must be offered. Completely different is the dress of the widow, as we shall now see.

Widows

A very poignant statement was made by Altekar when he remarked: "The position of the widow in society is one of the most important topics which the historian of woman has to discuss and elucidate. The treatment which she receives is often an index to the attitude of society towards women as a class."[106] I can follow this statement with another appropriate one by Swati Deshpande: "India, which has the dubious distinction of having the highest widowhood rate in the world, also has an inheritance law that's not hugely women friendly. India widows collectively outnumber the current Canadian population of 32.4 million, but the tribe suffers the ignominy of its rights being observed more in breach."[107] According to the 2001 census, there are forty-five million widows in India, forty million of whom receive no pension.

Traditional attitudes to women stem from the law books and the likes of Manu, who said:

> A virtuous wife should never do anything displeasing to the husband who took her hand in marriage, when he is alive or dead, if she longs for her husband's world (after death). When her husband is dead she may fast as much as she likes, (living) on auspicious flowers, roots, and fruits, but she should not even mention the name of another man. She should be long-suffering until death, self-restrained, and chaste, striving (to fulfil) the unsurpassed duty of women who have one husband.[108]

These tones of chasteness and austerity along with the inability to remarry have made the conservative widow's lot a harsh one. A widow is easily recognized by her dress and her lack of the auspicious ornaments and jewellery worn by the married woman. The *sindur* mark in the parting of her hair that signifies a woman's married status is also not there.

The Indian government has attempted to redress the appalling situation of many widows with legislation but, again, the massive gap between the theoretical law and what happens in practice does not ameliorate the lot of many widows. Cultural patterns – in which the Indian government does not wish to interfere – are set almost in tablets of religious and social tradition that are unbreakable. The Hindu Succession Act of 1956 stated that an intestate male's estate devolves equally on his sons, daughters, *widow* and mother, so the widow, in theory, inherits equally with others. However, a husband can make a will to leave his widow without anything at all. Subsequent Amendments to the Act from 2005 onwards attempted to equalize the inheritance of females with males. As the law stands now, a female has equal rights with a male in inheriting agricultural land and a discriminatory part of the law that prevented some widows from inheriting property if they remarried was removed. However, since the deceased male's property of a joint home is shared out between sons and daughters with one share allocated to him, the widow only gets a little of the whole – that share allocated to her deceased husband. The law has, says Meera Khanna "folds within folds of inequalities".[109]

Daughters should now inherit a share of the natal home alongside sons but they are often persuaded to will away their shares at an early age only to find when they are later widowed that they have nothing. The rationale for this is usually that they have been given their share as dowry and cannot expect more. In any case, the preference for sons still makes it likely that the males will be the ones to inherit, rather than daughters, especially if the father has made a will. When a man dies, the division of his property is immediate irrespective of the law, and the home in which his wife has lived is suddenly withdrawn, leaving a widow dependent, in the main, on her eldest son or sons. The extent of illiteracy amongst widows and the husband's ownership of her property in a patrilineal joint family, means that widows have very little access to any help from legal proceedings. A widow may not, in fact, have any record of her marriage and therefore no proof that she is a widow.

The lot of the widow is generally a harsh one: as Khanna rightly says, "widowhood is viewed not as a period in the life cycle of a woman, but as a personal and social aberration, to be devoutly wished away".[110] Widows are sufficiently abused to be branded as witches in some areas, 2556 being killed between 1987 and 2003 for supposed witchcraft, with a minimal punishment for the crime.[111] It is often said that the Hindu widow is physically alive but socially dead. Her life is expected to be religiously ascetic with a meagre vegetarian diet and the garb of the ascetic. In some cases in the past, her hair was cut, which still obtains occasionally in the present. Nothing about her appearance is expected to be attractive and the effect is to render a widow inauspicious, so much so that she is unable to attend special occasions – even if that happened to be the marriage of her own children: she is an omen of bad luck. While more moderate thinkers have pioneered for remarriage for widows – and there is no legal reason why they cannot remarry today – it is only among lower castes and tribes that remarriage occurs: for higher castes, it is rare. Such a custom is particularly pitiful when the widow is young and childless.

The widow is performing a kind of penance, a punishment for not acting in such a way when her husband was alive as to protect him with her devotion, religious rites and, as we have seen, *vratas*: a woman is never expected to outlive her husband. She is deemed to be sinful, evil, a creature carrying negative *karma* for which she must live the rest of her life to burn up. All the inauspiciousness of death surrounds her. As the other half of her husband, she must continue to pray for his welfare in his abode beyond death, in the hope that she will eventually be reunited with him. If she is lucky, then her sons will take care of, and provide for, her: again, she is a woman under the control of men. Widowhood is a great threat to a woman for even those in her natal home may not wish to have the economic burden or, indeed, the disgrace and bad luck of a widow in their home. She may be lucky enough to remain in her former husband's home, but her status vanishes and her daughter-in-law – she who was so dominated as a new wife – now has her turn to dominate. Of course, there are some women who refuse to adopt the widow's garb, who keep their toe-rings as a sign of their marriage and continue to wear jewellery, often out of necessity of having to work and support a family.[112] Women who spent a married life in the seclusion of *pardā*, may find themselves having to leave the protection of the males of the family in order to work amongst strangers. As Wadley points out: "Independence is not valued, and women state a clear preference to be a subordinate wife in a joint household."[113] A widow is highly dependent on her sons, if she has them. It is they that she hopes will support her in her degraded state as a widow. The young wife with no sons often has no such hope. Baker provides a very vivid description of the fate of a *Kṣatriya* widow:

> When a Rajput dies before his wife, she is subjected to a rigid ritual of mourning. She is expected to sit quietly for many months in a corner of the living room, sometimes hidden behind a curtain with her face completely covered. No other woman whose husband is still alive is allowed to see her face. Her only company, apart from her immediate family, is other widows. Her diet is kept to the bare minimum, just a little rice and water. She is not supposed to leave her position to relieve herself, a small pot being handed to her through the curtain. The clothes she wears for a specified time are of the same colour as those her husband wore when he actually expired. She takes no part in the elaborate funeral rites, although prior to the cremation she will take her farewell of him by walking backwards around his body. Twelve days after his death, all the widows in the neighbourhood come to lead her into the courtyard of her home where they ceremoniously smash the coloured wedding bangles she wears on her wrists and remove the gold pin from her nose. She is then dressed in black or white, the only colours she will wear for the rest of her days, and is led back to her position of isolation.[114]

The stark reality of a life to be lived without a husband is immediate for the wife left behind. Customs are different depending on caste and region. Baker describes, for example, how a *Vaiśya* Marwari widow living in Bombay had to have her hair cut very short and how the men in the family removed her jewellery with her beautiful hand-woven saris being distributed amongst her daughters.[115] Baker also describes a similar fate of widows in *Brāhmin* traditions in Tamil Nāḍu, who also have to have their hair cropped short.[116] The red *bindi* that married women wear on their foreheads is no longer worn by widows.

Remarriage for a widow usually depends on the tradition within her caste and it is *Brāhmin* widows who are the least likely – indeed highly unlikely – to remarry, reflecting the long tradition that was entirely against widow remarriage. It was simply regarded as not respectable if a widow married again and that tradition, rife amongst the upper class came to be adopted by lower castes also in an attempt to raise their own levels of respectability.[117] While widow remarriage was legalized in India as early as the mid-nineteenth century, tradition, respectability and family honour have held sway against the law, and the likelihood of widows experiencing what Baker so graphically described above is more the norm than any newly conjugal happiness. Amongst the lower castes, where historical tradition has not had the same influence, there is far more evidence of widow remarriage. There are exceptions, too, to the negative treatment of widows in some sects of Hinduism. In Śrī-Vaiṣṇava Hinduism it is believed that a male achieves the highest Heaven after death and that this is something about which the widow can rejoice: the widow is even regarded as auspicious in this case.[118] There are occasions, too, when widows remain in the family home and continue to be matriarchs who rule over their homes and the younger women of the family. We also have the exceptional Indira Gandhi, a widow who became India's prime minister in 1996. Fuller makes both these points but still comments that "widowhood consistently carries a powerfully negative symbolic load among Hindus".[119] Attitudes to widows and to their remarriage are changing but, like so many other facets of Hindu social and religious existence, encrusted layers of tradition and custom are hard to permeate.

Food: *Anna*

Food preparation, choice of foods, methods of eating and commensality are bound up in serious socio-religious customs of class and caste, as well as the enormous variations of regional praxis. Within the wide variations there are also traditional mores and taboos that pertain to regions, locales, families, religious sects and social environments. Additionally, individuals may have certain food customs in a religious setting and different ones in the home.[120] Louis Dumont's following comment highlighted only too well the enormity of difference between Hindu and western eating habits: "The fact remains that one can scarcely ever eat side by side with any but one's equals, that the host does not generally eat with his guests, and that meals are not those pleasant conversational gatherings with which we are acquainted: they are technical operations which leave room for only a limited margin of freedom."[121] The fundamental reason for the problems of commensality and traditions about food lies in the concerns for purity and impurity. When an individual is in contact with food – or the utensils used to prepare it – the relative purity or impurity of the person passes to the food. The purity of a *Brāhmin*, then, makes it possible for anyone to eat *Brāhmin*-prepared food. The impurity of a low-caste individual or a *Dalit*, makes it impossible for higher-caste individuals to eat that with which these low-caste individuals have had contact. The strictness with which such ideas are maintained will vary from region to region: the North, for example is slightly more tolerant than the South. Thus, some *Brāhmin* castes of northern India will eat meat and fish unlike the stricter observances of vegetarianism amongst *Brāhmins* of the South. Northern *Kṣatriya* castes will also eat meat, whereas northern *Vaiśya* castes are often stricter vegetarians than *Brāhmins*.[122] Even the *Laws of Manu* did not condemn meat-eating: it just made it more respectable not to eat meat. With much justification, then, R. S. Khare describes Hindu food, *anna*, as "the most intimate yet ubiquitously transacted bodily, interpersonal, social and spiritual substance".[123]

The ancient *Vedic* Hindu sacrificed an enormous number of animals, and it was this sacrificed meat that was then eaten. Animal sacrifice was a great part of religious ritual and gave to the slaughtered animal a certain religious status. Perhaps this is where the sacredness of the cow came about as Dumont suggested.[124] Certainly, the cow, as a grazing animal that produced milk, was more important alive than dead. In time, the cow became a sacred creature and its five products – milk, curd, purified butter (*ghī*), urine and dung – are still regarded as purifying. Cow dung is widely used as fuel, and urine could be utilized in the making of a washing product or as dye for ink. Even touching a cow is a means of purification. The cow is, thus, a sacred and protected animal, a symbol of non-violence, *ahimsā*, and it is a heinous crime to harm a cow. They can be seen roaming through the towns in India, grazing on grass verges or munching vegetables discarded by street sellers or even vegetables that are for sale. It is a creature that takes little yet gives a lot. The products of the cow – its milk, curds and *ghī* – are considered highly wholesome, *sattvic*, foods, whereas eating its flesh is the opposite and *tamasic*.

Those who are strict vegetarians find meat-eating totally abhorrent, rather like eating a corpse. Dumont, with some credibility, suggested that *Brāhmin* avoidance of meat may have been influenced by the ascetic tradition – that fourth stage of the stages of life in which the religious ascetic survived on fruits and herbs and lived spiritually without harming anything – as well as the influence of Buddhism and Jainism with their strict non-violence beliefs. Maybe, as Dumont suggested, many *Brāhmins* wished to emulate such respected spirituality.[125] The great diversity of customs regarding food means that it is rare to find wholly vegetarian or non-vegetarian castes.[126] And in this day and age, meat may be avoided for purely health reasons. Those beyond the caste system who are responsible for disposing of dead cattle and of turning their hides to leather are the dreaded impure at the opposite of the spectrum of *Brāhmin* purity. Those who are not vegetarians are generally averse to eating beef but in some regions like Bengal, most meats and fish are eaten. The prevalence of sacrifices to Kālī in Bengal means that a goat can be sent as a sacrifice to Kālī and returned as *prasāda* for the family to eat. Fish may be avoided in northern India on the grounds that Viṣṇu once incarnated as a fish and it would be sacrilegious, therefore, to partake of it. Generally, however, and certainly amongst high-class *Brāhmin* Hindus, vegetarianism became a symbol of superiority and purity, though with considerable variation.

From a religiously philosophical point of view, while food supports life, there is in food that particle of the ultimate Brahman that supports all existence. So food has "both gross (*sthūla*) and subtle (*sūkṣma*) properties, binding beings with their bodies and binding both of these to inescapable cosmic laws of *dharma* and *karma* that create and regulate food for all creatures."[127] Thus, there is a certain symbiotic relationship between eater and what is eaten. The author of the *Gītā* would probably have endorsed such a view. The *Gītā* links food with action: action > ritual action (*yajña*) > rain > food > beings (3:14), providing a cosmic link between food and the being who eats it. Chapter 17 of the *Bhagavad Gītā* classifies foods according to the three *guṇas* of *sattva*, *rajas* and *tamas*. *Sattvic* foods are those believed to increase life, strength, health, happiness and cheerfulness and they are "savoury, oily [milk, butter and cheese], substantial and agreeable" (verse 8). *Sattvic* foods include rice, grains, fruit and a good range of vegetables. *Rajasic* food is "bitter, sour, saline, excessively hot, pungent, dry, burning" and is said to "bring pain, grief and disease" (verse 9). Onions and garlic fall into this category and are avoided by many Hindus, though not, it seems, by *Kṣatriyas* of Rajasthan.[128] *Rajasic* food promotes the same quality as the *guṇa* – excitement, passion, anxiety, tension. Then: "Stale, tasteless, putrid, rotten and that which is refuse and impure is the food liked by the *tamasic*" (verse 10). Meat, stale foods and leftovers would be included in this category of *tamasic* food and, like the *tamas guṇa* that is the inert, dark and dull facet of life, will cause involution and stagnation. *Sattvic* foods, then, are the most pure, and raw foods being pure, may be given from a low-caste individual to, say, a *Brāhmin* who has performed some service. Perfect, *paccā*, food that is considered to be pure is parched grain or something fried in *ghī* which, since *ghī* is a sacred product of the cow, renders a food pure. Imperfect food is labelled *kaccā* and could not be passed from one caste to another. A foodstuff boiled in water becomes *kaccā* so, generally, *paccā* food is more versatile in commensality.

Food that is not cooked is less likely to be polluted, so uncooked grains may be transferred between castes. Cooked food, on the other hand allows impurities from the preparer to pass into the food and thus, to use the words of Jackson and Killingley: "To receive food from another person is to share, to some extent, in that person's nature."[129] Thus, as Khare succinctly puts it, for the Hindu, not only are you what you eat, but you eat what you are.[130] However, another highly polluting factor is saliva. Nothing should be eaten once it has been in contact with another person's saliva. Thus, if tasting a food while cooking, the spoon, or the like, cannot be returned to the food. We have seen in earlier chapters how *prasāda*, the food left over from offerings to deities is acceptable because it is from the gods. Similarly, the leftovers of a husband's food are customarily eaten by the wife, since the husband is her god.

The purity of the kitchen is meticulously maintained. There, shoes are never worn and the body is often purified by washing before entering it, particularly if the household shrine is in the kitchen. The higher the class, the stricter the observance of purity in the kitchen is likely to be. It is the women of the home who are responsible for the diet, being in charge of all food preparation and the keeping of fasts in the family. They ensure that the kitchen is kept thoroughly pure and that no one enters it with impurities such as leather. Visitors would not, normally, be allowed in a Hindu kitchen. A menstruating woman becomes impure and does not enter the kitchen or prepare food, though there are homes in which there may be no other option available for a woman, since males rarely cook in the home. It is the kitchen in which the woman is entirely autonomous. Nagarajan, in the context of Tamil custom, puts this beautifully: "The place where food is prepared is the center where all the family's ritual activities are commenced, maintained, and completed. In fact, the entire women's cooking area is the literal and metaphorical hearth – the spiritual and psychological core of the household and the most valued site for the production of auspiciousness."[131]

The princes and aristocracy of the past drank alcohol but it has been prohibited in the law books for the devout Hindu. It is believed to be a polluting substance that makes the drinker or seller of it highly impure and untouchable. As to water, it has similar caste restrictions as food and can be polluted by a lower-caste person: even if that person merely enters a room where there is water, it becomes contaminated by his or her proximity and has to be discarded. Wells are always a source of contention, *Dalits* insisting on their rights to draw water from them and caste Hindus resenting the subsequent pollution. A well can be purified after such contamination by a bucket of Ganges water or some drops of cow urine, but Baker offers an interesting comment here: "In desert areas where Untouchables have asserted their rights by insisting on drawing water from the communal well, Brahmins have been known to send a camel to fetch water from a well some miles away, to avoid polluting themselves."[132] The vessel that contains water is also an agent of impurity, especially if earthenware and in South India a *Brāhmin* will only accept water from a member of his own caste: customs are a little less rigid in the North.

In view of all the restrictions concerning purity and impurity, it is not surprising that eating habits are caste bound and food is not transferred from one caste to another, though there may sometimes be a downward movement of *jutha*, leftovers. Dumont referred to such practice as "the most convenient manifestations of the hierarchical principle".[133] Commensality is, therefore, always a problem and it may mean that special occasions have to provide different areas in which separate castes can eat. Frequently, in situations such as funerals, *Brāhmins* will cook the food and serve it, making sure that it is *paccā*; then, different castes are able to eat it, but high-caste *Brāhmins* may well distance themselves from such practice and lower-caste families will engage the services of lower-caste priests who are less traditional. At marriage feasts there may well be both *paccā* and *kaccā* foods, and Khare writes of "intricate food-ranking ritual schemes" that characterize weddings in North India.[134] Again, funeral feasts may involve segregation of castes to offset cross-caste pollution. In today's busy urban world, the maintaining of caste food restrictions is not easy and has had to become more relaxed. The food in some cafés and restaurants is often prepared by *Brāhmins* and they will treat preparation as a technical task, but it is well known that men away on business trips will be highly likely to indulge in eating meat and drinking alcohol. At the other end of the scale, the diet of the poorest *Dalits* is extremely meagre and while they would want to eat meat, many cannot afford it. Inevitably, in the busy post-modern world and city and town life, there is a greater relaxation in eating rules and people who would not in the past have eaten together have found it more expedient to do so in the ethos of working life. It is in the home where the usual traditions are reverted to, but changes are being accommodated. Food in Hinduism is much like centuries of Hinduism itself, and Khare pertinently comments: "If it has a deeply entrenched and restrictive caste–kinship–ritual core, then its culinary and gastronomic contours openly adjust, assimilate, and modify by regions and by changing social situations."[135] Nevertheless, external practices involving purity of food have a reciprocal effect on the inner purity of the eater: to ingest what is impure is to become inwardly impure.

Eating habits are very important. Only the right hand is used for eating; the left hand is used for unseemly actions such as the lavatory. Cutlery is absent in eating, and the food is scooped up in bread-like pancakes called *capātīs* or similar and eaten strictly individually. Saliva is polluting, so the moment the food enters the mouth it has been in contact with saliva and is rendered polluted: no one else should then touch that food. Such praxis means that a person who is eating cannot offer food to another, so he or she who serves the food remains ritually pure while others are eating so that they can be served. It makes sense with these arrangements to eat in successive groups. A resounding burp after eating suggests that the meal was enjoyable.

The woman of the home has much to consider in the well-being of her family and in large families the preparation of food is a long process and is conducted according to the traditions long-established in the family. The welfare of the husband, the wife's god, is particularly important and the dietary rules inject into a daily chore a religious ritual. Added to this are the *vratas*, the vows that women also make to promote the health and success of husband and family. Abstaining from eating but still preparing food for the rest of the family is the kind of self-sacrifice many women make as a part of their religious routine. What this chapter has explored is how religious tradition has so often shackled women's freedom in a predominantly overt patriarchal and patrilineal society. Great strides have been made by women to assert their independent identity as a gender that needs to be spiritually and socially free, but, I fear, there is a long, long way to travel before such freedom can be claimed by almost half of India's population. Bose, perhaps, has the appropriate final word when she says "the dominant force in the Hindu discourse of women has been one of overbearing control".[136] One wonders how India will face a post-modern future when shackled with such societal madness. The pen, searching here for historical truths that may inform the present day, is humbled by the experiential reality that seems shockingly mightier.

11
Sacred Times and Places

Festivals

Hindu religion is rich in life, colour and emotion and its festivals, in particular, are characterized by vibrancy, happiness, music, perfumed fires, countless candles, gaily-decked elephants, intensive rituals – all underpinned by varying amounts of spiritual needs and expressions at both the individual and communal levels. Many festivals are not only dedicated to the respective deities, but also reflect important events in the mythological narratives that are so endemic in Hinduism. Of the former, all major deities and many minor ones will have their respective festival days on which they are honoured, and as to the latter, the births of deities as well as famous events in their cosmological lives, their interactions with humanity and their victorious battles against the forces of evil will be celebrated. But it is not only deities that are the focus of festivals: sacred places like rivers and mountains and sacred creatures like cows and buffaloes may also be honoured at such times. Many festivals, though not all, are linked with the phases of the moon and with lunar or solar events.

There is great variation from region to region in the festivals that are celebrated and even pan-Hindu festivals vary considerably in the customs prevalent in the different locales. Furthermore, depending on the region, a festival with the same pan-Hindu name may have different durations and be based on variant or even totally different myths. A festival by the same name may focus on one deity in one area and a different deity in another. These different expressions will be informed not only by the geographical milieu but also by the immediate cultural beliefs and practices and by aspects such as sect, class and caste. All these factors point to a religion with more festivals than any other; some known widely, and others pertinent to a small locale or even a tiny village. It would be impossible in one chapter to cover all but a small fraction of the festivals in Hinduism and I can only illustrate the major features of the most well-known. My purpose here is more to explore the underlying religious and spiritual factors that inform some of the best known as well as to examine some of the main features. But it is important to bear in mind the differences that can obtain in the celebration of even one festival in nearby villages though, frequently, a group of villages may combine for such an occasion.

It is the larger temples that, in the main, have the wealth to have many festivals during the year; whereas smaller temples may have far fewer or even just one annually. Yet, there are pronounced differences between the celebrations of festivals in the North and South of India. In South India, the festivals in villages are mainly elaborate annual ones for tutelary deities of temples, but these are less evident in the North.[1] South Indian Hindu festivals focus greatly on the goddess and her special bond as protector of the community, whereas this is much less the underlying rationale of festivals in the North.[2] Since there are a greater number of temples in the South which, unlike the North, has been mainly free of invaders, there are likely to be a greater number of festivals, especially for village goddesses.

Festivals are often seasonal and suited to the seasons in which they occur. The hot, dry seasons will be characterized by certain festivals, while the rainy season that encourages poisonous snakes, scorpions and disease, when people feel insecure, will be reflected in different types of festivals. The rainy season is also a time when the deities are believed to rest and sleep, allowing demons and evil forces to come to the fore. Few festivals are aligned with the Gregorian calendar and those that are tend to be associated with more modern figures like Mahatma Gandhi, though solstices and equinoxes are fixed times for festivals. A solar day begins at sunrise and ends at sunrise the following day. It is the lunar calendar and the phases of the moon that inform the timing of most of the festivals. The moon's phases last for twenty-nine and a half days, from full moon to full moon, and so every two to three years, an extra month has to be added, otherwise festivals that should occur in the hot or rainy season will not do so. A whole lunar month is divided into segments with different deities being associated with different times and different days, like the fourth day with Gaṇeśa, the eighth with goddesses and the eleventh with Viṣṇu. Then, again, certain days, depending on the region, are associated with specific deities – Monday with Śiva, Wednesday with Gaṇeśa, Sunday with the Mother Goddess, and so on. The new and full moon occasions are regarded as especially important and are auspicious festival times. In the North, the full moon marks the end of a lunar month and in the South, it is the new moon that marks the end of a month. When the moon is waning, a full moon to a new moon, it is a "dark" fortnight, and when waxing, a new moon to a full moon, a "bright" fortnight.[3]

My purpose in this chapter will be to concentrate mainly on the pan-Hindu festivals and these are likely to be involved with the greater temples than the smaller village temples. Suffice it to say here that the smaller village festivals are times for a community in its entirety, a community joined with nearby communities, or even just a part of one community, to gather together for a festival that encourages identity, unity and solidarity amongst its participants, what Fuller describes as "one manifestation of the social significance of the local community".[4] People get caught up in festival activities even if they do not share the beliefs that underlie the events: it is by no means rare, for example, for Hindus to celebrate Christmas. Singing, dancing, fasting, feasting and an ambience of festive occasion is a daily occurrence in many parts of India. People may come from far and wide to celebrate: tradespeople line the streets to sell their wares, particularly the items and offerings necessary for individual *pūjā*, and at the greater festivals, the *mūrtis* of the deities will be processed through the streets to the accompaniment of drums, cymbals and conches. Normal boundaries of caste, sect and gender are broken down in many festivals, what Troy Organ describes as an opportunity for "rhythmic polarities",[5] when the prescriptiveness of *dharma* can, for once, be set aside.

Many of the pan-Hindu festivals are ancient; local ones perhaps less so. Some of these local festivals may have originated amongst the devotions of women, amongst those who habitually gathered together to practise *vratas*, vows, for the welfare of their families. Such community gathering then evolved into more general community festivals.[6] But such devotion underpins all festivals: they are times to express spirituality, focus on a special deity and honour it, and to receive *darśan* along with the blessing and protection of a deity. Festivals are times that open up intimacy between the divine and human worlds, between deity and devotee – characteristics that are the rationale of all the festivals outlined below. In what follows, I shall take a calendric approach to the major festivals beginning, though perhaps a little artificially, with the western conception of the New Year in January.

Lohri /Pongol / Makara-sankranti

The winter solstice late in December marks the point at which the sun begins to move northward heralding lighter and longer days. It is a fixed point in time and shortly afterwards, on approximately the fourteenth of January, the sun moves into Capricorn, called Makara, and a *sankranti* is the first day on which the sun moves into a new zodiacal sign. Thus, the festival is sometimes called Makara-sankranti. It is the time of the winter harvest, a time for kite flying by men and of giving sweets by women. Special foods are associated with the festival in different regions. Since it is the winter solstice and associated with the sun, the festival is connected with Viṣṇu as the sun-deity Sūrya-Nārāyaṇa. In the North of India, right up in the Punjab region, the festival is called Lohri and is characterized by the lighting of bonfires and the singing of popular folk songs. In the South, the festival is called Pongal and here it is really a harvest festival with the gathering in of rice and sugar cane. People eat boiled rice mixed with sugar syrup (jaggery), and since *pongol* means "boiling", the festival takes its name from this customary sweet rice eaten at the time. Cattle are particularly venerated in the South in this festival.[7] The *kolams*, or ground-rice patterns, popular in southern India are particularly evident at the Pongal festival, with elaborate patterns being produced. Vijaya Nagarajan describes them thus: "Drawing the *kolam* in rice flour becomes the event of the day, creating in the end a sense of fine white lace draping over every surface imaginable."[8]

Sarasvatī Pūjā

Sarasvatī is the Goddess of Learning, of the arts and music and at her festival in January–February, musicians and artists perform *pūjā* to her. Tradesmen may also place their tools of trade before her in order for her to bless their daily work. Sometimes, her image is replaced by a book or a pen at the festival. She is particularly venerated by students, who may find they are given a day's holiday at her festival. Sarasvatī Pūjā is a feature, too, of the later festival of Navarātri in September to October and so it has other names when it is celebrated earlier in January. The earlier celebration in spring tends to be mainly in regions like West Bengal and Bihar, where its timing in spring and on the fifth day of the month means that it is named the "spring fifth" festival, Vasanti-pañcamī. Yellow, *vasanti*, is the colour associated with spring, so many people wear yellow clothing on this festival day. It is very popular in the North as a household festival, but in the South tends to be confined to some temples.

Mahāśiva-rātri

Approximately in February on the thirteenth and fourteenth night of the new-moon day is the festival of Mahāśiva-rātri, which, as its name suggests, is associated with Śiva. Mahāśiva-rātri means "Great Night of Śiva" and is a more sombre festival when people fast throughout the day and night in a *pūjā* dedicated to the God. In this *pūjā*, his *liṅga* is painted and decorated, and then honey and milk, or the five sacred products of the cow, are poured over the top. Women process to the temples during the day to perform this rite, carrying a pot of water or milk, or perhaps flowers to put over the *liṅga*. For them, the well-being of their husbands is the main reason for their fasting and *pūjā*, but for unmarried women, it is the hope of a good husband that fills their prayers. Babb makes the interesting point that the weather is warming up at this time and some regard the festival as the beginning of the hot season. Pouring cool liquids over the *liṅga* symbolizes keeping the ferocity of this God, and the possible effects of his "heat", in abeyance.[9] Śiva was fond of intoxicating substances when in his ferocious modes and Mahāśiva-rātri is a time for some to imbibe *bhang*, the potent liquor derived from *cannabis sativa*: *bhang* is, in fact, produced at some temples and offered to devotees as *prasāda*. The day following the vigil is one of feasting.

Mahāśiva-rātri is one of the most important pan-Indian festivals for Śaivas and is also celebrated by many Vaiṣṇavas. Śiva's powers are particularly potent at this festival and since it occurs at the dark time of the month, this time is especially dangerous, when harmful forces abound. All other deities are believed to be weak at dark times, and Śiva, being the God so associated with the dark cosmic forces and with demons and hazardous creatures, is the only source of protection. He is said to perform his *Naṭarāja*, his cosmic dance of creation, preservation and dissolution at this time. The fourteenth night of every dark half of the month is a *Śiva-rātri*, but this occasion early in February is the greatest of them and the most dangerous. It is also said to be the anniversary of the time when Śiva married Parvatī, and is thus a mark of Śiva's part abandonment of his asceticism to become involved within the world. Purification by bathing is important at most festivals and especially so at this one. Such purification is preparation for the honouring of Śiva by singing his praises, chanting his many names or reciting the *Śiva-purāṇa*, and pilgrims will come from far and wide to attend at the most important sites and temples. The festival celebrated at Banāras especially attracts large numbers of pilgrims.

Holi

Holi is an immensely popular spring festival that occurs in February or March. It is very popular in the North and for many it is the New Year, but with different mythological origins informing its focus from region to region. It is not popular in the South, where it is unlikely to be celebrated. It lasts three or four days just before the new moon and is completely opposite in character to a festival like Mahāśiva-rātri, being riotous, noisy, totally lacking in any decorum and not displaying much spiritual character. While its origins are lost in the blur of the long ago, Organ thinks its origin may have been in fertility cults, particularly with the erection of a pole with its phallic symbolism around which the participants dance:[10] indeed, overt references to the phallus pervade the celebrations. Babb, in his research in central India, for example, says that a favourite rallying cry at Holi is "*maharaj land ki jai* (victory to the lord penis)".[11] One of the popular myths involved with the festival is that of a demoness, Holikā, who ate children. One day, a poor woman gathered the local women together and encouraged them to hurl at Holikā as much abuse as they could when she came to take a child. This had the desired effect and Holikā died of shame. However, perhaps the most popular myth, which also features the demoness Holikā, concerns her ability to walk through fire unharmed. Her brother was Prahlāda, who happened to be a devoted follower of Viṣṇu, much to the chagrin of his father who sought every way possible to kill his son, but such was Prahlāda's devotion that he always survived any attack. When Holikā picked up Prahlāda and walked into fire with him, the latter chanted the names of God and survived, whereas Holikā died. This myth may be behind the making of huge bonfires for Holi, these representing the fires in which the demoness was burned. Both these stories may inform the practice of hurling cow dung into the bonfires and shouting obscenities at them. On the other hand, when Kāmā, the god of love tried to pierce Śiva with his arrow of desire, Śiva burnt him to ashes, so for Śaivas, too, the bonfires would have considerable significance. The point is that everyone is included in Holi, whatever his or her usual social or religious nature.

Others celebrate Holi in memory of Kṛṣṇa, especially in connection with his many pranks with the cowherdesses, the *gopīs*, one of which was to throw coloured powder over them as an expression of his divine play, his *līlā*. At some of the Holi celebrations, images of Kṛṣṇa and Rādha are paraded through the streets. Holi occurs at the hottest time of the year and is characterized by "heated" behaviour, and practices are allowed that could not obtain at any other time. It is obviously easy to victimize someone with whom one has an old score to settle, and there is much obscene behaviour connected with phallic themes. There is a relaxation of caste rules and *Dalits* may be found chasing *Brāhmins* and labourer's wives beating the shins of their rich high-caste masters. It is also possible, it seems, that even an outcaste, a latrine sweeper, can be found chasing *Brāhmins*.[12] Women do not have to maintain their normal reclusiveness at this festival; meat can be eaten by vegetarians; pollution is not important; license and obscenity replace usual restrictions; and since the festival occurs at the hottest time of the year, people can let off steam! This is often assisted by drinking or making a paste of *bhang*.

The fires of Holi have something of the burning of the old and the welcoming of the new and therefore the festival has overtones of a New Year about it. Since it welcomes springtime, it is an outdoor festival and the fires of the home are extinguished and relit from the bonfires.[13] McKim Marriott described the experience of Holi: "As I stepped into the lane, the wife of the barber in the house opposite, a lady who had hitherto been most quiet and deferential, also stepped forth, grinning under her veil, and doused me with a pail of urine from her buffalo."[14] But when the riotous behaviour is over and the bonfires cease, more spiritual hymn singing and praises of the Gods take over. In Babb's view Holi has a "sense of catharsis and purging" in which evils of the past are swept away.[15] The reversed roles of the three-day celebration revert back to normal patterns of societal and religious behaviour: the pollution that qualifies the festival reverts to normal purity rules exemplified by the ritual bathing to cleanse away the pollution of the previous days. However, for a time during Holi, everyone becomes a *Śūdra* and "hierarchy is not masked but rudely shattered", as Babb puts it.[16]

Ugadi

Ugadi is the proper New Year festival in March or April for many Hindus in the South and is the real time for turning over a new leaf and for renewal and change. Houses are thoroughly cleaned and decorated with patterns of flour or rice, which is believed will bring good luck and happiness. Purifying bathing is important in the process of renewal, as are new clothes, some of the rich buying them for the poor as a means of acquiring merit for the coming year. Twice-born Hindus will renew their sacred thread at this time, and astrologers prepare their forecast of events in the coming year, forecasting how crops will fare in the fields or how disease might affect a region. A drink made of ingredients that symbolize life and renewal is popular. In some parts of the South, symbols of the Mother Goddess, particularly pots, are placed on poles above houses and directed towards the sun to attract rays of prosperity.

Rām Navami

Rām Navami is in March or April on the ninth day of the bright half of the month. The festival, as its name suggests, is associated with Rāma, the hero of the *Rāmāyaṇa* and is therefore very popular with Vaiṣṇava sects throughout the whole of India. It celebrates the birth of Rāma at Ayodhyā in northern India. Rāma is represented as a baby and placed in a cot, and typically baby foods are offered to him and received back as *prasāda*. Recitation of the beautiful tale of the *Rāmāyaṇa* would be essential. While the festival occurs at this time of the year, it is also celebrated later, in the autumn, as part of the nine-day festival of Durgā Pūjā and its associative celebrations and festivals.

Jagannātha

In around June or July, at the beginning of the monsoon season, a great festival takes place at Purī in Orissa in the north-east of India at the Jagannātha Temple. We get the English word "juggernaut" from this festival, for a massive chariot with huge wooden wheels is specially constructed and bears an image of Kṛṣṇa. His brother Balarāma (or Balabhadra) and his sister Subhadrā are also brought out of the temple on the following day and placed on separate chariots. The festival is the famous *ratha-yātrā*, "pilgrimage of the chariot". The chariots are pulled through the streets outside the temple by hundreds of people, for the carriages are massive, and all sorts of offerings from watches to coconuts are thrown on the chariots as they pass. They are accompanied by magnificently decorated elephants, thousands of pilgrims and many holy *sādhus*. It is a great honour to pull the chariots and it is believed that if one touches the ropes of the cart, *mokṣa* is achieved. Jagannātha means "Lord of the Universe", and is one of the many names of Kṛṣṇa, but at this time, he is accessible to all, even to the extent that people climb onto the chariots to touch the three deities. The dancers that accompany the procession, however, are as much Śaiva as Vaiṣṇava, illustrating the importance and popularity of this great festival.[17] The three images are paraded for all the spectators to have *darśan* and in this grand procession they are taken to a different temple about two miles away, where Jagannātha will stay for seven days, leaving a disconsolate Lakṣmī behind in his main temple. However, Lakṣmī leaves her temple on the fifth day accompanied by *deva-dāsīs* who sing of her plight to Jagannātha, eventually throwing dust in his face in his temporary temple. It is after this event, on the tenth day, that he and his accompanying deities return to take up residence with Lakṣmī in the main temple. Exactly the same grandeur and celebration accompanies the return journey. Jagannātha and his divine family will remain in the temple until the festival takes place once again the following year.

Darśan of Lord Jagannātha at this time is immensely special; the God is believed to be there in person, as Frédérique Marglin says, having had personal experience of climbing onto the *ratha-yātrā*, "he comes down, and is immersed in the middle of the people; he is available to everybody, without distinction".[18] The Jagannātha festival is preceded by a bathing festival during the dark fortnight at which the deities are taken out and bathed. It is this process that begins the cycle of renewal. The deities are bathed in the public eye, the water that washes them being passed to the public as *prasāda*. This process is a very special *darśan* of the deities. They are then returned to the temple and are believed to be in a state of "illness", being laid on the floor of the temple, with no *pūjā* being offered until the day of the new moon when the bright fortnight begins. It is then that the chariot festival proper begins, with the deities being renewed, freshly robed and ready to be seen by their devotees.[19] It is not just in Purī that this festival occurs, for there are other chariot festivals at other temples in India, though the one at Purī is the most spectacular and the most famous.

Viṣṇu's slumber

We come now to the rainy season, the season when the dry fields become green and the rain ripens the crops. While there is work to be done in agriculture and less time for festivals, it is also a dangerous time, an inauspicious, sombre and ominous time. In northern India, Viṣṇu, the God who sustains the universe is believed to sleep for the whole four months of the season, so he is not present to protect the world. This is the period from June to July, and it will be October or November before he wakes up. At one time, it would have been impossible to travel in view of the mud, so pilgrimages ceased, weddings could not take place, and territories came to a standstill. Modern communications have overcome the travelling but not the superstitions about this dark period. This affects the North of India more than the South, where Viṣṇu's slumber hardly features.

Nāga-pañcamī

During the rainy season in July and August comes the festival Nāga-pañcamī. The rainy season brings out the snakes, the *nāgas*, and this festival serves to appease the snake goddesses who may cause harm at this inauspicious time. It is a festival that is more popular in the South of India and cobras are given offerings of milk, but it is also found in the North under different names. Snakes are linked with the cosmic serpent, Śeṣa, on whom Viṣṇu rests. Kṛṣṇa, too, has associations with this festival in view of the myth of his destroying a serpent demon. Snakes were probably venerated by the indigenous tribal groups in India long before the arrival of the Āryans. They have always been closely associated with fertility, partly admired and partly feared. Farmers are expected to abstain from ploughing on this festival day in order not to disturb the snakes, and food and water may be left by snake holes to appease them.

Rakhi-bandhana

Also in July or August is the festival of Rakhi-bandhana, "protection tie", when sisters tie a *rakhi* on the right wrists of their brothers, who are seen as their protectors. The *rakhis* are attractively made, though not given without expectation of money in return. The festival takes place on the day of the full moon and is a time also when twice-born men, especially *Brāhmins*, in some regions renew their sacred threads. In an old myth, the *Vedic* god, Indra, was in danger of being slain by the demon Bali, but his wife tied a protective band on his wrist and his life was spared. According to other forms of the legend, she tied the amulet around the wrist of Bali, adopting him as her brother so that he would not kill her husband. In yet another myth, a queen of the gods tied a thread around Viṣṇu's wrist to ensure his protection in all her battles against demons. The key point of this festival and its variations in different parts of India is one of protection and security, again during the dark and inauspicious time of the monsoon season.

Gaṇeśa Catūrthi

In August or September, at the end of summer and early autumn, is the festival of Gaṇeśa Catūrthi. The elephant-headed god is immensely popular for anyone who needs success in life – students, business people, artists, artisans – all need the help of Lord Gaṇeśa, for their undertakings. Special images of the god are made in Mahārāṣtra, where the festival is extremely popular. These images are processed through the streets for the festival with competitions for the largest and best images and floats on which they are carried: they are then immersed in the sea some days hence at the close of the festival. Gaṇeśa is the son of Śiva and Parvatī and he is said to have been formed from the slough of skin that fell from her body when she bathed. Images of him at the festival are made of clay that has not been fired, resembling his birth, and these images dissolve readily in water. Popular stories from the *Purāṇas* related to Gaṇeśa are narrated during the festival as well as old and new myths. Such is the popularity of this festival that it has become pervasive in India, especially in the West and South and in Central India, though it is not celebrated in the North. People will have temporary images of Gaṇeśa in their homes and perform special *pūjā* to him for several days before taking their images to the nearest water for immersion. These immersion rites are accompanied by colourful processions, singing and dancing, sometimes with coloured powder thrown around. Royina Grewal makes the pertinent point here about this very unusual but very popular and pervasive God: "For his followers, Ganesha provides an anchor in a confusing, ever-changing world. He is the accessible god, compassionate and easy to please, who satisfies every human need, be it spiritual, emotional or material."[20] Gaṇeśa is a very modern God, despite his ancient mythological appearance, and the following comment of Nanditha Krishna is rather interesting in this respect: "Today's Ganeshas carry guns, kalashnikovs and nuclear-headed missiles, or sit in front of a computer."[21] It is a remarkable comment on what the needs of his devotees are!

Kṛṣṇa Jayānti

Also in August to September is the festival that celebrates Kṛṣṇa's birthday, Kṛṣṇa Jayānti, and it is celebrated by Hindus everywhere. It was believed that Kṛṣṇa was born at midnight in the prison in Mathurā where his parents were kept by his malicious uncle. He was born on the eighth night of a dark fortnight. It is customary to fast during the festival day. As a baby, Kṛṣṇa was fond of milk, curds and butter and in some customs, these are put in pots high up for young men to steal, just as Kṛṣṇa used to do. Centres like Vrindāvaṇa where Kṛṣṇa lived with the cowherds and *gopīs*, and Mathurā, his birthplace, are places of pilgrimage at this festival time. Since Kṛṣṇa is the focus of devotional Hindus, the festival features many of the myths about his life, devotional and emotional songs of praise and many pictures of the young baby in homes and temples. Kṛṣṇa loved to dance with the *gopīs* and so there is much dancing at the festival with enjoyment of sweet foods.

Durgā Pūjā, Navarātri and Dasahrā

A cluster of linked festivals occurs in September/October during autumn – mainly Durgā Pūjā, Navarātri and Dasahrā. *Durgā Pūjā* is the most prominent of these in northern India and is the occasion celebrating the slaying of the buffalo demon by the great Goddess Durgā. As a ferocious Goddess, she may be offered blood sacrifices on the occasion of this festival even, sometimes, though rarer since prohibited by the Indian government, a buffalo. Durgā Pūjā, popular in northern India, especially in Bengal, extends over ten days. Here in Bengal, Durgā is more likely to be celebrated as the beautiful Umā, the wife of Śiva who, at this festival, leaves her home and her husband in the Himālayas to return to her native home. Elsewhere, the festival is celebrated for four to five days. Where the *Devī-Māhātmya* recounting the Goddess's battles is read, this will take place over nine days, and her battle against the demon is re-enacted. In her temples, *pūjā* continues through the days and nights. Each day *pūjā* is offered it is addressed to different names of the Goddess representing her different forms. It is customary to fast and pray to the Goddess as Mother for a safe year ahead. Temporary clay images of Durgā attired for battle are made everywhere as part of the celebrations and in places like Kolkata these prolific images in the streets attract people from all regions. The images are sculpted according to prescribed traditions by artists skilled in the making of *mūrtis*, and the images will be temporarily imbued with life and the essence of the Goddess for the festival, before all of them are ritually immersed in the Ganges at the end of the festival, on the tenth day. Lynn Foulston portrays very vividly her experience of the festival in Kolkata:

> To visit Kolkata at the time of *Durga Puja* is to step into a different world. As darkness descends, the grubby streets and dilapidated buildings that once spoke of the opulence of this city are replaced by a wonderland of lights and sound. Excitement fills the air as thousands of people throng the streets. Dressed in their finest clothes and decked in gold, they wander from one magnificently decorated *pandal* (temporary pavilion housing huge tableaux of Durga and her children) to the next. The community face of the festival consists of hundreds of temporary buildings constructed of bamboo, cloth or other materials, some of which are replicas of famous temples or places of pilgrimage or simply famous buildings. These *pandals* are constructed solely to house the huge, fantastically decorated clay images of the ten-armed Durga slaying the buffalo demon, Mahisasura, and the other deities, Ganesa, Laksmi, Sarasvati and Karrtikeya, who surround her on either side.[22]

As Foulston points out, the *pandals* are highly inventive in their construction, one she witnessed being made entirely from sixty thousand vinyl long-playing and "78" records.[23] What is noteworthy, too, in her eye-witness research, is the "amalgamation of sacred and secular. While the foundation of this festival is religious, much of its outward appearance is now secular."[24] It is an interesting observation that can be applied to many festivals these days, with purely secular fairs being attached to many.

On the third day of Durgā Pūjā, a young and beautiful virgin girl is selected to be worshipped as Durgā. This occasion is Kumārī (virgin) Pūjā, and the young girl, finely dressed and ornamented is transformed to divinity for the occasion. If *pūjā* to her is correct, she will, depending on her age, bestow all kinds of benefits on those who worship her.[25] In Bengal, it is customary for married daughters to return to their natal homes for this festival, rather like Durgā is believed to return to her devotees for the duration of the festival. In southern India this virgin daughter represents the young virgin Durgā, the aspect of Durgā as a member of a domestic family.

David Kinsley was of the view that the worship of Durgā was at one time as a military Goddess who was propitiated for battle success; and the two festivals associated with Durgā Pūjā, Navarātri and Dasahrā, were originally one with Durgā Pūjā, the three being an extensive festival to promote success in battle.[26] Kinsley also noted connections with agriculture and fertility of the land in the *pūjā* rituals at her festival.[27] Popularly, Durgā is believed to reside in the Himālayas but is believed to come from her home there where she resides with Śiva, to visit her parents on the sixth day. This shows her softer side as Mother rather than her military prowess. Linked with Kinsley's suggestion of the fertility and agricultural nature of the Goddess, we seem to have a more mellowed Durgā than the ferocious Goddess of myth. Indeed, in Bengal, as Śiva's wife Durgā is a manifestation of Parvatī, the gentler wife of Śiva. Given this gentler nature, blood sacrifices may, in some cases, give way to a pumpkin as a substitute offering, and in parts of East India, the Goddess is represented by a sacred pot. Women can be seen carrying such pots on their heads: they place them in their courtyards and dance and sing around them.[28] Certainly, the undertones of agriculture and fertility are evident in the important installation of the pot, the *ghata*. It contains twigs from five different trees as well as Ganges water, with *betel* leaves at the top, rice and a coconut. Its decorated round-bellied shape with a narrow top are suggestive to many of the womb and fertility, and it is considered to be an appropriate symbol of the Goddess as Mother. Another incarnation of the Goddess is in a bundle of nine plants tied together by a priest and placed in the main temple with the same attention and adornments offered to a full *mūrti*. Again, the emphasis on agriculture and fertility is pertinent here.[29]

Whatever secular overtones to the festival, there is present throughout Durgā Pūjā the thought of the triumph of good over evil, whether that be the Goddess's slaying of the evil demon, or the ridding of evil from the community and the making of all things good. It should be remembered that Durgā Pūjā, Navarātri and Dasahrā occur during Viṣṇu's slumber, during what is really a highly inauspicious time, a time when the conquering of demons and malevolent forces is exigent. Durgā's presence at this time is an assurance that good will prevail. As Fuller comments, "Navaratri occurs close to the autumn equinox, the gods' midnight and the middle of the dark half of the year. One critical feature of inauspicious, dark periods is that they are preferred by demons, who are most active then, so that Navaratri once again occurs at the right time for Mahishasura [the buffalo demon] to gather his forces."[30]

Navarātri means "nine nights", the length of time during which Durgā Pūjā is celebrated and so it is easily linked with the Goddess's festival, but it can also be separate from it in some parts of India in that it is not the Goddess who is the central image of the festival. In Bengal, the festival is clearly Durgā Pūjā; in Gujarat and elsewhere it is called Navarātri and in northern India it is called Dasahrā, as we shall see. The ninth day of Navarātri for some is the festival of Rām Navami, the birthday of Rāma that we have already met above. Rāma had to rescue his wife Sītā from the demon king who had abducted her and needed the blessing of Durgā for this military enterprise. Because he wanted to commence battle at the end of the rainy season, he instituted a Navarātri in the autumn so that he could go into battle. Of the two festivals – spring and autumn – the latter has tended to become more popular. In northern India, Navarātri is associated with Rāma's victory over the demon king Rāvaṇa. The epic story of the *Rāmāyaṇa* is enacted or extracts from the epic are performed in what are known as *Rām-Līlā*, "Rāmā's play", by travelling actors who visit the villages to perform.

Navarātri is the name given, too, to a prominent festival in Madurai in Tamil Nāḍu, South India. Here, Durgā is known as Mīnākṣi and on the first day of Navarātri, a mobile image of her is placed in a shrine and *pūjā* offered her each night. On the eighth night, Mīnākṣi is depicted as slaying the buffalo demon. On the ninth night she is believed to worship her husband Śiva and in an unusual ceremony on the tenth night, her hair is symbolically washed. Navarātri is also an occasion for other goddesses to be venerated, like Sarasvatī, the goddess of learning and the arts and Saraswati Pūjā is celebrated on the first night of Navarātri. Minor goddesses pertinent to village cultures will also be honoured at this time, perhaps linked to Durgā. Then, too, it is a time for workmen to honour the tools of their trades and the objects essential to their livelihoods.

Dasahrā means "tenth day",[31] and is the final day of Durgā Pūjā when the *mūrtis* of the goddess are immersed in the river. At the Mīnākṣi temple in the South, Mīnākṣi is reunited with her husband Śiva and paraded in procession with him around the temple. In northern India, Dasahrā celebrates the beheading of Rāvaṇa by Rāma at the end of the battle in the *Rāmāyaṇa* and people make effigies of the demon and his brothers, which are publicly burned amidst great festivity. A *Rām-Līlā* that is performed in Delhi each year at the festival recites the story of Rāma and Sītā over the nine days of Navarātri and then, on Dasahrā, Rāma in the play shoots a lit arrow that sets fire to a huge bonfire – usually filled with fireworks – on which an enormous effigy of Rāvaṇa is waiting to be burned. Household deities are not forgotten on the tenth day and special *pūjā* will be offered them. The tenth is also a day on which, in some parts of India, wives worship their husbands, the latter being Rāma for the day. A wife will place her husband on an improvised shrine, wash his feet, put a *tilaka* on his forehead, garlands round his neck and give him offerings of food. Finally, she will bow to her husband in honour. Again, this group of festivals is associated with the triumph of good over evil. These festivals are a time of joy, a time when the monsoon rains are ending and the skies are blue.

Dīvālī / Dīpāvalī

Dīvālī or Dīpāvalī, "row or garland of lights", is celebrated in October or November. Northern India regards the festival as a New Year occasion, whereas elsewhere it is amalgamated with two other festivals in the main, Lakṣmī Pūjā and Kālī Pūjā. Dīvālī is mainly associated with Rāma and the point in the *Rāmāyaṇa* when he and Sītā returned home after fourteen years of exile. It is said that the inhabitants of Ayodhyā put lanterns in their homes and along the streets to welcome the couple. Thus, "garland of lights" is an apt name for the festival since families put rows of lamps, *dīpas*, outside their homes, and lights are floated on rivers and displayed at temples. Klaus Klostermaier offers the following nostalgic comment: "Countless little oil lamps on houses and temples and along rivers and roads softly illuminate the darkness of the star-studded tropical sky – a sight no one who has seen it could ever forget and every Hindu living abroad remembers nostalgically every year."[32] These little lamps are small clay bowls filled with *ghī* or oil with a burning wick. It is customary to put these mostly hand-made lamps in rows, rather like a garland. Modernity has meant that electric lights are now often used and light enters the festivities in the form of fireworks. The number of days over which the festival is celebrated will vary but will invariably include the new moon day. In some areas, Dīvālī lasts for five days and different myths are remembered on each of the days – Lakṣmī and Pārvatī as the givers of wealth; myths of Śiva and Pārvatī; Viṣṇu becoming the *avatāra* of a dwarf to defeat the demon Bali; the return of Rāma and Sītā to Ayodhyā; the visit of Yama the god of death to his sister resulting in brothers visiting their sisters or female relatives. Another custom of dice playing is popular in some regions. Legend has it that Śiva and Pārvatī were playing at dice and Viṣṇu helped Śiva to win. Dice playing commemorates this myth. Charlotte Vaudeville associates Dīvālī with Kṛṣṇa, and the myth of his lifting the mountain for cattle and inhabitants to shelter underneath when the god Indra, annoyed at being neglected, sent a deluge of continuous rain.[33] Southern Indian Dīvālī also celebrates Kṛṣṇa's defeat of the demon Nāraka on the first day of the festival.

As a New Year festival, Dīvālī is a time of renewal, a time for getting rid of the old and obtaining the new – clothes, utensils, business account books, settling debts and starting afresh. It is the traditional beginning of the financial year. Old quarrels are expected to be settled and forgiveness sought, and gifts and greetings cards are exchanged in a spirit of friendship, especially with the gathering together of families. Even ancestors of the dead are expected home for Dīvālī. But in villages there may be no connection with the major deities or the myths surrounding them, and caste customs with local festivities appropriate to a New Year may differ considerably in focus from the mainstream festivities of Dīvālī. Babb makes the rather interesting point that Dīvālī "is at least as much a state of mind as a concrete event",[34] and whether national, regional or local, it seems to be that Dīvālī expresses great personal hope, expectation of good things to come and of enjoyment of life in the present.

Lakṣmī Pūjā, the date of which varies,[35] is in itself a festival within Dīvālī, and for some, it is the most important celebration. Houses are cleaned and redecorated in the hope that Lakṣmī, the Goddess of prosperity, will enter them and grant the families blessings for the year to come. *Pūjā* to Lakṣmī takes place on the night of the new moon and *rangoli* patterns in some regions, *ālpanā* in others, are constructed on the floors in homes to welcome the Goddess. *Pūjā* to Lakṣmī is essential before *prasāda* in the form of Dīvālī sweets can be given to the children. Vaudeville notes that Lakṣmī Pūjā is a particularly favourite festival of merchant-class Vaiśyas who, she claims, "are largely responsible for making Dīvālī the most popular feast in Northern India".[36] Kinsley, too, noted the popularity of Lakṣmī with merchants, which is why businessmen focus on, and even venerate, their account books in the hope that their wealth will be maintained through devotion to Lakṣmī. The Goddess also protects homes from the returning dead and any malevolent spirits amongst them.[37] Gaṇeśa, who is also a god of prosperity, is very much associated with Lakṣmī at this festival. The lamps that are linked with Dīvālī are centred on Lakṣmī for many: they are lit to light the Goddess into homes and temples, again, in the hope that she will make the year to come a prosperous one. Many – usually only women – stay awake the whole night, leaving their homes brightly lit and the doors and windows open to welcome the Goddess.

In Bengal, a region particularly focused on the divine as female, the festival of Lakṣmī Pūjā occurs at the full moon in September/October, just after Dasahrā, and in Orissa, at the full moon a month later in November/December. The *ghata* associated with Durgā is also associated with Lakṣmī in Bengal, hinting at her connection with agriculture and fertility as well as wealth. In eastern India, in Orissa, it is the time of the rice harvest and the floor patterns to welcome Lakṣmī are made of rice paste. The Goddess's association with the harvest and wealth is to be seen in the symbol of her made out of the new crop of rice, coins, and gold decorations, all draped in a red sari. Offerings from the newly harvested rice are presented to this image of Lakṣmī. It is traditional for some to draw little footprints on doorsteps and floors, so that Lakṣmī is enticed into the homes.[38] A negative opposite of Lakṣmī, her sister Alakṣmī, is encouraged out of the backs of houses so that the home can be filled with the positive presence of Lakṣmī. Bengal especially celebrates the victory of Lakṣmī over Alakṣmī, who brings all kinds of unhappiness, poverty and hunger. Homes may not have images of Lakṣmī but earthen plates on which an image of her and her attendants is drawn, but there are also images of her in the many *pandals* that are set up for the festival. All these representations of Lakṣmī are immersed in water when the festival day comes to an end.

In Bengal, with its emphasis on the Mother Goddess, another festival that occurs at Dīvālī is *Kālī Pūjā*. The great temples of Dakṣineśvar[39] and Kalighat in Kolkata are the focuses of her festival *pūjā* at this time, but clay images of this black Goddess displaying her dreadful form are prolific in the cities during the celebration. Her presence in the temple clay image is ritually brought about by a priest. Her *pūjā* takes place after midnight with the sixteen offerings standard to *pūjā* everywhere, and include light, flowers, fruit, incense and a meal. Kālī has been traditionally offered animal sacrifice, usually goats, and the sacrifice of a goat is still part of the post-midnight ritual of the festival, though some communities and families have substituted a red pumpkin. At the close of the festival, the clay images are immersed in the river – a process lasting long into the following day, given the prolific numbers of images.[40]

Local village festivals

Village festivals more usually revolve around goddesses, the fierce and violent goddesses who act as protectors of their communities but who also can wreak havoc if not appeased. Times of disasters and disease might be the occasion for holding a festival rather than fixed times, though the latter has now become more the case.[41] Given the nature of these free, often unmarried and non-Sanskritized goddesses, they are believed to demand blood sacrifices, perhaps, as Kinsley suggested, either to appease them or to invigorate them.[42] And these festivals are occasions for normal societal rules to be ignored and more exuberant practices to emerge: "The village-goddess festival is often the time of undertaking heroic vows, which greatly heighten the aroused state of the village. Fire walking, carrying burning pots on one's head, and swinging while suspended on hooks through one's flesh are all common during these festivals and are associated with trance and possession."[43] Even those of the lowest castes of the village caste system have their own festivals: Viramma, Racine and Racine describe how the launderer caste in a village has a festival for their god who resides in their laundering oven. They can little afford the food for the festival and rely on donations from other, higher castes to be able to celebrate.[44]

The richness of festival celebration is not only based on mythological and legendary tales of the gods and goddesses, but includes also the more tangible anniversaries of famous founders of religious sects or exceptional leaders. Movements associated with Swami Vivekananda, Swami Prabhupada and Ramakrishna include major celebrations of their birthdays. Ramakrishna was closely associated with the Kālī temple at Dakṣineśvar, and had a vision of the Goddess there. His birthday is celebrated by a procession through the streets of Kolkata. The birth of Mohandas Gandhi is celebrated every October in a national holiday in recognition of his greatness and, for many, saintly nature.

Pilgrimage

Pilgrimage pervades all the religious and social strata of Hinduism. It is so pervasive that the whole of India is peppered with sacred places. Surinder Bhardwaj's comment here is very appropriate: "The holy places thus generate a gigantic network of religious circulation encompassing the entire Hindu population. Pilgrim 'flows' are the connecting links between the Hindu population and its numerous sacred centres."[45] More than any other aspect of Hinduism, pilgrimages gather disparate religious traditions into something of a unified whole. Jessica Frazier notes how ritualistic praxis is not so regionally different that pilgrims are at a loss in understanding ritual format in foreign regions: "Pilgrimage sites are a good place in which to observe the trans-regional continuity of ritual, and general patterns of temple ritual in most areas are similar enough that most Hindus in unfamiliar regions will know what to do when performing *pūjā* in the nearest temple. The common vocabulary and syntax form an important structure of continuity across ever more diffuse communities, countries and cultures."[46] Pilgrimages, it seems to me, supply a unifying factor to the immense diversity of religious beliefs and practices that pervade Hinduism, and the sites are, to use Surinder Bhardwaj's and James Lochtefeld's phrase, "reservoirs of Hindu beliefs".[47]

Pilgrimages have been an important part of Hinduism since ancient times, even though journeys were hazardous and incredibly long. Those who braved the pilgrimages could be subjected to disease, robbery and attacks by wild animals, but today, even though there are still some who prefer a spiritual journey by foot, modern communications and transport mean that the hardships of long ago need not be endured. For many, pilgrimage represents a spiritual journey into one's own self, whether travelling alone, or whether a group of people gather together to travel as an act of devotion. As was seen in chapter 8 there is no textual evidence for temples: they came about as sacred places to house *mūrtis* of deities in the devotional focus of Hinduism but, in becoming so, many became important centres of pilgrimage also. But added to such a development is the religious spirituality of India itself. Klostermaier puts this clearly when he says: "That space and time are permeated and filled with the presence of the Supreme is not a mere theological idea with the Hindus, it is a tangible reality in India."[48] The steady stream of pilgrims to sites in the whole of India is witness to the fact that God is believed to be everywhere and in all things. Some such pilgrim sites are constructed, others are natural phenomena but, either way, the pilgrimage site is believed to be sacred space, a place where the divine is particularly present. With the arrival of modern means of transport has come a greater emphasis on the power of pilgrimage as a religious and spiritual action, so much so, that more and more people undertake it: pilgrimage is immensely popular.

The usual Sanskrit term for pilgrimage is *tīrtha*, a word meaning "ford", or "crossing place", the point at which a river was crossed. The concept of crossing from one shore to another is as much a religious idea as a secular one; this shore being the mundane world and the other shore liberation into the divine world. Even holy people who help one cross from this mundane world to liberation are called *tīrthas*. [49] Then, too, the remains of water used to wash the feet of an image of a deity and then used as *prasāda* is called *tīrtha*.[50] Many sacred sites and temples are today on the banks of rivers and, from ancient times, rivers have been regarded as having special purification powers. But each *tīrtha* is sacred because there, the divine and human worlds coalesce; the transcendent becomes not just immanent but present. Such places supply an *axis mundi*, a pathway between Earth and Heaven.[51] *Tīrthas* are places of such sacredness and divine presence that whoever visits them acquires massive spiritual merit and, importantly, are a religious exercise open to any individual regardless of age, caste or gender. Another word associated with pilgrimage is *yātrā*, which more specifically means "pilgrimage" or "journey", and the two terms together, *tīrtha-yātrā* have come to mean "pilgrimage to a sacred place". Some *tīrthas* are literally at the crossing places of rivers, particularly at the auspicious confluence of two rivers, but wherever the pilgrimage site, the journey to it is expected to be a spiritual one that demands a certain amount of mental and physical discipline. Pilgrimages are rituals that are desirable but not obligatory: thus, they are undertaken on a very personal level.

Why so many places of pilgrimage originated is unclear. Naturally, it is human beings that seek to build temples to house the deities that they worship and the reasons for locating temples at different sites are various. To find sensible rationales for their origins is hazardous, as Bhardwaj warns: "The distribution of sacred places today represents the cumulative effect of the process of sanctification of certain selected locales over more than two millennia. Since the process of sanctification may have consisted of numerous elements, a single hypothesis cannot be expected to explain satisfactorily the distribution of sacred places."[52] One element that I think *is* relevant, however, is water, given the extent to which water is necessary not just for physical purification, but for inner purification also: the sacredness of rivers is suggestive that sacred sites along them is a natural outcome of millennia of regarding rivers as special and holy and their sources are especially sacred. We know, too, I believe, that certain geographical places inspire transcendent awe and must have done so to the mind long ago as they do today, and this factor, combined with mythological tales associated with an area in order to make tangible sense of that awe, must surely have played some part in the origins of some of the sites.

Natural sites such as mountains and rivers as well as unusual sites where rocks form strange shapes must have inspired mixtures of awe and myth. Even anthills are unusual enough to be sacred and many trees are deemed to be so. Such natural phenomena – be it lumps of rock, stones or clefts in rocks – are sometimes considered as actual manifestations of deities; the deity in reality. The summits of mountains were believed to be the abodes of the gods, especially in the spectacular Himālayan heights, but smaller hilltops may also be sacred sites. Pilgrimages to mountain tops often cannot take advantage of convenient transport and have to be made on foot: the more arduous the journey, the closer one comes to the divine powers that pervade the heights of the mountain, and to the gods themselves. Caves are especially sacred to those who worship the Goddess and Śiva: the warmth and shape of the cave is believed to be a natural *yoni*, the vagina and womb of the Goddess. For example, Mark Rohe describes a "tunnel-like cave named 'Garbh Joon' (womb-vagina) through which pilgrims squeeze as a sign of their faith and sinlessness", on route to the cave shrine of the supreme Goddess Vaiṣṇo Devī, almost six-thousand feet up a mountain in northern India.[53] Similarly, grottoes, gulfs and caverns are associated with Mother Earth. A whole region, like the Himālayas, may be regarded as a *kṣetra*, a "field", or area that is particularly sacred.

While there would have been a large number of pilgrimage sites that were part of Hindu orthodoxy, many sacred sites would have existed in popular praxis well before they became officially accepted into Hinduism. Since there is mostly some mythology underpinning an orthodox site as sacred, and *Brāhmins* were important in maintaining a particular pilgrimage site as orthodox by such myth, they were not too happy about *ad hoc* sites occurring over which they had no control and, indeed, could claim no fee for their services. A process of Sanskritizing of many of these was necessary in order to make them truly Hindu and that usually meant coming up with an appropriate myth for each in order to make a site legitimate. Thus, most pilgrimage sites will have a particular local and sacred myth, a *sthala-purāṇa*, that is associated with the site and with the presiding deity.[54] There are also likely to be links with holy seers and major theologians of the past. These textual supports lend authenticity to both deity and sacred place. Presiding deities will have a different name at each different site. Viṣṇu is known as Veṇkateśvara in the temple of the same name at Tirupati, for example, whereas elsewhere temples dedicated to him will have others of his names. Vasudha Narayanan puts forward a valid reason for such a practice: "The supreme being who is beyond human comprehension has, through its compassion, made itself manifest in human and worshipable image form just down the road in the local field or in the neighbourhood temple."[55] How far the local character of the deity is linked with a pan-Hindu deity is difficult to say, but the local deity surely has more meaning for the ordinary devotee.

Textually, pilgrimage sites are featured in several sections of the *Mahābhārata*, which also extols pilgrimage to as many sites as possible as a means of acquiring merit – and merit that is actually said to be superior to sacrifice.[56] The text is also important for supplying the oldest evidence for pilgrimage sites in the pre-Christian era.[57] Naturally, the *Mahābhārata* gives pre-eminence to those sacred sites that are concerned with its narrative, especially the great battle at Kurukṣetra, but it also names sites the length and breadth of India, only avoiding those areas where there were more alien wild forests of indigenous tribes.[58] Even today there are few, if any, pilgrimage sites in tribal areas that were originally pre-Āryan and have remained outside Hinduism. The other very pertinent source for indicating sacred places is the *Purāṇas*, though those that do are likely to have some bias in choice and there will be considerable variation in the lists that each gives. But the evidence from the *Purāṇas* is important because it lends orthodoxy to the many sites mentioned in them. And, if anything, the *Purāṇas* bear witness to the presence of God in all natural phenomena. The *Skanda-purāṇa* is particularly concerned with places of pilgrimage and contains many myths associated with the respective sacred sites. The *Purāṇas*, like the *Mahābhārata*, also, sometimes claim that pilgrimage is an alternative practice to *Vedic* sacrifice and is just as meritorious. Inevitably, however, the rise and decline of some pilgrimage sites has been fluid over the centuries; others are indelibly rooted into Hindu myth and culture.

People undertake pilgrimages for a variety of reasons. Festival time is especially important in that the temple presence of deities is transformed into mobile images of which the devotee can have *darśan*, and *darśan* is one important reason for pilgrimages at non-festival times, also. Then, too, there are famous sites associated with myths about the deities – famous battles with demons, birthplaces of deities, and the like. Some individuals have personal difficulties that the spiritual and physical journey to a sacred place may solve, and these might be very mundane problems such as a good future marriage, the need for sons, the need for a successful business, even the need for money. In expectation that a deity will grant what the devotee wishes, many will make a vow, a *vrata*, to undertake a pilgrimage to make their request more likely to be granted. Here, the *vrata* is a kind of bargain with a deity. There may be a sick member of the family at home, or the individual making the pilgrimage may need to be cured of illness. Requests to a deity are certainly common and some whose request is granted return on pilgrimage to thank the deity. Some families take their children to temples where their ancestors worshipped, to temples long associated with their families. Many simply want no more than a little peace in their lives. Others seek to purify their souls, to spiritualize the mundane. A pilgrimage is an accepted religious pathway to acquire religious merit, both for the present life and for a future one and, for its duration, the mundane things of life give way to a purely religious and spiritual time. While the householder pathway has always been highly praised in Hinduism, the ascetic life has been respected also, and pilgrimage permits the householder, especially, to leave the normal *dharma* of family life for a taste of the spiritually ascetic. The ascetic has the foremost goal of renunciation, whereas the one on a pilgrimage is usually more inspired by *bhakti*, devotion: however, he or she can share for a time the ascetic's abandonment of the mundane world. The *bhakta* may be able to experience, too, the kind of devotion that transcends the self – the true culmination of a real inward journey that corresponds to the physical journey and ultimate *darśan* of the pilgrimage.

Sacred sites are frequented by sacred men (and occasionally by sacred women); the holy men who have chosen to live their lives only for God. The ordinary individual finds himself or herself alongside such dedicated beings in a sacred place, a sacred space in which the divine is present: there has been a change from the profane to the sacred for the one on the journey. Removal of sin, or the burden of present *karma*, is a major motivator for a pilgrimage. Past sins are believed to be forgiven if a pilgrimage is successfully undertaken and the more arduous the journey, the greater the amount of sin removed. Bhardwaj terms such sacred places "high level" and believes that pilgrims to these sites are more motivated by the purpose of purification.[59] To die at a pilgrimage site is to free the soul from the body with the hope of no further rebirth as is the case at Vārāṇasī. Thus, death rites are often associated with sacred sites that are on the banks of purifying rivers, especially the Ganges, but other rituals of life-cycle rites may take place at pilgrimage sites. *Śraddha*, the rites for ancestors, are believed to be far more efficacious at a sacred pilgrimage site.

All kinds of different people, then, and for all kinds of different reasons engage in a pilgrimage. They are likely to prepare for a pilgrimage by first having a specific *intention*, a *saṃkalpa*. That intention has to be maintained on the journey and throughout the entire process: only then, through faith in the purpose and intention of the pilgrimage will its outcome be what the pilgrim wishes. Outward symbols sometimes represent the intensity of purpose. Pilgrims may have their hair shaved or cut and put on different clothing: these are statements that they are about to do something ritually and spiritually different. Indeed, some of the scriptures suggest ways in which a pilgrim should prepare himself or herself for the journey. Thus, a copper ring and copper bracelet are worn by some and perhaps red robes. While pilgrims should traditionally journey barefoot, far fewer do so in today's world. In general, luxury is not in the spirit of pilgrimage so any opulence should be avoided and sexual activity abandoned for the duration. The goal is one of spiritual gain that is out of the ordinary realm of existence.

I should so like to say that caste differences are waived in the case of pilgrimage but I am afraid that this is not always the case. There are instances where it would be impossible in the throng of pilgrims to avoid high and low castes coming into contact with each other. Bhardwaj notes that, especially in the case of shrines to the goddesses, all castes and scheduled castes have access to the inner shrines at pilgrimage temples and all of these individuals will receive *prasāda* from anyone, even if from a member of an unscheduled class.[60] Elsewhere, there may be a predominance of higher castes as, for example, Bhardwaj found with pilgrims to Badrīnāth,[61] and Bhardwaj admits that "the practice of touch pollution may have been responsible for making certain sacred places unappealing to the untouchable castes, no matter how near these may have been to their homes".[62] Remarkably, Bhadwarj's research concluded that "the higher the level of a holy place, the higher the proportion of ritually high-caste pilgrims".[63] Pilgrims of whatever caste are made exceptionally aware of the regional diversity of India in travel to a place of pilgrimage and yet at many sites hostels may well be caste differentiated. People may be obliged to walk together, but they do not usually eat together. Kinsley, too, found that at the great pilgrimage site of Vārāṇasī, "the twice born will undertake rituals that few low-caste people ever do or can afford to do. In Varanasi the former will usually perform rituals to their ancestors, whereas low-caste pilgrims generally visit the shrines of local saints or the temples of deities favoured by them or their social groups."[64]

Since pilgrimage centres focus mainly on a particular deity, it is to be expected that they are frequented mainly by devotees from the same sect.[65] A great centre like Vṛndāvana, where Kṛṣṇa is believed to have sported with the *gopīs*, is bound to be a major Vaiṣṇava centre, as are Gokula, Mathurā and Dvārakā that feature in the life history of Kṛṣṇa. Everything that is beautiful about Kṛṣṇa, his charm, his youthfulness and playfulness, his magical flute that called the *gopīs* and the soul, is believed to exist in the very essence of this whole area at Vṛndāvana. Then, at Gāyā, a two-foot long footprint of Viṣṇu, the *Viṣṇupada*, is said to have been left by the God when he visited the place. These kinds of sacred places are termed abodes, *dhāmas*, places specifically associated with certain deities. The sacred places in northern India that are associated with Kṛṣṇa, in particular, are called *līlābhūmis*, "play-grounds" or *līlā-sthalas*, "places of play". In the case of Kṛṣṇa, the whole land of Vraj (Braj) in the Gangetic valley in Uttar Pradesh, where he is believed to have lived, has become a sacred site in which the very ground is holy, and the dust from the place is reverently smeared on the forehead. The hill, Govardhana, which Kṛṣṇa lifted on one finger, and the pool where he bathed with Rādhā are whole areas that are holy. An example of a Śaiva-focused centre is a place like Banāras, which attracts Śaivas in view of its temple and great *Viśveśvara liṅga* representing Śiva. Śaiva pilgrimage sites are more widely known as fields, *kṣetras*.

Famous devotees who became saintly holy men are often connected with specific temple sites, sectarian associations with such temples being carried on by their disciples. Sri Ramakrishna, for example, was devoted to the Mother Goddess at the Dakṣineśvara temple in Kolkata, and his disciples are still there today. There are also smaller, modest sites that serve a particular group of disciples who are resident in the locale, in contrast to some great pan-Indian sites frequented by people of all religious affiliations. Small pilgrimage shrines may also be the focus of pilgrimage by those who are unable to travel great distances and whose choice of deity is catered for on a more local level: village goddesses are particularly applicable to this point and are the focus especially of the lower castes. Pilgrimage to such shrines is mainly with the motive of requests for personal help, whether that is material aid or the solution to a particular problem.[66] Some sacred sites are almost gender specific. Fuller describes pilgrimage to the temple of Aiyappan at Sabarimalai in the mountain range in the Western Ghats overlooking Kerala, in which women are almost entirely absent in favour of what he calls "the distinctively masculine, physically tough style of religiosity" that characterizes the male pilgrims.[67] Pilgrimage may be to a single site, but it is more likely to include a network of other sites, these being carefully mapped and well known throughout India. Such networks and circuits of sites are another factor that supports a unifying characteristic of pilgrimages.

Some interesting points have emerged from the research of Bhardwaj. First, there are more Śaiva pilgrimage sites than Vaiṣṇava, though I do not think this is indicative of Śaivism being more widespread in India than Vaiṣṇavism, as Bhardwaj does.[68] The proliferation of Śaiva sites in the South owes its fortune to the lack of invaders that the North suffered, as was the fate of Vaiṣṇava temples of the North. More accurate, I think, is his statement that "the association of sacred places with minor deities of Hinduism greatly increases at lower-level shrines" and it is the Mother Goddess that proliferates at these sub-regional shrines.[69] Given that the Mother Goddess is highly likely to be a pre-Āryan phenomenon, the high number of pilgrimage sites dedicated to her is a remarkable affirmation that indigenous religious beliefs have some legacy in the present day.

While not all *tīrthas* are associated with temples, it is very much the case that, where a site becomes sacred, a temple will be built on that site and will then become a focus for pilgrimage, but Kinsley's comment here is an apt one: "Although temples are often found in such places, the environment rather than the temple itself is usually the object of the pilgrim. The temple simply serves to mark, specify, or objectify the sacrality of the place so much as the place enhances the sacrality of the temple."[70] The many *svayambhū*, "natural", not human-made *liṅgas* of Śiva are perhaps examples of natural sites to which pilgrims flock for the sacredness of the place itself.

In the far North, the East, the West and the South are four famous temple sites, the four *dhāmas*, or divine dwelling places, which constitute the four major compass points and to which many devout Hindus hope to journey. They are particularly associated with the great theologian, Śankara, and he is said to have established famous monasteries in each. It is believed that if one can perform, in a clockwise and auspicious circular direction, pilgrimage to these four sacred places, then *mokṣa*, liberation from the incessant round of rebirths through union with God, is acquired. The northern one is Badrīnāth, a Vaiṣṇava sacred place high in the Himālayas and the source of the great River Ganges. This sacred place is open to pilgrims only in the summer months for in winter access to it is denied by heavy snows. In Orissa, in the East of India on the Bay of Bengal, is Purī, the place where the famous Jagannātha Temple sacred to Kṛṣṇa stands and where the equally famous festival takes place when the deities are towed on gigantic chariots. The temple complex here covers a whole block of the city and the Jagannātha Temple itself is the largest in India.

Right down in the South in Tamil Nāḍu is Rāmeśvaram on the ocean's edge, close to what was in ancient times Lanka, the island on which Rāma's wife Sītā was held captive. Rāma is said to have worshipped Śiva there in the form of a *liṅga*, believed to be a great *liṅga* of light that destroys all sins of one who beholds it. On the far West coast of India is Dvārakā on the coast of Gujerāt, where Kṛṣṇa built his great palace.

In addition to the four *tīrthas* above, there are seven famous places where one can gain *mokṣa*. *Ayodhyā* was Rāma's capital, and has been the scene of much animosity between Hindus and Muslims, since the Babri Masjid, a Muslim mosque, now stands on the site where Rāma is said to have been born. In the late twentieth century, thousands of Hindus from all parts of India carried bricks to build Rāma's temple there but they were stopped, leading to considerable bloodshed. *Mathurā* was the homeland of Kṛṣṇa and *Kāśī/Banāras/Vārāṇasī*, I shall come back to below. *Kāñcīpuram* is known as the southern Banāras, and is the "Golden City" with well over a hundred temples built in the southern style with massive *gōpuras*. *Dvārakā* is one of the major four cited above. *Hardwār* is at the foothills of the Himālayas just where the Ganges enters the northern plains of the country. Last is the ancient city of *Ujjain* in Madhya Pradesh and is another that claims to have Śiva's *liṅga* of light; it is essentially a focus for Śaiva pilgrims. These seven are specifically cited in scriptural texts as especially holy.

Although there are many *tīrthas* along the Ganges, three main ones are considered to be the greatest. Prayāga, now renamed Allahābad by Muslims, is at the confluence of the rivers Ganges and Yamunā – a highly auspicious site. Prayāga means "sacrifice", and according to Diana Eck, "it reminds us of the way in which pilgrimage to a sacred place came to be considered the primary substitute for the Vedic sacrificial rites."[71] Prayāga is known as the "King of *Tīrthas*". The ancient river Sarasvatī is also believed to be at the confluence of these rivers, though evident in the past, it is long gone. [72] It is here at this confluence of rivers that the great Māhā Kumbha Melā festival is held every twelve years and is attended by millions of Hindus. I shall return to explore it below. The other two are Gāyā and Kāśī or Banāras/Vārāṇasī. Gāyā, situated on a tributary of the Ganges, is in Bihar, on the edge of the plain of the Ganges and has long been a site sacred to both Hindus and Buddhists. It is Gāyā that is the best place for *śraddha* rituals associated with death rites to be performed, and many undertake a pilgrimage there for that purpose. Pilgrims bring the remains of the cremated dead – called "flowers" – to such sites. Death is one *saṃskāra* that is usually taken very seriously. The ritual is scripturally prescribed and complex,[73] and as Richard Barber points out: "*Shraddha* pilgrims come for a variety of reasons; they wish to express their devotion to the deceased; they regard the ritual as something which will bring peace and prosperity to their family; and they even use it as a means of warding off their fear of ghosts and of spirits."[74] To deposit the ashes of the dead in the river at Gāyā is an act that ensures a safe passage for the newly deceased or even complete liberation. By scattering the ashes in the river there, the debt that every twice-born owes to his ancestors is being met.

Vārāṇasī, Banāras (Benares) as it is known in the West, is also known as Kāśī and is the third of the three greatest *tīrthas* along the Ganges and a very ancient city. It is the most sacred *tīrtha* of all and is believed to contain all other *tīrthas* within its boundaries as well as the whole cosmos. Vārāṇasī is Śiva's permanent home and he is said to hold the city on the tip of his trident. The gigantic, never-ending and never-beginning *liṅga* of light is believed to have been located here and so Kāśī means "City of Light" and has become that fiery *liṅga*. However, there are twelve sites where Śiva's huge *liṅgas* are believed to have manifested themselves on Earth, and these are scattered throughout India. The whole microcosm of Kāśī is the macrocosm in miniature. In Eck's words:

> The eight directions are said to have originated in Kāśī, receiving their respective realms of sovereignty by establishing Śiva *liṅgas* in Kāśī. Similarly the heavenly deities who govern time are said to have received jurisdiction over time in Kāśī. The temples of all these deities, in addition to the temples of Viṣṇu, Durgā, Bhairava, Gaṇeśa, and all the gods, have their places within the patterns of Kāśī's sacred geography. At the center is the famous *liṅga* of Viśvanāth – Śiva as "Lord of the Universe." The whole of the city is protected by a grid of fifty-six Gaṇeśas, who sit at the eight compass points in seven concentric circles spreading outward from Viśvanāth.[75]

Many come to Kāśī to live and to die there, with the belief that at death they will be free; they will have realized *mokṣa*. The *ghāṭs*, or steps down into the River Ganges at Kāśī are well-known all over the world. They are used to enter the river for purification and to cremate and scatter the ashes of the dead. Jonathan Parry makes the point that cremation grounds are usually located at the outskirts of habitation but, at Banāras, the cremation *ghāṭs* are the focal point of the city – "the navel of Kashi" as he calls the site.[76] There are also hostels especially for the dying, and those who travel from all parts of India to die there are by no means few. As Kinsley put it: "The Ganges is understood to be a particularly accessible bridge from one mode of being to the other, a sure crossing point in the difficult transition from life to death or from bondage to liberation."[77] Such words show that the depth of belief in Hinduism is as relevant for death as in life. Fires at the *ghāṭs* burn constantly, maintained by the scheduled caste of *Doms*, who ensure that the sacred fire never goes out.[78] Given the number of people who are cremated there, a single fire hardly ever occurs. Since Vārāṇasī/Kāśī is a Śaiva place of pilgrimage it is mainly Śaivas who undertake pilgrimage to it, but it is immensely popular: devotees from all sects come there from all parts of India and there are many different shrines for the pilgrims to visit. Śiva is believed to keep Yama, the lord of death, at bay, which is one reason why those who die there are blessed with liberation after death, for Yama cannot place them in a new, reincarnated existence. Klostermaier graphically describes the city: "Banaras is filled with a peculiar atmosphere: death and life, piety and cynicism, asceticism and abandon, learning and superstition side by side; an illustration of the Lord of Kāśī who dispenses grace and terror."[79] While the site is ancient, temples there are recent, given Muslim domination in northern India for a long period, and it was not until the dawn of the eighteenth century that temples and shrines appeared at Kāśī. Such a fact is a clear indicator that a place can have greater sacrality than a building.

The great Golden Temple of Śiva at Kāśī, the Viśvanāth, is the most popular temple, built in the late eighteenth century in the centre of the city amongst the ancient streets. There are actually three Viśvanāth temples, the original one admitting *Harijans* in 1954, which upset some Hindus so much that a second was built to exclude them, and then a third one that was open to *Harijans*, foreigners and non-Hindus. As Barber comments in the light of this, "there is therefore no clear-cut attitude towards entry into the presence of God".[80] However, given the numerous different shrines in this city, and the highly auspicious nature of the river on whose bank it is built, there is much to attract all pilgrims, whatever their caste or lack of one. Eck's comment on Kāśī is the most apt, I think, in summing up the incredible sacred centre that it is: "Kāshī is the place where all gods and *tīrthas* abide, where all sacred waters flow. There is no other place in India that is host to the myriad sacred powers that have gathered in Kāshī. It is no wonder that Kāshī outweighed the heavens."[81]

Sacred sites dedicated to the Mother Goddess are legion, given that the innumerable local village goddesses are believed to be aspects of her *śakti*, her essence and power. Many of the sites dedicated to the female deities are believed to stem from the myth of Satī's body. Śiva, her consort, was so smitten by her death that he carried her through the universe, bewailing her death and devastating the world. Viṣṇu dismembered her body bit by bit with his discus, and the places where parts of her body fell became *Śākta pīṭhas*, "seats" of *Śakti*, the essence of the Mother Goddess, places where she makes herself manifest. Such *pīṭhas* are scattered throughout India, some more important than others, depending on the part of the body associated with the place, though different sites are known to claim the same parts. Noticeably, a Śiva *liṅga* is often found at the *pīṭhas* but is housed in a smaller shrine, emphasizing the superiority of the Goddess over her spouse at such sites. According to legend, the toe of Satī fell on the banks of the Ganges and it is there that the great Kālīghat Temple to Kālī was built. Originally called Calcutta, now Kolkata, this city is the focus of many pilgrims and has two temples dedicated to Kālī. The Kālīghat Temple is in the heart of the old city. Animal sacrifice is frequent to Kālī at the Kālīghat Temple, though some devotees and pilgrims symbolically sacrifice themselves to Kālī by touching the sacrificial post at the temple with their heads. For others, animal sacrifice is preferred. Foulston describes the scene at the temple:

> The temple complex of Kalighat is a world within itself. In one of the oldest areas of Kolkata where the streets are narrow and the houses dilapidated, the temple of Kali stands proudly, drawing crowds from all over India and, indeed, the world. During the hours when Kali's doors are open, the narrow passageways that circle her sanctum are thronged with devotees, *dhoti*-clad priests, beggars hoping for a meal, and those making a quick rupee by showing visitors around. The outside of the temple is often as busy as the inside, for many people bring their new vehicles, especially taxis and auto rickshaws, to be blessed by the priests.[82]

Such a colourful picture of the temple complex depicts the sight that greets pilgrims who visit Kālī's temple and the vibrancy and excitement of the ambience of the place is described well by Foulston when she says: "Strings of lemons and chillies, shiny and green, contrast with the blood red of the hibiscus; the air is pungent with the mingled smells of exhausts, cooking and incense. The temple is vibrant and alive, though with a slightly menacing air accompanying the fervent devotion of Kalī's many worshippers."[83]

The other Kālī temple a few miles North of Kolkata is the Dakṣineśvara, "Lord of the

South", Temple with its Kālī *mūrti* depicted as standing on the prostrate body of her consort Śiva. On the banks of the tributary of the Ganges are twelve shrines along the river, each containing a Śiva *liṅga*, but it is the female Goddess that dominates the city. Harding describes the ambience in the "lively lane" that leads to this sacred site: "The lane resembles nothing a visitor might expect of a modern city street. Yet, it is not so much the poverty and the somewhat chaotic conditions that catch one's attention. One is much more fascinated by the throbbing life in the lane that goes on without shame, indifferent to praise or criticism. Somewhat overwhelmed, one feels mysteriously drawn into the free spirit of the place where people, animals and things live and die, side by side, in unusual harmony."[84]

The *pīṭhas*, according to Kinsley, *root* a goddess in the earth itself, emphasizing a motherly, nurturing nature, a nature that is concerned with the mundane problems of her devotes. He made the interesting point that a *tīrtha* is a crossing place from this world to another, but a *pīṭha* "connotes a fixed point, and by extension the fixedness of the goddesses worshiped at these sites". Importantly, too, all these goddesses, whether at sites that are considered as *pīṭhas* or not, are linked and unified by the *śakti* essence of the Mother Goddess, Devī.[85]

One other pilgrimage site I want to mention here is the Mīnākṣi Temple at Madurai in the South of India. Mīnākṣi, "Fish-eyed",[86] is an embodiment of the Goddess and abides at the temple with her spouse, Sundareśvara. The city is built according to the plan of a *maṇḍala* with the Mīnākṣi temple at the centre. I mentioned this magnificent temple in chapter 8 in the context of temples, but it is worth repeating here the splendour of the four entrances into this temple with their massive towers, the *gōpuras*, that are intricately decorated. In the context of pilgrimage, those who travel to this special temple in the South will face an awe-inspiring spectacle of a tapestry in architecture on their arrival. John Koller superbly describes the sixty-two mile journey of members of a *Dalit* caste association to the Mīnākṣi temple for the great Chittarai festival, all on foot: "Walking along secondary roads and village trails, they joined together in singing the praises of God and recalling the stories of the wondrous deeds of the gods and goddesses made famous by the ancient singers and storytellers."[87] These pilgrims stopped at shrines on the way to perform *pūjā* and have *darśan* of the deities whose shrines they visited until, as Koller puts it, "their hearts brimming with devotion as a result of what felt like continuous *darśana* and unending *pūjās*, the pilgrims were prepared for the greatest of Madurai's seasonal festivals, the Chittarai festival."[88] Whether to a magnificent temple complex like the Mīnākṣi temple or to lonelier goddess shrines on the summits of hills and needing arduous climbing to reach them, these examples show that pilgrimage for most is a devotional act on the deepest level.

Tīrthas, then, can be temples, places, mountains, hills, caves, flowing water, forests, hot springs – indeed, the divine in India is almost everywhere. Additionally, people can become *tīrthas* in that the tombs of past saints of Hinduism, or the places where they lived become the foci of devotion especially for those who follow in their beliefs. An example here is the fifteenth/sixteenth-century saint, Caitanya, who founded the Gauḍiya Vaiṣṇava tradition of Hinduism. Caitanya is accepted by his followers as an *avatāra* of Kṛṣṇa. Then, too, *tīrthas* are frequented by *sādhus*, "holy men" and *saṃnyāsins*, those who are believed to be enlightened beings, never to be reborn. The sight of such men at sacred centres is a kind of *darśan* of its own.

Rivers

Rivers are a prominent feature of pilgrimage. The *Vedas* clearly accepted rivers as sacred, particularly the ancient Sarasvatī, which most claim no longer flows. Water means life, and rivers represent the life-giving nature of God. Flowing water not only washes and purifies outwardly, but is symbolic of inner spiritual cleansing. The banks of rivers are the favourite dwelling places of deities, of Hindu *gurus* and sages and have been the scene at which many Hindu scriptures have been composed. The Ganges, Gaṇgā, has been mentioned in so many contexts as the most sacred river in India. The ritual bathe, the *Gaṇgā snam*, is the main rite undertaken by pilgrims to Banāras. They walk down the crowded stone steps and embankments into the river at a place where *ghāṭs*, platforms at the river-side, have been purpose made for pilgrims to immerse themselves in the purifying river. Most pilgrims have their own prayers to offer at the *ghāṭs* of Mother Gaṇgā,[89] the prayers accompanied by a sense of relief that they will be answered and a sense, too, that sins have been purified. There are specialist *ghaṭias* there who provide all kinds of care for the pilgrims, some of whom return regularly to the same *ghaṭia.*[90] In one myth, the Ganges is said to have flowed in Heaven before descending to Earth, with Śiva breaking the tumult of her fall by allowing the massive waters to flow first through his matted hair. Pilgrims love her source high in the Himālayas and she flows through so many of the famous pilgrimage sites. It is dawn that is the most auspicious time of the day to bathe and as the sun comes up, people can be seen with their palms upraised in prayer. Others sit on its banks in the stillness of meditation, but there is much coming and going, bathing and praying, and the river itself is strewn with flowers and garlands as offerings to this great Goddess. Mother Ganges, Gaṇgā Mātā, is, what Diana Eck called "the liquid embodiment of *śakti*",[91] and pilgrims return home with a little of the sacred water of Mother Ganges so that the blessing of the Goddess is with them. In the *Agni-purāṇa* she is mightily praised:

> She should be worshipped. She yields enjoyment and liberation. The countries through which she flows are holy and excellent. The Ganges is the succour for the beings who resort to it always. . . . One who worships the Ganges for a month gets the fruits of all sacrificial rites. The goddess destroys all sins and confers (access to) heavens. One continues to stay in heavens as long as (his) bones remain in the Ganges. Blind people and others attain status with the celestials by worshipping her. The carrying of the earth dug up from the beds of Ganges destroys one's sins just as the Sun. (The river) purifies hundreds and thousands of holy men who look at it, touch it, drink (its waters) and repeat (the word) Ganges.[92]

So sacred is Gaṇgā Mātā that she can be ritually invoked into any other river or stream in India, or just a little Ganges water can transform another body of water into a sacred river or stream. Each wave of the Ganges is said to be a *tīrtha* and Eck offers a splendid comment on the impact of this spectacular river: "She carries an immense cultural and religious significance for Hindus, no matter what part of the sub-continent they call home, no matter what their sectarian leaning might be."[93] Mother Ganges, in fact, does not discriminate against any who bathe in her waters: whatever the caste, age, sect, gender, she accepts and nurtures everyone like a true Mother. Many holy men find spiritual solace in the quieter nooks and caves near her banks away from the popular *ghāṭs*. The other major sacred rivers are the Yamunā mentioned earlier that flows into the Ganges at Prayāga, having its source, like the Ganges, in the Himālayas, the Godavari, and the southern Kauverī in Tamil Nāḍu. Sacred pilgrimage sites may also be located on the sea, like Dvārakā, where Kṛṣṇa had his capital city, and Rāmeśvaram, both noted above. The auspicious estuary of the Ganges is on the Bay of Bengal.

It would be impossible to mention all the major sacred places that pepper Hindu India but I shall close those included here with three important sites in the South of India. The first of these is Śrīraṇgam, a *tīrtha* that is post-epic in time unlike *tīrthas* in the North.[94] I mention this site because of the size of the temple complex there, which is probably one of, if not the, largest temple complex in all of India. Śrīraṇgam is built on an island in the river Kauverī and this Vaiṣṇava *tīrtha* is visited by massive numbers of pilgrims from all over India. Śrīraṇgam covers a huge area and has seven concentric enclosures that brings into its confines most of the population around it. It is a temple town that even includes bazaars, banks and houses in its outer enclosures.[95] The Śrīraṇgam Temple is the focus of Śrī-Vaiṣṇava Hinduism that incorporates much of the *bhakti* fervour of the southern poet-saints, the Āḷvars, and shrines to these saintly devotees of Viṣṇu and Lakṣmī as to Viṣṇu's various *avatāras* are found in the temple complex. Another southern *tīrtha* of considerable repute and wealth is Tirupati in Andhra Pradesh. It is Viṣṇu who is the deity worshipped here in different temples housing his different manifestations. Since these temples are built on a hill, they were at one time only accessible by foot, though today, modern transport has meant that thousands more are able to visit Tirupati. It is customary here for women to sacrifice their long, dark hair at the main temple to Viṣṇu as Tirupati, Lord Ventakeśvara. Finally, Cidāmbaram in Tamil Nāḍu is the place where Śiva is said to have performed his cosmic dance.

The Kumbha Melā

The Kumbha Melā, popularly known as the *Kumbh*, takes place periodically and rotationally at four *tīrthas*, Prayāga, Hardvār, Nāsik and Ujjain, which means to say, once every twelve years at each of these sites. However, the Kumbha Melā at Prayāga, modern Allahābad on the banks of the Ganges and at that auspicious confluence of the Ganges, the Yamunā and the disappeared Sarasvatī, is the most important one. At this highly sacred *tīrtha* it is believed that a space opens up between this mundane world and the divine one. In the ancient myth of the churning of the ocean by the gods and demons, when the two sides quarrelled, the celestial bird Garuḍa flew away with the pot of nectar of immortality and it is believed a tiny drop of the nectar fell at the four *tīrthas*. A *melā* is a gathering, a fair, especially a religious fair, while a *kumbh* is a jar, in this case, the jar of nectar of immortality, though *kumbh* is also associated with the particular stellar constellation of Aquarius. The Ganges water is believed to be transformed completely into the nectar of immortality at the Kumbha Melā. The battle between the gods and *asuras* is a potent myth that surfaces again and again to provide the rationale for so many practices and beliefs in Hinduism, no less so at the Kumbha Melā. Because of the nectar of immortality, to be there at the Kumbha Melā is to have one's *karma* purified, one's sins forgiven, and a possibility of the immortality that the place imbibes.

The last Kumbh took place at Prayāga in January–February 2013. It was a Māhā Kumbha Melā, being the twelve-year occasion at the most sacred of all *tīrthas*. It lasted for fifty-five days and, as is usual, witnessed the largest gathering of human beings in one place in all time. Over the fifty-five days of the occasion, it is estimated that a hundred million people would have been there. Saints, renouncers, *saṃnyāsins*, *saṃnyāsīs*, and *sādhus* come from all over India, some leaving their lonely places high in the Himālayas for the occasion. Everywhere, their orange robes are conspicuous and while there are different sects of *sādhus* and *sādhuis*, female ascetics, there are many naked *sādhus* that cover their bodies with ash, the symbol of death and of having died to the world. Here in northern India, it can be very cold in the nights, and those who have no accommodation or no tent, have to sleep out beneath the stars in a vast encampment of over five miles square. Wealthier Hindus will usually provide food for the poorer and especially for the *sādhus* as a means of acquiring merit. *Sādhus* are not only associated with the more mystical, introspective strands of Hinduism, but may also be *bhaktas*, meditating on, for example, a glossy print of a chosen deity.[96]

Since a *melā* is a fair as much as a gathering, there are a surprising number of economic enterprises attached to the place.[97] It is a time when farmers can show their cattle or sales of agricultural equipment take place. Barber describes the scene vividly when he says

> the atmosphere was half that of a medieval pageant, as the *mahantas* passed in their baroque gilded bullock-carts, garlanded in the traditional fashion, and the naked, ash-smeared *sadhus* performed their strange feats, and half that of a vast fairground, with neon-lit displays by night and groups of entertainers by day. Sometimes the two merged imperceptibly: on the one hand, there were the religious minstrels, performers in a tradition going back for centuries, whose recitals of epics and songs in praise of the deities were rewarded by alms from the *sadhus* themselves, while on the other hand, as one of the religious leaders observed, there were *sadhus* whose acts belonged more to the theatre than to the world of ascetic yoga.[98]

The Kumbha Melā then, whether on the grand scale at the twelve-year Prayāga or at some of the more frequent occasions when one is held, is often seen as a commercial advantage for many who visit. Even prostitutes will move to a religious fair for the occasion of earning more.[99] Pilgrimage sites have always been areas for the less savoury types to visit. Such sites are places for secular activities, particularly at something on the grand scale of the Kumbha Melā, when it is a good occasion for thieves, tricksters and gamblers to make money: it is all part of the "colour" of the occasion.

Alongside its theatrical and commercial secularity, the purpose of the millions of pilgrims is to bathe in the Ganges in order to purify sins. People purchase marigolds and garlands of marigolds to offer Mother Ganges, and these are cast into the water after bathing. It is usual to pick up the Ganges water in cupped hands, offer it to the gods and then let it fall through the fingers. Many will be at prayer in the water; many will sing devotional songs, and some will dance. There are absolutely no constraints whatever on who enters the water to be purified by the Ganges and a western woman could find herself standing next to a praying naked *sādhu*. Here, gender, nationality, class and caste are waived. And yet it has to be said that sewage is pumped into the Ganges each day. While many pilgrims will not only bathe in the Ganges water but drink it, the more discerning are likely to hire boats to take them to the middle of the river where they can dip their hands into the water and simply touch it to their faces.

Although all those who attend the Kumbha Melā spend time in bathing in the Ganges as the central reason for their being there, and this can be done on any day, the highlight of the Kumbh is the mass bathing that takes place at the time coming up to dawn of the day of the new moon, though astrologically, there are a few other auspicious days for bathing. To bathe in the Ganges at the new moon, especially, releases seven generations of ancestors into Heaven. At this special time, it is the *sādhus* and holy men and women who form processions of about thirty-thousand individuals, some dancing and leaping as they process to the banks, watched by the many pilgrims. It is at this time of the new moon and at dawn, that the river is believed to be transformed into the nectar of immortality, and it is this that the thousands of *sādhus* and ascetic sects enter. The millions of spectators have *darśan* of these holy individuals all gathered together in a massive procession, the naked *nāga sādhus* leading all the others. Only when they have bathed, can the rest of ordinary pilgrims follow suit.

Conclusion

The Kumbha Melā brings together so many of the facets of Hinduism, not least the fervour and devotion with which so many Hindus will attend festivals and embark on long pilgrimages for the sake of their religion as well as the modernity that permits comfortable pilgrimage or even the scepticism that entirely eschews it. People can now stay in hotels at sites, not in the old pilgrim *āśrams*. Priests have as important a role at *tīrthas* as they have in temple and shrine worship, with their regular attendance on deities, and there are special priests, *tīrtha purohits* or *paṇḍās*, who officiate entirely in the context of pilgrimages for reasons financial or spiritual. Some of these *tīrtha* functionaries have records of the families they serve; especially the families or groups that return again and again to the same sacred place.[100] Sacred places are linked too with many of the life-cycle rites, particularly rites associated with the dead, but also with the *upanayana* ceremony of receiving the sacred thread. Brides, too, may take their purification bathe at a sacred site and many take their children to sacred sites for the tonsure ceremony. We saw in chapter 10 on women how important vows are for women's hopes for well-being of their husband and children. Vows to embark on a pilgrimage are an important part of the *intention*, *saṃkalpa*, of a *tīrtha-yātrā*. To be at a sacred place is, for a pilgrim, to be infused with the special divine ambience of the place; as Kinsley put it, "in one way or another they appropriate the power of the place and become renewed, refreshed, or 'reborn' as sacred beings, or beings who have come in close contact with sacred power".[101] Women, especially, have the freedom to travel on a pilgrimage that they do not have at other times.

Pilgrimage may be seen as a commercial enterprise for the great centres, but it is the journey that is in many ways central to the pilgrim. Like *pūjā* at its best, whether that is at a home or a temple, a roadside shrine or a *tīrtha*, there is a temporary suspension of the mundane for the spiritual and a movement from the profane to the sacred. Just as local and home ritual gathers people together to focus on the sacred rather than the worldly, pilgrimage gives individuals the opportunity to recognize the unity of faith, albeit with manifold expressions in the whole of India. Here is a chance to witness diversity but to remain at one with others who are expressing their devotion in *tīrtha-yātrā*. A pilgrimage is a physical journey, but it is also a journey into the inner self; a journey that has to transcend hardships in a gradual loosening of the material and mundane. It is not just the arrival at the goal that is the important point; it is the process of transformation that takes place during the journey. There will be many encounters with other Hindus who have different dialects, different ethnic origins, and who eat different food. There must surely be an increasing necessity for tolerance and shared understanding in the process that is a pilgrimage. Bhardwaj and Lochtefeld make a rather poignant comment when they say that "a person with faith gets the benefits of a *tīrtha*, while one without faith merely gets a bath".[102]

As was stated at the outset of this book, Hinduism is a bewildering complexity of widely different practices, beliefs, customs and traditions. Its classic accommodation of ideas, rather than the discarding of the old in favour of the new, has served to make it a religion of colourful and profound variety, rich in myth and containing the kind of breadth in its dimensions to cater for all levels of consciousness. Yet, despite such openness to the infinite paths to God, societal life, as we have seen in earlier chapters, remains mainly class and caste bound, so it would be true to say that while the paths to the divine are infinite, the *karmic* and *dharmic* placements of birth dictate, to a considerable extent, which of the multitude of paths an individual must take. This typifies the complexities of the religion rather well, illustrating the dualities and opposites that all manifest existence necessarily contains. Indeed, Hinduism seems to have every possible variable in its religious beliefs and praxis.

I recently had no more than a ten-minute conversation with a Hindu general practitioner of medicine here in Wales in the United Kingdom, a woman. Within those few minutes, I was able to establish that she belongs to a Scheduled caste. She had no conception whatsoever about *classes*, *varṇa*: for her, there are *Brāhmins* and everyone else. She had had an arranged marriage seventeen years previously, and had never set eyes on her husband before their marriage. Both her daughters will also have arranged marriages in time, and are eager for the occasion. She was twenty-five years old when she married and so had been able to study and gain her qualifications as a medic. She showed me the *tali*, the wedding pendant that she wears and never takes off: she knew the word *tali* but had a different name for it herself. It was a *triśūla* with a coconut underneath. DR M, as I shall call her, is a worshipper of Kālī. She eats meat, and her family in Tamil Nāḍu engages in animal sacrifice to the Goddess. Dr M's mother is a widow, as is her grandmother: one wears black and the other white. Dr M persuades her mother occasionally to wear coloured saris. Neither mother nor grandmother wears any jewellery and certainly not their *talis*. Dr M is keen for her two children to embrace their Indian culture, so she takes them to India regularly. My point in mentioning this brief meeting is that just a ten-minute dialogue with a person whom I had never previously met lifts the written word to the practical experience, creating valuable interchange between individuals. It is my hope that this present book will enable and enhance such dialogues, and open up experiential conversation between people of different cultures.

Glossary of Sanskrit Terms

The following is a selective list of the Sanskrit terms most frequently used in the chapters. Sanskrit consonants carry the vowel '*a*' with them, which is why transliterated Sanskrit words have so many '*a*'s. This '*a*' is normally short and pronounced like the *u* in English b*u*t. Where this is not so, here, and with other vowels, diacritical marks can be added in transliteration to indicate a change of sound. Sanskrit also has a number of aspirated words with an '*h*' following the consonant. When these combinations of letters occur, the reader is advised to separate the two consonants in order to obtain a more accurate sound. For example, *artha*, "wealth, success" is pronounced as *art* plus *ha* but since there are no diacritical indicators on the '*a*'s, both are pronounced as *u* – *urt-hu*. Such diacritical marks on vowels also help to indicate where stress on syllables is in a word. A simplified list of pronunciation of letters is as follows:

a	pronounced as in b*u*t
ā	as in f*a*ther
c	as in *ch*at
e	as in f*e*ll
i	as in f*i*t
ī	as in f*ee*t
ḷ	as in fab*le*
o	as in g*o*
ṛ	as in fu*r*
u	as in p*u*t
ū	as in y*u*le
ai	as in *ai*sle
au	as in v*ow*
ṃ	is a nasalized sound
ṣ and *ś*	approximately as in *sh*ip

abhiṣeka ritual bathing of a deity's image.

ācārya master, teacher, great theologian.

adharma what is not right and against the norms of society and religion; evil, the opposite of *dharma*.

Adi-Dravidas	former untouchables.
Aditi	*Vedic* goddess.
Ādityas	the sons of Aditī who personify aspects of nature.
Āgamas	"source" or "beginnings", what first came about: non-*Vedic* Śaiva scriptures bearing testimony to a personal deity.
Agni	*Vedic* god of fire.
ahiṃsā	non-violence.
Alakṣmī	the inauspicious sister of the Goddess of Good Fortune, Lakṣmī; she brings misfortune.
ālpanā	floor patterns made of rice paste.
Āḷvārs	"divers", devotional mystics who plunge into the divine.
anjali	a manner of greeting.
anuloma	marriage marriage that is "in the grain", between a man and a lower-caste woman.
Āraṇyakas	forest, wilderness writings; *Vedic* scriptures containing much mystical thought that overlaps with and prefigures some *Vedāntic* concepts.
āratī	part of ritual worship involving offering light, usually as fire, to a deity.
Ardhanārīśvara	iconic representation of Śiva as an androgyne, half female and half male.
Arjuna	one of the five Pāṇḍava brothers and the central human character of the *Bhagavad-Gītā*.
artha	wealth, success, social status.
Artha-śāstra	a treatise on the nature of *artha*, "wealth", by Kauṭilīya.
Āryans	"nobles", the race of people said to have infiltrated northern India in the second millennium BCE.
Ārya Samāj	late nineteenth-century Hindu reform movement.
āśramas	four stages of life – student, householder, forest dweller and renouncer.
asuras	demons, anti-gods.
Atharva Veda	one of the four *Vedas* that deals predominantly with incantations, spells and charms.
ātman	"self" but specifically the true Self that is the essence of all things and that is equated partially or wholly with Brahman.
avatāras	literally "descents", mainly of Viṣṇu in animal or human form.
Ayodhyā	the capital city associated with Rāma in the *Rāmāyaṇa* and subsequently a famous pilgrimage site.
Balarāma/ Baladeva/ Balabhadra	Kṛṣṇa's brother.
bhajan(a)s	hymns and devotional songs in praise of a deity
bhakti	loving devotion to a personal deity including reciprocal love of the deity.
bhakta	a *bhakti* devotee.

bhūtas	spirits
Brahmā	one of the triad of Hindu Gods with Śiva and Viṣṇu and responsible for the action of creation.
brahmacārin	celibate student in the first of the four stages of life.
brahmacarya	the state of celibate studentship.
Brāhmaṇas	commentaries on the *Vedas* and part of Sanskrit *śruti* scriptures that are textual manuals related to ritual.
Brāhmins	members of the highest class of the four classes of Hindus.
Cāmuṇḍā	an early name of the Goddess Kālī.
Caṇḍālas	the lowest caste of Hindus and outcastes.
capātīs	bread-like pancakes.
Dalits	"oppressed"; persons outside the caste system who were formerly known as untouchables.
dāna	giving, charity.
darśan(a)	viewing, sight of, audience with: a philosophical system.
Dāsas/Dasyus	the term in the *Ṛg Veda* used for non-Āryans, aboriginal and indigenous people.
deva-dāsīs	"servants of God", devotional temple dancers and singers.
deva-gṛha	"house of God", a temple.
Devī	Goddess.
-Māhātmya	important text extolling the Great Goddess.
Mahā-	Great Goddess.
dhāmas	"abodes", divine dwelling places and pilgrimage sites.
dharma	what is right socially and religiously; duty.
sādhāraṇa-	universal, eternal *dharma.*
sva-	"own" *dharma.*
varṇa-āśrama-	*dharma* pertaining to class and stage of life.
dharmaśālā	resting house for pilgrims.
Dharma-śāstras	law texts.
Dharma-sūtras	aphorisms, short statements, on a number of topics.
dhobī	washerman or woman.
drāviḍa	style of temple.
dupatta/orhna	the covering worn over the head by women.
dvija	"twice born", pertaining to the three highest classes of *Brāhmins, Kṣatriyas* and *Vaiśyas.*
advija	those not twice born.
gaṇas	ghouls, ghosts, demons in the entourage of Śiva.
ganja	a substance made from *Cannabis Indica* that is smoked.
garbha-gṛha	"womb house", the shrine housing a deity.
Gāyatrī Mantra	an important *mantra* from the *Ṛg Veda* that is chanted daily.
ghaṭa	pot representing a deity.

ghaṭias	specialist officials at the Ganges *ghāṭs*.
ghaṭs	sloping steps leading into the River Ganges built for worship and for cremations.
ghī	clarified butter which, as a product of the cow, is regarded as especially pure.
gopīs	"cowherdesses", especially those associated with Kṛṣṇa.
gōpura	towering gateway of a temple.
gotra	clan.
grāma	village.
-devāta	village deity.
gṛhastha	householder.
Gṛhya-sūtras	law texts associated with the householder stage of life.
guṇas	three strands or qualities – *sattva*, *rajas* and *tamas* – that are existent in all things.
nirguṇa	having no *guṇas*.
saguṇa	with *guṇas*.
Harijans	"children of God", the name given by Mahatma Gandhi to untouchables.
Harivaṃśa	a Vaiṣṇava text containing an account of the early life of Kṛṣṇa.
homa	sacred fire in the home.
iṣṭa-devatā	a personal deity.
Itihāsas	history and mythology in the two great epics.
japa	repetition of the name of a deity or of a *mantra*.
-mālā	beads used in meditative repetition.
jāti	birth, species, genus, type, caste.
jīva	individual, living soul.
jñāna	knowledge.
-kāṇḍa	knowledge portion of the *Vedas*.
jutha	leftover food.
kaccā	food that is impure and imperfect, unripe or uncooked.
Kāla	ultimate Time that is beyond normal time.
kalaśa	a husked coconut used in worship as an aniconic representation of a deity
Kāma	the god of love.
kāma	pleasure, especially sexual; desire.
karma	"activity", "action"; ritual action; the law of cause and effect by which an individual gains merit or demerit according to good or bad actions.
-kāṇḍa	the ritual action portion of the *Vedas*.
-yoga	the discipline of action without desire for results.
nitya-	obligatory daily ritual.

kauṣtubha	the jewel in the necklace worn by Viṣṇu.
kāvya	a poem.
keśānta kāla	ceremony marking boys' first shaving.
kīrtan(a)	ritual chanting in praise of a deity.
Kṣatriyas	the second highest class of Hindus, traditionally warriors, rulers and administrators.
kṣetras	pilgrimage "fields".
kula-devatā	family deity.
kumkum	vermilion powder used in ritual worship of iconic and aniconic representations of deities.
kurta-pajama	traditional male dress of trousers and long tunic.
lengha-choli	short-sleeved blouse worn by women.
līlā	divine sport or play.
-bhūmis	"play grounds" pilgrimage sites.
-sthalas	"places of play" pilgrimage sites.
liṅga	phallic symbol associated with the God Śiva.
lungi	southern-Indian lower-body garment for men.
Mahā-vidyās	ten Tantric goddesses.
Mānava-dharma-śāstra	the *Laws of Manu*.
maṇḍala	a diagrammatic, symbolic circle used for meditation ; a book of the *Ṛg Veda*.
vāstu-puruṣa-	a symbolic man used for the basic design of some temples.
maṇḍap(a)/maṇḍva	canopy under which a marriage takes place.
mandir(a)	temple; palace.
mantra	part of scripture or name of a deity used for meditation or ritual.
Manu-smṛti	The *Laws of Manu*.
Maruts	gods of the wind.
maṭhas	monasteries.
Mātṛkās	"Mothers", female powers emitted by the Great Goddess Durgā.
māyā	delusion; illusion.
mahā-	great delusion.
mokṣa	"release", liberation from the cycle of rebirths.
mudra	ritualistic hand position.
mūrti	image, embodiment, especially of a deity.
nāgara	temple design.
nāgas	snakes, serpents; naked ascetics.
Naṭarāja	the cosmic dance of Śiva that brings about the dissolution of the universe.
nirākāra	without form.
Nirṛti	a destructive *Vedic* goddess.

nivṛtti	inactivity.
niyoga marriage	the practice of surrogate husbands for widows.
Oṃ/Aum	the primordial sound from which all emerged; symbol of Brahman; a *mantra*.
paccā	food that is pure and perfect.
padma	lotus.
pallu	end part of a sari draped over the shoulder.
pañca-makara	five impure items in Tantrism.
paṇḍas	temple officials at pilgrimage sites.
pardā	"curtain", the practice of secluding women.
pati-vratā	a married woman who lives for her husband's happiness.
piṇḍas	balls of rice used to feed a deceased soul on its journey to the next life.
pitṛs	ancestors.
pitṛ-loka	realm of the ancestors.
pradakṣiṇa	circumambulation.
prakṛti	nature; manifested matter.
Mūlā-	Primordial Matter.
pramathas	malicious hosts connected with Rudra.
prānapratiṣṭhā	establishing the breath in the image of a deity.
prasāda	the "grace" of a deity given as the remains of food or other offerings to a deity.
pratiloma marriage	marriage of a high-caste woman "against the grain" to a lower-caste male.
pravṛtti	activity.
premā	love.
pretas	ghosts.
Pṛthivī	*Ṛg Vedic* goddess.
pūjā	worship, veneration, reverence.
pūjāri	priest at a temple or shrine.
Purāṇas	"ancient tales"; a class of *smṛti* scriptures.
purohit	family priest.
puruṣa	man; *Puruṣa-sūkta* the great sacrificial being of the *Ṛg Veda* from whom the cosmos, and the four classes were made.
puruṣārthas	the goals of human life – wealth, pleasure, what is right and liberation.
rajas	one of the three *guṇas* responsible for activity and energy in all life.
rakṣas/rakṣasas	demons.
rangoli	floor designs made with coloured powders.
rāsa/rāsa-līlā	circular dance.
ratha-yātrā	festival chariot carrying the image of deity.
ṛṣis	ancient *Vedic* seers.
ṛtu kāla	ceremony marking girls' first menses.

śabda	word, sound.
sādhaka / sādhikā	one who undertakes religious practice.
sādhana	religious or ascetic practice; fulfilment; pursuit of a goal.
sādhu	a holy man, usually ascetic.
sākāra	with form (of Brahman).
Śākta	devotee of the Mother Goddess in the Śākta sect of Hindusim.
śakta pīṭhas	the places where parts of Sītā's deceased body fell creating pilgrimage sites.
śakti	power, energy; the goddess in female form.
salwar	light loose trousers worn by women.
-kameeze	long loose-fitting tunic.
samādhi	stilled consciousness and deep, meditative concentration.
Saṃhitās	the "collections" of the *Vedas.*
saṃkalpa	intention.
saṃnyāsa	renunciation; the final fourth stage of life.
saṃnyāsin	renouncer.
saṃsāra	the cycle of births and deaths.
saṃskāras	life-cycle rites.
sapiṇḍī-kāraṇa	annual anniversary *śraddha* rites for the dead.
sapta-padī	seven steps taken during the marriage ceremony.
śāstra	scriptures, teachings, laws, rule books.
satī (the)	wife who immolates herself on her deceased husband's funeral pyre.
-mātās	"Mothers" who have not immolated themselves, but who have gained extraordinary powers.
sattva (adj. *sāttvikā*)	one of the three *guṇas* associated with light, spiritual evolution, what is good, truth, wisdom.
śikhara	a temple design resembling a mountain peak.
drāviḍa-	style of temple building.
smṛti	"remembered"; scripture that is not *Vedic* and that contains much devotional and popular material.
snātaka	one who has bathed at the end of *upanayana.*
vidya-	one bathed in knowledge.
śraddha	rites of offerings for the dead.
Śrī-vatsa	curl of golden hair on Viśṇu's chest, equated with Lakṣmī.
śruti	"heard", scriptures that have been cognized by the ancient seers.
strī-dhana	the gifts given to a bride at her marriage.
strī-dharma	the *dharma* of a wife.
Śūdras	those of the lowest and fourth class of Hindus who are not twice born.
sūtras	law texts.
sva-bhāva	"own being", one's innate nature.
sva-tantra	"own thread" referring to that which women are not expected to have.

tamas	one of the three *guṇas* and associated with dullness and inertia in the cosmos.
tapas	"heat", ascetic austerities.
tīrtha	"ford, crossing place" and pilgrimage site.
-yātrā	pilgrimage to a sacred site.
tri-guṇā	the three *guṇas*.
Tri-mūrti	the three Gods Viṣṇu, Śiva and Brahmā.
triśūla	the trident of Śiva and other deities.
tri-varga	*artha*, *kāma*, *dharma* as the three aims of life.
tulasī	the basil plant.
tyāga	renunciation, literally "ignoring".
Vaiśyas	the third of the four classes generally associated with trade.
vānaprastha	forest dweller, the third of the four stages of life.
varṇa	class, colour, covering.
catur-	four classes.
varṇa-āśrama-dharma	the *dharma* of class and stage of life.
vivāha	marriage.
vrata	a vow.
yajña	sacrificial worship.
yajñopavīta	sacred thread worn by twice-born Hindus.
yakṣīs	female spirits of the earth and trees.
yantras	mystical diagrams.
yoga	discipline.
yogin	a male practitioner of *yoga*.
yoginī	a female practitioner of *yoga*, especially in Tantrism.
yoni	the symbol of the female genital organ.

Notes

Introduction

1 Timothy Fitzgerald, "Hinduism and the 'World Religion' Fallacy" in *Religion* (London, San Diego, New York, Boston, Sydney, Tokyo, Toronto: Academic Press) 20 (April 1990), p. 101.
2 *Ibid.*, p. 110.
3 Brian K. Smith, "Questioning Authority: Constructions and Deconstructions of Hinduism" in *International Journal of Hindu Studies* (Illinois: World Heritage Press), 2, 3 (December 1998), p. 316.
4 Jessica Frazier, "Introduction: New Visions of Hinduism" in Jessica Frazier, ed., *The Continuum Companion to Hindu Studies* (London and New York: Continuum, 2011), p. 3.
5 Tracy Pintchman, *The Rise of the Goddess in the Hindu Tradition* (Albany, New York: State University of New York Press, 1994), p. 194.

Chapter 1 Fundamental Beliefs

1 Julius Lipner thinks that "Hindu" as a term originated from the "Indus" river, but was given by the Āryans themselves as early as the second millennium BCE to depict the whole area covered by the Indus and its tributaries, which they called *sindhu*. See "On Hinduism and Hinduisms: The Way of the Banyan" in Susha Mittal and Gene Thursby, eds., *The Hindu World* (New York and London: Routledge, 2004), p. 10.
2 Julius Lipner, *Hindus: Their religious beliefs and practices* (London and New York: Routledge, 1994), p. 1.
3 Herman W. Tull, "*Karma*" in Mittal and Thursby, eds., *The Hindu World*, p. 309.
4 Lipner, *Hindus*, p. 14.
5 *Ibid.*, pp. 5–6.
6 Lipner, "On Hinduism and Hinduisms: The Way of the Banyan", p. 24.
7 Troy Wilson Organ, *Hinduism: Its historical development* (London: Barron's Educational, 1974), p. 8.
8 See *ibid.*, p. 15.
9 Ram Gidoomal and Robin Thomson, *A Way of Life: Introducing Hinduism* (London, Sydney, Auckland: Hodder and Stoughton, 1997), p. 35.
10 S. A. Nigosian, *World Faiths* (New York: St. Martin's Press, 1994 second edn), p. 75.
11 Where Brahman is considered as greater than all the cosmos, the belief is *panentheism* rather than pantheism in which Brahman *is* the totality of the cosmos.
12 *Muṇḍaka Upaniṣad* 2:2:12, translator Patrick Olivelle, *Upaniṣads* (Oxford and New York: Oxford University Press, 1996), p. 274.

13 *The Bhagavad Gītā* 2:22, translator Jeaneane Fowler, *The Bhagavad Gita: A Text and Commentary for Students* (Brighton, Portland, Toronto: Sussex Academic Press, 2012), p. 28.
14 *Kaṭha Upaniṣad* 1:6, translator Olivelle, *Upaniṣads*, p. 232.
15 Chandradhar Sharma, *A Critical Survey of Indian Philosophy* (Delhi: Motilal Banarsidass Publishers Private Limited, 1987 reprint of 1960 edn), p. 19.
16 Wendy Doniger O'Flaherty, ed., *Karma and Rebirth in Classical Indian Traditions* (Berkeley, Los Angeles, London: University of California Press, 1980).
17 *Bṛhad-āraṇyaka Upaniṣad* 4:4:5, translator Olivelle, *Upaniṣads*, p. 65.
18 Jessica Frazier, "Introduction: New Visions of Hinduism" in Jessica Frazier, ed., *The Continuum Companion to Hindu Studies* (London and New York: Continuum, 2011), p. 5.
19 See Tull, "*Karma*", p. 327.
20 *Ibid.*, p. 326.
21 See Susan S. Wadley, "*Grāma*" in Mittal and Thursby, eds., *The Hindu World*, p. 431.
22 *Bhāgavata Purāṇa* 6:1:45, translator G. V. Tagare (Delhi: Motilal Banarsidass Publishers Private Limited, 1993 reprint of 1979 edn first published 1976), p. 779.
23 Barbara A. Holdrege, "*Dharma*" in Mittal and Thursby, eds., *The Hindu World*, p. 228.
24 See Gavin Flood, *An Introduction to Hinduism* (Cambridge: Cambridge University Press, 1996), p. 53.
25 For comprehensive and wide discussions of the nature of *dharma*, see Wendy Doniger O'Flaherty and J. Duncan M. Derrett, eds., *The Concept of Duty in South Asia* (New Delhi: Vikas, 1978).
26 *Bṛhad-āraṇyaka Upaniṣad* 4:4:6, translator Olivelle, *Upaniṣads*, p. 65.
27 *Ibid.*

Chapter 2 Scriptures

1 Michael Witzel, "Vedas and Upaniṣads" in Gavin Flood, ed., *The Blackwell Companion to Hinduism* (Malden, Massachusetts, Oxford and Victoria: Blackwell Publishing, 2003), p. 68.
2 See Gavin Flood, "Sacred Writings" in Paul Bowen, ed., *Themes and Issues in Hinduism* (London and Washington: Cassell, 1998), p. 132.
3 Witzel, "Vedas and Upaniṣads", p. 68.
4 *Ibid.*, p. 70.
5 Troy Wilson Organ, *Hinduism: Its historical development* (New York, London, Toronto: Barron's Educational Series, Inc., 1974), p. 81.
6 See for example 10:7:1–3, 22, 35, which hints at an underlying ground of all the gods and 19:71, which seems to hint at the *ātman* within that is Brahman.
7 Organ, *Hinduism*, p. 89.
8 Although the latest may be dated to about the first century CE, see Laurie L. Patton, "Veda and Upaniṣad" in Sushil Mittal and Gene Thursby, eds., *The Hindu World* (New York and London: Routledge, 2004), p. 47.
9 Ram Gidoomal and Robin Thomson, *A Way of Life: Introducing Hinduism* (London, Sydney, Auckland: Hodder & Stoughton, 1997), p. 58.
10 The four major compilers whose works are extant are Āpastamba, Gautama, Baudhāyana and Vasiṣṭha, each of which was a proponent of a particular *Vedic* school. For a translation of their texts, see Patrick Olivelle, translator, *Dharmasūtras: The law codes of Āpastamba, Gautama, Baudhāyana and Vasiṣṭha* (Oxford: Oxford University Press, 1999).
11 See Ludo Rocher, "The Dharmaśāstras" in Flood, ed., *The Blackwell Companion to Hinduism*, p. 110.

12 For an extensive analysis of these two epics and the *Harivaṃśa*, a Vaiṣṇava epic that deals with the creation of the universe on the one hand, and the early rural life of Kṛṣṇa, found in the closing books of the *Mahābhārata*, see John Brockington, *The Sanskrit Epics* (Leiden: Koninklÿke Brill NV., 1998) as well as *Righteous Rāma: The evolution of an epic* (Delhi: Oxford University Press, 1984), by the same author.

13 Bithika Mukerji, *The Hindu Tradition: An introduction to Hinduism and to its sacred tradition* (Amity, New York: Amity House 1988), p. 63.

14 See Surinder M. Bhardwaj and James G. Lochtefeld, "Tīrtha" in Sushil Mittal and Gene Thursby, eds., *The Hindu World*, p. 485.

15 Brockington suggests 500 BCE–300 CE, see *Righteous Rāma*, p. 1. See also Klaus K. Klostermaier, *A Survey of Hinduism* (New York: State University of New York Press, 1994 second edn), p. 83, who suggests the final redaction was in 400 CE.

16 Brockington, *Righteous Rāma*, p. 308.

17 See James L. Fitzgerald, "*Mahābhārata*" in Mittal and Thursby, eds., *The Hindu World*, p. 52,

18 Romesh C. Dutt, *The Ramayana & The Mahabharata* (London, Melbourne and Toronto: Dent, Everyman's Library, 1978 reprint of 1910 edn), p. 156.

19 John Brockington, *Righteous Rāma*, p. 11.

20 Originally, *avatāra* was used in the sense of *avatāraṇa*, "taking down" of oppression. See Fitzgerald, "*Mahābhārata*", p. 55.

21 See Jessica Frazier, ed., *The Continuum Companion to Hindu Studies* (London and New York: Continuum, 2011), p. 306.

22 Brockington, *Righteous Rāma*, p. 325.

23 For a detailed analysis, see *ibid.*, pp. 307–17.

24 Mukerji, *The Hindu Tradition*, pp. 72–3.

25 Though Rāma does bow to public pressure and banish Sītā twice as well as ambush the king of the monkeys in a rather dastardly manner.

26 Fitzgerald, *Mahābhārata*, p. 72.

27 *Ibid.*, p. 73.

28 *Ibid.*, p. 59.

29 Arun Kumar Mookerjee, "Dharma as the Goal: The Mahābhārata" in Krishna Sivaraman ed., *Hindu Spirituality: Vedas through Vedanta* (London: SCM, 1989), p. 133.

30 Kashi Nath Upadhyaya argues for a more genuine placement of the *Gītā* in the *Mahābhārata*, pointing out synonymy of language, phrases and ideas between both, as well as places in the *Mahābhārata* in which the *Gītā* is mentioned. He suggests that the *Gītā* is "an integral part of the *Mahābhārata*". See his *Early Buddhism and the Bhagavadgītā* (Delhi, Varanasi, Patna: Motilal Banarsidass, 1983 reprint of 1971 edn), pp. 6–7.

31 Juan Mascaró, *The Bhagavad Gita* (London, New York, Victoria, Ontario, Auckland: Penguin, 1962), p. 22.

32 Alexandre Piatigorsky in his introduction to J. A. B. van Buitenen, translator, *The Bhagavad Gītā* (Rockport, Massachusetts, Shaftesbury, Dorset, Brisbane, Queensland: Element, 1997), p. 3.

33 See John Brockington, "The Sanskrit Epics" in Gavin Flood, ed., *The Blackwell Companion to Hinduism* (Malden, Massachusetts, Oxford, Victoria: Blackwell Publishing, 2005 reprint of 2003 edn), p. 116.

34 The Pūrva or Karma Mīmāṃsā school, or at least its developing strands, possibly predates the *Gītā*.

35 For example, Sarvepalli Radhakrishnan, translator, *The Bhagavadgita, with an Introductory Essay,*

Sanskrit Text, English Translation and Notes (New York: Harper, 1973, and London: George Allen & Unwin, 1948), p. 14.

36 See Jeaneane Fowler, *The Bhagavad Gita: A text and commentary for students* (Brighton, Portland and Toronto: Sussex Academic Press, 2012), pp. xi–xlv.

37 John M. Koller, *The Indian Way: An introduction to the philosophies and religions of India* (Upper Saddle River, New Jersey: Pearson, Prentice Hall, 2006 second revised edn, first published 1982), p. 182.

38 Brockington, "The Sanskrit Epics" p. 128.

39 Klostermaier, *A Survey of Hinduism*, p. 82.

40 Velcheru Narayana Rao, "*Purāṇa*" in Mittal and Thursby, eds., *The Hindu World*, p. 98.

41 Freda Matchett, "The Purāṇas" in Flood, ed., *The Blackwell Companion to Hinduism*, p. 131.

42 See Thomas J. Hopkins, *The Hindu Religious Tradition* (Belmont, California: Wadsworth Publishing Company, 1971), p. 96.

43 Klostermaier, *A Survey of Hinduism*, pp. 96–7.

44 Matchett, "The *Purāṇas*", p. 130.

45 *Padma Purāṇa* II:71:18–19 translated by N. A. Deshpande, *Ancient Indian Tradition & Mythology*, vol. 41 (Delhi: Motilal Banarsidass Publishers Private Limited, 1990), p. 1174.

46 See Rao, "*Purāṇa*", p. 98. While five key subjects of content are not found to any great extent in the *Purāṇas*, there is, nevertheless, a focus on creation, and the Goddess is often projected as its source. Older ideas of creation are melded with conventions about creation at the time the particular *Purāṇa* was composed.

47 *Ibid.*, pp. 108–9.

48 Dominic Goodall and Harunga Isaacson, "Current Approaches: Tantric traditions" in Frazier, *The Continuum Companion to Hindu Studies*, p. 122.

49 Mukerji, *The Hindu Tradition*, p. 28.

Chapter 3 Class and Caste: *Varṇa* and *Jāti*

1 Dermot Killingley, "Modernity, Reform, and Revival" in Gavin Flood, ed., *The Blackwell Companion to Hinduism* (Malden, Massachusetts, Oxford and Victoria: Blackwell Publishing, 2005 reprint of 2003 edn), p. 519.

2 Sophie Baker, *Caste: At home in Hindu India* (London: Jonathan Cape, 1990), pp. 55–6.

3 John M. Koller, *The Indian Way: An introduction to the philosophies and religions of India* (Upper Saddle River, New Jersey: Pearson, Prentice Hall, 2006 second edn first published 1982), p. 95.

4 I have chosen to represent the priestly class with this spelling rather than *Brāhmaṇas* or similar, in order to avoid confusion with texts of the same name. *Brāhmin* is variously spelt in other texts.

5 See Klaus K. Klostermaier, *A Survey of Hinduism* (Albany, New York: State University of New York Press, 1994 second edn), p. 334.

6 Brian K. Smith, *Classifying the Universe: The ancient Indian varṇa system and the origins of caste* (New York: Oxford University Press, 1994), p. 8.

7 *Ṛg Veda* 3:34:9, translator Ralph T. H. Griffith, *The Hymns of the Ṛgveda* (Delhi: Motilal Banarsidass Publishers Private Limited, 1991 reprint of 1973 revised edn), p. 180. The word translated as "colour" here might equally well be "race": see Griffith's footnote to the verse.

8 *Ṛg Veda* 5:29:10.

9 *Ṛg Veda* 7:6:3, translator Griffith, *The Hymns of the Ṛgveda* p. 337.

10 *Ṛg Veda* 7:21:5, *ibid.*, p. 345.

11 There were many other hostile tribes mentioned in the *Ṛg* but it is the *Dasyus* that are the most

despised. For a summation of the *Ṛg Veda*'s account of them see Prabhati Mukherjee, *Beyond the Four Varṇas: The Untouchables in India* (Delhi, Varanasi, Patna, Bangalore, Madras: Motilal Banarsidass, 1988), pp. 18–19.

12 Ram Sharan Sharma, *Śūdras in Ancient India: A social history of the lower order down to circa A.D. 600* (Delhi: Motilal Banarsidass Publishers Private Limited, 1990 third revised edn, first published 1958), p. 20.

13 *Ibid.*, p. 30.

14 *Ṛg Veda* 10:90:1–3 and 11–12, translator Griffith, *The Hymns of the Ṛgveda*, pp. 602–3.

15 All other phenomena emerged in the same way from parts of Puruṣa, for example the moon from his mind, the sun from his eye, the sky from his navel, and so on.

16 *Chāndogya Upaniṣad* 5:10:7, translator Patrick Olivelle, *Upaniṣads* (Oxford and New York: Oxford University Press, 1996), p. 142. See also the *Bṛhad-āraṇyaka Upaniṣad* 4:4:6 and the *Śvetāśvatara Upaniṣad* 5:7.

17 Kenneth H. Post, "Spiritual Foundations of Caste" in Krishna Sivaraman, ed., *Hindu Spirituality: Veda through Vedanta* (London: SCM Press, 1989), p. 94.

18 It is no small wonder that the outcaste Dr Ambedkar who left Hinduism for Buddhism burned a copy of the *Laws of Manu* in public.

19 *Laws of Manu* 1:98–100, translators Wendy Doniger with Brian K. Smith, *The Laws of Manu* (London, New York, Victoria, Ontario, Auckland: Penguin Books, 1991), pp. 13–14.

20 *Laws of Manu* 1:28, 29, translators Doniger and Smith, *ibid.*, p. 6.

21 *Laws of Manu* 10:57.

22 *Laws of Manu* 9:335, translators Doniger and Smith, *The Laws of Manu*, pp. 232–3.

23 Baker, *Caste*, p. 51.

24 *Ibid.*, p. 121.

25 *Ibid.*, p. 49.

26 *Laws of Manu* 2:68, 2:146–8, 2:169–72.

27 Manu was against inter-class marriage but if it did occur then marriage of a high-class man to a lower class woman was better than a low-class man marrying a high-class woman. As we shall see later, Manu believed that castes came about because of such mixed classes.

28 John Brockington, *Righteous Rāma: The evolution of an epic* (Delhi, Bombay, Calcutta, Madras, 1985), pp. 317–18.

29 *Bhagavad Gītā* 3:5, translator Jeaneane Fowler, *The Bhagavad Gita: A text and commentary for students* (Brighton, Portland and Toronto: Sussex Academic Press, 2012), p. 53.

30 *Ibid.*, p. 78.

31 See *ibid.*, 18:41–5, pp. 288–90.

32 *Ibid.*, verse 47, p. 290. The same thought is to be found earlier in 3:35, where it is said that it is better to die following one's *dharma* than to adopt the *dharma* of another.

33 9:32–3, *ibid.*, p. 170.

34 1:40–44, *ibid.*, pp. 13–14.

35 Louis Dumont, *Homo Hierarchicus: The caste system and its implications*, translated by Mark Sainsbury, Louis Dumont and Basia Gulati (Chicago and London: University of Chicago Press, 1970 revised edn, first published 1966), p. 73.

36 Julius Lipner, *Hindus: Their religious beliefs and practices* (London and New York: Routledge, 1994), p. 113.

37 *Ṛg Veda* 7:103, translator Griffith, *The Hymns of* the *Ṛgveda*, pp. 384–5.

38 *Laws of Manu* 10:75– 6, translators Doniger and Smith, p. 244.

39 A detailed account of the daily routine of a temple priest can be found in Baker, *Caste*, pp. 124–6.
40 See André Béteille, *Class, Caste and Power: Changing patterns of stratification in a Tanjore village* (Delhi, Calcutta, Chennai, Mumbai: Oxford University Press, 1998 reprint of 1996 edn), p. 64.
41 Even to the extent that they have had to become outcastes: see Baker, *Caste*, pp. 54–5.
42 McKim Marriott, "*Varṇa* and *Jāti*" in Sushil Mittal and Gene Thursby, *The Hindu World* (New York and London: Routledge, 2004), p. 374.
43 Declan Quigley, "On the Relationship between Caste and Hinduism" in Flood, ed., *The Blackwell Companion to Hinduism*, p. 501.
44 *Ibid.*, p. 498.
45 Béteille, *Class, Caste and Power*, p. 77.
46 Baker, *Caste*, pp. 51–2.
47 Marriott, "*Varṇa* and *Jāti*", p. 375.
48 See Béteille, *Class, Caste and Power*, p. 95.
49 Sharma, *Śūdras in Ancient India*, p. 315.
50 *Laws of Manu* 9:322, translators Doniger and Smith, p. 232.
51 S. V. Ketkar, *History of Caste in India: Social conditions in India according to Manu* (New Delhi: Cosmo Publications, 1979 reprint of 1909 edn), p. 94.
52 Marriott, "*Varṇa* and *Jāti*", p. 376.
53 *Ibid.*, pp. 376–7.
54 Baker, *Caste*, p. 46.
55 *Ibid.*, p. 32.
56 Marriott, "*Varṇa* and *Jāti*", p. 377.
57 *Ibid.*, p. 378.
58 Sharma, *Śūdras in Ancient India*, p. 53.
59 *Ibid.*, pp. 39–40.
60 *Ibid.*, p. 79.
61 *Ibid.*, p. 268–9, though as Sharma points out, such kings and rulers may have been foreigners labelled as *Śūdras* because they did not support the role and power of the *Brāhmins*.
62 Still, there is some evidence from the *Laws of Manu* that *Śūdras* became sharecroppers and were given a percentage of the produce of the land. Their sheer numbers and the necessity of their working on the land must have meant some alleviation of their conditions. The growth of trade, too, must have meant a greater need for artisan crafts, and this would have helped the economic stability of some. Again, however, for most their lot was harsh but by the end of the Gupta period, wages seem to have improved and fewer *Śūdras* were reduced to the status of slaves. As to the status of women, I shall explore that in chapter 10.
63 Béteille, *Class, Caste and Power*, pp. 79–80.
64 According to Baker, "Handloom weavers are the second largest trained workforce in India and there are still ten million of them working today." See *Caste*, p. 103. Baker's book was published in 1990.
65 In Baker's book on *Caste*, she includes brilliant photography of members and scenes from different classes. Her photographs of a *Śūdra* weaving family show males of the family clearly wearing a sacred thread, traditionally the privilege of only twice-born Hindus. To date, I have been unable to contact the author about this point, but I refer the reader to the photographs of the weaver family in Andhra Pradesh opposite p. 104 and those that follow. Presumably, this is a classic example of the social rise of a low-caste group through taking on rituals of higher classes.

66 Baker, *Caste*, p. 99.
67 Blacksmiths and goldsmiths seem to have risen in status in some regions, see Viramma, Josiane Racine and Jean-Luc Racine, "High and Low Castes in Karani" in Ishita Banerjee-Dube, *Caste in History*, Oxford in India Readings: Themes in Indian History (Oxford: Oxford University Press, 2012 reprint of 2008 edn), p. 240.
68 Baker, *Caste*, p. 80.
69 Lipner, *Hindus*, p. 92.
70 Debjani Ganguly, *Caste, Colonialism and Counter-Modernity: Notes on a postcolonial hermeneutics of caste* (Abingdon, Oxon and New York: Routledge, 2005), p. 1.
71 Balmurli Natrajan, *The Culturalization of Caste in India*. Routledge Contemporary South Asia Series (Abingdon, Oxon and New York: Routledge, 2011), p. 1.
72 Jessica Frazier, ed., *The Continuum Companion to Hindu Studies* (London and New York: Continuum, 2011), p. 310.
73 Ganguly, *Caste, Colonialism and Counter-Modernity*, p. 3.
74 Post, "Spiritual Foundations of Caste", p. 89.
75 Buddhists, for example, are regarded by Hindus as a *jāti*.
76 Though see Dipankar Gupta's *Interrogating Caste: Understanding hierarchy and difference in Indian society* (New Delhi: Penguin, 2000). He believes that castes existed before any hierarchizing; their being endogamous, biologically discrete entities.
77 Manu considered some castes to have arisen through inter-marrying between pure and impure *varṇas*, some to have arisen through not observing sacred rites, some to have occurred through exclusion from their original group, some originating from slaves and others from outside the *varṇa* system.
78 This would apply to the economically advantaged in the case of the class system: see Béteille, *Caste, Class and Power*, p. 190.
79 See Dennis Templeman, "The Northern Nadars of Tamil Nadu" in Banerjee-Dube, *Caste in History*, pp. 93–6.
80 Asutosh Varshney, "Is India Becoming More Democratic" in Banerjee-Dube, *Caste in History*, p. 223.
81 Baker, *Caste*, p. 114.
82 *Ibid.*, pp. 166–7.
83 See Troy Wilson Organ, *Hinduism: Its historical development* (New York, London, Toronto: Barron's Educational Series, 1974), p. 191.
84 Natrajan, *The Culturalization of Caste in India*, p. 1.
85 Béteille, *Class, Caste and Power*, pp. 48–51.
86 *Ibid.*, pp. 54–5.
87 Ganguly, *Caste, Colonialism and Counter-Modernity*, p. 3.
88 Béteille, *Class, Caste and Power*, p. 55.
89 Kalpana Ram, "The Mukkuvars of Kanyakumari: On the Margins of Caste Society" in Banerjee-Dube, *Caste in History*, pp. 136–49.
90 Bithika Mukerji, *The Hindu Tradition: An introduction to Hinduism and to its sacred tradition* (Amity, New York: Amity House, 1988), p. 27.
91 Ganguly, *Caste, Colonialism and Counter-Modernity*, p. 5.
92 Or *antyavāsayin* "living at the end/beyond/outside", that is to say, outside the village or town.
93 Sharma, *Śūdras in Ancient India*, p. 145.
94 Gavin Flood, *An Introduction to Hinduism* (Cambridge: Cambridge University Press, 1996), p. 61.
95 Sharma, *Śūdras in Ancient India*, pp. 227–8.

96 In the Tamil area of India, the *Paraiyar* caste is responsible for village bands. Their contact with dead animals because of the dead animal skins of the drums means that they are regarded as untouchables. It is from the name of their group that we get the term *pariah*.

97 Béteille, *Class, Caste and Power*, p. 35.

98 Dumont, *Homo Hierarchicus*, p. 55.

99 Mukherjee, *Beyond the Four Varṇas*, p. 101.

100 *Ibid.*

101 Béteille, *Class, Caste and Power*, p. 197.

102 *Ibid.*, p. 50.

103 *Ibid.*, p. 91.

104 Baker, *Caste*, p. 54.

105 *Ibid.*, p. 153.

106 Viramma, Racine and Racine, "High and Low Castes in Karani", p. 242.

107 *Ibid.*, pp. 241–2.

108 *Ibid.*, p. 239.

109 The comment of a *Paraiyar* woman here is rather amusing: "We quietly borrow a razor from the barber in the ur and we quietly give it back to him, because if people ever knew that the same razor had shaved a Pariah and a Reddiar – ayoyo! There would be one of those arguments! That's impossible! But all the same, a barber agrees to it for some money or a little bit of grain." Viramma, Racine and Racine, "High and Low Castes in Karani", p. 240.

110 Susan S. Wadley, "*Grāma*" in Mittal and Thursby eds., *The Hindu World*, p. 433.

111 Viramma in Viramma, Racine and Racine, "High and Low Castes in Karani", p. 245.

112 Thomas J. Hopkins, *The Hindu Religious Tradition* (Belmont, California: Wadsworth Publishing Company, 1971), p. 126.

113 *Bhagavad Gīta* 9:26–32, translator Fowler, *The Bhagavad Gita*, pp. 168–70.

114 Organ gives a very moving account of this in *Hinduism*, pp. 365–6.

115 *The Guardian*, April 15 1994. The whole article is given in W. Owen Cole and V. P. (Hemant) Kanitkar, *Teach Yourself World Faiths: Hinduism* (London and Chicago: Hodder Headline Plc, 1995), p. 205.

116 Béteille, *Class, Caste and Power*, p. 45.

117 Mark Juergensmeyer, "The Lonely Modernity of Model Town" in Banerjee-Dube, *Caste in History*, p. 267.

118 Approximately 50% of central government jobs and educational placements are reserved for low castes; more in some southern states. See Varshney, "Is India Becoming More Democratic", p. 220. Many *Brāhmins* left South Indian states because of the difficulty in acquiring jobs. It is worth pointing out, too, that those who take up reserved places are unable to participate in political activism.

119 Ishita Banerjee-Dube, "Introduction" in Banerjee-Dube, *Caste in History*, p. xxxii.

120 Natrajan, *The Culturalization of Caste in India*, p. 5.

121 *Ibid.*, p. 6.

122 Banerjee-Dube, "Introduction" in Banerjee-Dube, *Caste in History*, p. xxvii.

123 Rajni Kothari, "Rise of the Dalits and the Renewed Debate on Caste" in Banerjee-Dube, *Caste in History*, p. 212.

124 Varshney's point is critical here: "*the incidence of voting is higher among the poor than among the rich, among the less educated than among the graduates, in the villages than in the cities*". See "Is India Becoming More Democratic?", p. 227.

125 *Ibid.*, p. 216.

126 *Ibid.*, p. 219.
127 *Ibid.*, p. 228.

Chapter 4 Stages of Life: *Āśrama-dharma*

1 *Bṛhad-āraṇyaka Upaniṣad* 3:5, translator Patrick Olivelle, *Upaniṣads* (Oxford, New York: Oxford University Press, 1996), pp. 39–40, my parentheses.
2 Patrick Olivelle, *The Āśrama System: The history and hermeneutics of a religious institution* (New Delhi: Munshiram Manoharlal Publishers Private Limited, 2004, first published by Oxford University Press, 1993), p. 19.
3 *Ibid.*, pp. 20 and 22.
4 *Ibid.*, pp. 110–11.
5 *Ibid.*, p. 26.
6 *Ibid.*, p. 60.
7 Walter O. Kaelber, "*Āśrama*" in Sushil Mittal and Gene Thursby, *The Hindu World* (New York and London: Routledge, 2004), p. 384.
8 Olivelle, *The Āśrama System*, p. 62.
9 *Ibid.*, p. 67.
10 Kaelber, "*Āśrama*", pp. 388–9.
11 R. P. Kangle, *The Kauṭilīya Arthaśāstra* (Delhi Motilal Banarsidass Publishers Private Limited,1992 reprint of 1986 edn, first published 1965), p. 151.
12 See Patrick Olivelle, "The Renouncer Tradition" in Gavin Flood, ed., *The Blackwell Companion to Hinduism* (Malden Massachusetts, Oxford and Victoria: Blackwell Publishing, 2008 edn, first published 2003), p. 278.
13 *Bhāgavata Purāṇa* 11:17:13–15, translator G. V. Tagare, Ancient Indian Tradition & Mythology Series, vol. 11, part 5 (Delhi: Motilal Banarsidass Publishers Private Limited, 1997 reprint of 1978 revised edn), p. 2012.
14 Olivelle, The *Āśrama System*, pp. 127 and 131.
15 *Ibid.*, p. 137.
16 Troy Wilson Organ, *Hinduism: Its historical development* (Woodbury, New York, London, Toronto: Barron's Educational Series, Inc., 1974), p. 203.
17 For these modifications, see Olivelle, *The Āśrama System*, pp. 161–73.
18 The eighth to ninth century philosopher Śankara, while favouring the fourth *āśrama* and the renouncer's life, mainly believed that the *āśramas*, like *varṇa* and all ritual, were unreal in comparison to the reality of Brahman.
19 Olivelle, *The Āśrama System*, p. 222.
20 Julius Lipner, *Hindus: Their religious beliefs and practices* (London and New York: Routledge, 1994), p. 93.
21 *Āśvalāyana Gṛhya Sūtra* 22:1–5, translator R. N. Dandekar, "Dharma: The First End of Man" in Ainslie T. Embree, ed., *Sources of Indian Tradition, Vol. 1: From the beginning to 1800* (New York: Columbia University Press, 1988), p. 225.
22 *Ibid.*
23 Thomas J. Hopkins, *The Hindu Religious Tradition* (Belmont, California: Wadsworth Publishing Company, Inc., 1971), p. 77.
24 In addition, the householder was expected to offer sacrifices to other semi-divine beings and to provide guests with hospitality.
25 Kangle, *The Kauṭilīya Arthaśāstra*, p. 153.
26 See Olivelle, The *Āśrama System*, p. 192.

27 *The Laws of Manu* 6:89, 90, translators Wendy Doniger with Brian K. Smith, *The Laws of Manu* (London, New York, Victoria, Ontario, Auckland: Penguin Books, 1991), p. 50.
28 *Laws of Manu* 3:77, 78, *ibid.*, p. 50.
29 *Laws of Manu* 6:2–4, *ibid.*, p. 116.
30 John Koller, *The Indian Way: An introduction to the philosophies and religions of India* (Upper Saddle River, New Jersey: Pearson Prentice Hall, 2006 revised edn first published 1982), p. 98.
31 *Laws of Manu* 4:257.
32 See Olivelle, The *Āśrama System*, p. 139.
33 Lipner, *Hindus*, p. 259.
34 Kaelber, "*Āśrama*", p. 400.
35 Gavin Flood, *An Introduction to Hinduism* (Cambridge: Cambridge University Press, 1996, p. 91.
36 Olivelle, *The Āśrama System*, p. 117.
37 *Saṃnyāsa* as a term seems to have originated in *Brāhmin* circles around the second century BCE. See Kaelber, "*Āśrama*", p. 396.
38 Olivelle, *The Āśrama System*, p. 194.
39 Kangle, *The Kauṭilīya Arthaśāstra*, p. 154.
40 Olivelle, *The Āśrama System*, p. 189–90.
41 Kangle, *The Kauṭilīya Arthaśāstra*, p. 154.
42 *Laws of Manu*, 6:35–7.
43 Olivelle, "The Renouncer Tradition", pp. 281–2.
44 See Kaelber, "*Āśrama*", p. 397.
45 *Laws of Manu* 6:45–9, translators Doniger and Smith, pp. 121–2.
46 *Contra* Louis Dumont's view that the renouncer establishes himself in individuality in contrast to the householder stage when he is one of a collective social grouping of *varṇa*. See *Homo Hierarchicus: The caste system and its implications* (Chicago: University of Chicago Press, 1980 revised English edn, first published 1966), p. 272.
47 Olivelle, *The Āśrama System*, p. 201.
48 A Hindu *Brāhmin* whom I met recently (as my surgeon!) told me that his great uncle entered a *maṭha* and at his death had a library of over twenty-thousand books. Clearly, his great uncle saw retirement and renunciation as a time to engage in academic spiritual activity. Incidentally, that great uncle of the Hindu *Brāhmin* was the renowned author and authority on Hinduism, particularly Śaiva Siddhanta, Krishna Sivaranam.
49 Hopkins, *The Hindu Religious Tradition*, p. 83.
50 Kaelber, "*Āśrama*", p. 396.
51 Organ, *Hinduism*, p. 195.
52 Hartmut Scharfe, "*Artha*" in Mittal and Thursby, *The Hindu World*, p. 250
53 Lipner, *Hindus*, p. 160.
54 Kangle, The *Kauṭilīya Arthaśāstra*, p. 1.
55 Scharfe, "*Artha*", p. 249.
56 R. N. Dandekar, "Artha: The Second End of Man" in Embree, ed., *Sources of Indian Tradition, Vol. 1*, p. 235.
57 Lipner, *Hindus*, p. 264.
58 *Laws of Manu* 2:224, translators Doniger and Smith, p. 40.
59 Olivelle, however, is of the view that a second century CE date for its compilation is more plausible, *The Āśrama System*, p. 152.
60 Klaus K. Klostermaier, *A Survey of Hinduism* (New York: State University of New York Press, 1994 second edn), p. 342.

61 Kangle, The *Kauṭilīya Arthaśāstra*, p. 12.
62 *Ibid.*, pp. 159–9. A *rakṣasa* is a demon.
63 *Laws of Manu* 2:2–5.
64 V. Raghavan, "Kāma: The Third End of Man" in Embree ed., *Sources of Indian Tradition, Vol. 1*, p. 255.
65 *Ṛg Veda* 10:129, translator Ralph T. H. Griffith, *The Hymns of the Ṛgveda* (Delhi: Motilal Banarsidass Publishers Private Limited, 1991 reprint of new revised edn 1973), p. 633.
66 *Bhagavad Gītā* 7:11, translator Jeaneane Fowler, *The Bhagavad Gītā: A text and commentary for students* (Brighton, Portland and Toronto: Sussex Academic Press, 2012), p. 132.
67 Dated, according to Dermot Killingley, to the fourth century CE, "*Kāma*", in Mittal and Thursby, *The Hindu World*, p. 265.
68 Klostermaier, *A Survey of Hinduism*, p. 483.
69 Raghavan, "Kāma", p. 257.
70 Cited in Koller, *The Indian Way*, p. 90.
71 Olivelle, *The Āśrama System*, p. 238.
72 Koller, *The Indian Way*, p. 88.
73 Doniger and Smith, translators, *The Laws of Manu*, p. xvii.
74 *Mahābhārata* Book 18, translator Purushottama Lal, *The Mahabharata of Vyasa* (New Delhi: Vikas Publishing House PVT Ltd, 1980), p, 370.
75 *Taittirīya Āraṇyaka* 10:79, translator Dandekar, "Dharma", p. 217.
76 *Bhagavad Gītā* 18:66, translator Fowler, *The Bhagavad Gita*, p. 298.
77 *Ibid.*, 18:45–8.
78 Edwin F. Bryant, translator, "The Song Goes Ever On: A Brief Look at the *Uddhava Gītā*", *Journal of Vaishnava Studies* 12, 1(2003), p. 20.
79 Roy W. Perrett, "Religion and Politics in India: Some Philosophical Perspectives", *Religious Studies* 33, 1(1997), p. 1.
80 *Ibid.*, pp. 11–13.
81 William S. Sax, "Conquering the Quarters: Religion and Politics in Hinduism", *International Journal of Hindu Studies* 4, 1(2000), pp. 53–4.

Chapter 5 Gods and Goddesses: Śiva

1 Wendy Doniger O'Flaherty, *Śiva: The erotic ascetic* (Oxford, New York, Toronto, Melbourne: Oxford University Press, 1981 reprint of 1973 edn), p. 21.
2 Namita Gokhale, *The Book of Shiva* (New Delhi, London, New York, Victoria, Toronto, Auckland: Viking, 2001), p. 7.
3 Devdutt Pattanaik, *Shiva: An introduction* (Mumbai: Vakils, Feffer and Simons Ltd., 1997), p. vii.
4 Robert Charles Zaehner, *Hinduism* (London, Glasgow, New York, Toronto: Oxford University Press, 1984 reprint of 1962 edn), p. 34.
5 See Mahadev Chakravarti, *The Concept of Rudra-Śiva through the Ages* (Delhi, Varanasi, Patna, Madras: Motilal Banarsidass, 1986), p. 39.
6 Wendy Doniger O'Flaherty, *The Rig Veda: An anthology* (Harmondsworth, New York, Victoria, Ontario, Auckland: Penguin Books, 1983 reprint of 1981 edn), p. 221.
7 *Ṛg Veda* 2:33, translator O'Flaherty, *ibid.*, p. 222.
8 *Ṛg Veda* 2:4, translator O'Flaherty, *ibid.*, p. 221.
9 Chakravarti, *The Concept of Rudra-Śiva through the Ages*, pp. 14–15.
10 *Ibid.*, p. 27.

11 *Śvetāśvatara Upaniṣad* 3:2, 3 and 7, translator Patrick Olivelle, *Upaniṣads* (Oxford and New York: Oxford University Press, 1996), p. 257.
12 *Ibid.*, 3:6.
13 *Ibid.*, 4:22.
14 *Ibid.*, 3:9.
15 *Ibid.*, 4:3 and 4.
16 Stella Kramrisch, *The Presence of Śiva* (Princeton, New Jersey: Princeton University Press, 1981), p. 44.
17 Chakravarti, *The Concept of Rudra-Śiva through the Ages*, p. 3.
18 Alain Daniélou, *The Myths and Gods of India* (Rochester, Vermont: Inner Traditions International, 1991 reprint of 1985 edn), p. 193.
19 Kramrisch, *The Presence of Śiva*, p. 8.
20 See Chakravarti, *The Concept of Rudra-Śiva through the Ages*, p. 41.
21 Kramrisch, *The Presence of Śiva*, pp. 74 –5.
22 *Ibid.*, p. 76.
23 T. S. Maxwell, *The Gods of Asia* (Delhi: Oxford University Press, 1998), p. 65.
24 *Śvetāśvatara Upaniṣad* 6:5–7, translator Olivelle, *Upaniṣads*, p. 263.
25 Chakravarti, *The Concept of Rudra-Śiva through the Ages*, p. 72.
26 Zaehner, *Hinduism*, p. 86.
27 Pattanaik, *Shiva*, p. 117.
28 Maxwell, *The Gods of Asia*, p. 44.
29 O'Flaherty, *Śiva*, pp. 84–9.
30 *Ibid.*, p. 89.
31 *Ibid.*, chapter 4.
32 *Ibid.*, p. 139.
33 *Śvetāśvatara Upaniṣad* 6:10–11, translator Olivelle, *Upaniṣads*, p. 264.
34 O' Flaherty, *Śiva*, p. 35.
35 *Ibid.*, p. 36.
36 Kramrisch, *The Presence of Śiva*, p. 82.
37 Daniélou, *The Myths and Gods of India*, p. 192.
38 Maxwell, *The Gods of Asia*, p. 45.
39 *Muṇḍaka Upaniṣad* 2:1:4, translator Olivelle, *Upaniṣads*, p. 271.
40 *Ṛg Veda* 10:136:1–7.
41 O'Flaherty, *Śiva*, p. 76.
42 *Ibid.*, p. 254.
43 *Ibid.*, p. 296.
44 *Ibid.*, p. 300.
45 Chakravarti, *The Concept of Rudra-Śiva through the Ages*, p. 107.
46 Wendy Doniger O'Flaherty, *Hindu Myths* (London, New York, Victoria, Ontario, Auckland: Penguin Books, 1975), p. 137 puts the date about the second century BCE.
47 *Ṛg Veda* 7:21:5 and 10:99:3.
48 Chakravarti, *The Concept of Rudra-Śiva through the Ages*, p. 109.
49 O'Flaherty, *Śiva*, p. 136.
50 Richard H. Davis, *Lives of Indian Images* (Princeton, New Jersey: Princeton University Press, 1997), p. 23.
51 *Ibid*, p. 33.

52 *Linga Purana* 1.75:21–2, multiple translators (Delhi: Motilal Banarsidass Publishers Private Limited, 1997 reprint of 1982 edn, first published 1973), p. 371.
53 O'Flaherty, *Śiva* , p. 257.
54 Kramrisch, *The Presence of Śiva*, p. 249.
55 O'Flaherty, Śiva, pp. 243–4.
56 Chakravarti, *The Concept of Rudra-Śiva through the Ages*, p. 66.
57 O'Flaherty, *Śiva*, p. 246.
58 See Alain Daniélou, *The Phallus* (Rochester, Vermont: Inner Traditions International, 1995, first published in French in 1993), p. 81.
59 Gokhala, *The Book of Shiva*, p. 51.
60 Kramrisch, *The Presence of Śiva*, p. 397.
61 *Ibid.*, pp. 298–9.
62 *Ibid.*, p. 283.
63 Maxwell, *The Gods of Asia*, pp. 58–9.
64 Satguru Sivaya Subramuniyaswami, *Dancing with Śiva* (India, USA: Himalayan Academy, 1993), p. xviii.
65 Stephen Cross, *The Elements of Hinduism* (Shaftesbury, Dorset, Rockport, Massachusetts and Brisbane, Queensland: Element, 1994), p. 38.
66 *Ibid.*, p. 40.
67 Maxwell, *The Gods of Asia*, pp. 57–8.
68 *Śvetāśvatara Upaniṣad* 6:9.
69 From the *Mahābhārata*, translator and editor Ainslie T. Embree, *The Hindu Tradition: Readings in Oriental Thought* (New York: Vintage Books, 1972, first published 1966), p. 236.
70 O'Flaherty, *Śiva*, p. 171.

Chapter 6 Gods and Goddesses: *Śakti* – The Divine as Female

1 T. S. Maxwell, *The Gods of Asia: Image, text, and meaning* (Delhi, Calcutta, Chennai, Mumbai: Oxford University Press, 1998), p. 99.
2 The *Devī-Māhātmya* forms part of an early *Purāṇa*, the *Mārkaṇḍeya-purāṇa*, but is probably an independent text and is treated and printed as such throughout India. While the *Purāṇas*, in the main, present the Goddess as subordinate to male gods, the *Devī-Māhātmya* is the first text to extol the Goddess as supreme, mainly in the form of Durgā. It is a text that is recited widely and is something of a *mantra* for many Hindus. Innumerable copies of it have been made and it also has a number of subsidiary limbs or *aṅgas*, for which see Thomas B. Coburn, *Encountering the Goddess: A translation of the Devī-Māhātmya and a study of its interpretation* (Albany, New York: State University of New York Press, 1991), pp. 99–117.
3 *Devī-Māhātmya* 11:6 translator Coburn, *Encountering the Goddess*, p. 74.
4 Coburn, *Encountering the Goddess*, p. 16.
5 Lynn Foulston in Lynn Foulston and Stuart Abbott, *Hindu Goddesses: Beliefs and practices* (Brighton, Sussex and Portland, Oregon: Sussex Academic Press, 2009), p. 1.
6 The Goddess Vaisṇo Devī, for example, is enshrined in a cave shrine almost six-thousand feet on a mountain in northern India as three stones (though no one seems to know which of the stones is the goddess). See Martin Edwin Rohe, "Ambiguous and Definitive: The Greatness of Goddess Vaiṣṇo Devī" in Tracy Pintchman, ed., *Seeking Mahādevī: Constructing the identities of the Hindu Great Goddess* (Albany, New York: State University of New York Press, 2001), pp. 55–9. Rohe comments: "She is, to her devotees and to pilgrims, the supreme Mahā-Devī incarnated and greater than all other deities" (p. 56), but she can be identified with any of the Great

Goddesses without confliction. As Rohe says: "Her unique identity dissolves into and merges with various other deities' identities" (p. 71).

7 Kathleen M. Erndl, "Goddesses and the Goddess in Hinduism: Constructing the Goddess through Religious Experience" in Pintchman, ed., *Seeking Mahādevī,* p. 201.

8 *Ibid.*, p. 202.

9 Sukumari Bhattacharji, for example, notes that one aspect of Lakṣmī was associated with a rice-growing agricultural people and so she was called Karīsinī, the cow-dung goddess, with sons who were mud and moisture. *The Indian Theogony: Brahmā, Viṣṇu &Śiva* (London, New York, Victoria, Auckland, New Delhi: Penguin Books, 2000, first published by Cambridge University Press in 1970), p. 161.

10 Devdutt Pattanaik, *Devi – The Mother Goddess: An introduction* (Mumbai: Vakils, Feffer and Simons Ltd. 2000), p. 8.

11 David Kinsley, *Hindu Goddesses: Visions of the divine feminine in the Hindu religious tradition* (Delhi, Varanasi, Patna, Madras: Motilal Banarsidass, 1987 first Indian edn), p. 178.

12 Pattanaik, *Devi – The Mother Goddess*, pp. 1–2.

13 *Ṛg Veda* 10:125, translator Ralph T. H. Griffith, *The Hymns of the Ṛgveda* (Delhi: Motilal Banarsidass Publishers Private Limited, 1991 reprint of new revised edn, 1973), p. 632.

14 Mandakranta Bose, *Women in the Hindu Tradition: Rules, roles and exceptions* (London and New York: Routledge, 2010), p. 15.

15 Lynn Foulston, *At the Feet of the Goddess: The divine feminine in local Hindu religion* (Brighton, Sussex and Portland, Oregon: Sussex Academic Press, 2002), p. 104.

16 Kinsley, *Hindu Goddesses*, p. 2.

17 See Tracy Pintchman, *The Rise of the Goddess in the Hindu Tradition* (Albany, New York: State University of New York Press, 1994), p. 97.

18 See Wendy Doniger O'Flaherty, "The Shifting Balance of Power in the Marriage of Śiva and Pārvatī" in John Stratton Hawley and Donna Marie Wulff, *The Divine Consort: Rādhā and the Goddesses of India* (Delhi: Motilal Banarsidass Publishers Private Limited, 1995 reprint of first Indian edn, 1984), p. 132.

19 Swami Chidbhavananda, *Facets of Brahman or the Hindu Gods* (Tirupparaitturai: Sri Ramakrishna Tapovam, 1974), p. 19.

20 Originally used adjectivally in relation to the gods, the word *śakti* became especially associated with the goddess as "the very foundation of all experience". Coburn, *Encountering the Goddess*, p. 19.

21 See Pintchman, *The Rise of the Goddess in the Hindu Tradition*, p. 5.

22 *Ibid.*, pp. 98–9.

23 *Ibid.*, p. 101.

24 Erndl, "Goddesses and the Goddess in Hinduism", p. 199.

25 Bose, *Women in the Hindu Tradition*, p. 5.

26 *Devī-Māhātmya* 4:11, translator Coburn, *Encountering the Goddess*, p. 49.

27 *Ibid.*, 10:4–5.

28 A point epitomized in the title of Thomas Coburn's *Devī-Māhātmya: The crystallization of the Goddess tradition* (Delhi and Columbia MO: Motilal Banarsidass and South Asia Books, 1988 reprint of 1984 edn).

29 Kinsley, *Hindu Goddesses*, p. 132.

30 C. Mackenzie Brown, with evidence from a philosophical section of the *Devī-Bhāgavata* known as the "Song of the Goddess", the *Devī-Gītā*, believes that the Goddess is posited as *nirguṇa* Brahman akin to Advaita Vedānta mingled with Tantric elements. The view of the Goddess

here is as a mysterious force by which she becomes manifest in the world. See his "The Tantric and Vedāntic Identity of the Great Goddess in the Devī Gītā of the Devī-Bhāgavata Purāṇa" in Pintchman, *Seeking Mahadevī,* pp. 19–36.

31 *Devī-Māhātmya* 1:78–9, translator Coburn, *Encountering the Goddess*, p. 37.

32 *Ibid.*, verses 75–7.

33 Usha Menon, "Mahādevī as Mother: The Oriya Hindu Vision of Reality" in Pintchman, ed., *Seeking Mahādevī,* pp. 37–8 and 42.

34 For an interesting analysis of the ways in which Sāṃkhya philosophy has had an impact on the theology of Śākta, see Nicholas F. Gier, "The *yogī* and the Goddess", *International Journal of Hindu Studies* 1, 2 (August 1997), pp. 265–87.

35 John Stratton Hawley, "Prologue: The Goddess in India" in John Stratton Hawley and Donna Marie Wulff eds., *Devī: Goddesses of India* (Berkeley, Los Angeles, London: University of California, 1996), p. 10.

36 Pattanaik, *Devi – The Mother Goddess*, p. 13.

37 *Devī-Mahātmya* 1:56, translator Coburn, *Encountering the Goddess*, p. 35.

38 *Devī-Māhātmya* 1:57–8, *ibid.*

39 *Devī-Māhātmya* , 11:4.

40 *Ibid.*, 11:31.

41 Tracy Pintchman, "The Goddess as Fount of the Universe: Shared Visions and Negotiated Allegiances in *Purāṇic* Accounts of Cosmogenesis" in Pintchman, ed., *Seeking Mahādevī,* pp. 90–1.

42 Kinsley, *Hindu Goddesses*, p. 143.

43 *Devī-Māhātmya* 11:3, translator Coburn, *Encountering the Goddess*, p. 74.

44 Coburn, *Encountering the Goddess*, p. 27.

45 *Ibid.*, p. 1.

46 See David Kinsley, *Tantric Visions of the Divine Feminine: The ten Mahāvidyās* (Berkeley, Los Angeles, London: University of California Press, 1997), p. 1.

47 *Ibid.*, p. 6.

48 *Ibid.*

49 Kinsley, *Hindu Goddesses*, p. 46.

50 *Kūrma-purāṇa* 1:12:53–4, translated and annotated by Ganesh Vasudeo Tagare (Delhi, Varanasi, Patna: Motilal Banarsidass, 1981), p. 91.

51 *Ibid.*, verses 48 and 49.

52 Kinsley, *Hindu Goddesses*, p. 50.

53 O'Flaherty, "The Shifting Balance of Power in the Marriage of Śiva and Pārvatī", p. 133.

54 Pattanaik, *Devī – The Mother Goddess*, p. 11.

55 Kinsley, *Hindu Goddesses*, p. 96.

56 See Thomas B. Coburn, "The Great Goddess" in Hawley and Wulff, *Devī : Goddesses of India*, p. 40.

57 See Bhattacharji, *The Indian Theogony*, p. 158.

58 *Ibid.*, p. 165.

59 *Devī-Māhātmya* 11:46, translator Coburn, *Encountering the Goddess*, p. 78.

60 *Ibid.*, verse 55.

61 Bhattacharji, *The Indian Theogony*, p. 174.

62 Kinsley, *Hindu Goddesses*, p. 100.

63 Although see Bhattacharji, *The Indian Theogony*, p. 167, where he suggests that she can be portrayed as a consort of Śiva in his more bloodthirsty aspects. Alain Daniélou also describes

her as a consort of Śiva, see *The Myths and Gods of India* (Rochester, Verrmont: Inner Traditions International, 1991 reprint of 1985 edn), p. 258.

64 *Devī-Māhātmya* 5:7.

65 See Maxwell, *The Gods of Asia*, p. 100.

66 Ajit Mookerjee, *Kali: The feminine force* (London: Thames and Hudson, 1988), p. 49.

67 *Devī-Māhātmya* 1:79–81, translator Coburn, *Encountering the Goddess*, p. 37.

68 *Devī-Māhātmya* 11:11 and 12.

69 Bose, *Women in the Hindu Tradition*, p. 31.

70 *Devī-Māhātmya*, 10:5.

71 Kinsley, *Hindu Goddesses,* pp. 151 and 155.

72 Stuart Abbott, in Foulston and Abbott, *Hindu Goddesses*, p. 109.

73 Kinsley , *Hindu Goddesses*, p. 158.

74 Mookerjee, *Kali* , p. 61.

75 David Kinsley, *The Sword and the Flute: Kālī and Kṛṣṇa dark visions of the terrible and the sublime in Hindu mythology* (Berkeley, Los Angeles, London: University of California Press, 1975), p. 82.

76 See *ibid.*, p. 94.

77 *Ibid.*, pp. 99–100.

78 *Ibid.*, pp. 101–2.

79 *Devī-Māhātmya* 7:6–9, translator Coburn, *Encountering the Goddess*, p. 61.

80 Kinsley, *Hindu Goddesses*, p. 119.

81 Mookerjee, *Kali*, p. 61.

82 Menon, "Mahādevī as Mother", p. 43.

83 *Ibid.*, p. 62.

84 Kinsley, *Tantric Visions of the Divine Feminine*, p. 87.

85 *Ibid.*, p. 89.

86 *Ibid.*, p. 88.

87 See Foulston, in Foulston and Abbott, *Hindu Goddesses*, p. 91.

88 Elizabeth U. Harding, *Kali: The black Goddess of Dakshineswar* (Delhi: Motilal Banarsidass Publishers Private Limited, 1998 Indian edn, first published 1993), p. 38.

89 See Hawley, "Prologue: The Goddess in India" in Hawley and Wulff eds., *Devī,* p. 11.

90 Menon, "Mahādevī as Mother", p. 43.

91 *Ibid.*, p. 50.

92 Kinsley, *Tantric Visions of the Divine Feminine*, p. 83.

93 Bose, *Women in the Hindu Tradition*, p. 34.

94 *Ibid.*

95 Kinsley, *Tantric Visions of the Divine Feminine*, p. 90.

96 Harding, *Kali*, p. 59.

97 Constantina Rhodes, "When 'God' is a 'Goddess': The Splendour of Laksmi as Supreme Reality", *Journal of Vaishnava Studies* 21:1 (2012), p. 9.

98 See Bhattacharji, *The Indian Theogony*, p. 162.

99 Kinsley, *Hindu Goddesses*, p. 27.

100 Bhattacharji, *The Indian Theogony*, p. 163.

101 See J. Gonda, *Aspects of Early Viṣṇuism* (Delhi: Motilal Banarsidass Publishers Private Limited,1993 reprint of 1969 edn, first published 1954), p. 213.

102 Rhodes, "When 'God' is a 'Goddess'", p. 14.

103 *Ibid.*

104 *Ibid.*, p. 18.

105 *Ibid.*, p. 21.
106 *Viṣṇu-purāṇa* 1:8:15 ff.
107 See Pintchman, *The Rise of the Goddess in the Hindu Tradition*, p. 148.
108 Foulston, in Foulston and Abbott, *Hindu Goddesses*, p. 27.
109 Bose, *Women in the Hindu Tradition*, p. 44.
110 Pattanaik, *Devi – The Mother Goddess*, p. 20.
111 Kinsley, *Hindu Goddesses*, p. 62.
112 I am privileged to be able to draw on the doctoral research of a former student of mine, Dr Lynn Foulston, for this section of the chapter. Her field studies in India have provided new insights into the nature of localized goddesses, and I am indebted to her for being able to use the resulting research, now in published form, *At the Feet of the Goddess*.
113 Foulston, *At the Feet of the Goddess*, p. 1.
114 See *ibid.*, pp. 188–9.
115 Foulston, in Foulston and Abbott, *Hindu Goddesses*, pp. 92–3.
116 *Ibid.*
117 Foulston, *At the Feet of the Goddess*, p. 83.
118 See *ibid.* pp. 78–9 and p. 90.
119 Jessica Frazier, *The Continuum Companion to Hindu Studies* (London and New York: Continuum, 2011), p. 278.
120 See Kinsley, *Hindu Goddesses*, p. 198.
121 Foulston, in Foulston and Abbott, *Hindu Goddesses*, pp. 86–7.
122 Foulston, *At the Feet of the Goddess*, p. 115.
123 *Ibid.*, p. 123.
124 See *ibid.*, pp. 100–101.
125 Frazier, *The Continuum Companion to Hindu Studies*, p. 262.
126 Shree Padma, "From Village to City: Transforming Goddesses in Urban Andhra Pradesh" in Pintchman, ed., *Seeking Mahādevī*, p. 116.
127 *Ibid.*, p. 117.
128 *Ibid.*, p. 120.
129 *Ibid.*, p. 133.
130 *Ibid.*, p. 139.
131 *Ibid.*, p. 142.
132 Pintchman, *The Rise of the Goddess in the Hindu Tradition*, p. 191.
133 *Ibid.*, p. 193.
134 *Ibid.*, p. 194.
135 Georg Feuerstein, *Tantra: The path of ecstacy* (Boston and London: Shambhala, 1998), pp. 268–9.
136 Texts date to the ninth century, but practices pre-date the texts: see Pintchman, *The Rise of the Goddess in the Hindu Tradition*, pp. 108–9.
137 Stuart Abbott, in Foulston and Abbott, *Hindu Goddesses*, p. 101.
138 Mookerjee, *Kali*, p. 68.
139 Kinsley, *Tantric Visions of the Divine Feminine*, p. 79.
140 A comment found in the *Nirvāṇa-tantra*, see Kinsley, *The Sword and the Flute*, p. 110.
141 Abbott in Foulston and Abbott, *Hindu Goddesses*, p. 126.
142 For the effects of meditation on the brain, see Jeaneane Fowler, "Spirituality" in A. C. Grayling and Andrew Copson, eds., *The Wiley Blackwell Handbook of Humanism* (Oxford: Wiley-Blackwell, 2015) in press.
143 See Coburn, *Encountering the Goddess*, p. 162.

144 Feuerstein, *Tantra*, pp. 61–2.
145 See Maxwell, *The Gods of Asia*, p. 102.
146 Feuerstein, *Tantra*, p. 116.
147 Kinsley, *Tantric Visions of the Divine Feminine*, p. 242.
148 Although Kinsley observed that *Tantric* texts are really written by males for males! See *ibid.*, p. 250.
149 Jason Burke, "Angered India demands change after gang rape exposes a society in crisis", *The Observer*, Saturday 29th December, 2012.

Chapter 7 Gods and Goddesses: Viṣṇu, Kṛṣṇa and Rādhā

1 Vaiṣṇavites are easily recognized by the V mark, or three vertical lines, on the centre of their foreheads.
2 According to Gonda, Viṣṇu may derive from *viś-* "to enter", or from *vi-aś-* "to reach, attain, fill, penetrate" or, similarly, from *viṣ-* with the idea of *vyāpti-* "pervasion". See Jan Gonda, *Aspects of Early Viṣṇuism* (Delhi: Motilal Banarsidass Publishers Private Limited, 1993 reprint, first published 1954), pp. 54–5. Ideas of "separating out" or "flowing powerfully" are both also suggestive of the ideas of pervasion, see T. S. Maxwell, *The Gods of Asia: Image, text, and meaning* (Delhi: Oxford University Press, 1998), p. 73, footnote.
3 A point made by Troy Wilson Organ, *Hinduism: Its historical development* (Woodbury, New York, London and Toronto: Barron's Educational Series Inc. 1974), p. 151.
4 Klaus K. Klostermaier, *A Survey of Hinduism* (Albany, New York: State University of New York Press, 1994), p. 241.
5 Gavin Flood, *An Introduction to Hinduism* (Cambridge: Cambridge University Press, 1996), p. 119.
6 See the detailed section on Nārāyaṇa in Benjamin Preciado-Solis, *The Kṛṣṇa Cycle in the Purāṇas: Themes and motifs in a heroic saga* (Delhi, Varanasi, Patna: Motilal Banarsidass, 1984), pp. 6–11.
7 Compare, for example, the *Laws of Manu* 1:10: "'The waters are born of man (*nārā*)', so it is said; indeed, the waters are the children of the primordial man. And since they were his resting place in ancient time, therefore he is traditionally known as Nārāyaṇa ('Resting on those born of man')." Wendy Doniger O'Flaherty, *The Laws of Manu* (London, New York, Victoria, Ontario, Auckland: Penguin, 1991), p. 4.
8 Sukumari Bhattacharji, *The Indian Theogony: Brahmā, Viṣṇu & Śiva* (New Delhi, London, New York, Victoria, Ontario, Auckland: Penguin 2000, first published 1970), p. 294.
9 Gonda, *Aspects of Early Viṣṇuism*, p. 60.
10 Benjamin A. McClintic, "The Implicit Power Behind Agni, Indra, Surya, and Others: Vishnu in the Vedic *Saṃhitās*", *Journal of Vaishnava Studies*, 21, 1(2012), p. 56.
11 See Gonda, *Aspects of Early Viṣṇuism*, pp. 11–16 detailing Viṣṇu's association with plants and trees.
12 *Ibid.*, p. 172.
13 Particularly with the sacrificial post, see Gonda, *ibid*, pp. 81–4.
14 See A. L. Basham, *The Wonder That Was India* (London: Sidgwick & Jackson, 1982 reprint of third revised edn, 1963, first published 1954), p. 300.
15 See Gonda, *Aspects of Early Viṣṇuism*, p. 105.
16 *Ibid.*, p. 107.
17 Maxwell, *The Gods of Asia*, p. 86.
18 *Ibid.*, p. 79.

19 See Alain Daniélou, *The Myths and Gods of India* (Rochester, Vermont: Inner Traditions International, 1964), p. 156.
20 See Gonda, *Aspects of Early Viṣṇuism*, p. 100.
21 *Bhagavad Gītā* 4:6–8, translator Jeaneane Fowler, *The Bhagavad Gita: A text and commentary for students* (Eastbourne, Sussex, Portland, Oregon and Vaughan, Ontario: Sussex Academic Press, 2012), pp. 74–5, cf. 7:24 and 9:11.
22 See Daniel P. Sheridan, *The Advaitic Theism of the Bhāgavata Purāṇa* (Delhi, Varanasi, Patna, Madras: Motilal Banarsidass, 1986), p. 60.
23 See Bhattarcharji, *The Indian Theogony*, p. 288.
24 Basham, *The Wonder That Was India*, p. 302.
25 Preciado-Solis, *The Kṛṣṇa Cycle in the Purāṇas*, p. 124.
26 Brian Collins, "*Avatāra* or *Cirajīvin*: Paraśurāma and His Problems" in *Journal of Vaishnava Studies* 21, 1(2012), p. 187.
27 Bhattarcharji, *The Indian Theogony*, p. 290.
28 *Ibid.*, p. 301.
29 Devdutt Pattanaik, *Vishnu: An introduction* (Mumbai: Vakils, Feffer and Simons Ltd., 2000 reprint of 1998 edn), p. 122.
30 See Preciado-Solis, *The Kṛṣṇa Cycle in the Purāṇas*, pp. 78–83.
31 See *ibid.*, pp. 19–37 for a comprehensive account of the speculations related to the origins of Kṛṣṇa in primary and secondary sources.
32 Organ, *Hinduism*, pp. 152–3.
33 Flood, *An Introduction to Hinduism*, p. 119.
34 Thomas J. Hopkins, *The Hindu Religious Tradition* (Belmont, California: Wadsworth Publishing Company, 1971, p. 105.
35 Preciado-Solis, *The Kṛṣṇa Cycle in the Purāṇas*, p. 77.
36 David R. Kinsley, *The Sword and the Flute: Kālī & Kṛṣṇa, dark visions of the terrible and the sublime in Hindu mythology* (Berkeley, Los Angeles, London: University of California Press, 1975), p. 17.
37 *Ibid.*, p. 56.
38 Sheridan, *The Advaitic Theism of the Bhāgavata Purāṇa*, p. 2.
39 *Ibid.*, p. 12.
40 Thomas J. Hopkins, "The Social Teaching of the *Bhāgavata Purāṇa*" in Milton Singer, ed., *Krishna: Myths rites, and attitudes* (Chicago and London: University of Chicago Press, 1966), p. 6.
41 See, for example, 4:7:30 where the sage Bhṛgu says that embodied beings do not understand the real nature of the Lord, which lies within beings.
42 Sheridan, *The Advaitic Theism of the Bhāgavata Purāṇa*, p. 23.
43 *Bhāgavata-purāṇa* 10:14:57, translator Ganesh Vasudeo Tagare (Delhi: Motilal Banarsidass Publishers Private Limited, 1994 reprint of 1988 reprint, first published 1978), Part IV, p. 1351.
44 *Ibid.*, 10:47:43, p. 1546.
45 Lee Siegel, *Sacred and Profane Dimensions of Love in Indian Traditions: As exemplified in the Gītagovinda of Jayadeva* (Delhi, Bombay, Calcutta, Madras: Oxford University Press, 1990, first published 1978), p. 22.
46 Nirad C. Chaudhuri, *Hinduism: A religion to live by* (Oxford, New York, Toronto, Melbourne: Oxford University Press, 1979), p. 274.
47 Robert P. Goldman and Sally J. Sutherland Goldman, "*Rāmāyaṇa*" in Sushil Mittal and Gene Thursby, eds., *The Hindu World* (New York and London: Routledge, 2004), p. 84.
48 Siegel, *Sacred and Profane Dimensions of Love in Indian Traditions*, p. 45.
49 *Ibid.*, p. 49.

50 Eric Huberman, "Rādhā: Beloved of Vraja" in Steven J. Rosen, ed., *Vaiṣṇavism: Contemporary scholars discuss the Gauḍīya tradition* (Delhi: Motilal Banarsidass Publishers, 1994, first published 1992), p. 336. For a translation of the *Rāsa-Līlā* see Graham M. Schweig, *Dance of Love: The rasalila of Krishna from the Bhagavata Purana, India's classic sacred love story* (Princeton: Princeton University Press, 2005)
51 *Ibid.*, p. 328.
52 *Bhāgavata-purāṇa* 10:29:10–11, translator Tagare, Part IV, p. 1435.
53 Schweig, *Dance of Divine Love*, p. 1.
54 Jessica Frazier, ed., *The Continuum Companion to Hindu Studies* (London and New York: Continuum, 2011), p. 265.
55 Huberman, "Rādhā", pp. 337–8. Indeed, in Bengal Vaiṣṇavism, all the *gopīs* are believed to be the *śaktis* of Kṛṣṇa himself.
56 Siegel, *Sacred and Profane Dimensions of Love in Indian Traditions*, p. 30.
57 *Ibid.*, p. 178.
58 *Ibid.*, p. xi.
59 *Ibid.*, p. 21.
60 *Ibid.*, p. 39.
61 Chaudhuri, *Hinduism*, p. 281.
62 Siegel, *Sacred and Profane Dimensions of Love in Indian Traditions*, p. 205.
63 *Ibid.*, p. 41.
64 Kinsley, *The Sword and the Flute*, p. 77.
65 *Bhagavad Gītā* 6:30, see Fowler, *The Bhagavad Gita*, p. 119.
66 *Ibid.*, 18:55–8, pp. 294–6.
67 *Ibid.*, 18:64–6, p. 298.
68 See Edwin F. Bryant, "The Song Goes Ever On: A Brief Look at the *Uddhava Gītā*", *Journal of Vaishnava Studies* 12, 1(2003), p. 15.
69 See Donna M. Wulff, "Consort and Conqueror of Krishna" in John Stratton Hawley and Donna Marie Wulff, eds., *Devī: Goddesses of India* (Berkeley, Los Angeles, London: University of California Press, 1996), p. 109.
70 See Kinsley, *The Sword and the Flute*, p. 41 note 70.
71 Rādhā is celebrated mainly in the North of India and since the *Bhagavata-purāṇa* is a southern text, this may account for the absence of Rādhā in it.
72 Tracy Pintchman, *The Rise of the Goddess in the Hindu Tradition* (Albany, New York: State University of New York Press, 1994), p. 160.
73 Wulff, "Consort and Conqueror of Krishna", p. 122.
74 Huberman, "Rādhā", p. 345.
75 Kinsley, *The Sword and the Flute*, p. 42.
76 Steven J. Rosen, "Preface" in Rosen, ed., *Vaiṣṇavism*, p. ii.

Chapter 8 Ritual in the Home and Community: Worship

1 Lawrence A. Babb, *The Divine Hierarchy* (Columbia: Columbia University Press, 1975), p. 32.
2 Gavin Flood, *An Introduction to Hinduism* (Cambridge: Cambridge University Press, 1996), p. 198.
3 C. J. Fuller, *The Camphor Flame: Popular Hinduism and society in India* (New Delhi, Harmondsworth, Middlesex, New York, Victoria, Toronto, Auckland: Viking, 1992), p. 60.
4 *Ibid.*, p. 61
5 *Ibid.*, p. 70.

6 Diana Eck, *Darśan: Seeing the divine image in India* (New York: Columbia University Press, 1998 third edn, first published 1996), p. 38.
7 *Ibid.*, p. 45.
8 Anuradha Roma Choudhury, "Worship" in Paul Bowen, ed., *Themes and Issues in Hinduism* (London and Washington: Cassell, 1998), p. 205.
9 Thomas J. Hopkins, *The Hindu Religious Tradition* (Belmont, California: Wadsworth Publishing Company, 1971), p. 113.
10 Vasudha Narayanan, "*Ālaya*" in Sushil Mittal and Gene Thursby, eds., *The Hindu World* (New York and London: Routledge, 2004), p. 463.
11 See Eck, *Darśan*, pp. 52–3.
12 A belief held, for example by the Śaivite Satguru Sivaya Subramuniyaswami, *Dancing with Śiva* (India, USA: Himalayan Academy, 1993), p. 317.
13 Narayanan, "*Ālaya*", p. 462.
14 Eck, *Darśan*, p. 7.
15 *Ibid.*, p. 38.
16 *Bhāgavata-purāṇa* 11:23:32–3, translated and annotated by G. V. Tagare (Delhi: Motilal Banarsidass Publishers Private Limited, 1997 reprint of 1978 revised edn), Part V, p. 2091.
17 For a comprehensive list, see Lynn Foulston, *At the Feet of the Goddess: The divine feminine in local Hindu religion* (Brighton and Portland: Sussex Academic Press, 2002), p. 126.
18 *Ibid.*
19 Akos Östör, "Cyclical Time: Durgāpūjā in Bengal: Concepts, Actions, Objects" in T. N. Madan, ed., *Religion in India* (Delhi, Bombay, Calcutta, Madras: Oxford University Press, 1994 impression, first published 1991), p. 177.
20 Devdutt Pattanaik, *Devi – The Mother-Goddess* (Mumbai: Vakils, Feffer and Simons Ltd., 2000), p. 99.
21 Foulston, *At the Feet of the Goddess*, p. 129.
22 *Ibid.*, p. 168.
23 Östör, "Cyclical Time", pp. 192–3.
24 Fuller, *The Camphor Flame*, p. 57.
25 Subramuniyaswami, *Dancing with Śiva*, p. 313.
26 Choudhury, "Worship", p. 203.
27 Hopkins, *The Hindu Religious Tradition*, p. 110.
28 Eck, *Darśan*, p. 33.
29 Subramuniyaswami, *Dancing with Śiva*, p. 331.
30 Foulston, *At the Feet of the Goddess*, p. 150.
31 Fuller, *The Camphor Flame*, p. 91.
32 *Ibid.*, p. 95.
33 Choudhury, "Worship", p. 208.
34 Sophie Baker, *Caste: At home in Hindu India* (London: Jonathan Cape, 1990), p. 42.
35 It should be remembered that so sacred were *Vedic* texts considered to be that women and low-caste individuals were at one time forbidden to listen to them.
36 Babb, *The Divine Hierarchy*, p. 116.
37 Eck *Darśan*, p. 46.
38 See Narayanan, "*Ālaya*", pp. 464–5 for the full hymn.
39 Fuller, *The Camphor Flame*, p. 74.
40 Babb, *The Divine Hierarchy*, p. 60.
41 *Ibid.*, p. 99 note 3.

42 Fuller, *The Camphor Flame*, p. 78.

43 Baker, *Caste*, p. 42.

44 *Ibid.*, p. 70.

45 *Ibid.*, p. 159.

46 Eck, *Darśan*, p. 6.

47 *Ibid.*, p. 3.

48 Pattanaik, *Devi – The Mother Goddess*, p. 97.

49 Tracy Pintchman, "Introduction" in Tracy Pintchman, ed., *Women's Lives, Women's Rituals in the Hindu Tradition* (Oxford and New York: Oxford University Press, 2007), p. 4.

50 Anne Mackenzie Pearson, *"Because It Gives Me Peace of Mind": Fasts in the religious lives of Hindu women* (Albany, New York: State University of New York Press, 1996), pp. 20–1.

51 R. Champakalakshmi and Usha Kris, *The Hindu Temple* (London: Greenwich Editions, 2001), p. 10.

52 Narayanan, "*Ālaya*", p. 455.

53 Jessica Frazier, ed., *The Continuum Companion to Hindu Studies* (London and New York: Continuum, 2011), p. 312.

54 *Ibid.*, p. 13.

55 Hopkins, *The Hindu Religious Tradition*, p. 109.

56 Champakalakshmi and Kris, *The Hindu Temple*, p. 14.

57 *Ibid.*, p. 27.

58 For an analysis of formal temple structure and the architectural development of Hindu temples, see Adam Hardy, *The Temple Architecture of India* (Chichester: John Wiley & Sons, 2007).

59 Nevertheless, there are remarkable variations. Despite prescriptive traditions for building temples, high in the western Himālayas where there has been proximity to Buddhist regions, temples may be found with *gōpuras* shaped like pagodas and containing *mūrtis* not dissimilar to Tibetan images.

60 Eck, *Darśan*, p. 91.

61 *Ibid.*, p. 59.

62 Foulston, *At the Feet of the Goddess*, p. 31.

63 Narayanan, "*Ālaya*", p. 466.

64 According to Klaus Klostermaier, since India gained independence, more temples have been built than in the previous five-hundred years. *A Survey of Hinduism* (Albany, New York: State University of New York Press, 1994), p. 312.

65 David R. Kinsley, *Hinduism: A cultural perspective* (Englewood Cliffs, New Jersey: Prentice Hall, 1993 second edn, first published 1982), p. 78.

66 Robert Levy, *Mesocosm: Hinduism and the organization of a traditional Newar city of Nepal* (Berkeley, California: University of California Press, 1990).

67 Babb, *The Divine Hierarchy*, p. 50.

68 Fuller, *The Camphor Flame*, p. 64.

69 For a full account of the role and functions of priests, see the account of those at the Mīnākṣī Temple at Madurai in C. J. Fuller, "Hindu Temple Priests" in Madan, ed., *Religion in India*, pp. 293–307.

70 Michael Witzel, "Macrocosm, Mesocosm, and Microcosm: The Persistent Nature of 'Hindu' Beliefs and Symbolic Forms" in *International Journal of Hindu Studies* 1, 3(1997), p. 517.

71 *Ibid.*

72 Baker, *Caste*, pp. 47–8.

73 Gaya Charan Tripathi's account of *pūjā* at the Jagannātha Temple supplies a balanced account

of overt ritual praxis alongside its mystical dimensions: see *Communication with God: The daily pūjā ceremony in the Jagannātha Temple* (Delhi: Indhira Gandhi National Centre for the Arts/Aryan Books International, 2004).

74 Babb, *The Divine Hierarchy*, p. 199. I have drawn on Babb's full description of the Baiga taken from his field research for the description of such a village priest. Babb gives a number of interesting cases that have been – it seems successfully – encountered and treated by one village priest, pp. 200–203.

75 For the ritual oppositions between right and left, see Veena Das, "Concepts of Space in Ritual" in Madan, ed., *Religion in India*, pp. 156–75.

76 Fuller, *The Camphor Flame*, p. 70.

77 Eck, *Darśan*, p. 49.

78 Babb, *The Divine Hierarchy*, p. 38.

79 Pika Ghosh, "Dance, Trance, and Transformation: The Art of Movement in Gaudiya Temples" in *Journal of Vaishnava Studies* 21, 2(2013), p. 100.

80 Vasuda Narayanan, "Performing Arts, Re-forming Rituals: Women and Social Change in South India" in Pintchman, ed., *Women's Lives, Women's Rituals in the Hindu Tradition*, p. 194.

81 *Ibid.*, p. 181.

82 André Béteille, *Caste, Class and Power: Changing patterns of stratification in a Tanjore village* (Delhi, Calcutta, Chennai, Mumbai: Oxford University Press, 1998 second edn, first published 1996), p. 46.

83 For a vivid account of the temple and its *pūjā*, see Elizabeth U. Harding, *Kali: The Black Goddess of Dakshineswar* (Delhi: Motilal Banarsidass Publishers Private Limited, 1998, first published 1993).

84 Sukumari Bhattacharji, *The Indian Theogony: Brahmā, Viṣṇu &Śiva* (London, New York, New Delhi, Victoria, Toronto, Auckland: Penguin, 2000, first published 1970), p. 306.

85 Frédérique Marglin, "*Jagannātha Purī*" in Steven J. Rosen, ed., *Vaiṣṇavism: Contemporary scholars discuss the Gauḍīya tradition* (Delhi: Motilal Banarsidass Publishers Private Limited, 1994, first published 1992), pp. 216–17.

86 Klostermaier, *A Survey of Hinduism*, p. 331.

87 See Stella Kramrisch, *The Presence of Śiva* (Princeton, New Jersey: Princeton University Press, 1981), "Appendix: The Great Cave Temple of Śiva on the Island of Elephanta", pp. 443–68, and plates 515ff.

88 Champakalakshmi, *The Hindu Temple*, p. 81.

89 George Mitchell, *The Hindu Temple: An introduction to its meaning and forms* (Chicago: University of Chicago Press, 1988 reprint), p. 14.

90 Frazier, ed., *The Continuum Companion to Hindu Studies*, p. 314.

91 Foulston, *At the Feet of the Goddess*, p. 33.

92 *Ibid.*, p. 34.

93 Narayanan, "*Ālaya*", p. 470.

94 Anuradha Roma Choudhury, "Sacred Place" in Bowen, ed., *Themes and Issues in Hinduism*, p. 251.

95 Narayanan, "*Ālaya*", p. 471.

96 Foulston, *At the Feet of the Goddess*, p. 43.

97 *Ibid.*, p. 58.

98 David Kinsley, *Hindu Goddesses: Visions of the divine feminine in the Hindu religious tradition* (Delhi, Varanasi, Patna, Madras: Motilal Banarsidass, 1987), p. 198.

99 Kinsley, *Hinduism*, p. 123.

100 Foulston, *At the Feet of the Goddess*, p. 144.
101 Kathleen M. Erndl, "The Play of the Mother: Possession and Power in Hindu Women's Goddess Rituals" in Pintchman, ed., *Women's Lives, Women's Rituals in the Hindu Tradition*, p. 150.
102 *Ibid.*, p. 152.
103 Sarah Caldwell, "Bhagavati: Ball of Fire" in John Stratton Hawley and Donna Marie Wulff, eds., *Devī: Goddesses of India* (Berkeley, Los Angeles, London: University of California Press, 1996), pp. 19–201 and by the same author, *Oh Terrifying Mother: Sexuality, violence, and worship of the Goddess Kālī* (Delhi: Oxford University Press, 1999).
104 Susan S. Wadley, "*Grāma*" in Mittal and Thursby, *The Hindu World*, p. 432.
105 *Ibid.*, p. 440.
106 Erndl, "The Play of the Mother", p. 203.
107 Babb, *The Divine Hierarchy*, pp. 137–8, with photograph.
108 Foulston, *At the Feet of the Goddess*, p. 137.
109 See Foulston's section on this, *ibid.*, pp. 133–40.
110 Bulbul Sharma, *The Book of Devi* (New Delhi, London, New York, Victoria, Toronto, Auckland: Viking, 2001), p. 149.
111 Frazier, ed., *The Continuum Companion to Hindu Studies*, p. 165.
112 Östör, Cyclical Time, p. 176.

Chapter 9 Ritual in the Home and Community: Life-Cycle Rites

1 Rajbali Pandey, *Hindu Saṃskāras: Socio-religious study of the Hindu sacraments* (Delhi: Motilal Banarsidass Publishers Private Limited, 1994 reprint of 1969 revised edn), p. 275.
2 Ralph W. Nicholas, "The Effectiveness of the Hindu Sacrament (*Saṃskāra*): Caste, Marriage, and Divorce in Bengali Culture" in Lindsey Harlan and Paul B. Courtright, eds., *From the Margins of Hindu Marriage: Essays on gender, religion, and culture* (Oxford, New York: Oxford University Press, 1995), p. 138.
3 Gavin Flood, *An Introduction to Hinduism* (Cambridge, New York and Melbourne: Cambridge University Press, 1996), p. 201.
4 Mary McGee, "*Saṃskāra*" in Sushil Mittal and Gene Thursby, eds., *The Hindu World* (New York and London: Routledge, 2004), p. 333.
5 *Ibid.*, p. 354.
6 *Ibid.*, p. 355.
7 See Pandey, *Hindu Saṃskāras*, p. 16.
8 *Ibid.*
9 McGee, "*Saṃskāra*", p. 333.
10 Gavin Flood, "Rites of Passage" in Paul Bowen, ed., *Themes and Issues in Hinduism* (London and Washington: Cassell, 1998), p. 256.
11 See *ibid.*, pp. 25–9.
12 Nicholas, "The Effectiveness of the Hindu Sacrament (*Saṃskāra*)", p. 155.
13 Most of the law texts on religion did not necessarily preclude women from access to *saṃskāras* except that, like the *Śudras*, *Vedic mantras* were not to be used. Both women and *Śudras* could, however, use *Purāṇic* material. See McGee, "*Śaṃskāra*", p. 336.
14 Flood, "Rites of Passage", p. 257.
15 Ram Sharan Sharma, *Śūdras in Ancient India* (Delhi: Motilal Banarsidass Publishers Private Limited, 1990 third, revised edn, first published 1958), p. 298.
16 Julius Lipner, *Hindus: Their religious beliefs and practices* (London and New York: Routledge, 1994), p. 264.

17 Sharma, *Śūdras in Ancient India*, p. 21.
18 Nirad C. Chaudhuri, *Hinduism* (Oxford, New York, Toronto, Melbourne: Oxford University Press, 1980), p. 202.
19 Chaudhuri commented that on certain days it is inauspicious to go in specific directions because they are, as he wrote, "spiked", or "speared". Thus, the West is spiked on Sundays and Fridays, the North on Tuesdays and Wednesdays, the East on Mondays and Saturdays and the South on Wednesdays and Thursdays. Travelling in these directions on these inauspicious days is believed to be fraught with danger. *Ibid*., p. 205.
20 Thomas J. Hopkins, *The Hindu Religious Tradition* (Belmont, California: Wadsworth Publishing Company, 1971), pp. 80–81.
21 A. S. Altekar, *The Position of Women in Hindu Civilization* (Delhi: Motilal Banarsidass Publishers Private Limited, 1995 reprint of second edn 1959), p. 7.
22 In some cases, a whole generation of ancestors for some southern Hindus. See Flood, *Hinduism*, p. 203.
23 Altekar, *The Position of Women in Hindu Civilization*, p. 110.
24 Gloria Goodwin Raheja, "'Crying When She's Born, and Crying When She Goes Away': Marriage and the Idiom of the Gift in Pahansu Song Performance" in Harlan and Courtright, eds., *From the Margins of Hindu Marriage*, p. 28.
25 Altekar, *The Position of Women in Hindu Civilization*, p. 4. However, the *Ṛg Veda* 8:4:6 has a prayer for the birth of sons and claims that birth of a girl is inauspicious. The *Atharva Veda* 6:11:3 recommends the "putting away" of a girl at birth.
26 *The Hindu*, www.thehindu.com/news/national/india-loses-3-million-girls-in-infanticide/article3981575.ece accessed 21/06/2013, and see the evidence also of Sophie Baker, *Caste: At home in Hindu India* (London: Jonathan Cape, 1990), p. 147 in the context of *Dalit* birth.
27 Library of Congress, Law Library, "Sex Selection & Abortion: India", 03/07/2013 www.loc.gov/law/help/sex-selection/india.php
28 "India: A dangerous place to be a woman", British Broadcasting Corporation Television (BBC TV), 27 June 2013.
29 Veena Talwar Oldenburg, *Dowry Murder: The imperial origins of a culture crime* (Oxford and New York: Oxford University Press, 2002), p. 4.
30 *Ibid*., p. 5.
31 McGee "*Śaṃskāra*", p. 341.
32 See Raheja, "'Crying When She's Born, and Crying When She Goes Away'", p. 26.
33 David Kinsley, *Hindu Goddesses: Visions of the divine feminine in the Hindu religious tradition* (Delhi, Varanasi, Patna, Madras: Motilal Banarsidass, 1987, first published 1986), p. 154.
34 Pandey, *Hindu Saṃskāras*, pp. 80–81 and *Laws of Manu*, 1:31.
35 McGee, "*Saṃskāra*", p. 342.
36 *Ibid.*
37 Lawrence A. Babb, *The Divine Hierarchy: Popular Hinduism in Central India* (New York: Columbia University Press, 1975), p. 75.
38 C. J. Fuller, *The Camphor Flame: Popular Hinduism and society in India* (New Delhi, Harmondsworth, Middlesex, New York, Victoria, Toronto, Auckland: Viking, 1992), p. 238.
39 Chaudhuri, *Hinduism*, p. 210.
40 Lipner, *Hindus*, p. 266.
41 Babb, *The Divine Hierarchy*, p. 77.
42 Pandey, *Hindu Saṃskāras*, p. 102.
43 *Ibid*., p. 106.

44 *Ibid.*, p. 112.

45 As exemplified, in the *Atharva Veda* 11:5:3, where the idiom of the student being an embryo within the teacher is found.

46 Pandey, *Hindu Saṃskāras*, p. 120.

47 Altekar, *The Position of Women in Hindu Civilization*, p. 19.

48 *Ibid.*, p. 24.

49 *Ibid.*, p. 23.

50 Pandey, *Hindu Saṃskāras*, p. 131. McGee notes that the thread seems originally to have been a garment worn on the upper part of the body during *Vedic* sacrifice. See her "*Saṃskāras*", p. 346.

51 For the full details of such symbolism see Pandey, *ibid.*, p. 132 and for a very detailed account of the ritual pp. 111–40. Extracts from the *Āśvalāyana Gṛhya-sūtra*, which details how the ceremony should be conducted, can be found in R. N. Dandekar, "Dharma: The First End of Man" in Ainslee T. Embree, *Sources of Indian Tradition, Vol. 1: From the beginning to 1800* (New York: Columbia University Press, 1988 second edn, first published 1958), pp. 224–6.

52 Pandey, *ibid.*, p. 133. The thread is worn over the right shoulder and under the left arm at funerals and simply hung around the neck during urination, defecation, or sex.

53 See, for example, the photograph of the Dashratha family from Andhra Pradesh in Baker's work, *Caste*, where the men in the *Śūdra* family of weavers are all wearing the sacred thread; photograph opposite p. 104.

54 Satguru Sivaya Subramuniyaswami, *Dancing with Śiva: Hinduism's contemporary catechism* (India: Himalayan Academy, 1993), p. 273.

55 Sarah Caldwell, "Bhagavati: Ball of Fire" in John Stratton Hawley and Donna Marie Wulff, eds., *Devī: Goddesses of India* (Berkeley, Los Angeles, London: University of California Press, 1996), p. 210.

56 Vijaya Rettakudi Nagarajan, "Threshold Designs, Forehead Dots, and Menstruating Rituals: Exploring Time and Space in Tamil *Kolams*" in Tracy Pintchman, ed., *Women's Lives, Women's Rituals in the Hindu Tradition* (Oxford and New York: Oxford University Press, 2007), pp. 88–9.

57 *Ibid.*, pp. 88–90. The *kolam* in front of a house also provides a "protective invisible, three-dimensional screen" that demarcates the profane inauspicious outside from the auspicious inside, so it may be used to divide the sacred/mundane space of kitchens, temples, something of a "crossing place", a ford, *tīrtha*, between the profane and sacred. See Nagarajan, p. 97.

58 Altekar, *The Position of Women in Hindu Civilization*, pp. 210–11.

59 Susan S. Wadley, "No Longer a Wife: Widows in Rural North India" in Harlan and Courtright, eds., *From the Margins of Hindu Marriage*, p. 99.

60 There were seven other types of marriages – giving a daughter to a priest; paying a token bride-price of a cow and a bull; the father giving the girl to a husband without dowry or bride-price changing hands; marriage between a male and a female who promised to be together; purchase of a bride; capture of a woman; capture of a woman who is drugged, deranged, drunk or asleep. See the extract from the *Āśvalāyana Gṛhya-sūtra* in Dandekar, "Dharma", pp. 226–7.

61 The custom of polyandry still obtains, it seems, amongst traditional tribal customs in isolated parts of the western Himālayas, and in the eastern Himālayas there are tribal groups who practise matrilineal customs. See Klaus K. Klostermaier, *A Survey of Hinduism* (Albany, New York: State University of New York Press, 1994), p. 187 and Jessica Frazier, ed., *The Continuum Companion to Hindu Studies* (London and New York: Continuum, 2011), p. 263.

62 *Manu-smṛti* 9:88–90.

63 *Ibid.*, 3:9.

64 *Ibid.*, 9:3, translators Wendy Doniger and Brian K. Smith, *The Laws of Manu* (London, New York, Victoria, Toronto, Auckland: Penguin Books, 1991), p. 197.
65 Altekar, *The Position of Women in Hindu Civilization*, pp. 354–5.
66 See Robert Jackson and Dermot Killingley, *Approaches to Hinduism* (London: John Murray, 1988), p. 89.
67 Vineeta Pandey, "Indian Women Push Back Marriage Age", 10/05/2011, www.dnaindia.com/india/1350166/report-indian-women-push-back-marriage-age See also timesofindia.indiatimes.com/2011-05-10/india/29527428 _1_child-marriage-ssa-icds
68 Asian Human Rights Commission, *India: A heartless nation for women*, April 16th 2013 www.humanrights.asia/news/ahrc-news/AHRC-PAP-001-2013 p. 5/9.
69 A. L. Basham, *The Wonder that was India* (London: Sidgwick & Jackson, 1982 reprint of third, revised edn, first published 1954), p. 153.
70 *Ibid.*, p. 154.
71 Altekar, *The Position of Women in Hindu Civilization*, p. 77.
72 Vishal Joshi, "Dalit locality attacked, water supply cut after inter-caste marriage in Haryana", *Hindustan Times*, 15/04/2013 www.hindustantimes.com/India-news/Haryana/Dalit-locality-attacked-water-supply-cut-after-inter-caste-marriage/Article1-1044879.aspx
73 Mattison Mines, "Hindus at the Edge: Self-Awareness among Adult Children of Interfaith Marriages in Chennai, South India" in *International Journal of Hindu Studies* 2, 2(1998), pp. 223–4.
74 *Ibid.*, p. 247 and *passim.*
75 Mark Juergensmeyer, "The Lonely Modernity of Model Town" in Ishita Banerjee-Dube, ed., *Caste in History: Themes in Indian history* (New Delhi: Oxford University Press, 2012, first published 2008), pp. 269–70.
76 Pandey, *Hindu Saṃskāras*, p. 182.
77 See AndrĐ Béteille, "Caste in Contemporary India" in C. J. Fuller, ed., *Caste Today* (Delhi: Oxford University Press, 1997), p. 165.
78 Oldenburg, *Dowry Murder*, p. 10.
79 *Ibid.*, p. 11.
80 *Ibid.*, p. 3.
81 Sudeshna Maitra, *Dowry and Bride Price.* Paper prepared for the International Encyclopedia of the Social Sciences, 2nd edn, 2007, p. 5.
82 BBC Television, "India: A dangerous place to be a woman".
83 Wadley, "No longer a wife", p. 97.
84 Nicholas, "The Effectiveness of the Hindu Sacrament (*Saṃskāra*)", p. 144.
85 Statistics from the National Crime Records Bureau, Asian Human Rights Commission, Meredith McBride, "India: A Heartless Nation for a Woman", 16/04/2013, p. 2. www.human-rights.asia/news/ahrc-news/AHRC-PAP-001-2013
86 "Indian dowry deaths on the rise", Telegraph Media Group Limited, 2013, accessed 21/06/2013 www.telegraph.co.news/worldnews/asia/india/9108642/Indian-dowry-deaths-on-the-rise.html#article
87 Maitra, *Dowry and Bride Price*, p. 4.
88 Babb, *The Divine Hierarchy*, p. 82.
89 Raheja, "Crying When She's Born, and Crying When She Goes Away", p. 24.
90 Babb, *The Divine Hierarchy*, p. 128.
91 Werner Menski, "Change and Continuity in Hindu Marriage Rituals" in Dermot Killingley, Werner Menski and Shirley Firth, *Hindu Ritual and Society* (Newcastle upon Tyne: S. Y. Killingley, 1991), p. 44.

92 Susan S. Wadley, "*Grāma*" in Mittal and Thursby, eds., *The Hindu World*, p. 434.
93 According to Raheja, however, once a bride is passed to the conjugal home, a certain amount of inauspiciousness passes with her. The woman is subject to polluting menses for many years, as also the pollution of childbirth. See Raheja, "Crying When She's Born, and Crying When She Goes Away", pp. 29–30.
94 See Babb, *The Divine Hierarchy*, pp. 83–4.
95 McGee finds many rites in the ceremony to be similar to those in *upanayana* – touching the heart as a symbol of intimacy; treading on a stone; holding hands looking at the sun; looking at the pole star; the use of a sacred thread are similar rites pertaining to the teacher–student and husband–wife. See McGee, "*Saṃskāra*", p. 345.
96 Baker, *Caste*, p. 15.
97 McGee, "*Saṃskāra*", p. 332.
98 Baker, *Caste*, p. 113.
99 Menski, "Change and Continuity in Hindu Marriage Rituals", p. 43.
100 Nicholas, "The Effectiveness of the Hindu Sacrament (*Saṃskāra*)", p. 156.
101 Lindsey Harlan and Paul B. Courtright, "Introduction: On Hindu Marriage and Its Margins" in Harlan and Courtright, eds., *From the Margins of Hindu Marriage*, p. 8.
102 Raheja, "Crying When She's Born, and Crying When She Goes Away", pp. 19–20, though Babb's research in Andhra Pradesh found that new brides made frequent visits to the natal home, see *The Divine Hierarchy*, p. 90.
103 Raheja, *ibid.*, pp. 33–5.
104 *Ibid.*, p. 40.
105 Pandey, *Hindu Saṃskāras*, p. 233.
106 www.advocatekhoj.com/library/lawareas/divadultery/4.php?Title=AdulteryDivorce&STitle=Adultery laws in India
107 Wendy Doniger, "Begetting on Margin: Adultery and Surrogate Pseudomarriage in Hinduism" in Harlan and Courtright, eds., *From the Margins of Hindu Marriage*, pp. 160–1.
108 Baker, *Caste*, p. 150.
109 See Altekar, *The Position of Women in Hindu Civilization*, p. 89.
110 Babb, *The Divine Hierarchy*, p. 82 note 2.
111 Nicholas, "The Effectiveness of the Hindu Sacrament (*Saṃskāra*)", p. 142.
112 *Ibid.*, p. 143.
113 *Ibid.*, p. 157.
114 Ram Gidoomal and Robin Thomson, *A Way of Life: Introducing Hinduism* (London, Sydney and Auckland: Hodder and Stoughton, 1997), p. 115.
115 Babb, *The Divine Hierarchy*, p. 91.
116 Shirley Firth, "Changing Patterns in Hindu Death Rituals in Britain" in Jackson and Killingley, eds., *Approaches to Hinduism*, p. 56. Firth's account of funeral rituals in India is extensive and well-documented and I have relied on her material in much of what follows. In addition, Pandey gives a more extensive account of death rites, see his *Hindu Saṃskāras*, pp. 234–74.
117 Babb, *The Divine Hierarchy*, p. 92.
118 Chaudhuri, *Hinduism*, p. 208.
119 See Firth, "Changing Patterns in Hindu Death Rituals in Britain", p. 59 for a range of suggestions of the rationale behind this practice.
120 Even in the case of Śaivas, according to Firth, see *ibid.*, p. 60. The *tulasī* plant is normally associated with Viṣṇu, not Śiva.

121 See Frazier in Frazier, ed., *The Continuum Companion to Hindu Studies*, p. 269.
122 Firth, "Changing Patterns in Hindu Death Rituals in Britain", p. 64.
123 *Atharva Veda* 18:2:7 translator McGee, "*Saṃskāra*", p. 353.
124 See Pandey, *Hindu Saṃskāras*, p. 256.
125 Firth, "Changing Patterns in Hindu Death Rituals in Britain", p. 78.
126 See Michael Witzel, "Macrocosm, Mesocosm, and Microcosm: The Persistent Nature of 'Hindu' Beliefs and Symbolic Forms" in *International Journal of Hindu Studies* 1, 3(1997), p. 504.
127 *Ibid.*, p. 265.
128 David R. Kinsley, *Hinduism: A cultural perspective* (Englewood Cliffs, New Jersey: Prentice Hall, 1993 second edn, first published 1982), p. 114.
129 McGee, "*Saṃskāra*", p. 354.
130 Troy Wilson Organ, *Hinduism: Its historical development* (Woodbury, New York, London, Toronto: Barron's Educational Series, Inc., 1974), p. 208.
131 Klostermaier, *A Survey of Hinduism*, p. 189.
132 Basham, *The Wonder that was India*, pp. 155–6.
133 Arun Kumar Mookerjee, "Dharma as the Goal: The Mahābhārata" in Krishna Sivaraman, ed., *Hindu Spirituality: Vedas through Vedanta* (New York: SCM Press, 1989), p. 128.
134 Paul B. Courtright, "*Satī,* Sacrifice and Marriage: The Modernity of Tradition" in Harlan and Courtright, eds. *From the Margins of Hindu Marriage*, p. 184.
135 Lindsey Harlan, "Satī: The Story of Godāvrī" in Hawley and Wulff, eds., *Devī*, p. 231.
136 Altekar, *The Position of Women in Hindu Civilization*, p. 121. See also his extensive coverage of the history of the *satī,* pp. 115–42.
137 *Ibid.*, p. 129.
138 Harlan, "Satī", p. 233.
139 Altekar, *The Position of Women in Hindu Civilization*, p. 139.
140 Klostermaier, *A Survey of Hinduism*, p. 374.
141 Julia Lesley presents a balanced account of the negative criticisms of the custom and a sensitive portrayal of the self-sacrifice of the *satī* for her own and her families' futures. See her article, "Suttee or *Satī*: Victim or Victor" in Julia Lesley, ed., *Roles and Rituals for Hindu Women* (Delhi: Motilal Banarsidass, 1992), pp. 175–92.
142 Courtright, "*Satī*, Sacrifice and Marriage", p. 189.
143 *Ibid.* pp. 189–90.
144 *Ibid.*, 190–1.
145 Harlan, "Satī: The Story of Godāvrī", pp. 235–6.
146 *Ibid.*, p. 242.
147 Altekar, *The Position of Women in Hindu Civilization*, p. 116.
148 McGee, "*Saṃskāras*", p. 338.
149 Pandey, *Hindu Saṃskāras*, p. 279.

Chapter 10 Women in the Home and Community

1 Mandakranta Bose, *Women in the Hindu Tradition: Rules, roles and exceptions* (Abingdon, London and New York: Routledge, 2010), p. 9.
2 Lindsey Harlan and Paul Courtright, "Introduction: On Hindu Marriage and Its Margins" in Lindsey Harlan and Paul Courtright, eds., *From the Margins of Hindu Marriage: Essays on gender, religion, and culture* (Oxford, New York: Oxford University Press, 1995), pp. 10–11.
3 Thomas B. Coburn, *Encountering the Goddess: A translation of the Devī-Māhātmya and a study of its interpretation* (Albany, New York: State University of New York Press, 1991), p. 172.

4 Jessica Frazier in Jessica Frazier, ed., *The Continuum Companion to Hindu Studies* (London and New York: Continuum, 2011), p. 300.
5 *The Laws of Manu*, 5:147–9, translators Wendy Doniger with Brian K. Smith (London, New York, Victoria, Toronto, Auckland: Penguin Books, 1991), p. 115.
6 A. L. Basham, *The Wonder That Was India* (London: Sidgwick & Jackson, third revised edn, first published 1954), p. 182.
7 *Laws of Manu* 3:55–6.
8 Tracy Pintchman, *The Rise of the Goddess in the Hindu Tradition* (Albany, New York: State University of New York Press, 1994), p. 198.
9 *Ibid.*, pp. 198–200.
10 A. S. Altekar, *The Position of Women in Hindu Civilization* (Delhi: Motilal Banarsidass Publishers Private Limited, 1995 reprint of second edn 1959), pp. 338–9.
11 See Katherine K. Young, "Theology Does Help Women's Liberation: Śrīvaiṣṇavism, a Hindu Case Study" in Steven J. Rosen, ed., *Women and the Worship of Krishna* (Delhi: Motilal Banarsidass Publishers Private Limited, 1996, pp. 235–7.
12 Altekar, *The Position of Women in Hindu Civilization*, p. 368.
13 James L. Fitzgerald, "*Mahābhārata*" in Sushil Mittal and Gene Thursby, eds., *The Hindu World* (New York and London: Routledge, 2004), p. 70.
14 John L. Brockington, *Righteous Rāma: The evolution of an epic* (Delhi, Bombay, Calcutta, Madras: Oxford University Press, 1985), p. 320 with dates pp. 307–17.
15 *Ibid.*, p. 322 with dates p. 316.
16 Frazier in Frazier, ed., *The Continuum Companion to Hindu Studies*, p. 288.
17 Joanna Liddle and Rama Joshi, *Daughters of Independence: Gender, caste and class in India* (London: Zed Books Limited, 1986), p. 57.
18 See Young, "Theology Does Help Women's Liberation", p. 271.
19 See *ibid.*, pp. 27–6.
20 At the time of the Partition of India, women sometimes committed suicide rather than be subjected to rape and abduction by Muslim men, but were occasionally pressurized by men of their family to do so in order to preserve family honour. See Veena Das, *Critical Events: An anthropological perspective on contemporary India* (Oxford, New York, New Delhi: Oxford University Press, 1999 reprint, first published 1995), chapter 3 *passim.*
21 Bose, *Women in the Hindu Tradition*, p. 154.
22 *Ibid.*, p. 151.
23 Satguru Sivaya Subramuniyaswami, *Dancing with Śiva: Hinduism's contemporary catechism* (India: Himalayan Academy, 1993), pp. 213 and 215.
24 Liddle and Joshi, *Daughters of Independence*, p. 192.
25 Cesar Chelala, "Rape and Gender Discrimination Related in India" in *The Japan Times* 25/04/2013, www.japantimes.co.jp/opinion/2013/04/25/commentary/rape-and-gender-discrimination-related-in-india#.UcRisfmkrp8
26 Meredith McBride, Asian Human Rights Commission, "India: A Heartless Nation for Women" 16/04/2013 www.humanrights.asia/news/ahrc-news/AHRC-PAP-001-2013
27 Liddle and Joshi, *Daughters of Independence*, p. 238.
28 Sophie Baker, *Caste: At home in Hindu India* (London: Jonathan Cape, 1990), p. 118.
29 Liddle and Joshi, *Daughters of Independence*, p. 12.
30 So, Altekar, *The Position of Women in Hindu Civilization*, p. 175.
31 However, some of the law writers – Vasiṣṭha and Yājnavalkya and even Manu – believed that women's impurities were regularly washed away during menses.

32 Altekar, *The Position of Women in Hindu Civilization*, pp. 194–5.
33 S. V. Ketkar, *History of Caste in India: Social conditions in India according to Manu* (New Delhi: Cosmo Publications, 1979), p. 119.
34 Vasudha Narayanan, "*Ālaya*" in Mittal and Thursby, *The Hindu World*, p. 450.
35 Cited by Laurie L. Patton, "The Cat in the Courtyard: Sanskrit and the Religious Experience of Women" in Tracy Pintchman, ed., *Women's Lives, Women's Rituals in the Hindu Tradition* (Oxford and New York: Oxford University Press, 2007), pp. 21–2.
36 Liddle and Joshi, *Daughters of Independence*, pp. 110–11.
37 *Ibid.*, p. 159.
38 Patton, "The Cat in the Courtyard", p. 21.
39 Shikha Dalmia, "Feminism Can't Cure India's Rape Epidemic", 19/06/2013 www.reason.com/archives/2013/06/19/feminism-cant-cure-indias-rape-epidemic
40 For an account of the political and nationalist movements in relation to women's rights in India from the nineteenth century on, see Geraldine Forbes, *Women in Modern India* (Cambridge: Cambridge University Press, 2004).
41 Klaus Deininger, Aparajita Goyal, Hari Nagarjan, "Women's Inheritance: Evidence from India", December 2010, www.voxeu.org/article/women-s-inheritance-evidence-india, and Javed Razack, "Inheritance and Succession, Rights of Women and Daughters under Personal Laws", www.lexorates.com/articles/inheritance-and-succession-rights-of-women-and-daughters-under-personal-laws/, accessed 21/06/2013.
42 Beina Xu, "Governance in India: Women's Rights", Council on Foreign Relations, March 2013 www.cfr.org/india/governance-india-womens-rights/p30041
43 Liddle and Joshi, *Daughters of Independence*, p. 131.
44 *Ibid.*, p. 152.
45 *Ibid.*, 144–5.
46 *Ibid.*, pp. 128–9.
47 Mary E. Hancock, "The Dilemmas of Domesticity: Possession and Devotional Experience Among Urban Smārta Women" in Harlan and Courtright, eds., *From the Margins of Hindu Marriage*, p. 61.
48 Cited in Meera Khanna, "The Voiceless Millions of Widows in India", 10/02/2010, p. 3 www.wunrn.com/news/2010/02_10_/02_08_10/020810_india3.htm
49 *Ibid.*, p. 4.
50 Rekha Singh, "Status of Women in Indian Society", www.bu.edu/wcp/Papers/Huma/HumaSing.htm, accessed 21 June, 2013.
51 Dalmia, "Feminism Can't Cure India's Rape Epidemic".
52 Sabrin Sidhu in British Broadcasting Corporation Television (BBC TV) documentary, "India: A dangerous place to be a woman", 27 June 2013.
53 Liddle and Joshi, *Daughters of Independence*, p. 138.
54 BBC TV documentary, "India: A dangerous place to be a woman".
55 Liddle and Joshi, *Daughters of Independence*, p. 141.
56 *Ibid.*, pp. 140–1.
57 *Ibid.*, p. 141.
58 McBride, "India: A heartless nation for women", pp. 1–2.
59 *Ibid.*, p. 2.
60 *Ibid.*, p. 3.
61 *Ibid.* pp. 3–4.
62 Dalmia, "Feminism Can't Cure India's Rape Epidemic", p. 1.

63 Evidence from BBC TV documentary, "India: A dangerous place to be a woman".
64 A fifth defendant was found hanged in his prison cell and another perpetrator was a juvenile who has already been found guilty and sentenced to three years in a correction facility.
65 BBC TV documentary, "India: A dangerous place to be a woman". A young girl was assaulted at 8.30 p.m. Despite being in a busy area, no one helped her and the men involved were able to continue their attack. But eleven men were arrested and convicted as a result, suggestive that the authorities are beginning to take sexual attacks and harassment more seriously after the December 2012 incident.
66 Saskia C. Kersenboom, "The Traditional Repertoire of the Tiruttani Temple Dancers" in Julia Lesley, ed., *Roles and Rituals for Hindu Women* (Delhi: Motilal Banarsidass, 1992), pp. 131–48.
67 Altekar, *The Position of Women in Hindu Civilization*, p. 357.
68 Susan S. Wadley, "*Grāma*" in Mittal and Thursby, eds., *The Hindu World*, p. 440.
69 *Ibid.*, p. 444.
70 See Young, "Theology Does Help Women's Liberation", pp. 261–3.
71 Bose, *Women in the Hindu Tradition*, p. 8.
72 David R. Kinsley, *Hinduism: A cultural perspective* (Englewood Cliffs, New Jersey: Prentice Hall, 1993 reprint of 1982 edn), p. 150.
73 *Ibid.*, pp.149–50.
74 Kathleen M. Erndl, "The Play of the Mother: Possession and Power in Hindu Women's Goddess Rituals" in Pintchman, ed., *Women's Lives, Women's Rituals in the Hindu Tradition*, p. 156.
75 *Ibid.*, p. 157.
76 Mary McGee, "*Saṃskāra*", in Mittal and Thursby, eds., *The Hindu World*, p. 355.
77 See Lynn Teskey Denton, "Varieties of Hindu Female Asceticism" in Julia Lesley, ed., *Roles and Rituals for Hindu Women* (Delhi: Motilal Banarsidass, 1992), pp. 211–32.
78 June McDaniel, "Does Tantric Ritual Empower Women? Renunciation and Domesticity among Female Bengali Tantrikas" in Pintchman, ed., *Women's Lives, Women's Rituals in the Hindu Tradition*, pp. 159–60.
79 *Ibid.*, pp. 165–6.
80 *Ibid.*, p. 171.
81 Kinsley, *Hinduism*, p. 138.
82 *Ibid.*
83 See Liddle and Joshi, *Daughters of Independence*, pp. 145–7.
84 Evidence from BBC TV documentary, "India: A dangerous place to be a woman", 27 June 2013.
85 Susan S. Wadley, "No Longer a Wife: Widows in Rural North India" in Harlan and Courtright, eds., *From the Margins of Hindu Marriage*, p. 95.
86 Liddle and Joshi, *Daughters of Independence*, p. 149.
87 *Ibid.*, p. 160.
88 Bose, *Women in the Hindu Tradition*, p. 139.
89 Wadley, "No Longer a Wife", p. 114.
90 Anne MacKenzie Pearson, *"Because It Gives Me Peace of Mind": Fasts in the religious lives of Hindu women* (Albany, New York: State University of New York, 1996), p. 18.
91 Kinsley, *Hinduism*, p. 139.
92 Pearson, "*Because it Gives Me Peace of Mind*", p. 18.
93 *Ibid.*, p. 19.
94 Kinsley, *Hinduism*, p. 139.

95 Pearson, "*Because it Gives Me Peace of Mind*", p. 27. For a detailed account of *vratas*, see also Bose, *Women in the Hindu Tradition*, pp. 138–44.
96 See Mary McGee, "Desired Fruits: Motive and Intention in the Votive Rites of Hindu Women" in Lesley, ed., *Roles and Rituals for Hindu Women*, pp. 77–88.
97 Bose, *Women in the Hindu Tradition*, p. 143.
98 Lawrence A. Babb, *The Divine Hierarchy: Popular Hinduism in Central India* (New York: Columbia University Press, 1975), p. 110.
99 Kinsley, *Hinduism*, p. 141.
100 Bose, *Women in the Hindu Tradition*, p. 139.
101 See Baker's example in *Caste*, p. 129.
102 Harlan and Courtright, "Introduction", p. 11.
103 Vijaya Rettakudi Nagarajan, "Threshold Designs, Forehead Dots, and Menstruation Rituals: Exploring Time and Space in Tamil *Kolams*" in Pintchman, ed., *Women's Lives, Women's Rituals in the Hindu Tradition*, pp. 90–1.
104 *Ibid.*, p. 91.
105 *Ibid.*
106 Altekar, *The Position of Women in Hindu Civilization*, p. 115.
107 Swati Deshpande, "Inheritance laws largely skewed against women" in *The Times of India*, 9 March, 2005, p. 1 www.articles.timesofindia.indiatimes.com/2005-03-09/mumbai/27857873_1_hindu-succession-act-inheritance-m-p-biria
108 *The Laws of Manu* 5:156–8, translators Doniger and Smith, p. 115.
109 Khanna, "The Voiceless Millions of Widows in India", p. 2.
110 *Ibid.*, p. 1.
111 *Ibid.*, p. 2.
112 Wadley, "No Longer a Wife", p. 100.
113 *Ibid.*, p. 100.
114 Baker, *Caste*, pp. 32–3.
115 *Ibid.*, p. 71.
116 *Ibid.*, pp. 133–4.
117 Altekar, *The Position of Women in Hindu Civilization*, p. 356.
118 Young, "Theology Does help Women's Liberation", p. 256.
119 C. J. Fuller, *The Camphor Flame: Popular Hinduism and society in India* (New Delhi, Harmondsworth, New York, Victoria, Toronto, Auckland: Viking, 1992), p. 23.
120 R. S. Khare, "*Anna*" in Mittal and Thursby, eds., *The Hindu World*, p. 417.
121 Louis Dumont, *Homo Hierarchicus: The caste system and its implications* (Chicago and London: University of Chicago Press, 1980, first published in French, 1966), p. 139.
122 Fuller, *The Camphor Flame*, pp. 93–4.
123 Khare, "*Anna*", p. 408.
124 Dumont, *Homo Hierarchicus*, p. 147.
125 *Ibid.*, p. 150.
126 Khare, "*Anna*", p. 415.
127 *Ibid.*, p. 411.
128 Baker, *Caste*, p. 29.
129 Robert Jackson and Dermot Killingley, *Approaches to Hinduism* (London: John Murray, 1988), p. 38.
130 Khare, "*Anna*", p. 414.
131 Nagarajan, "Threshold Designs, Forehead Dots, and Menstruation Rituals", p. 96.

132 Baker, *Caste*, p. 51.
133 Dumont, *Homo Hierarchicus*, p. 83.
134 Khare, "*Anna*", p. 419.
135 *Ibid.*, p. 415.
136 Bose, *Women in the Hindu Tradition*, p. 156.

Chapter 11 Sacred Times and Places

1 Chris J. Fuller, *The Camphor Flame: Popular Hinduism and society in India* (New Delhi, Harmondsworth, New York, Victoria, Ontario, Auckland: Viking, 1992), p. 129.
2 *Ibid.*, pp. 147–8.
3 For a clear and comprehensive account of the months and years, see Lawrence A. Babb, *The Divine Hierarchy: Popular Hinduism in central India* (New York: Columbia University Press, 1975), pp. 123–7, and Alan Brown, ed., on behalf of the Shap Working Party, *Festivals in World Religions* (London and New York: Longman, 1986), pp. 108–13.
4 Fuller, *The Camphor Flame*, p. 129.
5 Troy Wilson Organ, *Hinduism: Its historical development* (Woodbury, New York, London, Toronto: Barron's Educational Series Inc., 1974), p. 209.
6 See Devdutt Pattanaik, *Devi – The Mother Goddess: An introduction* (Mumbai: Vakils, Feffer and Simons Ltd., 2002 reprint of 2000 edn), p. 103.
7 Brown, *Festivals in World Religions*, pp. 114–15.
8 Vijaya Rettakudi Nagarajan, "Threshold Designs, Forehead Dots, and Menstruation Rituals: Exploring Time and Space in Tamil *Kolams*" in Tracy Pintchman, ed., *Women's Lives, Women's Rituals in the Hindu Tradition* (Oxford and New York: Oxford University Press, 2007), p. 99.
9 Babb, *The Divine Hierarchy*, p. 168.
10 Organ, *Hinduism*, p. 209.
11 Babb, *The Divine Hierarchy*, p. 171.
12 McKim Marriott, "The Feast of Love" in Milton Singer, ed., *Krishna: Myths, rites, and attitudes* (Chicago and London: University of Chicago Press, 1966), pp. 210–11, though see Babb's comment from his research in central India, which shows that where the gap is very wide, status difference is upheld, *The Divine Hierarchy*, p. 174.
13 Marriott, *ibid.*, p. 201.
14 *Ibid.*, p. 203.
15 Babb, *The Divine Hierarchy*, pp. 169–70.
16 *Ibid.* p. 174.
17 Anuradha Roma Choudhury, "Worship" in Paul Bowen, ed., *Themes and Issues in Hinduism* (London and Washington: Cassell, 1998), p. 226.
18 Frédérique Marglin, "Jagannātha Purī" in Steven J. Rosen, ed., *Vaiṣṇavism: Contemporary scholars discuss the Gauḍiya tradition* (Delhi: Motilal Banarsidass Publishers Private Limited, 1994, first published 1992), p. 217.
19 For an excellent and detailed account of this festival, see Frédérique Apfell Marglin, "Time Renewed: *Ratha Jātrā* in Puri" in T. N. Madan, ed., *Religion in India* (Delhi, Bombay, Calcutta, Madras: Oxford University Press, 1994 reprint of second, enlarged edn, first published 1991), pp. 197–211.
20 Royina Grewal, *The Book of Ganesha* (New Delhi, London, New York, Victoria, Toronto, Auckland: Viking, 2001), p. 146.
21 Nanditha Krishna, *The Book of Vishnu* (New Delhi, London, New York, Victoria, Toronto, Auckland: Viking, 2001), pp. 17–18.

22 Lynn Foulston and Stuart Abbott, *Hindu Goddesses: Beliefs and practices* (Brighton and Portland: Sussex Academic Press, 2009), pp. 156–7.
23 *Ibid.*, p. 157.
24 *Ibid.*, p. 158. Apparently, even the 2002 World Cup inspired the architects of one *pandal*, which was in the shape of a football and two 2007 *pandals* were inspired by the Harry Potter Books and the film *Titanic*! For a very detailed account of Foulston's witnessing of the festival, see Foulston and Abbott, *Hindu Goddesses*, pp. 156–69.
25 For a detailed description, see Elizabeth U. Harding, *Kali: The Black Goddess of Dakshineswar* (Delhi: Motilal Banarsidass Publishers Private Limited, 1998, first published 1993), pp. 124–5.
26 David Kinsley, *Hindu Goddesses: Visions of the divine feminine in the Hindu religious tradition* (Delhi, Varanasi, Patna, Madras: Motilal Banarsidass, 1987), pp. 110–11.
27 *Ibid.*, p. 111–13.
28 Pattanaik, *Devi – The Mother Goddess*, p. 106.
29 For a full description of the *ghaṭa* and the nine plants, see Foulston and Abbott, *Hindu Goddesses*, pp. 160–1.
30 Fuller, *The Camphor Flame*, p. 111.
31 Found with various spellings – Dassera, Dassehra, Dussehra, Daśahara.
32 Klaus Klostermaier, *A Survey of Hinduism* (Albany, New York: State University of New York Press, 1994), p. 327.
33 Charlotte Vaudeville, "Krishna, Gopāla, Rādhā, and The Great Goddess" in John Stratton Hawley and Donna Marie Wulff, eds., *The Divine Consort: Rādhā and the Goddesses of India* (Delhi: Motilal Banarsidass Publishers Private Limited, 1995 reprint of 1984 edn), p. 4.
34 Babb, *The Divine Hierarchy*, p. 156.
35 For example, September/October in West Bengal and Himachal Pradesh and November/December in Orissa.
36 Vaudeville, "Krishna, Gopāla, Rādhā, and The Great Goddess", p. 4.
37 Kinsley, *Hindu Goddesses*, pp. 33–4.
38 Brown, *Festivals in World Religions*, pp. 138–9.
39 For a highly detailed description of the festival at Dakṣineśvar see Harding, *Kali*, pp. 130–43.
40 Foulston and Abbott, *Hindu Goddesses*, p. 172.
41 Kinsley, *Hindu Goddesses*, pp. 204–5.
42 *Ibid.*, p. 205.
43 *Ibid.*, p. 206.
44 Viramma, Josiane Racine, and Jen-Luc Racine, "High and Low Castes in Karani" in Ishita Banerjee-Dube, ed., *Caste in History* (New Delhi: Oxford University Press, 2008), p. 241.
45 Surinder Mohan Bhardwaj, *Hindu Places of Pilgrimage in India: A study in cultural geography* (Berkeley, Los Angeles, London: University of California Press, 1983 reprint of 1976 edn), p. 7.
46 Jessica Frazier, "Introduction: New Visions of Hinduism" in Jessica Frazier, ed., *The Continuum Companion to Hindu Studies* (London and New York: Continuum, 2011), p. 11.
47 Surinder M. Bhardwaj and James G. Lochtefeld, "*Tīrtha*" in Sushil Mittal and Gene Thursby, *The Hindu World* (New York and London: Routledge, 2004), p. 501.
48 Klostermaier, *A Survey of Hinduism*, p. 311.
49 In Jainism, the spiritual masters were known as *tīrthāṇkaras*, "ford crossers", those enlightened individuals who had traversed the spiritual path for others to discover.
50 Bhardwaj and Lochtefeld, "*Tīrtha*", p. 480.
51 For an exploration of temples as bridges between the worlds of humanity and the divine , see

George Mitchell, *The Hindu Temple: An introduction to its meanings and forms* (Chicago: University of Chicago Press, 1988 reprint of 1977 edn).
52 Bhardwaj, *Hindu Places of Pilgrimage in India*, p. 85.
53 Mark Edwin Rohe, "Ambiguous and Definitive: The Greatness of the Goddess Vaiṣṇo Devī" in Tracy Pintchman, ed., *Seeking Mahādevī: Constructing the identities of the Hindu great Goddesses* (Albany, New York: State University of New York Press, 2001), p. 58.
54 See Vasudha Narayanan, "*Ālaya*" in Mittal and Thursby, eds., *The Hindu World*, p. 461.
55 *Ibid.*, p. 460.
56 Bhardwaj, *Hindu Places of Pilgrimage in India*, p. 29.
57 *Ibid.*, p. 15.
58 *Ibid.*, p. 56.
59 *Ibid.*, p. 162.
60 *Ibid.*, p. 152.
61 *Ibid.*, p. 176.
62 *Ibid.*, p. 191.
63 *Ibid.*, p. 227.
64 David Kinsley, *Hinduism: A cultural perspective* (Englewood Cliffs, New Jersey: Prentice Hall, 1993 reprint of 1982 edn), p. 115.
65 See, for example, the detailed analysis of Śaiva, Vaiṣṇava and Śākta pilgrimage sites in Alan E. Morinis, *Pilgrimage in the Hindu Tradition: A case study in West Bengal* (Delhi: Oxford University Press, 1984).
66 Bhardwaj, *Hindu Places of Pilgrimage in India*, p. 162.
67 Fuller, *The Camphor Flame*, p. 217.
68 Bhardwaj, *Hindu Places of Pilgrimage in India*, p. 92.
69 *Ibid.*
70 Kinsley, *Hindu Goddesses*, p. 184.
71 Diana L. Eck, "Kāshī: City of all India" in T. N. Madan, ed., *Religion in India* (Delhi, Bombay, Calcutta, Madras,1994 reprint of 1992 edn, first published 1991), p. 145.
72 But see Bhardwaj and Lochtefeld, "*Tīrtha*", p. 484, where they claim that it does flow in the monsoon period.
73 See Richard Barber, *Pilgrimages* (Woodbridge: The Boydell Press, 1991), pp. 99–100.
74 *Ibid.*, p. 99.
75 Diana L. Eck, *Darśan: Seeing the divine image in India* (New York: Columbia University Press, 1996), pp. 73–4.
76 Jonathan P. Parry, *Death in Banaras* (Cambridge: Cambridge University Press, 1994), p. 13.
77 Kinsley, *Hindu Goddesses*, p. 193.
78 For a discussion of the specialists and priests associated with the complexities of death rites, see Parry, *Death in Banaras, passim.*
79 Klostermaier, *A Survey of Hinduism*, p. 330.
80 Barber, *Pilgrimages*, p. 82.
81 Eck, "Kāshī", p. 147.
82 Foulston and Abbott, *Hindu Goddesses*, p. 197.
83 *Ibid.*, p. 198.
84 Harding, *Kali*, p. 3.
85 For an examination of the *śākta pīṭhas* in the context of Tantric beliefs and practices, see Dines Chandra Sircar, *The Śākta Pīthas* (Delhi: Motilal Banarsidass, 1973).

86 So named because just as a fish is believed to create life from spawn just by gazing at it, so Mīnākṣī brings to life the deep spirituality in all the devotees on whom she gazes.
87 John M. Koller, *The Indian Way: An introduction to the philosophies and religions of India* (Upper Saddle River, New Jersey: Pearson/Prentice Hall, 2006 revised edn, first published 1982), p. 7.
88 *Ibid.*, p. 8.
89 Rivers are mainly female (unlike mountains, which are male), their waters nourishing land and beings.
90 See Barber, *Pilgrimages*, pp. 82–3.
91 Diana L. Eck, "Gaṇgā: The Goddess Ganges in Hindu Sacred Geography" in John Stratton Hawley and Donna Marie Wulff, eds., *Devī: Goddesses of India* (Berkeley and Los Angeles: University of California, 1996), p. 137.
92 *Agni Purāṇa*, 110, translator N. Gangadharan, *The Agni Purāṇa, Part 11* (Delhi, UNESCO, Paris: Motilal Banarsidass, 1985), p. 328–9.
93 Eck, "Gaṇgā", p. 139.
94 See Bhardwaj, *Hindu Places of Pilgrimage in India*, pp. 34 and 64.
95 See R. Champakalakshmi and Usha Kris, *The Hindu Temple* (London: Greenwich Editions, 2001), pp. 71–5.
96 See Frazier, ed., *The Continuum Companion to Hindu Studies*, p. 159.
97 Some ascetic groups have financial interests in the local economy of the Kumbha Melā, which can lead to violent rivalry: see Bhardwaj and Lochtefeld, "*Tīrtha*", p. 496.
98 Barber, *Pilgrimages*, p. 101.
99 For the history of the Kumbh in relation to its political balances, see Kama Maclean, *Pilgrimage and Power: The Kumbh Mela in Allahabad 1765–1954* (Oxford: Oxford University Press, 2008). The 2013 Kumbha Melā cost the authorities 11.5 billion rupees (about $210 or £130 million) to organize but expected to generate about 120 billion rupees from the event. See Geeta Pandey, "India's Hindu Kumbh Mela festival begins in Allahabad", BBC News India www.bbc.co.uk/news/world-asia-india-21006259
100 Apparently, in some parts of India registers are kept by *paṇḍas* so that any pilgrim from the same ancestral home, *gotra* and caste, will have the same priest guide. See T. N. Madan, *Pathways: Approaches to the study of society in India* (Delhi, Bombay, Calcutta, Madras: Oxford University Press, 1995), pp. 121–2.
102 Kinsley, *Hinduism*, p. 115.
103 Bhardwaj and Lochtefeld, "*Tīrtha*", p. 495.

Further Reading

There are a number of **primary sources** that would cover the main aspects of this book. The important *Ṛg Veda* is translated by Ralph T. H. Griffith in *The Hymns of the Ṛgveda* (Delhi: Motilal Banarsidass Publishers Private Limited), reprinted in 1991 from a new, revised edition in 1973. In the series of Penguin Classics, reprinted in 1983 and first published in 1981, there is also Wendy O'Flaherty's *The Rig Veda*, which translates sections of the *Ṛg* thematically. Patrick Olivelle's new translation, *Upaniṣads*, published in 1996 by Oxford University Press (Oxford and London), as its title suggests, translates twelve major *Upaniṣads* with a lengthy introduction and additional notes on each of the texts. These texts cover the *Veda* admirably, but there are also anthologies that have selections from the *Vedas* and *Upaniṣads*. *Sources of Indian Tradition: Volume one from the beginning to 1800* edited and revised by Ainslie T. Embree (New York: Columbia University Press, 1988), has not only selections from the *Vedas* and *Upaniṣads*, but also detailed selections by V. Raghavan and R. N. Dandekar from *śāstras* on the four aims of life, *dharma*, *artha*, *kāma*, and *mokṣa*, which occurred in chapter 4. Wendy Doniger O'Flaherty's translation and edited work, *Textual Sources for the Study of Hinduism* (Manchester: University Press, 1988), has translations of sections from the *Vedas*, *Vedāntic* texts, the epics, *Purāṇas*, *Śāstras* and *Tantras*, in particular.

The *Laws of Manu* have featured widely in the chapters of this book and Wendy Doniger's translation with Brian K. Smith in 1991 by Penguin Books is an essential primary text for understanding the religious laws behind so many aspects of Hinduism. Patrick Olivelle has translated the works of the four major compilers of the *Dharma-sūtras* in *Dharmasūtras: The law codes of Āpastamba, Gautama, Baudhāyana and Vasiṣṭha* (Oxford: Oxford University Press, 1999). For a study of the Goddess, the *Devī-Māhātmya* is the outstanding scripture that propelled the Mother Goddess to the fore and Thomas B. Coburn's 1991 translation, *Encountering the Goddess: A translation of the Devī-Māhātmya and a study of its interpretation* not only has a translation of the text but also places it in its historical setting, discusses its commentaries and associative texts, and assesses its relevance in the contemporary world. For the *Bhagavad Gītā*, see my *The Bhagavad Gita: A text and commentary for students* (Brighton, Portland and Toronto: Sussex Academic Press, 2012). For a translation of the *Rāsā-Līlā*, there is Graham M. Schweig's work published in 2005 in Princeton by Princeton University Press, *Dance of Divine Love: The Rasa Lila of Krishna from the Bhagavata Purana, India's classic sacred love story.*

There are a number of **edited secondary sources on Hinduism in general** that the reader would find useful. Sushil Mittal and Gene Thursby's *The Hindu World* (New York and London: Routledge, 2004), is replete with works by contributors that will supply supplementary reading. Julius Lipner's introduction, "On Hinduism and Hinduisms: The Way of the Banyan", is a common-sense approach to the way Hinduism can be defined without deconstructing it to the point of nonsense.

There are articles on scriptures by Laurie Patton (*Veda* and *Upaniṣad*), James Fitzgerald (*Mahābhārata*), Robert Goldman and Sally Sutherland Goldman (*Rāmāyaṇa*), and Velcheru Narayana Rao (*Purāṇas*); while Barbara A. Holdrege, Hartmut Scharfe, Dermot Killingley and Klaus K. Klostermaier have covered the four aims of life – *dharma*, *artha*, *kāma*, *mokṣa* – respectively. Social action and social structure – *karma*, *saṃskāra*, *varṇa* and *jāti*, and *āśrama* – are dealt with by Hermann Tull, Mary McGee, McKim Marriott and Walter Kaelber, while food, the village, sacred space and pilgrimage are the concern of R. Khare, Susan Wadley, Vasudha Narayanan and Surinder Bhardwaj and James Lochtefeld. Barbara Holdrege also has an article on *Dharma*. *The Continuum Companion to Hindu Studies* (New York and London, 2011), edited by Jessica Frazier, takes a more thematic approach to the study of Hinduism, with a broader remit of such aspects as the history of Hindu studies, current approaches, research methods and regional perspectives in the field. The comprehensive *The Blackwell Companion to Hinduism* edited by Gavin Flood (Malden MA, Oxford and Victoria: Blackwell Publishing, 2005 reprint of 2003 edn), has a section on the Sanskrit textual traditions with articles by Michael Witzel (*Vedas* and *Upaniṣads*), Ludo Rocher (the *Dharma-śāstras*), John Brockington (the epics), and Freda Matchett (the *Purāṇas*). Of particular relevance to the chapters in this book would also be Patrick Olivelle's section on "The Renouncer Tradition" and T. N. Madan's "The Householder Tradition in Hindu Society".

Individual books on Hinduism are too many to list here, but I shall single out a few. Much loved by my students was always John M. Koller's *The Indian Way: An introduction to the philosophies and religions of India* (Upper Saddle River, New Jersey: Pearson, Prentice Hall). First published in 1982, the book was revised in 2006, and while it deals also with other Indian religions, I know of no other writer who can present Hinduism as sensitively, or get to the heart of the subject, like this author. Gavin Flood's comprehensive *An Introduction to Hinduism* (Cambridge: Cambridge University Press, 1996), is immensely thorough as is Klaus K. Klostermaier's *A Survey of Hinduism* (Albany, New York: State University of New York Press, second edn, 1994). Julius Lipner is a graphic and warm writer and his *Hindus: Their religious beliefs and practices* (London and New York: Routledge, 1994) is a superb book. A long-time favourite is always A. L. Basham's *The Wonder That Was India* first published in 1954 in London by Sidgwick and Jackson, revised in 1963 for the third time and reprinted in 1982. Similar is Thomas Hopkins' *The Hindu Religious Tradition*, which was published in 1971 in Belmont, California by Wadsworth Publishing Company.

Apart from entries in edited works on Hinduism several other works on **scriptures** need mention here. For the epics, two books by John Brockington are essential. The first covers both epics, the *Mahābhārata* and the *Rāmāyaṇa* and is *The Sanskrit Epics* published by Koninklÿke Brill NV in Leiden in 1998. The second is *Righteous Rāma: The evolution of an epic* (Delhi: Oxford University Press, 1984). **Class and Caste** have been widely studied. C. J. Fuller is editor of the book *Caste Today* published in Delhi in 1997 by Oxford University Press. Some papers in this book examine caste in urban and rural contexts in relation to Hinduism. Sophie Baker's *Caste: At home in Hindu India* is a very warm and readable account of individual lives in different classes in India supported by really superb photography. It was published in London by Jonathan Cape in 1990. Brian K. Smith's *Classifying the Universe: The ancient Indian varṇa system and the origins of caste*, published in New York by Oxford University Press in 1994, deals with class as a wider phenomenon than simply a stratification of society. An older book but one that has an important historical analysis of *Śūdras* is Ram Sharan Sharma's *Śūdras in Ancient India: A social history of the lower order down to circa A.D. 600* (Delhi: Motilal Banarsidass Publishers Private Limited, 1990 third revised edition, first published in 1958). A standard work on the subject of class and caste that cannot be ignored is that of Louis Dumont, *Homo Hierarchicus: The caste system and its implications*. It was translated from French by Mark Sainsbury, first published in 1966 and revised in 1970 by the University of Chicago Press (Chicago and London).

Another well-known work is *Class, Caste and Power: Changing patterns of stratification in a Tanjore village* written by André Béteille (Delhi, Calcutta, Chennai, Mumbai: Oxford University Press, 1998 reprint of 1996 edition). A much more recent book is Ishita Banerjee-Dube's edited work *Caste in History* in the series Oxford in India Readings: Themes in Indian History. It was first published in 2008 and has a 2012 reprint by Oxford University Press, containing many interesting articles. Of particular relevance would be the articles on caste in practice by Frank Conlon, Dennis Templeman, Raymond Lee Owens and Ashis Nandy, Shail Mayaram and Kalpana Ram. The section on caste in everyday life is also very relevant with entries by Viramma, Josiane Racine and Jean-Luc Racine on high and low castes in one area and Mark Juergensmeyer's interesting article "The Lonely Modernity of Model Town". There are also interesting sections on caste and politics and caste and colonialism. Rajni Kothari's entry "Rise of the Dalits and the Renewed Debate on Caste" is particularly useful for contemporary views of *Dalits*. For a contemporary and searching analysis of caste in the Routledge Contemporary South Asia Series, published by Routledge (Abingdon, Oxon and New York) in 2011, Balmurli Natrajan's *The Culturalization of Caste in India* provides a remarkable insight into the way in which caste is being accepted in post-modern India. Those interested in the four stages of life, the ***āśrama* system**, need look no further than Patrick Olivelle's superb study, *The Āśrama System: The history and hermeneutics of a religious institution*, first published by Oxford University Press in 1993 and then by Munshiram Manoharlal Publishers Private Limited in New Delhi in 2004.

Hindu deities feature widely in edited works on Hinduism in general, especially those noted above and since there are so many studies of the deities, I can only select a few here. The mythology surrounding **Śiva** is encompassed in the monumental work of Stella Kramrisch, *The Presence of Śiva*, published in Princeton, New Jersey by Princeton University Press in 1981. Similar is Wendy Doniger O'Flaherty's, *Śiva: The erotic ascetic* (Oxford, New York, Toronto, Melbourne: Oxford University Press), which was published in 1973 and reprinted in 1981. A historical analysis of Śiva from his roots as Rudra can be found in Mahadev Chakravarti's *The Concept of Rudra-Śiva through the ages* (Delhi, Varanasi, Patna, Madras: Motilal Banarsidass), published in 1986.

The range of studies of ***Śakti: the divine in female form*** is considerable and, again, I can only give a small sample here. Tracy Pintchman's edited work *Seeking Mahādevī: Constructing the identities of the Hindu Great Goddess* published in Albany, New York by the State University of New York Press in 2001, contains a wide range of entries on the Mother Goddess by Tracy Pintchman herself, C. Mackenzie Brown, Usha Menon, Mark Rohe, Sarah Caldwell, Sree Padma, Elaine Craddock, Jeffrey Kripal, Kathleen Erndl and Thomas Coburn. Tracy Pintchman's 1994 work, *The Rise of the Goddess in the Hindu Tradition* (Albany, New York: State University of New York Press), discusses the Goddess in female form chronologically right through from the *Vedas* to the *Purāṇas*. The late David Kinsley's *Hindu Goddesses: Visions of the divine feminine in the Hindu tradition* (Delhi, Varanasi, Patna, Madras: Motilal Banarsidass, 1987 first Indian edition), is well known. Lynn Foulston's 2002 study *At the Feet of the Goddess: The divine feminine in local Hindu religion* (Brighton, Sussex and Portland, Oregon) raises new perspectives on the ways in which local goddesses are viewed.

Two edited works by John Stratton Hawley and Donna Marie Wulff with some overlapping material are the earlier1984, reprinted in 1995, *The Divine Consort: Rādhā and the Goddesses of India* (Delhi: Motilal Banarsidass Publishers Private Limited) and the later, 1996, *Devī: Goddesses of India* published by the University of California Press (Berkeley, Los Angeles and London). A major study of the *Mahā-vidyās* was undertaken by David Kinsley in his *Tantric Visions of the Divine Feminine: The ten Mahāvidyās* published by the University of California Press (Berkeley, Los Angeles and London), in 1997. Earlier, with the same Press, Kinsley was also the author of the 1975 work *The Sword and the Flute: Kālī and Kṛṣṇa dark visions of the terrible and the sublime in Hindu mythology.* For an extensive view of Kālī, Elizabeth Harding has captured the whole ethos of ritual and festival surrounding the Goddess in her *Kali: The Black Goddess of Dakshineswar* (Delhi: Motilal Banarsidass Publishers Private Limited, 1998 Indian edition, first published in 1993). Also concentrating on Kālī is Sarah Caldwell's *Oh Terrifying Mother: Sexuality, violence, and worship of the goddess Kālī,* published in Oxford by Oxford University Press in 1999.

Sources on **Viṣṇu and Kṛṣṇa** are legion. The *Journal of Vaishnava Studies* is dedicated solely to Vaiṣṇava studies from ancient times to the present. It is published by Deepak Heritage Books in Hampton, Virginia. In an older source from 1954 and reprinted in 1993, *Aspects of Early Viṣṇuism* (Delhi: Motilal Banarsidass Publishers Private Limited), Jan Gonda examines all the roots of Viṣṇu from the ancient past. Benjamin Preciado-Solis' 1994 detailed study of Kṛṣṇa, *The Kṛṣṇa Cycle in the Purāṇas: Themes and motifs in a heroic saga* (Delhi, Varanasi, Patna: Motilal Banarsidass) is a very detailed study of the myths surrounding the life of Kṛṣṇa. Kṛṣṇa's love affair with Rādhā is immortalized in Lee Siegel's *Sacred and Profane Dimensions of Love in Indian Traditions: As exemplified in the Gītagovinda of Jayadeva* (Delhi, Bombay, Calcutta, Madras: Oxford University Press, 1990, first published 1978).

Ritual worship is encompassed in many of the above sources, especially those edited works on Hinduism in general. There are also field studies like Lawrence Babb's 1975 work, *The Divine Hierarchy*, published in New York by Columbia University Press, and Chris Fuller's later study in 1992, *The Camphor Flame: Popular Hinduism and society in India* (New Delhi, Harmondsworth Middlesex, New York, Victoria, Toronto, Auckland: Viking). Diana Eck's 1996 superb study, *Darśan: Seeing the divine image in India*, published in New York by Columbia University Press, reached its third edition in 1998. Very recent is Tracy Pintchman's edited work *Women's Lives, Women's Rituals in the Hindu Tradition* published in Oxford and New York by Oxford University Press, and Anne Mackenzie Pearson discusses fasts by women in *"Because it Gives Me Peace of Mind": Fasts in the religious lives of Hindu women* (Albany, New York: State University of New York Press, 1996).

There are now a number of excellent studies on **the Hindu temple**. R. Champakalakshmi and Usha Kris's excellent work on Hindu temples throughout India is supported by stunning photography. It was published in London by Greenwich Editions in 2001. Formal temple structure and the architectural development of Hindu temples has been studied by Adam Hardy in *The Temple Architecture of India* published by John Wiley and Sons in Chichester in 2007. This book also has excellent photography and very detailed illustrative drawings. George Mitchell's *The Hindu Temple: An introduction to its means and forms* is self-explanatory. It was reprinted in 1988 by the University of Chicago Press. A full account of the role and functions of priests exemplified at the Minākṣī Temple in Madurai can be found in Chris Fuller's "Hindu Temple Priests" in T. N. Madan, ed., *Religion in India* (Delhi, Bombay, Calcutta, Madras: Oxford University Press, 1994 impression, first published 1991), pp. 293–307. Gaya Charan Tripathi provides another example of ritual praxis at the Jagannātha Temple with a balanced account of overt ritual alongside its mystical dimensions in *Communication with God: The daily pūjā ceremony in the Jagannātha Temple* (Delhi: Indhira Gandhi National Centre for the Arts/Aryan Books International, 2004). Elizabeth Harding's *Kali*, noted above, also gives a vivid account of ritual at the Dakṣineśvara Temple.

Life-cycle rites (*saṃskāras*) are widely featured in general books on Hinduism. A comprehensive work on the subject, though somewhat dated is Rajbali Pandey's *Hindu Saṃskāras: Socio-religious study of the Hindu sacraments* (Delhi: Motilal Banarsidass Publishers Private Limited, 1994 reprint of 1969 revised edn). The study gives a highly comprehensive historical view of all the rites. Mary McGee's entry "*Saṃskāra*" in Mittal and Thursby's *The Hindu World*, noted above, is particularly good. In the context of marriage, Veena Talwar Oldenburg discusses dowry in her *Dowry Murder: The imperial origins of a culture crime* (Oxford and New York: Oxford University Press, 2002). Marriage in the life-cycle rites will overlap considerably with **women in the home and community**. Women's studies in relation to Hinduism have multiplied profusely in recent years and there are some outstanding contributors in this field again, too many to list here. An older book published originally in 1959 with a reprint of the second edition in 1995, is A. S. Altekar's *The Position of Women in Hindu Civilization* (Delhi: Motilal Banarsidass Publishers Private Limited. This work concentrates on the position of women in society historically from ancient times.

A sensitive study of women in Hinduism is to be found in Mandakranta Bose's recent work *Women in the Hindu Tradition: Rules, roles and exceptions*, published by Routledge (Abingdon, London and New York, 2010). Bose's study is an exploration of the parallel philosophical and social roles of the goddess as female and the female as mortal through an examination of authoritative textual evidence in an attempt to make sense of women's lives today. Lindsey Harlan and Paul Courtright are the editors of *From the Margins of Hindu Marriage: Essays on gender, religion, and culture* (Oxford and New York: Oxford University Press, 1995). The entries in this book are wide-ranging but especially relevant are those by Gloria Goodwin Raheja on dowry and the woman as a gift in marriage, Susan Wadley's entry on widows, and Paul Courtright's article on the *satī*. Joanna Liddle and Rama Joshi's *Daughters of Independence: Gender, caste and class in India*, published in London by Zed books, is a very intimate analysis of the many dimensions of the lives of women in India. It was published in 1986. Again, Tracy Pintchman's edited work, *Women's Lives, Women's Rituals in the Hindu Tradition*, is relevant here, particularly, entries concerning the ways in which women are empowered through their religious ritual praxis. *Roles and Rituals for Hindu Women*, edited by Julia Lesley, is similar. It was published in Delhi in 1992 by Motilal Banarsidass. Julia Lesley herself has an article in this work pertinent to the *satī*, "Suttee or *Satī*: Victim or Victor", pp. 175–92, where she presents a sound balance between the negative criticisms of the custom, but also a sensitive portrayal of the positive outcomes of the self-sacrifice of the *satī* for her own and her family's futures. John Stratton Hawley is editor of a comprehensive study of the *satī* in *Sati, the Blessing and the Curse: The burning of wives in India* (New York and Oxford: Oxford University Press, 1994).A more political perspective is undertaken by Geraldine Forbes in *Women in Modern India* (Cambridge: Cambridge University Press, 2004). Forbes studies women in colonial India from the nineteenth century on, especially women in the nationalist movement and in post-colonial India. The importance of the preparation of food in the lives and rituals associated with women is dealt with by R. S. Khare, "*Anna*" in Mittal and Thursby's *The Hindu World*, pp. 407–28.

Festivals are a feature of many general books on Hinduism. A clear and comprehensive account of the divisions of time informing festivals is to be found in Lawrence Babb's *The Divine Hierarchy*, pp. 123–7. A comprehensive coverage of the festivals themselves can be found in Alan Brown's *Festivals in World Religions*, which he edited on behalf of the Shap Working Party published by Longman (London and New York) in 1986. For **pilgrimages**, Surinder Bhardwaj's *Hindu Places of Pilgrimage in India: A study in cultural geography* (Berkeley, Los Angeles, London: University of California Press, 1983 reprint of 1976 edn) is very comprehensive and Bhardwaj has joined with James Lochtefeld to write the entry "*Tīrtha*" in Mittal and Thursby's *The Hindu World*. George Mitchell's *The Hindu Temple*, mentioned above, also explores temples as bridges between the worlds of humanity and the divine. A detailed analysis of Śaiva, Vaiṣṇava and Śākta pilgrimage sites in West Bengal has been undertaken by Alan E. Morinis in 1984 in his *Pilgrimage in the Hindu Tradition: A case study in West Bengal* published in Delhi by Oxford University Press. Diana Eck has a superb article in Madan's *Religion in India* entitled "Kāshī: City of all India", pp. 138–55 and a longer work, *Banaras: City of Light* (New York: Alfred A. Knopf, 1982). Jonathan Parry's *Death in Banaras* (Cambridge: Cambridge University Press, 1994), as its title suggests, focuses on those who visit Banaras at the close of life or for death rites and, particularly, on the specialists and priests associated with the complexities of death rites.

Index